A Tapestry of Jamaica

The Best of SkyWritings

Air Jamaica's Inflight Magazine

September 1972 – August 2002
Stories about People,
Sports, Music, Art, Culture,
Nature, History, Places,
Memories and Fashion
spanning 30 years of publishing.

Edited by Linda Gambrill
Designed by Mark Steven Weinberger

MACMILLAN
CARIBBEAN

Published by Creative Communications Inc., Limited, Kingston Jamaica
In association with Macmillan Publishers, Oxford England

Macmillan Education
Between Towns Road, Oxford OX4 3PP
A division of Macmillan Publishers Limited
Companies and representatives throughout the world

www.macmillan-caribbean.com

ISBN 1 4050 1189 0

First published 2003

Linda Gambrill, Editor
Mark Weinberger, Creative Director
Nadine Anderson-Cheng, Art Director
Dawn Pena, Administrative Assistant

SkyWritings is published bi-monthly for Air Jamaica Limited by
Creative Communications Inc., Limited
PO Box 105, Kingston 10, Jamaica W.I.

Creative Communications Inc., and Macmillan Education would like to thank all the copyright holders for giving kind permission to reproduce material within this publication.

All inquires should be addressed to the Editor, The Best of SkyWritings Magazine, PO Box 105, Kingston 10, Jamaica W.I.

Cover image
Malachi 'Kapo' Reynolds' painting of the hills of St. Ann was on the cover of the first issue of *SkyWritings* published in September 1972.

Printed and bound in Malaysia

2006 2005 2004 2003
10 9 8 7 6 5 4 3 2 1

Contents

PATRONS

MUSIC

MISS LOU

PLACES

FOOD

ROOTS

FASHION

PEOPLE

ART

SPORT

HISTORY

MEMORIES

CONTRIBUTORS

Foreword

A Tapestry of Jamaica, The Best of SkyWritings is the idea of Linda Gambrill, my wife and for a time, editor of *SkyWritings*. The project has taken her over a year from start to finish and required many full days and late nights to complete. The latest of these nights were spent by Mark Weinberger, who designed the book and was responsible for producing it, while Odette Dixon Neath, *SkyWritings'* dynamic editor, has been an invaluable rock to the project with her decisive guidance.

There are numerous people to recognize and thank for their contributions, including the editors, writers, photographers, illustrators and artists we have worked with over the years. The production team comprised: Dawn Peña, Nadine Anderson-Cheng, Laura Gambrill, Leeanne Bayley-Hay, AnnaKay Harrison, Leroy Edwards, Odette, Mark and ourselves. For guidance, encouragement and willingness to take us on as partners, we thank Macmillan Caribbean.

The task for the team was many-faceted: which articles to choose from of the over 1500 published; how to find the contributors for their permission to republish; designing the book for maximum impact and reader enjoyment.

Whilst often onerous and demanding, the project had one particularly satisfying dimension—everyone invited to participate agreed without reservation and many expressed their pride in being selected for inclusion in what they considered to be an important contribution to Jamaican literature.

Our gratitude is extended to those sponsors who supported the venture and had the vision to recognize how important a book of this content and calibre is on the fortieth anniversary of the nation's independence.

Finally, the loyalty and support of Air Jamaica has been an essential ingredient in making this book a reality. Thirty years ago when the airline decided it needed an inflight magazine, the management committed itself to a Jamaican publishing house, rather than its New York advertising agency, to create what ultimately became *SkyWritings*. The New Air Jamaica, under the dynamic leadership of Gordon "Butch" Stewart has enthusiastically endorsed that commitment.

This book and to all who have played a role in it, is an unqualified expression of our pride in and love for Jamaica.

Anthony A. Gambrill
PUBLISHER

Introduction

First published in September 1972, *SkyWritings* was conceived with two guiding principles: that Jamaica is a symphony of vibrant textures, and that there are many ways to tell our story.

We've always sought to be more than just another inflight magazine by creating an illuminating and entertaining exposition of real life in Jamaica. This book is a testimony to that vision.

Fortunately, over the past 30 years we've managed to woo an extraordinary number of some of the best writers, photographers, artists and thinkers in the Caribbean and around the world. We've also inspired ordinary people to share their own stories and therein lies the reward for producing 141 issues of the magazine: inspiring our readers to take second, and even third looks at Jamaica and their own experiences.

In truth, *SkyWritings* has made several editorial and design transitions, largely influenced by the culturally relevant themes of the day. Our first issue was published 10 years after independence in a decade characterised by the national pursuit of self-definition. Today, a technology-infused sense of immediacy and connectivity with the world around us has directed our work, giving credibility to the idea of a world family. So while Air Jamaica is now also the national airline of Barbados and Grenada, and our coverage has expanded to include much of the Caribbean, Jamaica is still our soul.

SkyWritings is the crossroads of everything from people and pop culture to history and fashion. The hook that pulls it all together is the idea that because of the inherent complexities of Jamaica and the Caribbean, life is good and our people are truly blessed.

Odette Dixon Neath
EDITOR SKYWRITINGS

Dedication

In dedicating this book I remember the wonderful words of Miss Lou:

Walk good on yuh way
an good spirit
walk wid yuh;
Walk good.

Love.

Linda Gambrill
EDITOR—THE BEST OF SKYWRITINGS

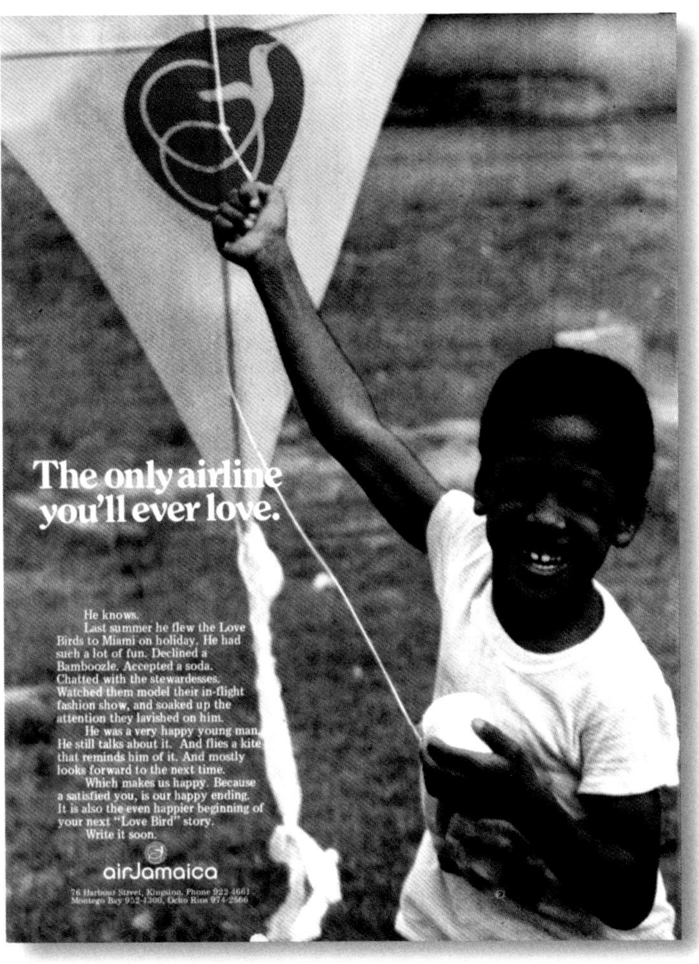

SKYWRITINGS ADVERTISEMENTS
September 1972
The first Air Jamaica magazine advertisement in *SkyWritings*.

AGENCY. CARTER GAMBRILL ROBINSON LIMITED
COPYWRITER. ADRIAN ROBINSON
ART DIRECTOR/PHOTOGRAPHER. MARK STEVEN WEINBERGER

Antigua • Barbados • Belize • Bonaire • Curaçao • Grand Cayman

The Vacation Innovators: Sandals and Beaches Resorts

Your connection to 17 of the most prestigious resorts on 5 of the most exotic islands in the Caribbean

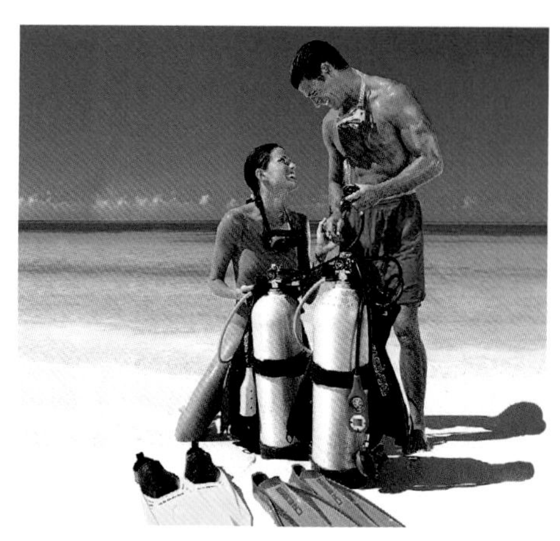

The first Sandals All-Inclusive resort for couples only opened its doors in Montego Bay, Jamaica in 1981 and since that time, Sandals Resorts have become the largest hotel operator offering high quality, beachfront ultra all-inclusive Caribbean vacations. There are now 11 Sandals resorts located on the exotic isles of Jamaica, Antigua, St. Lucia and the Bahamas and 6 Beaches resorts located in Jamaica and Turks & Caicos.

Voted World's Best Eight Years in a Row!

As the recipient of almost every industry award including World's Best All-Inclusive, Sandals is a diverse collection of eleven tropical hideaways created exclusively for two people in love on the enchanted islands of Jamaica, Antigua, St. Lucia and the Bahamas. As the world's best all-inclusive resorts, there's one thing that sets Sandals apart from all others -everything. The perfect stay includes unlimited gourmet dining and premium brand drinks, all land and water sports including golf*, scuba diving and state of the art fitness centers, plus the finest European spas** in the Caribbean.

Beaches For Everyone

In response to high demand from our guests who expressed a wish for a Sandals experience for everyone, not just couples, Beaches was created. There are four Beaches which provide a perfect vacation for everyone -families of all ages, couples and singles and which are located in Jamaica and the unspoilt Turks & Caicos. Beaches offers all the great amenities that Sandals is known for and also includes activities designed specifically for kids including: supervised Kids Kamp with Ultra Nannies, state of the art games centers, kids pool, teen discos and Pirates Island -the hottest family attraction with waterslides and 50's diner.

Beaches For Adults

2001 was a particularly busy year for Sandals and Beaches. Two resorts both located in beautiful Ocho Rios, Jamaica, opened their doors. These resorts are aimed at the adults market welcoming couples, singles and families.

Beaches Grande Sport Resort & Spa offers active amenities and true luxury for adults 16 years and older. Along with all the amenities, this PIRA (PADI International Resorts Association) Gold Palm Certified Resort offers a state of the art fitness center with personal trainers, yoga, pilates, kickboxing and much more.

Beaches Royal Plantation Golf Resort & Spa, a AAA Four Diamond luxury resort for adults 18 years and older, has become the first Jamaican hotel to be awarded the prestigious Five Star Diamond Award. This resort offers top shelf drinks, Beach Butler services offering services poolside to beachside, 24 hour room service and 80 suites- all with ocean view.

*Golf available at select resorts. **Spa services additional.

Sandals and Beaches Open Two More Resorts

Beaches Boscobel Resort & Golf Club the newest addition to the ever growing Beaches family resorts opened its doors in July 2002. Set on 10 beautifully landscaped acres, this resort features 230 luxurious oversized rooms and suites, 5 gourmet restaurants, 3 freshwater pools and 3 whirlpools, full array of land and watersports including scuba and much more. Golf is included for the entire family including golf clinics for kids at nearby Sandals Golf & Country Club.

Sandals has acquired its third luxurious resort in beautiful St. Lucia. **Sandals Grande St. Lucian Spa and Beach Resort** opened its doors in Summer 2002 as well. Already a AAA Four Diamond resort, this resort sits on a peninsula with the Caribbean Sea to the immediate North and the tranquil Rodney Bay to the South. All rooms offer breathtaking ocean views along with the best stretch of white sand beach and full exchange privileges including transfers to 2 neighboring Sandals Resorts.

1. Beaches Boscobel Resort & Golf Club aerial view. 2. Beaches Boscobel pool view. 3. Sandals Grande St. Lucian suite 4. Grande St. Lucian aerial view.

The Signature Spas At Sandals & Beaches Resorts:

Uniquely Pampering, Uniquely Caribbean

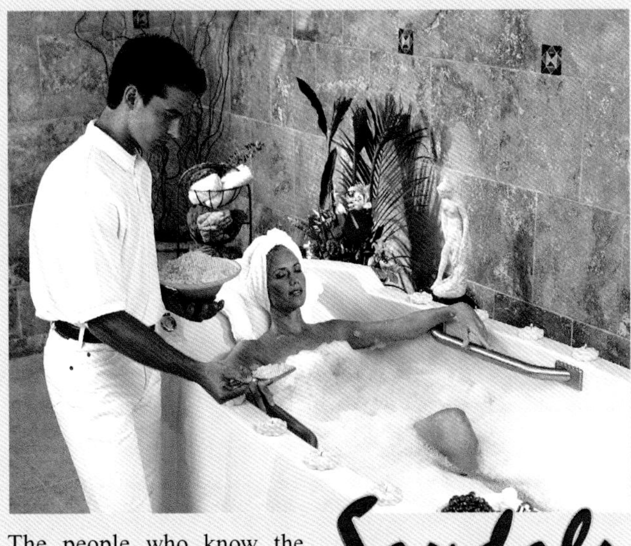

Sandals
SIGNATURE SPA COLLECTION

The people who know the Caribbean best -Sandals and Beaches Resorts- know that a true vacation is one that balances activity with relaxation to relieve the body, mind and spirit. With that philosophy in mind, Sandals has created a unique spa environment that is intimate, pampering and opulent, but never intimidating.

Each of the nine **Sandals and Beaches Signature Spas** offers a full range of classic European treatments with a uniquely Caribbean touch. Tropical flowers scent the air, while exotic, aromatic oils soothe the skin, remove tension and promote total relaxation. Just outside, white sand and turquoise waters prolong the feeling of relaxation and renewal.

The launch of the Signature Spa at Sandals Royal Bahamian Resort & Spa in Nassau in 1996 started a revolution in the world of luxury all-inclusive resorts. The readers of Condè Nast Traveler voted the Signature Spa at Royal Bahamian the "Top Caribbean Spa Resort" after its first year in operation and have done so year after year. Today, guests can enjoy world-class spa treatments at eight Sandals and Beaches Signature Spa resorts.

Sandals is the largest operator of luxury, ultra all-inclusive resorts in the Caribbean. Sandals has a total of 11 couples-only properties, including six in Jamaica, three in St. Lucia, one in Antigua and one in Nassau, Bahamas. Beaches Resorts, the newest addition to the Sandals family, welcomes singles, couples, families and friends. **Beaches** offers five locations: two in Negril, Jamaica, one in Ocho Rios, Jamaica, one in Providenciales, Turks & Caicos, and two in Ocho Rios, Jamaica, which are part of the new "adults-only" Beaches.

FOR MORE INFORMATION ABOUT SANDALS AND BEACHES RESORTS, CALL 1-876-968-4205 IN JAMAICA OR 1-800-SANDALS/1-800-BEACHES IN NORTH AMERICA OR VISIT WWW.SANDALS.COM/WWW.BEACHES.COM

Chairman, Michael Lee-Chin

National Commercial Bank, a company with a long and colourful history dating back to 1837, began a new era on March 19, 2002 when AIC Limited, Canada's largest privately held mutual fund company acquired 75% of the share holding in the bank from FINSAC. In the words of Michael Lee-Chin, AIC's Chairman, "we purchased NCB because we view it as a national treasure to which Jamaicans have a strong emotional attachment". With this parent, NCB is once again a strong and stable organization possessing the largest capital base of all banks in Jamaica. An exciting future of new products and service lies ahead, making it easier for customers to invest and obtain access to international fund management.

We offer a wide range of banking and financial services across our 50 plus island wide branch network. Additionally self-services are now conveniently supplied by our extensive network of over 90 Automated Banking Machines, which welcome Visa and MasterCard Credit Cards and Cirrus Plus Debit cardholders. NCB has been a pioneer in the credit card business and introduced Jamaica's first propriety credit card - KeyCard. The bank successfully forged strategic alliances with service providers such as Air Jamaica to launch the Lovebird KeyCard, and more recently the Travelmaster Credit Card, denominated in U.S. dollars through Air Jamaica's 7th Heaven Fly Free Programme.

Our core subsidiary companies comprise: Edward Gayle & Company and NCB Investments, which offer securities, brokerage, and investment management services (Investments in AIC's corporate funds can now be purchased directly from Edward Gayle); West Indies Trust Company offers pension administration and investment management services; Omni Insurance Services offers bank-assurance via its flagship product Omni; NCB Nominees provides registrar services, and we supply off-shore banking services via NCB Cayman.

AIC's and NCB's goals are to create long-term wealth for our clients and so help them achieve their ambitions. NCB's Private Banking business offers personalized service par excellence with confidentiality our trademark. The world-class fund management experience of AIC, aligned to the distribution capability of NCB and our rejuvenated focus on placing the customer at the centre of every thing we do, augurs well for the growth of financial services in Jamaica and the Caribbean - with NCB setting the pace.

COME BACK HOME

NCB

Your bank...Your future.

Email: ncbinfo@jncb.com • Website: www.jncb.com

Our Roots are Jamaican

Meeting the needs of Jamaican and Caribbean people in the region and abroad has been the objective of **Grace, Kennedy & Company Ltd**. since its inception in 1922.

We work towards this objective in several ways by offering quality goods and services –

BUILDING MATERIALS AND HARDWARE

- **Rapid & Sheffield**, which stocks first class brands of tools, equipment and hardware supplies -
  - for the professional builder and
  - for homeowners and householders working on home improvement projects.

FOOD

We distribute and export a wide range of products including familiar favourites such as –

- Vienna Sausages
- Mackerel
- Corned Beef
- Soups and Juices

And popular newcomers such as –

- Grace Coconut Water
- Grace Tropical Rhythms Juice Drinks
- Grace Pepper Sauces
- Grace Caribbean Combos
  (Easy to prepare rice and peas)

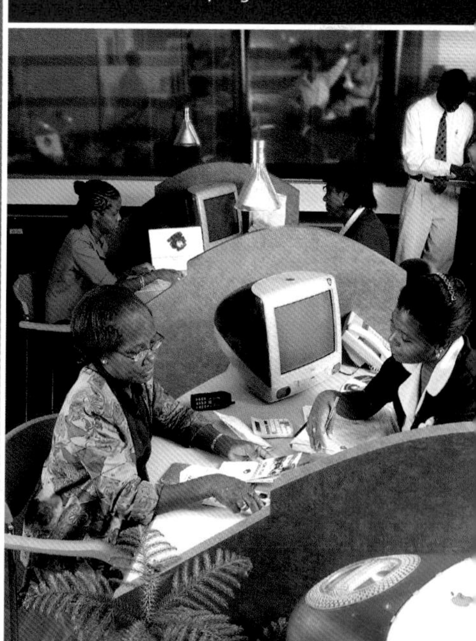

MONEY TRANSFER SERVICES

Western Union/Grace, Kennedy Remittance Services in Jamaica, Trinidad & Tobago and Guyana.

CURRENCY EXCHANGE SERVICES

FX Trader in Jamaica and Trinidad & Tobago.

Capital & Credit Merchant Bank

A success story of performance with integrity

Ryland Campbell

As 1994 dawned, so too was born a new institution which promised as its mission, "...Vision, Professionalism and Integrity, coupled with the provision of Superior Value-added Financial services of internationally competitive standards...." Today that promise has been fulfilled largely because of sound management, strategic financial focus, exceptional growth in profitability, our principles of professionalism with integrity, the trust and confidence by the investing public and the commitment and dedication of a cadre of dynamic and competent staff.

This is the story of Capital & Credit Merchant Bank (CCMB). A new and vibrant organization, that not only promised, but also in quick time delivered superior financial services, guided by a knowledgeable and trusted team of professionals and the words and spirit of the company's Mission Statement. It's a team which works hard at its stated mission of providing the best possible financial services of impeccable and "...internationally competitive standards to the benefit of the company's customers, employees, shareholders and indeed, the wider community."

It was a modest start, as the Bank began operating with an asset base of $30 million, making it the smallest of the thirty merchants banks operating in Jamaica at the time. Today, after just eight years of operation, Capital & Credit's Shareholders' Equity has surpassed $1 billion – a milestone for merchant banks in Jamaica – and the Bank has over $20 billion in Assets Under Management. Not bad for a little bank that dared and continues to so do.

Much of the Bank's success can be attributed to the guidance and stature of its Board of Directors; its Chairman, Ryland Campbell; its Founding President, Andrew Cocking, now Deputy Group President; and the financial expertise of it's current President and CEO, Curtis Martin. But these are just some of the personalities in this equation of success, each of whom would be quick to add that the Bank's success should be shared by the entire staff at all levels of the its operations.

Curtis Martin

Another key component in this success story has to be CCMB's savings and investment products that are geared to individuals and institutions alike. These include special products and services, including Tax Free Savings that are offered to non-residents, in particular Jamaicans who reside overseas. *

CCMB recently launched a new subsidiary aimed at offering investors a Bold New Step in Investment Opportunities - Capital & Credit Securities Limited (CCSL). Already the market response has been encouraging. CCSL makes its focus the offering to clients of Stock broking Services, Portfolio Management, Pension Fund Management and Investment Accounts, including its International Bond Account - a high performance instrument that affords investors a hedge against currency depreciation with higher yields than short term funds.

Although much has changed since the company started operations, it still maintains its passion for excellence through focussed leadership, transparency and Performance with Integrity. To this end, Capital & Credit employs research, market knowledge and astute management practices in the delivery of its wide array of financial services. Very soon, Capital & Credit Merchant Bank could be listed on the Stock Exchange as the company readies itself for becoming a regional player in the industry through strategic compatible partnership and alliances.

Growth, Performance and Continued Success continue to be the main goals of the Capital & Credit Financial Group, and Capital & Credit Merchant Bank, in particular, as the company redefines itself and sets new standards for achieving its stated goals, while remaining Financially Focussed.

ONE BEER ONE PEOPLE
Red Stripe
LAGER BEER
BREWED IN JAMAICA
LEVEL THE VIBES

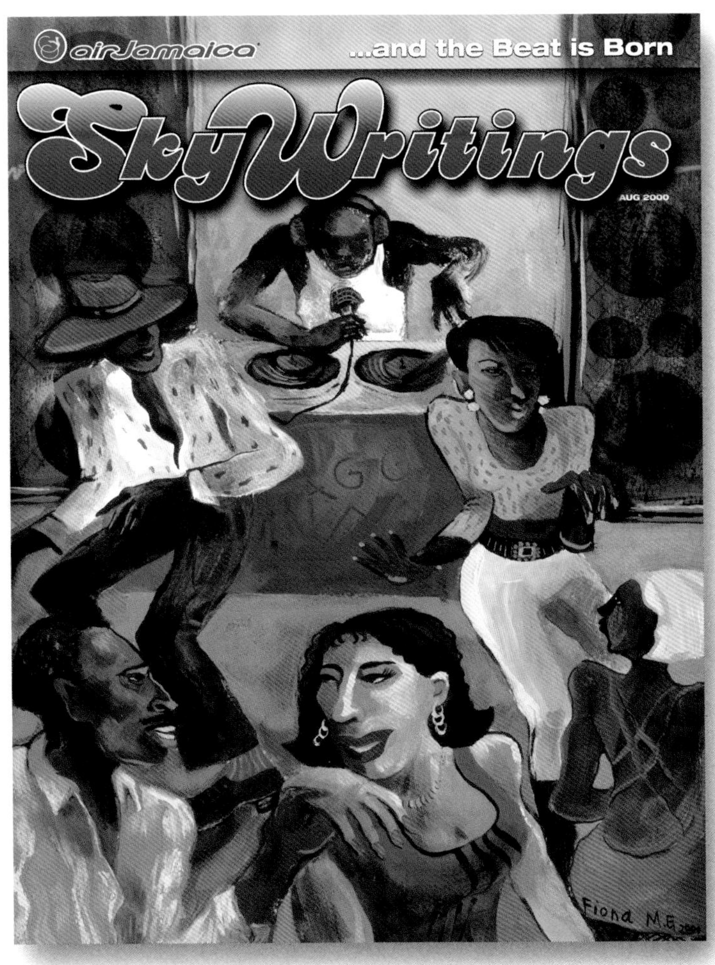

MUSIC

SKYWRITINGS COVER
August 2000
Capturing the essence of Jamaican sound systems. Energy in the dancehall.
©FIONA GODFREY

Folk Music Roots and Rhythm

SUZANNE FRANCIS-BROWN

To most people, Jamaican music is reggae and reggae is Jamaican music, and that's that. Little do they know that there is also a rich heritage of traditional sound and movement rooted deep in the island's history.

"The melody of Europe playing on the rhythm of Africa," is one way in which it has been described.

And indeed these two continents have provided much of the cultural background for a people largely descended from the Ibos, Mandingos, Yorubas, Fantis and Ashantis, but strongly influenced by mores of 17th, 18th and 19th century Britain.

Some features of each society have been preserved in a remarkably authentic manner, while others have blended into a creole form. Still others have disappeared altogether, victims of social change.

Jamaican folk researcher Marjorie Whylie describes the range of traditional forms as "a continuum with European features at one pole and African features at another, and then they're approaching along the continuum."

The forms extend from quadrille, once the rage of English and French ballrooms, to such African-derived, spirit-based religious cults as kumina and etu.

Along the continuum there is revivalism—an amalgam of Christian orthodoxy and African ancestor worship—John Canoe, which pulls on masquerade traditions in both Europe and Africa, and mento, a popular music form which developed as an extra figure to the quadrille and which has been used as a vehicle for protest, humour and examination of the human condition.

Much of the music has disappeared because its function has been removed, whether due to industrialization, spread of the electronic media, urbanization, or education which has often tarred such forms with the brush of ignorance.

This catalogue of dying or forgotten music includes a great many social and work songs.

There was a time in rural Jamaica when the moving of a house from one site to another, or the clearing of a plot of land or the 'selling' of the corn crop, called for communal effort accompanied by feasting and song.

The backbreaking work of hoeing, planting or harvesting a field under the broiling sun, or of breaking stones for surfacing the roadways, or digging the roads, was accompanied by songs which became chants as they braced men and women into the rhythm of the monotonous work.

"Hill and gulley ridah,
Hill an gulley, huh,
Hill and gulley ridah,
Hill an gulley, huh,
You bruk you foot, you tumble
down,
Hill and gulley, huh..."

The trials of the day and the relief brought by evening were also recorded in social songs:

"...All day we diggin road,
into de bwoiling sun,
All day we brukkin rockstone,
praying fe worktime dun.
Evening time,
Work is over now is evening
time,
Mek we dance pon mountain,
yes dance pon mountain,
Is evening time..."

Now the truck, the bulldozer or the tractor takes care of such tasks as home moving and. road digging, while the transistor radio accompanies men and women to work in the fields, and the strains of jukebox fill the air at night.

The village band which would have songs commemorating major tragedies or comic events, as well as older traditional music in their repertoire, has largely died out for lack of use.

So too have such evening activities as the 'pass the stone' game played to musical accompaniment:

"Go down a Manuel Road,
Gal an' Bwoy,
Fi go bruk rock stone;
Bruk dem one by one,
bruk dem two by two ...
Finger mash, nub cry,
'Member a game we a play.
Go down a Manuel Road,
Gal an' Bwoy,
Fi go bruk rock stone"

The situation also exists where the older folk in some areas have not passed on the music consciously, or where the younger ones have rejected it in favour of the bar and the jukebox, Marjorie Whylie explained.

"There is very little creative use of leisure time any more" she adds. "We have become a spectator people. You sit and you watch television or you go to the movies; there is no creating of the things for recreation. So much of the social music is disappearing".

Folk researchers lament the disappearance even while they understand it, and their major complaint has been the lack of proper documentation of the old forms so that they may be re-created even if only for historical purposes.

Olive Lewin, cultural officer in the Office of the Jamaican Prime Minister, says: "the music is going; it has to. It can't stay the same. But, we haven't taken enough notice of the forms and understood the sources".

Her particular concern is the social and religious forms which have not yet disappeared but whose chief proponents are getting old and only quick action in documenting their knowledge can prevent it dying with them, leaving the shell of the ritual but no understanding to give it substance.

"The lady who kept brukins alive died two years ago; the oldest living Nago died this year. It's criminal that no documentation has been done" she says.

Brukins Party is a form found in the parish of Portland, in eastern Jamaica and which celebrates the 1838 emancipation of slaves. It is still being kept alive by some although it has been superseded, islandwide, by Independence celebrations.

"Jubilee, jubilee, dis is di year
of jubilee,
Queen Victoria give we free,
Queen Victoria give we free,
Queen Victoria give we free,
dis is di year of Jubilee.
August morning come again,
August morning come again,
August morning come again,
dis is di year of jubilee.
Jubilee, jubilee,
Jubilee, jubilee."

Nago is a socio-religious tradition found only in one small district of Westmoreland, western Jamaica, and is derived from an archaic cult of the Yoruba people of Nigeria.

Another Yoruban-derived form, found in the western parish of Hanover, is etu, a socio-religious form based on a faith system where there is no actual spirit possession as occurs in many other cults.

Etu observances include 'set-up'—the process of sitting up on the night or nights following a death or, sometimes, before a wedding, for singing, dancing and feasting—and dinner feasts held to ensure success in particular matters of concern to a group or individual.

In etu, researchers say, the rhythms and the scale patterns on which the songs are built definitely point to an African heritage; however, research is insufficient.

The atchaka, an instrument made from a kerosene tin, and a drum called the ireh, are characteristic instruments at etu observances.

Gumbay is another traditional form with definite African antecedents—it's a cult of healing found in the south-west parish of St. Elizabeth, with music and movement led by the square-framed, hand-played gumbay drum.

Marjorie Whylie states that music linked to the celebration of death accounts for by far the majority of the traditional forms, and they vary from one parish to another. "It may be dinki minni which you find in the eastern part of the island, especially in the parish of St. Mary, and that involves dances which have role playing, ring play and that sort of thing" Miss Whylie explains.

One popular verse from dinki minni celebrations says:

"Rosibelle O, belle o, belle o,
Rosibelle O, belle O, belle O,
Rosibelle gawn a Madda
Morgan yard,
Rosibelle O, belle O."

Other observances linked with death include gerrah, the western part of the island's answer to dinki minni, tambo from Trelawny, and etu, as well as a form simply referred to as 'set-up' or 'nine-night'.

The musical content of these observances may vary from the religious base where choruses and hymns are sung:

"Sleep on, sleep on, sleep on
and take thy rest,
We loved thee true but Jesus
loves thee best,
Goodbye...Goodbye..."

to the tradition of calling for the food which a good host is bound to provide in generous quantities.

This is always done in song:

"From night me come yah,
me nuh see no housemaster,
Me a go mash up di house
and go way..."

The celebration of death seems to be linked with the African concept that death means passage to another level of existence, in the company of the ancestors; and the idea of a 'good funeral' is still strong among older people in some rural districts of Jamaica.

Two of the strongest of the old religious forms—as distinct from traditional religious observances like 'set-up'—are revivalism and kumina.

Revivalism is, the term applied to the amalgam of zion, which dealt with such heavenly spirits as the saints, angels and apostles; and pocomania (little madness) which dealt with the ancestral or ground spirits.

Many of the marked differences between these two have now disappeared making it almost impossible to find a purely zion or 'poco' group. But, the similar expressions of ecstacy of the group being controlled by the tempo of the drums, has remained.

The musical element of revivalism is singing accompanied by drums, usually a base drum and a rattling drum, suspended from the neck or shoulder and played by sticks.

Singing is generally in harmony, and often short verses from orthodox hymnals which are repeated constantly but with ornamentation and a phenomenon called 'tracking'. 'Tracking'—the speaking of a line by one person before it is sung by the group—started out as a purely functional exercise because so many members could not read.

Possession by a spirit is a familiar aspect of revivalism. Temporary possession is also a feature of kumina, and the adherents only convene for special reasons and not regularly as is the case with the revivalists. A play—the term used for observances involving singing, dancing and feasting—is made in celebration of an event, or to ensure success in a particular undertaking.

In kumina, the dancers move with a characteristic shuffling step, keeping their feet close to the ground, since this is the source from which the spirits will enter the body. The drums are hand played, with the drummers sitting astride their instruments. Each has a role, one playing a metronomic beat, another playing cuts to correspond to the presence of various spirits.

As such the drummers establish the lines of communication with the spirits, controlling the dance steps and, necessarily, occupying the central place within the circle of dancers. Percussion instruments are sometimes used to add texture and density to the music, and a 'shaka', or 'cata sticks' may be beaten on the body of the drum to produce definite patterns.

Kumina meetings also feature a king or queen who directs the proceedings, and senior members who are given duties. One popular kumina verse says:

"Di King and di Queen a go
reign,
Pembeleh,
Wah yo, wah yo, pembeleh,
Di King and di noble Queen,
Pembeleh,
Wah yo, wah yo, pembeleh..."

In kumina the songs are done in the vernacular, some in unison, others in a call and response pattern, and older songs which follow African scales and African melodic contours are often sung in African dialects or combinations of these dialects and the local vernacular. The African dialects have been traced by local researchers, and identified as coming from a tribe in the Congo, members of which are believed to have settled in Jamaica in the post-slavery period.

Some kumina group leaders can give translations of the African songs, while others can give the gist and still others have no understanding of the songs which form a central part of their ritual. Olive Lewin suggests that one reason for the lack of widespread in-depth research and documentation of the traditional music forms has been its divergence from the conventional modes.

"So the more culturally significant the music, the more difficult it is to transcribe it according to four lines and five spaces, crochets, quavers and semi-quavers" she says.

More information would therefore be available on work and dance music, such as quadrille which has European roots, than on the more African-derived forms like kumina.

Quadrille, found its way to the West Indian plantations via Britain. In Jamaica the original four figures were added to, and mento appeared—a form which took European melodic pieces, put syncopation to them and added the rhythm instruments.

Once a popular music and dance form, mento has been a vehicle of protest, recrimination, humour and examination of the human condition, and has similarities to the merengé of the Dominican Republic, gumbay of the Bahamas, rhumba of Cuba and calypso of Trinidad.

Mento has a clear, strong fourth beat, in a bar of four beats, and closely follows local speech patterns.

Guitars, banjos—as chordal or melody instruments—and rhumba boxes to provide the rhythmic impulse, are popular in mento bands. Drums are rarely found. Most instruments used for traditional music-making are home made, and vary according to the materials available, tradition, form and area. Some mento bands used metal graters of various sizes.

The bamboolin, a type of indigenous violin, is best known in St. Ann, northern Jamaica, where Jonathan Brown makes, plays and sells them by the famous Dunn's River Falls.

Fifes are made from bamboo, or even from PVC piping, and their tuning varies across the island, using the diatonic scale in the east, while not conforming in the west.

Bamboo stamping tubes—three or four joints of bamboo with the inner joints removed which, when beaten with a stone produces a booming sound—are found in Hanover.

The benta—bamboo with a string lifted from the membrane and played with a calabash to produce a singing note while sticks are beaten at the other end—is popular in St. Mary.

Various instruments are made from the calabash or gourd, these may be filled with seeds, stopped with cork and shaken in the palm of the hand or on the end of a stick.

Olive Lewin suggests that purpose is as important as form in categorizing Jamaica's traditional music, since the same words may appear in different contexts. "Rhythms differ according to purpose. The purpose is in the rhythm."

"It's like a cross" she adds. "I can put down two pencils and make a cross. If you're a Christian it has a certain significance, if you go further into religion you'll find the Pentecostals don't look at it the same way as Roman Catholics do".

"So it is with the music."

ORIGINALLY PUBLISHED JANUARY 1982

One Hundred Years Old and the

Alpha Boys Band Plays On...

DERMOT HUSSEY

Victorians would have called it a brave sight, thirty-odd boys of the Alpha band, seated under a spreading almond tree, possibly as old as the band itself—tooting clarinets, trumpets and trombones and saxophones in the gentle morning breeze.

Some are barely in their teens, mostly boys from what is politely called difficult social circumstances—petty crime, runaways from home and school. Often abandoned, they arrive at Alpha seeking care and protection, and are taught useful trades of printing and book binding, cabinet-making and in times past, shoemaking, tilemaking, blockmaking and pottery. It's music, however that's been the trick of the trades, and its subsequent skill has made the Alpha Boys School and band an unparalleled Jamaican and Caribbean experience.

A visionary Jamaican, Jesse Ripoll, in 1880 purchased 48 acres upon which the venerable institution stands, and four years later the Alpha Boys School was started, to be followed by the band, eight years later. Ever since, Alpha has benefitted from the progressive leadership of Roman Catholic nuns, an old order called the Sisters of Mercy. In May 1892 six sisters from Bermondsey came to Jamaica, and among those pioneers, was a Sister De Shantel who started a Drum and Fife Corps, conscripting tutors from the military to instruct the boys. Today, the Alpha Boys Band is an inexhaustible source of the best Jamaican musicianship.

No matter how disadvantaged any of the boys might have been initially, once they were given love and the security of a home, it is as if they channeled their frustrations into music, consequently their honour roll, is not only impressive, but seemingly endless: Leslie Thompson, Bertie King, Dizzy Reece, Joe Harriott, Harold McNair, Wilton Gaynair, Tommy McCook, Don Drummond, Rico Rodriquez, Eddy Thornton, Jo Jo Bennett, Jackie Willacy, Cedric

Procession at Winchester Park in 1937. Bamd master is George Neilson.

Brooks, Tony Gregory and Leroy Smart, and a fresh crop of talents from the 80s—Ian Hurd, Maurice Gray to mention two, who are keepers of the flame, the school's motto "Upward and Onward."

Another venerable tradition is its bandmasters, past graduates—legends like Rueben Delgado, Vincent Tulloch and Lennie Hibbert. They ensured that the standards were maintained and a code of discipline adhered to. The tradition is perpetuated by the current bandmaster, Sparrow Martin, a graduate and noted drummer. Under his direction, the band, a mix of saxes, clarinets, trumpets, trombones, euphoniums and percussion, start off "Two O' Clock Jump" tentatively, the tempo slightly off. Martin reigns them in, sets it right, and the boys take it from the top again. The trumpets and the saxes signature the classic big band tune to life. They ease into Glen Miller, reading their charts and playing accordingly.

The repertoire is flexible, 2,000 songs in demand of its busy schedule, and the anthems of the diplomatic missions in Jamaica, who engage the band on a regular basis for functions requiring them to ease from idiom to idiom effortlessly, as it does with pop and jazz, some tight classics, but is understandably at home with mento and reggae, for it's in the blood.

Fifteen year-old Alfred Poyster, plays four instruments, and is a long standing member of eleven years. He knows no other home but Alpha and the Band. "I like the standard of music we play," he says, "some of the music I like. I don't like some of the classics, like Beethoven and Mozart." Why? "Because it feels strange to me." Alfred sees a career in music. "I want to go as far as I can go, one more thing, I think the band needs more competition with other bands.

Conrad Heywood specializes in the trumpet as his main instrument, but doubles on guitar when necessary. He likes being in the band, and it has taught him a lot. He too, likes some of the music the band plays, "jazz and reggae, they are my two main music." What about classics and international pop? "I like them but I don't listen to them all the time."

Tassie Mohammed from the Turks and Caicos Islands, came to school in Jamaica, heard of the band and asked to become a member. "I think they are up to a good standard right now," says the fifteen year-old. "I play the drums, but if I had to pick another instrument... the bass, the keyboard and the saxophone."

"Really, I say to myself, I'm a reggae and soca drummer. I'm more of the pop kind. I don't really like the classics, I play some jazz, but I'm not really into the classics. To me its kind of dead. It doesn't have enough rhythm."

The Alpha Band, surprisingly, in spite of its long history has made only two overseas engagements, Miami in 1968, and Atlanta in June this year, but it has the most extraordinary outreach to past students and well-wishers, who are intensely loyal, especially if it was the only home they knew. Through them a lifeline of hard to get musical supplies is always coming in—reeds, oils, instruments. A recent well-wisher who learned of the band from a friend, has marshalled thousands of dollars worth of instruments from Germany. And when the link is broken, as in the case of Leslie Thompson, a brilliant graduate who died recently, had his trumpet bequeathed to the band. A graduate also never fails to pay homage to another institution within the institution, Sister Ignatius, who joined Alpha in 1939. She is the mother of the band, with a remarkable memory of its history and leading lights. She remembers the times when the boys had to use soap to mend instruments, and string to tie up broken keys. What was the special quality that made Alpha so musically influential? "I think. first of all, it was at one time, the only school that taught music as brass bands go, because I think that accounts for why it's been so popular and so well used, because the Military Band drafted from here, the Regiment Band drafted from here, plus all the leading orchestras during that time and still up to now."

Does Sister sees a difference between the present and the past?

"The difference now is really with the instruments, because in the thirties and forties we didn't have these amplifiers, keyboards, etc. Each individual stood on his own and I think that was a good thing, because it developed their tone and their self confidence, so that you found in the forties you had Little G McNair and Tommy McCook. I think the boys took their music very seriously and were very innovative, they didn't just stick to one thing, they tried different things.

Under the almond tree, Bandmaster Martin is putting the boys through a special programme to be played days later at the awards ceremony for the Musgrave Medalists (at which the band was awarded a Silver Medal). Listening to them glide from music to music, one gets the feeling that the next 100 years, would in effect be no greater a challenge than a long rehearsal.

Sister Regine and Sister Ignatius conducting a rehearsal of the Alpha Boys Band under the shade of the famous almond tree.

ORIGINALLY PUBLISHED
JANUARY 1993

Count Ossie and The Mystic Revelation of Rastafari

MARJORIE WHYLIE

The 'Rastafari' are a Jamaican millenarian cult whose doctrines of social rejection postulate a promised land in Africa in general (and Ethiopia in particular) where their earthly deliverer and leader Haile Selassie lives.

— REX NETTLEFORD, **MIRROR MIRROR**, WILLIAMS COLLINS AND SANGSTER (JAMAICA) LTD., 1970.

(FRONT ROW) Samuel Clayton; Samuel Williams (Count Ossie's son); Count Ossie; Fay Henry; Unidentified. (SECOND ROW) Tony Campbell; Leslie Samuels; Joe Rouglas; Richard Thellwell. (BACK ROW) Uriah Smith; George Clarke; Lord Bryner; Winston Smith; Cedric Brooks; George Dudley; Nambo Robinson.

In late 1970, a number of concerts took place at the African Cultural Centre in Kingston, featuring Kenny Terroade, Cedric 'Im' Brooks and the Count Ossie drummers. Together with other horn players, Brooks and Terroade and the drummers produced a fresh, new and exciting sound. It was out of this 'marriage' of drums and horns that the Mystic Revelation of Rastafari grew.

The music of the MRR is as Jamaican as the Rastafarian 'brethren' themselves. The rhythm owes much to Africa; the brass owes much to the liberalising influence of people like John Coltrane. But the total sound of the group is wholly indigenous—the combination of a driving pulse and a profound emotional conviction that their music speaks truly for them. The result is an erotic, prerational statement in music about a particular life-style. It is as multi-faceted and multi-textured as the society that is Jamaica. It's not surprising that the group has been acquiring a large following among Jamaicans of all walks of life. Already the MRR have a three-record album *Grounation*, to their credit. It's rambling, like their live performances, but there are intensely satisfying moments in it. And the word is spreading—the group has toured Trinidad, and there's a tour planned for the U.S.A.

This 'rasta' rhythm first came to public attention in the early sixties when Count Ossie provided background rhythms for the Ffolkes Brothers' "Carolina", a song which had a long stay at the top of the charts, and even today can still change a sedate party into a churning athletic mob—in Jamaican terms, 'a spot'.

Oh Carolina! Oh Carolina! The appeal of the music exists at the deepest level of the senses, for the MRR go back to ritualistic roots. The poly-rhythmic 'beat' is predominantly African. It seems to be a variation or a simplification of the 'kumina', an African-based ritual still thriving in the east of the island. The guiding hands are those of Count Ossie, who devised the whole rhythmic structure. If you can bear to listen to these drums analytically, instead of with the whole body and heart, you'll hear how complex that structure is.

First the repeaters, the smallest drums: dull beats on the third and fourth counts of each measure, played with the hands remaining on the drum-head for a moment after they fall, to stop the vibration. Then the bass drum, playing on the first beat only, but alternating between a deep tone and a note three or four semi-tones above—the drummer gets this variation by changing the position and attack of the single stick he beats with. And above all this steady pulse, Count Ossie plays the 'cuts', heavily syncopated, quick hands commanding a range of tones from the edge and tip of the drum.

Written in clean letters on the skin of the bass drum are the psalmist's words:

BEHOLD HOW GOOD AND HOW PLEASANT IT IS FOR BROTHERS TO DWELL TOGETHER IN UNITY! IT IS AS THE PRECIOUS OINTMENT UPON THE HEAD THAT RAIN DOWN UPON THE BEARD.

They say that music is 'the art and science of expression in sound,' the 'interaction of the basic elements of rhythm, melody and harmony.' The music of the MRR grows out of rhythm insistent and repetitious, hypnotic,—leaving room for complete freedom of melodic line, for improvisations and for meanderings round simple themes. A performance is an hours-long experience. It moves through gutsy singing, saxophones, trumpets and trombones played in abandon, and a driving beat.

The narrator is Ras Sam Clayton, who tells the audience what the group is about, and treats you to a little history and Rastafarian philosophy. The musical director is 'Im' Brooks. His range on the tenor sax is startling; and he also plays a satisfying flute. The style of the playing is loose, it makes for free experimentation. Sometimes the sound will be oppressive: it will talk of suffering and despair. At other times it will be plaintive, an expression of the faith of the 'Brethren' in their singular and moving vision of 'peace and love'. This music grows out of the deeply held religious, cultural and political beliefs of the people who play it. Perhaps that is why the group, splendid in informal surroundings, loses some of its fire on the concert stage. The music is personal, and the group doesn't ever rely on audience reaction; their enjoyment of the sound they make is total and complete. If you get to hear them, sit up close. You'll find it easy—and warm—to share their own experience of their music.

ORIGINALLY PUBLISHED SEPTEMBER 1972

Ska, Ska, Ska, Jamaica Ska

PATRICIA MESCHINO

"Not everybody can cha-cha-cha. Not everybody can do the twist. But everybody can do the Ska, it's a new dance you can't resist."

— THE SKA KINGS (1964)

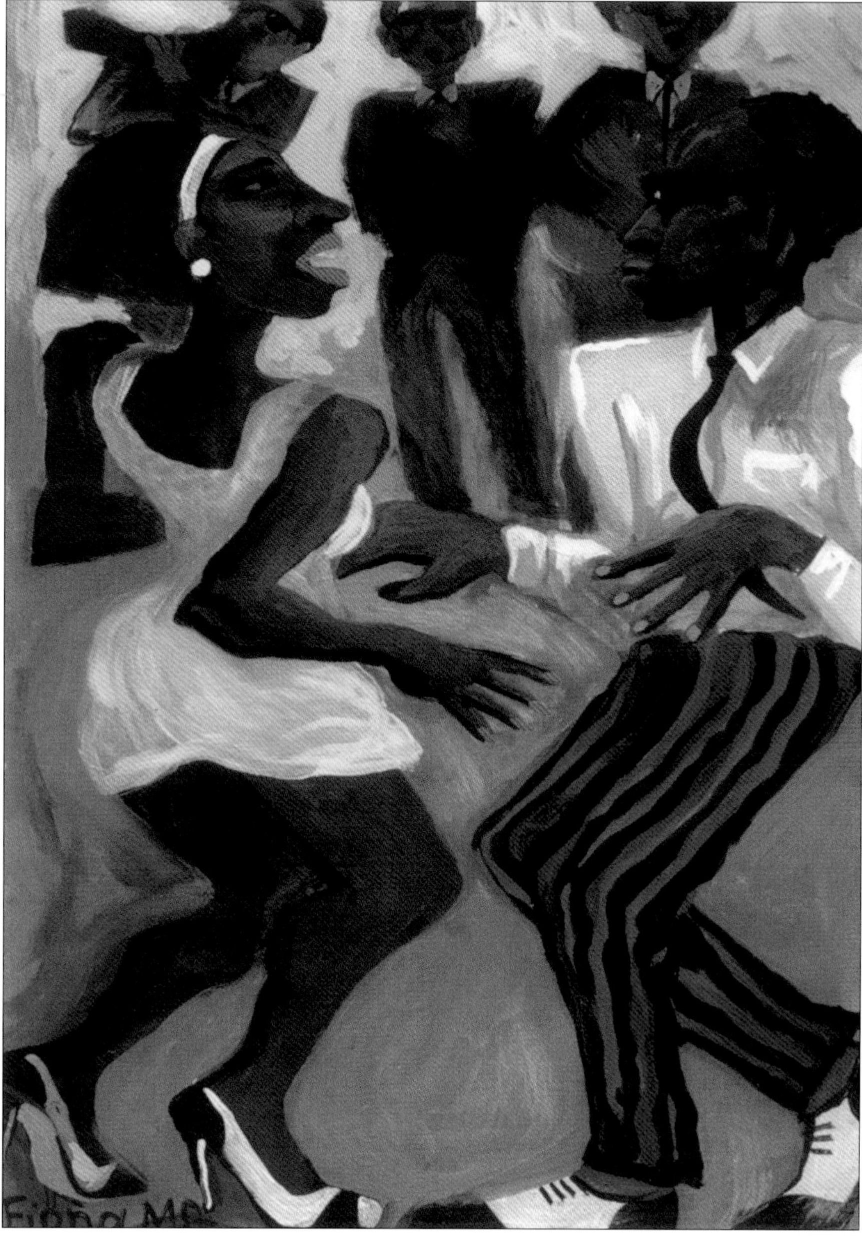

It was the first distinctive style of Jamaican music, synonymous with the proliferation of the island's vast recording industry. Created at the time of imminent independence from Britain, which was achieved in 1962, the music reflected the concerns and aspirations of a hardworking, proud and now liberated people.

"Ska, Ska, Ska, Jamaican Ska", a 12-bar blues shuffle accented on the second and fourth beats and a syncopated after beat provided by the guitar and piano, received its name from the skat, skat, skat sound of the guitar. Ska recordings ranged from the outrageous "El Pussycat"(never failing to elicit a synchronized "meow" from frenzied dancers) to the burgeoning early 60s Rastafarian fervor expressed on tracks named "Addis Ababa" and "Lion of Judah". Timeless ska instrumentals such as "Eastern Standard Time", "Rockfort Rock" and "The Guns of Navarone", indelibly etched into the collective subconscious of all Jamaican music lovers, seem to have always existed but it was 40 years ago when this enigmatic beat was born in economically depressed areas of Jamaica's capital city, Kingston.

Ska arose out of the need of sound systems (mobile discos) to find music suitable to the tastes of their patrons. Sound systems first appeared in Kingston in the late 1940s, bringing recorded music to those who couldn't afford to attend the live dance band sessions which were the rage of the era. Each sound employed a "selector" spinning records including indigenous Jamaican mento (folk music), Trinidadian calypso, Cuban rhumbas and especially American rhythm and blues, which Jamaicans had become acquainted with through (weather permitting) radio signals from Miami and New Orleans; these bawdier styles of music were preferred over the bland pop broadcast on the island's radio stations.

Competitive sound system owners would frequently travel to the American south in search of R&B 45's that had yet to be heard in Jamaica. Once these 45's were acquired, the selector would scratch off the record's label, concealing its identity because the "sound" with the broader collection of exclusive music was assured greater popularity.

In the late 1950s, as American musical tastes shifted from rhythm and blues to rock and roll, sound system operators experienced a shortage of music suitable for their clientele. Ever resourceful, these sound men—foremost among them the late Duke Reid (whose sound system was called "The Trojan"); Clement Dodd ("Sir Coxsone's Downbeat"); and Prince Buster ("Voice Of The People")—became producers, bringing Jamaican singers and musicians into local recording studios (circa 1957) and creating the shuffling rhythm and blues required to retain their audiences. It was Buster, lacking the funds to travel to America, who realized the success of the island's music depended on it sounding "more Jamaican". Jamaican session musicians slowly began altering the structure of R&B and these adjustments gave birth to ska. What distinguished ska from its American correlate was the incorporation of indigenous Jamaican elements: the banjo strumming of mento, the hand clapping of the revival church, the cadence of the Rastafarian "funde" drum, (all of which emphasize the offbeat) and the Latin influence from nearby Cuba. The powerful product of impoverished innovations, ska provided a voice for the shantytown dwellers and therefore was dismissed by local media. Thus, the evolution of ska was documented (some years later) primarily from the musicians and producers who were able to relate their experiences and of course, from the genre's substantial musical legacy.

It has been suggested that Coxsone Dodd encouraged guitarist Ernie Ranglin, (renowned jazz artist and a cornerstone of Jamaica's early recording scene) to emphasize the upbeat of the shuffle; however, it is drummer Lloyd Knibb (who played on most of the Jamaican recordings between 1962 and 1966) who is credited with giving ska its distinctive beat. Before Knibb, prominent drummers of the era, Arkland "Drumbago" Parks and Carlos Malcolm were bringing their kick drum down on the first beat; Knibb coupled the kick drum and the snare on the third beat and emphasized the change by dropping rimshots on the downbeat.

The Skatalites, a seminal dance band whose members doubled as studio musicians, can be heard playing on most of the significant Jamaican recordings of the 1960s (and on earlier recordings when several Skatalites were part of the band Clue J and the Blues Blasters). Formed in 1964, the influence of the Skatalites's recordings continues to this day, an incredible achievement considering they were only together for 14 months! Most of the Skatalites received their formal training at Kingston's Alpha Boys School, an orphanage and home for the underprivileged where music education is strongly emphasized. The group featured Tommy McCook on tenor sax and flute, the late Don Drummond (named by *Downbeat* magazine in 1960 as one of the best trombonists in the world) on trombone; Roland Alphanso on tenor sax; Lester "Ska" Sterling on alto sax; and Johnny "Dizzy" Moore on trumpet. The rhythm section included Lloyd Knibb on drums; Lloyd Brevette on bass; Jerome "Jah Jerry" Haines on guitar; and the signature piano and organ playing of the late Donat "Jackie" Mittoo. The Skatalites also featured four vocalists: Tony Gregory, Calypsonian Lord Tanamo, Doreen Shaffer and Barbados born Jackie Opel.

When the Skatalites disbanded, half the members formed the Soul Brothers and became the house band for Dodd's Studio One label while the remaining members called themselves the Supersonics and went to work for Reid's Treasure Isle label. Dodd produced the Wailers' (Bob Marley, Peter Tosh and Bunny Wailer) biggest ska hits, most notably 1964's "Simmer Down", which urged the "rude boys" to cool their violent ways. Other Studio One ska gems include child star Delroy Wilson's glorious "I Shall Not Remove", Toots and The Maytals' "Six and Seven Books of Moses" and Owen Grey's "On The Beach". Reid's Treasure Isle boasted Derrick Morgan's "Lover Boy", Stranger Cole's "Rough and Tough" and Justin Hinds and the Dominoes' "Carry Go Bring Come" among other ska classics. Other important ska producers included Chinese Jamaican Leslie Kong who enjoyed great success with Jimmy Cliff's "King Of Kings" and Derrick Morgan's (along with Millicent "Patsy" Todd) "Housewife's Choice" while brothers Justin and Duke Yap meticulous studio practices are credited with producing some of the Skatalites' finest instrumentals including "Confucious" and "Chinatown".

The king of ska producers however, was Cecil Bustamante Campbell, better known as Prince Buster. Buster's hits included Derrick Morgan's "Shake A Leg", "Lulu" and Eric Morris' "Humpty Dumpty". Buster also wrote and sang several ska chart toppers including "Madness Is Gladness"; "Wash Wash"; "They Got To Go"; and "Blackhead Chineyman" which initiated a very popular "musical war" with Derrick Morgan.

The organic single track recording process of the late 50s/early 60s with several musicians crowded into a small studio, improvising off of one another's solos and playing to a single microphone created unpredictable magic. "This music had spontaneity," says Chris Wilson of Heartbeat Records, the Cambridge Massachusetts record label responsible for reissuing classics from both Dodd and Reid. "Beyond spontaneity, these are timeless human songs with great feeling." Ska created a worldwide impact in 1964 when "My Boy Lollipop", sung by Millie Small and produced by Ernie Ranglin for Chris Blackwell, sold over 6 million copies and became a pop hit in both America and England. That same year, a ska delegation traveled to the World's Fair in New York City as a Jamaican tourism promotion. Small was the star of this ska entourage which featured Prince Buster, Eric Morris, Jimmy Cliff and Byron Lee and The Dragonaires. (The Wailers were branded as "rude boys", an unfit representation of Jamaican music while The Maytals and the Skatalites were perceived as "too religious", that is, Rastafarian and also unacceptable.)

The beat of Jamaican music slowed down in 1966, the drum and bass came to prominence and rock steady emerged; the shuffling ska beat became dormant in Jamaica, but resurfaced in other locations. In the late 1970s at the height of the UK's punk rock phenomenon, ska's resurgence arrived in the form of predominantly white bands such as the Specials, The Selecter, Madness (named after the Prince Buster hit) and The (English) Beat. England's top punk bands (the Clash, the Sex Pistols, etc.) interspersed reggae throughout their frenetic sets while English reggae bands (Steel Pulse, the Cimarrons, Aswad etc.) often shared concert bills with punk bands. These very disparate musical styles overlapped in their uncompromising lyrical assaults against the system (Steel Pulse's "Handsworth Revolution", Clash's "Guns of Brixton"), but overall they remained separate cultural and musical entities; attempting to find common ground brought about the creation of 2-Tone Records by one of the Specials' founding members, Jerry Dammers. "Our original intention was to find a midway point between reggae and punk," recalls Dammers, "but no matter how we approached it, the two styles didn't seem to mix." The solution was to reach back to reggae's roots, ska, and rev up the beat for the late 70s, the perfect complement for punk's combustible energy.

The 2-Tone concept was symbolized by a handsome black and white logo of a "rude boy"(drawn by Dammers, based on a photo of Peter Tosh from his Wailing Wailers days). The 2-Tone band's multi-racial lineups helped to promote unity at a time of heightened racially motivated attacks in England. 2-Tone became an international phenomenon, spawning fashion trends, generating major record label (Chrysalis) distribution and creating similar phenomena throughout Europe, Japan and the United States. This second wave of ska-mania brought the music of Prince Buster, Derrick Morgan, the Skatalites and other Jamaican ska greats to a younger generation of enthusiastic fans. With the demise of 2-Tone around 1986, ska continued, albeit with less fanfare, courtesy of bands such as Bim Skala Bim, the Untouchables, the Toasters and Fishbone. Today, the jazz/mento/ska underpinnings of England's Jazz Jamaica, melded into a style called "Skazz", have popularized very traditional Jamaican sounds throughout Europe but overall, the third wave of ska is physically and culturally miles away from its Kingston ghetto genesis. There are free-style jazz/hip-hop/ska bands, even Christian ska bands; the immensely popular American group The Mighty Mighty Bosstones describe their ska/hardcore/punk style as "Ska-core" while Spanish speaking groups are fusing ska with Latin pop into "Salska". Despite the grafting of various ska hybrids, the music of Prince Buster, Derrick Morgan, the Wailers and most certainly the Skatalites will always remain the root. "Those men made the music which set the foundation," said producer Clive Chin "and no matter what they try, they have to go back to the foundation, to mento and ska where it all started." In other words, "Skauthenticity"!

ORIGINALLY PUBLISHED AUGUST 1998

Byron Lee Thirty Years of Music

MIKE JARRETT

There is one name which will inevitably turn up in most any historical review of the development of Jamaican music. Byron Lee and his band, The Dragonaires have for thirty years been in the forefront of Jamaican music—recording it and playing it.

Journalist Mike Jarrett spoke to Byron Lee in his small, unpretentious office at Dynamic Sounds in the main industrial district of Kingston. This office, Byron said, was once used by Jamaica's present prime minister and former record producer, Edward Seaga. In that interview, on December 4, 1985, Byron Lee recalls highlights of his long career which saw not only the development of one of the region's finest dance bands but the building of one of the Caribbean's leading recording studios.

Mike Jarrett: Tell me, what do you regard as the major landmarks in your long career?

Byron Lee: I would say that this year has been one of our greatest years and we have reached another landmark in 1985. This is because we went to Trinidad (Carnival), played on the road alongside the top Trinidad bands in the road march. That in itself is a milestone... to allow a foreign band to come in and play with that select group of musicians in their biggest festival... that road march... we came out with honours.

In fact, when we passed through the Savannah, which is the judges' centre, Queens Park, and we said "Greetings from Jamaica", the entire stand rose with applause. It was something you'd have to see. And when you understand that they have never entertained a foreign band in that their major festival, it made us feel very proud.

We also went on a 26-city tour this year, which took us to places we had never been to before. Vancouver on the west coast of Canada, Calgary. In the United States we went to cities like Dallas, among others.

We were playing a Caribbean music, reggae but not just reggae. We were calling ourselves and advertising ourselves as a Caribbean aggregation.

MJ: Yours has been a long career, Byron.

BL: When I started in 1956, those were the days in Jamaica of great musicians, like Mapletoft Poulle, Graydon, Lennie Hibbert, Roy White, Sonny Bradshaw...it was the last days of the big band sound. Sound systems were taking over.

But I've always said that the band that I was most influenced by locally was a band led by Tony Brown. He had in his aggregation Ernie Ranglin.

On the other hand however, I was watching in the movies (rock & roll) bands like Bill Haley and the Comets, Little Richard. The Elvis Presley, twanging electric guitar era...it was just coming on.

It dazzled me. Not the old time sitting and playing, reading music sheets, straight up thing anymore. It had movement, sound, action. People were throwing the microphones around. Lighting.

I was, also influenced by people like Bill Doggett, Ernie Freeman.

At the same time we had the soul music thing like Sam Cooke, Jerry Butler, the Drifters, Ben E. King. And it was records that was creating that sound, not live music.

So I decided to buy myself a bass guitar... I think it must have been the first bass guitar to come into the Caribbean...

We started to play. House parties first. I was on the football team at St. George's College and that year we won three cups... that was the year of Carl Largie, Ken East, myself, Frank Watkins, Bobby Williams. And we used to celebrate at Emmet Park downstairs. That's how the band started.

MJ: And the name Dragonaires?

BL: Well, 'aire' is for music and the dragon came from the crest of St George's College, you know, St. George and the dragon. That was in 1956-57.

MJ: So what were your first engagements like?

We used to ring people and offer to play at house parties. They would say 'which band you have. Y'crazy. How much y'charge?' We'd say we don't charge, just some sandwiches. We used to be the intermission between recorded music.

After that we started playing for school graduations, anniversaries, fund-raisers.

Out of that we decided to go professional. That meant we had to set up ourselves properly, take on new equipment, adopt a professional attitude.

And that's how we started to play. Little by little we got into it. And Ronnie Nasralla and myself made a vow. At that time it was (on the marquee) 'Glass Bucket' in letters, little 'Ivor Graydon'; big, big 'Buccaneer Club', little 'Roy Cockbourne', big, big 'Bournemouth', a little 'Tony Brown'. I said no, no. We going' turn it around and put big Byron Lee and the Dragonaires and a little 'Glass Bucket' or 'Sombrero'.

MJ: Did that change anything?

BL: Well, right after that you had Kes Chin and the Souvenirs, the Vagabonds, Carlos Malcolm and the Afro-Jamaican Rhythms, the Skatalites, Granville Williams Orchestra, Lyn Taitt and the Jets, Tomorrow's Children, the Virtues, the Sheiks.... it was like a band explosion which took place.

MJ: Your band was also prominent in early attempts to put Jamaican music on the international music scene.

BL: Yes. A lot of people don't really realise that we actually helped, 'cause when Seaga (i.e. Edward Seaga, now prime minister) was minister of development and welfare in the sixties... but first let me go further back. He used to sit in this office here y'know. He built this place. He started West Indies Records. It was a little small then, just this front building.

So this is how I met him. The band used to play at Club Aleef, the Syrian club 'round by Derrymore Road and Joan Seaga, his sister, used to put on her fashion parade. And he came in as the MC, coat and carnation y'know.

So we are there playing 'Dumplin's. Afterwards he said he liked that tune and asked why we didn't record it. He invited us down to his offices... I didn't know he was in the recording business... he said come down and see him next week. So we came down here and he suggested that we record the tune down at RJR (radio station.)

MJ: That song was 'Dumplin's'?

BL: Yes, the first locally recorded song to reach number one on the local hit parade.

So we signed a contract with Eddie and after that we came out with a tune called 'Firefly jump-up'. That was recorded and mixed at JBC

(the other radio station) which Buddy Davidson, producer, mixed for us. He was at JBC. He used to sing in the band. He was the lead singer.

Then in 1962 (the year of Jamaica's Independence) he called me and Carlos... that time Carlos (Malcolm) and me licking hot now... Seaga said he wanted a sound which would be our national sound. Carlos did a lot of work with the mento... Rukumbine and all that. Seaga was interested in developing the ska which was being played in East Kingston.

MJ: That time, as I recall, ska was not really being played on the airwaves. It was really considered poor music from poor people.

BL: Yes. But he said go down there and bring it up town. Remember also it was his constituency down there.

So we went down there one night. I went down with Sammy Ismay (saxophonist), Ken Lazarus (guitarist and vocalist), Keith Lyn (vocalist) we all went down to Chocomo Lawn (one of Kingston's legendary dance halls out of which Jamaica's popular music form evolved) at Wellington Street.

When I looked at the people dancing this music...'Wash Wash,' with Prince Buster, music by Eric 'Monty' Morris, Stranger Cole, Jimmy Cliff. I marvelled, man. A great deal was happening in the music. I listened.

MJ: So you found something to take uptown?

Ronnie Nasralla worked up some simple choreographed steps and we decided to market the music. We were a little worried because the music still wasn't accepted uptown.

We put up posters with pictures of the whole band with "Ska Goes Uptown." We charged five shillings a head to go in.

More than 2,000 people turned up the night. We nearly dropped dead!

MJ: So when then did you go into the calypso music?

BL: Now that started when we went to Trinidad and we heard Sparrow's 'Dan Is The Man In The Van', 'Elaine, Harry and mamma' and songs like those. And we heard the motorcar brake drum...'the iron'... being used and we brought that (sound) back to Jamaica. That was in 1964. That simple instrument made the sound here for us. It gave us a trade-mark sound.

We took the iron from Trinidad but... we took our style as a show band there... musicians moving and swinging together, stopping together, flashing lights, that type of thing.

MJ: So when did you start building Dynamic Sounds?

BL: Towards the late sixties, 1966....one night we played at Club Maracas on the north coast and rains came and washed us out. We were playing for the gate (money). That turned into a two week rainy spell and for that period the band did not work. I said to myself: 'What kind of business this? When rain fall we don't work. Nobody gets paid.'

So we decided to build a studio on these premises. That time West Indies Records was still in the front building, but with George Benson (no relation to the jazz guitarist) and Bunny Rae in charge.

Later Johnny Nash came in and did 'Hold Me Tight' in that studio. He was the first foreign artiste to use our facilities.

By 1967, (the Mighty) Sparrow and myself did our first recording here, first album, called 'Sparrow Meets The Dragon'. That was on three tracks... two track stereo for the rhythm tracks and the voice on one.

Then there was a fire here. The property went up for auction and we consolidated our position here.

I was by then being handed the Atlantic label by the president of Atlantic, which did the *'Ska, Ska, Ska'* album.

MJ: It was then that you expanded the studio?

BL: Yes. We were told that if we set up an 8-track studio we would get foreign artistes interested in recording in Jamaica.

We did and Paul Simon came down and did 'Mother and Child Reunion' right here.

Shortly after that Jimmy Cliff wrote 'Wonderful World, Beautiful People,' and shortly after we did the movie score for *'Harder They Come.'*

MJ: So you were in the movies?

BL: Yes, but I must tell you that the band had previously been involved with another movie, the first Ian Fleming James Bond movie, *Dr. No*, most of which was shot in Jamaica. We were working alongside Ursula Andress and Sean Connery. That was much earlier however, in 1962.

In the early seventies the Rolling Stones came and did their album 'Goat's Head Soup'. Then came Elton John. Then the calls started coming in. We had to build another studio. So by 1973 we had two 16-track studios running.

Cat Stevens came; then the Electra group the Doors; then Roberta Flack came and laid rhythm tracks for body movements...more speaking and rhyming than melodies written down. We have seen a downturn in melodic writings, which suggests to me that there is no inspiration to write these tunes.

Now we are into an era where people rely on hit tracks...say you have a hit record, they take the backing tracks and record over it. So in fact what is happening is that the creative inputs are not as strong and they have taken the easy way out, giving way to a more commercial feel.

Today the industry is struggling to survive. What has made it great is that, still, reggae... Jamaican music, I should say, is popular abroad and getting its market share abroad. Returns are mainly from there. The local returns are nowhere near enough to suffice, considering the kind of outlay you must make to come up with good recordings.

MJ: And the band?

BL: Alright. In that period... the period now Mike, from I974 to 1979, 1980 I devoted myself entirely to work inside this company. So I took a backseat in the band and it did indeed suffer. We lost a little direction.

Those were the roughest days of the band. We lost personnel. Keith Lyn left, Ken Lazarus left, trumpeters left to go away (overseas), drummers left... I had the biggest rotation of drummers because what had happened was people were migrating.

Well, I am now back on the road with my band and I am happy. I feel that is where I belong. I like to see my music out there.

In 1986 I celebrate thirty years on the road. Sparrow gone thirty years in 1986 too and we're planning a big celebration. Me, Sparrow and the Merrymen from Barbados.

During the year we also want to tour the Far East. We have an offer to tour Japan and we are thinking about it. We also have an offer to go to Africa. Well it would be ten cities in Nigeria, Ghana, Cameroons... all through there .

MJ: How do you see the future of Jamaican music?

BL: My heart is still heavy that live music in Jamaica is still in the doldrums. It needs to come out. The young musicians must go out there and form bands and get energetic and people must help.

Inside here, by March, we plan to put in new state-of-the-art (record manufacturing) equipment, which means that we will be abreast with the best of New York City, cutting records as hot and as clean as them.

MJ: So Byron, In your thirtieth year of music things are looking brighter than ever.

BL: I think so.

ORIGINALLY PUBLISHED MAY 1986

The Profound Rhythms of Ernie Ranglin

PATRICIA MESCHINO

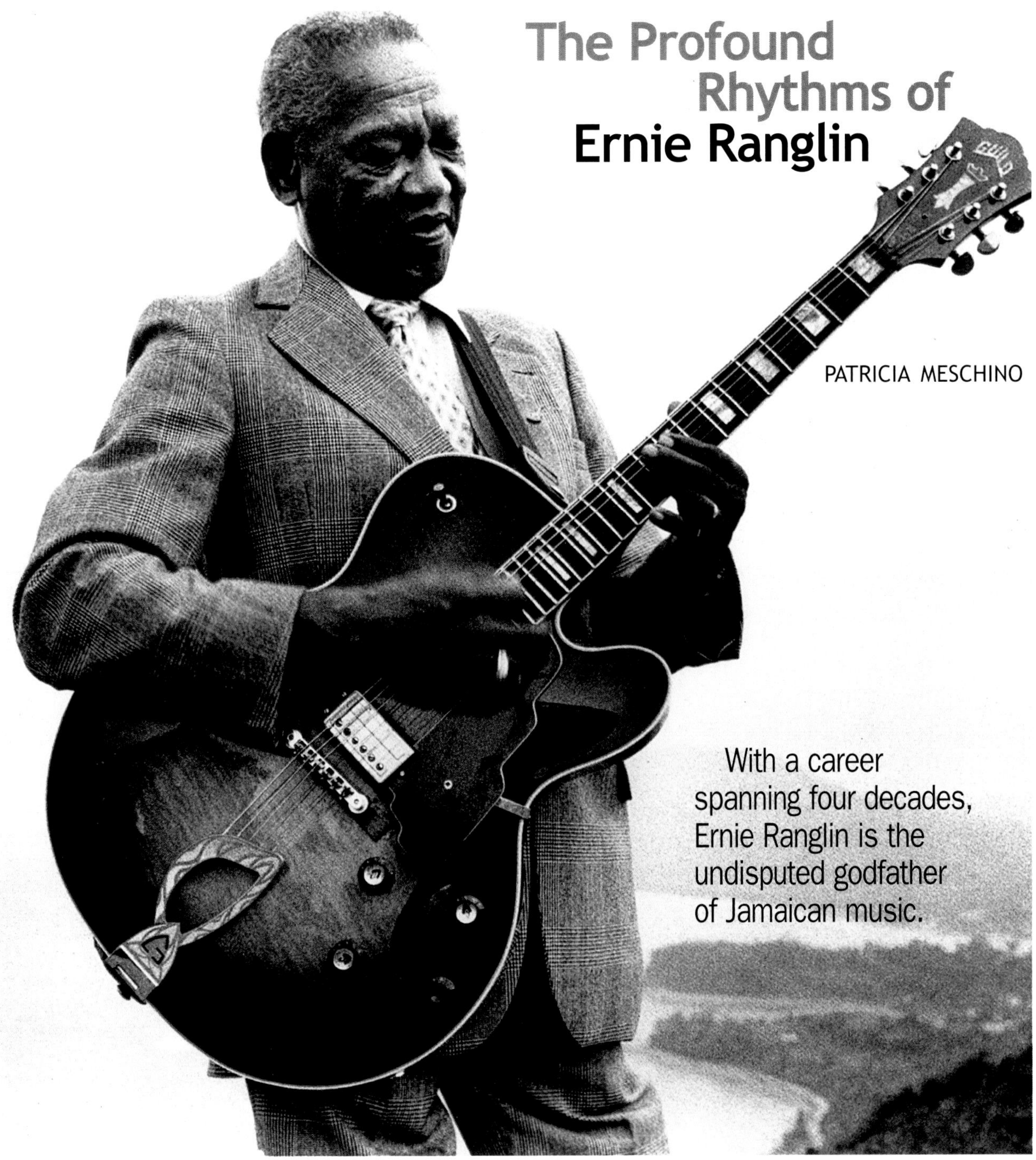

With a career spanning four decades, Ernie Ranglin is the undisputed godfather of Jamaican music.

Ernie Ranglin has played on innumerable recordings in a variety of styles, his nimble guitar wizardry greatly enhancing each effort. Born on June 19, 1932, in the remote district of Harrywatch in the parish of Manchester, Ranglin comes from a family of gifted guitarists; so impressed were his uncles with young Ernie's talents they bought him a ukulele at age four. By age 14, Ranglin's sights were already set on becoming a professional musician so he moved to Jamaica's (music) capital Kingston. Music lessons for Ranglin were primarily derived from guitar instruction books and watching musicians play at the dances which proliferated in the late 40s and early 50s in the economically depressed but musically thriving Kingston communities of Jones Town and Trench Town. Ranglin also played with friends who were attending the Stony Hill and Alpha Boys schools (including future Skatalite, legendary trombonist Don Drummond); he cites Cecil Houdini, an unrecorded Jamaican guitarist with whom he engaged in many long practice sessions, among his greatest early influences. While still a teenager, Ranglin joined the Val Bennett (the renowned Jamaican tenor saxophonist who passed away in 1991) Orchestra, playing a mixed bag of Cuban rhumbas, Broadway show tunes, jazz standards and mento (the Jamaican cousin of calypso) rhythms. Ranglin's outstanding musicianship and versatility was noticed by rival band leaders and by the early 1950s, he was recruited as a member of Jamaica's best known dance band, Eric Dean's Orchestra.

Ranglin was also listening to the Benny Goodman and Lionel Hampton bands where he first heard jazz guitar great Charlie Christian, another important inspiration in the development of Ranglin's style. Other significant influences for Ranglin include Billy Bauer and Lee Konitz, the Red Norvo Trio featuring Tal Farlow and later Barney Kessel and Les Paul. While on tour with Dean's Orchestra in Nassau, Ranglin was given a guitar by Les Paul who enjoyed his performance immensely and today remains among his biggest fans.

Ranglin went on to join the Baba Motta sextet, worked on the Caribbean cruise ship circuit and for a while joined the house band at the Jamaica Broadcasting Company. Shortly thereafter, he launched his solo career, performing at various hotels in Kingston and along Jamaica's north coast resort areas. In 1958, he formed his own group, the Ernie Ranglin Quintet, based at Montego Bay's Half Moon Hotel where he met Chris Blackwell who was developing a label specializing in the music of Jamaica, Island Records. Blackwell offered Ranglin the opportunity to make an instrumental record (with Ranglin on one side and Bermudian pianist Lance Heywood on the other) which became Island Records' inaugural release. Blackwell was so impressed with Ranglin's talents, he made him A&R man and arranger for his fledgling company.

Ranglin admits to having been a 'jazz purist' back then but realizing he had to eat, he journeyed into commercial music. Ska, the popular music of Jamaica in the late 50s through the early 60s, was the island's musicians' interpretation of American R&B which was broadcast in Jamaica (weather permitting) from radio signals originating in Miami and New Orleans; seasoned veterans like Ranglin became invaluable to Kingston's burgeoning recording scene. It has been suggested that Coxsonne Dodd, a major producer of the ska era with whom Ranglin worked extensively, encouraged Ranglin to emphasize the upbeat of the popular shuffle rhythm into a Jamaican boogie; the word ska was coined by musicians to describe the guitar's skat, skat, skat strum.

"In those days, we were listening to Bill Doggett, Louis Jordan, those guys who used to play shuffling rhythms," recalls Ranglin, amiably answering questions in the New York offices of Palm Pictures, Chris Blackwell's newly launched entertainment company. The silver-haired Ranglin exudes the warmth of a seldom seen but well-loved uncle or grandfather, his eyes twinkling gleefully even when recounting career lulls and scant financial remuneration despite myriad recording sessions. Ranglin consistently exhibits a humility refreshingly incongruous to his vast musical achievements. "We were trying to play in the same style but make it something different," he continued, "so I tried to put some jazz influence into it, to take it a step further."

Ranglin's diversity has graced several significant ska recordings, in particular, arranging and playing lead guitar on the Wailers' classic rude boy anthem, "Simmer Down." He also provided the somber guitar solos on the Wailers' "It Hurts To Be Alone" and "I'm Still Waiting". The Wailers weren't initially aware of Ranglin's stellar reputation but it wasn't long before Bob Marley became so enamoured with Ranglin's skills, he offered him a lifetime job as his teacher and musical director; due to other commitments, Ranglin was unable to accept the offer.

Chris Blackwell brought Ranglin and a little known teenaged singer named Millie Small to London in 1964 to record "My Boy Lollipop". The song's phenomenal success, earning the number two spot on the UK pop charts and selling seven million copies worldwide, brought ska to an international audience. The same year, Ranglin was voted Best Jazz Guitarist by England's Melody Maker Magazine and he did a nine month residency at London's prestigious Ronnie Scott's jazz club.

Ranglin went on to play guitar on the first reggae record, Toots and the Maytals' "Do The Reggae" among other classic Jamaican tracks and has recorded several critically acclaimed solo jazz albums. His celebrated 1996 *Below The Bassline* highlighted by fluid interpretations of cultural reggae anthems such as the Congo's "Congo Man Chant", The Abyssinians "Satta Amasagana" and Burning Spear's "Black Disciples" coupled with his own compositions "Surfin" and the title track introduced Ranglin's talents to a new generation of listeners while reacquainting him with long time fans in both the jazz and reggae communities. *Below The Bassline* was the inaugural release for Blackwell's Island Jamaica Jazz imprint.

While on tour in Africa with Jimmy Cliff in 1976, Ranglin met an unknown Senegalese singer named Baba Maal. Some 20 years later, Maal has emerged as the west African nation's premier entertainer and his *Nomad Soul* release, along with Ranglin's superb *In Search Of The Lost Riddim* are the debut releases for Blackwell's Palm Pictures. Ranglin returned to Senegal in 1997 to record *Riddim* with a host of Africa's top musicians including Maal, Mansour Seck on guitar and vocals and the remarkable vocal magic of fourteen year old female singer Cisse Daimba Kanoute. "I had always hoped to make a record in Africa, but it was a question of finding the time," explains Ranglin. "The music I have played over many years has shown me the connection to Africa, whatever style, jazz or reggae, the rhythms flow from the motherland."

The polyrhythmic drum patterns opening 'D' accord Dakar' commences *Riddim* musical odyssey, a journey as complex and culturally diverse as Africa itself. The reggae tinged "Nuh True", the energetic "Up On The Downstroke" and the stunning instrumental "Pili Pili", all written by Ranglin, concoct an intoxicating brew of jazz intuition, African tradition and Caribbean pop. Ranglin adopts a lilting, nearly classical approach on "Anna" and like finely cut crystal, his sensitive touch on "Midagny" gracefully reflects then offers a shimmering response to Seck's incandescent vocals. "Cherie", composed by Maal, features time honored percussion patterns embellished by Ranglin's kaleidoscopic melodies while Maal's vocals on "Minuit" resonate with the passion of African ancestors, stirred by Ranglin's nuanced textures and technique.

The sole accompaniment to Ranglin's astonishing guitar work here, perhaps the finest of his recording career, are traditional African acoustic instruments: The kora, a large hollowed gourd covered with cowhide, akin to a west African harp lute; the hoddu, a lute with three to five strings, considered the African ancestor of the banjo and sabar drums carved from hardwood, covered with goatskins and fastened with large wooden pegs; the djembe, west Africa's most recognizable drum and the tama, an hourglass shaped instrument also known as the talking drum.

Ranglin's Midas touch, honed over decades of varied musical experiences, sometimes gently floating above the percussive accompaniment, other times directly responding to the compelling vocals, seamlessly weaves *Riddim's* disparate elements into a delicately shaded, multicultural fabric.

According to Ranglin, the approach to making *Lost Riddim* was improvisational, with the musicians living as one extended family, engaging in one extended jam. Ranglin absorbed the surroundings and the rhythms then added his own impressions. "It was an experience I hope to have again," he says. "I felt immediately at home and I know that comes across in the music".

Whatever directions Ranglin chooses throughout his latest musical odyssey, in fact, throughout his entire career, his "riddims" are never, ever lost but consistently profound, following the right path, effortlessly connecting one musical destination in the African diaspora with another.

ORIGINALLY PUBLISHED FEBRUARY 1999

Stepping Razor

The Genius of Peter Tosh

OMAR DAVIES

COURTESY OF ©SONY RECORDS

Just over nine years ago violence silenced the voice of one of reggae's greatest artistes, Peter Tosh, christened Hubert McIntosh. Peter had a long history in the music business and his career went through many phases. He, along with Bob Marley and Bunny Wailer, were founding members of the Wailers, which to many students of Jamaican music made the greatest contribution to the development of popular music in Jamaica. Unlike Bob, Peter's music has never received the acclaim it deserves, and his forthright advocacy of the legalization of marijuana brought him into conflict with local authorities.

I have always found an attempt to compare the relative merits of Peter, as opposed to Bob or Bunny, to be a pointless exercise, as each in his own way made a monumental contribution to the music. First, there was Bob, the most prolific writer, initially of love songs and exhortations to dance and then later, as his horizons broadened, of songs of protest. Bunny, for me, was the mystic, with whom I will always associate the classic, "Dreamland." Then there was Peter, with the most powerful voice, and always the militant from the early days when he did a version of "Go Tell It On The Mountain." He was also the most accomplished musician of the three.

The early years of the Wailers demonstrated their attempts to simultaneously develop their own style, as well as to copy the stylings of American singing groups. In that regard, Curtis Mayfield and the Impressions had a profound impact on them. During that period, even whilst they recorded together, they each released singles for which each was primarily responsible with the other two providing harmony. From Peter, we had classics such as "Once Bitten, Twice Shy," "Funeral" (later re-recorded as "Burial"), "Stepping Razor" (written by Joe Higgs and later re-recorded for the *Equal Rights* album), "Mawga Dog", "Ha Fi Get a Beaten" and "Mark of the Beast". One cannot forget "Can't Blame the Youth" which inexplicably he never re-recorded. During these years, the group put out three albums—*The Wailing Wailers*, *Soul Rebel* and *Soul Revolution II*. The latter two were produced in collaboration with Lee "Scratch" Perry.

The signing with Chris Blackwell and Island Records in 1972 brought the Wailers great opportunities and exposure, but led, almost inevitably, to the disintegration of the group. The two Island albums, on which all three performed, were not commercially successful, but served as the launching pad for Bob's solo career, as the music world became aware of this "breath of fresh air" from this unique group. Whilst Bob dominated the first two albums, the cuts which were Peter's were reflective of what would continue to be dominant features of his lyrics; the fight against exploitation, and his call for unity among oppressed persons. Hence, "Stop That Train," "Four Hundred Years" lamenting the plight of blacks 400 years after slavery had been abolished, and "One Foundation." However, the most impressive output from that period was the song "Get Up, Stand Up," co-written with Marley which has become an anthem for protest groups worldwide.

By 1974, both Peter and Bunny had gone

on their own. Many of us lamented this development at first. However, the separation brought an unprecedented outpouring of creativity as the talent of each of the three was allowed unrestrained growth, even while reflecting their common roots. I feel that the three, individually and collectively, contributed as much to pop music as a more renowned group—the Beatles. Bob's development as a solo artist is well documented as he became and remains one of the pre-eminent stars in the history of pop music. The fact is that Peter's output deserves far more acclaim than it has received and this article is an attempt to bring some attention to the efforts of his prodigious talent.

His first solo album, *Legalise It* was done for Atlantic. It reflected a theme which he pursued to his death—that marijuana be legalised. The album was adequate but not outstanding, although it demonstrated the wonderful harmonization between Peter and Bunny on cuts such as "When the Well Runs Dry". The second and last album for Atlantic, *Equal Rights* remains to me the finest reggae album ever made. There is simply no bad cut on it; in fact, there are perhaps too many good songs. After nearly 20 years of listening to it I still have difficulty in deciding which is my favourite piece although the screaming lead guitar on "Stepping Razor" still gives me a thrill. At the same time the deep bass line and the stuttering organ on the title track, "Equal Rights" with Tosh in a relaxed vocal mood, must not be under-estimated. But where do you rank "African" which has inspired so many in their search for their heritage? Or where do you put the assertive "I Am That I Am"? If you have never listened to this album, you owe it to yourself to spend 45 minutes doing so. I am convinced that you will come away totally captivated by Tosh's lyrics, vocal talents and equally by the tightness of his backing band.

After these two initial albums with Atlantic, Tosh signed with Rolling Stones Records and this gave rise to two albums: *Bush Doctor* and *Mystic Man*. This period was characterized by two important developments. The first was the formation of Tosh's backing group Word, Sound and Power including Sly Dunbar, Robbie Shakespeare and Mickey Chung, together with the Tamlins on backing vocals. The second development was an increased number of live performances. On their best night, there was no better live act in music at that stage.

During that period there was collaboration with Mick Jagger and Keith Richards, with Jagger sharing lead vocals on "Don't Look Back" and Richards playing guitar on various cuts. Of note in this period were the reggae-disco hit "Buckingham Palace," the chest-beating "I'm the Toughest" (an adaptation of the old hit by James and Bobby Purify, "I'm Your Puppet") and a personal favourite, the hymn-like "Jah Seh No."

Following this period with Rolling Stones records, Tosh moved to EMI and this led to four albums: *Wanted, Dread & Alive, Mama Africa, Captured Live* and *No Nuclear War*. There are several classic hits from this era but one remains a favourite of mine: "Rastafari Is." It was done originally for *Wanted: Dread & Alive* and redone live on *Captured Live*. This cut combines reggae rhythms, Nyabinghi drumming with a blues-rock guitar with amazing results. In fact, "Rastafari Is" indicates how true rastas are able to combine their enjoyment of music with the worship of the Creator, without falling prey to the false divisions which inhibit more traditional believers.

Whilst Tosh's recordings remain with us, to me his greatest talent was demonstrated in his stage appearances. I have already made reference to the tight aggregation which he put together as Word, Sound and Power. However, perhaps because of his great music talent, even when he lost Sly, Robbie and Mickey Chung, and they were replaced by lesser lights, he was able to harness new people into an aggregation which seemed to give nothing away in a comparison with the original group. In terms of his live performances, his greatest attribute was the element of surprise. You never knew how he would make his entrance; you never knew how he would be dressed; you never knew what new arrangements he would try; but lastly, you never knew what he would say.

Among his live shows, which I had the privilege of witnessing, three confirmed in my mind Tosh's greatness as a stage performer. The first was the Peace Concert held at the National Stadium in 1978, where he not only gave a scintillating performance, but lectured the huge crowd, including the prime minister and the leader of the opposition, on the social ills afflicting the country. At first, I was angry at his outburst, but two questions from a friend silenced me. First, what had he said which was not true? Second, if Tosh did not raise these questions, who would?

The second was at the first Reggae Sunsplash, held in Kingston in 1980. For some reason there was a delay in bringing Tosh on stage and so the crowd became restive. However, in addition, Sly and Robbie, together with most of Tosh's band, Word, Sound and Power, had backed most of the preliminary groups, including Black Uhuru and the Tamlins. I had become somewhat bored with the sameness of the band's playing, and so I worried that Tosh's performance would seem like a continuation of what had gone before. How pleasantly surprised were we! When Tosh came on stage, the band took on a totally different sound and he proceeded to give a performance such as we had never seen before from a Jamaican artiste.

The third great local performance, turned out to be his final one in Jamaica. This was in December of 1983 at the Pulse's Super Jam concert. Among the preliminaries were Gregory Isaacs and the Skatalites. Following these acts, there was a lengthy band change made worse by the fact that Tosh's lead guitarist was nowhere to be found. Tosh came on stage after midnight to what was initially a sullen and unresponsive gathering. After about three songs, he had us eating out of his hands. Many would have been well satisfied if he had stopped after five songs. But he went on and on, prancing, playing the congos and his custom built guitar. It was the total performance and it is one that anyone who was present, still talks about to this day.

With time, as his records are listened to and younger artistes get tuned in to his music, Tosh will receive his due credit which, by and large, has not been given to date. His achievements were not due solely to his god-given capabilities but also to the work he put in as a musician. Allan "Skill" Cole, Bob Marley's friend and confidante, and now coach of the Arnett Gardens football team, the area where the Wailers grew up, has told me that in his assessment, Tosh's greatness lay in his skill as a musician. "Skill" says that Peter could play any instrument he put his hand on. In a letter to me in the mid 70s, Peter indicated that no less a star than Eric Clapton had asked him to tour with him and teach him to play the reggae rhythms. Few people know that Tosh played guitar on the Eric Gale Album, *Negril*.

I have deliberately tried not to engage in the useless comparison with Bob or Bunny, but simply to encourage those who may not have seriously listened to Tosh to begin to do so. If you are totally new to his music, I recommend that you start by getting a copy of the album *Equal Rights*. I guarantee that after listening to it, you will be hooked for life. In any event, I have learnt that within the next few months, two new box sets featuring Peter's music will be released worldwide.

Perhaps the music world is belatedly coming to acknowledge the talent of one of its real geniuses—Peter Tosh.

ORIGINALLY PUBLISHED APRIL 1997

Giving Thanks and Praise

OMAR DAVIES

Most readers will be familiar with the music of Bob Marley and to a lesser extent that of his fellow founding members of the Wailers, the late Peter Tosh and the sole surviving member of the original group, Bunny Wailer. However, very few would be acquainted with a particular aspect of their musical output—their songs of praise. The fact is that these three musical geniuses, initially as a group, and later as solo artistes produced an amazing body of religious music which has received very little recognition.

I have become very interested in this area of the group's output for two reasons. The first is that, as a fan of the Wailers, individually and collectively, I have a deep appreciation for all their music. In the second place, sometime ago, when I was writing an article on the work of Tosh, I devoted some attention to an analysis of his "songs of praise." Once my interest was aroused, it struck me that there was need for work on the similar output from Bob Marley and Bunny Wailer, as well as that of the original group.

The first set of religious songs by the Wailers are versions of traditional Negro spirituals and hymns. The lead in these songs is carried mainly by Bob or Peter, although Bunny is featured as back up vocalist and later on in his classic album *Blackheart Man*, he does perhaps the best version of "This Train".

I do know how the songs which they covered were selected but the influence of the Pentecostal Church is evident in Bob's version of "Wings of a Dove" and "Nobody Knows the Troubles I Have Seen". However, also interesting are the versions of "The Lord Will Make a Way Somehow" and "Let the Lord be Seen in You". Peter's contribution in this early period included "Amen" and a strident version of "Go Tell it on the Mountain".

"This Train" was obviously a favourite of the group. There is Bunny's interpretation on his *Blackheart Man* album and there are several other versions with which I am acquainted, including one recorded in Sweden by Marley where he accompanied himself on acoustic guitar. Yet another twist is added when he uses "This Train" as the take-off to create "Where is My Mother?"

The final song from this grouping worth mentioning is "Sinner Man", initially recorded by Peter and Bunny. Over time, this song reflected not only progression in Peter's musical ability but the changes in his socio-political view of who was the "Sinner Man".

It is not possible to definitively address the temporal sequencing of the various recordings of songs of praise made by the Wailers. Nonetheless one can clearly identify a set of cover versions as opposed to a collection of songs which were adapted, secular to religious and religious to secular, whereby members of the group modified a basic melody or set of lyrics for the purpose of advancing a particular message.

The first example indicates how a traditional English song—"London is Burning"—was used by the three members of the group in two diametrically different ways. Bob took the melody and added to it the lyrics in praise of marijuana to create "Kaya". Either the original adaptation or the updated version, which was the title track of one of his Island album is a classic. Interestingly, the same melody was used by the group, but by drawing on the concept of the fire "consuming" London, a new song is created. There are two versions. On the first, "Fire, Fire", Peter takes the lead and although there is an implicit reference to a day of reckoning, it is not clear who stands in judgement. The second version, "Love Fire", is by Bunny and in it he proclaims "Jah Love is Like a Burning Fire". The adaptation by Bunny so impressed the British group, Simply Red, that they demonstrated the most sincere form of flattery by imitating Bunny, breath by breath, in their own cover version of his recording. I have often wondered whether the members of Simply Red know the origins of the song.

For the Negro spiritual "Sinner Man" there is another interesting evolution and adaptation. The first step in the process was the cover version by Peter and Bunny. This was followed by the change when the object of derision and condemnation was no longer the Sinner Man but became the Downpresser Man. The first version of "Downpresser Man", still made reference to him fleeing from the Almighty on Judgement day. The culmination of the adaptation/conversion was a strident protest song against oppression on Tosh's *Equal Rights* album.

The discussion of the way in which the members of the group each modified a song brings into sharp focus their common musical "training" and socialization during their critical formative years. Apart from "This Train" and the varying adaptations of "London is Burning", there are many phrases (several biblical in origin) and ideas which are common to the lyrics of songs each composed following the breakup of the group. Consider, for example, the lines:

"The lips of the righteous teach many
But fools die for the want of wisdom"

They first appear in "Wisdom" a song from their period as a group, with Bob singing lead. They also feature later in Bob's "Stiff Necked Fools" (*Confrontation* album/CD) and Peter's "Fools Die" (*Wanted, Dread and Alive* album/CD), following the breakup of the group.

The third example of adaptation mixed with creativity is Bob's version of the country and western song, "Crying in the Chapel", which was turned into a major hit by Elvis Presley. This song is changed to "Selassie is the Chapel". What is most fascinating about Bob's conversion of a plaintive song into one of praise to Selassie, is that it represents one of the earliest public statements of the group's commitment to the Rastafarian faith. This commitment was to lead to the blossoming of their creative talents and over time yielded some of their more impressive compositions. Research needs to be carried out on the influence of the "Elder" Mortimer Planno, not only in adapting this song, but more generally in developing the theological "reasonings" of the group as they converted to the Rastafarian faith.

One of the earliest examples of original creativity in a song of praise by the Wailers is Bob's "Thank You Lord". It is a beautiful song in which Bob expresses thanks to the Almighty for all the simple blessings. It is an important development of the music of the Wailers in terms of original compositions.

The final example of adaptation/ creativity has assumed larger than life proportions, to the point of being named the song of the 20th century by the BBC. I refer to Marley's adaptation of Curtis Mayfield hit, "People Get Ready" which became "One Love". Hailed internationally as an infectious expression of hope, joy and optimism, the refrain leaves no doubt the basic thrust of the song : "Give thanks and praise to the Lord and feel all right."

The Wailers as a group and individually produced a body of songs, reflecting their deep immersion in the Rastafarian faith and the proclamation of Haile Selassie as the Almighty. The songs which were created in this period must be seen in a context. The period, beginning in the early to mid-sixties, was one during which young people throughout the world were challenging accepted positions of the status quo. In both North America and Western Europe, musicians played a critical role in the challenge. The part played by singers and musicians in the American Civil Rights struggle is worthy of special note. It is during this period that Bob Dylan wrote the classic "Blowing in the Wind." Later on, the protest against America's involvement in the Vietnam War was given musical expression in such songs as John Lennon's "Give Peace a Chance" and his hauntingly beautiful "Imagine".

The spirit of protest was also abroad in Jamaica and the Wailers were prominent in questioning, amongst other aspects of the status quo, the justice and educational systems as well as accepted religious beliefs. A natural extension was an increasingly militant Pan-Africanist stance, extolling black pride and dignity. This Pan-Africanist socio-political position itself complemented their conversion to Rastafarianism which views Haile Selassie as Almighty God. The songs which demonstrate their commitment to the faith amongst the most impressive in the extensive body of compositions by the Wailers. For completeness, "Selassie is the Chapel" is included as well as the early production by Tosh in collaboration with U Roy, entitled "Earth's Rightful Ruler".

Most of these pieces are drawn from the period following the break-up of the original group. One exception is "Rastaman Chant" which was included in their second Island, LP/CD *Burnin'*. Subsequently the compositions are individual pieces with Bob and Peter having the greatest number. There are many classics contained in this grouping. From Bob we have, "Give Thanks and Praise", "Forever Loving Jah" and the musical dismissal of non-believers who questioned the relevance of the Rastafarian faith following Selassie's death—"Jah Live." Finally the reassurance to all Rastafarian believers that in the end, Jah will be waiting "I Know".

It is not possible to comprehensively review all of his religious works of Peter Tosh in praise of Jah but worthy of special mention would be "Igziabeher (Let Jah be Praised)", "Jah Guide", "Create", "Jah Say So" and "Rastafari Is". Bunny was not as prolific as either of his two colleagues but there are also significant songs from his body of compositions, including "Amagideon", from the *Blackheart Man* album.

What is striking about this body of work from the three artistes is that it was presented without apology as a natural part of their repertoire, both in terms of recorded music and in live performances. This is significant for a host of reasons but amongst them is that it is a clear indication of the extent to which they regarded their religious beliefs as an integral part of their being and hence their audiences had to accept them on these terms. This was evident, even from the way in which their stage performances were initiated with greetings in the name of "Jah Rastafari, ever living, ever faithful." Not to be ignored is the fact that their music was changing, reflecting several influences. For one, there was increased exposure internationally to other musicians and musical styles. An additional interesting development was the mixing of the reggae rhythms with the Nyabinghi drumming and the blues guitar riffs of Al Anderson, Junior Marvin and Donald Kinsey. This combination is reflected in tunes like Bob Marley's "Babylon System", "Time Will Tell" and Peter Tosh's "Rastafari Is".

In reflecting on this body of work and its integration in their performances and recordings, it would make them unique amongst international pop artistes. I cannot think of any other groups or individual artistes who unapologetically used their performances, in front of what would be termed secular audiences, to consistently expound their religious faith. What is clear to me is that the message of Rastafari was being presented and taught by the Wailers through their music with uncompromising sincerity.

It somewhat surprising to me that the Christian churches, particularly those in the Caribbean, led by more radical "liberation theologians" have not sought to incorporate adaptations of some of these composition into their worships services. Perhaps the sharpness of the criticism of many traditional Christian beliefs contained in some of these compositions represents too great a barrier to such assimilation.

Whatever the reason, these songs of praise remain a permanent testament to the individual and collective geniuses of these artistes and deserve a greater acknowledgement.

This is an edited version of the paper "Giving Thanks and Praise (The religious music of the Wailers)" presented at the Institute of Jamaica.

ORIGINALLY PUBLISHED AUGUST 2001

On The Road With Bob Marley

DERMOTT HUSSEY

"How can a big music come from a little island?" Not even Bob Marley would have had the answer in 1975, as he was about to give the world some of Jamaica's finest hours.

Never before had a talent, mistakenly called Third World in origin, had so much First World impact. Neville Garrick, graphic artist and designer of several of Marley's important albums, was a member of that great crusade which took Jamaican culture to dimensions a million times greater than its beginnings.

The year was 1975, and in a colonial manor in Kingston, Bob Marley and a backing band with the original name of the Wailers, as well as Neville Garrick, were putting together what Marley had liked to call his army in service of a general. The ghetto had crossed the border uptown. In the sprawling yard, Marley was surrounded by musicians and brethren who had found a resting place from the tribalism of the ghetto. Youths from warring political factions could find relative safety in the yard, teaming with excitement, football and music.

Dermott Hussey: As you embarked on the Natty Dread tour, did Bob have any idea of how it was going to be, or was he feeling his way?

Neville Garrick: He was feeling his way. He was always sure he could increase his audience, but his whole thing was that he was carrying this message of Rastafari to the people. I think that was his driving force, even moreso than the music. At that time he was young and bubbling and enthusiastic, really going more on the attack. I always felt him to be a man with a mission, more than a man waiting to see something happening.

One of the first concerts we did was the Schaefer Music Festival in Central Park. It was crowd of about 15,000 people. I was amazed. Bob stole the show. I think it was the show that really launched Bob Marley in America, because we were doing small gigs on that tour.

(TOP LEFT) On stage in the foreground with sons Stephen and Ziggy. (ABOVE AND AT RIGHT) Portraits of Bob Marley candid and in concert.

Everywhere we performed, was sold out. The following year when we came back to the Roxy in Los Angeles with the Rastaman Vibration album tour, the celebrities came out. When I checked backstage, the Rolling Stones couldn't get in. In the audience there were people like Bob Dylan, Stevie Wonder, Herbie Hancock, George Harrison, Ringo Starr, Dr. John and Billy Preston. I came backstage and found them in the dressing room. The next day, the *Los Angeles Times* said "Bob Marley has arrived".

DH: Did the European leg of the Natty Dread tour have the same kind of reception?

NG: In Europe, the response was always 25% more than the US audience. I remember in Norway, and that might have been a later tour, possibly 1978, people stood up in the rain for Bob's longest concert ever, which was about three hours, until we literally ran out of music. When Bob played the Lyceum on that same Natty Dread tour, there were so many people that the London Fire Brigade had to hose people off the theatre door.

DH: In Jamaica Bob had pretty much led his own life, on his own time. How much did that alter once he was on tour?

NG: Well Bob was a man, whether people knew it or not, who dealt with discipline. He had an army side of him. He dealt with touring in a very disciplined way, more than a fun way. Before we went on tour, we would be running for at least 3 months, just getting ourselves physically conditioned. He carried that right through to the point where he took a cook on tour with him. Rehearsals, sound checks, getting to the venues on time...those were the things that he focused on. It was fun, but it was business as well. What the gate receipts were, he would check with the road manager. He always kept abreast, like the general really running the show. Bob liked to get information, he was a man who never liked you to come around him and have nothing to say. He also liked to write on tour. In the early days we did a lot of touring by bus, so when we spent three or five hours on a bus, he would play dominoes or sing or read his bible. I know he made quite a few songs, or even lines from songs on the bus. I found him to be a perfectionist in terms of what he was carrying to the people on tour. He treated every audience like a brand new audience who had never seen him before, even if he came to that city six times. I heard him say to people in the band that musicians were in the audience so don't play off key. He was playing it so fine tuned that he wanted all his musicians to be correct.

DH: Audiences were in awe of him, but how was the press responding to him then?

NG: It was a breakthrough—the image, dreadlocks, rasta, the rebel...here Bob made his key shots were his interviews. His interviews were so good that they got front page coverage in the music press. He would get most of the covers and two or three pages. What he was talking about, Tom Petty nor any of the guys were saying it. With Bob's whole sense of reasoning. He ended up interviewing most of the interviewers. Bob showed the power of the media, because the media was in love with Bob Marley. He used to say, "If I sell as many records as the amount of pictures taken of me, I'll be a rich man", and laugh while they were taking pictures.

DH: When did things begin to get really large, in terms of multiplying so many times more with larger audiences and so on?

NG: Ironically, that was in 1976 after the attempted assassination. That's the time Cindy (Breakspeare) had won Miss World, and the time when he went to England. Some of the tabloids had linked Cindy to Bob, so he became more of a household name.

The Miss World competition was in November, and the assassination attempt was December 3. We kind of went into hiding because of the whole shooting affair, but by doing so, a whole mystique developed. When Bob was first sighted in London, it was a big rahtid thing. We were in London for about two months keeping it quiet, low profile, and we were in the studio most of the time, but a journalist saw us and she couldn't hide it.

DH: Live at the Rainbow in England in 1977 was one of his most exciting shows. Do you have any special recollections of that concert?

NG: At the first show at the Rainbow, somebody gave Bob a red, green and gold shawl, and I said jokingly "Skipper you should go on stage so". He threw it across his face and the music started du-du-du-dum—we started "Natural Mystic". Now nobody had ever heard "Natural Mystic" because this was off *Exodus*, a brand new album. The whole stage was dark blue. Bob came out, and I hit him just on the head with a spotlight, so it's like you couldn't tell what it was. The place got crazy. "There was a natural mystic blowing in the wind..," and he flashed off the shawl. He went from that in "So Much Things To Say", "Heathen", "Guiltiness", just like it's on the album. The people were dumbstruck, and Bob misread it, but the people were in awe because they had never heard it before. Minds had been blown, so they couldn't react. They clapped but then he called for "Lively Up Yourself", which they loved, and they tore down the whole place.

He was very clever and very conscious of his shows. Once the band settled down, he would soar like a bird, singing lines that he never sang before in a song.

DH: How did audiences in the world at large react to him?

NG: In 1979, we attempted our first world tour by going to the east, Australia, the west coast of the United States, Hawaii, Canada, Europe and ended up in Africa. All his tours had impact, but we had now reached international status. Bob was no longer music news, he was hard news. We went to Japan first, which was really a mind-opener for me. On arriving we had an immediate press conference. They wouldn't even give us a chance to settle in the hotel. From we arrived there was 100 journalists, a big long table with Bob and members of the group, cameras flashing, and everybody sticking their microphones in his face. It was amazing as an onlooker. What I found was that Japanese journalist asked the most important and really relevant questions. The Japanese seemed to focus more on the Rastafarian culture. They asked very searching questions. The concerts were all sold out, and in meeting the Japanese kids and listening to them in the audiences, I realised that these kids learnt English by listening to the songs that they liked. It was a way of them getting interesting in learning English. They could sing the words of the song, but they wanted to know what they meant.

When Bob sang "No Woman No Cry", he could break and just make the audience sing a verse, which he did in phases, because they knew the words to the songs. The response we got from the Japanese, was the best responses we got from a country we only went to once. We went to New Zealand after, and that was another first. This was staged at a race track and we wondered where the stage was going to be. A 40 ft. Mercedes Benz trailer truck drove up, opened its side panels, everything came out on hydraulics, a complete 40 x 30 stage with lights. In less than 3 hours we had a stage ready to go, and we had an audience of about 25,000 people.

DH: Was Australia just as warm?

NG: The response in Australia was overwhelming. In Brisbane a lot of white kids came back to the hotel after the show, the following day to meet Bob. They were spellbound, and stayed for as long as five hours. Others kept coming, and those who came before wouldn't leave, until parents started phoning the hotel looking for their

Chant Down Babylon Coming Home to the Hip Hop Nation

As the 20th century heads for the finish line, and a the dawn of a new millennium, Bob Marley may yet realize his greatest dream, breaking through to black America—a wailing rastaman, challenging his people, however fractious, to unity.

Island Defjam's release of *Chant Down Babylon*, produced by Stephen Marley, and featuring some key songs by his father, interpreted by some of the foremost talent in the hip-hop nation, will bring Marley home.

I believe the message had long been read by urban black America, and white America too, but to what conscious extent, few of us are aware. Indeed, dreadlocks are widely popular, but that may be nothing more than a fashionable trend. In hip-hop, however, he has sainthood. A writer, Tour, in his article in the New York Times "In the End Black Men Must Lead," says "Our path to nationhood has been paved by a handful of fathers: Mohammed Ali with his ceaseless bravado, Bob Marley with his truth telling rebel music, Huey Newton with his bodacious political style, James Brown with his obsession with funk".

"Play I on the R&B
Want all my people to see
We bubbling on the top 100
Just like a mighty dread"

That verse from "Roots Rock Reggae" on *Rastaman Vibration*, Marley's fourth international release, demonstrates that he had longed for recognition in that market, and more importantly, that without that market, his life's mission would have been unfulfilled. Historically, white American youth, particularly at the college level, had been aware of Marley's message from the mid-seventies, when rock music had co-opted reggae in the United States. In the 1970s international record company executives were looking for a distinct identifiable new sound or trend, but Marley could not crack the US mass market, despite considerable promotional effort. Reggae was too politically laced, too religiously unorthodox, but despite these obstacles, reggae moved into the American and British mainstreams, and heavily influenced the music of later generations.

Stephen Marley is seeking to do the same for a new generation, who might have missed the message. The songs take on fresh meaning, and during their recording, some magical things apparently happened; alternative vocal tracks were taken from the original Island recordings, and worked well with remixes; new beats give Marley a contemporary sound, while several rappers spin a new narrative inspired by Marley's original message-Erykah Badu's soulful mourn on *No More Trouble*, Guru on *Johnny Was*, Rakin's rap on *Concrete Jungle*, Busta Rhymes as Busta Rhymes on *Rastaman Chant*, Lauryn Hill's rapture on *Turn The Lights Down Low*, and M.C. Lyte's rhyme on *Jammin:* "Those that claim but really don't know the game/Bob Marley learn the man behind the name."

– DERMOTT HUSSEY

children. Every now and then I would say is so and so here. The kids would say, "Mom we can't leave now", until several parents decided to come for their children, and when they came they were captivated by what was going on.

Instead of grabbing the kids and leaving, they stayed for a half an hour, because they knew they had questions to answer when they took the kids home. It fascinated me because it showed that the present generation, probably because of Bob playing a Pied Piper, will be able to look and understand other cultures, and work together instead of trying to divide.

DH: What were some of Marley's most outstanding concerts?

NG: In 1979 Bob did a free concert called Amandala in support of the SWAPO guerrillas at Harvard Stadium. To me it was one of his most outstanding concerts. Bob was a person who came up and sang. He never really talked that much, but this day, Bob was like a preacher. It's a few times I've ever seen him preaching a sermon to the people. He was ad-libbing like never before, songs like words from "Redemption Song" started at that show. That's the first time I heard Bob sing "Emancipate yourself from mental slavery". We had Patti La Belle and Dick Gregory who was so overwhelmed that when he met him he bowed and kissed Bob's hand. "No Woman No Cry" was one of his really classic deliveries. That show was videotaped, but never released so the world might still have a chance to see that show. Another show was the Black Music Convention of, I think, 1978. Bob performed as the headline act. This was like Bob's introduction of black America on that entertainment level, because all of them were there, and Stevie Wonder was moved once more, because it had been on about three occasions that Bob had performed and Stevie was in the audience, and after Bob was into the set, Stevie just said, "Take me up to the stage". He came up and did about three songs with Bob that night. In fact Bob said after the show that Stevie had so much innocence in him. He hugged Bob and started singing. Bob said when he touched him, it was like a baby. Another memorable moment was in the winter of '79, which was our only winter tour ever. We went into North America, east and west coast, promoting *Survival*. We had had time over the years to sit back and study and there was a most elusive market, and that was the black market believe it or not. This was something Bob wanted badly. We were sweetening the music with more R&B flavour, just to win that audience, because the message was for them. The feedback we were getting was that the music was being played mostly on white FM stations, so we weren't getting through. It was also partly the fault of the black media as well, which was not picking up on us. Bob was getting front page of *Harpers Bazaar*, which was a woman's magazine, but we couldn't get an article in *Ebony*.

Bob turned down one date at Madison Square Gardens for five nights at the Apollo, doing two shows a night. In money terms what we earned was equivalent to one night at Madison. The Apollo was rammed every night. The lines would wrap around the block where the Apollo was, and older folks who I spoke with, were saying that they had never seen Harlem like that since Marcus Garvey. At the midnight show you could still find 30% white people would drive up to Harlem to see Bob Marley. So, although we went into Harlem, it wasn't 100% black. On that same tour we went to Chicago, and the black community came out and responded to Bob. People came and invited him to a naming ceremony. He went but didn't realise that he was the one going to be given the name. They went through a whole African ritual and Bob was given the name "The Chosen One".

DH: What was your first tour of Africa?

NG: A positive thing out of the Survival tour was that we met the daughters of the president of Gabon, when we performed in Los Angeles, and they made us have our first trip to Africa in 1980. They were impressed and said they wanted us to perform for their people, so Bob consented to do two free concerts for just expenses. Two weeks after we met them, we were on an aircraft heading for Gabon. Zimbabwe was later in the year on April 18th. Gabon was a tremendous experience. We kissed the ground. It was the first time we set foot in Africa. Since it was the government inviting us, we got full red carpet treatment and were guests of the president.

After Gabon we came back home and finished the *Uprising* album. While completing the album Bob got an invitation to Zimbabwe's independence celebrations, but we got to understand that Bob alone was invited, but he replied to the president pointing out that he was not just an individual, but part of a family, and an organisation. They replied saying that they understood, and that even if Bob did not perform, he would have been an official guest, but they didn't see the value of it promotionally. Bob said, "Alright, I'm going to do it myself."

He decided to take the whole band and 32 tons of equipment. When Chris Blackwell saw Bob making this move, Island eventually chipped in about $90,000 when they realised that this brother was taking his money, about a quarter million dollars, to set the thing up. From England we landed at Nairobi airport in Kenya, and an emissary came from Prince Charles saying that he wanted to meet Bob Marley, and if Bob could come out to his private place. Bob said, "If the Prince want to meet I, tell the Prince to come down here." You know that the Prince never showed. That meeting never happened."

When we came off the plane, it was red carpet all the way into Customs. On each side of the red carpet was the entire Parliament except Mugabe. It was like we had to walk the gauntlet of bear hugs, and "Welcome brother". When we reached customs, the people outside were looking to see Bob. They tore down the gate, and the airport went into disorder.

Close to midnight when Bob was to perform, before the clock struck 12, we started the music, but we could hear pandemonium outside the stadium.

Apparently there were some guerrillas who had come from a nearby camp, but they could not get in. Eventually they were let in, and the community decided to come in with them them. They started firing tear gas, but the wind took the tear gas right into the royal box. Order was eventually restored and Bob came back with "I Shot The Sheriff". Bob also gave a free concert after the ceremony. It was his high point there. When he sang "Zimbabwe", people were jumping and singing it. We played "Zimbabwe" for about 15 minutes straight.

The Uprising tour which followed in support of the album was, unknown to us, his last.

DH: What made that so special?

NG: It was a tour of records. Since we had been to Europe several times before we could compare audience attendance and sales. For instance we started in France, and in three weeks Bob had sold 350,000 copies of the *Uprising* album. One of the biggest audience ever. We had been using Average White Band as an opening act for us, but they were having problems because whenever you toured with Bob Marley, people came to see Bob Marley and not the opening act, so Average White Band was being stoned with eggs and tomatoes while the people chanted Marley...when Bob hit the stage and said "greetings in the name of...," 111,000 people responded. I was about 35 feet up in the air in a lighting tower. We had filled the National Stadium and the playing field. When Bob did "Redemption Song," everybody who never had a candle held their lighters up.Some started to light bonfires in different parts of the stadium. Bob tore the place down, he was more than a star. Right now Elvis Presley is the most famous person in music, but I think Bob will outlive Elvis Presley. He was more than a troubadour, he was a folk hero. "Jailhouse Rock" can't hold you as long as 'Emancipate yourself from mental slavery.'

ORIGINALLY PUBLISHED DECEMBER 1999

Jimmy Cliff
The African Ambassador

TREVOR FEARON

From the outset you notice his eyes. They glow. They transform this soft-spoken, lean figure of average height in a manner that you suspect must have characterised many of the notables of history.

He is musing on the November 1982 World Music Festival held in Montego Bay: an event that brought together artistes and groups as diverse as the Grateful Dead, Peter Tosh, Aretha Franklin, the B-52s, Rick James, Skeeter Davis (yes, Skeeter Davis!), Gladys Knight and the Pips and many others...

"It shows the long way that Jamaican music, reggae music, has come—to reach the point where it can touch and attract so much other music. Because, it was reggae music that brought them here".

Jimmy Cliff pauses, thinking perhaps of the many years that Jamaican artistes had fought their uphill battle for recognition; the years when local radio stations virtually ignored its presence and the 'sound systems' of the dance hall were their only vehicle; the years when Jamaican music had only a cult following overseas, and the few North American and European radio deejays who did play the music would routinely play it for a laugh ("just listen to this rubbish"); the grudging acceptance as the unmistakable gifts of such giants as Cliff and Marley were finally recognised, and as more and more foreign artists began using the rhythms in their own music; to today, when reggae is no longer, for a large segment of the international music market, an item of curiosity.

For Jimmy Cliff it has been twenty-one years: a performance span equalled by few other Jamaican artistes; a span that almost precisely equals the birth and growth to maturity of the Jamaican music form. And along the way, his contribution to this growth has been among the most outstanding. Because, whereas other giants such as Bob Marley and Peter Tosh in large measure pursued and represent the uncompromising militancy that many outside of Jamaica assume to be synonymous with reggae, Jimmy Cliff represents an equally important facet: he is the deeply spiritual balladeer sincerely persuaded of the hearing and rapturous power of love.

In the end, the fact that both paths draw upon and lead inexorably back to Africa is perhaps not surprising. Alongside their pre-eminent statures in their homeland, Cliff and Marley have been accorded virtually hero status in many African nations for their support in their respective ways, of the struggles for human rights and justice.

It is not a struggle with which, on a personal scale, Cliff is unfamiliar. Like many would-be artistes, he left his rural village of Somerton, outside of Montego Bay, for Kingston to pursue his church-choir nurtured dream of being a recording artiste. Like Ivan, the frustrated singer-songwriter he was to play a decade later in what is acknowledged to be the best-ever Jamaican film, *The Harder They Come*, he was to find that the path was anything but easy. What with the fact that the local recording industry was in its nascency, a local popular music industry was almost non-existent, and the fact that the first wave of producers were not by and large noted for their honesty.

In retrospect, Cliff believes that those and other factors, such as the prevailing preference for American music ("...If you wanted to get anywhere locally, those days you had to be singing American-type music") directly led to the creation of the first modern authentic Jamaican popular music form—then called ska. Out of the frustrations, he believes, came "a cry for acceptance".

"I wanted acceptance. I wanted respect. I wanted justice. I wanted equality. And it was out of these feelings on the part of us artistes that reggae music came. We created a beat, something identifiably Jamaican."

And, while he notes that "the spirit out of which it came is not yet satisfied…the need for acceptance, identity, respect and love are still not satisfied (and) we will continue to be creative," for Jimmy Cliff the intervening years have brought some measure of success.

A number of his songs, such as "Wonderful World (Beautiful People)", "Many Rivers To Cross", and several others have become virtual classics of the genre. His artistry has earned the respect of a broad cross section of the Jamaican community—for instance, one of the most acclaimed pieces in the repertoire of the renowned Jamaica's National Dance Theatre Company, is the stirring tribute to Cliff. He has received a number of the island's most prestigious honours, culminating (so far) in his being chosen for 1982 Norman Manley Award for Excellence, arguably the most coveted commendation locally, equalled or surpassed only within the entire artistic arena by honours granted to the incomparable Louise Bennett or (posthumously) to Bob Marley.

The Award for Excellence, presented to Cliff by another personality with fortright views and who has had a long Jamaican association—singer/actor/activist Harry Belafonte—was, Cliff admits, one of the most moving moments of his life. Many in the large, cheering audience wept with the artiste as, for once, he struggled to find words to express himself. Giving up, he went into song, and his emotion-filled "Many Rivers To Cross" was perhaps his most moving performance ever.

"I felt joy. It was appreciation…it was showing that your work has been observed and has been appreciated. It gives me strength to go on."

"An ambassador is one who moves from place to place on missions for his people. And my people are not only Jamaican but African." Jimmy Cliff takes very seriously the concept of being 'the African Ambassador.' The term itself, he says, is one that was first used to describe him during his many tours of that continent. Perhaps more than any other West Indian personality, he has been taken to heart by multiple thousands of listeners there, ever since his first visits in 1974.

"I am most popular in the so-called Third World countries—like across Africa or in Brazil. They understand my message much more than in Europe or in North America—although I find that the young people in Europe and North America who are much more interested in truth and rights are very open to my music.

"When I am in Africa I am completely at home." Indeed it is not every artiste that will be welcomed at the airport by a head or deputy head of state as Cliff has been in Africa, or who will be the guest of honour at a state ceremony as has been Cliff's experience. President Kenneth Kaunda of Zambia in fact wrote and read a poem he had written in praise of the Jamaican artiste at a packed state ceremony held in his honour in Lusaka.

"The president said, 'Inspire the world Jimmy, inspire us, inspire Africa, set us on fire.'" In Zimbabwe, the deputy prime minister told him, "Jimmy, you can build empires. I can only look after my people in these regions."

In Cliff's opinion, it is the spirit that dwells in him and in a few other artistes that has been struggling in their own respective countries for their rights, that has been recognised. "President Mugabe of Zimbabwe recognised how powerful, positive and profound an effect Bob Marley had on the people of Zimbabwe during their struggle and that's why he extended a personal invitation to him to come for their Independence celebrations," he asserts.

That same spirit, he finds, has also been communicated among 'New World' areas with significant African cultural influences. In Brazil, for instance, a country that Cliff terms a significant link in the African chain of continuity, he feels equally at home.

"When you go to Bahia for instance, you think that you are in Benin (Nigeria) or somewhere like that. And I walk around in the ghettos there and hear them playing "Bongo Man" or "Love I Need" and more of my music - and they don't even speak English—and I think that it can't be a coincidence." In some way, he believes, his music is helping in the task of reuniting the consciousness of the scattered peoples of Africa. As he says, "We are the same people just connecting with each other again." And his role in effecting these linkages, he thinks, justifies the appellation placed on him by some African enthusiasts—the African Ambassador.

In his role is an (albeit youthful) elder statesman among Jamaican artistes, Cliff's thoughts on the situation of Jamaican popular music and its influences overseas are given from a base of experience.

"It has certainly grown," he notes. "One of our earlier handicaps was that there weren't enough people writing, enough people creating, in the early stages.

"Now, both in terms of the writing and the music, there are quite a few youths now doing songs of the highest international standards." He dismisses the suggestion that with increasing popularity, as evidenced by the many non-Jamaican artistes utilizing the rhythms in their own compositions, much of the potence of the music will be lost.

"They are using a rhythm, a beat. But reggae wasn't born or created out of that. It was first the spirit, the cry for acceptance, and the expression of the struggle of a people.

"So others take the beat and sing their lifestyle to it. But the message of life which was born out of the creation of this music, they are not able to carry that, they have never lived that. A music form can be taken by anyone, but the feeling out of which it was born cannot be so easily taken."

By extension, he does not believe that reggae is going to make the type of break-through that many in Jamaica may be anticipating: "We are not going to have the breakthrough that say, Latin American music had some years ago, or say, the twist fads or crazes. Those music will come and go, but reggae is a people music. It moves with the people. So that even though acceptance has tripled or quadrupled in recent years, it will never be treated by most people as an 'in thing.'

"It's like the difference between buying something to take and place in your home and just buying something to use and throw away. It's deeper than entertainment. It's the sentiment of life. And it goes beyond the concerns of most other music. It is concerned with life."

And it is this concern, he believes that enables an artiste like himself to communicate with so many at so many different levels.

"I am from the so-called ghetto. But having being born to be the ambassador, I communicate with all people because love is at the base of all that I am dealing with. Love is my foundation. Therefore I love the rich because they are lonely and I love the poor because they are so many. Heads of state and people from the ghetto invite me into their homes—it shows that I am on the right track."

"I try to show the rich not to worship creation but to worship the Creator. I am angry at the way they step on the poor, but it is not my duty to hate. I still show them love, but I show them that I am angry at the way they use their position and wealth to keep down the poor."

"Love is positive. Hate destroys. Love and you can make your enemy bow…"

And so the African Ambassador, the Ambassador of Love, pursues his calling.

ORIGINALLY PUBLISHED APRIL 1983

Jamaica's black art genius

DAVID KATZ

Lee "Scratch" Perry is a mass of contradictions. He is a devout Rastafarian who believes in extra-terrestrials, has proclaimed his children "angels" in the biblical sense, and advocates black supremacy while living with his wealthy European wife in Switzerland. He is also one of the few creative forces in popular music to truly deserve the title of living legend, and his contribution to the Jamaican music scene is immeasurable.

Perry's ceaseless creativity has resulted in some of the most startling and original sounds ever recorded on the island of Jamaica, and the uniqueness of his vision has found resonance in music forms around the world. He was actively involved in every major change of style on the island from the pre-ska days before independence to the "golden age" of roots reggae at the end of the 1970s, until a drastic personal metamorphosis saw him spending lengthy periods abroad. Later projects recorded in Jamaica and elsewhere have continued to be marked by the individualism that has always set his material apart, though Perry's focus has largely shifted from the determined logos of the production sphere to the arcane chaos of performance and spectacle. Scratch's singular and atypical trajectory has been motivated by a burning desire to create unique and inspiring music, and a parallel journey has given rise to a limitless effort to elevate the Almighty—a saviour Perry seeks to perpetually serve through his art.

Though he once claimed to come from Jupiter, his earthbound arrival came in the rural town of Kendal, Hanover in 1936, where his father was a road contractor and the rest of the family worked the land; money and food were perpetually short, and existence defined by a ceaseless toiling. Lee dropped out of school at age fourteen, preferring to attend domino tournaments; his mastery of wild dance steps then brought him fame at competitions held in the surrounding parishes, and it was music that inspired him above all else from his youthful days. Towards the end of the 1950s, Perry was employed as a tractor driver to assist in the development of Negril; he married a woman of Indian descent in the town of Little London and was baptised into the Church of God, but ultimately heeded his musical calling by travelling alone to Kingston circa 1961.

Duke Reid was then the reigning champion of sound, but Reid only wanted to take Perry's lyrics and use them for better established artists, so "Little" Lee went to work for the opposition, joining forces with Coxsone Dodd, who was then something of an underdog; the more democratic nature of Coxsone's set up was clearly preferable. "I'll never be a big man," Perry explained, "and I wasn't with Duke for that long, because, you couldn't take the pressure with Duke. He's a boss, but there was no boss around at Studio One."

Perry performed a variety of duties for Dodd and became a significant force in the establishment of Studio One, rising from an errand runner and delivery hand to vocalist, percussionist and auditions supervisor, but Scratch eventually tired of Dodd taking the glory and drifted away from Studio One in 1966 after voicing over thirty of his own songs and bringing artists like Toots and the Maytals to prominence.

Scratch was briefly an in-house producer for West Indies Records Limited, but was removed from the position by the better-connected Bunny Lee. Scratch then worked on prime rock-steady nuggets for Prince Buster and Joe Gibbs, and began forging new styles in conjunction with singer and promoter Clancy Eccles, who was then releasing music from the corner of a tailor's shop he operated a few doors down from Prince Buster on Orange Street. Perry's most significant partnership came with engineers Lynford Anderson and Barrington Lambert at WIRL, out of which the Upset label was formed, but the intricacies of such partnerships always proved to have their limits, so Scratch moved on to form his own Upsetter label in 1968, eventually moving to the premises of Buster's former record shop at 36 Charles Street. An early sortie as an independent producer was "People Funny Boy," a landmark recording in its fusion of the African-inspired beats of pocomania; its peculiar cadence would put forward the sound that became known as reggae, launching Perry as a formidable production force.

With his Upsetters backing band—initially an offshoot of the Supersonics featuring bassist Jackie Jackson and pianist Gladdy Anderson-Scratch concentrated on instrumental work, scoring his first international hit in 1969 with "Return of Django". The song's sustained UK chart position saw Perry travel to Britain for a six week tour, backed by a new set of Upsetters that included the rhythm team of Family Man and Carlton Barrett. It was this younger band that joined with Bob Marley and the Wailers under Scratch's direction in 1970 for a series of classic recordings, yielding hits like "Duppy Conqueror", "Mr Brown" and "Small Axe". Perry completely restructured the group's sound in this period, and prepared them for the international stardom they would achieve upon signing with Island in 1972.

Scratch then became an in-house producer at Dynamic Sounds, creating outstanding work with artists like Junior Byles; "Beat Down Babylon" remains a rasta anthem, and "Da Da" was a successful Festival song competition entry. "What attracted us to Lee Perry was that he had tremendous talent," explained Dynamics' boss Byron Lee, "he could recognise a hit before it was recorded." Despite the benefits of such an arrangement and the top quality equipment at his disposal, Perry tired of relying on others, and eventually opened a four-track recording studio at his home in Washington Gardens; it was operational by the end of 1973 and would soon be associated with the most serious and radical works created in Jamaica. By this point, Perry was fully experimenting with the dub form, creating startling new mixes of earlier material on ground-breaking albums such as "Cloak and Dagger" and "Blackboard Jungle Dub."

Though initially stocked with sub-standard equipment, Scratch was always able to conjure a magical sound at his now legendary Black Ark studio. "Mine wasn't professional machines, they were only toys," Perry explains. "Not even Errol Thompson who build the studio can't do nothing in there. Even the great King Tubbys come in there and don't know what to do." It was on such limited gear that Perry recorded Susan Cadogan's version of American soul smash "Hurt So Good" in 1975; though not a big seller in Jamaica, the song hit the pop charts in Britain, and the UWI librarian found herself flown to London for an appearance on 'Top of the Pops.' With cash generated from that hit and Junior Byles' "Curly Locks", Perry upgraded his studio facilities and launched into a heavier, more complex sound; this attracted interest from Island Records, who began licensing Scratch's material abroad in 1976.

As his commitment to the Rastafari faith deepened, Scratch recorded exceptional album works such as Max Romeo's *"War in a Babylon"*, Junior Murvin's *"Police and Thieves"* and the Congos' debut *"Heart of the Congos"*; he made George Faith a major star with the soulful "To be a Lover" and furthered the dub cause with the Heptones on "Super Ape". Perry also collaborated with rock artists John Martyn, Robert Palmer and Paul McCartney. He also produced a record in London by punk group The Clash, leading Bob Marley to voice "Punky Reggae Party." But after a radical Nyabinghi group installed themselves at his studio, a number of pressures took their toll, as various musicians and unknown gunmen made financial demands on Scratch; too much bad wine, rum and ganja also brought unpredictable behaviour, culminating in the demise of the Black Ark in 1979 and its eventual destruction in the early 1980s. It was a time of turmoil for Perry and his family, and would result in his eventual exit from Jamaica.

Since then, Lee Perry has largely abandoned music production, recreating himself as an abstract vocal wordsmith and musical shaman; his nomadic wanderings have seen periods spent in the USA and Europe. Since the late 1980s, Scratch has made an extraordinary comeback: his work with inventive English producer Adrian Sherwood won him a whole new audience overseas, as did collaborations with Simply Red and the Beastie Boys; his long-standing partnership with London's Mad Professor, a producer and engineer of Guyanese origin, has seen a dependable series of live performances and adventurous album collaborations. He has since toured the world as a vocalist, performing regularly in Europe, North America, Asia and Australia.

Now that Perry is in his mid-sixties, the world has finally taken note of his incredible achievements and given him belated accolades.

Scratch is often overlooked in his native land. "Jamaican people never like my music until foreign people start to like it," he recounts grudgingly. "Jamaicans never like my music until white people start to like it." Despite this general lack of recognition, Lee Perry continues to spend much time in the land of his birth; he insists he "never really left Jamaica", and hopes to eventually rebuild his studio in Kingston.

ORIGINALLY PUBLISHED DECEMBER 2000

THE ESSENTIAL PERRY

TOP TEN ORIGINAL ALBUMS

1. **Best of Lee Perry & The Upsetters Vol. 1** [aka Clint Eastwood] (Jet Star PT 1023). Early vocal and deejay gems from the Reggae Boys, Count Sticky, U Roy with Count Ossie and Peter Tosh, plus plenty of hefty organ workouts from the Upsetters. Recorded circa 1969-70. 2. **Bob Marley & The Wailers: Soul Revolution I & II** (Trojan TRLD 406). Classic vocal work and impressive proto-dub instrumental package, showing the strength of the young Wailers at the dawn of the 1970s. 3. **Junior Byles: Beat Down Babylon** (Trojan TRL 52/TRLS 253) Heartfelt protest music from one of reggae's most under-rated legends.Recorded 1970-72; reissue has bonus tracks from1973. 4. **Blackboard Jungle Dub Upsetter** [aka Upsetters 14 Dub Blackboard Jungle] (Upsetter/Clocktower, etc SCR1/CT 115). First true masterpiece of dub, circa 1974. Check for the Coxsone repress with all 14 tracks in true channel-separated stereo — a noisy repress, but in the incredible original format. 5. **The Upsetters: Super Ape** [aka The Upsetters: Scratch the Super Ape]. (Island ILPS 9417). A startling whole of organic dub unity; the high point of dub at the Black Ark studio in 1976. 6. **Max Romeo: War In A Babylon** (Island ILPS 9392). Romeo's most successful and politically relevant album to date. Recorded in 1976. 7. **Junior Murvin: Police And Thieves** (Island ILPS 9499). 1977 Social commentary from one of Jamaica's all-time greatest singers. 8. **The Congos: Heart Of The Congos** (Blood & Fire BAF 9) Ethereal harmonies and religious allegory set to cow sounds and other startling effects. 9. **Lee 'Scratch' Perry & The Dub Syndicate: Time BoomX De Devil Dead** (On-U Sound ON U 43). One of the most captivating post-Ark discs, Scratch in fine vocal form in London in 1987, co-produced by Adrian Sherwood with strong musical backing from the core of the Roots Radics. 10. **Lee 'Scratch' Perry & Mad Professor: Black Ark Experryments** (Ariwa ARI 114). The most autobiographical and coherent of Perry's many discs with the Mad Professor, recorded in London in 1995.

Music is the life of Beres Hammond

PATRICIA MESCHINO

"Making songs is as sacred as making babies," says Beres Hammond, whose impassioned, signature strain of lovers rock has led to innumerable romantic unions and undoubtedly the conception of many children. "Every time I travel, I hear some really lovely stories, people come up to me and introduce husband, wife and kids and explain it's because of a particular song they got together, because of Beres Hammond's music."

The power within Beres' music to bring people together and start families lies in the singer's emotive convictions, displayed throughout a career comprised of personalized, well-crafted music. Breaking up is hard to do but staying together isn't so easy either and Beres Hammond's music expresses the resolve of a man who's been hurt by love but is ultimately strengthened and enlightened by such character building episodes, songs conveying realistic portrayals of relationship complexities. He does not create, as his song titles "Sweet Lies", "Double Trouble" and "Too Sweet Love Affair" testify. "I'm not gonna sing I'll climb the highest mountain and I'm not gonna swim the deepest sea either," he asserts (although on "Full Attention" he asked "should I stand in the middle of the road and let something run over me?). "If you want to jump overboard sweetheart, I'd advise you not to because I'm not gonna jump after you. I'd throw a rope overboard and say if you have a change of heart, see if you can hold on to this but I'm not gonna jump after you. So my music is like that too, I just keep it real."

Beres Hammond's music is about as real as it gets in reggae or in any other genre. The prolific singer/songwriter's granular delivery embodies the spiritual fervour within the secular ballads of Sam Cooke, the romantic cool and social conscience of Marvin Gaye in the 1970s and especially the "Pain In My Heart" passion of Otis Redding; each of these late American sweet soul music icons profoundly influenced Beres in his youth.

The ninth of ten children, Hugh Beresford Hammond was born in Annotto Bay in Jamaica's garden parish of St. Mary, on August 28, 1955. As a precocious youngster, Beres made regular trips to Jamaica's capital city Kingston to mingle with the singers who frequented the downtown record shops. His favourite Jamaican artists of the era were Ken Boothe, Leroy Sibbles and in particular the king of Jamaican rock steady, the great Alton Ellis, "who reassured me that I should use melody in my style."

After graduating from school in the early 70s Beres entered several local talent shows; he joined the Jamaican fusion band Zap Pow as lead singer in 1975. Beres remained with the group for four years (recording the albums *Zap Pow* (Mango, 1978) and *Reggae Rules* (Rhino Records, 1980) while simultaneously pursuing solo recordings until he realised that he "couldn't serve two masters." Beres' 1976 debut solo album *Soul Reggae* (Aquarius Records) produced by his friend Willie Lindo sold well throughout Jamaica but he soon surpassed that success with the R&B flavoured single "One Step Ahead" which held the number one spot on the Jamaican charts for three and a half months. The frustrations of attaining hit records without monetary compensation (due to Jamaica's chaotic, sometimes exploitative music industry infrastructure) led Beres to drop out of the music business, regroup and form his own record label/production company, Harmony House, in the early 80s. "At the time I didn't have a clue about what a production company was," Beres laughs, "but the guys I was recording for all had them so I thought if I'm going to get along in the business, I need one too."

Beres' Harmony House debut single "Groovy Little Thing" marked the first time he reaped financial returns from his music and commenced a succession of hit reggae records

for various producers. The singer's 1987 hit "What One Dance Can Do" produced by Willie Lindo became a dancehall anthem in Jamaica (and in Caribbean communities throughout North America), entered the pop charts in England and elicited a spate of answer records including Beres' own "She Loves Me Now." More hits followed for Beres including "All Because I'm Lonely." "Emptiness." "Settling Down," "Single Girl (Cat and Mouse)," but even greater success occurred in 1990 when Beres joined forces with his longtime friend producer Donovan Germain of Kingston's Penthouse Records. Donovan asked Beres to record vocals over a dancehall reggae rhythm track he had created. Although Beres barely remembered recording "Tempted To Touch," the song shot to number one on reggae charts everywhere as did the subsequent hits "Is This A Sign," "Respect To You Baby" and "Feeling Lonely," from the singer's Penthouse album *A Love Affair.* With his hits played in regular rotation on Jamaica's brand new all reggae radio station, IRIE FM, Beres Hammond was now, after almost 20 years in the music business a bona fide, island wide phenomenon with reggae producers based in Jamaica and the United States clamouring to work with him.

Attired in his trademark glasses, a white polo shirt, khaki pants, leather sandals and a blue "Sean Jean" baseball cap, Beres reflects on the triumphs and travails of his music and life (the two are synonymous for him) in the state of the art recording studio at his home nestled in the hills of St. Andrew, Jamaica. Indeed, when he isn't touring Beres spends everyday "except Sunday when we break for rice and peas" in his studio "voicing" singers and laying down his own tracks. What distinguishes Beres' studio from Kingston's numerous recording facilities is that his is a live music studio. "It's tight knit like a home vibe," Beres explains as he lights a Craven "A" cigarette, "It's very small but the kind of connection the musicians experience when they come in here, they don't want to leave. That's the kind of vibe computer music can't give you, four or five musicians in the studio vibeing each other, each one telling the other, yeah, you should play this right here. It's real music when everyone is sharing ideas together it feels warmer, like a man and woman should start dancing, getting closer and that's what music should be all about. I am proud to say that when this studio was finished (approximately three years ago), the first time we tried it out, it had sort of a perfect sound," says Beres, a beatific smile illuminating his full black beard. "In my head I knew the sound would come out like this but when you hear it for the first time you think, hey, I don't even want to touch a button. I want the sound to remain just like this because it's really warm and beautiful, the album can testify to that."

The album is the February 2001 release *Music Is Life* (Harmony House/VP Records) the first Beres Hammond album recorded at his (home) studio. Showcasing Beres' smoky, soulful delivery which tenderly caresses each note, *Music Is Life*'s production shimmers with lilting lovers rock rhythms anchored in a drum and bass foundation, the rockin' steady strum of the rhythm guitar, fluid horn arrangements and sweet percussive accents. *Music Is Life*, incredibly, remains the number one album in Jamaica at the time of this late November writing, propelled by the phenomenal success of two Beres produced singles, "They Gonna Talk" recounting a predestined, against-all-odds romance and "Rock Away" which celebrates music of a bygone era. Both songs offer unforgettable melodies, straight from the heart lyrics and soothing celestial reggae tempos. "Rockaway" has been on the charts for almost a year, spending a month at Number One in Jamaica and the rest of the time lodged in the number two position. "That song is reminiscing on songs themselves from the 60s and 70s, when music had so much contribution to peoples lives and a reflection in people's way of thinking," Beres confesses. "Music can do what a politician can't do or the pastor in church and I'm saddened by the fact that a lot of the folks who are producing music can't see that. The generation that didn't actually experience that time, I'm just hoping this song will give them a hint of what that was about. For it to be on the charts for that period of time, I think the purpose has been served."

In his April 2001 concert at the Hammerstein Ballroom in Manhattan, Beres sold out the cavernous venue, attracting more than 3,000 reggae fans with scalpers commanding as much as $250 for a single ticket! In superb form Beres delivered many hits from his vast repertoire spanning four decades, accompanied by an audience that enthusiastically sang along, word for word to tunes such as "She Loves Me Now," "Falling In Love," and "Rock Away." Wyclef Jean's guest appearance performing his duet with Beres "Dance 4 Me," (from *Music Is Life*), featured a rap which summed up the feelings Beres inspired among the Hammerstein Ballroom audience and for most reggae fans: "Beres Hammond, that's the real thing; all you fake singers out there, bow down to the legend."

"The venue couldn't hold the amount of people and that made me feel good," Beres humbly notes, "It tells me that good work pays off, it might take some time but it pays off eventually."

ORIGINALLY PUBLISHED FEBRUARY 2002

Monty Alexander

PATRICIA NESCHINO

"Its back to the future," says Monty Alexander, the master pianist, pointing to Jamaican roots, by his introduction of a mento band at two of his most recent performances, particularly, the Air Jamaica Jazz and Blues Festival.

While we mistakenly perceive mento as the music of the past, rather than the music of the future, this is the Jamaican stream of musical consciousness that shaped Alexander's music and our collective lives. Even the most contemporary DJ is perhaps unaware that the stream too is part of his consciousness. Mento music remains an untapped resource, a fresh musical treasure that the world is yet to discover. Similarly, in next door Cuba, The Buena Vista Social Club, with its own grand masters, have also made Cuban roots music, "the son", irrevocably a music of the future, not the past.

After 55 recordings, Monty Alexander in his most recent works began a turn to his homeland, a journey that another celebrated Caribbean man, poet Aimé Césaire spoke of in "Return to the Native Land."

> "Those who have never invented
> neither powder or compass,
> Those who could harness neither
> steam or electricity,
> Those who explored neither the
> seas nor the sky,
> But those without whom the earth
> would not be the earth."

It was a kind of Jamaica that moulded the raw talent, the gift to play the piano naturally, almost instinctively, and with a passion and curiosity for music. It made the young Monty slip away from Jamaica College and find his way to the early recording studios: Federal and Studio One. The sessions were chaotic, but of a divine order. Alexander as a 15 year old found love and camaraderie with the big guns: Don Drummond, Roland Alphanso, Aubrey Adams, Dizzy, Johnny Moore and Ernest Ranglin. It was a time of spontaneous music, when daily a street of strivers would come into the studios with their songs, face the mike and begin to sing. Someone in the band would start a little riff, "take it up a key, its too low", the drummer starts playing a little backbeat, the song was recorded two or three times and that was it.

The acceptance by his seniors gave Monty confidence, a pre-requisite for any endeavour; an essential ingredient in playing a note and feeling good about playing it. Those sessions, combined with hotel and stage show performances, developed Monty quickly. By the time he migrated to the United States at age 17, he was able to strike an immediate chord with musicians in Florida—a reassurance of the confidence to get ahead, while leaving the Jamaican cultural kit bag for a while. But not for long, for that dimension is now expressed musically in a raft of images, rhythms and colour, that Alexander draws on inexhaustively in the international scene where he records and works. It is how he has tempered that with a brilliance of technique, a jazz that swings ferociously, without the complexity of the bop and groove that is Jamaican.

"Stir it Up", the music of Bob Marley, his latest CD is Monty Alexander's recognition of what the world has given high honour. For several years Monty has regularly recorded a Marley song, "Stir it Up," as a full work of select Marley songs interpreted by Alexander and a jazz trio and reggae rhythm section. The two cultural streams merge and separate while Alexander sits on the rhythm like a heartbeat, celebrating the best of Jamaica by the best.

ORIGINALLY PUBLISHED APRIL 2000

Sets in the City

PATRICIA MESCHINO

In the early 90's, Thursday nights in Kingston meant just one thing to me, House of Leo, and many of my visits to Jamaica were extended to accommodate a night at this open-air dancehall Mecca. Located on Cargill Ave and Half Way Tree Rd. at the intersection of uptown and downtown, classes would converge, observing or participating in some of the most colourful and controversial cultural expressions the island has ever produced. The array of vendors lining the House of Leo entrance hawking everything from "Wrigleys" and "Craven A" to jerk chicken and fried fish, were nearly as entertaining as the dancehall celebrities inside sporting outrageous (for the females X-rated) fashions while demonstrating new dance steps (World Dance, Bogle, Tatty) with the resident sound system, Stone Love, spinning dancehall reggae at deafening decibels.

Appalling to some, quite appealing to others, House of Leo was the focal point of Jamaica's last great organic music scene. When the venue was sold to a born-again Christian whose beliefs didn't justify renting to the dancehall massive, the decline of the outdoor dance began in the city, stifling the creativity in dancehall reggae and its most important component, the sound system.

"I don't think that era will ever come back again," observes Winston "Wee Pow" Powell, founder of Stone Love Movement, Jamaica's most successful sound system which has been operating for 28 years. "That's what's killing a lot of (reggae) artists today, there's not these sounds for them to go and test their skills on. The city is what makes things happen in Jamaica and those open air dances are a spring board for new deejays and singers, more creativity, more dances, more vibes, more new talk for the selector, more everything."

The sound system is the bloodline coursing through every phase of Jamaican music from mento to Y2K dancehall. Rudimentary sound systems first appeared in the late 1940's, pre-dating Jamaica's voluminous recording industry as well as precipitating its development. Kingston's live music scene was thriving in the forties with big bands (such as the Eric Dean's Orchestra) playing a jazz/swing style that dominated the nightclubs while smaller combos offered a mixture of jazz, Cuban rhumbas and mento, a Jamaican folk music comparable to Trinidadian calypso. The sound system emerged from Kingston's dance band environment in the city's most economically depressed areas; early "sounds" were actually PA systems used for political rallies consisting of a record player, a small amplifier and a pair of speakers. The introduction of improved amplifiers in Jamaica around 1947 revolutionized the concept of playing recorded music for parties, enhancing the musical rather than the vocal output. Sound system dances soon became an extremely popular Kingston night life activity, delivering a varied musical selection dominated by R&B and bebop which Jamaicans had become familiar with through radio signals beamed in from southern American cities. The shuffling rhythms and gritty vocals in the music of Shirley and Lee, Ruth Brown, Fats Domino and Louis Jordan was even more appealing to the masses than the music played by local dance bands and certainly preferable to the insipid pop (Patti Page, Pat Boone etc.) broadcast on the island's only radio station at the time, RJR. Inexpensive and easily accessible, the sound system provided entertainment for the poorer inner city populace and additional income for vendors selling refreshments.

"I did a lot of social work coming up in the "sounds" taking guys from the street who are doing wrong and telling them they can do this," recalls Clement Seymour "Sir Coxsone" Dodd, among Jamaica's most important musical pioneers who cites the sound system as a positive social force. "The sound system was really a means of earning for a lot of people in Jamaica; a lot of folks had parties and were able to accumulate some cash or travel to England."

Born in Kingston some 68 years ago, Clement Dodd, an accomplished cricket player, was given the name "Sir Coxsone" after the Yorkshire cricket team's star batsman. His interest in music began at age 14 when he developed a fondness for jazz, bebop and big band music.

In the early 1950's Dodd answered a call for short contract sugar cane cutters in the American south. Before he left Jamaica, Dodd noticed businessmen like Stanley Motta and Tom The Great Sebastian (among Jamaica's earliest sound system operators) placed their speakers pumping out hit records in front of their business establishments as a way of attracting customers. Believing there were future financial opportunities in the acquisition of audio equipment, Dodd bought a PA system, turntables and a receiver while living in America which he shipped to Kingston, along with a box of records.

Upon his return to Jamaica, Dodd assembled his equipment and began spinning records in his mother's grocery store. "Folks would come from all directions to buy at my mother's store, just to hear the music," Dodd recalled in his Brooklyn record shop, Coxsone's Music City, "and that was a sign of what was to come". Dodd brought out his sound system, which he called Downbeat, for his first session in 1952. "The venue was in Kingston at Mountain View Road and Windward Road, and from the success of it, I decided to keep more parties. As time went on I had so many bookings for my sound, I had to acquire another set of equipment and we started playing on the outskirts of town. We would sell tickets, provide transportation and leave Kingston with three or four busloads of folks."

Early sound systems incorporated the talents of a "selector", who played the records and a deejay whose playful word patter between tunes and clever rhymes over instrumentals thrilled the revellers who came to eat, drink and dance to their favourite tunes. Pioneering deejay Winston "Count Machuki" Cooper (1924-1994) began his career emceeing or deejaying with Tom The Great Sebastian before moving over to Coxsone's Downbeat. Winston "King Stitt" Spark, the first deejay to have a hit record, learned his craft apprenticing with Machuki; both derived their spoken-word style listening to the animated catch phrases of American disc jockeys. "We never have the kind of equipment these guys have now, never have any headphone to cue up the record; we had to show our skills like lifting up the needle and dropping it in the right groove of an LP," Stitt reminisced in a 1995 interview with Kingston writer Howard Campbell. "But the funny thing is we were better than the sounds of today...because it come down to skill."

By the late 1950's, sound systems dances had proliferated to other parts of the island; sound men would place their equipment on trucks, touring the island's bucolic parishes, their bass heavy output reverberating from crowded urban centers to sparsely populated areas.

The fierce competition between sets of the era developed into the exhilarating, sometime violent practice of sound system clashes, with two or more sounds vying for vinyl supremacy. Rival selectors in their quest for musical dominance, would repeatedly fly to America, ("riding plane like bus"), scouring record bins in search of the exclusive R&B shots that would ensure large audiences as well as clashing victories. Once these records were secured, the labels were soaked or scratched off to protect their identity from spies sent by opposing sound operators. Coxsone's"Downbeat" and Duke Reid's "Trojan," each powerfully amplified sets, engaged in the period's most formidable battles. A chronicled clashing tale involves the song "Later For Gator" by Willis Jackson, also known as Coxsone's Hop; Duke Reid tried for months to uncover the record's identity and eventually secured a copy; he played it against Dodd at one of their clashes and Dodd was so shocked, it is said, he nearly passed out!!

"I think one of the great films still to be made about Jamaica is the sound system man," offers Dermot Hussey of Jamaica's RJR Global Beat. "It's a fascinating history, something that we just missed, the territorial wars, it's like warlords, science fiction almost, in a musical sense".

The advent of rock and roll and the smoother edge adopted by black American music in the early 60's created a dearth of records suitable to sound system patrons tastes. This prompted innovative sound men, foremost among them Coxsone, Reid and later Prince Buster, to bring musicians and singers into the recording studio and produce their own records. The result was an indigenous interpretation of R&B which increasingly developed a stronger Jamaican identity incorporating mento's banjo strumming, the cadence of the Rastafarian "funde" drum, the hand clapping of the revival church (all of which emphasize the offbeat) and the influences of nearby Cuba which became known as ska; intended exclusively for sound system play, these ska recordings proved so popular, the sound men decided to release them to the public, commencing Jamaica's prolific recording industry.

Sound systems have come a long way since Duke Reid/Coxsone Dodd and the single turntable. Today's top sets are touring entourages spinning records in New York or London nearly as often as they do in Jamaica. The sets utilize thousands of dollars worth of equipment which includes mixers, preamps, power amps, synthesizers and keyboards (for sound effects) and as many as 48 speaker boxes each made to exacting specifications to enhance reggae's forceful basslines. Sound men also spend thousands for clashes, arming themselves with a set's most effective weapon, the potentially lethal custom made dub plate "specials", acetate recordings "voiced" by popular artists lauding a specific sound system or deriding an opponent. It is the sound system selector's strategic sequencing of specials interspersed with rare records, mock news bulletins (usually announcing the demise of a rival "sound"), sirens and other dramatic sound effects as well as the selector or emcee's clever commentary that determines which sound wears the crown.

The frequency of sound system clashes has diminished along with the vibrant open air sound system dances featuring live deejays of the Reid/Coxsone, (1970's) King Tubby's Hi Fi/U Roy, even the Stone Love/House of Leo era due to a combination of escalating violence and a Night Ordinance Act restricting the playing of loud music. Today, sound systems spin the latest dancehall alongside hip hop primarily in nightclubs and at private parties and as a result, the quality of Jamaican music has suffered: not a single deejay's career has "bus" with the force of a Buju, Beenie or Bounty. None in the last five years, the final days of Kingston's invigorating, if sometime problematic, dancehall environment.

"I goin' on 11 years in this and it decline man, it decline," says Ricky Trooper formerly of Killimanjaro sound system. Ricky left 'Jaro last year to form his own set, Sound Troopers and he remains one of the most feared "clashing" selectors. "Hear what happen now.... when the sound system thing run the right way it was more competitive. You used to have new artists on the scene because the sound system was one of the main arteries for them. It's not run 'pon them level there again, it's a corporate thing, this man say him control the business so him not play this sound here, not give them a second chance at this title... We kinda keep that side of the business (clashing) rolling...Metro Media nah play inna clash dance. Stone Love don't play inna clash dance. A man go to a dance and it's the same set of music them hear over and over again, the next sound comes, play same songs so you have no competitiveness in it."

"A change must come," insists Phillip Smart who worked alongside King Tubby as an engineer. In the late 60's, Tubby created dub plate specials with the vocals sporadically dropped out, allowing resident hometown deejay U Roy to establish a toasting style far more sophisticated than his predecessors. "When Tubby's was playing, deejays get to hold the mic in the dance, try their stuff so someone can hear them. That lived until the 80's and the Stone Love era and the specials took over and regressed the sound systems. I don't know if it will come back the way it was in that era but maybe some new innovations will take place and the people will feel the business again... today they don't see reggae music as a viable way to make a living."

ORIGINALLY PUBLISHED AUGUST 2000

Up on the Downbeat

The Phenomenon of Stone Love

DIANA THORBURN

What is Stone Love? It's the most powerful, most popular sound system in Jamaica, the Caribbean, and some parts of the world.

On any given night Stone Love sets will be spinning the latest dancehall songs—and more recently hip hop mixes—in Beverly Hills, California, London's East End, and Asylum Club in Kingston, Jamaica. At the turntable, belting out hypnotic chants and sounds on the mike will be Wee Pow, Rory, Cancer, Billy Slaughter, Neco, Geefuss, Swamp Thing, or Bill Cosby. These are Stone Love's selectors, many of them named by Rory, one of the more enigmatic members of Stone Love, and certainly the most famous.

The dancehall is big in Jamaica. No, bigger than big. It is massive. Dancehall music and the DJs who perform it, are, as a young Jamaican politician recently said, the most powerful media through which young people receive messages about who they are and what they should do. The power of the message aside, dancehall has also "gone abroad"—far, far abroad. Stone Love has already toured Japan, and, as this article is being written, they are on a tour of Europe where they'll play in Italy, Spain and Germany. Last year in Cannes, Stone Love introduced thousands of people to reggae and dancehall at MIDEM, the world's largest music trade show. Engagements in New York, Toronto, Florida and London are weekly events. How did this phenomenon start? In the early 1970s, a guy calling himself Wee Pow had a small home component stereo set that he was dying to play at one of the many parties in the Molynes Road area, where he was from. These parties were the original "dancehalls"—where people went to lime, mingle, and shake their groove thang, mainly to reggae music. Wee Pow went to all the parties, often in the company of popular singer Hopeton Lewis, who was Wee Pow's first motivator to start playing on the street himself.

When he eventually did start playing at parties, he had one box. The runnings were hot and cold, constantly changing directions. Was his a soul set or a strictly reggae set? It had to be one or the other, but Pow wasn't sure. Along with the changes in the music were changes in the name of the set, even naming it after himself, but that too went out the window. (Sets were usually named after one's birth sign, and Pisces had already been used.) Eventually the name Love kept coming back, and, to be unusual, he put Stone in front of it, and the rest is history. Nobody liked the name at first and pushed for Pow to change it, but it stuck.

In the beginning, the small unknown set called Stone Love played mainly uptown, not high uptown, but certainly not downtown. But Wee Pow wanted to take Stone Love downtown, into the ghetto, where the popular sets ran. Soon, the first gig was lined up by the promoter Sassafrass, who organized for Stone Love to play at a bar session on Manaltry Lane off Half Way Tree Road.

Fast forward to 1983. Bamboo Lounge. Semi-uptown Kingston. Major clash between Stone Love and Champagne Disco ("a wicked sound no one ever hears about," according to its former owner). Both were small sets—Champagne had but five boxes, Stone Love four; both were eager to make that big break to stardom. The man spinning for Champagne is Rory, "the funky kid", known to be one of the best mixers in town. The strength of the clash weighed heavily on who could spin the best reggae, and that was Stone Love's domain; Champagne could master disco and pop. Champagne had an uphill task, but they were on home turf. Who won the clash depends on who tells the story, Wee Pow or Rory, but both will agree that it was that night that began the union which was the first step in Stone Love making it to the big time.

After the clash, Wee Pow, recognizing Rory's skills, asked him to send him a trained mixer to join his set. Three months later, Pow ran into Rory and asked where the promised youth was; Rory presented himself. From then on, there was no turning back. Stone Love was on its way to to dancehall legend.

Moving around between Manaltry Lane and Admirals Pen Road, it wasn't until 1985 that Stone Love began to carve its niche in the hard core of the dancehall, with a Monday night session at Torrington Bridge, and on a Wednesday night when Classique—the ruling sound at the time—was on tour. Classique was also the first sound to record and play dubplates. Another selector, Cancer, joined Wee Pow and Rory. Stone Love had by this time started to get a good name around and the first signs of their popularity showed when the Manaltry Lane crowd followed them down to Torrington Bridge just to hear them play. Well, one day Classique went on tour and stayed too long. When they came back, Stone Love ruled the dancehall. (And eventually came to dominate the dub plate scene too.)

From there the dates started rolling in, increasing year by year. By 1990, Stone Love was considered one of the biggest of the sets, along with Jammy's, Stereo One and Metro Media. But violence in the inner city forced them out of Torrington Bridge, further uptown, to Cross Roads, where their regular set was Thursdays in front of the old State Theatre. It was also around this time that uptown folk began to frequent the dancehall, mainly following Stone Love. (Wee Pow attributes this to the presence of Rory, who is considered pretty much an "uptown yout'". Rory claims they got popular uptown through playing gigs with Ambassador Disco, then a popular uptown set.) Within a year the crowd outgrew that location, and they moved to a Thursday set at Tropics in New Kingston.

Somewhere around this time, Wee Pow made the "policy decision" that Stone Love was going to go "clean". No more bigging up the violence in the dancehall, no more playing records which glorified or incited violence, and a tamer approach to the sexually-laden lyrics and vibes that the dancehall and its music have been heavily criticized for. The break from the norm—for gun talk and explicit language are par for the course in the dance—had to be done slowly. As Pow puts it, "we had to grow up at some time... but it was a hot mantle to hold. I decided, as senior selector, that we had to take a stance, to make a commitment. We're not 100% clean, but we're cleaner than most." Besides the flack from the patrons of the dancehall, as well as the artistes themselves,

there simply was not much music for them to play if they were to maintain their position. But there lies the power of Stone Love—the artistes soon began to change their style, and their lyrics, because if they didn't, they would get no play from Stone Love.

After the Tropics date, Stone Love moved to playing on Thursday nights at House of Leo off Half Way Tree Road, which then became one of the main attractions in Kingston's night life. Again the violence became a problem, with fighting in the dance itself, and House of Leo was locked down.

But Stone Love has kept growing. The "demise of the dancehall" has not stopped their booking calendar from getting fuller and fuller, and the selectors from being busier and busier. There are now seven selectors, and all are deployed, sometimes with a rookie or two to help out. Part of the reason for this is the international attention which dancehall began to demand in the early 1990s, which, though waning now, is still strong. Tours abroad have now become a standard feature of their engagements. Stone Love even cut its own record, which made it to No. 6 on the British reggae charts. The other new development is the phenomenon of clubs playing dancehall, with a designated dancehall night in most of the popular nightspots in the Kingston Corporate Area. Another factor is the popularity of dancehall uptown. Since 1991, when Stone Love played their first uptown dance, they are now regular attractions at "all-inclusive" parties which cater mainly to the middle class. The open air dancehall still thrives in the country parts (i.e., anywhere out of town), but in Kingston, Stone Love can only be found at special fetes, or in the clubs.

Even the demise of dancehall music itself has not changed Stone Love's popularity. Yes, the music is getting stale, yes, it needs to be revitalized, yes, the artistes are their own biggest enemy. But it isn't dying, it is in transition. Hip hop and some of the "new" traditional reggae are creeping in, along with influences from other musical genres, changing the way the dancehall rocks. But it still rocks, and powerfully so. "Stone Love's strength lies in Wee Pow's creativity, and the effort he puts into it all," says Cancer, who has been with Stone Love for 11 years, and, as a "senior selector" often keeps an eye on things when Wee Pow can't be there.

In an age where to be a selector or a DJ is the goal of many young Jamaican men, to be a Stone Love selector is the ultimate, the apex of one's career. But it's a rough life—playing sometimes seven days a week. You have to love the music, they all say. But for Wee Pow it's not just a matter of coming out every night to play. He is also the brain and the brawn behind Stone Love. He is involved in every single aspect of running the sound—the maintenance of the equipment, recording the dub plates, managing the bookings (now with the help of a booking agent in New York), handling the publicity, fending off persistent journalists. For a selector as popular as Rory, who is the most-requested selector in Stone Love, it means being on a plane as much as being on the ground, and living out of a suitcase. They will arrive on an evening flight from New York and head straight out to May Pen to play a set that very night. Then leave the next day for London. Yet you ask any of them how long they see themselves doing this, and the answer is the same: "To the def' (death)." Stone Love is life itself.

ORIGINALLY PUBLISHED AUGUST 1998

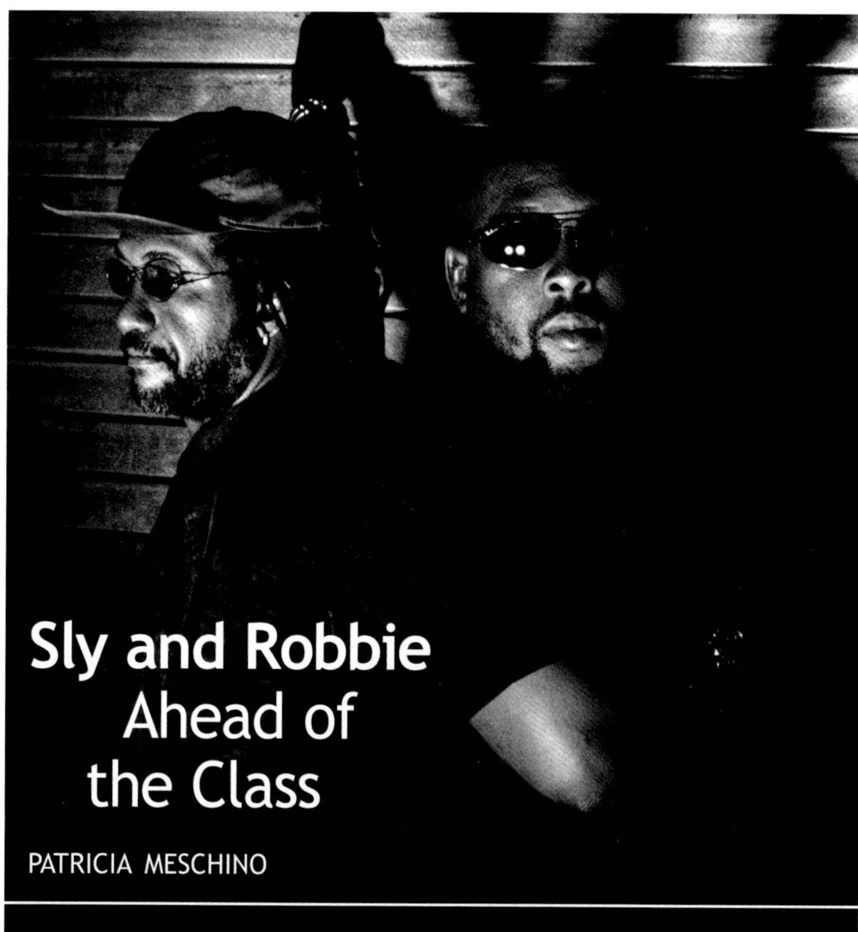

Sly and Robbie Ahead of the Class

PATRICIA MESCHINO

Jamaica's premier production duo still riddim rockin' after all these years

You can hear it in No Doubt's single "Hey Baby" but it's somewhat disguised by the ska-rock band paradigms, breakneck speed playing and the near blinding allure of platinum blonde lead singer, Gwen Stefani. The deejay break delivered by Bounty Killer brings the listener closer to it, but even the Killer's imposing Jamaican dancehall stature is only tangentially related to this ever-evolving, awe-inspiring chapter in the book of reggae. It is the thunderous sound of reggae's foundation, the durable drum and bass.

When Stefani repeatedly instructs "girls say, boys say", invoking all ages to forget their troubles and dance, besides her bandmates she is also supported by Sly Dunbar and Robbie Shakespeare, the architects who helped restructure, solidify and later modernize reggae's foundation. When No Doubt, admitted dancehall reggae fans, decided they wanted an authentic Jamaican sound for their *Rock Steady* album they came straight to Jamaica's 'Riddim Twins' who served as producers for two of Rock Steady's tracks: "Underneath It All" and "Rock Steady". With the popularity of the "Hey Baby" single, which reached number five on the Billboard Pop Charts and number two in England, reggae rhythms incomparably Sly and Robbie's proves they haven't lost their mainstream appeal.

Working with internationally prominent non-Jamaican artists is nothing new for Sly and Robbie. Since the early 1980s, the twosome's signature drum and bass playing and equally stellar production skills have been utilized by such diverse luminaries as folk/rock icon, Bob Dylan, 1980s punk rock diva, Cyndi Lauper, and jazz keyboard virtuoso, Herbie Hancock. Sly and Robbie have repeatedly demonstrated their dexterity in successfully balancing Jamaican drum and bass sensibilities with (non) Jamaican artists distinctive musical identity.

"Producing a foreign act is fun but serious," explains Robbie Shakespeare prior to an evening recording session at Kingston's One Pop studio. "They come to us because they're looking for something that's different; it's reggae but they want something a step above what they have and that's the challenge for us. It's like making a cake—you don't want to add too much sugar or too much egg or anything, you want it to be just right. Every thing has to blend in."

"We listen to everything that happens musically we don't care who it is or what is playing and I think that's what keeps us going. Some people play football but my hobby is to sit and listen to a lot of music," adds Sly, regarding the duo's unparalleled success.

Sly Dunbar started playing drums at age 15, his drumming style influenced by Lloyd Knibbs of the seminal ska group the Skatalites while Robbie was taught to play bass by Aston 'Family Man' Barrett. It wasn't however until in 1972 while each was playing in different bands in adjacent Kingston clubs that Sly and Robbie would meet. Robbie went to hear Sly's Band, Skin, Flesh and Bones and was immediately impressed by Sly's drumming style; Sly went to hear Robbie's Big Relation band and was equally excited by his approach. "I started asking him questions about the basslines he was playing and we realized we had some of the same ideas, so we started working together," says Sly.

The Riddim Twins were first united as a recording studio team when the Hookim Brothers, Joe Joe and Ernest of Kingston's legendary Channel One studios selected Skin, Flesh and Bones as the musical foundation of the group that would become the Revolutionaries. In contrast to previous sessions where musicians played primarily for the accompaniment of singers, these recording sessions were directed by the musicians, which precipitated the development of diverse styles and more intricate musical structures. Sly began tinkering with the sound, doubling up the drumming with what sounded like rim shots. Basically, he took a disco drum pattern but played it in a reggae tempo in what became known as the "rockers" style; the bass player he was continually teamed up with for these sessions was Robbie Shakespeare.

Soon Sly and Robbie were heavily in demand, however, they quickly grew dissatisfied with the way many producers wanted their music recorded, particularly the drum and bass so they set up their own Taxi label to record the musical ideas that other producers had rejected. The Riddim Twins invited their friend Gregory Isaacs into the studio for their first session and the resultant song "Soon Forward", became the Taxi label's first number one single.

The duo then joined Peter Tosh and his Word, Sound and Power band for a 1978 world tour. At the time Tosh was signed to Rolling Stone Records and on this tour he was the opening act for superstar rock bands including Foreigner,

Journey and the Stones themselves. The response to the Riddim Twins drum and bass was good but the duo felt something was lacking.

"We were playing reggae but we realized that people didn't get into it because it was so heavy," Sly recalls, "so we said how can we get that reggae sound really cracking when we play in a situation in front of 50,000 people? After the Tosh tour I started experimenting with open snares, trying to make the reggae sound more powerful, to get that aggressive edge."

Sly and Robbie decided their experimentally aggressive sound was best suited for a Kingston-based vocal trio named Black Uhuru whom they had begun recording. Black Uhuru's streetwise rasta image, their roots music with a swagger, was a perfect match for the duo's soul shaking almost intimidating reggae style. "Black Uhuru was a tough group," explains Robbie. "Touring with Peter we used to hear rock and roll that was kind of tough, so we tried to mix the rhythm just as tough for Black Uhuru, mostly adding dem kind of rock and roll guitar with a Jamaican rough tough attitude, rude boy style."

"When we started with Black Uhuru we were trying to structure a young Motown in terms of production and creating an identifiable sound," adds Sly. "We were feeling the music a different way and we were playing what we felt, without boundaries or limitations." From the initial Uhuru album, 1979's *Sensemillia* to 1985's *Anthem* (winner of the inaugural reggae Grammy) reggae had never sounded like this before. "What people loved about Black Uhuru were the live performances," Sly proudly recollects. "When they listened to the record and then came to see us live, they couldn't believe it; everyone wanted to know how we got that sound."

Throughout the 1980s, there were hit records and the critical accolades; a sense of originality dominated the decade in recordings for reggae stars such as Yellowman and Bunny Wailer, and international artists ranging from Nigeria's Fela Kuti to Japan's Ryuichi Sakamoto. They were the first Jamaicans to be nominated for an R&B Grammy in the instrumental category for the track "Bass and Trouble" (from their 1985 album *Language Barrier*). While their 1988 production of Maxi Priest's "Wild World" hit number 25 on the US pop charts and number two in England leading to a collaboration with pioneering hip hop artist KRS-1 on 1989's rap and reggae fusion "Silent Assassin".

The Riddim Twins' success accelerated in the 1990s with their 1994 production of Chaka Demus and Pliers mega hit, "Murder She Wrote", which rocketed to international popularity on the strength of it's rhythm track named "Bam Bam", based on a Toots Hibbert song. As the producers of Chaka Demus and Pliers *All She Wrote* album (Island Records) Sly and Robbie would make history again: for the first time six songs from a reggae album went to the top 40 in the British pop charts paving the way for dancehall deejays and their rhythm tracks' mainstream acceptance.

As the 20th century came to a close, Sly and Robbie rode a revitalized wave of dancehall hits producing several chart topping singles including Beenie Man's indomitable "Foundation", Bounty Killer's "Fed Up" and the wildly popular "Mission Impossible" theme while their remix of The Fugees "Fu Gee La" became one of the pair's best selling singles to date; they also produced the title song for Palm Pictures' successful film *"Dancehall Queen"*. In 1999 the dynamic duo secured their second reggae Grammy for the album *Friends* which featured several artists including Maxi Priest and Simply Red's Mick Hucknall who made reggae-tinged covers of songs by Cole Porter, The Rolling Stones and 1960s Jamaican hits.

Sly and Robbie are currently recording the *Friends* sequel featuring Beres Hammond and Horace Andy along with Wyclef Jean and Bounty Killer. They are also at work on the debut album for Abijah, the promising newcomer whose single "Revelation" and concert performances in Jamaica have garnered extremely enthusiastic responses.

Robbie views his long time partnership with Sly and their staggering musical achievements in much the same way: "We have respect for one another, as musicians and as human beings and if you don't have respect it nah go work. Me enjoy how him play and I guess him enjoy how me play too."

"Sometime God put two people together," adds Sly, "and just the way we could talk about music from when we first met, we have the same attitude and approach towards playing. Our aim is to get the music to a certain level and our mind is focused like we are one people."

ORIGINALLY PUBLISHED AUGUST 2002

How Does Reggae Music Define Jamaica

PATRICIA MESCHINO

Ziggy Marley

"When you think of London, you think of Big Ben, Paris it's the Eiffel Tower, New York it's the skyline although that's been dramatically altered due to recent events. But when you think of Jamaica, it's the natty dreadlocks flashing him locks and playing his guitar," offers Clyde McKenzie, public relations director of Kingston's Shocking Vibes record label which launched Beenie Man's career in 1986 and continues to guide his professional path. "Reggae is Jamaica and Jamaica is reggae. There is no other music so identified with one country."

More than its magnificent Blue Mountains or verdant Fern Gully, more than the clock tower in Kingston's Half Way Tree or the statue of national hero Sam Sharpe in the center of Montego Bay, more than Miss Lou or Nanny, even more than it's national dish ackee and saltfish, Jamaica is defined by it's reggae, a music that has been exalted and embraced by everyone from African freedom fighters to American ad execs. But how does reggae define Jamaica? Is it the vocalists' distinctive accent utilising colourful local expressions? Is it the soul shaking basslines or the one-drop drumming echoing the tempo of life on the island? Or do the synthesized dancehall rhythms bearing names such as "rice and peas" and "fiesta" more accurately define a 21st century Jamaica? The obvious polarities of Burning Spear's spiritual incantations reverberating through the hills of St. Ann and the insolence of deejay Elephant Man's lyrics are but diverse chapters in the book of

Jamaican identity that is revised almost as quickly as a new chapter is written.

Since a signature, indigenous sound emerged from Kingston ghettoes in the late fifties, Jamaican music has been through various permutations from ska to rock steady to dub to reggae to it's latest innovation dancehall. The island's sound systems (or mobile discos), a definitive phenomenon unto themselves, have been central to each phase of the music's development. In their early stages sound systems, consisting of a turntable and a set of speakers, popularised music throughout the island but especially in the trend–setting capital of Kingston. Attending sound system dances became an extremely popular night life activity in Kingston's economically depressed areas because the sound system selectors played a variety of music dominated by rhythm and blues which Jamaicans had become familiar with through (weather permitting) radio signals from Miami and New Orleans. Far less expensive than hiring a live band, the sound system was an easily accessible form of entertainment for the poor inner city populace and provided additional income for vendors selling food and drink.

The shift in popular American music towards rock and roll in the early sixties created a dearth of R&B records acceptable to Jamaican sound system patrons tastes. Thus many sound system operators, including Coxsone Dodd and Duke Reid quickly became producers, bringing musicians into makeshift recording studios and creating a distinctive version of R&B which became known as ska. "In those days, we were listening to Bill Doggett, Louis Jordan, guys who used to play shuffling rhythms," recalls guitarist Ernest Ranglin. A veteran of Jamaica's many jazz/swing bands of the 1950's, Ranglin admits to having been a "jazz purist" back then but realising he had to eat, he journeyed into commercial music and became invaluable to Kingston's burgeoning recording scene. Ranglin was the resident guitarist for Federal Records but moonlighted for other record labels' sessions (including Coxsone Dodd's Studio One and Duke Reid's Treasure Isle). Ranglin was also the first A&R man for Chris Blackwell's Island Records label and is deservedly regarded as the godfather of Jamaican music. "We were trying to play in the same style as R&B," says Ranglin of ska, Jamaica's first truly defining sound, "but make it something different, something unique for Jamaica." Among his innumerable ska recording sessions, Ranglin played lead guitar on the Wailers (Bob Marley, Bunny Wailer, Peter Tosh) classic 1964 rude boy anthem, "Simmer Down" which called for calm among dissenting youth, defining an era of ghetto upheaval in a newly independent Jamaica.

"I was 14 years old, stealing out of school and playing on those sessions," explains Kingston–born piano virtuoso Monty Alexander. "Those sessions were the spirit of Jamaica, the sound was so real and so raw." An internationally–renowned jazz pianist, Alexander has played with Frank Sinatra among other American music icons but his recent recordings have celebrated his Jamaican roots. "I did a record a few years ago called *Caribbean Circle* (Cheske Records) where I bring back my childhood. I play old time mento (Jamaican folk music) songs, I talk about the Carib Theater and the way I did it, you feel the Jamaican spirit." As the title of Alexander's 2001 release *Goin' Yard*

Coxsone Dodd

10 Best THE EARLY DEEJAYS

In the early 1970s, the role of the deejay was elevated from incidental sound system figure to major recording star, once Duke Reid placed U Roy's fluid toasting atop his old rock steady hits; other inventive sound system chatters like Dennis Alcapone, Big Youth and I Roy further elevated the form. These toasters' dynamite command of the rhyming microphone would later be greatly emulated in hip-hop, ultimately spawning what is perhaps the most popular music style in the world.

Artist	Album	Label	Comment
1. U Roy	Version Galore	[Virgin]	Fluid toasting from the great U Roy; the tunes that kicked off the deejay explosion.
2. Big Youth	Screaming Target	[Trojan]	Killer set produced by Gussie Clarke; brought deejay albums to another level.
3. I Roy	Presenting I Roy	[Trojan]	Another excellent set from Gussie; Roy's clever tongue raises the deejay platform.
4. Dennis Alcapone	Forever Version	[Studio One]	Hard hitters from a suave toaster.
5. Prince Fari	Message From The King	[Virgin]	Meditative chants over heavy rhythms.
6. Tappa Zukie	Man A Warrior	[Klik/MER]	The fiery debut from a very youthful Tappa.
7. Prince Jazzbo		[Clocktower/Black Wax]	Ital Corner (aka Natty Passing Thru) Toasts of tribulation over thick-as-molasses Lee Perry rhythms.
8. Jah Lion (aka Jah Lloyd)	Colombia Collie	[Island/Mango]	Humour and gravity from the late Jah Lloyd, graced by Perry's inimitable touch.
9. Big Youth	Natty Universal Dread	[Blood And Fire]	Incredible three CD box set of prime youth material-all killer, no filler.
10. I Roy	No Check Me With No Lightweight Stuff	[Blood And Fire]	Collects the best of Roy's stylish rhyming deliveries.

(Telarc Records) implies, he honours the defining sounds of his homeland, covering Bob Marley's "Exodus" and the late musician Augustus Pablo's "King Tubby's Meets Rockers Uptown", a tribute to the late engineer/sound system operator King Tubby (a.k.a. Osbourne Ruddock, the creator of dub). "Put King Tubby's dub records on and immediately you feel Kingston, Jamaica," explains Alexander, "the raw aspects of what it is, the essence and the soul of it. I feel King Tubby's groove so I was motivated to play that for this new record because King Tubby DEFINES Kingston Jamaica!"

King Tubby's Hi Fi was the first sound system to play dub plate "specials" with the vocals sporadically dropped out of reggae hits, the rhythm stripped down to an intermittent strum of the rhythm guitar, the reverberation of a keyboard riff or a thunderous bassline. The simplified dub tracks allowed deejays such as U Roy (Ewart Beckford) to establish a vocal style far more sophisticated than his predecessors Count Machuki, King Sporty and King Stitt, deejays who rose to prominence with lyrical rhymes confined to between song patter or a quickly chanted phrase over a song's

instrumental break, working with Coxsone's Downbeat sound system. U Roy and later I Roy, Big Youth and others were the first deejays to lyrically "toast" over the rhythms, telling stories and providing commentary in a style which provided the root from which American rap flourished.

Jamaican sound systems, ska, dub and deejay's are defining elements in the island's musical culture; Jimmy Cliff's dramatic portrayal of Ivanhoe Martin in the 1972 film *The Harder They Come* and it's powerful assorted reggae artists soundtrack album were pivotal elements in exporting another defining aspect of Jamaican music to the world. But the single figure identifying reggae, the Rastafarian way of life and Jamaica for most people is Bob Marley. During his lifetime, Marley's island nation was a source of fascination to an international musical community. What was it about Jamaica that shaped Marley's progressive lyrics, which utilised colloquial terms to express profoundly global ideals? Many visitors arrived in Jamaica to explore the birthplace of Marley's genius; expecting a tropical paradise, some, instead, encountered harsh political realities, a curious juxtaposition of an English colonial past and a vibrant yet troubled post independence identity and great disparity between the island's poor and it's privileged. These conditions as well as Jamaica's urban volatility and rural mysticism defined Bob Marley's music.

Since Marley's death in 1981, his life and music have been redefined countless times, serving multiple purposes both within and outside of Jamaica. "Now they trying to say my father's this and my father's that, but in the early days it was a continuous fight, dig!" exclaims Bob's eldest son Ziggy Marley. "Now everybody is jumping on the bandwagon, *Time* magazine (which cited Bob's 1978 "Exodus" as the Album of the Century) but when he was here singing the music there was a fight, trust me! If it weren't for the people then he wouldn't be where he is today. In Jamaica, Bob Marley couldn't get his songs on the radio. Today, the tourist board, they just give you part of the man, not the parts they don't like, they don't say anything about the ganja smoking. It's like "One Love" that's the only song they push...why don't they push "Africa Unite"? There's nothing about the "Rat Race"! It's very important to raise our consciousness beyond these limitations; there's no more class, no more race and no single definition of reggae."

As significant as Marley's messages of freedom, spirituality and equality remain, the musical component supporting his sentiments played a crucial role in his defining Jamaica for a worldwide populace. Marley's international conquest was spearheaded by an army of talented musicians comprising of the Wailers band with brothers (the late) Carlton Barrett, drums and Aston "Family Man" Barrett, bass, serving as the infantry's core members. "Family Man and Carly played a very important part in our father's music which is their music," observes Ziggy. "My father could always change other people for guitar and keyboard but drum and bass, he can't change that!"

Indeed reggae's essential ingredient in defining Jamaica is the bass, which captures the island's haunting beauty, its leisurely pace yet boisterous tension. For more than four decades "Family Man" Barrett has remained a stalwart figure in popular Jamaican music, his definitive melodic basslines providing the primary element of reggae's roots rock solid foundation. "I always key my bass playing to who I am backing," he says. "I make sure that they are flowing, that the music is swinging its way around them and that they vocally float on top of that." Family Man remains the musical director of the Wailers who continue touring the world while his indelible basslines are dependably recycled into hits for emerging reggae stars (his pumping bassline from Marley's 1972 classic "Stir It Up" provided the anchor for Junior Kelly's Y2K breakthrough hit "If Love So Nice").

Family Man's pioneering style has influenced all reggae bassists, most notably Robbie Shakespeare who along with his partner drummer Lowell "Sly" Dunbar are responsible for revolutionizing reggae's sound in the late seventies. Sly and Robbie garnered a formidable reputation as musicians especially through touring with Peter Tosh in 1978 as principal players in Word, Sound and Power. However the duo received even greater acclaim for their production/musician work with the trio Black Uhuru (lead vocalist Michael Rose, Ducky Simpson and the late Puma Jones) hailed as the greatest hope for maintaining reggae's international following after Marley's passing.

At the time, Sly and Robbie were attempting to structure a Jamaican Motown, in terms of defining their own distinctive reggae groove. Indeed, from the first Uhuru album, 1979's "*Sensimilla*" to 1986's Grammy winning "*Anthem*", reggae had *never* sounded like this before: the "Riddim Twins" brandished their drum and basslines so forcefully they could have been charged with assault! "We were feeling those songs in a different way," recalls Sly, "and people loved Black Uhuru's live performances. We used to play in New York at the Ritz to see if we could shake something down from the roof and when we see things start to drop, Robbie used to look at me and say here it comes! That sound kept pounding inside of you for at least an hour after the concert finished!"

Sly and Robbie glean their inspiration from diverse musical genres and from everyday Jamaican life. "When you're in the ghetto 'pon a corner on a Friday night and you come out of a session you are looking for ideas everywhere, people walking, you just look and incorporate it when you play," explains Sly. "Robbie would play a bassline around the way a woman walks down the road and I play the drums representing somebody walking, buck their toe and start to tumble." Sly laughs, pauses, then continues. "You can see that reggae defines Jamaica by looking at other music, even rap. In America a lot of singers make records with rappers and that's a Jamaican originated thing. The singing and deejaying that was created by U Roy deejaying and the Paragons singing on Duke Reid's label, the bass and drum thing, dropping out instruments and leaving the vocals, that is a total Jamaican thing. Reggae has taken a lot of ideas from American music too, but we recreate an original concept and turn it around. Reggae also defines Jamaica by the originality of the people; we've hung on to reggae and nobody can take that from us and say we didn't create it."

Any discussion of reggae's role in defining Jamaica must include today's dancehall, music dominated by deejays chanting over synthesized, sparse reggae riddims. Dancehall deejays primarily express themselves in local patois and are many times criticised for materialistic concerns, x-rated chat and exaltation of inner city violence. While the image and music of Bob Marley defines Jamaica for the worldwide community, the inner city grit of deejays Bounty Killer and Elephant Man may provide an equally viable, albeit troubling, definition of the island, although their interpretation of Jamaica has limited international acceptance. Deejay Merciless finds little difference between the clashing words, aimed at opposing deejays, that made him the sensation of Sting 2000 and the work of Bob Marley; both he says, are taken from a shared Jamaican experience. Bounty Killer draws a comparison between his profuse cursing on stage and the expletives underscoring the scathing social commentary of the late Peter Tosh. Many, however, find such analogies erroneous and offensive.

"What is happening in the dancehall now, the kind of debase behaviour and the moral sacrilege taking place on stage," observes popular sing-jay Tony Rebel, "it is a reflection of what is happening overall with the system that is in place and how it relates to the majority of the people. Was it created out of a need to help these people or was it created to suppress them?" Rebel, an uncompromising proponent of culturally uplifting lyrics has proved that positive lyrics do yield hit songs: at the time of this writing his song "Just Friends" a duet with singer Suede, held the number one position on the Jamaican charts for several weeks. "All of that negativity is coming through in the behaviour pattern of the people where people are recognising that certain things are not beneficial to them and that there is one law for the rich, one for the poor. At the same time, other people are saying we know this country has great potential and if a proper system is in place this country can be a haven."

In 1993 Rebel released his chart topping "Sweet Jamaica" an anthem providing one of the island's most accurate definitions. He recites a few lyrics: "help me big up Jamaica, land of wood and water/the system might not be proper but we still love the vibe, the food and the culture/it's a nice place to live, sweet Jamdown, the only problem is dollars can't run." "You bring forth all aspects and within that last sentence there is hope," Rebel reasons, "if that's the problem at least we're identifying it, then we can solve it. If you listen to a variety of songs, you'll hear different descriptions of the country because the music is a reflection of society but society does mirror what comes through the music because the music is very influential. So the definition of Jamaica through reggae is what is good, what is bad, what it was, what it is and especially how you'd love to see it."

ORIGINALLY PUBLISHED DECEMBER 2001

10 Best CONSCIOUS NEW ROOTS

'Slack' records depicting sexual themes and boastful 'gun talk' lyrics, which seemed to glorify violence, became the reigning fashion in the Jamaican dancehall by the early 1990s. Garnett Silk ushered in a new cultural renaissance from 1993, singing themes that echoed those expressed at height of reggae's international acceptance in the roots era of the late 1970s. Luciano, Everton Blender, a reformed Tony Rebel, plus veterans Cocoa Tea and Yami Bolo, are among those to push forward this new wave; other more radical voices have come from the 'Bobo Dread' community (that is, followers of Rasta Elder Prince Emmanuel Edwards) have risen in the form of Anthony B, Sizzla and Capleton. As reggae rose to once again embrace input from live musicians (with new music now often made by an exciting combination of live and digital sounds), Jamaican music reached new heights of international popularity.

Artist	Album	Comment
1. Garnett Silk	It's Growing [Digital B/VP/Vineyard]	A spiritual voice from within the dancehall; the one that kicked it all off.
2. Luciano	Messenger [Island Jamaica]	Message music with broad appeal, produced by Fatis Burrell.
3. Sizzla	Black Woman And Child [Brick Wall/Greensleeves]	The most thoughtful lyrics and best delivery from the sizzling one, its rhythms built with care for Bobby Digital.
4. Bushman	Total Commitment [Jammys/Greensleeves]	Excellent lyrics, and a fine delivery with shades of Luciano; sterling production by Jammy.
5. Anthony B	Universal Struggle [Jet Star]	Strong lyrics, original approach; one of the best from Star Trail.
6. Everton Blender	World Corruption [Greensleeves]	Meaningful lyrics and delivery; another treat from Star Trail.
7. Morgan Heritage	One Calling [Greensleeves]	Internationally successful and with good reason. Jammy and crew provide the beats.
8. Junior Kelly	Juvenile [Jet Star]	Original sing-jay with good lyrics.
9. Sizzla and Bredren	Liberate Yourself [Kariang]	Disc one is Sizzla, disc two is conscious vocal and deejay work from others.
10. Various Artists	The Herbalist [Xterminator]	Great weed anthems from Fatis' camp.

So What's Up With Shaggy

PATRICIA MESCHINO

It's a rare occurrence for a reggae song to top the Billboard Hot 100 (singles) Chart but Shaggy's anthem of denial "It Wasn't Me" from his latest album "Hot Shot" (MCA Records) has reached that premier position. Another track from "Hot Shot" "Angel" recorded with Shaggy's longtime spar Rayvon reached #9 on Billboard's February 17 Hot 100 Chart, designated as the chart's greatest gainer. Adding to Shaggy's astonishing accomplishments, "Hot Shot" has now surpassed triple platinum (over 3 million) sales, reaching the number one slot on the February 17 Billboard 200 Album Chart, sliding past England's fab four, The Beatles' "1" and beating Jennifer Lopez's "J.Lo" out of the top position.

For Orville Richard Burrell, known to millions of fans worldwide as Shaggy, mainstream success is nothing new: among his many achievements, Shaggy previously reaped double platinum sales for his 1995 album "Boombastic" which also earned the music industry's most prestigious honour, The Grammy for Best Reggae Album. Although most artists would be kicking back, revelling in their recent chart topping triumphs, for Shaggy, it simply means he has to accelerate his efforts.

"It's overwhelming," Shaggy sighs. "It's almost like waiting to exhale, as much as things are flying right now, I'm still wondering if things could go wrong. I was asked by the president of MCA the other day, 'when are you going to start enjoying this?' and I said there's no easing up; there's a lot to be accomplished and I feel if I ease up right now, something is going to go wrong."

Born in Kingston, Jamaica on October 22, 1968 and nicknamed after Shaggydog the Scooby Doo cartoon character, Shaggy moved to Flatbush, Brooklyn, North America's largest enclave of Caribbean immigrants, at age 11. Shaggy first displayed his musical skills while attending Brooklyn's Erasmus Hall high school, chatting lyrics "deejay" style in the lunchroom and accompanying himself with rhythms pounded out on wooden benches. Shaggy honed his deejay skills along Brooklyn's dancehall circuit as a member of the Ruff Entry crew which was comprised of deejays Redd Foxx, Bajja Jedd, Screechy

Dan, Nikey Fungus and singer Rayvon along with radio disc jock/producer Shaun "Sting" Pizzonia. The Ruff Entry crew plied their trade at Brooklyn clubs including the President's Chateau, the Village Hut and the infamous Biltmore Ballroom "where we dodged bullets and ducked behind the turntables" quips Shaggy. "We did all those places back in the day and that gave us the rawness of what we're doing now," explains Rayvon who has only missed one tour in Shaggy's hectic globe trotting schedule which has included dates in eastern Europe and the Middle East. "We don't really need the fanciness of a big show to rock the crowd," Rayvon continues, "we just come out there and stick it to the crowd just like back in the day and we've never gotten booed 'cause we work hard out there."

By age 20, Shaggy had released his first singles "Man A Mi Yard" b/w "Bullet Proof Buddy" followed by "Big Hood" and "Duppy or UglyMan". His next single "Mampie", produced by Sting reached number one on the New York reggae charts while his subsequent release "Big Up" recorded with Rayvon topped the reggae charts in both New York and Jamaica, a rarity for New York based reggae artists.

"It was a challenge for a New York artist to get a hit anywhere in America because Jamaica is the core where the music comes from," Shaggy explains. "The radio deejays would normally be looking for songs that came out on seven-inch out of JA, they weren't paying attention to New York artists so that in itself was a struggle. What gave us a little leverage, Dahved Levy (a popular radio personality) was on Kiss FM (a New York urban station) and Sting was the deejay on his show and he played our songs; that was a big plus for us."

Shaggy's burgeoning success on the New York City dancehall circuit coincided with his enlistment in the U. S. Marines where he served in the Persian Gulf War. Shaggy returned to North Carolina's Fort Lejeune; and would frequently commute 18 hours round trip to Brooklyn just for the opportunity to juggle the mike in the dancehall. Despite his devotion to his craft, Shaggy never contemplated making a living from his music until he met his future manager Jamaican-born Robert Livingston. Livingston learned the rigours of the music industry travelling as a roadie with Gregory Isaacs in the late 70s/early 80s. "Sting and I looked at it as a hobby, a ghetto fabulous thing, a way to get pocket money and a couple of chicks," Shaggy laughs, hastening to add, "hey, we got more chicks then than we get now! But Robert thought of it as a business; he said hey, you guys got something."

"When I met Shaggy I said this guy has a look, he has the right attitude and I think he could be the s**t," explains Robert Livingston in his characteristic, no nonsense style, an amalgamation of Kingston grit and NYC record industry hustling. Robert had managed Super Cat for several years guiding the popular deejay's career through many successful phases until their relationship soured. "When Shaggy came to see me, I wasn't even thinking of working with anyone because I just finished working with Cat.

Sting had created a rhythm called "Bedwork Sensation" (also the name of a song by Baja Jedd), an eclectic mix incorporating everything from the Peter Gunn theme to a Motown drum riff into an irresistible ska tempo. When Shaggy heard it, he got the idea to cover the Folkes Brothers' 1959 Jamaican hit "Oh Carolina." "I didn't know the words to the song because even when you listen to the original, you can't understand what the hell they're saying," Shaggy states, "so I put my own words to it. It's a good song but I didn't think it was the greatest song in the world. To this day its still one of the bigger puzzles of my career to say wow, how did that hit?"

Shaggy's version of "Oh Carolina" hit hard, especially in England where it became one of the biggest selling records in that country's history. According to Robert Livingston, when he heard "Oh Carolina" he thought, "I could use this song to change the whole music business. I started thinking how should I break this guy? Should I use the market here (America) or go somewhere else and bring him back and that's what I did. Livingston brought the record to the UK's most successful reggae record label, Greensleeves and persuaded them to release it. Through the concerted efforts of Greensleeves, Livingston and Shaggy (who spent a great deal of time in England promoting the single. "Oh Carolina" became the first reggae record to reach number one in England since Ken Boothe's "Everything I Own" in 1971, removing Michael Jackson from the top of the charts. "Shaggy entered the British charts at number one, ENTERED!" Livingston emphasizes. "C'mon, that's a big achievement, knocking Michael Jackson out of the number one spot! The irresistibly quirky single, delivered in Shaggy's inimitable Jamaican patois which is easily understood by most non-Jamaicans, catapulted the deejay to international stardom, selling over 600,000 copies in England and reaching number one in several European countries. Virgin Records International signed Shaggy for the largest sum any reggae artist had ever received, 1.5 million pounds (approximately $2.4 million US); in America Shaggy's debut album *"Pure Pleasure"* (Virgin Records) which featured "Oh Carolina" exceeded sales of 500,000, earning the ex-marine gold record status.

In 1995, Shaggy's single "Boombastic" (from the album of the same name) ranked among the top five records in America for the year, selling over two million copies. *"Boombastic's"* 1995 Grammy for Best Reggae Album placed Shaggy in the elite company of Shabba Ranks as the only dancehall deejays to have won Grammy Awards (Shabba earned his in 1991 and 1992). Shaggy's following album for Virgin, 1997's *"Midnite Lover"* did not measure up to Virgin's expectations; despite the Grammy and the millions *"Boombastic"* had earned for Virgin, Shaggy was dropped from the label. "I felt betrayed," Shaggy says forthrightly. "When you give your heart and soul to a company, you think you're working on building a career but I guess they didn't look at Shaggy as a career artist. In some respects I can't blame them; if you look at reggae music and dancehall artists, they're really isn't a huge success story of longevity and continuity. When it happened, it was a shock and I went into some kind of depression. I'm sure the industry looked at Shaggy as he's washed up, it's over. Creatively, it made me a little disoriented to figure out where my direction is. I had to become really strong and use the negativity as a stepping stone. I fired back and it paid off!"

Shaggy signed with MCA Records who released "Hot Shot" in August 2000. "Hot Shot" has sold faster than hot bread due to the popularity of "It Wasn't Me"; throughout the song, Shaggy offers shrewd counsel, (deny, deny, deny!) despite the strong evidence against distraught singer Ricardo "RikRok" Ducent whose woman has caught him in compromising circumstances with the girl next door.

RikRok: "She saw the marks on my shoulder"

Shaggy: "It wasn't me!"

RikRok: "Heard the words that I told her"

Shaggy: "It wasn't me!"

RikRok: "Even caught us on camera"

Shaggy: "It wasn't me!"

RikRok: "Heard the screams gettin' louder"

Shaggy: "It wasn't me!" "To be a true player you have to know how fe play/never admit to a word wha she say," Shaggy advises.

"It Wasn't Me" was "discovered" on the internet by a radio disc jock in Hawaii who downloaded it from Napster, a world wide web free song sharing service. He played "It Wasn't Me" on the air and received an instantaneous, very enthusiastic phone reaction from his listening audience; several other stations throughout the US tested the song in their markets and quickly added it to their playlists. "I was just lingering and all of a sudden Shaggy said this kid here can sing, he can write, let's work with him and then all of a sudden, boom, "It Wasn't Me" happened; this type of situation happens everyday, it's a typical Jamaican story!" RikRok offers as his explanation of the song's popularity. "The song connects because it's a great story," comments Shaggy. "It touches home, every one has either been in that situation or knows someone who has...it's very candidly done, it's funny...although it's not pretty. It's not derogatory, but initially I thought we'd get a lot of backlash from women." (The straightforward counteraction to "It Wasn't Me", "Son of a B***h" (Big Yard) recorded by Marsha and Lady Saw, written by Shaggy, RikRok and Dave Kelly, provides, as it's title indicates, an uncensored, veritable female perspective on the situation)

Shaggy's affable personality, tireless work ethic and ability to seamlessly fuse elements of popular (American) music into dancehall reggae and even more significantly fuse dancehall reggae into popular American music has established him as a bona fide star. What is most satisfying about Shaggy's success with "It Wasn't Me" and "Angel" is that despite the pop context in which the songs have been heard (the album has yet to make an appearance on the Billboard reggae charts) Shaggy's vocals are delivered in an uncompromisingly Jamaican deejay style. "That's shows you!" exclaims Robert Livingston, "people will embrace it once they get to hear it and you have to find ways to get them to hear it. We never started promoting the record in the r&b market because the r&b market started saying Shaggy is a pop artist. But r&b fans buy Shaggy's music; urban fans buy Shaggy's record so the only way for us to get Shaggy's record played is to start where he gets the most love. Then once he gets popular everybody will play him."

In an another very significant breakthrough for Jamaican music, Shaggy along with Rayvon and RikRok will embark upon a summer stadium tour with two of America's most popular groups the Backstreet Boys and Destiny's Child along with Jessica Simpson. Shaggy has been assiduously preparing for this momentous career opportunity for several years. "When I went to Brazil on tour with Maxi Priest, I saw him playing in front of 40,000 people who didn't speak his language," Shaggy recalls, "and I couldn't even remember Maxi Priest being played in the dancehall; that's when I got the whole picture. I said this is bigger, this is what I want. From that point on, that's what I've been striving for. Now I've got something to prove, to go down in the history books as someone who contributed to the upliftment of Caribbean music. Sting and Robert and the team, they share that vision and have made this whole thing happen."

ORIGINALLY PUBLISHED APRIL 2001

The Gentleman Rude Bwoy David Rodigan

NAZMA MULLER

Roots rockin' British radio is warming rainy London nights with sultry reggae rhythms and while David Rodigan may not be Jamaican born, he's acquired everything else to make his ascension to reggae royalty bona fied.

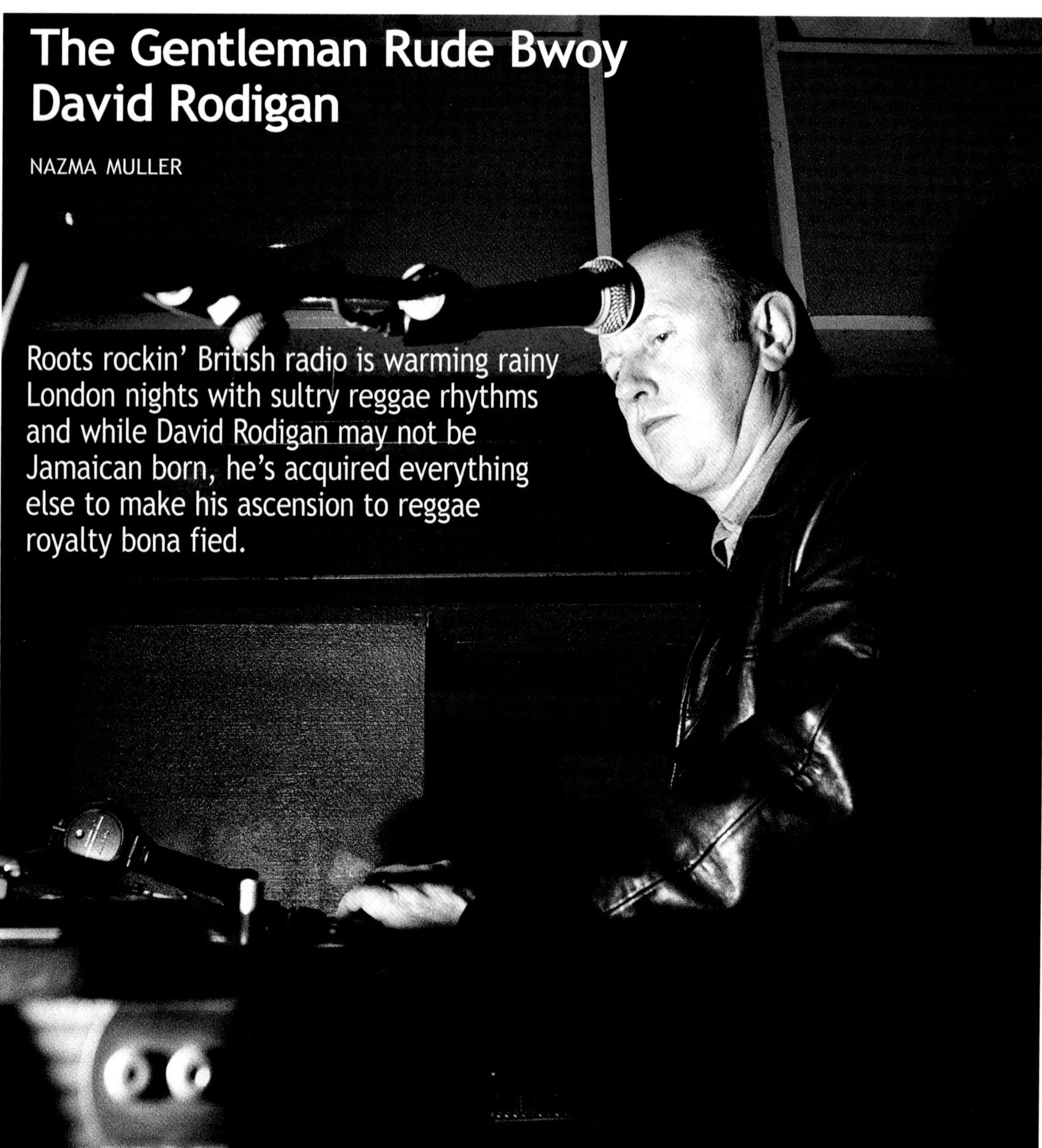

It's a dreary Sunday night in London, the air chilly even for mid-July. But on the radio, "The sun is shining, the weather is sweet—makes you want to move your dancing feet..." Sandwiched between Beethoven on a classical music and Britney Spears on the innumerable pop station, Bob is singing sweet songs of melodies pure and true on Kiss 100.

It's 10 p.m. and for the next two hours, Jamaicans across London will be back a yard, imagining themselves in a session in Rae Town, a warm, aromatic breeze blowing, a Red Stripe or Guinness in hand, all de man dem heads bobbing along to an old-time something from Dennis Brown. "Roddy, yuh a dub-wise smaddy!"

It's a hail-up to the radio DJ, a slice of a "dubplate" slipped in smoothly at the end of a Sanchez number. Only the wickedest of selectors have dubplates and you have to be respected by reggae artistes for them to do a remix of their songs bigging you up. Roddy is David Rodigan, and he has a dubplate mix that includes Luciano, Buju Banton, John Holt and Wyclef Jean.

Roddy is definitely "smaddy" in the dancehall. He is also white, middle-class and British. Short and balding, he is the most unlikely-looking selector. But don't be taken in by his looks or the English accent (Oxford, no less). Rival sound systems have made the mistake, and barely survived the sound clash to tell the tale of the Gentleman Rude Bwoy who slaughtered them with big tunes.

Listen carefully and you will hear the tiniest of lilts, a relaxed mellowness to his vowels. It's from 40 years of listening to reggae, 20 of them as a selector, 15 married to a Jamaican.

Rodigan's street cred as a selector is impeccable: every Wednesday night he pulls a crowd of hardcore, homesick yardies at Subterania, a reggae club in Ladbroke Grove. They are not allowed to smoke weed when he's onstage. If he smells it, he stops the show—and no bottles are pelted.

To 21-year-old Bill Cosby, an aspiring selector with the infamous Stone Love sound system, "Rodigan is a maestro. Him in a class by himself. He can put a tune together, he can handle him business. He's a veteran, like Bob Marley."

That this young Jamaican selector considers Rodigan a guru whose style and knowledge must be respected seems merely an inevitable continuation to an amazing journey that began in the late 1960s.

Born in 1951 in a military hospital in Germany to Scots-Irish parents, Rodigan was raised in North Africa until he was eight, when he came to England. Like any teenager, he was into rebel music. In 1960s England that included reggae.

"We were young mods," Rodigan recalls. It's a Wednesday night and we're sitting outside Subterania in his Mercedes-Benz. "We were crazy about Stax, Otis Redding and Marvin Gaye, James Brown, Curtis Mayfield and equally crazy about this new, young music from Jamaica which was underground. You know, you couldn't go to a club and not hear it."

He contracted ska fever. The music was raging through the underground scene; but it hadn't hit, and wouldn't until Millie Small's "My Boy Lollipop" in 1967-68.

"It was great dance music! And it still is." Left to Rodigan ska would still be on Top of The Pops every week. "Ska has this tremendous energy and passion in it," he says earnestly. "It's irresistible. It's impossible to hear it and not want to dance. And that was what appealed to us most of all. Although we didn't understand patois, we understood the sense and feeling of the pieces. That was the attraction."

But there was, unfortunately, life beyond the record player. After his first year at university, Rodigan dropped economics and switched to drama and the history of theatre later taking a job as an actor in a repertory company in north England. Way into the seventies, he worked as a jobbing actor, moving from company to company.

But he was still hooked on Jamaican music. His friends had outgrown their ska phase and moved on to glam rock and Abba; while Rodigan was still collecting 45s of rock steady, rockers, roots and culture and reggae.

A hobby had mutated into an obsession. "Without fail, wherever I was, whichever theatre I was working for, whichever part of the country, I would either get back to London the Saturday night after the show or I'd have friends send me a mail order list and I'd keep up to speed with all the records."

Finally, Rodigan had to face the music. "It was when I was unemployed that I first started to come to terms with my addiction," he said half-seriously. "I realised I was a reggae junkie. I couldn't let this thing go, it was part of my life."

He began to hitchhike from London to Oxford with a bag of reggae records. There was a sizeable Jamaican community in Oxford with its own sound systems. The fellas from the systems would meet him at the bus garage in Oxford every week and Rodigan would tell them what was hot, what to buy. If they didn't like it, he promised, he'd exchange it the following week. "Eventually I went big time," Rodigan laughed, "I got a market stall."

Meeting Bob Marley didn't help his addiction. In 1974, he and his girlfriend went to see Bob at his very first show in London. The first song the Wailers did was "Rastaman Chant", a non-stop flight to Nirvana for the massive crowd. At the end of the show Rodigan knew there was no way he was going to get past the hundreds of fans waiting outside the stage door. He and his girlfriend left. "I came out and walked down Fulham Palace Road until I saw this enormous cloud of smoke come out of a

From cheers, screams and hollers, recalls Rodigan, "a deathly silence descended upon the masses". Mouths dropped. No! A white man! The crowd stared in disbelief: this could not be David Rodigan, the voice they listened to every week, regular as church.

shop doorway. When the smoke cleared, there was Bob Marley on the end of a big spliff." Rodigan stood frozen, his mouth dropped open and he squeaked, "That's Bob Marley!" He was stupefied. He didn't know what to do or say. His girlfriend stared at him. "What do you mean?" she said. "Go and say hello. I've heard you going on for years about this man. Go and say hello."

So Rodigan walked up to Bob and said, "You don't know me but I know you"—or something equally inane."I just want to say thank you," he continued, mouth dry, heart palpitating. "I've waited so long for this night. I was in that ram jam session and it was just absolutely brilliant and thank you for everything." Bob replied, "One love. Rasta!" shook Rodigan's hand. A car roared up and he got into it. And as the car drove off, Bob Marley turned round and waved at a dazed David Rodigan out the back window. The stunned teen just stood there, waving back.

Four years later, the path to meeting Bob a second time opened up. The presenter of Reggae Rockers, a BBC radio show, left. Rodigan's girlfriend pretended to be him and wrote a letter to the producers saying he was the best thing in reggae fandom, and they should invite him to an audition for the slot. Fifteen minutes into the audition however, the interviewer stopped Rodigan and said, "I'm terribly sorry to have to stop this interview, but I'm afraid we can't offer you the job because you're the wrong colour."

Rodigan didn't get upset; he knew where the guy was coming from. "I understood perfectly because there was I, a white person, wanting to present a black music programme." It was hard enough for black people to get jobs in the media then, Rodigan didn't want to take one of the few they had a right to.

But when the BBC producers played the tape of his audition to Jamaicans in the industry, they told the producers to hire him; he knew what he was talking about. They thought he was black. Rodigan ended up co-hosting the show with a Jamaican, Tony Williams.

A year later, he went over to Capital Radio in a permanent slot, presenting Roots Rockers, which ran for 11 years. It was shortly after joining Capital that he made his first public appearance.

A big show was being held at the Apollo Club in Willesden, one of the oldest black clubs in London. The show had been billed to the max, and he walked onstage to face a room packed to the rafters. From cheers, screams and hollers, recalls Rodigan, "a deathly silence descended upon the masses". Mouths dropped. No! A white man! The crowd stared in disbelief: this could not be David Rodigan, the voice they listened to every week, regular as church. The MC whispered to him, "If you don't say something, this place is going to explode!"

As Rodigan started to speak, he could see people closing their eyes, trying to match this white man's voice with what they knew from the radio. They opened their eyes, still disbelieving. And then he played his signature tune, "Mash Down Rome" by Michael Prophet, and that was it. Bedlam broke out. The place went wild, and Rodigan knew he had them. The music was in control, and it didn't matter the colour of the person playing it.

Around this time, Rodigan made his first pilgrimage to Kingston. "I had landed. The next thing I knew I was in Orange Street. I was standing outside Prince Buster's record shop. I was in Waterhouse, 18 Drumbley Avenue. King Tubby's studio. I met the King. I was in the King's throne room. The legendary Osbourne Roddock, creator of dub music. Prince Jammy was there. I met Sugar Minott, Jah Youth, Bunny Wailer, Gregory Isaacs, it was just endless. It was like, Wow! I was meeting all my musical heroes."

Back in London, he met Bob Marley again. He had gone to Island Records' office where Marley was rumoured to be hanging out, having just returned from Zimbabwe's independence celebrations. Rodigan spotted him coming down the stairs, surrounded by his ubiquitous entourage. The two were introduced by an Island official. But instead of shaking Marley's hand, muttering a platitude and then begging Marley's manager for an interview, as was the custom, Rodigan said to the superstar, "Will you come on my show on Saturday night?" There was a collective gasp at his audacity. Minders looked uncomfortable and mumbled that he wasn't doing interviews. Bob Marley looked at Rodigan, looked around at a couple of his people and then back at him and said, "Ahright."

Sure enough, the following Saturday night, Marley showed up at Capital Radio's studios. Rodigan took him into a small room before the show and said, "Bob, I don't want to talk about politics, religion or anything like that. I just want to talk about the music. Is that okay?" Marley grinned and said, "Yes!" So they talked about music, and the tunes Marley made and why he made them. "I was nervous as a kid," says Rodigan. "My voice was like (he squeaks in a falsetto), 'Bob Marley, oh my god!'I was shaking like a leaf. I could hardly cue up the records. It was 1980 and I was interviewing Bob Marley. It doesn't get much better than that."

In 1983 Rodigan returned to Jamaica to do a series of broadcasts for Capital. He met Barry Gordon, a popular Jamaican radio DJ, and invited him to be on his show. Barry G returned the compliment and asked Rodigan to appear on his show. The two sat down in the studio. The news was on; they were going live in a few minutes. Barry G turned to Rodigan and said, "Forget being my guest. This is a clash!" As Gordon explains: "We Jamaicans love competition. So it was natural for me to inject a level of competitiveness into everything. Here was this DJ who was so big in the UK—I felt I had to see what he had. He was so wrapped up in the music, why not expose him to the very discriminating Jamaican audience?" Rodigan went into shock; but managed to stay calm. "I knew what it involved: you had to play a tune just as good as or better than the tune that's just been played. It was a bit like a jigsaw, you had to find a way out of that, and to carry on building the jigsaw." The next day, Rodigan and Barry G were the talk of Jamaica.

Sir Rodigan, as he has been dubbed, is an unworldly yet clever selector. And the key to his cleverness is his knowledge of the music. As legendary producer Coxsone Dodd, now 70, and one of Rodigan's own heroes, said: "He was one of the persons who caused a lot of Jamaican DJs to start collecting the music. In sound clashes he was more knowledgeable, because of that everybody try to compete with him. And when it come to selecting, he's very good. I'm very respectful of him, because he plays the music, he doesn't go into the politics."

Barry G is still amazed by Rodigan's devotion to the history of reggae and his willingness to learn the history and origin of a song. "He makes it his duty to experience it; he has mastered it. He can be selecting Jamaican music for Germans and he can tell them where bauxite is mined, where Bob Marley grew up, the history of Port Royal, where to get fish and bammy. This is a man who has no connection with a place other than through the music and he has taken the time to learn the culture."

And that is saying something. As well known as reggae is, Jamaica—its people and its culture—can still elude and bemuse the most earnest of wannabes. David Rodigan is no wannabe. As far as Jamaicans are concerned, he's not only on the inside, he's ranking. Come down, selector!

Check out Rodigan's dubplate mix from Buju Banton, Freddie McGregor, Luciano, Bounty Killer, Gregory Isaacs and Wyclef Jean at www.rodigan.com which also carries his Kiss show live (also on kissonline.co.uk) as well as videos of sound clashes.

ORIGINALLY PUBLISHED AUGUST 2002

MISS LOU

LOUISE BENNETT

The Hon. Louise Bennett-Coverley, O.M., O.J., M.B.E., Hon. D. Litt., is Jamaica's most popular folklorist. Her collection of dialect poetry has captured the essence of the Jamaican spirit and culture.

The Honourable Miss Lou

SANDY McINTOSH

It would take a brave person to deny that Jamaica's most cherished national treasure is the Honourable Miss Lou, Louise Bennett.

Sitting in her semi-enclosed office at the dreamhouse she and her husband, Eric Coverley, restored from a ruin in Gordon Town, she remembers the days when the Jamaican dialect was literally scorned.

Her determination to fight this scorn, she says, was inspired by the people she grew up with, and the wide cross-section of people who would visit her mother's dressmaking parlour. "Most of the people I really loved were people who talked the dialect, and I couldn't see anything wrong with them."

Neither could she see anything wrong with the other aspects of Jamaica's indigenous life which were given so little credence by those who believed that "real" culture had to be imported.

"I have always been fascinated by everything that was truly "Jamaican" Miss Lou adds, "and I was upset that we were not learning more about it."

"I just love Jamaica. I feel this country has given so much to all of us. I have a feeling about people; I must judge people not by how much education they have, but by the type of people we are. I feel the unwashed slaves left us a lot through their suffering, and joy, too. They found a lot of time to create. We have really created a whole new culture from the British, the Spanish, the Africans—all the people who came together to make Jamaica and with especially strong African undertones."

The drums of pocomania which evoke a 'night sound' almost as regular as the crickets and the tree frogs, set the young Louise on an islandwide research programme.

"I made my mother tell me of any relatives she could think of, and I'd go and spend time with them all over the country, and I went to all the poco meetings I could find."

She also trekked to settlements such as Accompong and Maroon Town, often riding mules along otherwise inaccessible terrain, to delve into the culture of the Maroons.

Today, youngster on this quest would probably have little trouble getting a research grant. But in Louise Bennett's youthful days, she was regarded as 'plain mad' and irresponsible. What was more, her research and writing could not earn her a living at that time.

People visitng her mother would insist that Miss Lou was wasting her time.

The fact that she was able to persevere and carve out a career for herself as a multi-talented pioneer in Jamaica's cultural development was due in no small way to her mother's dogged support and faith in her. Another guiding light has been her husband, Eric Coverley, well known fine artist and theatrical personality who contracted her for her first stage performance 43 years ago for the queenly fee of one English guinea!

Not a person to stay down for long, she also found much strength during her struggle in the very culture she was living to highlight.

She remembers her grandmother quoting the Jamaican proverb "God brush fly fe tump-a-tail cow." (God will help when there seems no way).

Other local proverbs reminded her: "Dark night get him peenie wallie (firefly), sun hot get him shady tree" and "every chain no fe rolling calf," (sometimes your fear is greater than the reality). Or "God roll thunder fe mek mozella (a type of grain) grow."

Courage also came from her religious faith—as she says when things go wrong, "I just pray, I'm a praying soul. My mother was a praying soul and she brought me up that way." A Presbyterian who also gains strength from Unity teachings, married to a Wesleyian and whose ten adopted children are Catholics, she adds, "I go to all the churches though I don't feel now that I must go to church to pray...."

She had begun to score a breakthrough with her dialect verses when they started appearing in Jamaica's newspaper, the *Daily Gleaner* and she found people acting them out in community festivals. Repeatedly, she found herself being asked to be a judge at these occasions. It was then that she felt the need for more training so, she went off to study at RADA on a scholarship.

Three months after her arrival she joined other West Indian students recording Christmas greetings for broadcast at home. But, instead of the conventional lines, she gave a mini-performance, with verses such as "Mi darlin' fren', mi journey end, me ketch a London Town!" Among those in the studio who got a thrill from hearing her was the manager of the BBC overseas section who promptly signed her up to do a 'live' West Indian radio programme. Her typical dialect verses on the West Indian London scene heard on the programme (*Caribbean Carnival*) had people queueing up in the snow to see it. And so she found that as a fledgeling first year student, she had copped a prize regarded as an ultimate goal by graduates!

Today, Miss Lou is still writing, always in dialect, and now mostly in prose. Her radio and television shows, dramatic triumphs, international performances, have brought her a success which has done little to set her apart from the people who regard her as very much their own. They shout to her in traffic, come up to offer her jokes to add to her repertoire, and in her hill top village regard her as a favourite neighbour.

Though her popularity can make things a little difficult sometimes, she says, "I am very grateful and very humble that it happens at home."

ORIGINALLY PUBLISHED AUGUST 1981

Ring Ding

LOUISE BENNETT

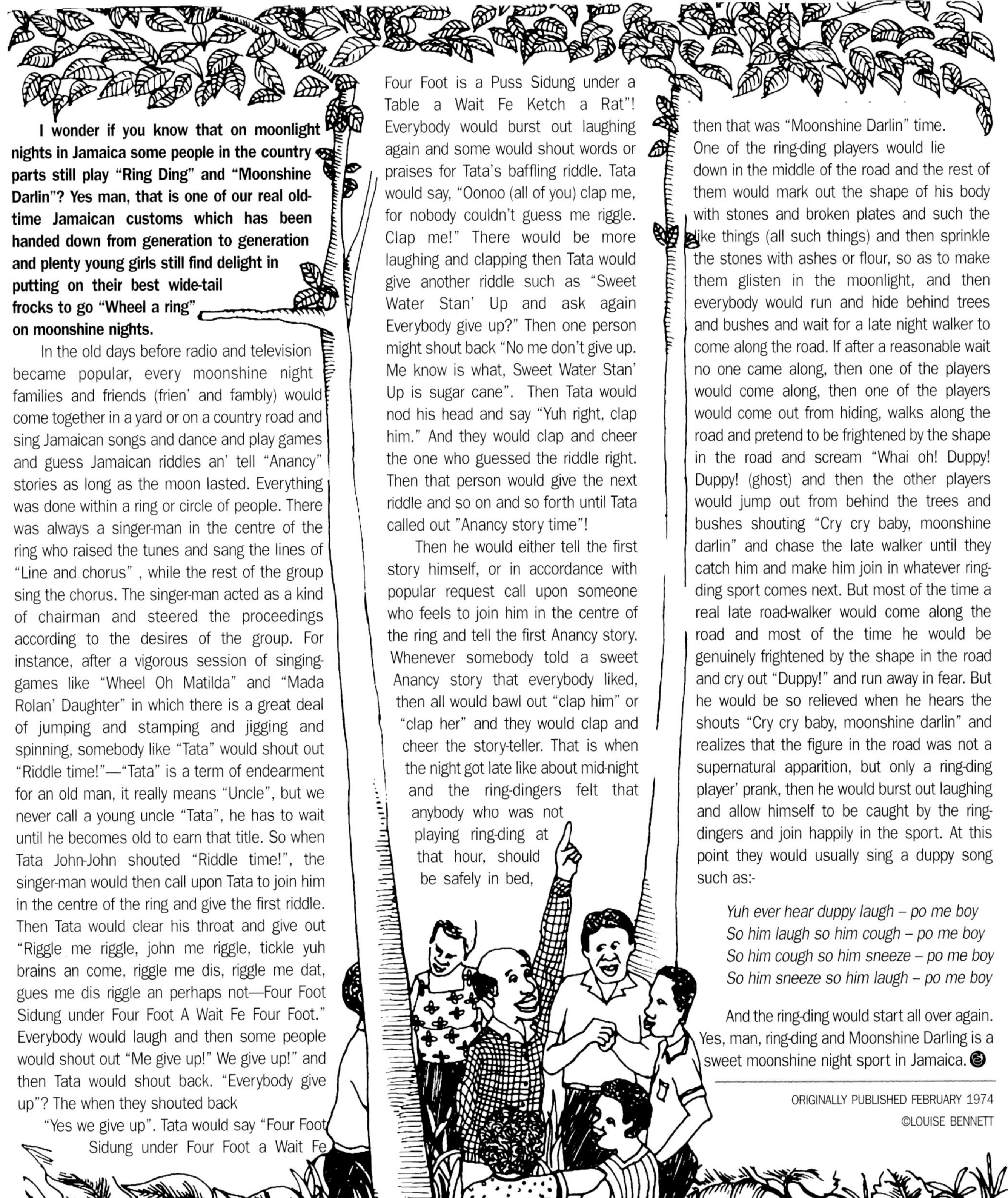

I wonder if you know that on moonlight nights in Jamaica some people in the country parts still play "Ring Ding" and "Moonshine Darlin"? Yes man, that is one of our real old-time Jamaican customs which has been handed down from generation to generation and plenty young girls still find delight in putting on their best wide-tail frocks to go "Wheel a ring" on moonshine nights.

In the old days before radio and television became popular, every moonshine night families and friends (frien' and fambly) would come together in a yard or on a country road and sing Jamaican songs and dance and play games and guess Jamaican riddles an' tell "Anancy" stories as long as the moon lasted. Everything was done within a ring or circle of people. There was always a singer-man in the centre of the ring who raised the tunes and sang the lines of "Line and chorus" , while the rest of the group sing the chorus. The singer-man acted as a kind of chairman and steered the proceedings according to the desires of the group. For instance, after a vigorous session of singing-games like "Wheel Oh Matilda" and "Mada Rolan' Daughter" in which there is a great deal of jumping and stamping and jigging and spinning, somebody like "Tata" would shout out "Riddle time!"—"Tata" is a term of endearment for an old man, it really means "Uncle", but we never call a young uncle "Tata", he has to wait until he becomes old to earn that title. So when Tata John-John shouted "Riddle time!", the singer-man would then call upon Tata to join him in the centre of the ring and give the first riddle. Then Tata would clear his throat and give out "Riggle me riggle, john me riggle, tickle yuh brains an come, riggle me dis, riggle me dat, gues me dis riggle an perhaps not—Four Foot Sidung under Four Foot A Wait Fe Four Foot." Everybody would laugh and then some people would shout out "Me give up!" We give up!" and then Tata would shout back. "Everybody give up"? The when they shouted back "Yes we give up". Tata would say "Four Foot Sidung under Four Foot a Wait Fe Four Foot is a Puss Sidung under a Table a Wait Fe Ketch a Rat"! Everybody would burst out laughing again and some would shout words or praises for Tata's baffling riddle. Tata would say, "Oonoo (all of you) clap me, for nobody couldn't guess me riggle. Clap me!" There would be more laughing and clapping then Tata would give another riddle such as "Sweet Water Stan' Up and ask again Everybody give up?" Then one person might shout back "No me don't give up. Me know is what, Sweet Water Stan' Up is sugar cane". Then Tata would nod his head and say "Yuh right, clap him." And they would clap and cheer the one who guessed the riddle right. Then that person would give the next riddle and so on and so forth until Tata called out "Anancy story time"!

Then he would either tell the first story himself, or in accordance with popular request call upon someone who feels to join him in the centre of the ring and tell the first Anancy story. Whenever somebody told a sweet Anancy story that everybody liked, then all would bawl out "clap him" or "clap her" and they would clap and cheer the story-teller. That is when the night got late like about mid-night and the ring-dingers felt that anybody who was not playing ring-ding at that hour, should be safely in bed, then that was "Moonshine Darlin" time. One of the ring-ding players would lie down in the middle of the road and the rest of them would mark out the shape of his body with stones and broken plates and such the like things (all such things) and then sprinkle the stones with ashes or flour, so as to make them glisten in the moonlight, and then everybody would run and hide behind trees and bushes and wait for a late night walker to come along the road. If after a reasonable wait no one came along, then one of the players would come along, then one of the players would come out from hiding, walks along the road and pretend to be frightened by the shape in the road and scream "Whai oh! Duppy! Duppy! (ghost) and then the other players would jump out from behind the trees and bushes shouting "Cry cry baby, moonshine darlin" and chase the late walker until they catch him and make him join in whatever ring-ding sport comes next. But most of the time a real late road-walker would come along the road and most of the time he would be genuinely frightened by the shape in the road and cry out "Duppy!" and run away in fear. But he would be so relieved when he hears the shouts "Cry cry baby, moonshine darlin" and realizes that the figure in the road was not a supernatural apparition, but only a ring-ding player' prank, then he would burst out laughing and allow himself to be caught by the ring-dingers and join happily in the sport. At this point they would usually sing a duppy song such as:-

Yuh ever hear duppy laugh – po me boy
So him laugh so him cough – po me boy
So him cough so him sneeze – po me boy
So him sneeze so him laugh – po me boy

And the ring-ding would start all over again. Yes, man, ring-ding and Moonshine Darling is a sweet moonshine night sport in Jamaica.

ORIGINALLY PUBLISHED FEBRUARY 1974

"Fe We"

LOUISE BENNETT

Meck me tell yuh Jamaican dialect. You notice the title of this article? Well that's how we say "our" in Jamaica dialect; "fe we." When we want to say "this is ours," we say "dis a fe we." "Mine" is "fe me," "yours," "fe yuh" and "theirs" is "fe dem." You get it?

Alright me dear, (we like to call people "me dear" when we like them, it's a term of endearment and "me" means "my"). Well, as I was saying, the Jamaican dialect is the language that most Jamaican people ("smady") talk, most of the time, some Jamaican people talk some of the time and all Jamaican people can understand all of the time. Most of the words in the Jamaican dialect come from English words, but it is not easy for any outsider or foreign person to recognize all the English words in the Jamaican dialect when they listen to Jamaicans talking.

Oh no, it's not easy to understand at all, but it is nice to listen to and as we Jamaicans say, "it sweet fe talk." You notice the "fe" again? Well this time "fe" means "to"—"It sweet fe talk." Don't bother to feel confused about "fe" because "fe" has only two meanings "to" and "for."

When we want to say "For better for worse," we say "Fe betta fe wussa." Yes me dear, "worse" is "wussa" and "worst" —"wussara." Some of our Jamaican dialect words sound just like whatsoever we are talking about looks like. For instance if someone is "out of order" and behaving badly, we say they are "boogoo yagga." If someone is sweet and lovely and kind, we say they are "boonoonoonoos. "If a place is untidy we say it is "chaka-chaka."

You hear the vitality in the words—boogoo yagga, boonoonoonoos, chaka-chaka. Don't it make you feel to laugh too?

Well, the Jamaican dialect is full of humour and wit and vitality and the whole thing started during the slavery time, when most of our African ancestors who came to Jamaica as slaves were from the Ashanti tribe and talked the Twi language. But our English forefathers, who were the slave owners, couldn't understand what our African ancestors, (the slaves) were saying to each other when they talked in Twi, yuh se (you see). So the English started to force the Africans to stop talking their African language altogether and to learn to talk only the English language.

What a jeopardy to freedom of speech! Lawks! How could the African slaves mock and jeer and pass remarks about the English slaves owners in the English language without the English understanding them? Wat a ting! (What a thing). But our African ancestors were crafty you know, yes man; they decided to disguise up the African language inside of the English language, in such a way, that the English still would not be able to understand them, if they did not want to be understood! Yes sir, the Africans would speak the English with the strong accent and word construction of their native tongue, and when our English forefathers (the slave owners) thought that our African ancestors (the slaves) were really being creative and ingenious!

That's how the Jamaican dialect was created and through the centuries all the people of many different nationalities who have lived in Jamaica, the Spaniards, East Indian, Chinese, Jews, French and so on contributed more and more word and phrases to the Jamaican dialect. We were even able to save a few Arawak words for our Jamaica dialect. For as you know the Arawaks were the very first inhabitants of the island when Columbus discovered it and the name Jamaica is an Arawak word meaning "Land of Wood and Water."

So anytime we hear anyone call our Jamaican dialect "corruption" of the English language we just laugh after them and say that if that be the case the English language must be a corruption of Norman French and Latin and all the other languages that the English say English is derived from. Wat a joke! So walk good fe now, yes "walk-good" means "good-bye," and we have a little Jamaican song what say:

Walk-good on yuh way an
good spirit walk wid yuh;
Walk good.
Walk-good, good fallow
yuh,
if yuh jus' walk-good.

Ah gone! (I am gone).

ORIGINALLY PUBLISHED SEPTEMBER 1972

Introducing Bredda Anancy

LOUISE BENNETT

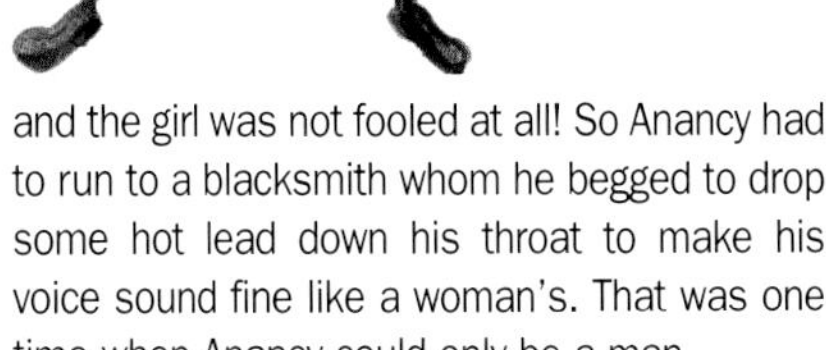

Our Jamaican folk-stories are called Anancy stories. Anancy is an Ashanti (West African) Spider God, but most Jamaicans know and love him as the 'trickify' little spider-man who speaks with a lisp and lives by his wits, who is both comic and sinister, the hero and villain of Jamaican folk-stories.

Some people feel that Anancy points up human weaknesses and shows how easily we can be destroyed by our greed, or stupidity or by putting out trust and confidence in the wrong people and things. Some people feel that Anancy shows in his stories the survival tactics employed by the weak in society in order to combat the strong. Some others feel that Anancy is just a lazy, lying, deceitful, envious and down-right wicked, good-for-nothing creature. But all agree that he is a lovable rascal.

Most Anancy stories have songs and these have been the true lullabies to many Jamaican children for generations. Each Anancy story ends with the phrase "Jack Mandora me no choose none" which means, 'Jack Mandora'—doorman, keeper of heaven's door; "me no choose none"—it is not of my choosing or I take no responsibility for the tales I have told!

We call Anancy "Bra Nancy" or "Bredda Nancy" (Brother Anancy), or just plain "Anancy" and when I was a little girl, there were no stories in the world I loved as much as Anancy stores. All the stories that were in the pretty foreign books with the pretty coloured pictures didn't 'sweet me' (appeal to me) like the Anancy stories which my grandmother and my great-uncle and my friends at school told me.

We used to swap Anancy stories with each other during recess time and lunch time and those of us who knew plenty Anancy stories and could tell Bredda Nancy stories "sweet", were very popular with our school mates. We were always certain of a big audience during the story-telling sessions and all the listeners became part of the story-telling too, because we all knew the little spider-man so well, with "his cunny look" (cunning eyes) and "him tie-tongue talk" (his lisp) and "him trickify laugh"—"kya, kya, kya".

Bredda Nancy's laugh was infectious and whenever he laughed, we would laugh too. In fact, there was a great deal of laughter during the telling of Bra Nancy stories, for Anancy never really cries, he only "form cry" (pretends to cry) and he never really gets angry, he only "form vex" (pretends to be angry).

The strongest and most endearing feature of Bredda Nancy is his sense of humour. Bra Nancy injects humour into everything. Even when Anancy is doing wicked things, like the time when he was beating poor Billy Goat, who was wrongfully accused of stealing a bunch of bananas, which we know was stolen by Anancy himself. Anancy's tactics were so comical as he shouted "yuh shteefin' shteef yuh!" (you thiefing thief) that we found ourselves laughing with Anancy instead of sympathizing with Bredda Billy Goat.

We were fascinated by the little spider-man with his many arms and legs and his magical powers. Oh yes, Anancy is a magic man! We know that we could never be like him and we had better not try any of Anancy's tricks, for he is magic and we are human.

Before telling Anancy stories during the daytime we had to "mash ants" (kill an ant) or our mothers could turn into "bankra-baskets" and never become human-beings again!

Anancy is greater than all the other heroes in the other stories. Every existing custom is said to have been started by Anancy ("is Bra Nancy meck it"). He could get himself and other people in an out of trouble like magic. He could become any-body he wanted to be anytime he wanted—well not quite anything, there are just one or two little times when Anancy could only be a man.

Like the time when he was trying to steal away a pretty young girl by pretending to be her mother and singing the secret song which her mother used to sing for her daughter to open a secret door. But when Anancy started to sing the secret song, his voice was a man's voice and the girl was not fooled at all! So Anancy had to run to a blacksmith whom he begged to drop some hot lead down his throat to make his voice sound fine like a woman's. That was one time when Anancy could only be a man.

But most of the time Anancy could change himself into what he wanted—a young girl sometimes, an old woman sometimes, or even a little baby!

Like the time when Anancy's wife was working for a rich and wicked old man who wouldn't pay her any money until she could guess his secret name. So one day Anancy told his wife to dress him up like a baby, sling him on her back and take him to work with her. Mrs. Anancy did as she was told. When they got to the rich man's house, he was sitting on his verandah rocking and fanning himself and Mrs. Anancy begged him to allow her to leave her baby on the step of the house until she was finished working. The rich man agreed and Mrs. Anancy went about her business.

Anancy started to cry like a baby, first quietly and then louder and louder. His screams became so shrill, that the old man bent over to look at the baby and Anancy screamed and bared his teeth in the old man's face. The old man was so frightened that he shouted, "Poor me Seckery! Look wat me live to see. Young baby with big mouth full up with long yellow teeth! Poor me ole Seckery!" He called for Mrs. Anancy to come an take up her baby. When she came and bent over the baby, Anancy whispered, "Him name Seckery".

So, of course, that evening Anancy's wife was able to guess the rich man's name when mean old Seckery reluctantly gave her a big bag of money with all the back pay in it, the baby-Anancy jumped off her back and the man-Anancy picked up the bag of money, put it on his head and laughed—Kya, kya kya kya!

Jack Mandora me nuh choose none.

ORIGINALLY PUBLISHED SEPTEMBER 1977

"Miss Lou" in London

LOUISE BENNETT

When I go to London you see, I always dress for comfort, I never dress for style. So anytime you buck me up on a London street, be it spring, summer, autumn or winter, I look like a walking monument blotted with clothes, merino and sweater, and cardigan, and head-scarf, and throat-scarf and coat, and stocking, and high boots making sure that I feel warm and comfortable, mmm.

I like to walk along a big London street like Oxford Street in the day time and see the thick crowd of people going and coming in and out of stores, and in an out of buses and cars and taxies. Yes sir, I always like to just stand up round by Oxford Circus there and watch the different nationality people pass by and guess to myself which part of the world they come from! You can meet up people from every nation in the world any day of the week in London.

I like to sample the London restaurants too, mmm, and try out all the different nationality foods and don't ask if you can't find food from all over the world in London! Yes man, you can find East Indian, Chinese, Greek, Italian, Syrian, West Indies, and English food too of course, though to tell the truth, the only English food that I really like is 'fish and chips'. Yes you can find any type of nationality food you want in London and you don't have to pay any big money neither. You can be walking along a street with big stores and big restaurants and big banks and big cinemas and big bright lights and all of a sudden you just turn a corner and you land up into a little dark street with little shops and little stores and little restaurants with nice food at very reasonable prices. But I still feel that the East Indian food in London is nicer than East Indian food in any other part of the world. Yes me dear, when I taste a certain type of dahl, curried-lamb, paratha and chapati and such the likes East Indian foods, I know that I am in London. Water come a me mout' (my mouth waters).

Another thing that makes me know that I am in London is when I find myself in a long queue moving orderly and peacefully along to a bus-stop or a ticket window or a shop counter.

Oh, yes me dear, English people like line-up fe true, and especially London people! Of course, the queue does make things run more smoothly, but to tell the truth, sometimes you can waste plenty time in a London queue. Oh yes, supposing you are queuing up in a bread-shop, don't bother to bawl out and ask "Do you have any rye-bread?" and expect anybody to answer you before its your time to get served you know, oh no, everybody just looks on you with scorn and nobody will answer until when your time comes to be served, and then when you ask again "Do you have any rye-bread?" the shop assistant might say "No madam" and he is finished with you! Mmmm, thats how you

waste time in a London queue. One night, in the shillings and pence time you know, I was going to a cinema and I saw a long queue outside the theatre and I wanted to know if the feature film had started yet, so I walked up to the door-man and said "Please can you tell me if the feature-film has started?" The man didn't even look at me, he just said, "loidy, get in the one-and-noin queue". I said, "But if the feature film has started I won't go in, for I haven't got time to stay for the later show." The man put on a stern look on his face and said "Loidy, toik my advice, get in the one-and-noin queue." Well I stood in the one-and-nine-pence queue for about twenty minutes only to find when I got up to the ticket window that the feature-film was about half-way gone! See here, I did feel to brain the door-man with me shoes heel, but as I am not a violent person, I didn't.

I always feel care-free and adventurous in London, all like when I board a double-decker bus and relax with a cigarette upstairs and pick chat with other passengers on the bus. You know what? I find that though the English people might look forbidding, their curiosity is stronger than their reserve and as soon as they realize that they can understand what you are saying to them they start to question you. Yes man, they ask you all kinds of questions. The first one usually is "How long have you been in England?" Well, I usually answer "two weeks", and you can bet that the English person's next utterance will be "Two weeks! You learn English very fast!" Then I would laugh and tell them that I am from the West Indies, and I can never forget an English woman saying to me at that point "West Indies?" Oh you must be very proud of Mahatma Gandhi!" and when I explained that Mahatma Gandhi was from the East Indies and I am from the West Indies, the lady smiled and said "Oh yes, I know all about your people, I once met a very interesting fellow from Uganda." What a joke! Plenty English people still don't know the difference between the East Indies and the West Indies and they blissfully mix up Africa and India with the Caribbean Islands!

One day after I had finished explaining all about the West Indies to a nice English gentleman in an Italian restaurant in London, he introduced me to a friend who came in as "Miss Bennett from South Africa, Jamaica." Ah me dear, I get plenty jokes in London, and I don't know if it is my luck or if its a formula or what, but anytime I ask a London policeman the way to anywhere, the bobby always smiles at me kindly and say, "Loidy go stroight, first on the left, second on the roight, you can't miss it," and some how I never have! Yes man, London sweet me!

ORIGINALLY PUBLISHED JULY 1974

MYAL

LOUISE BENNETT

"Bitter cerassee can cure nearly everything.
Chainy-root an strong-back wi gi yuh stamina.
Daily-cup a garlic-tea wi bring dung blood-pressure.
Ginny-grass an lime-leaf wi cure yuh fever.
Pepper-leaf and castorile wi bruk you bwile dem.
Divi-divi gargle wi cure yuh sore troat."

The belief in bush medicine, the curative powers of plants and herbs, is very strong in Jamaica and it all began with myal.

Myal is the practice of bush-medicine. It comes from the African word "Maye", meaning sorcerer or wizard. The myal-healer, male or female, (myalist) must master the knowledge of the curative powers of plants and must use this knowledge for good only. In this sense, the myalist is the direct opposite of the obeahman who is best known for using "duppy" (spirits or ghosts) to do harm to others. Yet, the myalist must also have complete knowledge of the methods of the obeahman in order to counteract evil.

The cotton tree, which is the counterpart in the West Indies of the sacred akata of Ashanti religion, played a vital part in the practice of myalism and also of obeah.

Champong Nanny, Jamaica's best-known Maroon warrior-woman, was said to be a great myalist. According to legend, in the famous battle with the British in 1738 at Accompong, Jamaica, when the Maroons were outnumbered at one point and it seemed as if victory would go to the British that day, Champong Nanny tore off her clothing, rubbed her body with a certain myal-plant and stood on the brow of a hill inviting the soldiers to fire at her. The legend goes that the bullets bounced off her body, back to those who fired them, wounding the soldiers. The British fled in terror from the scene and victory went to the Maroons.

But it is believed that because Nanny used her myal powers to hurt people that day, she lost all her powers of myalism.

In the seventeenth and eighteenth centuries, the practice of myal flourished in Jamaica. But, there were never more than a few real practitioners at any one time because the role of the myal-healer was a demanding and strenuous one, both morally and spiritually.

The myal-healer was the leader of the cult and was called "myal-man" or "myal-woman." The followers of the cult were called "myal-bredda" (brother) and "myal-sister."

To be initiated into the myal-cult as a healer, one had first to do a long period of study with an established myal-man, or woman, learning about the curative powers of herbs, plants and trees, until the teacher felt the learner was ready for the initiation ceremony.

Then, at the "myal-grung" (place of worship), the myal-breddas and sisters would robe the "learner-healer" in white from head to foot—a white turban for his head and white wraps for his body. After the ceremonial robing, he was given to drink a potion of "gumma," a species of callaloo, (spinach) juiced and mixed with white rum. Following this, the breddas and sisters would form themselves into a circle around the learner-healer and to the vibrant rhythm of the kbandu drums would begin the vigorous myal-dance, chanting, spinning and leaping.

The words of the chant were very African in sound:

"Qulama, baynah, luban baynah,
Quluma, lanumba baynah..."

The learner healer was made to keep dancing until he was "possessed" by the myal-spirit and fell to the ground ("drop a grung") and to all appearances seemed lifeless. He had to remain in this state, "rooted" to the ground for at least seven days. If he came out of this 'state' before seven days, he was disqualified as not possessing the right qualities for a myal-healer.

During the time of "rooting" or "lock," the learner-healer is carefully watched and tended by the brothers and sisters of the cult. The learner-healer at this time is supposed to be communing with the myal-spirit and receiving higher instructions from them about the secret powers, both good and evil, for curing and healing the sick in body and spirit and never using these powers to harm or revenge anyone, no matter what the temptation.

At the discretion of the myal-priest (head-healer) after a minimum of seven days "rooted," the initiate is ready for "revival," and in the midst of drumming, dancing and chanting, he or she is first disrobed and anointed with the juices of certain herbs and then a second potion, the mixtures of which until today is kept secret, is forced down his or her throat. Gradually, the initiate returns from the spirit-world, chanting and prophesying. The words are followed closely with reverence as, messages from a higher sphere. He or she is then given a strong "bush-bath"—a bath with a certain quantity of special herbs.

Because of these "revivals" from the spirit-world, the myalist gained the reputation of being able to raise people from the dead.

The cotton tree, which is the counterpart in the West Indies of the sacred akata of Ashanti religion, played a vital part in the practice of myalism and also of obeah. This tree was revered as the dwelling-place of both good and evil spirits - myal duppy (good spirits) and obeah duppy (bad spirits)—over which the tree had supreme control. Both the myal healer and the obeahman knew the secret rituals through which the cotton tree would permit the spirits to do the bidding. The tree would permit those who cast evil spells to remove the evil spells if they wished but evil-doers were not permitted to make contact with the good spirits (myal-duppy) of the tree. So, though the obeahman had power to remove evil spells he had no power to reverse the cure of the myalist.

An obeahman would cast an evil spell on a person by driving a nail into a cotton tree, calling upon an evil spirit to order a person's shadow to leave their body and dwell in the cotton tree.

The myalist would counteract these spells by taking the victim of the spell, dressed in a white robe and white turban, to the cotton tree and there make sacrifices of food and drink, such as white rice cooked without salt; rum, eggs, and a live chicken which would be killed and the blood sprinkled at the root of the tree. The myalist would then fill a gourd with water, hold it up to the tree, and with loud chants and strong, leaping movements, order the shadow out of the tree and into the gourd. The gourd was then covered and taken to the home of the shadowless person whose turban would be removed ceremoniously by the myalist, dipped in the water and the turban put back on the person's head. In this way the shadow was returned to its owner.

After the cotton tree ritual, the myalist would always prescribe "bush-medicine" and a "bush-bath" for the patient. Sometimes the medicine would be herbs juiced, put in a bottle and buried in the ground for nine days before being taken in small doses. Sometimes, herbs steeped in rum, or boiled and taken as tea for a specific number of days.

It was very difficult to remain faithful to the principles of myal because of the temptation to use its powers for personal gain or revenge. It is said that some myal-healers who lost their powers became obeahmen.

Today, the practice of myal in Jamaica is almost dead, but the belief in "bush-medicine" and "bush-bath" is as strong as ever. It is quite natural for a Jamaican to tell you...

Rat-aise an Sinckle-bible cure you
sore-foot.
Duppy-Cho-cho wi wash weh bad-luck.
Susumba leaf, Susumba pill wi wash out
you system.
Ginger-root and Mint-tea fe gas an
flatulence.
Broom-weed an Periwinkle
fe palpatation.
Love-bush tea fe mirasme baby.
Semi-contract pull out cole (cold)
outa baby.
Sour-sap leaf good fe pain-a-joint.
Majo-bittas and Rice-bittas cure yuh
billiamness.
Donkey-weed and Pull-me-coat fe
pain-a-belly.

ORIGINALLY PUBLISHED MAY 1980

Folk Medicine

LOUISE BENNETT

The use of folk medicine is still very strong in Jamaica. Belief in the curative powers of Mother Nature, and the conviction that knowledge of these powers was revealed to our ancestors and handed down from generation to generation to provide healing and balm for the human being, is deeply rooted in the Jamaican culture.

In many Jamaican homes today there is a special corner, on a shelf or on a table, in a cupboard or in a drawer, where the bottles and phials, jars and boxes of "house remedy" or "yard remedy" are kept, used when necessary and carefully replenished from time to time.

White over-proof rum usually forms the base for most "house-yard home remedies". Some of the bottles would contain "rubbings" such as, scorpion steeped in rum for soothing painful joints (pain-a-jint) and relieving muscular pains and arthritic condition...young snake steeped in rum used for the same ailments. White (young) cockroaches steeped in rum to relieve pain-a-aise (ear ache). Both the roach and the snake must be put into the rum while they are alive for best results. Other bottles would contain bissy (kola-nut) steeped in rum which is considered an antidote for all forms of ptomaine poisoning and stomach upsets. A few leaves of ganja steeped in rum for colds and fever, belly-aches and all manner of minor complaints. Asafetida is mostly steeped in water and used for flatulence. The boxes and jars would contain things like dried pomegranate-skin, dried fowl-gizzard, a few fowl-feathers, dried ginger-root, pieces of stale bread the mildewed portion of the bread would be used to make "bread pills" for colic (severe belly-ache) to make poultices for boils and to be applied to old sores to remove 'dead-flesh'.

Usually there is some corner of the yard called the "bush-tea patch", the "bush doctor" or "the yard hospital" where all kinds of herbs and cacti are grown—"sincle bible" (aloes), tuna (cactus), red water-grass, jack-'na-bush, ramgoat dash-along, broom weed and other plants which are supposed to have medicinal values.

Before calling a doctor it is often customary to try a little "yard remedy". If someone is suspected of having say, mumps, the first thing done is to make certain that it is really mumps by giving the patient a half of a lime to suck on and, if that causes great pain and almost unbearable burning in the throat, you then proceed to treat the patient for mumps. One method is to get some warm wood-ashes, spread it on some green 'river-tobacco,' leaf and tie it on to the jaws of the person with a large white 'kerchief or piece of white cloth, and "mumps fly!" The patient makes a quick recovery. Another house remedy for mumps is

If someone is suspected of having whooping cough, the best "yard remedy" is to get a cane-piece rat and use it to make a soup and feed this to the patient.

to use a fowl-feather to apply some warm castor oil on the swollen area... If someone has measles, the burnt-corn remedy is tried first. A cob of corn roasted until burnt, then the grains are shelled and put in a glass of water, allow to soak awhile and settle and the liquid given to the patient... another "house" or "home" remedy for measles is the tamarind-bush tea and tamarind-bush bath. Boil some leaves from the tamarind tree in water, feed the liquid to the patient, a cup-ful at a time. To speed up the recovery, bathe the patient in the same brew at least twice a day—morning and night. Dried fowl gizzard and dried pomegranate skin are considered very good "house" remedies for vomitting. They can be boiled together or separately and the liquid given to the sick person, two tea-spoonfuls to begin with and one tea-spoon at intervals until the vomitting stops. Another 'sure' remedy for vomitting is a dose of bissy steeped in rum. A dose is usually two to three tea-spoonfuls.

On some occasions after one has been to the doctor, it may be felt that certain "house" remedies are necessary to effect a complete cure. For instance, if one has been in a car accident or a fight and has been badly shaken up, bruised, or battered, he is never considered properly attended to, at times even after being hospitalized, until he is given a dose of young calabash, roasted and juiced and mixed, with a little castor oil to 'purge out' the 'bruised-blood' from the system.

If someone went to the doctor and was told that he had an ulcerated stomach, whatever the doctor prescribed, some families would first try a little "house remedy"—one that is felt to be a 'sure cure' for ulcerated stomach. They would get a piece of "sinckle-bible" (sempervive-aloes) cut into half-inch cubes and slide a few pieces two, or three times a day down the throat. If this is done faithfully for at least two weeks, the patient might find there is no more necessity for the doctor's prescription.... Another "home remedy" for ulcerated stomach is the molasses treatment. A teaspoonful of unrefined molasses is put into a half pint of milk and taken three times daily. This is considered another 'sure cure' with marked improvement within a month.

In the old days the kitchen cobweb figured strongly in folk medicine, but since the cobweb must come from a kitchen with an open wood-fire and the cobweb must be very black with soot and smoke, it is not very widely used these days, but kitchen cobweb was used to make a tea and given to mothers with new-born babies to drink every morning for nine mornings after the birth. This makes the mother pass out all impurities from her body, restores her strength and keeps her in good health for the next baby....

If someone is suspected of having whooping cough, the best "yard remedy" is to get a cane-piece rat and use it to make a soup and feed this to the patient.

For sprains, it is customary to soak leaves from the custard-apple tree in black vinegar and use it to bandage the sprained area. This will "draw out" the pain and heal the sprain.

There are "yard remedies" which seem to be based purely on superstition. For example, if one gets stuck by a rusty nail, he should toss the nail into an open fire and the injured spot will heal without further medication. For someone suffering from fits (epileptic seizures) try to lay them in a bed and place a hot clothes iron, preferably an iron, underneath the bed then place a door key in the patient's hand and the seizure will gradually pass and the patient usually falls asleep. A common practice to get rid of nausea is to break a matchstick or piece of dried bramble in two pieces and put a piece behind each ears. This will also get rid of muscular spasms. For instance when running or jogging, if one should feel a sharp pain in the side or leg, the matchstick or dried bramble behind-the-ears method is said to cause the pain to go away almost immediately.... If one is prone to land or sea-sickness a few layers of newspaper folded and placed next to the skin on the abdomen and on the back will allow them to travel in comfort without a trace of nausea (no bad-feelins at all). For ague, a door-key placed in the afflicted person's hand and held tightly will cause the ague to go away.... Many people will swear that to cure colic—severe abdominal pain—is to pick two roots of broom-weed, hold one in either hand, put your hands behind your back and tie the two roots together behind you, then boil the knotted roots and give it to the sick person to drink.

It is maintained that if the roots are not tied behind the back the cure will not be effective.... There are those who say that an easier method of curing colic is to have the sick person pass his hand under his arm and inhale it. This is also a common method of getting rid of nausea, vomitting and even insects stings.... There are several different "yard remedies", for colic ailment common among children who tend to over-eat fruits in season and indigestable mixtures of food, (mango season is colic time).

Screams of "green bush! green bush!" are sure to chase away wasps and bees. The moment the insects hear the cry of "green bush" they fly away because they know that stinging has no effect when those they sting use the "green bush" antidote. Three green leaves picked from any three different plants, crushed together and rubbed on the stung spot will prevent swelling and render the sting harmless. Those who neglect to use the three-green-bush remedy, have been known to suffer the discomfort of swelling and pain.

If one is stung by a scorpion, the scorpion should be crushed and the scorpion fat"—the substance that comes from the insides—rubbed on the forehead of the stung person. This will prevent them from from ever being stung by a scorpion again, as they are bound to see the insect, overpower it and kill it, before it gets a chance to sting them.. Whether or not a person is stung by a scorpion, the 'fat' rubbed on their forehead will make them immune to scorpion stings.

These are only a few of our Jamaican folk medicine practices which still play a fascinating and vital role in the Jamaican folk life. The large areas dealing with the supernatural, duppy, (ghosts) obeah (witchcraft) myal, undoing evil cannot even be touched here.

There is a Jamaican proverb which says, "God roll t'under fe meck mosella grow", mosella is a yam which grows to huge proportions and provide large families with big meals at little cost. Thus, "the Divinity uses His powers to take care of the weak and needy." Those who practice folk-medicine, often quote this proverb. "God roll tunder fe meck mosella grow."

ORIGINALLY PUBLISHED JULY 1983

Gran-Market and Christmas Market

LOUISE BENNETT

Everyday is market-day in Jamaica but Christmas-Eve day is the Grand Market day when every market-place becomes a "Gran-Market."

From early morning on Christmas Eve both town and country-people begin to "pull foot" (make tracks) for Gran-Market. In the old-time days before trucks and buses were prevalent, it was a pretty sight around the Jamaican country-side to see the procession of market-vendors carrying "food-kinds" and "fruit-kinds" to sell at the "Gran-market". Men, women and children with bottle-torches in their hands would light-up and before-day darkness, and pretty-up the procession with bankra-baskets on their heads, full of oranges and grapefruits and tangerines and ripe bananas and green bananas, callaloo and okra and chocho, escallion and tomatoes and all kinds of food and fruits and vegetables.

The donkeys came with their hampers loaded with 'hard-food', like yam and yampie and coco and sweet-potatoes and breadfruits and green plantains and bundle upon bundle of sorrel.

Sorrel is the Christmas-blooming red plant which Jamaican-people love to boil down with ginger and mix with sugar and spices to make the sweet Christmas-time drink. Lawks, wat sweet like sorrel at Christmas-time! The then flowers-vendors would make the "Gran-market" procession joyful to behold with their baskets and buckets full of all the pretty Christmas flowers like bougainvillea and poinsettia and hibiscus and marigold and roses of all colours.

Anything you want to buy, you can get to buy at "Gran-market". Lace and cotton, silk and satin, beads and chains and rings, bangles and spangles and dolly-play-things! Cook-food and fresh-food and sweetie and fruits, dressing clothes and drudging-clothes, all at the "Gran-market". When I was a little pickney we used to go from market to market to feast our eyes on all the pretty things that you never see in any market on any other day by "Gran-market" day. Then, the crowds of buying and selling people were bigger and thicker than any other market-day crowd of people.

Lawks me dear, we used to enjoy pushing through the crowds and those days when we spend our little money we could come home with our hands full-up and baskets full-up with Christmas niceness.

Then in the old-time "Gran-market" days, Jamaica country-people always have a Christmas-cow procession too, yuh know! Mmmmm, the cows used to parade from the cow-pens to the market –place with their heads dressed up with pretty

Christmas flowers. The cow-drivers were called "whooping-boys" because they always go "whoops" as they drive the Christmas-cow down to "Gran-market".

Through we don't have any Christmas-cow procession nowadays, still and for all, around Christmas-time plenty Jamaican people still swear that they can hear the duppies (spirits) of the long-time "whooping-boys" all over the countryside going "whoop" every "Gran-market" soon-a-morning. True, true. Well then, big crowds of people would follow the Christmas-cow procession, laughing and talking and dancing and singing songs like:

Nuff Christmas-cow a parade tru de town,
Beef ina market a sell bit a poun'
Rookoombine ina Christmas
time, Rookombine.

Yes me dear, they would sing about the nice fresh beef they were going to buy at Christmas-market on Christmas morning for Christmas morning was a real "beef-market" morning. In country and town we always have Christmas-market on Christmas morning for Christmas-market is a real big celebration place, especially for children to jump and prance and blow fee-fees and horns, blow up balloons and burst balloons, and burst clappers and light starlights and redlights and bluelights and bawl out "Christmas!"

When I was a little pickney on the way to Christmas-market we were bound to meet John-cunu dancers (Christmas masqueraders) with Ass-head and Actor-boy and Grass-boy and Kookoo and Jack-in-de-green and we would jump up and chant "Ass-head come and gone, Jack-in-de-green as go buss him calla, brrrrr!" Sometimes we would pretend that we were afraid of the "Ass-head" and he would run us down until we give him a hapenny or a penny and then he would cut-figure (dance) to the John-cunu music for us.

Down at the Christmas-market we would buy wangler and cut-cake and grater-cake and asham and cockshan and such-the-likes nice things, while the parents and other big people buy beef and fancy cake and wish one another "Merry Christmas." 'Cocksham' is what we call "pop-corn" nowadays. Plenty snow-ball carts used to be down at the old-time Christmas-market because we could make plenty noise and bawl out "Christmas!" on the top of our voices an go for boat rides an dance when the music-ban played. Nobody ever told us to be quiet or 'stop de nize' down at Christmas-market.

So although every day is market day in Jamaica, yet still and for all the "Gran-Market" Day and Christmas-Market Day are the sweetest market days of all.

ORIGINALLY PUBLISHED OCTOBER 1978

Old-Time Jamaican Country "Wedden"

LOUISE BENNETT

There is a wedding here today,
There is a wedding here today
The wedding cakes are on parade,
There's a wedding here today.

If you are passing through a Jamaican country village and see a procession of young women all dressed in white, some with what from a distance looks like high, bulky head-dresses with veils falling unto the shoulders, and others with white-veiled objects in their hands and all singing, don't panic, what you are witnessing is the "cake parade" for a real old-time Jamaican country wedding. This is one of the customs handed down from generation to generation, ever since Emancipation in Jamaica.

The old-time country wedding is very rare these days but, some young couples love to carry on this tradition. Once a couple has taken the decision to have a real, old time country wedding they must first select a "wedden godmadda" and a "wedden godfada", both usually well-versed in all traditional trappings. The wedding godmother is chosen by the bride-to-be and the wedding godfather by the groom-to-be, and it becomes the responsibility of these two to plan the wedding and to see that everything proceeds according to tradition.

There are five traditional customs. All very special features of an old time country wedding —choosing the wedding godmother and godfather; the booth building function (the reception is always kept up in a "wedden booth" built in the yard of the parents or relatives of the bride or groom-to-be, wherever is more convenient), the cake parade, the cake-bidding and the "turn-thanks" day.

Once the wedding godparents are chosen the parents and relatives of the bride-to-be give whatever money they can afford for the wedding to "wedden godmadda", the parents of the groom-to-be give their money to the "wedden godfada".

The "wedden godmadda" chooses volunteers from among the relatives and friends (frien' and fambly) to help with certain functions, then the preparation for the big day begins.

Wedden godmadda goes with the bride-to-be to select her entire bridal outfit. She decides how many bride's maids there should be and the colour of their dresses. She sees to the making of the bridal gown; sometimes she makes it herself. (The wedding clothes are always in the latest fashion and have nothing to do with traditions.) The godmother is responsible for dressing the bride on her wedding day and providing the bridal bouquet, arranging for the baking of the cakes (sometimes she bakes them herself) and the cake procession, and she supervises the decoration of the 'wedding table'.

The wedden godfada takes charge of the planning for most of the recreational side of the wedding-reception. He helps the groom to choose his suit, arranges for the village band or music-men to play at the reception and collects the money from the groom and his relatives for drink, taking sole responsibility for supplying cane-liquor, rum and all the liquid refreshment for the occasion. He also arranges for the making of the show bread. No old time Jamaican wedding is complete without a show bread, an elaborate bread of plaits and twirls and loops with a bird on top to signify 'peace' or two birds for 'love'. The most important tasks of the "godfather" are to conduct the booth building and cake bidding ceremonies. The godparents accompany the couple to select the wedding ring.

The booth-building is always done on the night before the wedding and it's a lively and vigorous affair. The booth builders sprinkle white-rum on the site where the booth is to be erected, this to appease the spirits who live in the earth, for disturbing their dwelling-place, even for so short a time. The booth is usually dismantled within a few days after the wedding.

After the 'sprinkling', post holes are dug and white-rum thrown into each hole, the posts are firmly planted into the ground with much singing and bantering. The favourite 'post planting' song is:

"Hosanna, mi buil' me house oh, ha ha

"Me buil' it pon a rockygroun', ha ha
"De breeze can't blow it down, ha ha
"It buil' pon a rocky groun', ha ha."

While some men are 'planting posts' and tieing beams, others will be choosing strong coconut-boughs for the roof. Women and children will be plaiting coconut-fronds and preparing the "buna", the matting around the trunk which holds the beams to the posts, and the boughs to the beams for the roof. Still others will be preparing food for the workers, with others juicing canes, using a home-made cane-mill, to provide drink for the booth-building ceremony and the wedding reception.

In the meantime, the godmother and godfather would have taken the bride and groom-to-be to some quiet spot for counselling on the pleasures and perils of married life. At the end of the counselling and on joining the workers, they are greeted with shouts of playful banter and love songs like:

"Darling don't tell no lie
Swear to love me till I die
Cause I want to marry you."

Warning songs like:

"Teet'an tongue mus' meet,
But blood noh haffe draw oh!"

(There must be disagreement or argument at times, but there need not be violent quarrels and fight).

The bidding ceases and the wedding godmother unveils the centre cake and amidst much clapping and cheering, presents the bidding plate and money to the couple.

Teasing songs like:

"Yes me lady, yes married lady
Han' full a ring an she can't do a thing!"

The wedding booth is completed and decorated amidst much singing, feasting and dancing.

The wedding day is a busy one for the wedding godmother, in contrast with the wedding godfather who only has to accompany the groom to the church, preside over the wedding reception, cake bidding and quadrille dancing.

On the morning of the wedding day wedden godmadda all dressed in well starched white apron and colourful bandana—plaid head-tie, and her chosen helpers veil the wedding cakes, using net. After this the godmother with her helpers proceed to the wedding booth, where she supervises the decorating of the wedding table using ferns, wild flowers and the fruits in season. Places are left for the cakes and show bread and at the head of the table, where the bridal couple will be seated, the bidding-plate is set on a bed of ferns surrounded by flowers.

At this point the wedden godmadda leaves her table helpers for she must hurry to the church to see how well the relatives and friends are carrying out her instructions as they decorate the altar. Then it is back to her home to get the cake procession started before she dresses the bride in her "lama" (fineries)—her long wedding gown and wedding veil, her bouquet of roses and always a leaf or two of sweet-basil, or noo-noo bush in her shoes or stockings for good luck. The godmother seats the bride in the front room with a relative to 'fan' her while she quickly 'freshens' up. She will also arrange the bridal procession and sees that everything is 'boonoonoonoos' (beautiful and in order). After the marriage ceremony the wedding godmother will give the order for the newly weds to be taken on a "drive-out" around the village. The villagers will get a glimpse of the pair and the wedding party will get to the booth before the bridal couple arrives.

The cake bearers selected by the godmother for the procession must be young, unmarried women all dressed in white. There are never less than twelve girls in the procession even if there aren't twelve cakes. The centre cake is usually three tiered.

The centre cakes are always carried on the heads and the side cakes in the hand. The shortest girl carries the top cake on her head and leads the procession, walking along in front; behind her are four girls walking in twos with side cakes in their hands; then comes the tallest girl walking along with the bottom centre cake on her head. Behind her are four girls walking in twos with either cakes or flowers in their hands, and behind are two girls walking side by side, one with the middle-centre cake on her head and the other with the show bread in her hands. They travel through the village from the godmother's house to the wedding booth singing and chanting "there's a wedding here today." Villagers, invited and uninvited guests usually join the procession through the village to the wedding booth, but the uninvited guests never enter the booth.

The cake bearers place the cakes on the table in the space provided for then and remain in the booth singing and chanting until the wedding godmother returns from the church ceremony. She unveils the side cakes and the show bread, the centre cakes remain veiled.

When the bride and groom return from the church the wedding godmother, and the cake bearers meet them at the entrance singing "Behold the bridegroom cometh," lead them to the booth and seat them at the head of the table. The singing and chanting continue while congratulations and blessings are offered to the couple.

Now the wedding godfather takes charge. After inviting the parson to bless the table he raises his hands and, in a strong authoritative voice declares "I bid (whatever amount he wishes) that this beautiful cake be not unveiled". The bidding ceremony has begun and there is much excitement as others join in bidding "that this beautiful cake be unveiled." With each bid, the bidder walks up and places some money on the bidding plate. Everyone comes prepared to give whatever they can afford, and often the money put down bears no resemblance to the bid made. But each bidder is expected to add humour and sparkle to the function by bidding much more than he puts on the plate.

The bidding is a lively and entertaining affair and when the wedding godmother feels that the money is sufficient to give the couple a start in 'married life', she shouts "I bid that this beautiful cake be now unveiled". The bidding ceases and the wedding godmother unveils the centre cake and amidst much clapping and cheering, presents the bidding plate and money to the couple. The top and middle cakes are removed and the wedding godfather calls upon two of the cake bearers to cut the bottom centre cake. The one finishing first is supposed to get married before the other. The wedding godmother and the cake bearers proceed to cut up the cake, sharing it around, the bridal couple receiving the first slice to share between them. Wine is poured from cooling jars and wedding godfather calls upon the many speech makers.

Speeches are usually long and full of humour and good counsel, most of them ending with, "I hope you live like Isaacs and Rebecca." At the end of the speeches wedden godfada shouts "quadrille!" The village band strikes up the tune of the first figure and the bride and groom lead off in the dance. The first set of quadrille dancers are members of the bridal party. During the dancing "wedden godfada" cuts a portion of the show bread into slices and each unmarried young man is expected to buy a slice of the bread and present it to the girl of his fancy. This is a very popular feature of the old time Jamaican country wedding; the money from the show bread is given to the newly weds as ''brawtah" (extra).

After the sixth figure in the quadrille there is a break for dinner. Mannish water (a soup) is served first, then curry-goat and rice, fricasee-chicken and rice-and-peas, roast breadfruit, roast yam, boil banana and run-dung, cane-liquor, rum, ginger-beer! The wedding godmother packs baskets full of the best dishes and beverages for the bride and groom to take home and both godparents accompany the newly weds to the gates of their future home. Here they must spend the first night of marriage.

The first Sunday after seven days of marriage is called turn-thanks day. The newly married couple and their wedding godparents must attend a service at the church where the marriage took place to give thanks to God for their union. As they leave the church the wedding godmother takes the right hand of the bride, the wedding godfather takes that of the groom and join them together saying:'

"We hand you over to one another, go and live like Isaacs and Rebecca."

ORIGINALLY PUBLISHED JANUARY 1981

Like Old Time People Say

LOUISE BENNETT

JAMAICAN PROVERBS	LITERAL TRANSLATION	MEANING	ENGLISH EQUIVALENT
Roas' one lef' one till a mawnin.	Roast one and leave one for the morning.	Don't put your whole capital in a single speculation.	Don't put all your eggs in one basket.
Call puss massa, him nyam yuh.	If you call a cat master he will eat you.	If you belittle yourself, people will take advantage of you.	Don't make yourself a mouse or the cat will eat you.
No put yuhself ina barrel wen matches box can hole yuh.	Do not put yourself into a barrel, when you can hold into a matches box.	Do not over estimate yourself.	Don't over-rate yourself.
Do something before sinting do yuh.	Do something before something does you.	It is better to take precaution against a thing.	Prevention is better than cure.
Howdy an tenky no bruck no square.	How-d' do and thank you do not brake a square.	There is nothing to be lost by behaving in a courteous way.	Courtesy costs nothing,
Yuh sleep wid dog yuh ketch dog flea.	If you sleep with a dog you will catch his flea.	You will be punished or rewarded according to your actions.	Show me your company I'll tell you who you are.
Mawger cow a bull mumma.	The meagre cow is the bull's mother.	Everything has to have a small beginning.	Great oaks from little acorns grow.
So cow a grow so him nose hole a open.	As the cow is growing his nostrils are getting bigger.	The longer we live the more we learn.	Live and learn.
Dog wag him tail fe suite him size.	The dog wags his tail to suit his size.	Adjust your expenditure according to your resources.	Cut your coat according to your cloth.
Teck sleep mark dead.	Take sleep to mark death.	If you are warned beforehand that something is going to happen take all necessary steps in advance.	Forewarned is forearmed.
Bare foot man noffe mash macka.	A man who is bare footed must not step on prickles.	People whose own conduct is open to criticism should not criticise the conduct of others.	Those who live in glass houses must not throw stories.
Braggin ribba nebba drawn smady.	A bragging river never drowns no one.	A man who utters threats in a loud voice, or is given to noisy boasting need not be taken seriously.	Barking dogs seldom bite.
A sabe-so meck meck-so tan-so.	It is understanding that make an influential person powerful.	One's knowledge is responsible for one's position. Accomplishment depends on understanding.	Knowledge is power.
Bignado an cocoa head no deh a barrel.	Showing off and no food is in the barrel.	They brag most who can do the least.	Empty vessels make the most noise.
Braggadosha meck monkey play figgle ina dog doorway.	Fool hardiness makes monkeys play a fiddle at a dog's door.	Dogs attack monkeys refers to those who take stupid chances.	Fools rush in where angels fear to tread.

ORIGINALLY PUBLISHED JULY 1973

Noh Lickle Twang!

LOUISE BENNETT

Me glad fe se's you come
back bwoy,
But lawd yuh let me dung,
Me shame o' yuh soh till all o'
Me proudness drop a grung.

Yuh mean yuh goh dah 'Merica
An spen six whole mont' deh,
An come back not a piece betta
Dan how yuh did goh wey?

Bwoy yuh noh shame?
Is soh you come?
Afta yuh tan soh lang!
Not even lickle language bwoy?
Not even little twang?

An yuh sista wat work ongle
One week wid 'Merican
She talk so nich now dat
we have
De jooce fe understan?

Bwoy yuh couldn' improve
yuhslef!
An yuh get so much pay?
Yuh spen six mont' a foreign, an
Come back ugly same way?

Not even a drapes trouziz? or
A pass de rydim coat?
Bwoy not even a gold teet or
A gole chain roun yuh t'roat.

Suppose me las' me pass
go introjooce
Yuh to a stranga
As me lameted son wat lately
Come from 'Merica!

Dem hooda laugh afta me, bwoy
Me could'n tell dem soh!
Dem hooda sey me lie, yuh was
A-spen time back a Mocho.

Noh back-ansa me bwoy, yuh talk
Too bad; shet up yuh mout,
Ah doan know how yuh an
yuh puppa
Gwine to meck it out.

Ef yuh want please him meck
him tink
Yuh bring back something new.
Yuh always call him "Pa" dis
evenin'
Wen him come say "Poo."

ORIGINALLY PUBLISHED JULY 1983

Jamaica Oman

LOUISE BENNETT

Jamaica Oman cunni' sah!
Is how dem ginal soh!
Look how long dem liberated
An de man dem never know!

Look how long Jamaica Oman
Mada, sista, wife, sweetheart,
Outa road an eena yard deh pon
A dominate her part!

From maroon Nanny teck
her body
Bounce bullet back pon man,
To wen nowadays gal-pickney tun
Spellin-Bee champion.

From de grass-root to de hill-top
In Profession, Skill an Trade,
Jamaica Oman teck her time
Dah mount an meck de grade.

Some backa man a push,
some side a
Man a hole him han',
Some a lick sense ina man head
Some a guide him pon him plan!

Neck an neck an foot
an foot wid man
She buckle hole her own,
Wile man a call her "so-so rib"
Oman a tun backbone!
An long before Oman Lib,
bruck out
Over foreign lan'
Jamaica female wasa work
Her Liberated plan!

Jamaica Oman know she strong
She know she tallawa,
But she no want her pickney dem
Fe start call her "Pupa".

So de cunni' Jamma Oman,
Gwan like pants-suit is a style,
An Jamaica man no know
she wear
De trousiz all de wile!

So Jamaica Oman coaxin
Fambly Budget from explode,
A so Jamaica man a sing
"Oman a heaby load!"

But de cunni' Jamma Oman
Ban' her belly, bite her tongue,
Ketch water, put pot pon fire
An jus' dig her toe a grung.

For "Oman luck deh a dungle"
Some rooted more dan some,
But as long as fowl a scratch
dungle heap
Oman luck mus' come!

Lickle by lickle man start
praise her
Day by day de praise a grow,
So him praise her, so it
sweet her,
For she wonder if him know.

ORIGINALLY PUBLISHED NOVEMBER 1972

Miss Lou "Any which part mi live—a Jamaica mi deh!"

MERVYN MORRIS

The latest honour to Miss Lou is our Order of Merit, restricted to a small number of Jamaicans—not more than 15 living members at any time—who have achieved "eminent international distinction". Jahan Ramazani, in *The Hybrid Muse*, considers her "a major anglophone poet of our time." In *Come Back to Me My Language* Edward Chamberlin observes: "More than any other single writer, Louise Bennett brought local language into the foreground of West Indian cultural life." Miss Lou (the Honourable Louise Simone Bennett-Coverley, O.M., O.J., M.B.E., Hon. D.Litt.) has been internationally recognized as a distinguished writer, performer and scholar of Jamaican culture for many years—at least since 1965, when she made an impact on the Commonwealth Arts Festival in Wales.

She was international long before that. In 1945 on a British Council scholarship she entered the Royal Academy of Dramatic Art in London, and soon had a BBC programme of her own. She came home to Jamaica in 1947 but went back to England in 1950 to work again for the BBC, in charge of "West Indian Guest Night." She performed with repertory companies in Coventry, Huddersfield and Amersham. She moved to New York in 1953 and, after various jobs, gradually returned to theatre work. She and Eric Coverley co-directed a folk musical called "Day in Jamaica" which moved around Episcopalian church halls in New York, New Jersey and Connecticut.

In 1954 she married Eric Coverley in New York. On their return to Jamaica, in 1955, she worked for the Jamaica Social Welfare Commission as Drama Officer, travelling throughout the island, continuing the serious study of Jamaican folklore and oral history she had begun in the early 1940s. She lectured on drama and Jamaican folklore for the Extra Mural Department of the University College of the West Indies. She has been a generous resource person for many scholars of Jamaican folklore and language, including one recently puzzled by "Eh-heh" and "A-oah." ("Eh-heh" sometimes means "Yes" but—depending on tone and context—may sometimes imply "Of course" or "Serves him right." "A-oah" is often an expression added for emphasis, usually after a statement of defiance; but may sometimes play as "Now I understand. So that's what you mean!").

One day many years ago, as a teenage author of stilted verse in standard English, she was struck by a vivid remark in the Jamaican vernacular, and started writing in creole. (Jamaican creole, Jamaican dialect, "nation language", patois, Jamaica talk: what most Jamaicans speak has been called by various names. The terms most often employed by Louise Bennett herself are "dialect" and "our Jamaican language"). In 1968 she told Dennis Scott she had wondered "why more of our poets and writers were not taking more of an interest in the kind of language usage and the kind of experience of living which were all around us, and writing in this medium of dialect instead of writing in the same old English was about autumn and things like that."

Born in Kingston, in 1919, she was from early critical of the black self-contempt often induced by colonial experience. Talking with Don Buckner, in 1976, she recalled: "When I was a child nearly everything about us was bad, yuh know. They would tell yuh seh yuh have bad hair, that black people bad... and that the language yuh talk was bad. And I know that a lot of the people I knew were not bad at all, they were nice people and they talked this language."

She helped Jamaicanize the pantomime, now only distantly related to its English antecedents of the early 1940s. She wrote some of the scripts and contributed to others, and until 1976 was one of the focal personalities in the annual show. From 1966 until 1982, often three times a week, she composed and delivered *Miss Lou's Views*, topical four-minute radio monologues. From 1970 until 1982 she hosted *Ring Ding*, a weekly television show for children, in which children performed and were reminded of various elements of Jamaican folk culture. She and her husband migrated from Jamaica in the early 1980s (to Fort Lauderdale and then to Toronto), but she insists that her cultural identity has always travelled with her. "Any which part mi live —Toronto-o! London-o! Florida-o!—a Jamaica mi deh!" (No matter where I live—Toronto, London, Florida—I am in Jamaica!).

Some of her work may be sampled in recordings, such as audio-cassettes called *Yes M'Dear: Miss Lou Live* (Island Records) and *Lawd...Di Riddim Sweet* (Sangster's), and a video, *Miss Lou and Friends* (Reckord films). The books by her most readily available (all published by Sangster's Book Stores, Kingston, Jamaica) are *Anancy and Miss Lou* (Anancy stories), *My Aunty Roachy Seh* (monologues) and two collections of poetry, *Jamaica Labrish* and *Selected Poems*.

ORIGINALLY PUBLISHED MARCH 2002

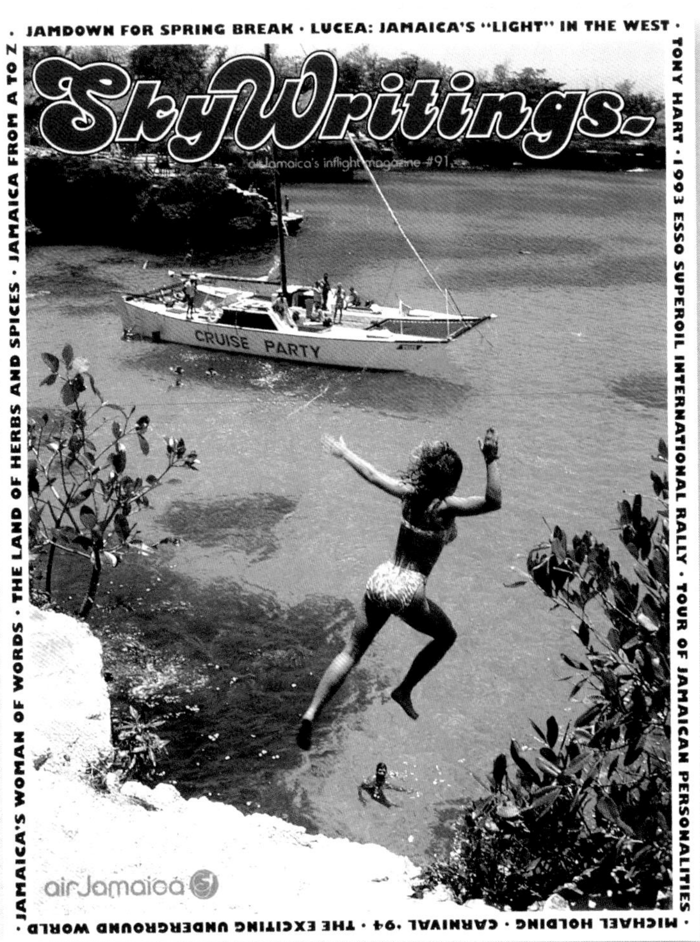

PLACES

SKYWRITINGS COVER
March 1994
Spring Break in Negril.

Trekking Over The Blue Mountains

ALAN EYRE

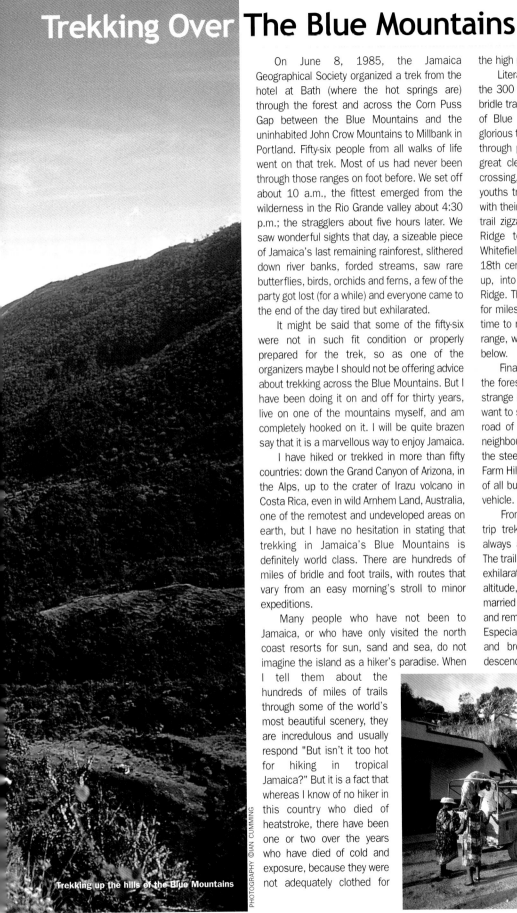

Trekking up the hills of the Blue Mountains

On June 8, 1985, the Jamaica Geographical Society organized a trek from the hotel at Bath (where the hot springs are) through the forest and across the Corn Puss Gap between the Blue Mountains and the uninhabited John Crow Mountains to Millbank in Portland. Fifty-six people from all walks of life went on that trek. Most of us had never been through those ranges on foot before. We set off about 10 a.m., the fittest emerged from the wilderness in the Rio Grande valley about 4:30 p.m.; the stragglers about five hours later. We saw wonderful sights that day, a sizeable piece of Jamaica's last remaining rainforest, slithered down river banks, forded streams, saw rare butterflies, birds, orchids and ferns, a few of the party got lost (for a while) and everyone came to the end of the day tired but exhilarated.

It might be said that some of the fifty-six were not in such fit condition or properly prepared for the trek, so as one of the organizers maybe I should not be offering advice about trekking across the Blue Mountains. But I have been doing it on and off for thirty years, live on one of the mountains myself, and am completely hooked on it. I will be quite brazen say that it is a marvellous way to enjoy Jamaica.

I have hiked or trekked in more than fifty countries: down the Grand Canyon of Arizona, in the Alps, up to the crater of Irazu volcano in Costa Rica, even in wild Arnhem Land, Australia, one of the remotest and undeveloped areas on earth, but I have no hesitation in stating that trekking in Jamaica's Blue Mountains is definitely world class. There are hundreds of miles of bridle and foot trails, with routes that vary from an easy morning's stroll to minor expeditions.

Many people who have not been to Jamaica, or who have only visited the north coast resorts for sun, sand and sea, do not imagine the island as a hiker's paradise. When I tell them about the hundreds of miles of trails through some of the world's most beautiful scenery, they are incredulous and usually respond "But isn't it too hot for hiking in tropical Jamaica?" But it is a fact that whereas I know of no hiker in this country who died of heatstroke, there have been one or two over the years who have died of cold and exposure, because they were not adequately clothed for the high mountain trails on February nights!

PHOTOGRAPHY ©IAN CUMMING

Literally from the front door of my home on the 300 foot contour at Salt Hill, St. Andrew, a bridle track runs a clear twenty miles to the top of Blue Mountain Peak (7402 feet). It is a glorious trail, this one, plunging down 2500 feet through pinewoods and coffee groves into the great cleft of the Yallahs valley. By the river crossing, you will very likely find a group of youths trying to scoop jonga (a small crayfish) with their hands from under the rocks. Then the trail zigzags up the great shoulder of Sheldon Ridge to Torre Garda and the hostel of Whitefield Hall, once a famous plantation of the 18th century coffee era, then on and up, and up, into the cloud-forest heights of Portland Ridge. There mossy forest enshrouds the hiker for miles, opening up dramatically from time to time to reveal spectacular views of range upon range, with towns and villages of the plains far below.

Finally, it emerges from the ferny gloom of the forest on to the windswept peaks with their strange dwarf, almost alpine, vegetation. If you want to shorten the walking distance, there is a road of sorts as far as Whitfield Hall and its neighbour plantation of Abbey Green, although the steep, corkscrew climb from Hagley Gap to Farm Hill is a bit scary and beyond the capability of all but a late model car or a four-wheel drive vehicle.

From Abbey Green it is a twelve mile round trip trek to "The Peak" – which in Jamaica always and only means Blue Mountain Peak. The trail is well maintained, and it is a steep and exhilarating ascent of nearly 3000 feet relative altitude, but it is not a mountain climb. My married daughter did the trek when she was five, and remembers it still as a peak point in her life. Especially the part after her brother dropped and broke the flashlight and they had to descend the trail in darkness, groping along and

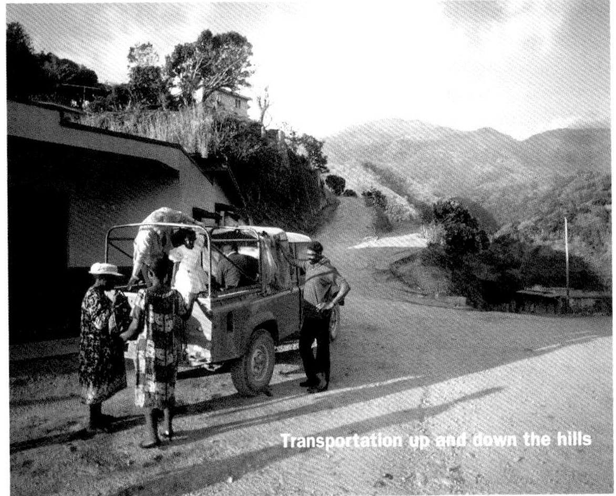
Transportation up and down the hills

A view at the top of Blue Mountain Peak

calling out to each corner and hazard of the way!

Trekking over some of the lower ranges of the Blue Mountains can begin as close to town as the suburban Papine and Gordon Town minibus termini. From both of these places, just a few minutes from downtown Kingston or Half Way Tree, a fascinatingly complex network of bridle trails, for the most part well maintained and used by locals, spreads out over the circle of mountains surrounding the Jamaican capital. You can climb to the height of Flamstead, once the lookout point from which Horatio Nelson and other British naval officers surveyed the Port Royal base and its approaches far below, sending their messages by mirrors. It was at Flamstead that the American commander of the Alabama in 1863, Raphael Semmes, wrote "In those mountains of Jamaica I was in an entirely new world, and was enchanted with everything I saw." Most hikers who reach Flamstead today feel much the same.

This same trail from Papine goes on to Bellevue, owned by the University of the West Indies. This famous 18th century coffee estate, renowned then for the particularly brutal treatment meted out to the slaves who lived and worked there, is now a lovely, quiet retreat where academics are supposed to be able to think clearly and without distraction. Perhaps the most popular trek in the whole Blue Mountain region, and certainly one of the most scenic, leads from Gordon Town up to the gorge of the Hope River to the Newcastle army camp. If you are feeling vigorous you may wish to continue to the top of Catherine's Peak (5056 feet), the mountain which so dominates Kingston but is itself now dominated by its tall radio antenna.

One of the best centres for exploring the Blue Mountains on foot and with backpack, or by horse or mule if you prefer, is Pine Grove Hotel and Chalets, efficiently and warmly operated by Mrs. Maria Thwaites. Hiking trails radiate from the magnificently sited hilltop hostelry in all directions: you can choose up or down, for you won't find much level land in these mountains, but remember if you go down first, to surrounding places with sweet names like Guava Ridge and Mavis Bank, Content Gap and Orchard, Pompey's Hut and Misty Valley—remember that you will need at least twice as long in time to walk back up again, a substantial meal at Marcia's cloud-kissed restaurant is certainly the best end to any trek through the Blue Mountains.

There are many unexpected bonuses for the hiker on the Blue Mountain trackways. You can explore, and even camp in, one of the famous old 18th century coffee factories at Clydesdale. The technology of those times is evident in the now rather battered water wheel and pulpery. In its heyday, just after the Haitian Revolution, when white planters fled Haiti and brought their expertise to Jamaica's Blue Mountains, almost every slope was covered with coffee bushes, not with the pines and eucalyptus and wynne grass pastures of today. In the National Library of Jamaica there is a large and beautifully coloured survey map of Clydesdale as it was in slavery days. It was from hillsides such as these that the coffee houses of Europe obtained their supplies; for a time Jamaica was the world's largest exporter, and so popular did West Indian coffee become that the satirist Alexander Pope could quip:

"Coffee which makes the politician wise, and see through all things with his half-shut eyes."

However, the coffee plantation is not merely a part of the history of the Blue Mountains: it is a dynamically growing industry in 1986.Some of the most interesting hiking trails lead to presently active coffee factories such as Moy Hall, Mavis Bank, Silver Hill and Wallenford, all of them in superb mountainscape settings. Here you can follow the laborious, centuries-old processes whereby the red-ripe cherry coffee is prepared for export as the premium aromatic coffee bean in the world.

Another centre from which trails lead in many directions is Hollywell, a few miles from the prominent army camp at Newcastle. With a bit of luck or better than average skill at map reading, you can find the Cascade, Jamaica's second highest waterfall, plunging sheer off the north slope of Hartley Hill (4363 feet). Even if you get lost in the attempt, the result will not be a disaster, for you will find instead ferny dells and glades, and paths that offer sudden breath catching vistas of mist-shrouded peaks and even sometimes the blue Caribbean in the far distance. And nowhere in the Blue Mountains, except at the highest elevations and on the wild, totally uninhabited northern slopes in rainy Portland, are you far from some road or far settlement where hospitable country-folk are certain to guide and assist you.

No trek through the Blue Mountains is complete without a visit to Cinchona Botanic Gardens. Half a dozen trails converge there, and it is one of the most spectacularly situated tropical botanic gardens in the world, a floral jewel on the mountains. After a morning climb to 5000 feet, to share a picnic lunch amid juniper, camphor, cork oak and mulberry trees, and absorb the billowing cloudscapes and vistas of range upon range to Kingston and the sea is to sensitive Jamaicans and visitors alike an unforgettable, almost mystic, experience.

There are a few trails only suitable for trekkers with experience and stamina, and just one or two require advance preparations as for a minor expedition; these should never be attempted by one or two persons alone, or without competent local guides. However, some of these are superb. One is the Corn Puss Gap trail mentioned at the beginning of this article. Another is the wild, romantic path that leads from Windsor in Portland to the site of Nanny Town. Cleared occasionally, but quickly reconquered by the rainforest, this is a historic trackway used in the early 18th century (before the 1734 "peace" treaty) by Quao and by their Maroon warriors who from their remote stronghold at Nanny Town resisted enslavement and British colonialism for over a hundred years. Another historic site, extremely difficult to reach, is the lair, high on the upper slopes of the Queensbury Ridge of Blue Mountain Peak, of Three Finger Jack, another freedom fighter whose exploits coloured Jamaica's past.

Here are ten of the most popular trekking routes through the Blue Mountains. It should be understood that, although representative, these are selected trails only, and there are many more which the enterprising hiker can discover from the Survey Department 1:500,000 or 1:12,500 topographic map series of Jamaica, or from helpful local informants. In the latter connection, remember that "a few chains" may actually mean several miles while "just round the corner" may be slightly less. "Not far" can be several hours' trek.

Whitfield Hall

Stony Hill—Hermitage—Dick's Pond—Hollywell Forest Park—Newcastle—Gordon Town (18 miles). This route passes one of the reservoirs for Kingston, some beautiful protected rainforest with tree ferns, and also some badly despoiled areas in the Hope River valley.

Hollywell Forest Park—Middleton Gap—Moodie's Gap—Mount Airy (10 miles). This route follows logging roads all the way, much of the distance through commercial forest. There are magnificent views of two big valleys, those of the Buff Bay and Ginger rivers.

Mount Airy—Mount Telegraph—Long Road (11 miles). Another picturesque route mainly through commercial forest, but with exceptionally fine vistas of the north coast.

Gordon Town—Sugar Loaf—Content Gap—Top Mountain—Cinchona (13 miles). This route is very popular with youth clubs and school parties, and the trail is often quite busy on public holidays and weekends. Some fine views at the higher elevations.

Cinchona—St. Helen's Gap—Moore's Gap—Vinegar Hill—Chepstow (16 miles). A beautiful but rather lonely trackway which was originally made for military purposes but was used a century ago by peasant carrying produce across the mountains on pack mules. An open-air market was held for many years at St. Helen's Gap. Many forest areas along the trail are presently being cleared for coffee cultivation.

Gordon Town—Flamstead—Bellevue—Mount Rosanna—Governor's Bench—Lime Tree—Orchard—Mavis Bank (10 miles). Many fine views of the south coast. Less lush and more open than the other routes.

Pine Grove—Guava Ridge—Bellevue—Mount Dispute—Lucky Valley—Newstead Cane River Falls (13 miles). An interesting trek which includes forestry plantations, peasant farming, gypsum mines, and a waterfall (now unfortunately often dry) once frequented by Three Finger Jack.

Mavis Bank—Sheldon-Penlyne Castle—Abbey Green—Portland Gap—Blue Mountain Peak (16 miles). This is the famous "Peak Trail", and two days are obviously essential for the round trip if it is to be more than an endurance test. Sunrise or sunset from the Peak is a never-to-be-forgotten climax.

Cinchona—Westphalia—Arm Hill—Abbey Green—Radnor—Hagley Gap—Arntully—Moy Hall—Cedar Valley (14 miles). A varied and very scenic trek along the southern slopes of the Grand Ridge of the Blue Mountains. Several old and presently active coffee estates are passed along the way.

Bath Fountain—Corn Puss Gap—Millbank (14 miles). Only for the fit. Passes through almost virgin rainforest. Impassable during and after heavy rains. A much easier but somewhat less scenic route is Bath village-Hayfield-Cuna Cuna Pass-Millbank (13 miles).

ORIGINALLY PUBLISHED MAY 1986

Mountain Beauties

BEA LIM

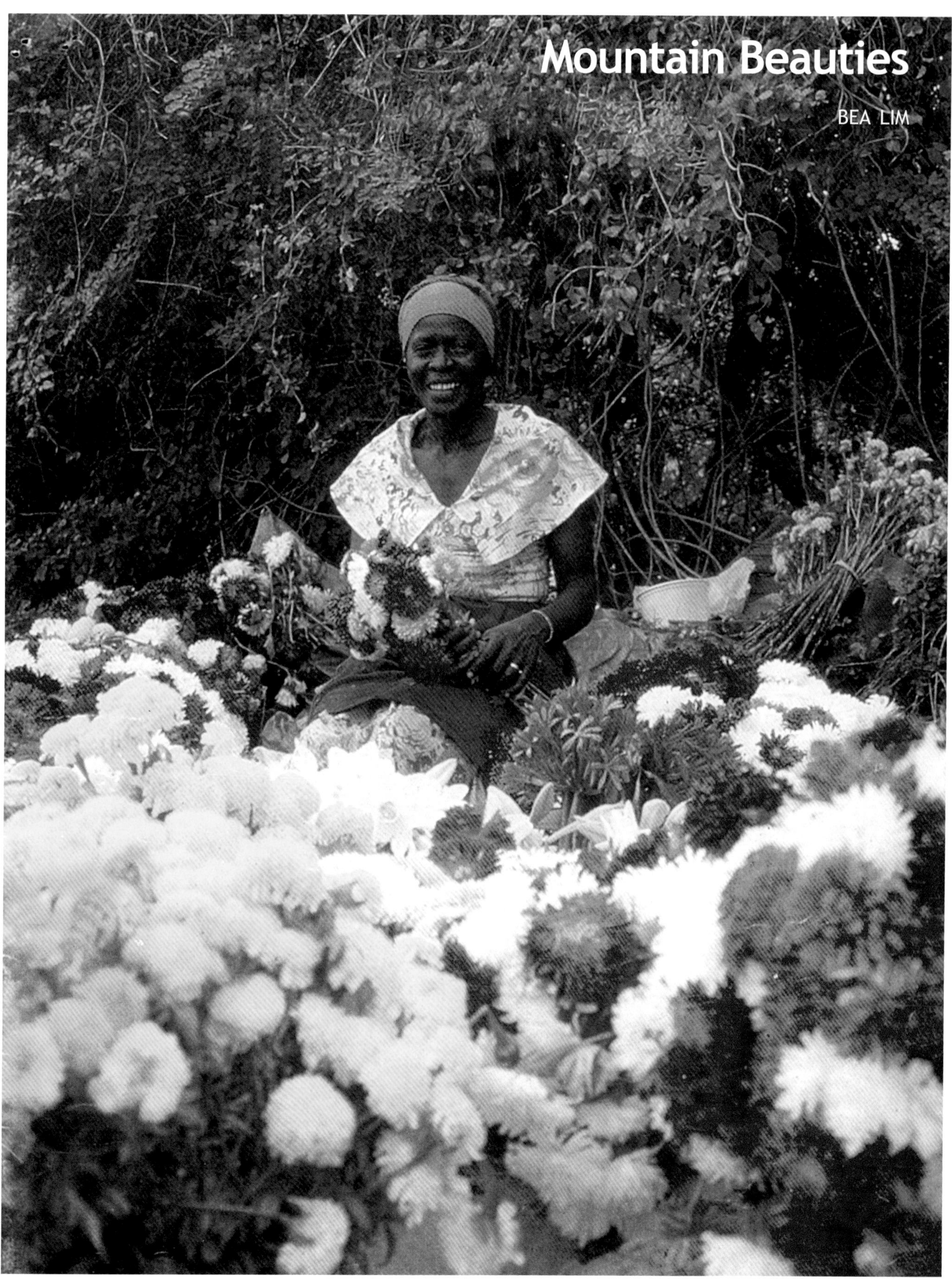

Her flowers are fresh. The morning is beautiful. And a handsome stranger is telling Doris Mothersill she's pretty. Joy!

She's a celebrity in her own right! Doris Mothersill. From larger-than-life portraits across Jamaica and in several countries around the world, her smiling face looks out at you. At her feet—buckets of mountain fresh cut flowers—gladioli, asters, marigold, lilies and carnations brought from the hills of St. Andrew to charm city dwellers.

From a rural village, half-an-hour ride from Kingston and tucked in the foot hills of the Blue Mountain, not one but five Mothersills journey every Friday and Saturday to sell flowers on the sidewalks of St. Andrew. At the corner of Ruthven and Trafalgar Roads—Doris, Kathleen and Joyce Mothersill along with friend Icilda Gordon are part of the Friday-Saturday landscape. It's been so for nearly 30 years.

A stone's throw from the famous Devon House, at the corner of Devon and Hope Roads, sisters Sylvia and Hazel lend colour to the city sidewalk as they too peddle fresh cut flowers.

It was the Jamaica Tourist Board that first caught the Mothersill smile, appended the lines quoted at the beginning and used it to win friends for Jamaica. Artists have painted the Mothersills and their flowers. The most recent being Susan Alexander who included a portrait of the flower sellers in an exhibition to celebrate her 30 years in Jamaica. Photographs...there have been many.

It's a long way from Maryland in the St. Andrew hills to the sidewalks of Kingston with boxes and buckets of flowers. But behind the weekly trek to Kingston is a story, repeated several times over, one of the hardiness and resilence of the folk who live in rural Jamaica, particularly those who eke out a living from the steep hillsides.

The hill farmers, or small farmers, or 'cultivators' as they are colloquially called are Jamaica's breadbasket. On plots of land carved out of the steep hillside, they grow root crops, legumes and vegetables that are the staples in many a Jamaican diet. These small farmers, most with large families, journey to the cities and big towns on weekends to sell their crops or, they sell to higglers who come to their villages and even on their farms to procure foodstuff.

These farmers work hard and at times the rewards are small.

In the upper reaches of the Blue Mountains they grow not only food crops but flowers. Jamaicans love beautiful things and a flower garden or a rose bush is the prized possession of many a householder. To supplement this they also buy freshly cut flowers.

Far up in the Blue Mountains roses, lilies, asters, gladioli, marigolds and carnations thrive in the cool, mountain air. Some years ago one Mothersill came up with the idea of collecting these mountain blooms and selling them to the 'flower-starved' dwellers on the plains. And so a weekly ritual began.

At daybreak each Wednesday during the lily season (February to July) five Mothersills set out from Maryland up a steep mountain path. The route winds through pine forests that lead into Hollywell (a recreational park maintained by the Government's Forestry Department) and on to Hardwar Gap in the adjoining parish of Portland.

At Hardwar Gap they meet the flower farmers who grow these beautiful lilies—red hypiastrum, the deep blue agapanthus, the fragrant white Bermuda or Easter lily and the pure white Eucharist lily. The flower sellers lovingly collect the lilies, carefully tie them together with banana bark strings and pack them in boxes.

From years of trading, the 'flower merchants' have built up a strong friendly relationship with their 'clients'. So, it is not unusual after the sales are concluded to 'take tea' in one of the small mountain cottages or for the visitors to share the contents of their flask and their sandwiches.

A little gossip, some catching up on the test happenings and it's down the slopes with the flower cartons on their heads. Back home in Maryland the flowers are placed in water to keep them fresh until selling time on Friday.

Thursday, like clockwork, the Mothersills board the 7 a.m. bus bound for Mavis Bank, also in the hills. The bus rounds many a tortuous curve, labouring on each bend, but affording the rider a breathtaking view of the mountains on every turn all the way to the bustling centre of Mavis Bank.

Flowers thrive in the districts that cover this mountainside. Villages with names like Content, Cascade, Guava Ridge, St. Peter's and Clydesdale. They've been growing there for decades.

For more than 300 years Jamaica was an English colony and the English are reputed to be the world's greatest flower lovers. Seeds were brought from England and planted in the gardens of the coffee plantations that dotted the sides of the Blue Mountains in the 1800's. Many of these garden flowers have gone to seed, an example, the blue ageratum, and their blooms cover the slopes of the mountain - 'garden escapees'. Others like the aster, marigold, gladioli, rose, and recently, the chrysanthemum, have proven to be popular commercial flowers and, as a result, the farmers of Mavis Bank grow them in their cool, moist, hill country.

The Mothersills are familiar faces to the growers of these areas. Here life is a two way street. They rely on each other to keep the trade growing. In Mavis Bank the Mothersills will walk to the nearer farms and collect their flowers or meet the farmers in the square and transact their business. Once again flowers are bundled, tied, placed in cartons and no sooner it is time to board the old bus for the return trip to Maryland. The Mavis Bank flowers bunch the mountain lilies in water to await the next day's trade.

It surprises a lot of Kingstonians to find that they awake on a Friday morning to find the Mothersills in their familiar places on the sidewalks of St. Andrew. Flowers not sold on Friday are kept by kind city neighbours until Saturday.

Business is usually brisk. City housewives, and many men too, look forward to having flowers fresh from the mountains every week. Saturday's over and it is back to the hills and to their very large families.

For the Mothersills and so many other hill dwellers, this is the life... food and flowers for many a harried city folk.

ORIGINALLY PUBLISHED JANUARY 1983

A Kingstonian Remembers

CALVIN BOWEN

Kingston today is a far different place from the one that I knew as a boy. To begin with, old-time Kingston was a much smaller place than now. There was no Barbican or Beverly Hills, no Harbour View or Mona and no Portmore—the new satellite city to the southwest in St. Catherine.

The city was much confined with the limits of Constant Spring and Papine at the upper outskirts and at Rockfort and Spanish Town Road at the eastern and western ends.

Much of the populace—that is about a quarter of the one-million-plus that it is now—lived in the city proper, on Hanover Street, Duke Street, East Street, Church Street and Orange Street.

Very few traces of these former homes—some of them splendid mansions—remain today. But in their time they represented the height of residential living in the city.

Some other roads, such as South Camp Road and Waterloo Road in the east, also served as residential areas; but the main concentration was in what is now regarded as downtown Kingston.

One of my earliest memories was living on Waterloo Road in the east. It was far from being the built-up area that it is today, and Rollington Pen (as it was then called) had many an open land above Giltress Street.

Franklin Town was another area that was being developed as a middle-class residential centre, and Newton Square was coming into its own as a place of fine houses. Bournemouth and Springfield were yet to be.

To the west, the famous Smith Village (now Denham Town) was the domain of the working-class, along with such well-known places as Jones Pen (now Jones Town), Trench Town, Rose Town and all that cluster of urban villages that remain a feature of Kingston today.

At the heart of the city were places like Brown's Town, Allman Town, Admiral Pen, Passmore Town, and Rae Town—some of which underwent transformation as the city became more modern and more populous.

Another early memory was living on Tower Street, just east of Hanover Street, and going to a kindergarden at the northwest corner of Hanover Street and Barry Street—a school that has long disappeared.

Later, I was to go to St. Aloysius Boys School, on East Street, another city landmark that has disappeared. The "big" school then was Central Branch (better known as Conversorium) on lower Church Street, which has been re-located uptown.

Kingston today, with its high-rise office buildings and multi-storey apartment blocks, is a far cry from those early days of the 1920's which I recall.

But perhaps the most significant difference between then and now is the transportation system. Those were the days of the tram-cars and the horse-drawn buses, or buggies as we knew them. Motor buses and taxis were to come much later.

The main tram-lines ran from the foot of King Street to a number of outward points. The principal routes were Constant Spring, Hope (Papine), and Rockfort, where the termini were.

In between were the East Street route, which ran along Harbour Street and had its western terminus at Orange and North Streets, and its northern terminus at Cross Roads. The South Camp Road line ran between downtown Kingston and Cross Roads.

For many of us Kingstonians of the day, the favourite was the Avenue Line which ran a circuit around downtown Kingston, traversing Harbour Street, Tower Street, then through Rae Town into Paradise Street, Victoria Avenue, East Queen Street, and King Street—a round trip that was, for many, a Sunday afternoon's delight.

Buggies were a luxury, affordable mostly by the well-off. Rich Syrian and Chinese merchants were their principal patrons.

When the motor buses came, one of the earliest operators was the legendary James F. Gore, whose name is associated with so many business ventures of early Kingston. His buses ran along Windward Road to and from downtown, and set a pattern from which others followed.

Later came the white ("chi-chi") buses, and those miniature public transport vehicles, called "scrambolas", the forerunners of today's mini-buses.

Another development which was to play a notable part in the modernisation of Kingston was the establishment of the motion-picture theatres. Palace Theatre, at South Camp Road and Victoria Avenue, was one of the earliest, along with the Movies Theatre, in Cross Roads, now only a memory.

Later were to come the Gaiety Theatre, on East Queen Street; the Rialto, on Windward Road; the Majestic, on the Spanish Town Road; and some smaller ones. The magnificent Carib Theatre came even later, to be followed by the Regal and the State, also in Cross Roads; and the Tropical, on Slipe Road, now no more.

These were the days before television when "going to the pictures" was a popular evening's activity, especially when there was an exciting serial running. Ice-cream parlours provided another "after-hours" social life. I remember a famous one, Da Costa's, on Victoria Avenue.

Let us not forget the stores. King Street was then the big shopping centre, with such notable places as Metropolitan House, later called Nathan's, at the north-western corner with Barry Street (now no more); Bon Marche, at King and Harbour Streets; Sherlock and Smith, on King Street; and London Shop, happily still with us.

Landmarks of their days were Times Store, Justin McCarthy, Garden Grocery, Kinkead's, Gore's, Community Store, Chemical Hall, most of them gone the way of antiquity. Issa's, a modern department store, also came and went.

At the foot of King Street stood the famous Victoria Market and the equally famous Victoria Pier, the landing place of royalty and other distinguished visitors to the island. The market had a later existence as Jamaica's first Crafts Market, now removed to another site; as the pier has been.

Another landmark which has gone is the old Gleaner building on Harbour Street, now replaced by, an imposing successor on North Street.

One of the most memorable land-marks, however, was the Myrtle Bank Hotel which from its waterfront site on Harbour Street commanded an international reputation as Jamaica's "Grand Hotel". Constant Spring Hotel and South Camp Hotel were other landmarks, now also gone.

As the business centre of Jamaica, Kingston was a hospitality town in those days for out-of-town visitors. A few of these remain, like Portland House, at East and East Queen Street. But famous in their day were the Commercial Hotel, at Duke and East Queen Streets; and Arlington House, on East Queen Street.

Warden Court, on South Camp Road, now the home of the Adult Literacy Movement, was another of these old-time hostelries, others of which were on Duke and East Streets, as well as on South Camp Road and on Half Way Tree Road.

Melrose Hotel, on Duke Street, came and went; as did the Flamingo Hotel, in Cross Roads (now a health centre), and Mimosa Lodge, which became the Kingston Hotel and is now a nurses training home.

Restaurants included such well-patronised places as Peggy Brown's, at King and Harbour Streets; and the Esquire, at Tower Street and Oliver Place. Chinese Commercial (now Sterling's) is a pioneer still going strong.

And, of course, there were the bars. Dirty Dick's, at Port Royal and Orange Streets, was perhaps the best known; but equally famous was Al Bar on Church Street; Cock of the Walk, at Half Way Tree; and Sloppy Joe's, in Cross Roads, still holding its own as a popular drinking spot.

Special mention must be made of the Tally-Ho, favourite resort of journalists and politicians alike; now, alas, no longer with us. And a passing salute to the Jamaica Arms, a happy combination of bar and restaurant, which started on Harbour Street then moved to Port Royal Street, before bowing out.

A feature of old-time Kingston which has also disappeared are the wharves. The old finger piers, stretching from Breezy Castle in the east to the western end of Port Royal Street, were in their time an integral part of the Kingston scene.

Their replacement by modern ship terminals at the western outskirts of the city, where a new maritime complex was created at Newport East and West, marked a distinct change in the appearance of the city, a change that was to be accentuated by the creation of the modern complex of shops and offices and a hotel (the Oceana) on the Kingston waterfront.

Another "new look" that came was the building of New Kingston, also a complex of shops and offices and hotels in uptown Kingston, which replaced the old Knutsford Park Race Course. The old Kingston Race Course remains, but is no longer a race track.

Transformed like most of Kingston, this one-time centre-piece of Kingston has become National Heroes Park, a mausoleum of the nation's heroes, and a memorial to their greatness; the site also of the Cenotaph, remembering those who died in the World Wars I and II (and which once stood on Church Street, between Barry and Tower Street).

Kingston has indeed undergone many changes, and bears little resemblance to the place I knew as a boy—a boy who once lived in a small two-bedroom house on the old Royal Mail Wharf premises, where now stand the proud edifices of the Bank of Jamaica and the Scotia Bank Centre, two outstanding symbols of modern Kingston.

ORIGINALLY PUBLISHED AUGUST 1988

Historic Kingston Churches

Some Places of Worship in the Old City of Kingston

MARGUERITE CURTIN

Shortly after the earthquake of 1692 had devastated the town of Port Royal, the parish of Kingston was created out of part of the older and larger parish of St. Andrews. The parish of Kingston was only six square miles in size and within its boundaries the town of Kingston was laid out on approximately one square mile.

The established church of the British colony was the Church of England, the state church, thus the Parish Church of Kingston was intended to serve the English officials and residents living in both the parish

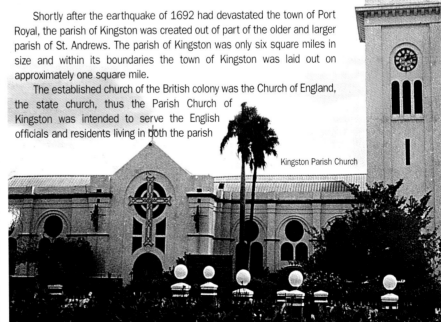

Kingston Parish Church

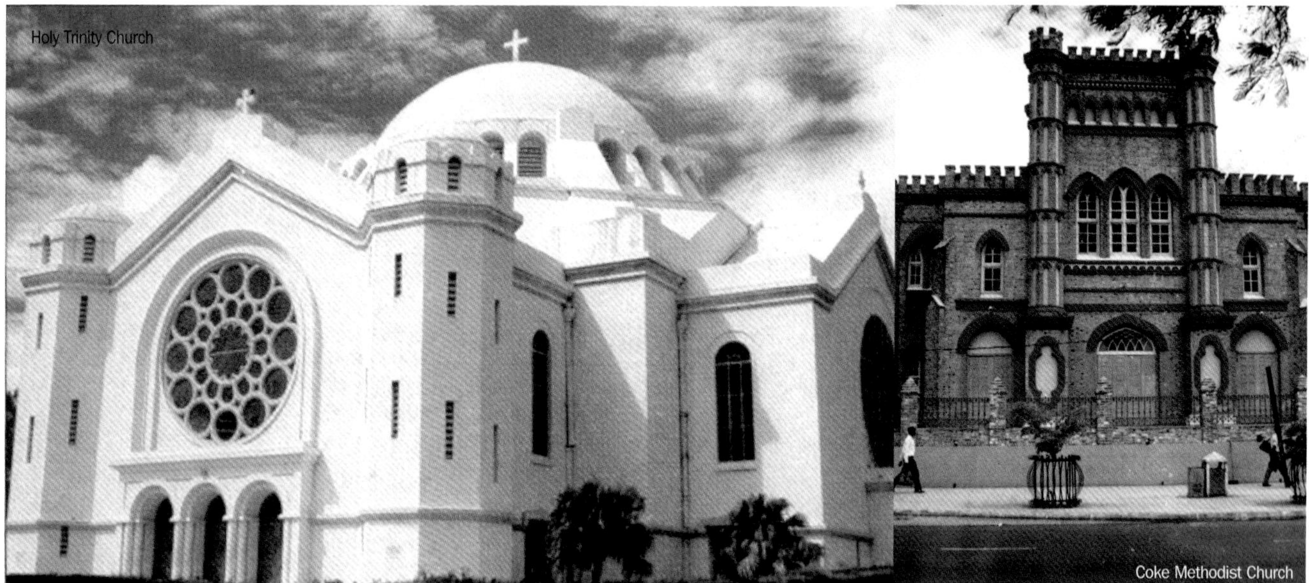
Holy Trinity Church

Coke Methodist Church

and "towne". With the rapid growth of the congregation of the Parish Church, Chapels of Ease, namely St. George's and St. Michael's were built to "ease" the congestion at the main church.

As the right to freedom of worship was one which Jews of Jamaica had secured in the early years of English rule, the Jewish community in Kingston was able to establish its own synagogues, just as it had done previously in Port Royal.

In spite of the disapproval and often open antagonism of the authorities, such as the city magistrates, several dissenting sects began to make their presence felt in Kingston in the latter part of the eighteenth century... Methodists, Presbyterians and Baptists, particularly Native Baptists, who in spite of much persecution would sometimes preach on the Race Course just north of the city.

For some years Catholics had worshipped secretly in two private chapels but the arrival of French refugees and their slaves in the 1790s spurred them on to obtain permission from the authorities of the island to establish a public place for French, Spanish, Irish, and English Catholics to worship.

For three hundred years Kingston's churches have contributed to the colourful life of the city of Kingston. They are monuments representing the faith and sacrifice of devout congregations who in spite of the ravages of hurricanes and the destruction of earthquakes have sought to rebuild, preserve and maintain these places of worship for posterity. We have selected just seven of these for further mention.

The earliest grave on the Kingston Parish Church site bears the date 1699 and it is most likely that a wooden building was first erected until a more permanent structure could be built. In 1701 the deed conveying the land to the church wardens was discharged and in that same year, a rector was appointed for the parish.

The Synagogue

Some writers like James Knight (1746), described the parish church as "a handsome building"; Edward Long effusively referred to it as a "large elegant building", while others with a more discriminating taste, like the architect James Hakewill (1820), referred to it as "a convenient structure, but without any pretensions to architectural beauty". The present structure was built after the 1907 earthquake; its consecration took place on January 17, 1911. But regardless of opinions as to its architectural style, or as to the structural changes which have taken place over the centuries, one fact is certain; the parish church has always been integral to the life of the city of Kingston. As early as 1816, the writer Monk Lewis described the church "full to overflow with black people". Some would stay all Sunday for fear of being excluded from evening service; here the christenings, marriages and burials were performed. By 1826, the congregation had increased still more, the church being thronged every Sunday morning, mainly by free people of colour and free blacks.

The history of the Kingston Parish Church is the history of Kingston in a nutshell. It reflects moments of joy and sorrow in its people's lives: a founder's day service for students of an old Kingston school...wedding bells for a beauty queen and a minister of government...a tragic Christmas morning when a boat capsized in the harbour and 26 people lost their lives....It celebrates, too, the creativity of the artist: in the Lady Chapel is the Pieta by Susan Alexander and the Madonna and Child by Osmond Watson, while in the nave is the carving of the Angel by Edna Manley. Gifts such as the statue of St. Thomas from the Syrian community, and the statue of Our Lady from the Chinese community are reminders of the affection which the people of Kingston feel for their parish church.

On the eastern side of St. William Grant Park (formerly the parade ground and later Victoria Park) stands Coke Methodist Church named after Dr. Thomas Coke, founder of the Methodist Mission in Jamaica.

The first chapel, which was really a remodelled merchant's house, opened in 1790 on the same site. These were perilous times for Dissenters and missionary activity was much frowned upon by the authorities. So great was persecution during the latter part of the eighteenth century that eventually Coke Chapel was forced to close its doors as a grand jury in the city found it "injurious to the general peace and quiet of the said town". After seven years Coke Chapel opened its doors once more. The congregation had trebled!

Like most Kingston churches Coke Methodist Chapel suffered severely in the earthquake of 1907. The present building was erected after this disaster.

Many an aspiring politician has used its steps as a platform for expressing his political convictions. This was especially so in the 1930s, during the early days of the labour movement.

The rebuilding of Holy Trinity Cathedral, the mother church of the Catholic community on North Street, was of immense significance to the psyche of the inhabitants of Kingston. Suddenly on January 14, 1907, earthquake and fire had destroyed their city.

Just five weeks after the disaster, on February 21, Colmar House, a property at the eastern end of North Street (the city's northern boundary) was purchased for the erection of the new church. It adjoined Winchester Park, already the headquarters of the Jesuit community.

There were those who complained that the new church was out in the country and, indeed, it was some distance from the original Holy Trinity which had stood on the north western corner of Sutton Street and Duke Street, where the Government Printing Office stands today, and which was now a pile of rubble. (The first church had been founded in 1810 by a Spanish merchant who was resident in Jamaica, and a Augustinian friar from Vera Cruz. Originally it was a modest brick building but by 1907 it could accommodate a congregation of 2,000 and was regarded as one of the most stately churches in the island.)

As the new edifice, covering an area of 12,000 square feet on North Street, rose in its "grand simplicity of the pure Byzantine style" the people were in the tiptoe of excitement" as the day for the dedication approached. Finally, on February 5, 1911 the solemn dedication took place. Thousands of people, clergy and lay, attended including the governor of Jamaica, Sir Sydney Olivier, and many of the "elite of the island".

St. Peter's Church, Port Royal

The courageous leader of this challenging task was Bishop F. C. Collins, S.J.D.D. Funds were raised both locally and abroad; generous donations providing all that was needed to make the church ready in such a short time.

St. Andrew's Scots Kirk or Scots Church was erected in 1814 by public subscription. On November 30 of 1813 a group of citizens had met at the Kingston Court House and had agreed to help to build a Presbyterian place of worship in the city. Before the end of December 1813, Eight thousand one hundred and one pounds had been collected for the building fund.

James Delaney's design was accepted on February 4, 1814. The building was to be an octagonal one with a gallery supported by mahogany pillars with Ionic or Corinthian capitals. In 1821, James Hakewill, a visiting artist, referred to the Kirk as "the handsomest building in Kingston".

Like so many of the churches of Kingston, considerable remodelling took place at the Kirk as a result of the 1907 earthquake. Some walls were so unsafe that the height of the original building had to be reduced.

In 1939 the congregation of another Presbyterian church, St. Andrew's Kirk on East Queen Street, joined the congregation of Scot's Kirk, thus forming the St. Andrew's Scots Kirk.

Throughout the years the Kirk's contribution to music, especially choral music, has been considerable. Since 1947 its choir, the St. Andrew Singers, has been giving regular recitals. The Kirk possesses one of the finest organs in the Caribbean.

Among the many interesting symbols to be found in the Synagogue on Duke Street are two perpetual lights which burn on either side of the Ark. They are reminders of the union of the Sephardic and Ashkenazi congregations which eventually took place in April 1921. As far back as 1883, however, a group of Sephardim and Ashkenazim had founded the United Congregation of Israelites, purchased a site (29,000 sq. ft.) at the corner of Duke and

St. Andrew's Scots Kirk

East Queen Street Baptist Church

Charles Streets, and built a fine brick synagogue in the Byzantine style. "Kahal Kadosh Shangareh Shalom" (i.e. "Holy Congregation—Gates of Peace") was the name given to this united synagogue.

But among the 2,000 Jews in Kingston in the 1880s there was a large number of both Sephardic (Spanish and Portuguese) and Ashkenazi (English and German) who refused to unite and kept to their separate congregations. For many years, therefore, there were three congregations, not two or one.

The "fearful earthquake" of January 14, 1907 badly damaged all three synagogues. Quickly the congregation of the United Israelites began rebuilding their Duke Street synagogue in the earlier design but with reinforced concrete, not brick. The architects were Henriques Bros. On March 28, 1912, the restored synagogue was rededicated. On that occasion the governor of the island, Sir Sydney Olivier was among those present.

East Queen Street Baptist Church was started by the Baptist Missionary Society of Great Britain in the year 1816. It was not, however, the first Baptist Church in the Kingston area as Baptist witness began in Jamaica with the arrival of George Lisle. A former slave and pastor of a church in the United States, Lisle came to Jamaica with his wife in 1782. Shortly after, some of his church members followed him to Jamaica and helped him build a church on the outskirts the city in the vicinity of Elleston Road and the road now called Victoria Avenue (opposite the present Sinclair's Garage). At length these Native Baptists set up their congregation on Hanover Street.

George Lisle and Moses Baker were nevertheless responsible for the arrival of the English Baptists as it was in response to their appeal to the president of the Bristol Baptist College that this second set of Baptist dissenters set about their mission on the east side of Queen's Street. By 1822 the actual building was dedicated on January 22. It was said to have seating accommodation for 2,000 and at that time had membership of 2,937—the largest membership of any Baptist Church in the world then.

The building was extensively damaged in the earthquake of 1907 and the minister in charge of the church actually had to have a leg amputated as a result of the quake. In spite of hurricanes, especially the 1951 hurricane, this important city church has continued to keep its building in good repair.

Some eighteen ministers from England served the church over a period of 142 years. Finally, in 195S, four years before Independence, the first Jamaican was appointed minister and this trend has continued to the present day.

Port Royal was part of the parish of Kingston since 1867. Prior to the earthquake of 1692 there were two Anglican churches in Port Royal: St. Peter's and St. Paul's. St. Peter's was flattened to the ground by the tremor, while St. Paul's was submerged under water and sand, its site not being investigated by archaeologists until the 1960s.

The men responsible for the rebuilding of St. Peter's on its old site in 1726 were John Clark and Louis Galdy. Little if anything is known about John Clark but there is much to find out about the Galdy brothers, Louis and Lawrence, who some years before had been expelled from Montpelier, France, because of their Protestant religion.

In the churchyard of Port Royal, is the famous grave of Louis Galdy. His incredible escape at the time of the earthquake is recounted on the tombstone: swallowed by the earth he was then spewed into the sea and picked up by passing ship. Few, however, remember that St. Peter's Church is itself also a fine memorial to Louis Galdy.

The interior of the church is interesting with its carved organ loft, brass chandelier given by William Terry in 1743 and its precious communion silver which includes a chalice, a plate and a flagon.

Another reminder of this Anglican church's Huguenot connections is a fine marble relief done by Louis Francois Roubiliac, sculptor (1695-1762).

Also on St. Peter's walls are several eighteenth century memorials: some are poignant reminders of how tragic and brief life was for many a young midshipman who ventured into the fever ridden tropics.

Historic St. Peter's still serves the Port Royal community and visitors to the town are welcome to share in its worship on any Sunday.

ORIGINALLY PUBLISHED MARCH 1993

Kingston Billy

BARBARA GLOUDON

Have you ever stopped to consider the phenomenon of the Kingston goats? If you haven't, imagine you're a tourist, newly arrived in the island...

So now you've landed in Kingston, Jamaica's capital. Sunshiny. Warm. Pungent. With the vigorous vibrancy of any metropolis...take it or leave it.

From the Norman Manley International Airport, you drive into the city, making your way along what's popularly known as the Palisadoes Road, along the Rockfort Road, maybe up Mountain View Avenue or along Victoria Avenue until (like some other streets in Kingston which change name before you get to the other end) it changes its name to East Queen Street.

The smells, the sounds, the sights are different...and no sight more different than the goats in the streets.

Goats in the streets?

You must be kidding...pardon the pun and all that...but whaddya mean goats?...In the middle of the city?

Smile...You're in Kingston now.

The goats of Kingston are part of the city's ambience, man. Nobody seems to know who they belong to, but obviously they have some sense of belonging. They have somewhere to come from in the morning and somewhere to go at the end of a long, hard day of scavenging garbage cans; in the exhausting pastime of dodging the wheels of vehicles and in the demanding profession of producing more and more kids to skip between the wheels and to scavenge in the garbage cans.

No fooling. They come out in the morning...from wherever. By the time the work-bound traffic builds-up on the major streets, the goats are ready "for work" too. Mother goats and the kids. Maybe poppa is indeed in there, somewhere, a real "rammie". Macho. Smelly.

With utter disdain for the speeding vehicles,

the goats make their way across the roads, heading for their feeding grounds...hedges, garbage cans and rubbish heaps, in between dodging wheels.

Jamaican drivers are alleged to be among the world's worst...or so some people say. With all that, you see a dead goat only occasionally. The Kingston Goat is a master at manoeuvering in traffic. He/she begins from a position of disdain. Obvious contempt for all that vehicular stuff. Shall the goats inherit the earth...?

The step off the sidewalk, in what the British call a crocodile...one behind the other. The line spreads sideways sometimes but the protocol demands that the leader is followed. Road safety rules advise that when crossing the road "Look right, look left, look right again." Go tell that to the goats. They look in one direction—straight ahead. Tough on drivers whose brakes are not what they should be and lose the filling from their their teeth in the crunch. But like Billy Goat Gruff and all that trip-trap from tales of childhood, the Kingston goats go tripping across. Brakes squeal, the air is thickened with curses... Somebody's goat's been got...and it is not the goat!

Safely on the other side, the Kingston goats begin their day's work. And they work hard. Overturning garbage cans. Chewing on anything.

Dieticians will tell you that every balanced diet must have a spot of green in it. Goats know this and go to work on hedges, as well as the garbage.

One of our horticultural legends is that privet, that prickly, tough scrub (used as a hedge) is a deterrent to intruders. Sez who? Goats adore it.

They "cleanse the palate" in the middle of their never-ending meal with a hearty round of privet. Thorns and all.

Evening comes on... and the goats head for home.

Where to?

Well, there's speculation. Some say: Version 1: They belong to some syndicate which has trained them to forage and return by evening. Version 2: They belong to no one but themselves and. somewhere in the city, there is a whole sub-division where nothing but goats live. Version 3: They share a sub-division with human syndicate which sends them out to work each day. But for what reward?

Well, let's not forget that Jamaica is the land of curry goat, pungent goat meat stewed in a fiery, peppery potage, joined in wedlock to steaming white rice" with "fingers" of boiled green bananas. That's what goats are for, in case you come from another planet.

An awful lot of curry goat gets eaten in our homes and restaurants and at parties and sporting events and wherever there is merriment, all over Kingston and the rest of the island. How much do the goats of Kingston contribute to these acts of national conviviality? Everyone knows that the real curry goat recipe demands that it is the kids which go into the pot. Maybe the older ones walking the streets of Kingston are only doing their thing until the time comes to make more kids.... for the perpetuity of curry.

The street goats, you should understand, are not the elite of our island's goat population. Lest it be forgotten, pedigree goats are regarded as genuine economic contributors. Officials have been known to officiate at the handing over of imported goats for economic self-help projects for rural youths. Such goats and the handers-over can be assured of media attention but the Kingston goats...well... there's no record of the press...being stopped for them.

Nobody can break the stride of the Kingston goats and so they trod on, day by day, showing more order and discipline than many human beings.

The city of Kingston might do well to adopt a member of the species as official mascot.

After all, if Mayor Koch can be seeking an official mascot for New York City, what's wrong with Kingston? An official mascot would not be the only common denominator between the two places.... Whatever NYC comes up with, we think the Kingston goat is a winner.

ORIGINALLY PUBLISHED JULY 1984

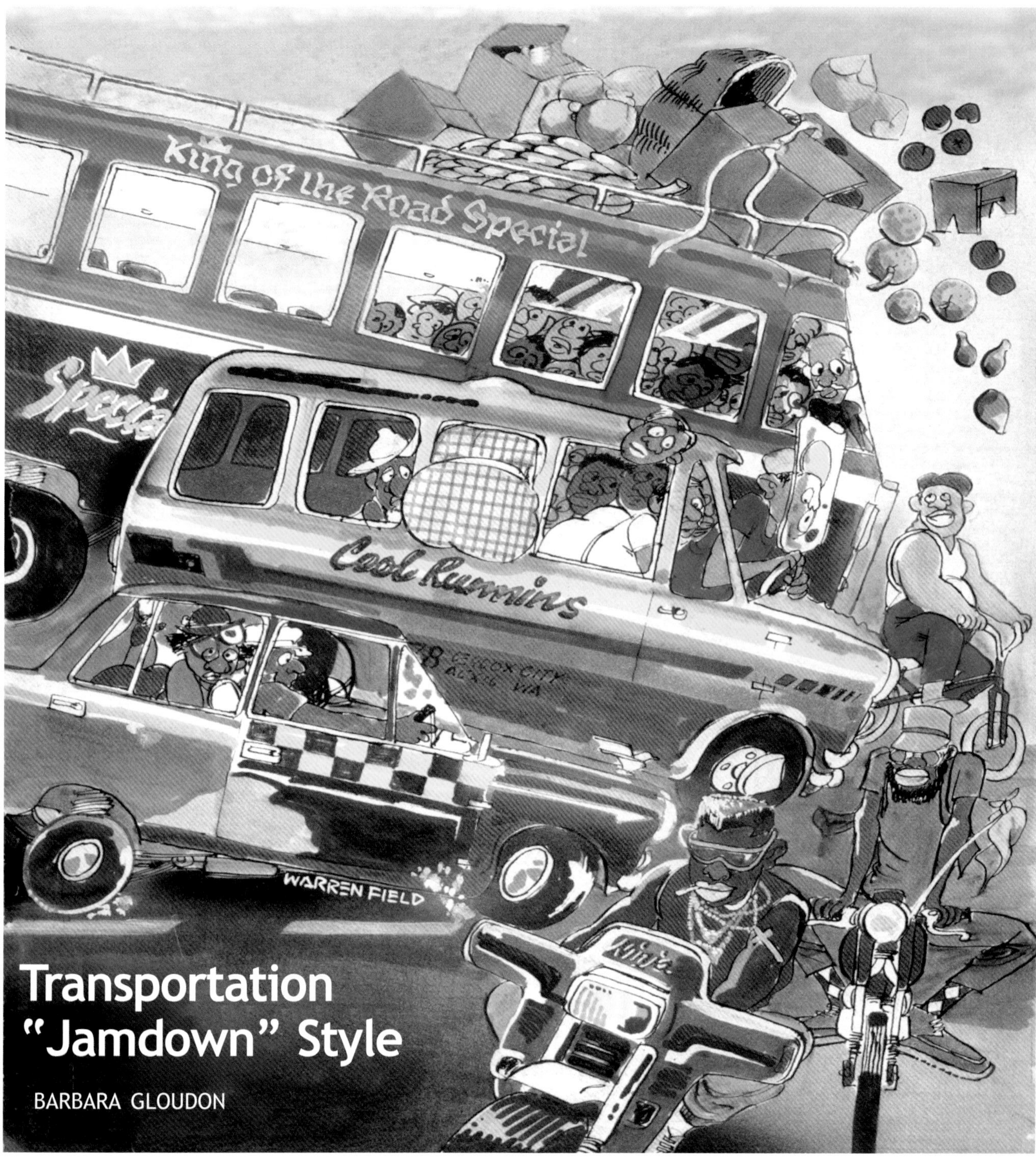

Transportation "Jamdown" Style

BARBARA GLOUDON

"Come eena dis... Cross Roads... Cross Roads.. one more, driver."

Technically, it is not possible to get one more living soul into the vehicle. The ductor (conductor to the uninitiated) is hanging from the steps by the tip of his sneakers. A lady with a basket eases her rump painfully on the edge of the steel holding a seat together. Three small children, tucked neatly into a little space, like socks in well-packed suitcase, squirm and try to get a bit more air.

The school boy, his shining morning face long since dulled, hangs on to the nearest form of support which turns out to be a sensitive portion of a lady's anatomy. The hapless lad gets his first real biology lesson and a fabric-covered denunciation to go with it.

Up front, the driver polishes his mirror-lensed glasses, cracks the sound system a little higher, puts in a tape from a reigning dancehall deejay, and urges the beautiful young lady beside him to "Move up, mek smaddy else get space." She does so willingly. It is a privilege to be asked to sit beside the driver. Secure in the knowledge of her accolade, the sweet young thing hitches up her skirt and comes closer.

The driver "crack de music higher." Some of the passengers approve. Some don't. Those who don't choose carefully the moment and the method to show their disaffection. To do otherwise could mean a shortened journey.

Those tuned in to the dancehall riddim ask the driver for some more volume, especially if the song is "rude" (risque to you). Out on the step, his fingers inter-laced with currency notes, folded length wise and damp with the sweat of toil, the ductor tells the driver "Take it away..."

The bus tears away from the stop, a vibrating package of human organism, fully on the go, bobbing and weaving through the traffic. Then the ductor yells "One stop..." One more stop. One more passenger. One more moment in the life and times of a Jamaican mini bus.

Colourful, yes. Picturesque, yes. (There's even a T-shirt immortalising the Jamaican Mini-Bus Ride). But the island's traffice authorities, the police department and commuters are not amused. The mini-bus system has become a nightmare. Not a day goes by, but there are soul-searching, complaints on call-in radio programmes, letters to the press, even denouncements from the pulpit about the mini-bus chaos. Meanwhile back at the bus stop, the ductor knocks the side of the bus and tells the driver to move out... one more time.

Mini-buses are a comparatively recent phenomenon in Jamaica. Before that, transportation Jamdown style, was a horse of another carriage. Yes, there were horses and carriage. In particular, there were buggies—light little vehicles with a kind of rumble seat at the back, providing opportunity for small boys to run after the buggy, then hop on for an unscheduled ride. This gave rise to the cry "lick a back, driver, lick a back," an exhortation, usually given by some envious/unsympathetic passerby. This was licence for the driver to use his whip indiscriminately to dislodge the intruder who would have no recourse, but to wait for the next "hop."

With time, the buggy died. Horses reverted to running at the race track. The buggy is known now only in obscure folk songs... "De buggy bruck, de buggy bruck, de buggy bruck and de horse fall down..."

In recent times, some tourism properties have revived the horse and buggy as a visitor attraction and shades of Central Park—one bride made the local news headlines recently when she opted to travel to church for her "million dollar wedding," horse and buggy style.

After the buggy, came the tramcar, running their stately way on trolley lines up and down the city. They too added to Jamaican folklore in the poems and jokes about the beauty seat—the one which had its back to the driver and faced all the other passengers. The legend is that only the beautiful would be so "barefaced" as to sit looking at everyone else. The tram car has its place in history. In this the 50th anniversary of nineteen thirty eight, the year which marked the start of the Jamaican labour movement, tram cars were an integral part of that scene.

Like shadows in a silent movie, they glided among the workers roaming the streets seeking justice. Tram cars provided the children of the day with all the adventure of a horse chase in a cowboy movie. It took will to run along smartly and to hop on and off the tram step. It took cunning to insert oneself between the rows of adults to avoid paying the fare. What would Kingston's street have been if the trams had been kept? A tourist attraction like San Francisco?

Like some determined secret which refuses to be hidden, the tram rails, buried beneath layers of asphalt on certain Kingston streets, work their way to the surface from time to time. The young go by, unaware of what they signify. For the old, they invoke nostalgia of an age they knew.

After the trams came the Chi-Chi Bus... Big Leyland giants from the factories of "Mother England." They were fitted with hydraulic doors which hissed and wheezed when opening. Jamaican words, say the linguists, are onomatopoeic... they resonate with sound. So it was logical that the buses became known by the sound made when doors were opened i.e. "chi-chi." The street language also called them "Weedy" buses, immortalizing the English official who presided over the bus company in those days.

The big buses and the public had a love-hate relationship. We bitched when they were overloaded. We grumbled when they were late. We, all of us, had clear ideas on how to improve the system... We hated when the crews went on strike...

Until there came the day when divestment of public enterprises became priority on the national agenda. The bus company (Jamaica Omnibus Services) closed and the mini-buses arrived proliferating from one end of the island to another. Franchise holders, awarded packages (packaged routes) became part of the national language. So too did "Quarter Million," the alleged cost of one of the new Coaster buses. And so began a whole new chapter in transportation folklore...

There's a Jamaican folk saying "if crocodile come up from river bottom and tell yuh say river bottom dark believe him." There's also the companion piece "Rock stone a ribber bottom nuh know say sun hot." Being roughly translated —only those in the situation can tell you how it is...

No words can adequately describe a mini-bus ride... The speed... the proximity, the flesh and scent, the leveling-crushing experience of unsolicited biological proximity to total strangers. Yes—so it is in a subway train at peak hour, but I contend—the train is bigger, man...

And the language has a rhythm of its own "One stop driver..." which, being translated means "stop for another passenger..." The names of the vehicles...Kung Fu... Exterminator... Western Flyer... Vibrator... corruptions of the most unimaginable sources. For most imaginative, I choose Prince Macho Perry. Took a while to figure it out, though. Think I've got it now.. Prince Machiavelli?

And what about Enforcer One and Two? And the Don? And Walk Though—the latter a humble rattle trap which could pass for a bread van. You enter and exit by a pair of doors at the back... walk through if there's space.

Every route has its Walk Through and its Don—the sleek and shining prince of them all. From time to time, the powers that be make a grand pronouncement then try to remove the Walk Through. But even as the Don flashes by, you will see one stealthy old pensioner, one pock marked Walk Through, without a fashionable radio and tape deck trying bravely, stuffing gratefully one more passenger into the sardine pile.

While there is colour and humour in the mini-bus business, it can get too colourful and too dangerous. After one accident too many recently there was flurry of training of bus crews and enforcement of laws regulating the state of the vehicles and prohibiting over-loading. When it got too much, the crews rebelled. They withdrew not only their services but their enthusiasm. Anguished commuters, stranded one more time, protested. An accommodation was reached. The cycle began again. "Cross Roads... One stop.. Hey babee, come eena dis... Going your way... Move up to de front... Right through driver... Come up closer babee.. Crack de music higher..."

ORIGINALLY PUBLISHED AUGUST 1988

Bob Marley's Heritage
Trench Town Culture Yard

ELENA OUMANO

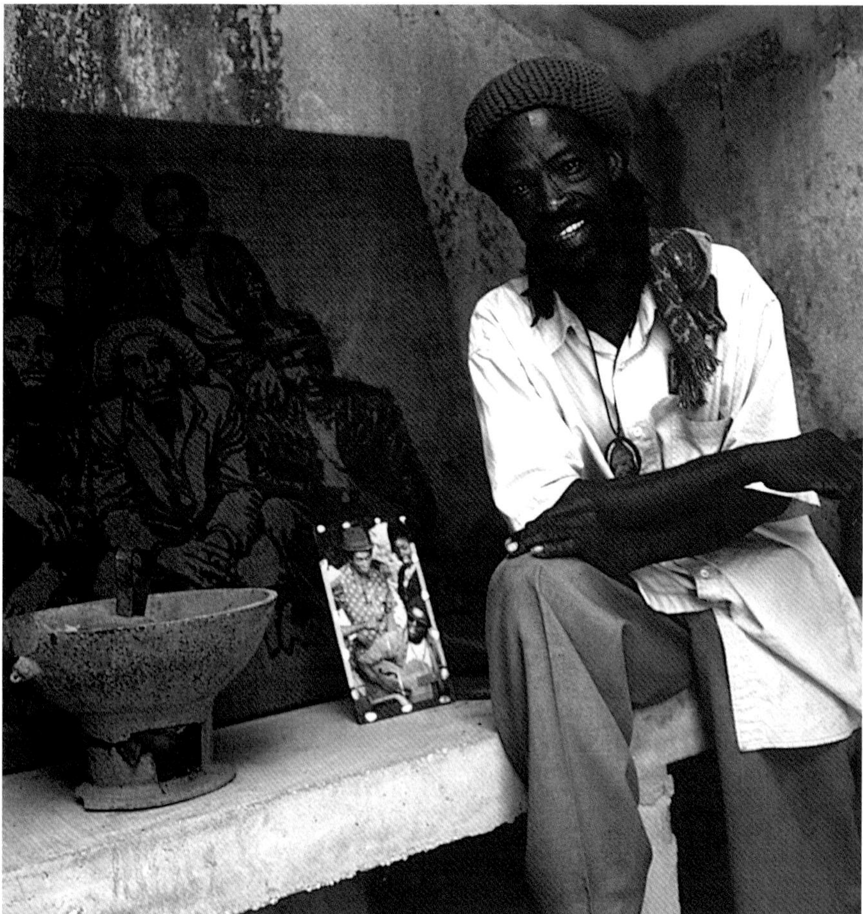

(THIS PAGE) Tourguide Magnus Skeen; (OPPOSITE PAGE) Vigo "Donovan" Smith at the entrance to the Trench Town Culture Yard; Marley's mentor Vincent "Tata" Ford, who co-wrote *No Woman No Cry*.

The way to Trench Town is not marked by the breathtaking sea vistas and wild outcroppings of arching ferns, trees and brilliantly colored flowers that you see along the way to Jamaica's more established tourist destinations. Yet man-made beauty is everywhere: rose vines trained to trail over pock-marked concrete walls; red, green and gold lettered expressions of unity and portraits of community leaders decorating the facades of crumbling buildings.

It is here you'll find the Trench Town Culture Yard, a shrine to the musical and cultural world leadership of singer Bob Marley and to roots, rock, reggae as a carrier of knowledge.

On February 6, 1999—what would have been the 54th anniversary of the late reggae king's birth—England's Prince Charles and other dignitaries gathered at the Yard at Kingston's Lower First Street. Under a brilliant tropical sun, they inaugurated the Trench Town Culture Yard, Jamaica's first inner-city heritage tourism project. In the sixties and seventies, this humble government housing project transformed into the epicenter of an overlapping series of musical and cultural epiphanies that changed not only Jamaica but also the world. Though Trench Town and neighboring urban areas have suffered since that first reggae flowering, the community is restoring its position as a tiny but potent pocket of spiritual richness and a testament to the indomitable Jamaican spirit.

You can't talk about reggae without mentioning Rastafari, and it was in this Yard where the music took as its message Rastafari's Garveyite point of view. Today, the Yard is known far and wide as a "rasta" and reggae mecca, a must-see attraction for millions of international music fans and believers. This is the place to pay homage to Marley and the other Wailers—Bunny Livingston and the late Peter Tosh—as well as to many more seminal figures of reggae music and culture. Joe Higgs, Toots Hibbert of Toots & The Maytals, the Wailing Souls, and countless others made music and "sighted up" Rastafari in the Yard's inner courtyard. And that philosophy spread throughout the world through the universal language of music, reminding everyone that we are one people, ruled by the power of "Jah love" and deserving of equal rights and justice.

As you approach the Yard in Trench Town, the red, green, and gold rasta-reggae motif overpowers the concrete grey. Green and gold Jamaican flags wave from the tall poles and the gaily-colored fence that border the Yard's entrance. A banner strung across the poles announces "The Oneness of Trench Town Community" to remind all who enter, "United we stand...divided we fall." A garden on the left, filled with local artist Stoneman's stunning found sculpture and assemblages, catches your eye. More art is housed in a room in the left-hand row. To the right, a row of rooms house the Casbah Restaurant and the bar. One of several trained tour guides from the community escorts you between those front rooms into the Yard's square-shaped inner courtyard. A small stage for live concerts now stands at one end. In a corner is the rusted-out carcass of the blue Volkswagen bus that carried the Wailers to performances around the island during the 60's. Three more rows of what were originally single room family dwellings describe the Yard's inner boundaries. One room now houses the Culture Yard's crafts workshop, where women of the community knit and crochet red, green, and gold tams, scarves, and other items; another, a museum of Wailers and reggae memorabilia; a third, the gift shop. Miss Brady's former home now contains a glass showcase protecting the battered acoustic guitar on which the teenaged Marley and his slightly older mentor, Vincent "Tata" Ford, wrote "No Woman No Cry," one of the world's most poignant love songs. It begins with the lines, "I remember when we used to sit/inna government yard in Trench Town." Tata and Marley were inspired when a sobbing Miss Puncie ran from the room to the right that she shared with her common-law husband, Piper Saunders, and their eight children. It is the last song Bob ever played on that guitar.

Bob and Tata wrote "No Woman" in the tiny "kitchen" in the back row, where Ford prepared food for the Yard's youth. At night, he and Bob practiced on that guitar, using a tattered music

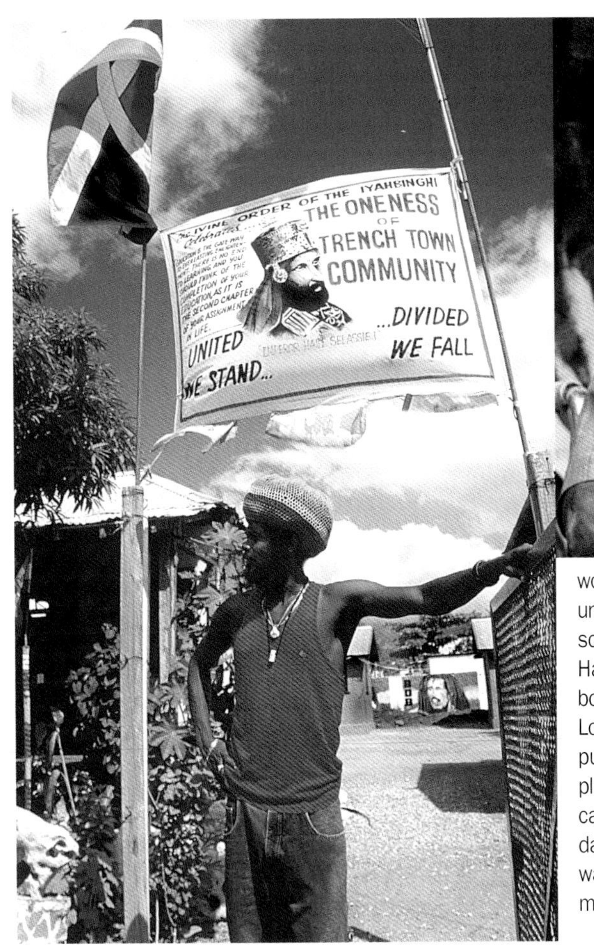

instruction book they read under the weak light of an oil lamp, a homemade contraption that's little more than a rag wick soaked in kerosene. When the "tining" light gave out, they took turns sleeping on the kitchen's narrow cot. But if a young girl named Rita Anderson (who later became Mrs. Marley) was visiting, Tata ceded his resting place to the courting couple.

The Yard was originally part of a housing scheme erected by the British in the thirties and forties, before Jamaica's 1962 Independence. When Cedella Booker and her small, wiry son, christened Nesta Robert Marley, received word that they were moving to Trench Town in the late fifties, it was as if they'd won the lottery, so prized were these communal urban projects by Jamaica's less privileged.

With most rooms opening up onto the courtyard, the first sight of the morning was your neighbor. And with each room home to as many as 14 family members, much of the Yard's life took place in the courtyard, where everyone shared cooking, bathing, and washing facilities. Neighbors became family and took care of each other as such.

On washdays, when the courtyard was crisscrossed with lines of drying laundry, Miss Lou might burst into a church hymn; Miss B would join in, then Miss Monica, until the entire Yard swelled with song. On weekends, Mr. "Big Hand" carried his turntable and boxes of vinyl records down to Lower First Street, rigged up his public address boxes, then plugged into a light pole. Everyone came to Lower First Street to dance and party because the Yard was known far and wide as a music yard.

Until 1970, you could gaze from the back of the Yard straight through from "First Street to Seventh Street," as Bob sings in "Trench Town Rock." After the success of his 1973 *Catch A Fire* Island Records debut, Bob moved "uptown" to a former great house at 56 Hope Road, now the site of the Bob Marley Museum. But Marley never abandoned Trench Town. Whenever he returned to Jamaica from a tour abroad, his first stop was always the Yard, where he could sit in the courtyard and reason with his longtime breddren. During one of his last visits before his 1981 passing, Marley told these men—most of whom still live in Trench Town—to prepare themselves. One day, the world would come to them, to witness where the legend began.

"This is 'Rich Town,'" says Piper Saunders today, "rich in music and people. Feel that cool breeze blowing? That's his presence."

A concrete wall that went up during the political turmoil of the 70's now blocks the view from the back of the Culture Yard. Thanks to the dogged efforts of the community to restore the Yard, other buildings, and construct a school, study center, and a medical clinic, Trench Town's family feeling is returning, and that wall has transformed into a symbol of renewed unity and hope. It bears the inscription of a verse from Marley's "Tribute To Trench Town" and local artist Lloydie's powerful mural paintings of Bob, Peter, Bunny, and the late Raphael "Med Gong" Smith.

Together with his brother Michael Smith, chair of the Trench Town Development Association, Med Gong was a driving force behind the Yard and this community's recovery. Other Jamaicans have also contributed. They include Jamaica's Governor General, Howard Cooke; the Jamaican Product Development Company [TPDco], the Jamaica Tourist Board [JTB]; Sister Grace Yapp of the Franciscan Ministries; architect Christopher Stone; Gloria Palomino; and the three young Australian owners of Rockhouse Hotel in Negril, on Jamaica's western shores.

"Whenever someone comes here, they feel the spirit from back then," says Smith. "You can't get that spirit anywhere else. You know right away that this is 'it,' where it all comes from. People actually get on their hands and knees and crawl into the courtyard. Some don't even need to hear about Bob Marley. They just want to spend five minutes in the kitchen where Bob and Tata wrote music, played guitar, and slept."

For Smith and the community, the work is about even more than restoring a cultural dream. The pride and happiness written on the shining faces of Trench Town's children is their greatest reward.

As you finish touring Marley's home and reggae's birthplace, those children are returning from school, dressed neatly in tan uniforms and carrying school satchels. The sound of their play fills the air, blending with the steady, rhythmic cross-currents of the Nyabingi [Rastafarian] drummers who gather in the Yard's front garden every day, under the spreading shade of a stately tree. This simple concrete and wood communal housing project has become a kind of holy place, an internationally-recognized monument to the power of people united as a force for positive change.

ORIGINALLY PUBLISHED FEBRUARY 2001

Sybil Hughes of the Mayfair Hotel

SONIA GORDON

The Mayfair is a small 32-room hotel tucked away in the cul-de-sac of West Kings House Close. I am here to interview Sybil Hughes, owner and operator of the hotel, and I hesitate on the threshold of a large airy room which doubles as a living-cum-dining-room-cum-private-office. From a passage to the right, a tall, fair lady approaches wearing a severely tailored linen dress. Her only adornments are small pearl earrings and a cluster of pearls at her throat.

"Come in, come in, my dear. Have a seat. Would you like some tea?" I accept, and she gestures as we seat ourselves at a table covered with papers, magazines, books and phones and says with a gentle laugh, "You'd never believe this is a dining table, would you!" The laugh and disarming manner are characteristic of the interview. Not that she can't be serious. She just does not appear to take herself too seriously. She is informal and unaffected with a wry sense of humour. As we talked she fields constant phone calls and deals with occasional staff queries calmly and decisively.

Sybil Ryan Hughes is originally from Cayman, and a hint of Cayman accent remains, overlaid with Jamaican inflections in her speech. She speaks in an extremely soft voice in rapid, staccato bursts and her conversation on how the Mayfair got started is interwoven with side excursions into events of the time.

It was while she was working as accountant "for a big company, for years and years" that her husband kept urging that they should buy a small hotel. "It was his idea, really, and I loved it because I kept a house that was never empty... I mean we had open house all the time." Her husband, Jim, was an electrical engineer. "That's what his people wanted him to be, but he didn't want to be. So after that he registered to train as a chef. And so we had the three things that we needed most. He was the chef and engineer and I was the accountant, and so we started.

"When we heard about this property everything had been sold. A syndicate had bought the whole eight and a half acres and were cutting it up into housing lots. There was no street or anything here except the old house. The man who'd bought the old house visualised it as it was with the long driveway going out to West Kings House Road and when he found that he was going to have a street in front of his house, he didn't want it, so we bought the house."

Showing great foresight and resourcefulness, Sybil then got the names of all the other property owners and approached them with a plan. "I checked to find out whether they were going to live in their houses or rent them because if a man lives in his house, he takes care of the garden and it's o.k. But if he rents it sometimes it can be, you know, really a disaster to the neighbourhood rather than something nice." She asked for a first option to buy in time, in return for which she would rent the properties on their behalf, collect the rents and do all the property management for free.

"They agreed and I had proper papers made up". Within three months and before the Hughes had completed the purchase of their first property, the owner of the adjoining lot decided to migrate and sell his interests. "So that is what we did in May 1965. We started renovating the old house, the street was being put in, this house (where we are sitting) was being built. We had a house in Hope Pastures then and we were both working but we came down every day to check. To make a long story short we opened on January 19, 1966 with not one guest!" she laughs cheerfully, "but that night we got one and it was too funny because he turned out to be my cousin from Cayman and he didn't know that I had a hotel!"

So how did the Mayfair get going? "Well in 1966 we had the Commonwealth Games. The Sheraton was there—all the hotels were full. They had big bookings. Well we never had one booking because we were not on the map—the street had just been put in. We were not in the telephone directory because the directories were printed in November and we opened in January so while we had a telephone we were not listed and what else—oh! We had no money to advertise!" this sounds like a recipe for disaster but, again, she laughs cheerfully.

"We started with 10 rooms. I think there were four full-time staff and two part-time staff. I continued working because my salary had to pay them. My husband left his job, he stayed home and when I came home in the evening, I took over from him! I didn't need much sleep, you see. I've never needed more than three hours a night..."

The Commonwealth Games saved the day for the Hughes however. They got two bookings from the overflow at the other hotels; a couple of newspapermen from England. Eventually they got others and before the games started they were completely full. But it was the combination of the newspapermen and Mrs. Hughes' hospitality that rally pulled it off. "The Games finished at around 11 p.m. and by the time they had relayed their stories to their papers and got back here it was after 12. So I asked them what they had eaten and they said oh, they'd picked up this and got that so I said "Oh no! Well tomorrow morning I'll give you a nice lunch to take with you and when you come back tomorrow night, you'll get a full course dinner," and this is what happened. "My dear, the first night they had that. The second day they telephoned and asked if they could bring some more newspaper people, and we ended up feeding 32 newspaper people in our dining room at 12 to 1 o'clock in the morning, from soup to dessert, and we never looked back after that. We are still getting people coming from it, you know! We get people from Finland, from all over Europe. Then we got some really good breaks. *Vogue* and *Harpers Bazaar* came to Jamaica to do photos and we got pages of coverage. And then we stared advertising."

When questioned whether they had entertained any famous clientele she is, I suspect, deliberately vague no doubt because the thing they would treasure most is their privacy. "Oh, we've had a few," she said airily, then laughed "They're all the same… there have been very, very few people that I've had that I feel, really, I could have done without, but then if I hadn't had them I wouldn't appreciate how good the others were, you see!"

The Mayfair has continued to prosper with the largest concentration of visitors drawn from Europe and the Caribbean, much of it repeat business. It also does a fair trade in American businessmen particularly in July and August. "It's funny," she says "but those are the busy months in Kingston although they are the hottest, because the businessmen come and bring their wives and children."

"We have a real international group," she continue, "Germans, Dutch, Greek, Russians. We had two Russian couples recently and another seven for holidays. Japanese, Italians." It sounded like a convention of the United Nations. But then Sybil Hughes was also, until very recently, president of the International Club, a club formed 50 years ago by another well-known Jamaican, Violette de Barovier Riel. The International Club awarded Mrs. Hughes a certificate of merit for outstanding service and she remains their vice-president.

She has also relinquished her position as chairman of the Kingston area of the Jamaica Hotel & Tourist Association (JHTA) but remains a councillor of that group. "I want to give my hotel more time," she explains. She is vice-president of the Jamaica Federation of Women and is very active on behalf of her church, the St. Andrews Scots Kirk. "I'm a director of the Caribbean Hotel Association and I do my own marketing." As she said earlier, she needs very little sleep.

When asked her views on the future of the hospitality industry in Jamaica, this indefatigable lady was very optimistic. "I think Jamaica has every thing to gain and I think our people are beginning to realise that we need tourism. You go into the hotels now and the staff bends over backwards with few exceptions. I think Jamaica has a bright future where tourism is concerned."

As proof of this belief she has expansion plans for the Mayfair in '93. "I have 32 rooms and two houses that are not in the system yet. I'm hoping to have them in the system this year and also to put up six more rooms this year." She is also beefing up the water supply by adding additional holding tanks as a buffer against future droughts.

Sybil Hughes did not get to this point by resting on her laurels or by being pessimistic. But perhaps there is more to it. Does she still find it interesting and enjoyable after all these years or despite the long hours and the problems? "Oh yes," come the ready reply. "I'm always in trouble. The problems, I just…" She smiles then adds, "Let me tell you—I put everything in God's hands and I don't worry about a single thing under the sun. My dear, I have miracles happening everyday of life. Every single day of life." Perhaps that's the real answer.

ORIGINALLY PUBLISHED MAY 1993

Treasure on the Beach

ODETTE DIXON

Hellshire is Kingston's most popular beach. Located on St. Catherine's south coast, Hellshire is approximately thirty minutes drive from Kingston by way of two routes: the Portmore-Kingston Causeway and the Mandela Highway through Gregory Park. Mecca for Kingstonians of every social strata, Hellshire serves up a veritable slice of Jamaican life. The special treat is fried fish laced with onions and peppers, served with bammy (a savoury cassava cake) or festival, a faintly-sweet fried dumpling. Sundays at Hellshire may feature dancehall music, played by one of Kingston's premier sound systems.

On this day, you can get the best of two worlds: the beach with friends and the dancehall.

It is a shack with a multi-coloured zinc roof. There is no flooring, only furrowed sand that's just been raked. The rickety formica-topped tables have been wiped and at the base of each is a lignum vitae branch, a natural pest control to keep away flies. In a corner, Carol is slicing onions and fiery hot Scotch Bonnet peppers into a bowl of vinegar: Welcome to a little shack of a restaurant on the curve of Hellshire Beach in St. Catherine.

Just outside the shack stands Cutie, the owner, head cook and bottle washer of this popular fish joint. The epitome of a creole mama, she leans against the side of a boat

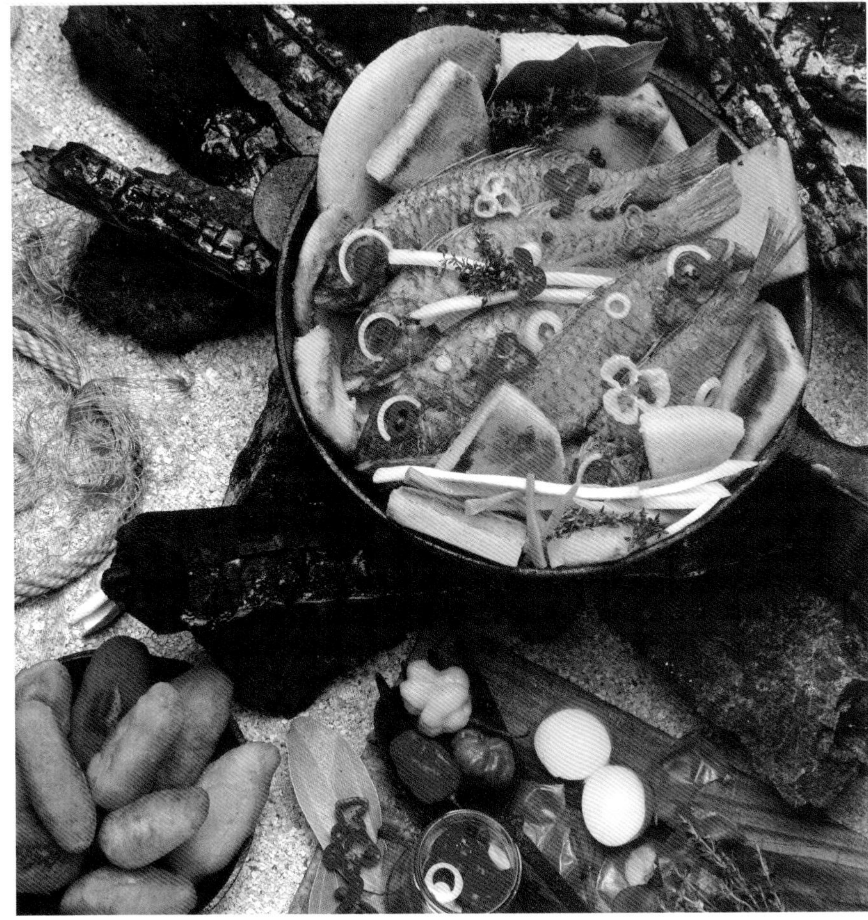

named "Big Wave" arguing with the fisherman. On the sand at her feet is a rusty old scale and fish. Lots of fish. There are rainbow-hued parrot and pewter turbot. Pink snapper and silver jack. After haggling a few more minutes she heaps the fish into a straw basket and bellows for her son David to take the catch into the restaurant.

And so begins this Sunday. From 5:30 in the morning to the wee hours of the night Cutie cooks and serves up classic Jamaican seafood in this tiny shack on the beach. The fare is spartan: fried or steamed fish, grilled lobster, fish tea, bammy and festival. There are no variations and no specials. Her husband, Junior, along with her two children, serve alternately as waiters, maitre'd, and chefs in the restaurant but the operation and personality of the place is solely Cutie's.

To everyone she is Cutie, plain and simple. Her defiant features have been passed to Carol her daughter and also to David. She claims not to remember her birthday, and will only say that she was born on Laws Street in downtown Kingston. Her hair is parted into large plaits that frame her face and when she speaks, strikingly white teeth flash against her ebony skin. As a hefty woman, there is no need for her to assert her presence, but she does this anyway by yelling at everyone and everything. "If you no watch these children is you one work the whole day," she confides. Carol is commanded to speed up slicing the onions and peppers. A few boys from around the beach are tasked to scaling the fish and David is dispatched to meet the drinks truck. Cutie has been running her restaurant for fifteen years. "Me use to come out here and help me Auntie on the weekend. When she leave and go to foreign, she leave the business with her husband but him joke it out. Me take it over and so it been going all this time," she says.

Since that time there have been storms and Hurricane Gilbert, robberies and a fire. The shack itself has been moved six times. "You see that coconut tree?" she says as she points fifty yards down the beach to a coconut tree stump, "that tree used to be behind the shack. But true as to how the beach keep washing away we got to keep moving back and back." Beach erosion is of as much concern to her as soil erosion is to a farmer. The thousands of people who visit the beach each weekend occasionally mutter to themselves how far the beach has come up and then they go home to land-locked bliss. Cutie however watched the shore with a cautious eye. With the help of the Urban Development Corporation and the Hellshire Citizen's Association, vendors on the beach have organised themselves into a grassroots environmental team. Like Cutie many of them are now aware of their responsibilities to the area in which they live and work.

Before anything, Cutie is a mother. Although a hard task master, she feels that by driving the work ethic into her children she is preparing them for the realities of life. "You want to see that my mother and father never did have nothing to give me. Carol and David grow up and see the business, but them must know that is work me work to get it, and they have to work to keep it."

Cutie admits that she made mistakes with Carol, as there were times when she should have been in school but she was at her mother's side helping around. At eighteen and with scant schooling, Carol certainly knows how to total a customer's bill, and her destiny it seems, will be to walk and work her mother's path. On the other hand, David carries the dreams of academia for this family. He is attending high school in Kingston, and at his tender age of fourteen he wants to be an architect. With all her might, Cutie aims to make this dream come true. From this rickety board shack on the beach will come a great builder. This is the essence of the Jamaican Dream. As the flames of the wood fire dance, Cutie places a large, black griddle in the centre of the heat. A family has just ordered fish and festival. Cutie deftly slices each fish and rubs a mixture of salt and pepper into the gashes. "You see this fish eye how it clear?" she shouts to no one in particular, "make sure when you buy fish the eye crystal clear. Never you buy a cloudy-eye fish. That is as stale as they come." And with that she slides each fish onto the griddle, and into a bubbling sea of hot oil. Meanwhile, Carol pinches small pieces of dough out of a cheese-cloth covered pan and swiftly kneads a dozen of her famous festivals. In reply to a questioning glance Cutie snaps, "Don't even ask what in festival. Everybody know but what they don't know is the technique to make it."

With time, customers stream in and by eleven o'clock the shack rings with loud music and chatter, and reeks of suntan oil and beer. Most of the customers appear to be regulars but there are a couple of first-time diners as well. The crowd is mostly made up of upper middle-class scions who have barreled through the sand in four-by-four vehicles. Seated well apart from the crowd is a very young girl escorted by a middle aged man. Cutie glances at Carol and they both roll their eyes. Later, she explains that the restaurant is the favourite haunt for older men squiring young girls. "Way out here, the only friends they will see is those that doing the same thing. And they won't see their wife unless she on a bad move too!" she laughs. Cutie's husband Junior is a quiet man. He sits beside the too-loud stereo changing the radio stations as soon as there is a commercial break on each. Throughout the day he reaches into the old upturned refrigerator for beer or soda as each customer desires. Occasionally he disappears to return with fresh cases of drinks but mostly he just sits there on the stool. He watches everything and everyone in the restaurant, and though he sees a lot he speaks very little. Cutie and Junior have been together for twenty years and have been married for six. There seems to be a mental synchronicity between them, the kind of togetherness that comes when two people have lived a life of challenge and still manage to care for each other.

A small young woman in a trendy bikini has just walked in and she is now pointing in the cooler at the fish she wants. When asked if Hellshire is too far to drive for breakfast, she replies emphatically, "No, no, no. I know this may sound trite, but Sundays and Cutie are inseparable. You know when I got married I didn't bother with a stuffy reception? No man, we all just drove out here and limed until two in the morning." As she says this, Cutie manages a half-smile. In her own aloof way she is basking in the praise.

It is now six in the evening and the beach has become quiet. Cutie is sitting on a stool ardently watching Carol as she does what she herself has been doing for the past fifteen years. "Right now, I know that I must ease up and let Carol know some of the work I did know, but I can't leave this place," she says as she surveys the roof of the shack. Carol is confident that she will be as good as her mother, if not better. "Well for one thing," she says as she glances cautiously at Cutie, "I won't be as miserable as her, but I will still get things done."

Cutie has recently managed to buy a boat and hire a fisherman. She is also part-owner of the "Big Wave." Although the business does well, Cutie has no intention of leaving the house she lives in a few yards from the restaurant. There are a few determined patrons who wake her up at any hour of the night and drag her half-asleep to the restaurant. She admits that she doesn't mind, but will only provide this after-hours service for a few special customers.

Cutie says that in the early days, the motivation for her hard work was her children. Now she works because this is all she knows how to do. This woman does not like to relax, and within a few minutes she is up and charging. Her boat "The Cooler" has come in. As she bustles down to the beach, her daughter Carol can be heard shouting, "David, bring the basket!" And so with the strength of her voice, Carol proves that she is poised to step into her mother's footprints in the sand. ☻

ORIGINALLY PUBLISHED SEPTEMBER 1991

The Oldest British Cathedral in the West

JOY SCOTT

Its stately, majestic red-shingled steeple with a weathervane on top is a landmark in Jamaica, its mellow, weather-beaten bricks bearing silent testimony of the proud history of this ancient cathedral.

The Caribbean is regarded as the 'Cradle of Christianity in the Western World' and the St. James Cathedral in Spanish Town is a monument to this claim. It is the oldest British cathedral, over 300 years old.

Built on slightly raised ground in the south-eastern section of the town, the cathedral was built on the foundations of the Spanish Chapel of the Red Cross, destroyed by Cromwell's troops when the British came to Jamaica in 1655. An Anglican church was built on the spot and on December 20, 1655, Charles II signed its charter. A violent earthquake destroyed the building in 1712 but it was rebuilt two years later. It is this structure which stands today.

Cobbled flagstone leads to the narthex or portico. Here, to one side on a table rests a large leather-bound visitor's book which has been in use since 1968 and has been signed by people from all over the world.

The floor of the nave, the main part of the building, is inlaid with marble tablets beneath which rests the remains of long-departed souls. The walls of the cathedral are spread with monuments to governors of Jamaica, rich planters, soldiers, statesmen, patriots, physicians and "gentle ladies." The works of the famous sculptors of the day are displayed in these marble monuments include that of Bacon, Wilton, Steell and Westmacott.

The English sculptor John Bacon, who also did the Rodney statue in the town square, sculpted the monument to the Earl and Countess of Effingham. The earl came to Jamaica in 1790 as governor and 19 months later, his wife, Catherine, died at sea on a voyage for her health. Five weeks later, the heartbroken Earl died. He is buried in her grave in the cathedral.

The memorial to Sir Basil Keith, who died in 1777, was done by Joseph Wilton and that of the Countess of Elgin, who died in 1843 is the work of Sir John Steell.

Polished mahogany pews, some with the names of families inscribed, fill the spaces on both aisles. A rail separates the altar from the rest of the church.

In the bema on an altar table covered with a white lace cloth rests a golden cross flanked by two golden candlesticks.

An impressive stained glass window dominates the eastern section and immediately below that is a beautiful altar piece—a painting of the Last Supper.

The cathedral's silver communion plate consists of three complete sets and a number of odd items. The oldest vessel—a flagon—dates from 1685 but was refashioned a century later.

The cathedral is in a cruciform and there are two small chapels at each transept. The entire furnishings of one chapel were donated by a lady in memory of her mother.

At the top of the nave are the pulpit; the Lord Bishop's Chair and three chairs for the Suffragan Bishops of Kingston, Mandeville and Montego Bay.

The cathedral celebrated its tercentenary in 1970 and a huge wooden cross was erected after travelling across the island to each Anglican church.

The choir loft, located at the back of the church, contains the powerful three-manual, 300 year old pipe organ. Each year the cathedral choir presents an oratorio from the great masters. Last year Beethoven's "The Mount of Olives" was performed at Easter and Handel's "Samson" will be presented at Christmas. In addition, organist, Trevor Beckford, gives an organ recital each November in which the mellow tones of the organ and his dexterity provide a pleasing treat for music lovers.

There are many stories connected to the old cathedral. One such is about willow trees planted by brides in the churchyard. According to former Canon B.C. Jones, for those marriages which went well the willows flourished but for those where there were problems and even divorce, the trees died.

Another story is about one man who accepted a bet that he could walk the length of the cathedral and back, at midnight, alone. Despite visions of the churchyard filled with tombs dating back centuries, he almost accomplished the task. But, at the front door, his coat caught on a nail and after frantically failing to dislodge it, screaming for help from the ghosts which were after him he dropped dead—from fright.

ORIGINALLY PUBLISHED APRIL 1984

A Walking Tou

ANGUS MACDONALD

Anglers Club, otherwise known as McFarlane's Bar, dates back to around 1750 and still provides a service in Port Royal square.

Three hundred years ago Port Royal was the "richest, most wicked and sinful city in the world." A home port for some of the most evil pirates who ever plundered the Caribbean—with the richest sea routes in existence. Port Royal is today a sleepy little town rich only in history. Its streets, along which the most feared pirates of the mid to late seventeenth century who roamed from one ale house to the next—along which noble and gallant sea warriors, then engaged in building an empire for England, left their footprints—are now all but deserted.

Those historic days are far behind but the buildings—the old naval hospital; the fort which helped defend its captured riches and the sovereignty of the island of Jamaica; the church; the old gaol—all stand as monuments to the heroic, swashbuckling days when Port Royal was the base from which England launched its challenge to Spain and later France, for mastery of the world.

ORIGINALLY PUBLISHED OCTOBER 1984

Old gaol in Gaol Alley. This structure dates back to around 1710.

The old Naval Hospital, built around 1818. The iron staircase, although not located at the exact point indicated in this drawing, is of the type to be found elsewhere in this old structure.

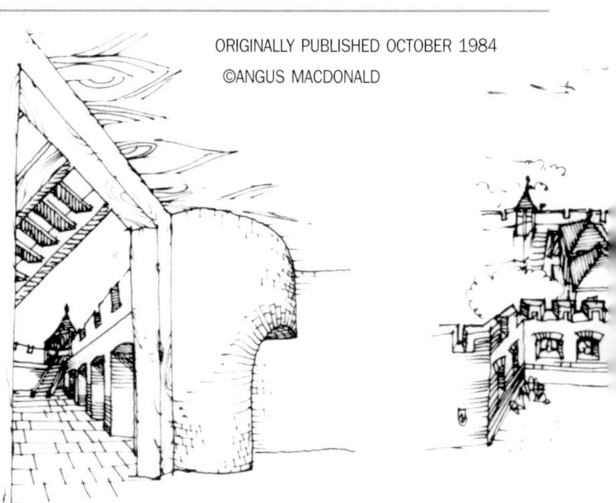

"The Quarterdeck", Fort Charles, dates back to around 1728.

# of Port Royal

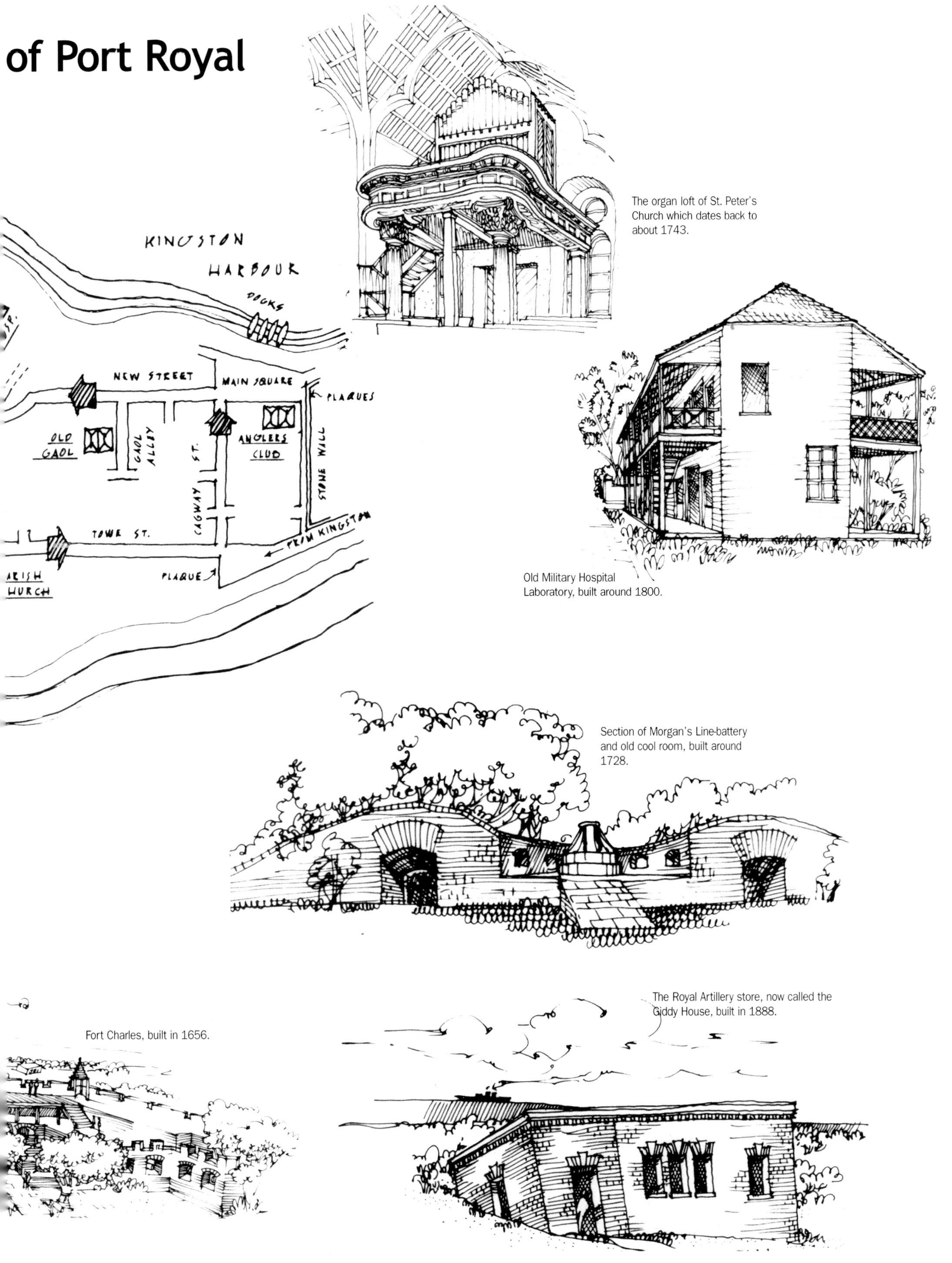

The organ loft of St. Peter's Church which dates back to about 1743.

Old Military Hospital Laboratory, built around 1800.

Section of Morgan's Line-battery and old cool room, built around 1728.

The Royal Artillery store, now called the Giddy House, built in 1888.

Fort Charles, built in 1656.

The Heritage of Spanish Town

MARGUERITE CURTIN

Spared by hurricane and earthquake, but singed by fire, the ancient township of Villa de la Vega continues to survive, even though threatened by the onslaught of the twenty-first century. Enigmatically, she waits for the revelation of her fascinating story.

Spanish Town, as the name implies, is a Spanish town. In 1534 the Town of the Plain was laid out by the Spanish colonists from the abandoned settlement at Sevilla la Nueva on the north coast of the island. Looking southwards, they climbed the diabolically steep mountain range which peaks at Mount Diablo, and passed through the treacherous river gorge, at last reaching the ideal open spot on the bank of the Rio Cobre.

But the site predates Spanish settlement. Preliminary digs in this archaeologically rich town reveal Arawak remains, possibly related to the largest-known Amerindian settlement in Jamaica, situated six miles east at White Marl, Central Village. Spanish Town can, therefore, be regarded as the oldest continuously inhabited town-site in Jamaica.

Twenty years after the founding of Villa de la Vega by the Spanish, houses of tile and stone began to replace the earlier wattle and daub huts. A stone monastery and a stone church were built. Eventually there were five religious institutions: an abbey, two monasteries (Franciscan and Dominican) and two hermitages, one devoted to our Lady of Bethlehem, and the other to St. Jeronimo. Life may not have been as idyllic as that of the picture painted by Vazquez de Espinosa, a Carmellite Friar, who writes in praise of the township by "the crystaline waters" of the Rio Cobre but it would seem that the early inhabitants of "La Vega", as they called their town affectionately, lived in tolerably happy circumstances. There were factions and friction between governors and ecclesiastics, as well as the ever-present possibility of raids from English, French and Dutch privateers, but on the other hand, there were governors who managed to take several constructive steps. For example, Fernando Melgarejo de Cordoba (1596-1609) set up the Archives, while Alonso de Miranda (1607-1611) besides building the monastery of St. Francis and repairing the Cabildo's meeting hall, was responsible for laying out the town's streets. Spanish Town is a classic model of a Spanish township: a quadrangular plan—streets in a grid pattern around a central Square (the Plaza Mayor).

Certainly the former inhabitants of Sevilla la Nueva, the first Spanish settlement in Jamaica, wished to have buildings of elegance in their new town also. Findings of the historian, Sylvia Wynter, indicate that Arawak craftsmen actually became highly skilled masons in the period of early Spanish settlement (1509-1534). In fact, at one time there were only Arawak masons left on the island. Prof. Wynter tells us of a former Arawak cacique who is known to have worked on the church at Sevilla la Nueva. His baptismal name was Juan de Medina. Did he ever work on a building in Spanish Town? Answers to questions such as this one could, indeed, further understanding of Spanish Town's early years.

The English historian, Edward Long (1774) mentions that he actually saw in Spanish Town stone remains of Spanish buildings that were too large to be incorporated into English dwellings. As a result of what he saw, Long concedes that the structures erected in the Spanish period were executed "by no mean artists".The Spanish historian, Francisco Morales Padron, in his important work, *Jamaica Espanola,* (Seville 1952) provides us with the name of a master mason who was contracted to work in La Vega. His name was Yusepe Perez. Further research may well throw light on the various techniques used by early Jamaican stone masons and on their traditions, some of which may well have survived to this very day.

In 1655 when Oliver Cromwell's Western Design failed to take the island of Santo Domingo, Admiral Penn and General Venables turned to the island of Jamaica rather than return empty-handed to England. Landing at Passage Fort the Puritan forces marched into Spanish Town and seized it. Long reports that "handsome houses" still existed there in spite of previous raids of marauding pirates. The best of these houses were then chosen by the English officers of the conquering army; private soldiers were quartered in others; while the remaining houses were left to go to ruin. Long insists that "history does not mention that the English destroyed the (Spanish) houses".

Many of the existing houses in Spanish Town today are on Spanish foundations but what is more, some of the apparent Georgian houses may well have a Spanish core disguised beneath an English overlay. Long writes at length about the design of houses in Spanish Town. He favoured Spanish design over "the modern" (1774). Spanish houses were "excellently contrived"—though small. Alterations and "considerable additions" by the English newcomers transformed the original structures into roomy and commodious dwellings with piazzas on the street's edge. Gradually the now fashionable sash windows and "jealousy shutters" replaced the little turned pillars and "upright shutters" of Spanish windows. And so the Spanish houses were totally disguised thus contributing to the architectural uniqueness of Spanish Town.

Officially the English called their newly acquired capital, St. Jago de la Vega, but in everyday parlance it was simply, Spanish Town. For 217 years this inland town was to be their civic and administrative centre (1655-1872). Port Royal, across the harbour, was the centre of trade until the disastrous earthquake of 1692; several English residents of Spanish Town had wharves and houses in this great trading depot. With the destruction of Port Royal by the earthquake, however, the town of Kingston, which would one day challenge the hegemony of Spanish Town, began slowly to take shape on the Liguanea Plain. Later it was to become in the eyes of most Spanishtownians "the Resort of all the disorderly and mischievous part of the community, both Natives and Foreigners".

In the meantime, Spanish Town, the older city, enjoyed the status accorded to it as the capital of a valued sugar colony. The govemor's residence, Kings House, on the western side of the Square was described by Long as "the noblest and best edifice of the kind, either in North America, or any of the British Colonies". On the northern side of the square the memorial to Admiral Rodney commemorating his victory over the French at the Battle of the Saints in 1782 was a reminder to all of Britain's naval supremacy. On the eastern side of the square, the oldest building of this civic group (1762) housed the colony's House of Assembly. Maintaining the southern side of the square was the court house (1819)—destroyed by a fire in 1986. Southwest of this city-centre was the immense barracks (c 1791) erected under the supervision of the royal engineer on the seventeenth century parade ground. This immense barracks, one of three in the world built in this design, needs urgent restoration now.

The economy of Spanish Town centered around those who had business in the capital city—officials, civil servants, military personnel, members of the House of Assembly and Council, lawyers, the judiciary, and dignitaries of the church. There were slaves and a slave market; Jews and a synagogue. Markets teemed with meat and produce and tradespeople such as tailors, seamstresses and shoemakers enjoyed prosperity. The fashionable had to be fitted out for the grand balls, concerts and routs. There were dancing masters and dancing classes; a theatre and newspapers. The *St. Jago Intelligence* was the name of one newspaper and the *St. Jago Gazette* another. Williams Daniels, a journeyman who once worked in the printery of Benjamin Franklin in Philadelphia, was publisher of the *St. Jago Gazette* until the time of his death. By the same token, however, when the city's decline set in these people were among the first to feel the hardship most keenly. In 1865, for example, there were 91 shoemakers, 127 tailors and 772 seamstresses in an adult population of 3124, many of whom "were without sustenance". But in the days before, when the city flourished and swelled with those who came from all over the island to attend the House of Assembly, or the Supreme Court in the latter months of the year, the story was one of prosperity for many tradespeople and artisans.

The journal of Lady Nugent gives an interesting picture of life in early nineteenth century Spanish Town. Wife of the governor, Maria Nugent, an American woman, spent much of her time, when she was not travelling about Jamaica, in Kings House, Spanish Town.

Many fine examples of Jamaica Georgian and Victorian architecture still remain intact; elements of civil, military, ecclesiastic, commercial and domestic architecture blend together producing the interesting and unique character that is Spanish Town's. For example, the feeling of intimacy on King Street, one of the best preserved streets, contrasts with the overwhelming impact of space which is experienced in the Square. And always there is the element of surprise. Interspersed between important buildings of the state were houses of urban dwellers, built on a smaller scale but with the same exquisite craftsmanship in the tradition of Spanish Town artisans. (In 1865 there were 150 carpenters and 60 masons in the city.)

In many ways, Spanish Town is the history of Jamaica in a nutshell. Until the rival maritime city of Kingston became the capital in 1872 all the political and legal decisions affecting the life and development of the island and its people were made in Spanish Town. Here on the steps of Kings House, the proclamation abolishing slavery was delivered at midnight on August 1, 1834. Over the centuries countless Jamaicans have made their way to Spanish Town, the most famous perhaps being Paul Bogle who led a deputation from Stony Gut in 1865 to Governor Eyre in Kings House to seek better conditions for the people of his parish, St. Thomas.

Numerous also have been the visitors from abroad who stayed in Spanish Town for one reason or another—Hans Sloane, Admiral George Rodney, Captain Bligh of the "Bounty", and Simon Bolivar, to name a few. From Passage Fort they rested at the Ferry Inn by the Fresh River and travelled in to Spanish Town.

Today, the thirteen-mile journey between Spanish Town and Kingston takes but twenty minutes. In the days before the coming of the motor car, the journey was a three-hour one by carriage. With each passing year the distance which once separated Spanish Town and Kingston becomes less and less. Indeed it would seem that by the end of the twentieth century the rival cities will have become one metropolis on the Liguanea and St. Catherine plains.

For those who have been fortunate enough to encounter the marching bands of Spanish Town, their fanfare which echoes through the streets not only recalls the pomp, and celebration of Spanish Town's rich historic past but also affirms that this living city promises to be in the future a vibrant cultural centre in which archaeological and archival research will play a vital role.

It is now up to Jamaicans to bring about the conservation and restoration of this historic gem; to halt its deterioration and preserve a city whose history and architecture are important not only to the heritage of this hemisphere but also to the world.

ORIGINALLY PUBLISHED JUNE 1989

A Fishing Village

MARY LANGFORD

A hundred years ago life in Jamaica was quite different to the life which we take for granted today. Being a small hilly island, it was a great deal easier to travel by schooner than by horse and buggy. Consequently the more important towns were on the coast and geared to accommodate sea-going craft of various sizes and descriptions. There would be ocean-going vessels engaged in the export of sugar and bananas and the import of manufactured goods; there would be sailing ships which carried people and provisions from one town to another; and of course there would be the humble canoe used by the local fishermen. Freshly caught fish, crabs or lobster could be bought at the seaside most any day of the week. Over the last fifty years all this has changed. Container ships go to Kingston; the banana boats go to only a few ports; the bauxite companies make their own arrangements; and different types of automobiles and trucks carry people and agricultural produce to the urban centres speedily along widened asphalted road. Improvements in transportation have led to a marked decline in the use of the numerous bays dotted around the island. Although still as beautiful as ever, most bays are no longer scenes of lively activity.

However, if the adventurous visitor would like to know more about where Jamaicans live and how they earn their living, exploring the coastal villages—especially those on the South Coast—can prove very rewarding. There are several such villages along the stretch of coast between Black River and Alligator Pond. Parotee Bay, Billy's Bay, Treasure Beach, Calabash Bay are all worth visiting, but Great Bay has changed the least in the last fifty years. In spite of the introduction of electricity, a piped water supply and asphalted roads, Great Bay more than any other of these fishing villages maintains the ambiance of Jamaica in the early years of this century. Perhaps this is because the road actually ends at Great Bay; there is no road over the great bluff that forms the eastern side of the bay. On the other hand, the special atmosphere which characterizes Great Bay may be due to the people who live there. It is said that they are the descendants of shipwrecked sailors probably English or Scottish, judging by the surnames common to the area. All of the older families are fair in complexion with curly blond hair. They are hard-working and honest with an unusual degree of self-confidence and independence, who rear goats, sheep and cattle. It is a dry area but the livestock can always drink water from the ponds which, although often low never, seem to dry up completely. Lignum vitae, thatch palm and dogwood trees grow everywhere in the sandy soil. Cassava, escallion, melons and peppers are easily cultivated and find a ready market. Most of the older houses and shops are constructed of wattle and daub with thatched roofs, but this method of building is giving way to concrete blocks and zinc sheets. There is even a small supermarket and motel at the end of the road, but neither are crowded. The churches of Great Bay are better patronized. There is a small Seventh Day Adventist Church, a Grace and Truth (Plymouth Brethren) meeting place and a Salvation Army outpost. A strong sense of genuine and practical religion motivates the inhabitants of Great Bay.

Having said all this, the really important thing about Great Bay which makes it worth visiting and writing about is that it is a Jamaican fishing village. The sea dominates life in Great Bay. In the old days nearly every family owned a canoe adzed out of a silk cotton tree. These canoes went to sea propelled by oars and sailed without compasses. Even now very few of the fishermen use a compass for navigation. Many however have discarded their wooden canoes for larger craft of similar shape manufactured from fibre glass and powered by 40 horse-power outboard engines. With supreme faith in their engines, most of the fishermen do not even bother to take a stand-by sail or oar. Life jackets are never seen.

There is no pier at Great Bay. The men going to sea must wade out to their boat, steady it, stow their accoutrements, secure the engine and then wait for the right moment to clamber aboard. Some fishermen troll just outside the bay, others go as far as the Outer Banks eight or ten miles off shore to drop their pots, or collect them as the case might be, while others journey to the Pedro Cays, the waterless islands that lie fifty miles south of Portland Point.

The really big event of the week is the return of boats from the cays. Not only do they bring news of family and friends who sometimes stay out there to fish for three months at a time, but thousands of dollars worth of fish. By general consensus women are not allowed to visit the cays. Life out there is hard but the fishing is good. In the old days runners would carry the fresh fish in baskets on their heads and immediately set off for towns 10 or 15 miles away. Now vans and pick-ups with cold boxes wait for the arrival of the boats, buy what they think they can sell and quickly speed away to Montego Bay or some other urban centre. Sometimes the lobsters are not sold immediately but stored in cages anchored in the shallow sea as they must be kept alive until actually put into the pot.

On days when the weather will not allow small craft to venture out, there is much to be done on shore. Fish pots, made of thin sticks and galvanized mesh wire, have to be laboriously fashioned in such a way that the unsuspecting fish glides in through a large opening which gradually narrows and so they are unable to find a way to regain their freedom. Seines and smaller nets used to catch shrimps and fish nearer to shore also have to be made or mended. The process of setting and drawing a seine which is actually a large open-ended net fitted with floaters, is an exercise which invariably attracts attention. First, the seine is loaded into a canoe after one end has been made fast to a point on the shore. The men in the canoe then paddle slowly out into the bay in a wide semi-circle paying out the net as they go. At last the other end is brought back to shore and the net is ready to be drawn. After a while a dozen or so men and teenage boys take up their positions along the ropes and slowly, very slowly, drag the net onto the beach. The women and children then eagerly cluster around picking up, selecting and purchasing whatever they consider to be worthwhile. At some fishing villages further along the coast, it is claimed that quite big snappers can be caught in the seines, but mostly one sees sprats and other "trash" fish useful for boiling a delicious fish tea. Regardless of what is brought in, the whole business of drawing a seine provides a morning full of anticipation and excitement with the opportunity for much friendly chatter and revelry.

With all this fish around, the birds which feed on fish will soon be noticed flying low over the sea and suddenly diving. There is the brown pelican, commonly known as Old Joe and the frigate bird which is also called a man of war because it tries to take away the fish which the other birds have caught. Flocks of Captain Lewis can be seen circling for hours over currents where they think fish are feeding. Like the birds, small boys also want to catch at least one fish, so they get their bait, prepare their hook and line and set off to the rocks where they perch precariously for hours. Quite large king fish and barracuda have been known to be hooked off these rocks.

At night, when it is calm enough some of the men take to their boats and go several miles out to enjoy an evening of "drop fishing." From the shore, the light of their boats is easily seen appearing and disappearing as the boat rides the swells of the waves. On clear nights, ashore or at sea, the stars are brilliant and it is fascinating to try to identify the various constellations. You are lucky indeed if you can actually see the Southern Cross.

Everyone in Jamaica knows something of Black River, formally a prosperous logwood shipping port; and has heard of Treasure Beach the south coast seaside resort of families living in Malvern and Mandeville. The great cattle properties of St. Elizabeth, Pepper, Goshen and Gilnock now are just names of places which are connected to the bauxite mining; Lovers Leap (Yardly Chase) provides a magnificent view of the southcoast; and God's Well (Guts River) east of Alligator Pond is surely the clearest and most beautiful stream on the island. All these places are worth the effort you have to make to find them but if you can journey "to the end of the road" you will be rewarded by finding for yourself a piece of Old Jamaica.

ORIGINALLY PUBLISHED NOVEMBER 1993

PHILIP GOSSE
1810 – 1888
Liliaceae.
Icacinaceae.
Plumbagin-
aceae.
Thunbergia.
Rubiaceae.

Exploring Philip Gosse's Jamaica

IAN ROBINSON

Today, I want you to accompany me to what we in Jamaica call "bush" with the aim of visiting sites associated with Philip Gosse, who came to Jamaica in 1844 as a naturalist collecting and painting plants, insects and particularly, birds. While he did some painting here, most were done after he returned to his home at Poole, Dorset in England.

He no doubt acquired his painting skills from his father who was a successful miniaturist who did portraits for lockets. His father did well enough to have Philip educated in Latin, Greek, math and his favourite subject, natural history.

Having tried his hand in North America, Philip came to Jamaica, and on his journey, he met fellow passengers who were Moravian missionaries, and who, being dispersed over the southern half of the island, were well disposed to helping him during his travels. Soon, he was staying with a Mr. and Mrs. Colman at Bluefields House, which is our starting point.

It was from Bluefields House, once a guest house, and now a private home, that Gosse ventured up into the hills, went wading in the Black River Morass (swamp) and visited fishermen along the coast. The English name of Bluefields may have been a corruption of the name Blaufelt, a Dutch pirate who sailed from this area to harass the Spanish treasure fleets as did Henry Morgan who assembled his fleet here before sacking Panama in 1670.

Peculiar place names abound in this area. Calder Shafston, is a great house perched on the hillside above Bluefields. Historically, its prosperity was based on the pimento tree; its berries used for condiments and its oil for deodorants. Today, Calder Shafton is a guest house but you might need Gosse's horse to reach it as I understand the road is a bit of challenge. Gosse indeed rode through here as he scaled Bluefields Mountain to emerge at Content—which we will also visit, but by a longer and, I hope you will find, interesting route.

As we proceed westwards, a new road carries us away from the beach making it more pleasant especially since you can buy food, often cooked and served from boats which have been converted into kitchens. The main favourites, cassava bammies fried crisp along with fried fish, were inherited from the Taino, the Amerindians who originally inhabited Jamaica. You may also find jerked chicken, fish and pork—'jerking' being a way of roasting with lots of herbs over a pimento log fire. This tradition found its way down from the Maroons, escaped slaves who hid in the mountain recesses of Cockpit Country.

As we drive along the coast road, we seem to be gradually edged into the placid sea by the hills. We pass Friar Cap Point at Mearnsville, but when we reach Cave, where Gosse collected specimens of different fish, we turn right and start our zig zag assault on Bluefields Mountain. The views are going to be worth it all I assure you!

Within minutes we pass the entrance to Chebucktoo Great House, also a private home. The name to me sounds African, which gives me the excuse to tell you about a group of people in the next valley who are descended from the

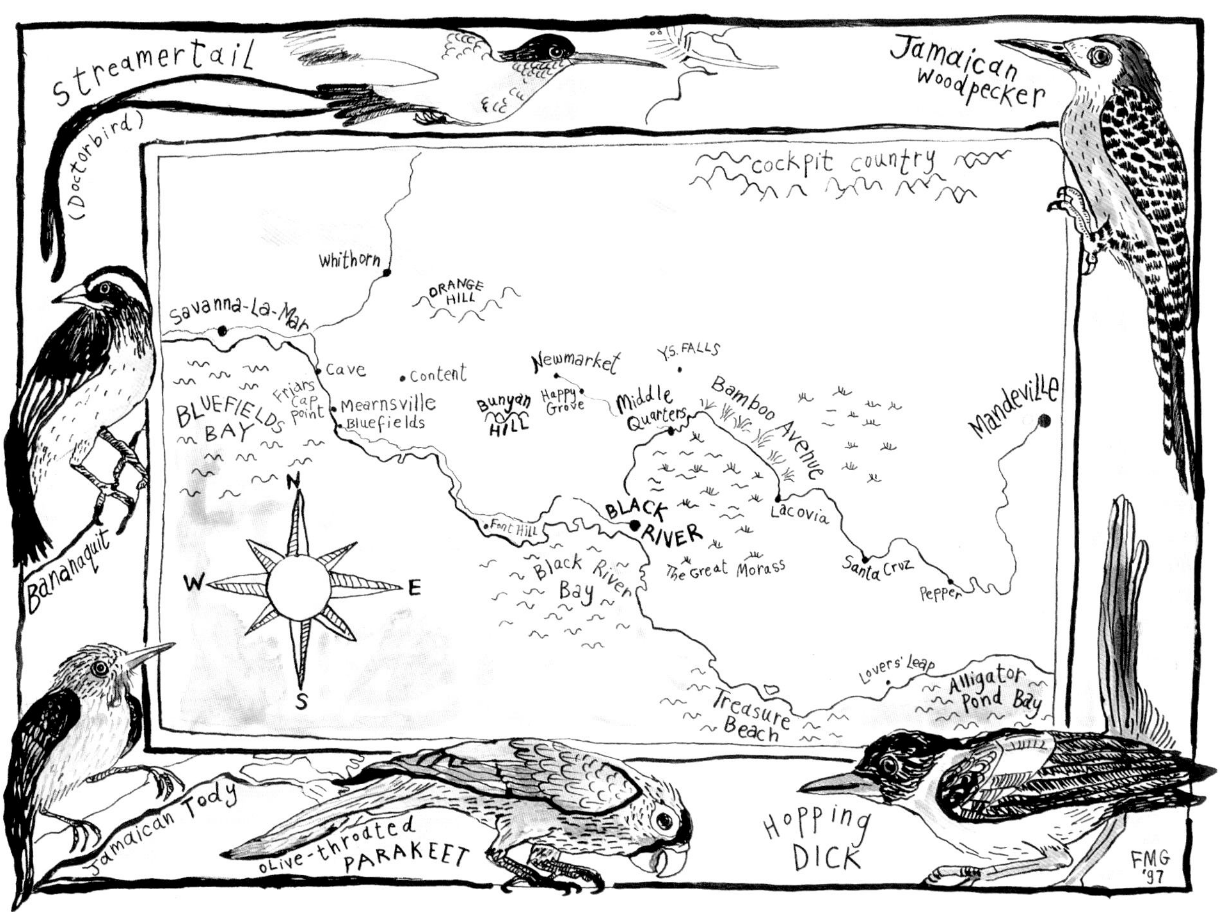

Nagos, a sub-tribe of the Yoruba, who settled here. They came in 1840, after slavery was abolished, and were the forerunners of indentured workers, most of whom later came from Ireland, India and China. They worked on the sugar estates for something like five years in return for their passage. The older folk in the neighbouring village of Abeokuta ("under the rock" in the West African tongue) can still speak a few Yoruba words and have distinctive folk tales and dances.

The types of trees and plants we see on the roadside have not changed much since Gosse's day, except that there were more of them then! It was in the late 18th century that the planters imported trees such as the breadfruit, mango, logwood (the only dye which could make silk really black) and many more to add to the indigenous trees such as pimento, annatto (used even today as a safe red dye for foods), trumpet tree and the cassava plant.

Do stop on the wider sections of the road and enjoy the views: eastward to Black River and westward to Savanna la Mar (simply "Sav" to the locals) with Negril off in the haze.

Soon you will be in Kentucky. Back in Gosse's time it was owned by a Frances Jones who had 59 slaves processing the property's pimento. Ask a passing local to show you the pimento tree; crush its shiny dark green leaf and smell the allspice fragrance which is reminiscent of four spices: cinnamon, cloves, pepper and nutmeg—not bad value for money!

Our next stop is at the highest point in western Jamaica at 620m or 2020 ft for the unmetricated among us. Grinding your way up the hill you will reach a large concrete water tank; here in the countryside water is collected from a concreted hillside catchment. Around the corner you will find the Steel family who will be glad to show you, what at first appears to be no more than a rocky outcrop. As one gets closer, its lichen covered pink rocks take on a man-made form. Mr. Steel tells me that it used to be a Baptist chapel, but, unfortunately, the Baptists know nothing about it. They believe that the first Baptist chapel in Westmoreland was built in 1827 at Ridgeland, way across the parish. The stone door jams have the words "Bunyan Chapel" carved into them. A date on the keystone would be helpful, but is most likely somewhere under the pile of stones we are standing on! My latest inspiration is that since there is a Plymouth Brethren chapel just down the road, perhaps it was moved after a hurricane or something. I waited, and waited one Sunday to speak to an elder, but it seems to have been an all day service, and I gave up!

Interestingly, Gosse joined the Brethren soon after returning to England, so maybe he was converted here and sent money to set up the chapel.

Make a point to climb the hill and enjoy the views: to the northwest you will see Dolphin Head Mountain behind Lucea while to the east lies firstly Spur Tree ridge which you have to ascend to reach Mandeville and if it is a clear day, with some imagination, or a couple of Red Stripe beers, you can see the majestic Blue Mountains which tower over Kingston.

At the Brethren chapel we can take a right turn to Content, one of many such named villages in Jamaica, but this is where Gosse would have emerged on his ride from Calder Shafston. Turning back, we push on to the DeLeon's Holly Hill and Hopewell until we almost reach Darliston, the largest town in this area. You can pop into town for a quick look around and some refreshment, but we are turning right and heading south to Newmarket. We will pass Happy Retreat, Vile Hill, Lenox Bigwoods, Joe Williams Bigwoods, Hopeton stopping at Mt Carmel's hilltop Moravian Church. What evocative village names. We bypassed another village called Helter Skelter!

Newmarket, as its name describes is a market town most likely dating from the time of the American War of Independence when we were not allowed to trade with the "enemy." Stewart Town in St. Ann, and possibly Newmarket, were developed to make the plantations self sufficient, the food being grown by former slaves who had gained their freedom.

If you had attempted to visit the town back in July 1979 you would have needed a boat. At that time a depression sat over the area for four days dropping 1.5m of rain. Being limestone, the countryside normally soaked up the rain like a sponge. This time it seems that there must have been a collapse in an underground cabin, causing all the water to backup and flood the town to its roof tops for some 18 months. Then, rowing boats were the only way to cross the town, but the town seems to have picked up where it left off and it's business as usual!

Beersheba, which we missed near Newmarket, and Happy Grove which we pass though next on our way down to Middle Quarters, were created by missionaries to house the newly freed slaves in 1838. Sometimes the villages were named after the English sponsor, a missionary or some biblical name.

What goes up, must come down. As we descend we emerge at Middle Quarters, home of the "pepper swimp" (shrimp) which are caught in the adjacent morass. Buy some, but you will need a drink again to temper the fire!

The village name is a reference to the fact that this area was known as Suriname Quarters. In 1679 settlers came here from Suriname (Dutch Guiana) when it was being exchanged for New Amsterdam (New York) with the English, giving the Dutch a South American base. History has proved it not to have been a very good swap for the Dutch!

Now we are back down on the coast road again. You can turn left and enjoy Bamboo Avenue on your way to Mandeville, or turning right will take us to Black River and Bluefields.

In June 1846, Philip Gosse sailed from Port Royal bidding adieu to kind friends and finally leaving this lovely island. His name is perpetuated in Jamaica by the Gosse Bird Club while his famous etchings of Jamaica's birds have been superseded by Bond's *Birds of the West Indies* and Downer and Sutton's *Birds of Jamaica*.

Happy exploring following Gosse's footsteps and as we say in Jamaica "walk good!"

Philip Henry Gosse

(1810-1888) was one of the foremost naturalists of the 19th century working in and around the British Museum during his time. He visited Jamaica for 18 months in 1844-1845. During this time he was able to lay some of the foundation upon which later naturalists have built and developed present knowledge of Jamaica's history. Gosse worked mainly in the Bluefields area on the south-west coast of the island. His visit inspired him to write a number of books which have been recognized today as ornithological classics. These include: *The Birds of Jamaica*, published in 1847, *Illustrations of the Birds of Jamaica* in 1849 and *A Naturalist's Sojourn in Jamaica* in 1851. A more recent publication, *Gosse's Jamaica 1844-45* was written by Gosse and edited by D. B. Stewart. This publication is of particular interest to bird lovers and contains the most interesting parts of the *Birds of Jamaica*, as well as portions of *A Naturalist's Sojourn.*

ORIGINALLY PUBLISHED JUNE 1997

The Poet and The Preacher
Falmouth's Curious Heritage

ED KRITZLER

My Dream Is Of An Island Place
Which Distant Seas Keep Lonely.
A Little Island On Whose Face
The Stars Are Watchers Only.
— ELIZABETH BARRETT BROWNING (1806-1861)

England's Romantic poet wrote these lines in 1838 after her Uncle Samuel died, leaving her his Jamaican properties. Although she never visited the island, her town house and the surrounding village of Falmouth appear frozen in time, in a somnolent state of decay—as if awaiting her loving spirit to bestow on it a kiss of restoration.

Think of Colonial Williamsburg just prior to restoration and you have a good image of Falmouth. This coastal town, 22 miles east of Montego Bay, was founded by Elizabeth Barrett's grandfather Edward in 1790. He drew up the town's plans, sold off lots to his neighbours—the proprietors of area sugar estates—and kept the waterfront for himself. What remained, he donated for building a church, courthouse and public gardens.

For the next half century, Falmouth stood as the wealthiest New World port south of Charleston, South Carolina. At a time when the epitome of English wealth made one "as rich as a West Indian planter," Falmouth's mercantile glory was expressed in its architecture, a display of Georgian designs considered among the finest anywhere beyond Britain; such were the blessings of sugar. Jamaica was then the world's leading producer of the sweetener and most of it was grown and processed by some 28,000 slaves on 88 plantations near Falmouth.

When Elizabeth was 14, her Uncle Samuel resigned his seat in Parliament and moved to Jamaica with his family to manage properties he had inherited. The poet had always been close to her father's brother and they carried on a regular correspondence. When her tyrannical father cut her out of his will for running off with Robert Browning, her uncle cushioned her with his Jamaican legacy, the port of Falmouth, its wharves, and the family townhouse, all of which allowed her to be financially independent.

In 1830, the *Jamaica Almanac* made particular note of Falmouth's "superb, elegant, and substantial" town houses and merchant homes, claiming that the bustling port "yielded to none in its social urbanity." However, it was not to last. With the freeing of the slaves, Falmouth went into a precipitous decline—plantations were abandoned, and with them, commerce dried up. The internationally read *Falmouth Post* ceased publication, and the port's leading citizens returned to England or moved across the island to Kingston. Only the buildings remained. However weathered and worn, most of the present town's edifices—the churches, police station, post and tax offices, court house, and many shops and homes—date from the time when Elizabeth was the town's reigning (if absentee) land owner.

The seaside port is a half-hour drive east of Montego Bay. The coast highway takes one past some of Jamaica's finer hotels, golf courses, small sandy beaches and two restored Great Houses that once belonged to the family—Cinnamon Hill and Greenwood. The first is where Elizabeth's father Edward, the notorious tyrant of Wimpole Street, was born, and is now the private residence of singer Johnny Cash. Five miles further, on a hillside overlooking the sea, is the Greenwood mansion with its spacious ballroom built by Edward's cousin Richard to entertain guests after he became Speaker of Jamaica's House of Assembly. It has been impressively restored and refurbished, and is open to visitors.

A walking tour of this Rip Van Winkle town is being organized by the Hon. Roylan B. Barrett, the Custos of Trelawny Parish of which Falmouth is the capital. (Note: the title Custos signifies an honorary post as the Queen of England's representative, a lifetime appointment.) Custos Barrett—"call me Roy"—is a Falmouth born attorney. He is responsible for much of the volunteer work in the parish, heralded especially for initiating counseling services in the town to help citizens with almost any problem. Roy, a black man, is a distant cousin of the Barretts who never let colour interfere with their conjugal desires. "I could be one of their great-great slaves" he says jokingly. Indeed, most descendants of the family in Jamaica are people of colour.

Beginning in January, visitors will be met in the town square by two student guides to be shown sites spanning the rise and fall of Falmouth's prosperity—the waterfront pier where slaves were sold, and the church where their freedom was proclaimed. Other stops are a military fort, now a school where young boys climb atop huge cannons that once defended the town, a police station with 4 ft. thick stone walls that once contained the explosive experiments of the famous Jewish chemist, David Lindo, and alongside privately owned townhouses, is a cluster of brightly coloured small houses, the restored homes of ex-slaves who had purchased their freedom. The hour walk-about will bring visitors to a private garden for an English tea hosted by "Auntie Olga," known for her ginger jelly, pepper jam and delicate scones.

In the 18th century, when sugar was said to be "King", the Barretts were Royalty, and Falmouth was their Court. Elizabeth's forebearers shaped and mis-shaped their world,

The Baptist preacher William Knibb declared at the stroke of midnight, August 31, 1838, "...the monster is dead." Slaves then proceeded to bury their chains, shackles and leg irons.

> "...Falmouth stood as the wealthiest New World port south of Charleston, South Carolina."

blending sugar, slavery and political power into "one of the great West Indian family fortunes." Along with their neighbour John Tharp, whose Good Hope Estate has been transformed into a five star resort, the Barretts owned the most land, the most slaves, and produced the most sugar. Family members held the highest political offices, bought and sold Africans, freed their colored children, sent slave ships to Africa, sugar to Britain and rum to New England. In 1826, they owned 25,000 acres, 3,376 slaves and 17 sugar estates, sugar, slaves, land and political power were the pillars of Barrett wealth. But in a climate where one was either for or against slavery, their quasi-liberalism was a weak link. Samuel and his cousin Richard were "enlightened" slave owners—they outlawed the whip, schooled slaves, allowed religious instruction, and extra time off for married couples. But coming events would make their good intentions irrelevant.

In 1824, a Baptist missionary from England, the Rev. William Knibb, came to Falmouth to bring christianity to the slaves. He preached christian brotherhood, equality before God, and a religious vision that was shared by the Barretts, who befriended him. Opposing him were the planters who believed it was not possible to be both a good slave and a good christian. They were right. The planters saw Knibb's orations as naive and inflammatory. In 1832 they arrested him for inciting the slaves to rebellion in what was called the Baptist War.

The slave revolt in January, 1832 was fed by a rumour that their freedom had been granted but kept secret by their masters. Cane fields were burned; great houses and sugar works were destroyed. Fifteen whites were killed. When the revolt was put down, 300 Africans were hung as a reprisal. Knibb was sent to Montego Bay for trial where Samuel Barrett wrote to him: "We are prepared to testify to your peaceable character as a Christian." Richard Barrett's political clout secured his release. "...it is my firm conviction" Richard wrote, "that religion had nothing to do with the late disturbances, on the contrary, its absence was a chief cause of them."

Knibb was exiled to England. At a crowded London meeting, he decried the brutal suppression of the slave revolt and warned a racial war was in the offering. Hooded members of the Colonial Church Union—Jamaica's equivalent of the Klan—had set Knibbs' church ablaze, along with 19 other churches, and

(OPPOSITE) William Knibb Memorial Baptist Church. (ABOVE) A. Duperly print of Market Street, c1840. (RIGHT) Rafting on the Martha Brae. (FAR RIGHT) A restored great house.

beaten up many missionaries. In England, the abolitionists demanded action. Parliament responded with The Emancipation Act of 1833, abolishing slavery with a provision that delayed full freedom for five years. On the eve of Emancipation Day, Knibb, who had returned to Falmouth and rebuilt his church, welcomed a crowd of 6,000 slaves to a midnight mass. When the church bells rang in a new day—August 31, 1838—the preacher cried: "The Monster is Dead!" and led the free men outside to bury their chains and leg irons in the churchyard.

When her mother died in 1828, Elizabeth Barrett, 22, the oldest of 11 siblings, became the family caretaker and mainstay of her father. What started out as an affectionate bond between them was to tighten into a stranglehold. She was always sickly, having been diagnosed at 14 with a "nervous disorder" and prescribed opium; henceforth, she was addicted to morphine and had a chronic lung ailment. When not caring for the family, she retreated to her bedroom, composing the poems that won her acclaim. One day, she received a letter from the poet Robert Browning who boldly wrote: "I love your verses with all my heart Miss Barrett—and I love you too." The next day she confided to a friend that his letter "threw me into ecstasies." So began a romantic courtship and 15 years of wedded bliss.

The couple settled in Florence, Italy, entertaining literati at their villa, but Jamaica was never far from her thoughts. She asked that her wedding announcement read "...of Wimpole Street and Cinnamon Hill, Jamaica," and wrote her brother there: "You would smile to see how interested I have grown in the Jamaica crops." She confessed little desire to meet her fellow planters, whom she referred to as "white savages." Still, she had hoped to visit Jamaica but owing to her fragile condition, she changed her mind: "Had I gone, it would have killed me."

Jamaica's rulers who oversaw the policy of emancipation were opposed to it. Forced to pay wages, the planters looked to recoup their "loss" by charging their ex-slaves rent. The Ejection and Trespass Acts gave owners the right to evict them from their homes, and to arrest any who refused. They assumed the former slaves, having no place to go, would be unwilling to leave their cottages. It was a serious miscalculation.

Knibb, addressing 2,500 former slaves in Falmouth, said: "if the planters are blind to their own interests and drive you from their properties, there is plenty of land in Jamaica you can resort to." The visionary preacher, whose home, church and furniture are preserved in Falmouth, had hit upon a scheme that became known as the Free Village Movement. By droves, the ex- slaves deserted the estates. Sugar production fell an astonishing 72 percent. By 1847, 140 sugar estates and 465 coffee estates were abandoned. By then, Knibb estimated there were 200 free villages throughout Jamaica, and "in Trelawny, the parish in which I live, there were 23 free villages." In 1859, the *New York Times* correspondent reported 50,000 ex-slaves had settled in these villages, and that they represented "an independent yeoman class." Outside Falmouth are five villages founded by Knibb—Martha Brae, Granville, Refuge, Kettering and Alps.

Elizabeth's brother who managed her properties, encouraged the ex-slaves to stay on. His treatment of them was as sanguine as it was paternalistic—he called them "my pet Africans." But he was a kind and generous employer, and when other estates floundered, his continued to show a profit. When it too began to fail, Elizabeth acknowledged "the late bill has ruined the West Indian. Nevertheless, I am glad, and always shall be, that the Negroes are free."

In later years, when the abolitionist cause took fire in the United States, Elizabeth wrote anti-slavery poems. Like Harriett Beecher Stowe's Uncle Tom's Cabin, Elizabeth's poem, "The Runaway Slave," written from the point of view of a female slave, gained wide popularity. Today, only the cut stone walls remain of her town house in Falmouth. A lintel over the doorway, with the engraved date 1799, is a reminder of the town's prosperous beginnings when slavery was not yet the moral issue that would freeze the town and engage its two most memorable citizens, the preacher and the poet.

ORIGINALLY PUBLISHED JANUARY 2001

Wild Nature in the Cockpit Country

SUSAN KOENIG

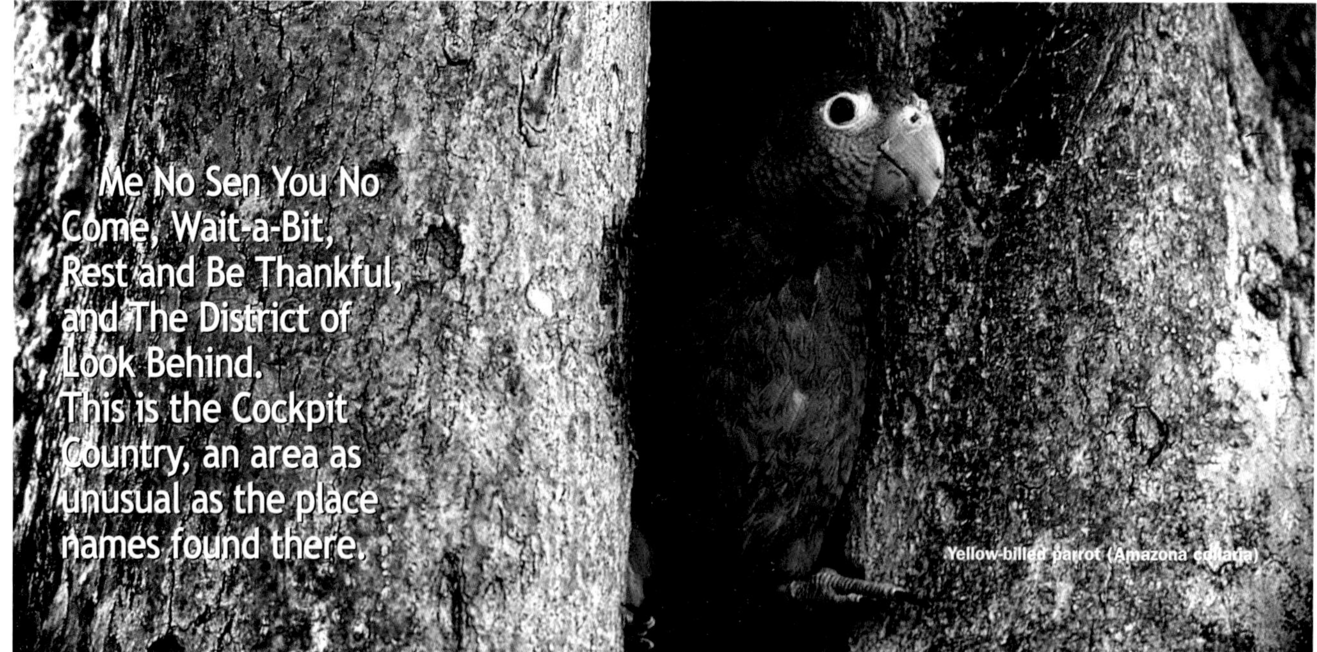

Me No Sen You No Come, Wait-a-Bit, Rest and Be Thankful, and The District of Look Behind.
This is the Cockpit Country, an area as unusual as the place names found there.

Yellow-billed parrot (Amazona collaria)

Imagine more than 300 square miles of thickly-forested inverted egg cartons and you begin to get a picture of the Cockpit Country. Now imagine trying to get around this place where steep, conical limestone hills surround valleys hundreds of feet deep—the "cockpits" for which the area is named—and you will understand why not many settlements appear on the map.

Left to its rugged isolation, the Cockpit Country is like an island within the island. It is home to over 100 species of plants that exist nowhere else in the world and provides important refuge for much of Jamaica's wildlife. Here can be found the giant swallowtail butterfly (largest in the Western hemisphere), the croaking lizard (actually a gecko), peenie wallie (a large beetle with luminous "eyes"), whistling frogs, and both the black-billed and yellow-billed parrots. In fact, nearly every bird species endemic to Jamaica is found there. This is especially notable as Jamaica today, with 27 endemic bird species, boasts more than any other Caribbean island, including much larger Cuba and Hispaniola.

The dramatic sweep of the Cockpit Country, which sprawls across west-central Jamaica's parish of Trelawny and reaches into the eastern edge of St. James and the northern tip of St. Elizabeth, can be appreciated on flights between Montego Bay and Kingston. While visitors to the interior are few, many people go to Windsor Cave, located in the northwest corner of the region near the headwaters of the Martha Brae River, for an easily accessible opportunity to experience the Cockpit Country. A short walk around a typical limestone "egg carton" hill leads to the cave entrance where the breeze of cool cave air, constantly flowing through the entry way, is welcome relief from the Cockpit Country's heat and humidity. Inside, light from the entrance reveals stalactites, stalagmites and other erosion-sculpted formations. A major attraction is the harmless colony of bats that hang upside down amid the limestone crags. The cave actually is the daytime roost for over a million bats. These nocturnal mammals are a critical part of the complex Cockpit Country ecosystem, feeding on insects and helping disperse seeds.

Black-billed Parrot (Amazona agilis)

Outside, along the path back to the road, a number of the region's bird species can be seen including smooth-billed anis, the "John Crow" (actually turkey vultures, but nicknamed for a fiery preacher because of the bird's red head), streamertail hummingbirds (locally called "doctorbird"), Jamaican orioles, cave swallows, Jamaican todies and black-billed parrots.

Parrots are the reason I came to the Cockpit Country. Jamaica is one of only two Caribbean islands to have two native parrot species: the black-billed parrot and the yellow-billed parrot. Both are endangered and both live in the Cockpit Country. Although yellow-billed parrots are also found in the John Crow and Blue Mountains of eastern Jamaica, the Cockpit Country is the largest region where both species co-exist and is the major stronghold for black-billed parrots. For several years I have been working with Jamaican colleagues, conducting research on the parrots' natural history that will help in their conservation.

Surprisingly little is known about these parrots and their habitat. Filling in the gaps in our knowledge is a major goal of the Jamaican Parrot Project, an international collaboration between the US-based Wildlife Preservation

Trust International (WPTI), Jamaica's Gosse Bird Club, the oldest ornithological association in the Caribbean, and the Natural Resources Conservation Authority (NRCA), the government agency responsible for protecting Jamaica's wildlife. NRCA already is planning to use the data gathered in this study to assist in planning a national park in the Cockpit Country to protect the threatened birds of Jamaica.

Why have Jamaica's parrot populations declined over the decades? One reason is loss of habitat. Black-billed and yellow-billed parrots are what are known as secondary cavity nesters. Rather then hollowing out their own nesting holes in trees, as the Jamaican woodpecker does, they instead search out existing cavities such as those created when tree limbs break during tropical storms and hurricanes. As branch stubs or main tree trunks slowly decay, they form the deep, dark cavities in which the parrots like to nest. The parrots depend on the large, old trees of the forest to raise their young, as well as for food and shelter. Large-scale clearing of forest, whether for urban development, industry or agriculture, reduces the total area available for the parrots to live. Selective logging of larger trees for lumber removes trees most likely to have suitable nesting cavities.

Another serious threat to the parrot's survival in the wild comes from humans and their long fascination with keeping parrots as pets. While indigenous people kept them as pets and even traded them to buccaneers who carried them back to Europe, never in the history of man have we seen the numbers of parrots—hundreds of thousands worldwide—being trapped and traded each year as we have in the last three decades. The demand for parrots as pets is an important factor in the decline of many different species of parrots throughout the world.

Many people may not be aware that Jamaica's parrots (as are all of Jamaica's bird) are protected under the Wildlife Protection Act of 1974. It is illegal to purchase or to offer for sale either species of parrot and a special permit is required from the NRCA to keep a parrot. Few parrot owners (not just in Jamaica) likely know just how their pets were taken from the wild. To get young birds poachers cut holes in nest trees to remove nestlings, destroying the possibility of a cavity being used for future nesting, or fell a nest tree hoping that at least one young bird survives the fall. Adult parrots are captured by spreading vegetable gum from either the breadfruit tree or naseberry tree along the branches of ackee trees during ackee season. The parrots' feet get stuck to the branches and their feathers become smeared with the gum, leaving them unable to fly so they are easily caught. This actually can be more damaging than poaching chicks from nests as it removes important breeding birds from the wild population.

We need to learn a lot about these parrots, such as what they eat, when they breed, what are the threats to chicks' survival and how they deal with the changes in their habitat. In order to study the parrots and truly learn about them, we must live in their world. Sadly, the life of a field researcher is not as glamorous as television nature documentaries lead you to believe. In an ideal world we would sit under birds' roost trees just before dawn, watch them shake the morning dew from their feathers, and they burst from the canopy squawking as they fly off for their first meal of the day. Later we would see them feed on favoured foods or gently preen their feathers. When an afternoon rain shower arrives, we would watch them ruffle their feathers and bathe, all the while calling to neighbours with raucous vocalizations.

Jamaican Oriole (Icterus leucopteryx)

The reality is that, more than not, I stumble up hillsides before dawn with a flashlight to an area where birds were calling the night before. Amid swarms of mosquitoes I try to spot the green birds among the thick green foliage. Imagine looking for a single green mango in a 50 foot tall tree—this is what it is like trying to find a parrot perched silently in the forest. When they do vocalize, it is to alert a mate that it is time to fly away. Usually this is when I am half-way up a hill after picking my way through a craggy limestone valley. Watching them fly overhead, I cannot help but feel they are taunting me with the fact that wings are more useful than legs in the Cockpit Country.

Afternoon rains arrive quickly and suddenly in the Cockpit Country as warm moist ocean air drifts in and collides with the cooler air of the forest. You hear the rain first—and ever louder racket—like standing under a waterfall, which is just how it feels when the torrent arrives. I usually have just enough time to pull a poncho from my backpack, though it doesn't really offer much protection. The only thing to do is wait out the storms which, during the rainy season, can dump several inches in just an hour and turn trails into mudslides. As quickly as a storm develops, trade winds blow away the clouds and once again, the brilliant blue Jamaican sky is overhead. Somewhat soggier, I continue my search for parrots. Fortunately, my spirits do not get as dampened as my body. Perhaps best is the thrill of watching a youngster leave its nest on its maiden flight, knowing that is survived the cold rain that dribbles into a less-than-well-protected nest cavity, predators and poachers for the illegal pet trade. These all-important glimpses of how many survive, where they fly, and what they eat are so crucial to our understanding, and ultimately protecting, the parrots and their habitat.

The Cockpit Country is a perfect example of the earth's remaining wild places which so intrigue us today. Most have survived because of their remoteness of inaccessibility. As more people become interested in visiting these places we must carefully examine how this can be done and still preserve their natural wildness, which is what attracts us to them in the first place. The solution for the Cockpit Country, as it is for many places, will be to carefully plan and control access to select areas. This will allow more people, including future generations, to enjoy the Cockpit Country's natural wonders—its unique landscape, rich plant life, diverse wildlife—while preserving the rest from intrusion that could upset the delicate balances necessary to sustain the whole ecosystem.

ORIGINALLY PUBLISHED FEBRUARY 1998

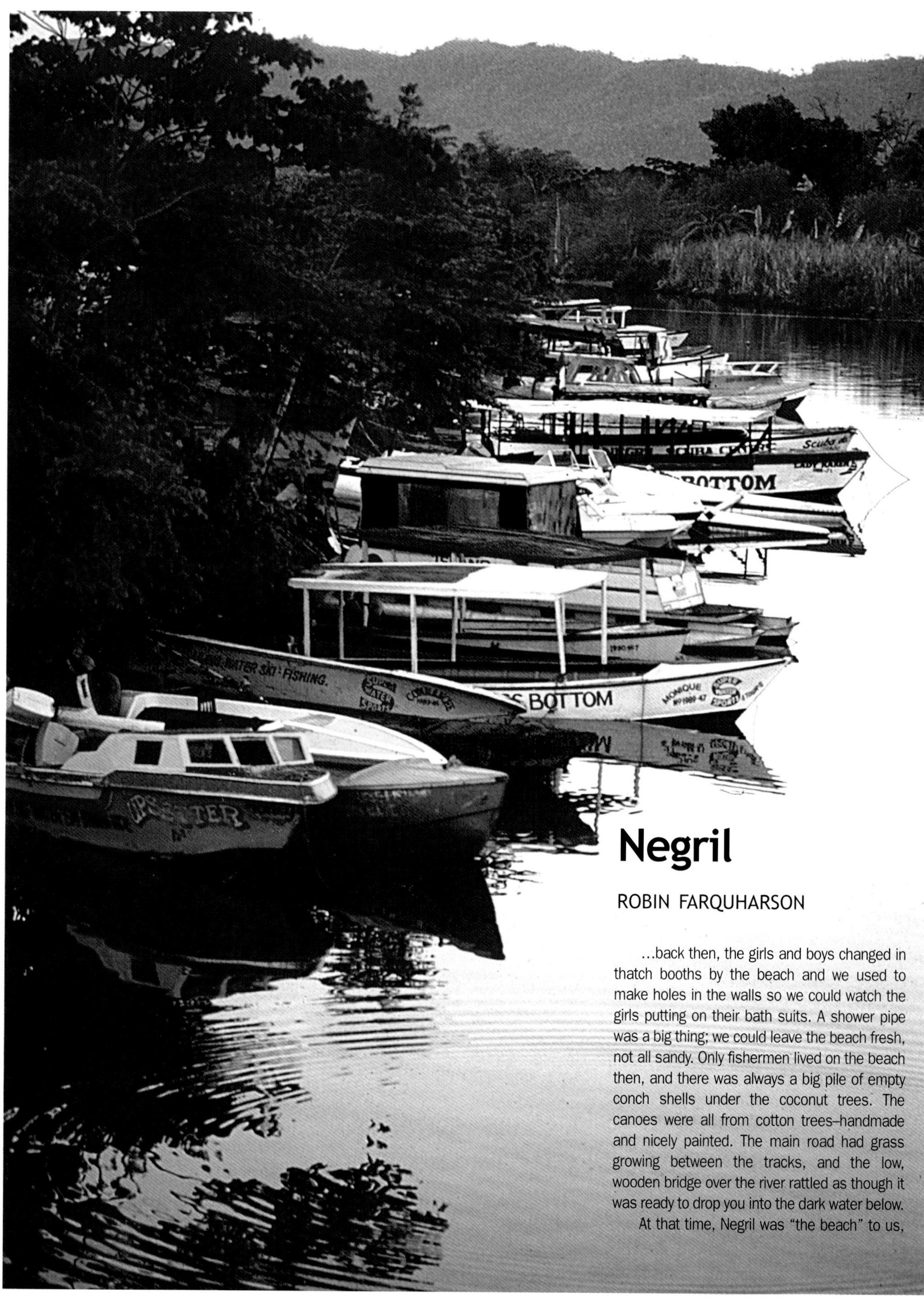

Negril

ROBIN FARQUHARSON

...back then, the girls and boys changed in thatch booths by the beach and we used to make holes in the walls so we could watch the girls putting on their bath suits. A shower pipe was a big thing; we could leave the beach fresh, not all sandy. Only fishermen lived on the beach then, and there was always a big pile of empty conch shells under the coconut trees. The canoes were all from cotton trees–handmade and nicely painted. The main road had grass growing between the tracks, and the low, wooden bridge over the river rattled as though it was ready to drop you into the dark water below.

At that time, Negril was "the beach" to us,

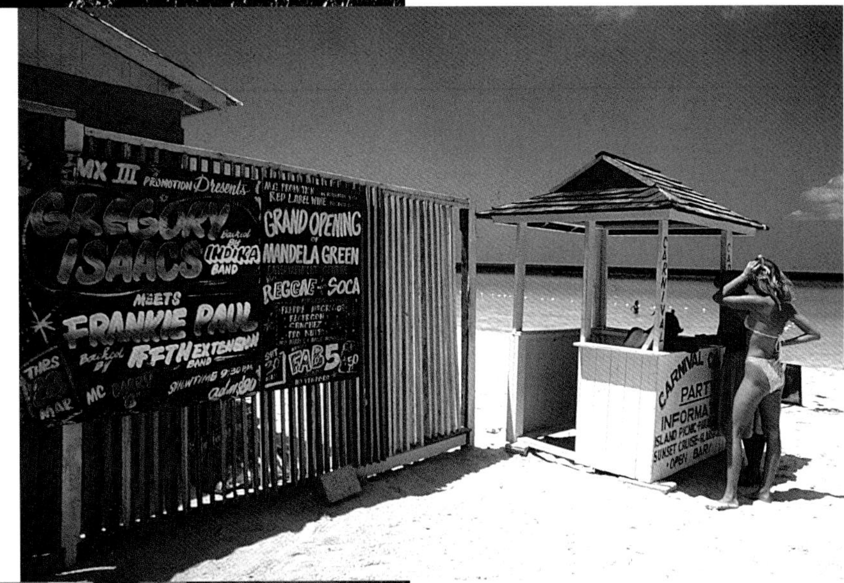

(ABOVE) The great morass.

(RIGHT) On the beach at Alfred's Ocean Palace

(BELOW) "Mr. Jahbah" himself, famous for his "ital" vegetable patties.

(OPPOSITE) Early morning on the Negril river.

and we went as often as we could. Especially when someone was having a party and there would be plenty of breadfruit, rice 'n peas, pear and plantain to go with the chicken. Those were simple days and none of us dreamed of what Negril would become...

Happily we can see that for all the growth and change in Negril, certain aspects remain the same as ever—the sun, the sea and the clean air, as health-giving and delightful to visitors of today as before in simpler times.

ORIGINALLY PUBLISHED JULY 1991

Mt. Zion United Church

JEAN MIRANDA

"A silent sentinel over the past, A mute witness to a period of intense human tragedy and human triumph, a monument...."

It's still standing after 138 years, a tribute to man's triumph over cruel circumstances.

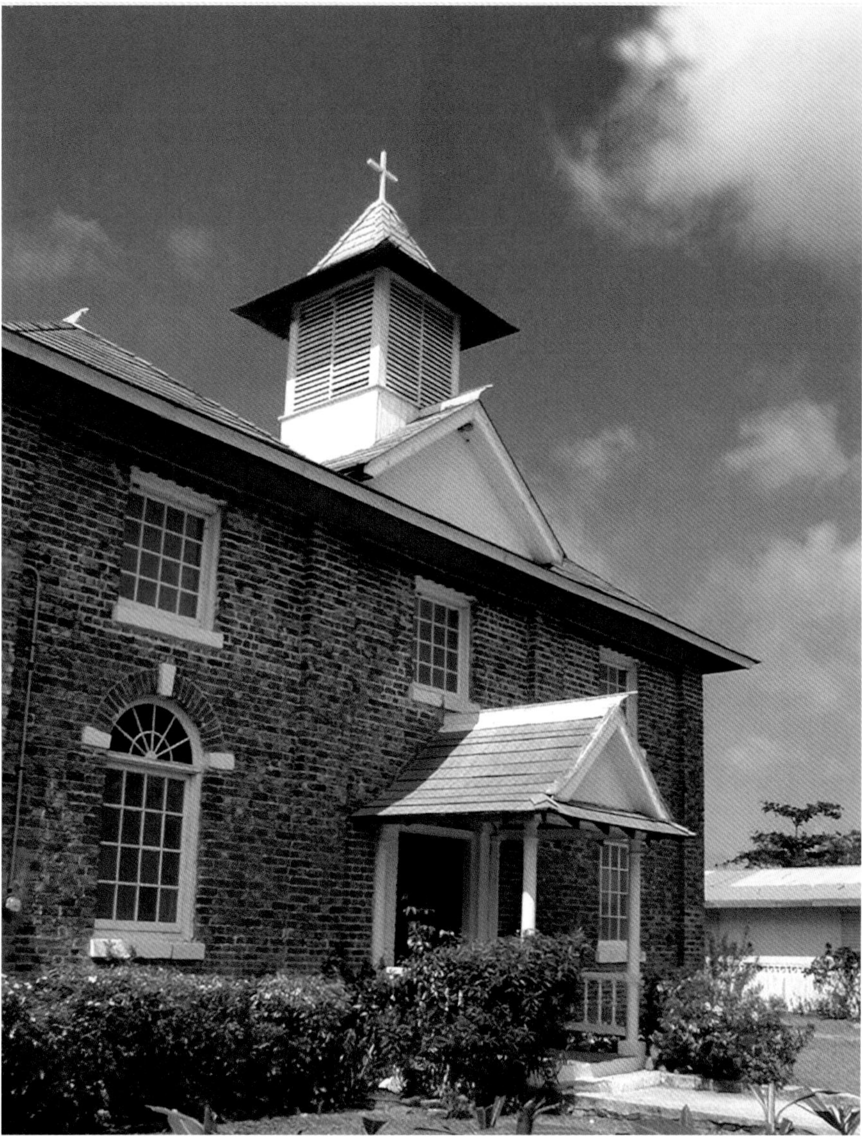

Mt. Zion United Church, as it is known today, graces the crown of a hill not far from Montego Bay. Behind it is a range of higher hills; before it the sea and on either hand richly cultivated country.

To get to the 'Mount' travel eastwards along Sunset Avenue going away from the town. The landmark for your turning point is the Rose Hall Country Club and Golf Course to the right with the Great House rising behind them. Make the right turn and keep going all the way, past the Great House entrance and up. The road winds, it's up hill all the way and the rural folk will see to it that you are on the right track.

The story began when slavery was still very much a part of the Jamaican scene. The first stone was laid in January, 1837, amidst much solemnity and great ceremony. For the occasion a cross-section of people assembled, and they marched three abreast around the grounds.

In his book "Twenty-nine years in the West Indies and Central Africa", Mt. Zion's first minister, the Rev. Hope Waddell wrote: "Thus we took possession of it in the name of the Lord, and by prayer, after several appropriate addresses consecrated it to his service".

The Rev. Waddell had earlier arrived in Jamaica and was fired with the zeal to begin a mission. He started his church and a year later it was completed, in time for the day in August when slavery in the British colonies was abolished.

An old member of Mt. Zion Church, a church elder for many years, tried to jog his own memory to recall the early days at Mt. Zion as told by his mother. He is 82 and Thomas Sacott ("Old Tom") remembers being told that the church took nine years to build. But that nine years we were told stretches from the period a mission began at Cornwall, some distance away, to when when Rev. Waddell and his faithfuls secured a piece of land on Easthams estate and started the church that is now standing.

"Old Tom" remembers well that the slaves played a very valuable part in the building of the church. He's rather explicit in telling that in those days there was no cement, so it was necessary to make your own mortar to hold the bricks together. The mortar worked, for although Mt. Zion Church was closed and declared dangerous in 1966, it was the woodwork that had failed, not the brick walls.

Mt. Zion lies beyond that famous (or infamous) Rose Hall Great House. It's plainly visible from the air sitting atop that hill. Indeed, it is conspicuous even from the sea. It was the people, Rev. Waddell wrote, who thought that Mt. Zion was a fitting name for their church.

History recalls that the grounds had to be enclosed by a wall. So, voluntarily, people of all ages worked to finish the stone wall. The story goes that a great grandmother, too, would have her stone in the wall and she came with three generations of her children to do so.

After the stone laying and construction of the outside wall the building came to a halt. Good stones were not easily obtained, wood was perishable and the site was difficult to reach because the roads were steep and bad. It was a long period of inactivity.

But, said Rev. Waddell, the Lord interposed and helped them out of their difficulties. Bricks were made available and so was a trained bricklayer.

"Old Tom" said his mother told him how the slaves, at the end of their day's work on the estates, journeyed down to Tavern where the ships docked. There they collected the bricks used as ballast in the ships arriving from Liverpool for sugar. And, they cheerfully walked the many miles carrying stones for their church.

A neighbouring planter gave the minister the services of an English bricklayer, and also provided labourers, cattle, carts, some bricks and even lime (calcium oxide) burnt on his estate.

The old people in Mt. Zion say hat the bricks are held together by mortar made from lime, ashes and molasses. Row after row went up under the guidance of the bricklayer. It was only the carpentry that proved to be a headache.

Rev. Waddell wrote that he procured the materials from neighbouring towns, engaged workmen and superintended the wood work himself. Aid came by way of an English carpenter who came on Saturdays to direct the "important parts".

Mt. Zion was finished at the end of June, 1838. It stood there—66 feet long and 48 feet wide with a gallery, and capable of housing 800 people "of all ages". The Minister was rightly proud of the cost... only 1,500 pounds "from the purchase of the ground to the hanging of the bell".

The bell, incidentally, is said to be a gift from Rev. Waddell himself. "Old Tom" said that the adventurous who would wish to climb up to the belfry can see the initials "HDW" etched on the bell—they're Rev. Waddell's.

Describing the last building days, Rev. Waddell said they were the busiest of all. "Lamps had to be lighted to finish the work and sweep the house and have it ready for public dedication the next day. At last all was ended; the people gave three cheers, shook hands, wished each other good night and morrow and departed contented and happy".

An entry by the reverend gentleman in his diary is quite interesting. It said: "The house of God was built without injury to man or beast, and without a single case of intoxication or even the use of rum on the ground". (If you meet a Jamaican ask him what happens before a building goes up, and what takes place at the end. He will tell you that rum—over-proof at that—is an important part of the ceremony at the start and the finish).

July 1 was consecration day and more than 1,000 people came to join in the worship. Rev. Waddell records that two ministers helped him on that day and a collection of forty pounds was made.

From his little house below the church on the hill "Old Tom" and the oldsters like him gaze and remember. The church had a steel rod, he said, to ward off lightning. It extended the full height of the church and was buried underground with a chain attached. He added, the church of his parents and his generation had weathered many a storm and earthquake. "It's solid" he says.

But in 1966 things changed at Mt. Zion. An army of termites feasted on all the wooden portions of the building. Making the situation worse was a faulty gutter-bed system and several leaks which caused the timber to be water-soaked. Historical documents record that the termites and water were too much for the virgin timber. Following imspections by the minister in 1966, Rev. T. Phillips, church officers, and five architects, Mt. Zion Church was declared unsafe and the building closed. That was in April, 1966 and the congregation moved to the school house.

The debate which followed was whether to rebuild or restore the church. Whatever the decision, it would take a sum much larger than members of the congregation could find on their own. Friends of Mt. Zion, hearing of the congregation's plight, started a building fund with a donation of $350 and a promise to contribute regularly until the church was restored. At the end of 1967 they had contributed $1,100 and, combined with members' efforts, more than $2,000 was realised. So, demolition of the old church began.

John Rollins, owner of Rose Hall and a long time friend of the community, made one of his frequent trips to Mt. Zion as the demolition began. Learning that the old church wasn't being restored he indicated his willingness to further assist the project financially. He guaranteed repayment of a loan which was to be on a joint basis between the congregation and himself.

So the demolition plan was shelved and restoration began in February 1968. Another friend of the church guaranteed a second loan at the bank, and the contractor Mr. E. A. Fray, did the work "in the spirit of a friend".

Mt. Zion owes the success of its restoration project to people like Messrs Rollins and Fray. To Heinz Simonitsch who aided financially and gave his advice freely; and to his wife who gave the hymn books. To Frank Pringle who supplied earth; to Paul Methuen who gave the altar cloth and pulpit curtains; to Mrs. Rollins who presented an organ to the congregation. To Mr. Harold Simpson who worked on the plans and to Messrs A. D. Campbell and M. Dyer who stood by them and saw the project through.

Mt. Zion Church from the inside is worth seeing any day. The high-up pulpit with its mahogany rails and lectern, all beautifully carved and with turned pins, is testimony of craftsmanship of the highest calibre and many, many years old. The straight-backed chairs which grace the platform are years old, and solid mahogany. Curved arms and turned, slender pins add to their beauty. The church boasts a high ceiling; tall, natural-colour wooden pillars go from floor to ceiling. Light is admitted from all sides through the twelve high glass windows topped with stained glass. And, at the entrance of the church is the elegant stairway that leads to the gallery.

The elders will even show you their visitors' book, a record of the pride of place their church has enjoyed over many years.

The bell atop Mt. Zion church still calls the people from the surrounding districts to worship today, just as it did 138 years ago. They come from Chew Stick, Tryall, Rose Hall, Cornwall, Spot Valley, Kings Gate, Rose Hill, Lilliput, Long Bay, Flower Hill, Barrett Town, Palmyra, Dover, Little Ease, across the hills to participate in services. "Old Tom" still sits on his verandah at the foot of the hill and gazes, upwards. To him his church means many things: it is a memorable and holy link with the past; an example of fine craftsmanship of more than a century ago and a monument to the freedom gained by his parents and many like them.

ORIGINALLY PUBLISHED FEBRUARY 1977

What To Look For Under The Sea

RALPH ROBINSON

Deep water sea fan with black coral, sponges and Chromis fish.

A splendid example of a natural, balanced ecosystem, Jamaica's fringing reefs represent an ancient association of marine organisms that have been in existence for millions of years. Living corals form pleomorphic colonies, dendritiform to solid, almost spherical, in design. Multicoloured sponges, anemones and sea fans attach to the coral outgrowths, while small creatures seek food and refuge in the rocky hollows and crevices.

Living within the coral itself, minute plant cells called zooxanthellae contribute to the reef-building process, and are the main source of colour in the coral communities. Since these micro-organisms require light in order to live, hermatypic, or reef-building, corals are found generally at water depths of less than 100 feet. In this bluish zone only the diver, freed from the terrestrial world about by a self-contained air supply, can truly experience the wonders and intricate beauty of the reef environment.

Down to around 30 feet, elkhorn coral forms extensive beds that stretch unbroken for miles, its palmate branches confirming to the direction and intensity of the water currents that bathe it and bear its food. Staghorn coral, a close relative, possesses easily broken tips, and is more susceptible to wave action. Hence, it is found in slightly deeper water, and does not extend to the surface. Reaching a height of 10-12 feet, star coral boulders provide a haven for a multiplicity of marine organisms, such as encrusting algae and sponges, and fastened sea fans and feather stars. Marine crustacea, such as shrimps and spiney lobster, shelter beneath the overhangs, while precariously perched coral crabs delicately glean surface algae with their massive pincers. Sergeant majors and trunk fish nibble the algal mats, and pugnacious little damselfish dart about valiantly defending their territory against all intruders.

Another name for the majestic pillar coral is cathedral coral. Encountered usually as a solitary colony, well away from the main reef mass, divers pay homage as they approach the gothic spires. Tiny fish, with rainbow colours, frolic at hide and seek among the sturdy, though slow-growing, branches, and octopus retreat by squeezing their boneless bodies through very small openings in the algal draped limestone.

Brain coral, as its name suggests, resembles the exterior of the human brain. Coral cups fuse to form sculptured rows and channels which, by nightfall, will support a myriad of hungry, plankton-feeding polyps. Set among the larger coral masses may be found a variety of smaller species, such as finger and flower coral, as well as a host of others, forming colourful moulds a foot or more across.

Distantly related to the hard corals, stinging corals are of similar appearance. They are widespread in shallow waters, and occur in abundance on eroded reef tops, wrecks and pilings. The polyps are small, and there are no visible coral cups, which accounts for the smooth appearance of the colony. Jamaican "fire corals" are armed with special protective

polyps which, if brushed against by unprotected skin, may inflict quite a painful sting that can itch for several days. Light gloves are recommended if you intend to handle rocks and coral.

Located among the reef building corals are what may appear to be elaborate flattened or feathered plants. These are in fact living animals called soft corals, and include the gorgonian sea fans, sea whips and sea feathers. Gorgonian corals inherited their name from the mythical Gorgons which had snakes for hair, and all who looked upon them were turned to stone! Unlike the hard corals, the skeletal core is flexible in these organisms, and the whole colony bends and undulates with the movement of water around it. Gorgonians occur in shades of purple, blue, green and orange, and may be found at all diving depths. Precious 'black coral', is well known to sub-aqua enthusiasts in Jamaica.

Whenever there are rocks, shells, submerged timbers or corals to provide suitable attachment, sponges abound. These come in a variety of sizes, shapes and colours, depending on the local conditions. In fact, it was not until the mid-eighteenth century, when internal water currents were observed, that the true animal nature of sponges was clearly established. Large barrel varieties, measuring five feet or more, are quite common on the walls of Jamaican reefs, and are capable of filtering several hundred gallons of water each day in order to obtain food and oxygen. In contrast, encrusting sponges such as 'chicken liver' form only shallow moulds, and exploit the space of crevices and other confined areas.

Often found crawling on the surface of sponges is the elegant bristle worm, or 'sea forty legs' as it is colloquially referred to in many Jamaican coastal communities, presumably after its land-based cousin. Admire, but don't touch since the lateral while bristles of these worms are its protective armament against would-be predators. Among the most beautiful of the sedentary worms to be found on our reefs is the plume, or Christmas tree worm. It extends its elaborate, twin-spiralled crown into the water in order to trap plankton. Any threat of disturbance and the crown is retraced instantly.

Tube-dwelling worms are also found in the sandy flats that separate the coral buttresses, as well as in the soft, white sands that extend from the shoreline to the reef. Turtle grass affords stability and support within the substratum, while also providing food and refuge for a great variety of marine organisms.

(ABOVE) Orange cup coral.

(BELOW) Spotted moray eel and reef urchin

Starfish, brittle stars, sea urchins, conchs. Helmets, even sea turtles, are all to be found associated with this particular habitat. Green turtles, although actually brownish in colour, are not uncommon among Jamaica's reefs, and average 100-200 pounds in weight. Happily these beautiful animals are now protected from hunters by Jamaican law.

Related to the sea urchins and brittle stars are the sea cucumbers. Milky white, and brown specimens graze the bottom sand using their tentacles, apparently oblivious to anything that is going on around them. Although there are no sea snakes in the West Indies, the spotted snake eel, after found gliding across the flats or through coral rubble, may be confused with such. Reaching a length of two to three feet, Jamaican snake eels are not aggressive and may be gently handled with safety.

There are close to seven hundred species of fish associated with the coral reefs in our area, but some of them are small and may live in the sand, or take refuge by day in coral recesses. An occasional glance by the enthusiast under rocks and ledges is often rewarded through sighting of nocturnal species such as squirrel-fish and iridescent cardinal fish. Further investigation of the many coral tunnels and caves that penetrate the reef will usually reveal other nocturnal fish, such as glasseye snappers, bigeyes and glassy sweepers. These provide colour and lustre against the pale backdrop of coral limestone.

Peacock flounders are the most common flatfish in Jamaica waters, and are certainly the most ornate. Partially buried in fine sand or among sea grass, they measure about a foot long, and when swimming may be identified by their distinctive markings of bright blue spots

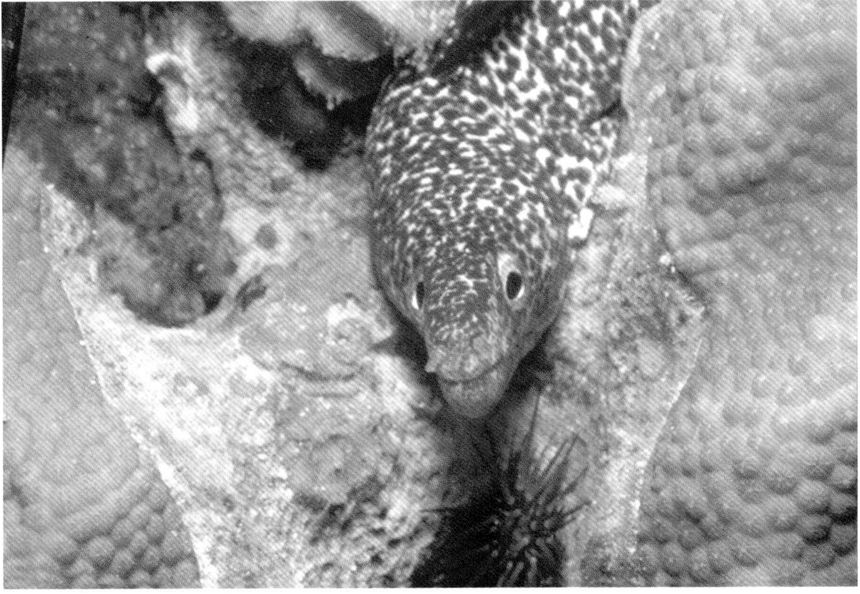

Red night shrimp on sponge with watercress algae and coral

and rings. Similarly, spotted eagle and sting-rays are often encountered in this shimmering, sandy environment, and are most easily identified with moving.

Sand divers, or lizardfish as they are often called, are a very common sight on sand or pebble bottoms. They are raptorial feeders, and often occur in large numbers where there are schools of fronts or goatfish above. Lizardfish have been known to consume prey only slightly smaller than themselves. They are easily approached, but dart off at astonishing speed when disturbed or in pursuit of prey.

By far the most common and widespread eel living among the corals is the spotted moray. Protruding from holes or coral recesses, often with mouths open, their long needle-sharp teeth present an awesome sight to the uninitiated! However, these fish are largely nighttime feeders, and secretive by nature. Specimens grow to about four feet in length, and can be approached quite safely to a similar distance.

Associated with Jamaican reefs is a multiplicity of brilliantly coloured fish which provide yet greater adornment to the coral seascape. Stoplight parrotfish daintily graze on exposed coral polyps, while varieties of butterflyfish, chromis, hamlets and wrasse flit about in search of small morsels to supplement their diets. Drums, so-called because of the sounds they produce, are not uncommon on Jamaican reefs, and the larger, spotted form may be encountered as solitary individuals under coral ledges. One of the most common and easily identified of our angelfish is the rock beauty. Fairly easy to approach, this fish has discrete yellow and black markings with brilliant blue flashes on the upper and lower parts of the eye. Angelfish are probably the least fearful fish on the reef, and represented by tangs, ocean surgeons and doctorfish, possess a characteristic sharp 'scalpel' at the posterior end and should be handled carefully. Groupers are not uncommon, and the carnivorous coney exhibits a versatile range of colour phases, ranging from the reddish-brown to yellow.

Frequently found suspended head down among the corals to avoid detection, the slender trumpetfish appears lethargic. However, its protrusible snout displays great alacrity at capturing small fish and crustaceans. Trumpetfish are very timid, and will turn away from curious observers.

When scuba diving among Jamaica's reefs, it is not unusual to encounter a shoal of small barracuda, or even come face to face with a fearsome-looking five feet specimen! The writer has known them to lurk nearby, casually observing his moments, or even approach and circle with mouths agape! However, divers not involved in spearfishing activities have little to fear from these impressive rogues of the sea.

Although sharks do not live on the reef, they visit occasionally. One of our most frequent callers are the nurse sharks, which may reach a length of 10-12 feet. They are found usually in shallow water resting motionless on the bottom. Nurse sharks are not aggressive creatures, but are best left undisturbed. A more casual visitor to our vicinity is the giant manta ray, or devilfish. Propelled by graceful undulations of their wing-like pectoral fins, mantas has been sighted, mouths open and straining plankton, in the clear, azure waters off the forereef.

The rich experiences that result from exploration of Jamaica's underwater gardens never fail to leave a lasting impression on the minds of these who go there, and will, undoubtedly, form the basis for a return visit, very soon.

ORIGINALLY PUBLISHED JUNE 1989

Into The Valley

ANDREW SMITH

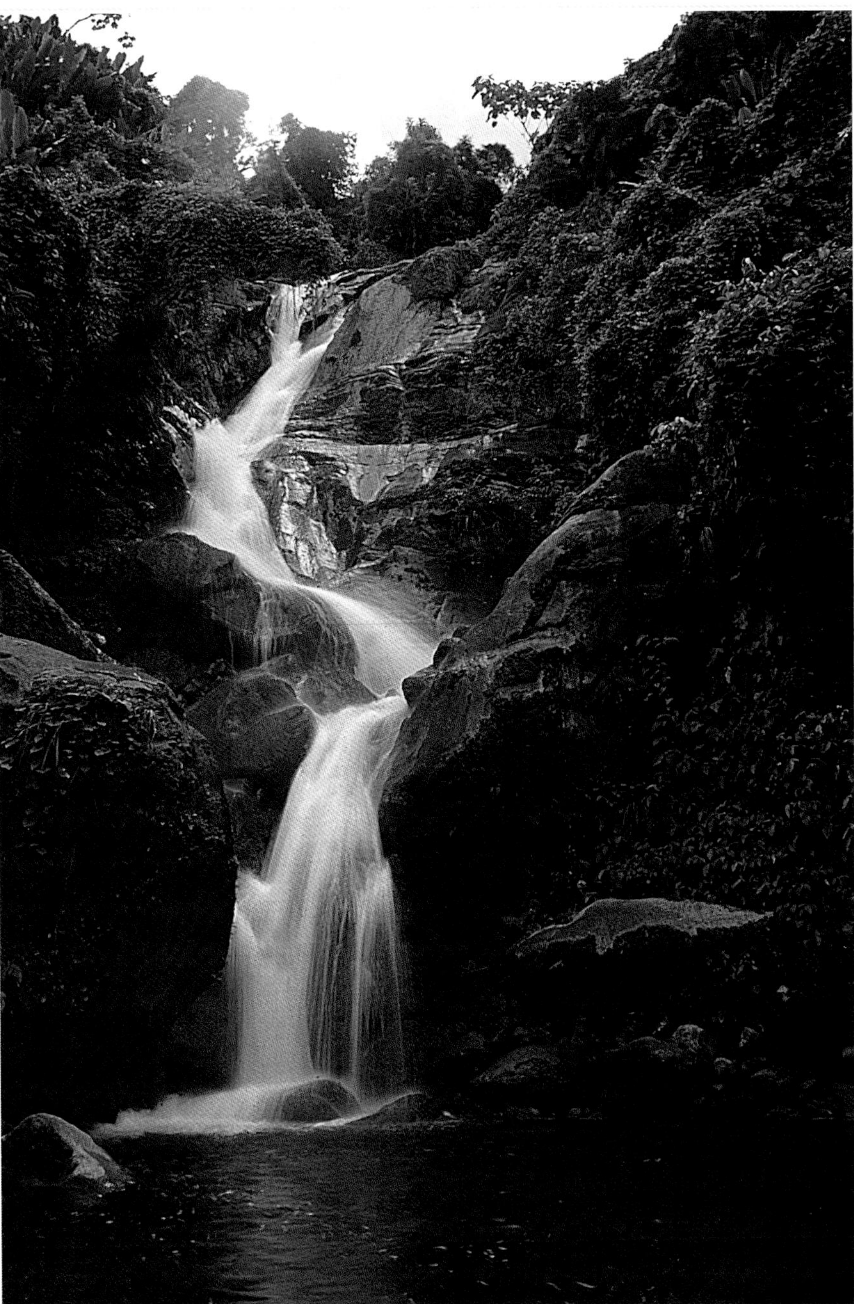

Nestled between the Blue Mountains and the John Crow Mountains in Portland is a valley which is as beautiful as it is inaccessible. Nature rules in the Rio Grande valley, one of the most fragile and relatively untouched corners of Jamaica. The few visitors who have experienced "The Valley" leave overwhelmed by its majesty and grandeur.

The John Crow Mountains lie to the east of the valley, a range of sandstone and shale with a limestone plateau capping the top. It is on these steep slopes that one discovers the spectacular falls of White River. The south-eastern slopes of the Blue Mountain range are located to the west of the valley. Here volcanic agglomerations pepper the swiftly flowing tributaries, creating an obstacle course which tests the senses of balance and co-ordination.

A variety of features attract the intrepid explorer to the valley. Experienced hikers rate the paths which criss-cross the two mountain ranges as among the most challenging in Jamaica. The presence of wild hogs and endemic wildlife such as conies, birds, snakes and the elusive giant swallowtail butterfly (*Papilio homerus*, the largest butterfly in the western hemisphere) have attracted many naturalists to this living laboratory. For those interested in local history, Maroon villages dot the mountains as they have for over a century.

I have been fortunate enough to have visited the valley every year since I first discovered it six years ago. I have gotten my feet (and other parts) wet hiking up White River, Bruk Foot River (aptly named), Cocoa Spring and Lime Bush River. Paths traveling to Crown Land, Level Ground and through Cuna Cuna Pass have all taken their toll on me, while the blissful walk to Bowden has allowed me to be at peace with myself.

Millbank has been the main base of my expeditions into the surrounding mountains. A ranger station of the Blue & John Crow Mountain National Park, as well as the Rio Grande research station are both located here. The latter was established by Dr. Eric Garraway, an entomologist who has spent the last few years studying *Papilio homerus* and other butterflies in the valley. Both local and foreign scientists have made use of this facility as the base for various forms of research.

Before going on any of the trails, stop by the ranger station and inform them of the trail which your guide shall be taking you on. Always remember that you are privileged to experience the wonders of a very fragile and unique ecosystem in which live species of flora and fauna found nowhere else in the world.

From Millbank, adventurous hikers have many trails to choose from, depending on their level of experience and fitness. Most of the trails which are located on the mountain ranges are transient at best, due to the very heavy rainfall experienced in the valley. Only those regularly used by the farmers are kept cleared, further reinforcing the need for a capable local

trail, which include Maroons and slaves. After this half day sojourn, hikers are welcome to soak in the warm mineral springs at Bath.

If you wish to opt for a more physically taxing, but also a more psychologically exhilarating hike, you may choose trails on either the John Crow Mountains or the Blue Mountains. Trails on both ranges are quite difficult, due to the steepness of the slopes, the density of the vegetation, and the presence of swiftly flowing, boulder-ridden mountain streams.

As you climb higher up-slope, the natural forest regains its dominance, and as such the bio-diversity increases. Wild pine, tree ferns, blue mahoe, Santa Maria, fig trees, trumpet trees, and mountain guava are just a few species which support ubiquitous epiphytes, lianas, ferns, mosses and toadstools. Blue herons and mountain doves are a few species found by the streams and in the dense vegetation. As you hike on the trails, you may be passed by farmers accompanied by packs of dogs hunting for the wild boars which populate these mountains and other wild places of Jamaica. These tusked feral descendants of pigs brought by the Spaniards in the sixteenth century are one of the chief sources of meat in the upper Rio Grande valley. It is these animals which were the origin of Jamaica's famous jerk pork. Its exotic taste is reason enough to visit the valley.

However, one of the most exciting sights is seeing the giant swallowtail butterfly soaring above the forest canopy. With a wing span of 15 cm, this endemic specie is one of the most sought after butterflies in the world by collectors. This is in spite of being protected internationally under the Convention of International Trade in Endangered Species and locally under Jamaica's Wildlife Act. Unfortunately, attempts to establish an ongoing research project on the status of *Papilio homerus* have been stalled due to lack of funding.

guide. Errol Francis, one of the best guides in the valley lives in Millbank. He has the uncanny and necessary ability to find or create a trail when none appears to exist—a vital consideration when you have been hiking up treacherous slopes for six hours and need to get back to Millbank before night falls.

The most relaxing walk is along the main road across the parish border into St. Thomas. You experience the friendliness of the villagers of Millbank as you stroll along this road unaccompanied and at your own pace, easily striking up conversations with farmers and ebullient school children. As you leave Millbank, the flora and bird populations increase in tandem. Endemic species such as hummingbirds, woodpeckers and todies as well as transient migrants such as warblers can be seen.

Extending your trek along this path through Cuna Cuna Pass will take you into Bath in St. Thomas. This well established, historical trail takes hikers through the forest to the site of one of Jamaica's oldest established mineral baths. As you hike, your guide will be able to inform you of the activities of past users of this

On the John Crow Mountains is a tributary which is known locally as White River. Previously, either wading across the Grande or jumping from one stone to another was the only means of getting to the other side. Although this does give you practice for later on in your journey it can lead to a thorough soaking if you are not careful, as I have personally experienced.

Fortunately a bridge which was decimated in 1976 is being repaired and is scheduled to be operational in early 1997.

Errol has guided me and my friends up White River three times and every time I swear (among other things) that it shall be my last time, due to the physical challenge intrinsic in hiking up these slopes. Many times Errol's versatility with his "lass" (machete) has proved indispensable, especially when we are engulfed in dense vegetation with no apparent way out. Of course, we could always take the "shorter" route up river, which involves negotiating our way around boulders which would dwarf any NFL linebacker.

Whenever I hike up White River I constantly question my sanity. Maybe I am a shutter-masochist who derives pleasure from exposing myself (and my film) to the most rugged terrain in Jamaica in order to record the beauty of this island's wild side. This is definitely the case involving the spectacular waterfalls found on White River. After hiking and cursing for hours I hear the thunder of water descending towering escarpments. I am then left speechless as I turn a bend in the river and behold the power of nature's creations in the form of the first fall of White River. The exact number of falls on this river is unknown and due to the fragility of the ecosystem hikers are not allowed past this fall. Still, after hiking up-slope for hours all you should really want to do is dive into the plunge pool and cool out.

For those not inclined to hiking up mountain slopes in search of hidden waterfalls, the social history is an education in itself. People have been living in the valley since slavery, as evidenced by the names of villages such as Cornwall Barracks and Moore Town. The former was a slaves barracks, and the latter is one of the few original Maroon settlements found in Jamaica. Monuments to Jamaica's only National Heroine, Nanny of the Maroons are located at Moore Town.

Motor vehicles can be utilised to get to these villages, but, if you want to truly experience the flavour of the land, you may hike from Millbank to Moore Town via Ginger House and Cornwall Barracks as I did. The return trip takes a day and a guide is not absolutely necessary, as most of the time you are walking on the main road and the mountain paths that you'll take are well-defined. Much can be learned from the villagers, who I found friendly and willing to impart the oral history of the villages, such as details of the historical animosity between residents of Maroon and slave villages.

Presently, the residents of the valley concentrate on farming, as they have for centuries. Obtaining a livelihood in the valley can be difficult due to the closeness that Man lives with nature here. Prolonged rainfall often results in the erosion of the main road in the valley, loss of crops and earth movements of sometimes immense proportions, all of which hinder the potential development of the valley.

In spite of these difficulties, the resilience of the citizens of Millbank and the rest of the valley has been shown by their involvement in the formation of Valley Hikes. Valley Hikes was established in order to sustainably develop the valley by providing eco-tourism packages. Residents, such as Errol, who understand and love the land which they inhabit have been the driving force behind the activities of Valley Hikes.

It is extremely important for visitors to the valley to support its residents, both human and otherwise. Too many of Jamaica's wild places have been destroyed by over-exploitation for tourism. When this is done, our unique bio-diversity is lost forever. Future generations may never able to experience the joy of sighting *Papilio homerus* in the wild, or taste wild boar meat.

In order for places like the Rio Grande Valley to maintain its fragile ecosystem and the tenuous but vital link between Man and nature, all visitors must be environmentally responsible. Do not destroy or take any living thing with you, and do not leave behind anything not found therein. It is only by exhibiting such behaviour that we shall forever be able to enjoy Jamaica's hidden places.

ORIGINALLY PUBLISHED APRIL 1997

Morris Cargill on Ian Fleming

The public image of the late Ian Fleming was, and still is, that of a ruthless adventurer with a highly-developed taste for good wine, good food, and bad women. This comes, I am sure, from the habit people have of identifying an author with the leading characters from his books. In fact, Ian Fleming bore little relation to James Bond, except, one might say, in a Walter Mitty sense; for the author was a failed 007, as I will tell you about in a moment; and his palate was hardly able to distinguish the difference, or perhaps just didn't care to do so, between filet de sole bonne femme and plain roast beef.

In my view, however, the great disparity between Ian Fleming and James Bond was all to Ian's credit. He was a man with a gift of making friends and keeping them. All of us, who were Ian's friends, would uncomplainingly go to dinner with him at Goldeneye in spite of the fact that we knew that we should have to sit on very hard seats and eat an almost uneatable dinner cooked by his loyal and adoring housekeeper whose only departure from being the most estimable of women was that she couldn't cook. We all took the precaution of having a snack at home before we left.

Interior of Goldeneye

ALBERT R. BROCCOLI PRESENTS PIERCE BROSNAN AS IAN FLEMING'S JAMES BONE
GOLDEN
No limits. No fears. No su

Ian Fleming

The beach at Goldeneye

Ian's only resemblance to James Bond was that he was tall and very strong. His older brother, Peter, had preceded him at Eton, where he had chalked up a fine scholastic record, and Ian felt then, as he was often to feel in later life, that he could not compete with him in this area. So Ian concentrated on games and at these he was enormously successful, becoming Victor Ludorum for two years running—a feat which has never been equalled. It is not surprising that this tall, strong and handsome young man was later to catch the eye of the remarkable Sir William Stevenson.

William Stevenson, one of whose comparatively small ventures was the establishment in Jamaica of the Caribbean Cement Company, was a man of extraordinary talent. At the start of World War II he was a wealthy and respected businessman with interests in many parts of the world. When Churchill came to power, he asked Stevenson, whom he knew personally, to set up an elaborate system of espionage for Britain, which Stevenson achieved with such brilliance that even the U.S. Secret Service came to rely on him.

One of Sir William Stevenson's projects was a school for spies which he had set up in Canada and Stevenson personally selected Ian Fleming for special training as a killer spy. This training involved, among many things, vigorous physical discipline. In one of the final tests, the trainee was handed a loaded revolver and told to go to a certain room at a certain hotel. He was told that he was to kick the door down and kill the occupant.

There was no bluff about the loaded revolver. What the trainee was not told, however, was that the man in the room would be expecting him, and had the unusual knack of dodging revolver bullets. The trainee was also not told that his entire performance would be followed on closed-circuit television.

As his teachers watched, Ian was then approaching the door, revolver in hand. At the door, he hesitated. He then walked a few footsteps back down the corridor and then, after seeming to be lost in thought he went to the door once again. Once again, he hesitated. Then, with a sudden motion he put the revolver in his pocket and came away.

Back at "school" Ian was very frank about it. He could not, he said, bring himself to kill a man in cold blood. He continued after that failure to do intelligence work for the navy. But it

was routine stuff, and had nothing to do with exploits à la Bond.

JAMES BOND,
his code 007
The double "0" means he has a license to kill when he chooses... where he chooses... whom he chooses!
NOW HE IS A FLESH AND BLOOD EXPERIENCE ON THE SCREEN!
IAN FLEMING'S
Dr. No
THE FIRST JAMES BOND FILM ADVENTURE!
CARIB TODAY
4:30 & 8:30 P.M.
SEE THESE JAMAICANS IN THE FILM:
BYRON LEE & The Dragonaires

It was during the war while Ian was stationed in Bermuda but was on a visit to Jamaica, that he saw the twenty acres of Goldeneye with its small private beach and resolved to buy it. The name of the land before Ian Fleming changed it to Goldeneye, was Rotten Egg! He built upon it a solid big highly unimaginative house, and after the war ended he made Goldeneye his winter home. At this time, he had managed chiefly, by being fast on his feet, to remain a bachelor, and so far as anybody knew, he entertained no plans whatever for marriage.

But the beautiful and clever Lady Rothermere, the wife of the press lord for whose newspaper Ian had gone to work after he came out of naval intelligence, had other plans for him. As Annie Rothermere put it to me "I took one look at that beautiful hunk of man and decided he was going to be mine." So she divorced her husband, and in due course married Ian at the parish church in Port Maria. And that, really, was how the James Bond books began according to Ian, "it was just after my marriage to Annie that I began to write my first novel. I had to do something to take my mind off matrimony."

Ian Fleming at his desk at Goldeneye

And so it was that every year, for thirteen years, Ian came to Goldeneye and wrote a new James Bond thriller in three months.

It is not surprising that many of the scenes in these books, and many names of people and places, are taken from Jamaica. He would borrow his friend's names quite shamelessly. I appear as a journalist in one book and as a judge in another. The Reynold's bauxite installations at Ocho Rios appears in *Dr. No*. And, of course, there were always the consultations with his friends. On one occasion Noel Coward who had been given the proof of one book to read, complained to Ian that he had made the sun rise in the west, for it was little details like that Ian often got wrong. Ian agreed to change the location so as to get the sun rising at its proper point in the compass simply, I think, to please Noel, for as Ian put it "the bloody reader oughtn't to have the time to pick up things like that if the story is going fast."

On another occasion Ian told me that he had run out of kinky sexual situations (most of which, I think, he got out of Havelock Ellis) and what was he to do. Had I any ideas? he asked me. I suggested that he have his couple doing it absolutely straight, in the customary position because the new, generation of young people, fed upon pornography in glorious technicolor would be completely shocked by normality. This delighted Ian, but I do not think he followed by advice except in one or two very brief entanglements.

In the year before Ian's death, he and I had decided to write a book together on Jamaica, describing all the places and people we most loved. Alas, this project never came to pass, at least not in that form. Ian had one heart attack from which he recovered and was told by his doctors that he must slow down, give up smoking, drink very little and, in fact, look after himself. But this Ian refused to do. He loved his scuba-diving, his brandies-and-soda and his active life too much to live, as he called it, a living death. His second heart attack came in Jamaica. He lingered on for weeks and was finally flown back to England, where he died.

Ian Fleming, the most loyal of friends, was a gentleman in the true meaning of that very tired word. It is not much known, that he was also in some way a very uncertain man, unsure of himself and his own accomplishments. As I wrote earlier, he felt himself overshadowed by his older brother Peter, who had always been regarded as the bright member of the family, in contrast to Ian who, at Eton and for a short time afterwards, often seemed to be getting himself into embarrassing scrapes.

Annie, in spite of her love for Ian, did not help much in this regard. An elegant and witty woman, she had a house in London to whom all the great in politics and letters, came to one time or another. Indeed, in the thirties, forties, and fifties, it was the only "Salon", properly so called, left in England, and it is not too much to say that England was to a great extent ruled from her drawingroom. Ian, though an intelligent man, was no intellectual, and he hated the kind of entertainment which Annie thrust upon him and what he called the "constant nattering of the politicians and the dons." He felt too, that his Bond books, thumping best-sellers though they were, were regarded with contempt by most of the people Annie entertained.

In the end I think he was a very lonely man. I don't think, had he lived, he would have written any more Bond books. His last was his thirteenth, and six months before he died told me, with a sad and rather weary shrug of the shoulders, that he thought he would never finish it, and had been caught upon a treadmill of his own success. And that, indeed, was the simple truth.

ORIGINALLY PUBLISHED AUGUST 1980

Port Antonio
Redefined and Rediscovered

LAURA GAMBRILL

When the going gets tough A-list celebrities, adventurous Europeans and Kingston-fleeing locals go to Port Antonio.

Their reasons: lots of tranquility, welcoming people and plenty jerk pork. Rustic from pillar to post, demanding visitors need not apply. From the get go, you will learn that "Porty" offers the increasingly scarce luxury of a simple holiday amidst tropical splendour rather than your typical commercialized, Riviera-esque fun. Choose to disappear into the landscape or become part of it and still not get fussed over. The general feeling here is: Harrison who? Dress-code what? Quiet nights and sun soaked days top off the bill. Every Jamaican knows it's virtually written in stone — Porty *is* all-natural.

And yet, curiously, its this very same no frills atmosphere that is putting Porty on the map as Jamaica's next hub for hip. Recently Porty became home to the trendy G-Jams

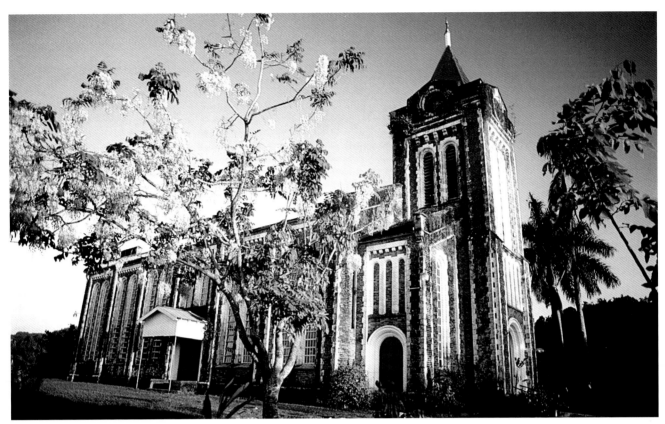

(OPPOSITE PAGE) Climb a hill and put Port Antonio into perspective, a view from Bonnieview; Raft away the day on the Rio Grande; Ready when you are.
(this page) Keeping faith at Portland Parish Church built in 1840; Folly lighthouse.

recording studios (hosting heavyweights No Doubt and Gorillaz) and in June 2002 it will see the completion of a new deluxe marina in time for the Tall Ships race. Don't expect however, that these developments mean the roads in what is probably *the* off-road adventure capital of Jamaica, will become a four lane highway any time soon. Thanks to Port Antonio's trademark dose of daily 'liquid sunshine', bad-ish roads in and around Porty are a standard which one local asserts (not in an unfriendly fashion), "have become the challenge you have to be willing to deal with in order to get here. It keeps the people who probably won't like Porty anyway (because this is part of Porty's vibe), out."

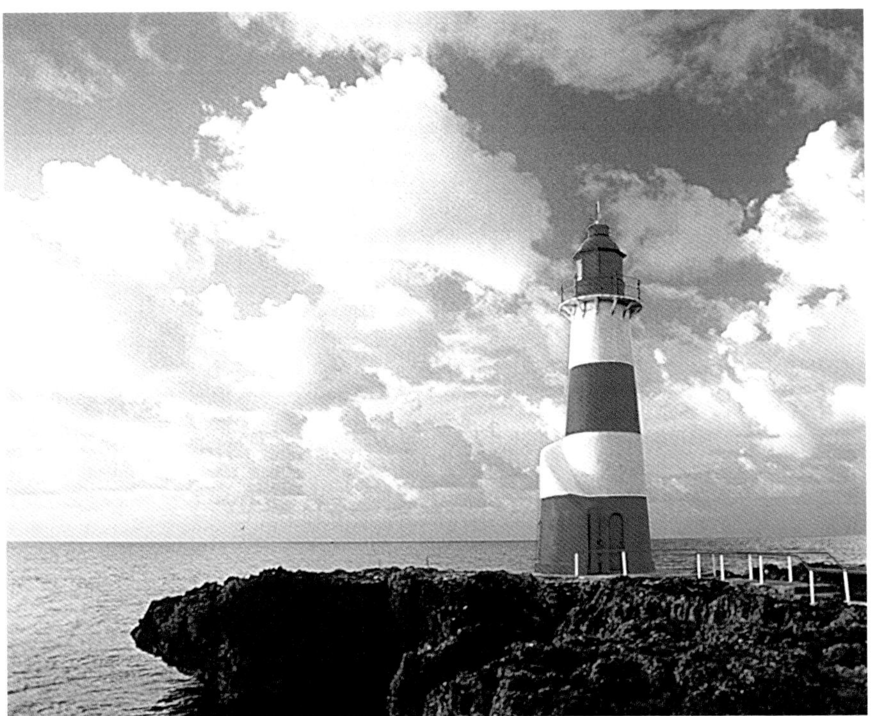

Call it self-preservation or telling it like it is—Port Antonio has remained this way since the days of Errol Flynn and is not about to change. Old world charm means most of Porty's visitors stay in guesthouses in town or at classic small hotels on the beach. It also means seeing relics of the past in the form of traditional Jamaican architecture and what used to be the holiday homes of some of America's richest families still around, offering a sometimes eerie, if not just false impression that the place isn't still the stomping ground of the rich and famous.

Still it's the anonymity and personal touch you can't package or create that gives Port Antonio its unique edge, not to mention that it's one of the best places in Jamaica to see nature's bounty in all her glory. From rainforest to the Blue Hole, from river rafting to Boston Bay's delicious jerk pork—the best thing about Port Antonio is that you don't have to be a celebrity to feel like one.

ORIGINALLY PUBLISHED FEBRUARY 2002

Natural Living at Tamarind Hill Farm

MARGUERITE GAURON

Some never discover "The Land of Milk and Honey" nor do they find true love. Only a very lucky few find both in their own little Garden of Eden, where fresh springs bubble out of the verdant tropical jungle to form natural ponds, flowering trees feed thousands of honey-producing bees and pineapples flourish naturally on an 18-acre organic farm in Jamaica's Blue Mountains.

For Joanna Bulova (of the famous Bulova watch family) and her enterprising Jamaican husband, Vincent Slimforte, Tamarind Hill Farm, at Tom's Hope in Portland's lush Rio Grande Valley, represents a healthy business that evolved from a love of nature and each other.

Joanna was born in England of Austrian parents, who moved to New York when she was just a baby. A psychotherapist by profession, today she has happily adapted to a completely new way of life as a keeper of bees, rabbits, birds, fish and creatures of the wild.

She shares her strong environmental commitment with her husband who was born in the Rio Grande Valley, of East Indian parents. His family migrated to England when he was 11 and he later joined the Royal Air Force (RAF), specializing in the operation of large computer systems. On retirement, he moved to the Caribbean island of Nevis where he bought property and managed a hotel.

They were both single, with grown-up families, when they met in Nevis in 1988. Joanna's family had owned a winter home there for many years and she came to visit them. After meeting Vincent she spent the succeeding year commuting from New York to be with him. She finally rented out her apartment and moved to Nevis in 1989.

One of the highlights of their sojourn in Nevis was the adoption of a pet pig. They called him "Rover" and "He was just like a dog," reminisces Joanna. The couple concur that one of the most difficult aspects of leaving Nevis was parting with Rover.

In 1990 Vincent took Joanna on a visit to Jamaica. "We found relatives and we loved it," they recall. The next move was to buy the Tamarind Hill property and begin to build a house. They were married by a local Baptist minister in a small riverside community called Fellowship in July 1991.

Joanna Bulova Slimforte with her beloved rabbits.

With the house still unfinished, they rent a tiny gingerbread farmer's cottage. Cooking is done in a rustic open-air kitchen over glowing wood fires fueled with waste wood from the property.

"We are almost entirely self-sufficient," says Vincent. The property produces organic fruit and vegetables, including pineapples and other crops indigenous to the area. Fish are reared in natural ponds, fed by fresh mountain springs, and some of the catch is shared by wild water birds which frequent the wetlands on the farm.

Rabbit-rearing is another venture, and Joanna is a leading promoter of natural honey, as she actively organizes community training workshops and field days to encourage local farmers to become involved with bee farming as a source of income generation. Bees in this part of the world feed on wild blossoms from redwood, sweetwood, palm trees, orchid trees and other exotic flora. Developing a healthy bee population contributes to the protection of biodiversity and the natural propagation of healthy food crops in the Rio Grande Valley. The Tamarind Hill Honey label is smartly displayed in leading supermarkets.

Joanna and Vincent invite visitors to enjoy their organic farming project as an eco-experience. The farm is an officially-declared bird sanctuary and abounds in rare and exotic species. Visitors can wade in the Sandy River, tour the rabbit nursery and fish ponds, bird-watch and inspect the apiary.

From computer engineering and psychotherapy in London and New York, to the simple life on a hillside farm in rural Jamaica, surrounded by birds, animals, natural foliage and love, this couple enthuses: "We couldn't be happier."

ORIGINALLY PUBLISHED APRIL 1998

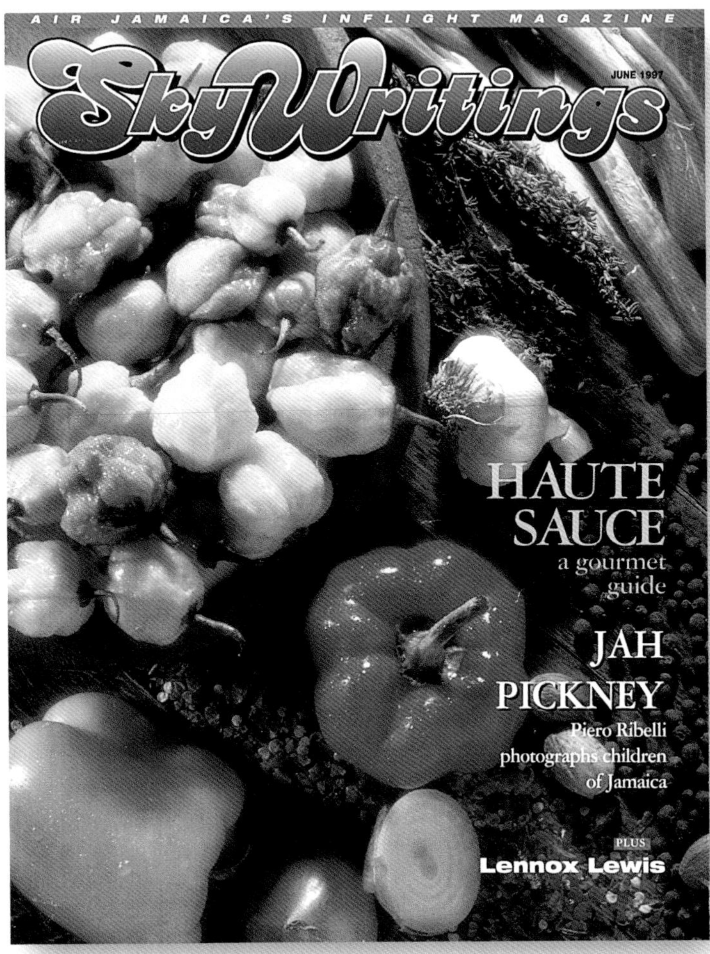

SKYWRITINGS COVER
June 1997
Savouring the power of peppers.
©FRANZ MARZOUCA

In Celebration of the Patty

BARBARA GLOUDON

There is a story going around somewhere that the Jamaican patty owes its origins to the Cornish pasty, a kind of meat and vegetable pie, which would've been introduced to the island by English settlers or travellers way back in the time when Britannia ruled the waves and cane fields. Whatever the origin, all I know is that a Jamaican patty is ours, a distinctive feature of our culinary heritage, often imitated but never duplicated.

I believe that we erred as a nation when we did not include the patty (along with ackee and saltfish, rice and peas and jerk) on our national Coat of Arms. After all, the Arawaks and the pineapple no longer run tings and as to the crocodile, whenever we see him (usually in a canal at Portmore) we certainly don't invite him to dinner. The patty would be far more reassuring, trust me.

For better, but never worse, it has become a national symbol, a touchstone, especially for Jamaicans exiled, for whatever reason, on distant shores. Even those who have shaken the dust off their feet from our Island of Challenges are never happy until they have located the nearest patty shop in their new homeland. But no matter what patty shops are abroad, savvy travellers will return from a visit to the Rock with a couple dozen patties destined for the microwave.

What then, is the secret of the patty? What is the power which it exerts over us? Some people take it very seriously indeed. A gentleman of unabashed Victorian upbringing was heard denouncing an upstart, a "hurry come up" who was "exhibiting himself" as a man of substance in a certain corner of Foreign. He also happened to be the proprietor of a baking establishment. Faced with one of the man's displays of self-importance, our Jamaican gentleman gave him short shrift. "He should be tried for treason. The man makes the worst patties in the world."

Real men might not eat quiche but any red-blooded Jamaican man recognizes the virtue of a hot patty alongside a cold Red Stripe. Some people feel impelled to add the adjective "beef." This is quite unnecessary. With a real patty, you shouldn't have to ask "Where's the beef?" I know that in an age of beta-carotene and free radicals, red meat is high on the list of undesirables, but patties filled with substances other than beef should not lay claim to the name.

If you insist, you may partake of envelopes of pastry filled with red peas, split peas, chick peas or some other form of legumes...calaloo, cabbage or other vegetable matter. While these may be nutritionally correct they are not patties. Pastries yes, but patties, no. And what of the bona fides of chicken and lobster patties? These are not to be admitted into the inner circle as legitimate members of the patty family either.

Okay, okay, but please understand that they're so treated only because their contents have some weight, some substance. But let's get down to the meat of the matter...the qualities of a real patty.

ONE—The crust must not weigh heavily

upon the digestive system. Light and flaky are attributes to be encouraged.

TWO—In the contents the gravamen, the real beef, must reflect the virtues of a seasoning hand, an understanding that skellion and thyme, onion and good country pepper, in appropriate quantities, enhance the flavour of ground beef.

THREE—The temperature of a real patty is served hot, not lukewarm, certainly not cold. The steam must rise from the very core of its being when teeth make the breakthrough from crust to filling. It is not only hot by name, but hot by nature. A cold patty is an insult to sense and sensibilities. Cocktail patties tend to fall into this category. They're often served anything but hot.

FOUR—How to eat a patty.

I know this girl who always splits the patty open at the seam, exposing the rich, steaming, meaty filling. She knows the precise moment when the meat is cool enough (not cold) to close up the crust and enjoy. She defends this method by reminding that there is no greater pain than having the roof of one's mouth seared by a really hot patty. Others find their enjoyment in modest-sized bites, blowing in between each one, alternating with sips of some appropriately cold brew.

It has come to my attention that some reckless persons have taken to "invading" the patty by opening the crust and inserting slices of cheese, bacon or some other "foreign substance" upon the beef. It makes for "good eating," or so they say. I have no urge to prove them right although I will admit to the knowledge that patties can claim legitimate relationships with other edibles.

There was, for instance, the patty and cruss of another era. "Cruss" (or crust, if you must) was a crisp fold of pastry shaped to nestle the patty in its warm embrace, sold from a "patty pan" a two-tiered tin box equipped with hot coals to heat the precious contents. There is also that old standby, patty and coco bread still known today (thank heaven). For my money though, a good patty should stand on its own merits. No need "to gild the anthurium," as a philosopher friend of mine would say.

One final word of advice... Whatever you do never, ever be seen eating a patty with a knife and fork... not even at a black tie affair. (You should be so lucky!).

ORIGINALLY PUBLISHED APRIL 2001

In Search of the Perfect Patty

ALEX D. HAWKES

Its marvellous filling typically consists of cubes of meat, diced white potatoes (called "Irish", or "Irish potatoes" in Jamaican marketplaces), onions, and sometimes turnips, all with suitable seasonings. But no one is really sure about the name...anymore than anyone is really quite certain about just what goes into an authentic Jamaican patty.

The pastry crust must, for the connoisseur, be flaky and lightly browned, either with yellow food colouring or, if you are a purist, with a dash of the liquid made by steeping some of the scarlet seeds of the annatto, an elegant small bushy tree with pretty big pink blossoms and prickly pods which turn red when mature. The filling for the customary patty contains finely-minced beef, perhaps with a chunk of fully-ground lean pork, for added flavour. Some onions or escallions are sometimes put into the mix, along with a bit of filler, in the form of leftover bread.

Then comes the vital addition of the "seasonings", which usually include a grand series of often-secret spices, but more publicly-acknowledged garlic, salt, ground black pepper, Jamaican pimento (allspice) and, perhaps, sweet green peppers. The final addition during the mixing and blending of the filling for the Jamaican patty is a lesser, or greater, involvement with one of the hottest of all volcanic bush capsicum peppers in the world, of which there are many varieties used in authentic Jamaican cuisine.

The Scotch Bonnet comes in several colours, from waxy yellow to green or splendid scarlet. Country pepper can be any one of a formidable series of capsicums; and some people opt for the slender little bird pepper, the green ones usually being hotter than the vivid Christmas-red ripe ones, these so fiery that care must be taken to remove all of their seeds and inner ribs with care, for in preparation, some people even get a rash on their fingers through absorption of the juices. But an addition of these hot peppers, usually prepared and minced after seeding and de-veining, is essential for culinary success.

The filling, generally prepared by professional "patty-makers" in our best known establishments throughout the island, is put into the pastry circles, then folded over, and the edges crimped with a moist fork. These are then baked "just until done", as one of the Kingston experts in this delicacy informed me. He would never use such a modem culinary apparatus as an oven timer, for he has been baking and making his sought-after patties for more than twenty-five years. He knows precisely what should go into both the pastry and the "special filling"; and he knows exactly how hot this big oven should be, by testing the heat with his fingers before the big trays of patties are put in. And, of course, he knows just when to remove the baking trays, after the filling has settled a bit and when they can safely be taken out to be kept hot in the patty warmer, a glass-fronted case which is kept in many Jamaican shops and bakeries.

ORIGINALLY PUBLISHED FEBRUARY 1977

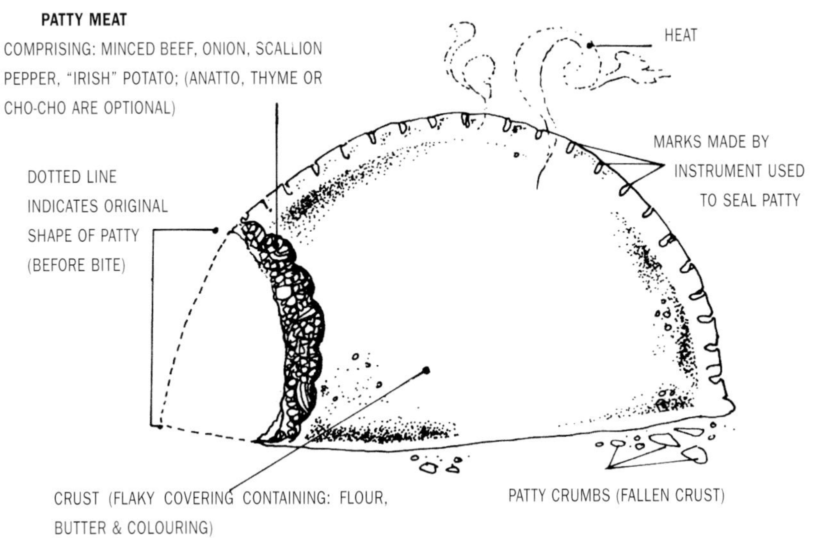

Love At First Bite

Childhood Memories of Mango.

BARBARA GLOUDON

"Me nuh drink cawfee tea, mango time
Care how nice it may be, mango time
Inna de height a de mango crop
When de fruit dem a ripe and drop
Wash yuh pot, tun dem down, mango time."

(JAMAICAN FOLK SONG)

Summer holidays couldn't come fast enough for me. As soon as school "let out," and as soon as I could persuade my mother to entrust me to the tender mercies of Mr. Mahoney's truck and the assorted array of persons who journeyed from country to town to do their shopping, I was off and ready to run like leggo beast (if my grandmother would let me) in the depths of Hanover Bush.

The days of fishing of janga (crayfish) in the river, the sweet taste of rose apple pulled from the trees by the river bank, the luxury of gorging on breadfruit (one each for man, woman and child) roasted at the fireside while the hot pot cooked, were all treats of a Jamaican midsummer child's holiday—but not complete unless it included as many visits as possible to mango bush.

Black mangoes, better known as Blackie, grew in rich profusion, burdening the branches, falling to the ground to create a thick carpet of the little green-skinned fruit and the thick yellow juice of those which didn't survive the fall. One season, my cousins and I had a contest to see who could eat the most Blackies at one sitting. I believe I accounted for 48—a cool four dozen. Well, they are small fruits after all—just enough to fit into the mouth, where the tongue slips the sweet sticky flesh from the seed which can be saved for a thorough going over until it emerged almost bleach white.

But there was no time to clean the seed in the mango eating contest. I don't recall if I was the winner with 48 to my credit but I have not forgotten the mother of all belly aches which afflicted me later in the day. My grandmother felt quite justified in administering a wash-out (cerasee tea, or was it castor oil in cream soda?) That came long before the obligatory treatment at the appropriate time—the end of the holidays, just before I was packed off back to Town to face the deprivation of City Life, cleansed of all the excesses of summer feasting.

You thought that after gorging on the 48 Blackies and enduring the Washout, I would play ease-up with the mangoes for the rest of that season? Yuh mussi mad. What were summer holidays for, but to bring the abundant mango crop under control? Furthermore, Blackies were not the only mangoes in the Bush. There were many varieties, such as:

Hairy mangoes, which I became entangled with only as a last resort. I hated the feel of the "hairs," the stringy strands which prevailed after the pulp was eased from the seed. That's why they called them Hairy, yuh nuh!

Robin mangoes, found in St. Elizabeth (my home parish). A faint but distinctive perfume permeated the flesh, reached after tearing through a slightly leathery skin. I used to boast to my Hanover cousins that I was one up on them. My parish grew Robin—theirs didn't. That didn't stop them in the least, for they had Kidney mangoes appropriately shaped like the organ culled from some poor unsuspecting goat or pig which has sacrificed for the family protein stock, appropriated by our thieving holiday hands, roasted with salt over a quick fire, then passed from burnt finger to burnt finger as we cousins shared one more round of midsummer contraband.

By the end of the summer, we were as fat as Governor mango, deserving of the insult: "Yuh big and so-so." The plump fatness of Governor mango was a reference to the "bigness" (not so much size as importance) of the governor who "ruled" in colonial splendour at the time. Beefie mango—a smaller cousin of Governor, fleshy and thick, generously shared. First you sliced off the two jaws then the sections around the sides. You reaped a lot of "meat" therefrom. Even the seed which remained had enough substance clinging to it to make the sharing worthwhile. "Dem neva call it beefi fe nutten."

Sweetie—about the size of a big "fowl egg," right sized to slip inside your cheek, so it bulged like you were afflicted with gum-boil. But Sweetie was sweet and very obliging. You could stash away quite a few before Mummaw (grandmother) discovered that you were once again up to "your leggo-beast Kingstonian behaviour," spoiling your appetite before supper.

Turpentine mango must have been invented

by a cabinet maker to cure wood. Didn't cross the road for too many of those. The taste reminded of the smell of furniture polish. Figure that out. And then there was Number Eleven, which, it is said, was so named because it was part of Captain (Mutiny on the Bounty) Bligh's stock of plants brought to these parts, known only by number. (I don't know if is true. So me buy it, so me sell it).

Let us speak now of the aristocrats of the mango family. Julie, Bombay and East Indian. Those were *Town* mangoes, hybrids, carefully cultivated, grafted matings of lesser with greater stocks, to create the favoured choice for high-table feasting.

Julie and Bombay and East Indian didn't grow in Mango Bush. There were too refined, too stoosh. You wouldn't find them in the crocus bags of the women who journeyed to mango bush in the hills of St. Andrew, to reap from the trees leased for the season. That's how it is in mango bush in the hills. The vendors contract with the tree owners to take off the season's crop, for a price. Never mind that people call the crop "common mangoes." They sold well in the market or by the roadside, holding pride of place especially in July and August.

The women come to the hills by bus, armed with big baskets bound with hefty lengths of crocus bag or coarse cotton. When the baskets are filled to capacity, the fabric is used to tie up the load, then it is down the hill to await some passing truck or bus, heading for market gate. These days, when the mango women gather early July and August by the side of the road leading to mango bush, they discuss how the mango trees are fast disappearing, cut down to make way for houses and other developments. Progress some call it. You mean we might never see mango bush again? No more Blackie and Hairy, Robin and Kidney, Governor and Beefie? God forbid!

These days when, summer comes, the price we pay for being adults is work instead of unending holidays. No visits to Mango Bush. Instead, we stop by the market where the smell of mango juice evokes childhood memories and the prices invite cardiac arrest. What you mean $40 for one mango? Yuh damn mad! I don't care if it is one of the new-style made for export, big as Governor washing tub used to be. Okay, so it has a name—Tommy Atkins. Who is he? You still insist on $40 for one mango? In my granny days, that could buy out a whole mango bush. Okay, let me try it. Gosh!—it's heavy. Is for sure I couldn't eat 48 of these, not in any Mango Bush!

ORIGINALLY PUBLISHED JUNE 1998

MANGO & CREAM CHEESE ROULADE
Chef Louis Bailey, Air Jamaica

INGREDIENTS:
4 slices mango
2 oz plain cream cheese
lettuce to garnish

METHOD:
Cut firm ripe mango into thin slices. Spread chilled cream cheese onto slices and carefully roll into "roulades." Arrange the roulades on a bed of lettuce.
SERVED CHILLED.

SMOKED TILAPIA WITH MANGO AND OLIVES
Chef Dennis McIntosh, Ciboney Ocho Rios

INGREDIENTS:
5 oz tilapia fillet, boneless and skinned
juice of 1 lime
1 sprig of thyme
pimento leaves
lime leaves
1 heart bib lettuce
1 escallion, chopped
1/2 sliced mango
4 black olives, halved
1 oz oil & vinegar
salt & pepper to taste

METHOD:
Season the fish with lime juice, escallion, thyme, salt & pepper. Place the fish on a wire rack and put the rack inside a pot lined with pimento leaves and limes leaves. Do not add oil! Cover.
'Smoke' the fish for about 10 minutes or until cooked. Cool the fillet and arrange on a plate with heart of lettuce, olives and sliced mango. Combine the oil & vinegar dressing and lime juice and drizzle over the fish.
SERVES ONE.

MANGO & PINEAPPLE PUNCH
Chef Dennis McIntosh

INGREDIENTS:
1/2 pineapple, peeled and diced
8 oz mango nectar
8 oz pineapple juice
16 oz coconut water
4 oz sugar
4 oz dark rum
juice of 2 limes

METHOD:
Blend pineapple and mango juices, sugar, coconut water and lime juice until smooth. Add rum and pour over ice. Garnish with pineapple and mango slices.

MARINATED SHRIMP WITH MANGO ON LETTUCE LEAVES
Chef Norma Shirley, Norma's at the Wharfhouse and Red Bones, the Blues Cafe.

INGREDIENTS:
2 cups coconut milk, well stirred
24 large shrimp, peeled and deveined
7 tablespoons fresh lime juice
1-1/2 teaspoons sugar
2 tablespoons diced red sweet pepper
2 tablespoons diced yellow sweet pepper
4 tablespoons finely chopped red onion or white ends of escallion
1/4 medium scotch bonnet pepper, or to taste
1/2 cup finely diced firm ripe mango
1-1/2 tablespoons fish sauce (available in specialty stores)
Mixed lettuce leaves

METHOD:
In a saucepan, simmer coconut milk over a medium heat. Add shrimp and poach them until they turn pink (approximately. 5 minutes). Remove shrimp and place in a bowl, in a medium bowl toss all other ingredients together with tablespoons of the coconut milk poaching mixture. Toss shrimp into the mixture.
Cover and chill for 6 hours.
To serve, divide lettuce equally on plates and top with shrimp mixture.

MANGO AND CHOCOLATE MOUSSE
Chef Steve Sowa, Sandals Ocho Rios

INGREDIENTS:
10 egg yolks
6 oz sugar
vanilla essence to taste
1 oz gelatine
8 oz whipped cream
1 cup mango puree
1 cup melted chocolate

METHOD:
Whip egg yolks with sugar and vanilla over boiling water until temperature reaches 140ºF. Dissolve gelatine in a little hot water and add to egg mixture. Allow to cool and fold in whipped cream. Divide mixture into two and mix mango puree with one part and melted chocolate with other. Divide into molds or terrines and chill. Turn out onto plates and decorate with chocolate and mango sauces, chocolate curls and diced mango.

Meet the Breadfruit

ALEX D. HAWKES

Visitors to Jamaica are invariably very impressed by the luxuriant tropical vegetation which they see on all sides. Towering coconuts and other palms, huge mango and guango trees, and immense buttressed cotton trees. And almost everywhere, the uniquely spectacular breadfruit.

Though one of Jamaica's commonest trees, the breadfruit is also one of its more unusual species, with an exotic history and considerable importance in the island cuisine.

The breadfruit tree is a very impressive one, sometimes to sixty feet tall, set with fantastic lacquered rich-green leaves a foot or more in length (rarely to almost three feet!), each with conspicuous lobes of handsome pattern. Some bright souls have suggested that these leaves were those sported by Adam and Eve, since they would be much more effective than a diminutive leaf from a fig tree. The individual flowers of this species are tiny, and in the male, spikes are borne in tightly packed club-like structures; these are on occasion pickled or candied by good local cooks, with interesting edible results. The rounded heads of female flowers in time develop into globular or vaguely oblong fruits, these measuring up to a maximum of about eight inches in length and six inches in diameter. In weight, they range from two to about ten pounds apiece, latter specimens being known more in the Pacific islands than hereabouts. The bright or yellowish green rind, often sparsely mottled with brown when mature, is set with blunt projections, or rarely, in some special variants, with abbreviated thorns. The usually sizeable median core is surrounded by white or yellowish firm pulp. This is the edible part. The huge fruit, generally unpeeled, is roasted over charcoal or less desirably in the oven, and consumed with lots of butter; made into crisp chips for snacking with rum cocktails or the lovely island beer, Red Stripe; stuffed with piquant meat mixtures; made into hearty soups or chowders; and into dessert puddings touched up with coconut milk and tropical spices.

Breadfruit is high in carbohydrates and rich in availability of vitamin C and thiamine, so it forms a distinctive and valued substitute for potatoes, yams, rice, and other starchy crops. When properly prepared, the flesh of certain varieties has much the texture and flavour of firm bread, hence the origin of the name.

In fact, during the height of the summer breadfruit season, sales of commercial baked bread in Jamaica fall off noticeably!

In this island, this tree is so common and widespread that many people consider it obviously indigenous, but such is not the case. The species artocarpus communis, of the same immense largely tropical botanical family as the commercial fig, giant banyan, India-rubber tree, and the allied edible jackfruit, has been cultivated by man since prehistoric times. In fact, like a number of our crops, such as corn, rice and the coconut, it is not today known authentically in the wild state. The tree's original haunts are presumably Malaysia, whence it was transported to the various insular groups of Micronesia and Polynesia by the incredible oceanic migrations of the early peoples.

There are countless variants—throughout the Pacific and Tropic Asian areas, with some thirty-one distinct named forms being know in Tahiti alone. The most prized of these are totally without seeds, so that their propagation is of necessity by root suckers or cuttings, or by circumposing (air-layering). Some of the seedy breadfruits are valued for this characteristic, since the angular seeds when roasted or boiled are very flavourful, much reminiscent of temperate zone chestnuts.

In the year 1787, Captain William Bligh went to Tahiti, in the Society Islands of the Pacific, to collect fruit and vegetable plants which were thought to be cultivable in the West Indies, particularly Jamaica. He was in command of H.M.S. Bounty. The story of this expedition is well known, with its mutiny of the crew and his being set adrift with 18 men in an open boat, to sail some thousand miles prior to reaching land again. Bligh persevered, however, in 1793 he succeeded in bringing living plants of the breadfruit, plus many other species which are now commonplace in the island, to Jamaica. The rooted cuttings were planted out at Bath, now in the eastern parish of St. Thomas, the second oldest botanical garden in the hemisphere.

Soon the breadfruit spread throughout the island, though the slaves for some fifty years would not eat this strange fruit which grew on a tall tree and which had to be cooked like a vegetable, since they had nothing comparable either in Africa or here in the West Indies. So the pigs fattened on the fallen cannon-ball-shaped fruits. Following the abolition of slavery, breadfruit became gradually accepted as an important foodstuff for the freed men in their villages.

Interestingly enough, the National Fruit of Jamaica, the ackee, also involves Captain Bligh. Its botanical name is blighia sapida, and it was brought from West Africa at an early date on a slave ship. Its cooked fruit often with salt codfish, is today a staple of the Jamaican diet. But oddly enough the ackee is considered poisonous in almost all other parts of the Caribbean, and is never eaten.

Bligh's breadfruit is very much a tropical tree. In Miami, where so many exotic tropical species succeed in an essentially sub-tropical climate, the breadfruit will not even grow outdoors, the slightest low temperatures causing it to drop all of its foliage and in time perish. One horticultural friend there, though, has erected a costly glasshouse, especially designed to accommodate his prize breadfruit, which grows well and indeed produces its attractive tasty fruits annually. At Key West, not too much further south than Miami, the tree thrives outside, several huge old specimens fruiting copiously and regularly.

Tinned breadfruit is exported from Jamaica, and can be obtained in gourmet shops overseas, but the texture and taste of this canned product is not much like that of the fresh fruit, direct from the huge tree, in a Jamaican garden!

ORIGINALLY PUBLISHED MARCH 1973

Jamaican Ginger

The Connoisseur's Choice

NORMA BENGHIAT

The ginger plant, zingiber officinale, of which the rhyzome is the edible part, is native to South East Asia. It was one of the earliest oriental spices known to Europe. It was initially introduced there in its dried form, even before the Roman period. By the Middle Ages it was a very popular spice, not only as a flavouring, but as a medicine against the plague or black death, as it produced a certain amount of sweating which was considered a good sign. It is now known to modern medicine as a stimulant to the gastro-intestinal tract and as a counter irritant. It is also reputed to be an aphrodisiac.

Because of the long life factor of the rhyzome, the Spaniards were able to introduce it to the West Indies without much difficulty, where it thrived beautifully in its adopted home. Ginger made its first appearance in Jamaica in about 1527 and by 1547 it was a well established spice and was exported to Spain.

The two known varieties of ginger in the island are the white or yellow tumeric ginger and the royal blue or flint ginger. The interior of the rhyzome of the latter, has a bluish tinge but it is of a poorer quality and yield.

The Jamaican ginger is well known to connoisseurs for its rare mild, subtle flavour, for its pale yellow colour and for its high oleoresin content. Because of its unique qualities derived from a combination of climate, soil and type of cultivation—it fetches the highest price on the world ginger market.

Ginger plays an important part in the spicing of the dishes of the south east Asian countries, India, China, Malysia and the Phillipines. However in Europe, America and Canada this spice is chiefly used in the flavouring of sweets, such as gingerbread, biscuits, cakes, puddings, creams, sauces and drinks-such as ginger ale, ginger beer, wines, possets and porter. The use of ginger in Jamaican cooking follows the European influence.

Christiana is the centre of the ginger industry in Jamaica. It is a mountain town of great charm perched on a ridge some 2800 ft above sea level. The mean temperature is 69°F (20.6°C), which is delightfully cool for Jamaica. In the past, before the expansion of hotel rooms on the north coast, city dwellers as well as people from the hot plains below spent many happy holidays in such cool hill towns. To meet the demand for accommodation, two small hotels were built, the Savoy and the Villa Bella, which are still in operation although now almost forgotten.

Ginger thrives on the slopes around the Christiana areas, where it is planted in rotation with red peas (red kidney beans) and Irish potatoes. Planted in May-June it is reaped mainly between December and January. The planted rhyzomes produce new "hands" which are often referred to as "barampas".

Traditionally, ginger has been exported in its dried form, which means that the ginger has to be peeled, a most laborious task washed with lime or lemon juice to improve the colour and then dried. A new market has developed for split, unpeeled and dried ginger. This however, fetches a lower price.

A visit to the home of a ginger grower revealed the process in action. Several women were deftly peeling the ginger with special ginger knives with thin shaped blades. A good peeler can peel as much as 40-50 lbs. of ginger in a day. The peeled, washed ginger was placed on stiff mats made of dried fern stems, corded together. These mats were placed on platforms raised several feet off the ground and positioned to catch the maximum of sunlight—it needs between seven to ten days for drying to a 10% maximum moisture content. At the first sign of rain—which is fairly often—the mats are rolled up stacked and removed to a safe place under cover; for should the ginger get wet during the drying period, discolouration caused by fungus would ruin it. The skins are used in the manufacture of soft drinks or for the production of ginger oil.

ORIGINALLY PUBLISHED AUGUST 1986

Herbs and Spices

DIANE ROBERTSON

Over the years, Jamaica's ethnic customs have led the way to creative cooking. We have produced a very exciting and unusual array of dishes like the popular jerk chicken, mackerel run-down and our national dish, ackee and saltfish. Our secret? Experimentation with different combinations of herbs and spices.

Here is an introduction to a few popular herbs and spices and the recipes we use them in, for you to try.

PIMENTO

Pimento berries (allspice), known as Jamaican pepper, are dark reddish brown seeds, aromatic when fresh. The name allspice is given because it has the scent of cinnamon, cloves and juniper berries. The seeds are used locally for pickled meats and soups, and in folklore medicine it is highly recommended for diarrhoea and upset stomach; even pre-menstrual pains. Also, the pimento seeds are used medicinally to make a stimulating plaster for back pains.

Here is a recipe for old time pimento liqueur (otherwise known as pimento dram), which is still served particularly for the "over eaters."

INGREDIENTS

4-5 cups ripe pimento berries (usually gathered between July – October)
5 cups of Jamaican white rum
2 cups of lime juice
10 cups of water
2 cups of sugar
4 ounces cinnamon sticks

METHOD

Wash pimento berries and place in a large earthenware jar with rum and lime juice in order to macerate for a week. At the end of the week, strain the pimento liquor through a piece of muslin cloth taking care not to crush the berries. Discard the berries. Boil the sugar, water and cinnamon to make a syrup. Cool and stir. Add syrup to the strained liqueur. Mix well and strain again. Store in clean dark bottles and place away from the light for maturity.

SORREL

The period December to April has always been recognized as the beginning of our "sunny winter season." With Christmas in its midst, traditional cuisine with fruits and herbs of the season are still enjoyed today, with changes made to suit the times. Here is one such recipe for the Jamaican sorrel (hibiscus sabdariffa) drink which folklore medicine recommends for stomach acidity and as a diuretic.

INGREDIENTS

8 cups sorrel petals
2 ounces grated ginger
12 cups boiling water
Orange peel (dried)
Sugar for sweetening to taste

METHOD

Place sorrel and crushed ginger and dried peel of orange into a pot of boiling water. Macerate for 12-16 hours. Strain, sweeten to taste, and bottle. For preservation keep in refrigerator. Add an ounce of white rum to each quart bottle.

GINGER

Ginger is reported to be very effective for motion sickness and for general well-being. Here is a receipe for ginger beer which is one of those delicious concoctions created in the sixteenth century. It is a home-brewed drink, formerly sold in the marketplace.

INGREDIENTS

1/2 cup honey
3 cups sugar
1/2 lb ginger
1/2 cup lime juice
4 quarts water
1 cup yeast (if available)

METHOD

Grate ginger or crust and place in a large bowl. Add lime juice. Pour boiling water over it. Mix yeast with a cup of the sugar. Pour 1/2 cup water over mixed paste.

When ginger mixture is warm, add the yeast paste and stir. Cover and let it stand for three days. Skim, strain, and sweeten to taste. Keep in refrigerator. Serve chilled.

There is another simple method used as well.

INGREDIENTS

1 sprig of peppermint
3 cups sugar
1/2 lb ginger
1/2 cup lime juice
4 quarts water

METHOD

Pour boiling water over ginger in a large bowl and leave for six hours. Strain, add lime juice, sugar and sprig of mint. Sweeten to taste, bottle & refrigerate.

ORIGINALLY PUBLISHED MARCH 1994

Bread Jamaican Style

NORMA BENGHIAT

There was a time when we had numerous small bakeries producing several types of bread and sweet soda cakes. Popular breads include "Krispi crust," coco bread, grotto (a square bread), steam bread (with a soft texture), pork bread with the same texture as hard-dough, the national favourite, but with little bits of pork included, plait bread (a form of show bread), peg bread, wholewheat, sandwich, and french breads.

The sweet breads and soda cakes included raisin breads, Easter buns, ginger nut, served like a peg bread, for which Valentine's Bakery was famous; ginger bread which was very moist; soda cakes such as bullas, "mess around" (like bullas), made with molasses but lighter in colour, with a sprinkling of sugar on top, and totos—made with spices and coconut. Jackass corn, a very tough biscuit, was also popular.

Many of these breads have disappeared with the closing of several of the small bakeries and the amalgamation of some of the larger ones in the fifties. Some breads have thus virtually disappeared often because the recipes have died with the owners. In our march towards modernization, many of these breads have been replaced by soft, sliced breads—white, "whole wheat" and bran, more amenable to higher degrees of mechanization. The hard dough bread has thus become our most popular bread.

Hard-dough bread is a dense bread of uncertain origin—possibly Cuban. It appears that the dough break machine, important in its achieving the right texture, is utilized only in Jamaica, Cuba and Haiti. On a visit to Spain in 1986, I was pleasantly surprised to encounter in the Andalusian towns of Toledo, Cordoba, Seville and Cadiz, the identical hard dough, but made into rolls instead of loaves.

Some pastry shops are reviving the making of breads of the past such as the coco and plait breads.

However, breads made at home can be infinitely better than the shop baked variety. There exists a limitless variety even within the limited scope of the type of flour and ovens available. It is therefore surprising that more people do not make their own breads.

The Bakers Expo, held earlier this year, was made memorable for me by the participation in particular of a small bakery from Jamaica's North Coast which is maintaining a very old tradition.

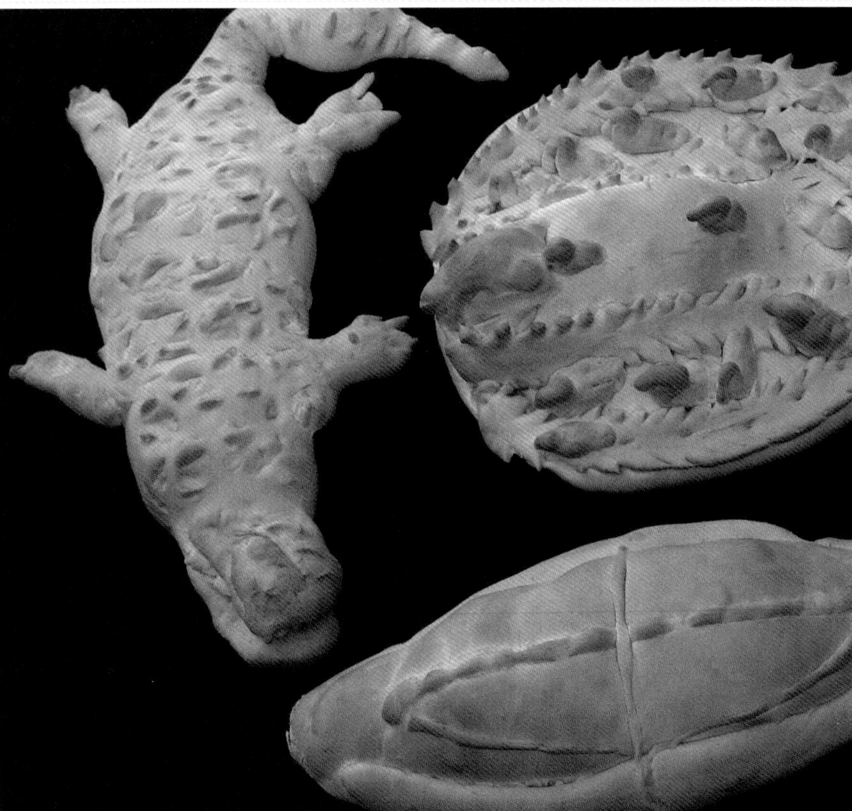

Don C's Bakeshop in Annotto Bay, operated by Donald and Joyce Chung, has been in operation for only four months. It was formerly Chang's Bakery. It started to produce show breads as part of their line of baked products.

These show breads are made from hard dough. Some are as large as 24" by 15". They are generally quite flat and are decorated to depict one of several themes. Doves for peace, the duck for prosperity, the duck and dill for a large family, the alligator for reverence, the mongoose for the Crop Over, the man and woman for weddings, the airplane for travel; the crown bread for riches and the open bible with inscriptions for religious ceremonies.

These show breads used to play an important part in celebrations in the rural areas. Each theme depicted the particular celebration.

I am told that in the old days at country weddings, the show bread was kept in a private room. All guests wishing to see it were obliged to pay. The significance seems to be tied up in ritual practices pertaining to the warding off of the evil eye.

A revival of these labour-intensive pieces of art indicate that people are willing to pay for them and small bakeries are willing to produce them.

The history of bread and its ingredients is worth looking at.

Although wheat came to be the dominant cereal flour for bread making in Jamaica, the New World already used the indigenous corn as a staple in the diet of North and Central American Indians. The bread made from the cassava root was similarly a basic food of the South American and Antilles Indians.

The bammy or cassava bread of the Arawak Indians is to this day, made by the same method used for centuries by them. This was the principal starch and bread used during the Spanish occupation.

Although wheat flour was introduced later during the British period, it continued to form an important part of the diet of the population.

Before the discovery and manufacture of compressed yeast, various forms used for brewing and baking were produced from an assortment of mashed grains, malted barley or rye, boiled potatoes and flour or anything that would produce a good ferment.

Soda leaven breads were very popular in Jamaica before the days of refrigeration and the introduction of yeast.

ORIGINALLY PUBLISHED MAY 1987

Quintessential Blue Mountain Coffee

DWIGHT WHYLIE

The best Blue Mountain coffee comes from a labour of love.

The panorama from the cottage window 1300 metres up made my eyes and spirit smile. A wide deep valley with little dots of houses, tufts of coffee, bamboo and other trees, and a profusion of wildflowers and other shrubbery.

There was a hush to my city-dweller's ear, which slowly recognised a constant chorus of birds, insects, wind and rushing water. The only intruding sounds were occasional vehicles on the road above, and distant planes. Fog and cloud gave us time before curtaining the view while my wife Joan and myself sipped welcoming cups of coffee.

The cottage is the home of Alex and Dorothy Twyman, and is on Old Tavern Estate, where they and their son David grow their coffee. Alex runs the farm. David dries and stores the beans, and Dorothy roasts them to order, and does the packaging. They then send them off to the four corners of the earth. I called it organic coffee, but delightfully honest Twyman quickly corrected me. To be organic, he counselled, he would have to use no chemicals at all. He uses as little as possible, and only when absolutely necessary.

Twyman finds his way along the miles of paths on his 140 acres in a Land Rover, two small John Deere tractors or two water-booted feet. The paths and roads were hand-cut by a local self-taught man who walked the land, studied the contours and the soil, marked out the route with pegs, and led the crews which carved them into the mountainside. The road to the processing yard accepts only serious off-road vehicles. Citified SUV's don't even ask.

At the processing yard is the Old Tavern building which appears on their logo, as well as the ruins of an earlier 18th century building. The coffee trees which surround it are all of the arabica variety, as are all the trees in Jamaica. Those in the vast plantations of Brazil, for example, are mostly robusta variety. Arabica came originally from Ethiopia through the French West Indies to Jamaica.

Coffee growing got a tremendous boost two

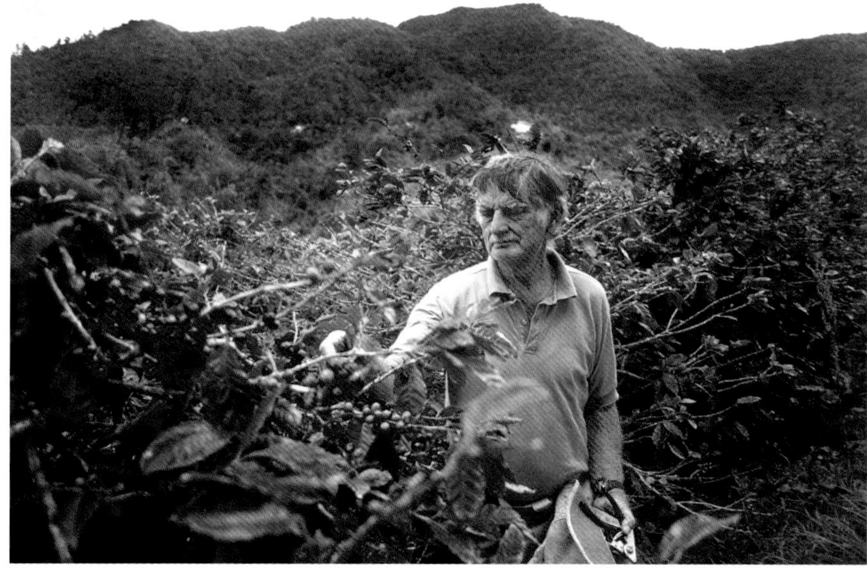

centuries ago after the Haitian revolution forced French planters to flee to Jamaica. By 1814 Jamaica was the biggest coffee producer in the world, with a reputation for quality as well as quantity. But production declined over the next 25 to 30 years, leaving abandoned farms all over the mountains. One result is that only in the higher reaches are any extensive areas of original forest found.

The bright shiny red coffee berries, about the size of cherries, grow on trees which would shoot up to fifty feet if allowed. Alex keeps his at around six feet maximum and prunes them to branch horizontally. This makes picking the berries easier for the local ladies he hires year round to do most of the work on the farm. They pick steadily from November until May, filling their sacks with berries, which are then washed and bad ones separated in the same process. The bad ones called "lights", float. The good ones sink.

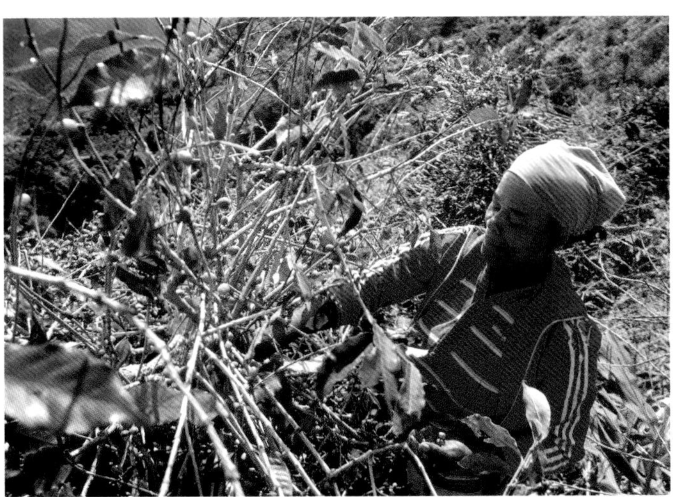

The ladies also pot the seedlings he grows himself from selected berries, use them to replace sick or dying plants, and nurture them to bearing. They apply compost and chicken manure to mature plants. That compost is made up of wood chips made from culled plants and trimmings, as well as the skin, pulp and hulls from the harvest berries. Inside that shiny red skin is pulp and a bean which is usually in two hemispheric segments. A mechanical pulper removes skin and pulp with a knobby rotating drum and spits out the beans.

In addition to cutting the paths and bushing the spaces, the men do limited chemical fertilising, using mainly urea, and a blend of micro-nutrients which occur naturally in the soil, notably zinc. (Depleted zinc is believed to be one of the causes in the catastrophic decline in production in the early 19th century.) They mainly use the more efficient folia method which feeds the tree through a spray on its leaves rather than through the soil. Coffee is about 70 percent self-pollinating; the bees and other insects increase that percentage considerably. The 40 acres not in coffee are full of birds and friendly insects who help control the bugs who make war on the coffee.

The worst of these is the coffee berry borer. An outright kill needs a deadly chemical trade named Endo-sulfan. The workers inspect constantly and pick off and destroy infected berries before another generation is launched to spread the problem. Alex has used Endo-sulfan in the past, but not for two years now. The Coffee Industry Board is trying out a biological control agent. It is a tiny parasitic wasp which uses the borer, the way the borer uses the berry.

After pulping, the beans are washed and fermented for 18 to 24 hours depending on the temperature, then drained and bagged for son David to haul to Kingston for drying on a barbecue. This is not a grill. It is a large flat concrete floor where the wet beans can be spread thinly for the sun to suck them dry. When dry, he puts them in storage to rest for two months, to allow internal flavours to develop. They then go to the Coffee Industry Board for hulling, electronic sorting to get rid of the bad beans, and for final polishing. At that stage, the Board export some of these "green" beans on behalf of the Twymans.

David keeps what the family needs, and holds them in Kingston to avoid the humidity and low temperatures of the mountains, until they are ready for roasting. He takes enough home to Mom for her to roast and dispatch quickly. Dorothy roasts them in a room in the cottage a small batch of 2-3 kilograms (4-6 pounds) at a time. The cups we had were brewed from beans roasted and ground in the hour before we arrived, and sweetened with their honey.

The Twymans dispatch their coffee by couriers around the world. They won the right to do direct single-estate marketing after years negotiating with the Coffee Industry Board. This allows them to control the process from seedling to roasted bean. They are the pioneers and many skeptics have since come around to their way of thinking.

The best Blue Mountain coffee remains the best in the world for a few simple reasons in Alex Twyman's opinion: "Unlike most lesser coffees growing in brighter warmer climates, an almost unique mix in the Blue Mountains of acid shale soils, low temperatures, and little sunshine, slow down the maturation of the coffee. The bean has time to become harder, denser and more flavourful." And he adds: "We do all the wet processing of our Blue Mountain coffee in spring water as fresh and pure as any in the world. It comes from our own spring above the yard."

Kenneth David of the industry bible *The Coffee Review* described Twyman's Blue Mountain coffee as, "The quintessential balanced, classic Caribbean cup." Martha Stewart simply called it: "Virgin coffee!" in a postcard she sent after she visited the Twymans.

Says Alex, "Good coffee is like fine wine. It grows in very similar conditions, and needs even more caring human attention than wine to make it great. Both are equally vulnerable when they reach the table. They both deserve the same discerning care in preparation, so treat them as partners in enhancing a good meal and the fellowship which goes with it, and they will reward you wonderfully."

ORIGINALLY PUBLISHED JUNE 2000

In Search of the Original "Jerkers."

NORMA BENGHIAT

In the last 20 years the widespread proliferation of "jerk stands" throughout the island has put jerk pork, once a scarce commodity, within reach of everyone. But little is known about its origin and importance in the history of the island and in particular the Maroons. For they were the ones who created this magnificent mouth-watering delicacy which was only available to the rest of the population when the Maroons sold it outside of their towns and settlements. The recipes vary from township to township and from person to person but the Boston area in Portland is considered by many to be the best jerking place.

A visit to Colonel C.L.G. Harris of the Eastern Maroons of Moore Town provided the real key to unravelling the mystery and mystique surrounding this famous regional speciality. Cassidy (Dictionary of Jamaican English) says that "jerk" is the English form of a Spanish word of Indian origin, meaning to prepare pork in the manner of the Quichua Indians of South America, and indeed all the Indians, Arawaks and Caribs who inhabited the Caribbean smoked their meats on a raised platform from which the word "barbecue" has come. This method of preserving meat was adopted by the Europeans and the word buccaneer was derived from the French "boucanier" which meant "to cure by smoke". These early buccaneers were in fact not plunderers as they were later to become—but smoked meat to sell to passing ships bound for the Spanish Main.

The Spaniards introduced cattle, hogs, fowls and other animals to Jamaica. So from this time, there was an abundance of wild hogs which were constantly hunted for lard which the Spaniards used heavily in their cooking.

Slaves were introduced from as early as 1517 and when the island capitulated to the British in 1655 most of the Spaniards fled to Cuba and their slaves fled to the interior mountains. The question has always been posed whether they were joined by any remaining Arawaks.

Norma Benghait (LEFT) along with Col. Harris and Judy Allison, honorary Maroon in front of the Nanny Monument at Moore Town.

The freed slaves fed themselves by hunting and planting food crops in the interior mountains. A formidable number of Maroons, fugitives from the Spaniards in the south Clarendon area, were lead by Juan de Bolas who eventually surrendered when promised freedom and pardon for offences. These Maroons were engaged by the English to hunt down runaway slaves. When their leader defected, the rest it appears settled near to towns and did not return to the mountains.

The drive from Kingston to Port Antonio takes you over the Junction Road into St. Mary, then along the coast.

We were guided by Mrs. Judy Allison, honourary Maroon, who guided us through the town and onto the road leading up to Moore Town. In fact it is the same road that one drives up to get to the starting point for rafting. We climbed up the mountain, discovering that around each bend of the road were spectacular vistas of the rugged interior mountains across the beautiful Rio Grande. One of these views we later learnt was Nanny's look-out point.

Nestled in a small valley surrounded by mountains and through which a small tributary of the Rio Grande flows, Moore Town gives the feel of tranquility that is so peculiar to the Jamaican countryside.

The visitors' book showed that many had recently been there, from as far afield as Japan and one wonders if a small museum would not boost the tourist potential of this unique area.

Col. Harris said that lands were given to the Maroons very far apart, some to the east—Portland—and others in Trelawny, to the west. He thinks that this was a deliberate policy to separate the strength of the Maroons. When the second Maroon war was started by the Trelawny Maroons an honourable settlement was reached with Walpole but Governor Balcarres tricked them and their lands were taken away and they were sent to Nova Scotia and then to Sierra Leone. Songs composed on the spur of the moment commemorate the uprisings.

Col. Harris further said that the slaves during the Spanish period were not treated as badly as after and that nothing has come down (to them) to say that the Maroons were runaway slaves from the Spaniards.

The Maroon men would journey very far into the Blue Mountains in those days, almost into St. Andrew.

Stray dogs were sometimes taken in and became the pride of the hunters fleet. What they used mainly in those days was the "junga"—a long spear which would be thrown with unerring skill. "When we went to the bushes", he said, "we would let go the dogs and as they were highly trained they could immediately smell the quarry at a distance. If you had many dogs you would not let go all at once as some were the greatest trackers, others were the catchers so that you would know when to let go this and when to let go that".

They would also set traps. One method used was to tie a rope onto a very flexible branch with a noose on the ground so that when the pig stepped on it, it would fly up catching the pig's feet. Another way was to dig holes along the path the pig had to take, cover it over skillfully with leaves and sticks which would give way under the weight of the pig.

There was once some men who reported that they could not bring back all the pigs cornered, so successful were their methods. Depending on the number of men hunting they could kill from 4-6 pigs.

Col. Harris indicated that the buccaneers used to dry their meat in the sun, but the Maroons preserved theirs by smoking. Baskets of meat were hung over wooden fires in the kitchen to be cured and used when needed. This was not regarded as jerk.

Jerking on the other hand was done over an open fire and the method is exclusively Maroon.

The patta is a platform built with four sticks of the desired height staked into the ground. On this long sticks of pepper elder or fiddle wood are placed. A fire of dry wood would be made under the "patta" and allowed to burn to coals. In the meantime, the meat is prepared - all the bones are taken out and the meat cut several times across, but not the skin.

"The times when the people used to come so much, they would ask for the jerk bones first as these were so tasty", said Col. Harris.

Lowering of the patta is done when the coals are very low by getting four pieces of string and tying one each to the four sides of the patta and the four cross pieces and so it is lowered. They also roasted yam foots in the charcoals. These were the nicest yams, so floury, and the drippings from the fat on them made them delicious when done. The yams were scraped when done and put back on the coals and they were just as if baked.

"Jerking was just a part of life in Moore Town, done mainly on a Friday for sale on Saturday. Then too if somebody was having a "set up" or any kind of festivities, someone would be sure to be there to sell jerk."

Col. Harris reminisced about the making of sausage. "They make the sausage when they jerk and it is more expensive than the jerk. You get a piece of the large intestine and wash it properly. The women wash it and turn it over using a stick so that the inside can be properly cleaned. They get some of the meat and chop it up, and season it with escallion, thyme, pepper and every sort of condiment. Beef thyme was also used to season the jerk and the escallion and thyme but the basic condiments were salt and pepper and the pimento when they could get it. They used to use another fragrant bush which I have forgotten the name of and perhaps, is a secret and should not be told. They used it when it was not the wild hog. The meat of the latter was red and this bush would give the domestic pig the same red colour."

Although some people use the blood to mix with the seasonings for the jerk the Maroons never used it. It was given to the dogs. The seasoning was an art in itself said Col. Harris. "You get the coarse salt and grind it fine in the mortar and to get it finer they would fill a bottle of water and grind it finer. Then you add bird pepper and Scotch Bonnet peppers and beat it together like you are mixing cement and sand—you have to know the right proportions and there were people noted for making this resulting paste called "coir". People would eat this paste like a condiment. You rub this into the flesh already prepared. They would use wild cinnamon or bitter wood also and if they got pimento they would use this also. The skin part was not cut at all, but left whole. The meat was put on the patta skin down to start with then at about half way it was turned over.

"But before turning it over a piece of fat is used to rub the meat side—this is to ensure that the meat remains free of burns and is succulent and brown, with no cracks, for the man who jerks and has cracks in his meat is considered a novice".

The Maroons also had another way of cooking pork called "roasin". This was done not exclusively, but for most weddings.

It was first parboiled, drawn and stuffed with white yams mashed and well seasoned. A guava or lime was put in its mouth and roasted on a spit. Colonel Harris said that these white yams could be kept for a long time and they were often kept under one's four-poster bed.

The intetehs were specially woven carriers for the jerk pork, which the Maroons often sold at the market.

These are intricately plaitted palms made into containers to carry the jerk—with the bottom end wider than the top and flatish so that the meat can be pushed in, like a pocket.

The second way of carrying the pork is to use what is called the cabbage skin or the canda. This is the sheathing part of the mountain cabbage palm. The heart of the thatch is also eaten and this is one of the reasons to which we ascribe the strength of the Maroons in those days, also the eating of the "cacoon"—a dark brown nut, the kernel of which is eaten.

The front of the palm falls off when it reaches a certain age. It is pressed with weights or stones and then sewn with vines—this makes an instant inteteh whereas the other has to be made.

Henry Gosse also leaves us with a description of a Maroon jerk seller in his writings, 1851.

"He was generally seen in the towns armed with a fowling piece and cutlass, and belts that suspended on one side, a large plaited bag known as a cuttacoo, and on the other, a calabash, guarded with a netted covering, in which he carried his supply of water. On his back braced round his shoulders, and suspended by a bandage over the forehead, was generally seen the wicker cradle that held enclosed a side of jerked hog, which he sold passing along, in measured slice to ready customers, as an especial delicacy for the breakfast table".

Colonel Harris indicated that the proliferation of jerk stands everywhere started when many Maroons began to live outside the settlements. Boston jerk pork is reputed to be the best in the island. And it is from this first stand that jerking really became known to many non-Maroon Jamaicans. But even before this, and it continues to this day, various settlements in Portland and Boston, sell their jerk pork at the Port Antonio Market. This is where it was first sold outside of the Maroon settlements.

A visit to Boston proved quite successful as there was a large amount of jerking taking place. We visited the "Stanley Duncan Jerk Pork Stand" and spoke to Carlton Allen, Everton Williams (Skinny) and Mike Kensington.

They said that they knew that jerk pork was a Maroon speciality but that they had learnt the art of preparing it—and their jerk pork was considered to be the best!

Here is their recipe for the seasoning:

2 handfuls of pimento (allspice) berries.

2 lbs. hot pepper (Scotch Bonnet and birdpepper)

1/2 lb. ginger

1 oz. wild cinnamon

1/4 lb. thyme

1/4 lb. black pepper

1-1/2 lbs. salt.

The Maroons jerked pork because that was what was available to them but we have seen the method and seasoning used also to prepare chicken and fish. The drum chicken, a version of jerking has now become very popular.

However the quality and art of jerking does vary considerably and some, Colonel Harris would surely agree, are only novices at it.

ORIGINALLY PUBLISHED JUNE 1988

Jerk

HELEN WILLINSKY

The same method of jerking applies today as it did in the seventeenth century. There are jerk huts everywhere in every town, every village, in every city in Jamaica. As people circle the huts the cooks bellow out "Which jerk yuh wan try...taste mine!" Although jerk seasoning was traditionally made into thick pastes, people now find liquid marinades easier to work with. Today jerk chicken has become more popular than the original jerk pork. Anywhere in the world where there is an enclave of Jamaicans, New York, London, Miami along with dominoes, and Red Stripe, you will find jerk chicken!

To me, Jamaican jerk cooking is the perfect reflection of the island lifestyle—spicy, sweet, charismatic, and hot. But all these concoctions can be made at home so that you can come up with your own version of jerk. So you see, you don't have to go to a Jamaican jerk hut to enjoy it. You can make it in your own kitchen. Here are some of my recipes for you to enjoy with your friends and family long after you have left Jamaica.

Jerk Marinade

1 onion, finely chopped
1/2 cup finely chopped escallion
2 teaspoons fresh thyme leaves
1 teaspoon salt
2 teaspoons sugar
1 teaspoon ground Jamaican pimento (allspice)
1/2 teaspoon ground nutmeg
1/2 teaspoon ground cinnamon
1 hot pepper, finely ground
1 teaspoon ground black pepper
3 tablespoons soy sauce
1 tablespoon cooking oil
1 tablespoon cider or white vinegar

Some people find marinade more convenient to use than spice pastes. This marinade is more liquid than a paste, but not as liquid as most marinades. The flavour of the marinade may strike you as a little harsh when you first mix it, but I assure you, the flavours will all blend and mellow as the meat cooks. To increase the heat of this rather mild marinade, add hot pepper sauce. If you want less heat, remove the seeds and membranes containing the seeds from the pepper before grinding them.

Mix together all the ingredients. A food processor fitted with steel blade is ideal for chopping and combining. This is an excellent marinade for chicken, beef, or pork. Store leftover marinade in the refrigerator in a tightly closed jar for about 1 month.

Yield: About 1-1/2 cups.

Jerk Rub

1 onion, finely chopped
1/2 cup finely chopped escallion
2 teaspoons fresh thyme leaves
2 teaspoons salt
1 teaspoon ground Jamaican pimento (allspice)
1/2 teaspoon ground cinnamon
4 to 6 hot peppers, finely ground
1 teaspoon ground black pepper

Pastes made of spices, herbs, and onions are the authentic jerk flavouring method. You rub the paste into the uncooked meat to add flavour. This is a medium-hot paste; it can be made hotter with the addition of more hot peppers or hot pepper sauce. If you want less heat, remove the seeds and membranes containing the seeds from the peppers before grinding them. Scotch Bonnet or habanero peppers are preferred, but you can substitute the milder, more readily available jalapeno or serano peppers.

Mix together all the ingredients to make a paste. A food processor fitted with a steel blade is ideal for this. Store leftovers in the refrigerator in a tightly closed jar for about a month.

Yield: About 1 cup.

Jamaican Jerk Barbecued Ribs

1 cup jerk marinade
1 tablespoon sugar
2 tablespoons red wine vinegar
4 pounds pork spareribs
About 1-1/2 cups barbecue sauce

In this recipe, I combine the jerk flavours with barbecue sauce. The sauce, added during the final 15 minutes of cooking adds a delicious crust to the succulent ribs. Any store-bought barbecue sauce will do.

Combine the jerk marinade, sugar, and vinegar. Add the ribs and turn to coat thoroughly. Marinate in the refrigerator for at least 4 hours.

Prepare a fire in the grill. When the coals have burned down, rake the coals to the sides. Set a drip pan in the centre of the grill and arrange the coals around it to provide indirect heat. Place the ribs on the grill over the drip pan, and cook for 1-1/2 hours, turning and brushing frequently with the marinade. Brush the ribs with the barbecue sauce during the last 15 minutes of cooking. Serve with rice and peas and a salad. Add lots of brightly coloured napkins, a Jamaican Red Stripe beer, and reggae music.

Yield: 4 servings.

David's Jerk Chicken

1/2 cup store-bought homemade Jerk Rub
1 onion, finely chopped
1 fresh hot pepper or 2 tablespoons hot pepper sauce
1 sprig fresh thyme, finely chopped
2 escallions, finely chopped
1 chicken
cut into serving pieces.

David's Jerk Chicken is a very special concoction. He starts with a prepared jerk sauce, which one can buy at a supermarket. Then he adds his own ingredients to make it exactly as he wants it: a little more chopped green onion, some thyme, more hot pepper. Finally, he sniffs and says,"Aha! This is it." He knows he has the right mix just by smelling the spices and seeing the consistency he likes. He rubs his chicken with spice mix and lets it marinate for 4 hours before putting it on his grill, which burns a combination of coals and pimento wood. Mix together the jerk seasoning, onion, hot pepper sauce, thyme, and scallions. Rub the chicken well with jerk paste. Allow to marinate for at least 4 hours in the refrigerator.

Prepare a fire in the grill using a combination of coals and pimento wood. If you don't have pimento wood, substitute apple wood or hickory, or build a fire with just charcoal. Place the chicken on the grill over white hot coals. Jerk (cook) over very slow fire for about 1 to 1-1/2 hours, turning every 10 minutes or so. The chicken takes on a very dark colour when done. David's Jerk Chicken is cooked over an open fire with the grill at a height of about 1-1/2 feet above the fire. At no point is the grill closed.

Serves 6.

ORIGINALLY PUBLISHED APRIL 1998

Drum Chicken

CHERRY BRADY

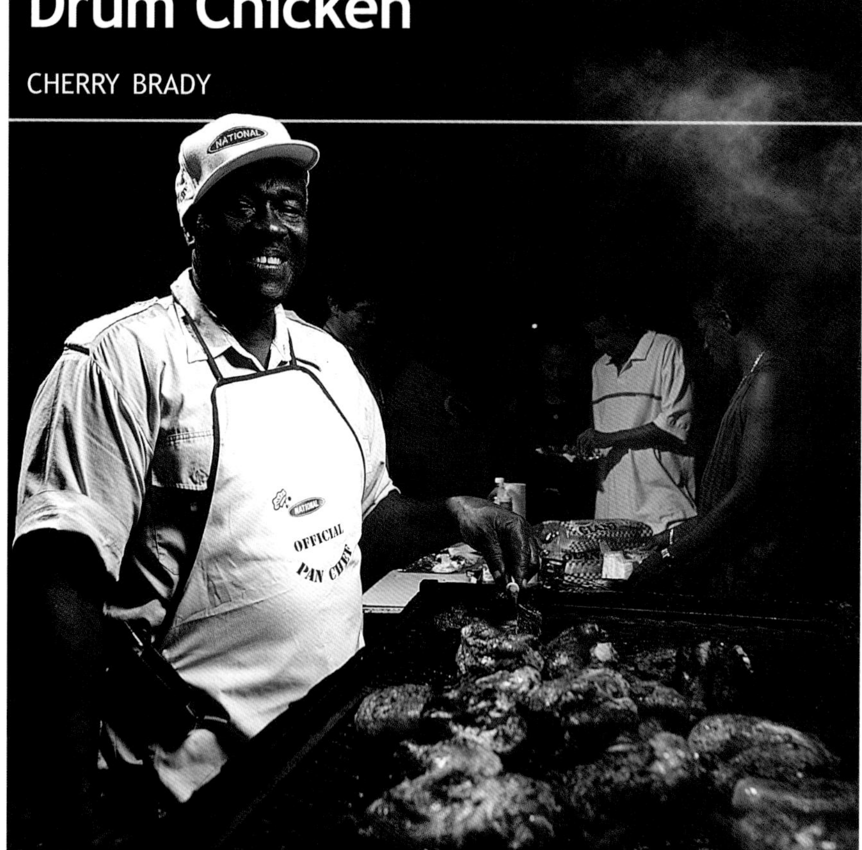

If Colonel Sanders had tasted "**Drum Chicken,**" Kingston Jamaica, not Kentucky, would have been the centre of the instant chicken dinner empire.

So, what is "drum chicken"? Strangely enough, it has its origins in "jerked pork" (not at all related to the beef jerky popular in the western regions of the United States).

Jerked pork had its own beginnings in the eastern parish of Portland, Jamaica, where wild boar once roamed the tropical rain forests of the Blue Mountain range.

The Maroons were descendants of the men and women who escaped slavery when the British captured the island from the Spanish one day in 1655. They were later joined by escapees from the British plantations (but that is another story all in itself). They developed the technique of "jerking".

The wild boar would be cut into manageable strips, seasoned heavily with spices and hot peppers (a wonderful preservative in the tropical heat) and slowly cooked over coals between strips of green wood from the pimento (allspice) tree. The result was a spicy, slightly smoke-scented delicacy which came to be known as "jerked pork."

Eventually, the long-tusked wild boar got virtually "jerked" out of existence, to be replaced by the lowly domestic pig.

Portland's "Jerked Pork" was universally recognised as a culinary triumph—best consumed with a hunk of hard-dough bread and an ice-cold Red Stripe beer.

As regional dishes have a way of doing, jerked pork spread to the capital city, Kingston.

One account has it that an enterprising Portlander set up his jerk pit adjacent to one of Kingston's popular watering holes, the Revolution Lounge. Whether the jerked pork or the Revolution Lounge became the greater attraction is best left unsaid. Later, the master jerker offered "jerked chicken" as a secondary product. Instant success!

And now, jerked pork and jerked chicken pits are as ubiquitous in Jamaica as souvlaki stands in Greece. But the jerk pit has major disadvantages. It needs a permanent spot and enormous quantities of green pimento wood - which wasn't quite all right for our pimento exporting industry or the environment.

Some say it was a man named Manley (not the leader of the opposition) who first combined the portable features of the barbecue with the seasonings of the jerk and invented the off-spring—DRUM CHICKEN.

Scores of drum chicken sellers set up business along a major arterial road, the Red Hills Road, the nightclub strip of Kingston. Initially, they did battle with the public health inspectors who were dutifully ensuring that the public got a healthy, wholesome product. Some of the drum chicken entrepreneurs, no doubt having heard of the philosophy of "getting Government off the backs of private enterprise", fought back—even to the point of an inspector being physically attacked by a "Drummer" wielding a hot drummed chicken.

Public health officials and consumer vigilance have kept drum chicken an acceptably hygienic product, and now even the most persnickety will snack on drum chicken.

The drum chicken business has developed beyond the point of "one man with his drum on his back."

At dusk (drum chicken is never available during the day) a youngster appears with the drum and a bag of coals. He gets the fire going. Half an hour later, the chef arrives (sometimes' even attired in chef's hat and apron). The first batch of chicken which has been marinated for an entire day in a seasoning mix of salt, pepper, pimento and escallions is laid on the grill. Then the drum, puffing smoke like a steam engine as the coal-man dashes water over the flaming coals to maintain an even temperature, advertises the readiness of the first batch.

Only then does the "boss" arrive. He is in charge of cash collections.

The first car soon pulls up, "Give me half-a-chicken deh nuh Bossy!" (Translation: "Please may I have a helping of one half of a chicken, Sir.")

Others will argue this point vigorously, but for sheer style, personality and a darned good "drum" chicken, I rate Jambo's International Chicken Snacks (on the Red Hills Road) and Hopeton who sells his "Drum" outside Northside Plaza on Old Hope Road.

Some others ruin their "Drum" by slathering ketchup over a perfectly good "drum."

And also on the Red Hills Road, while you may be waiting for your drum chicken to have its final sizzle, have a cup of soup from "Boo the Fish Man" who sells fried fish and bammy right next to Jambo's International.

ORIGINALLY PUBLISHED JULY 1983

Sweets for My Sweet

ENID DONALDSON

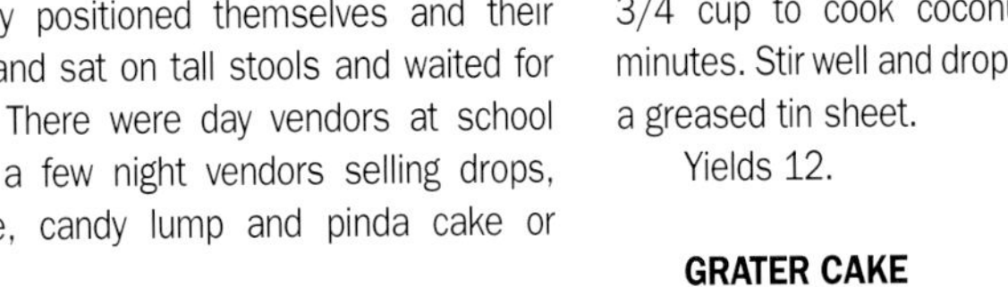

Most palates have a passion for sweet treats and happily, here in Jamaica we have some wonderfully innovative ways to feed that passion. A mention of fun names like "Bustamante Backbone," "Crepe Sole," "Gizzada" or "Pinch-me-round," "Bulla," "Coconut Drops" and "Grater Cake" have many of us thinking of our dear grandma's warm, aromatic kitchens and send us packing to the nearest supermarket to find mass market versions of these traditional Jamaican sweet treats.

As small as the island is, sweet treats tend to be known by different names in different areas. In rural districts the tendency is to name the treat after individuals, perhaps because the streets were neither named nor houses numbered, so it was easier finding Miss Emma to sample her drops or Mass Johnny for his bullas.

Recipes were passed on by word of mouth so whereas some exactness got lost in the exchange, others gained because of the informality of the medium. Ovens in the country were nearly all made of wood and lined with metal. More sturdy ones were constructed with red bricks, to give a more even heat. The ever-ready Caledonia Dover stove known as an American stove helped to keep the home stocked with sweet treats. At nights ripe bananas rested overnight in the Caledonia stove to capitalize on the residual heat which was just enough to shrink the bananas for making banana figs.

Many of our sweet treats use coconut as a base, among them gizzada or pinch-me-round, and busta backbone, coconut chips, coconut toast and a quick and easy pastry shell. Most of these treats were not expensive to make because the ingredients were home grown.

Farmers with a sugar mill would puncture a dry coconut at the two "eyes" at the top, wash it well and allow the coconut to fill up with boiling "new sugar," as the cane juice boils to form a sugar head. This "new sugar" or "wet sugar" is made from raw cane juice and contains all the rich nutrients from the cane. It is supposed to be good for nervous conditions.

In the old days, there were vendors who sold these treats, but they did not walk with their wares. They positioned themselves and their candy box and sat on tall stools and waited for the traffic. There were day vendors at school gates and a few night vendors selling drops, grater cake, candy lump and pinda cake or wangla.

Bullas have as many recipes as cakes, and it is said if you are making a cake and it falls for whatever reason or let's say it gets a bit doughy it is called a bulla. An insult in Jamaica is also called a bulla. This sweet cake is one of the only sweets Jamaicans eat with avocado.

Crepe sole is like a bulla with extra soda. It looked like the rubber sole of the two shilling and sixpence "puss shoes," a soft low-cut version of today's sneakers. Busta Backbone, a dark, tough sweet is made from grated coconut and wet sugar. The late Sir Alexander Bustamante, one of our National Heroes and Jamaica's first prime minister, was known for his firmness of character hence the name of the sweet. Busta entered the trade at a farthing each (four for one penny wrapped in skimpy grease proof paper and very chewy). (How much more do you expect for a farthing?) There is a Jamaican saying "nothing for nothing and very little for shilling" but the price of Busta made it very popular.

Here are the recipes for three classic Jamaican sweet treats.

COCONUT DROPS

2 cups diced coconut
1 tsp powdered ginger or 1 tsp grated root
1 tsp vanilla
1 lb brown sugar
1 pinch salt

Combine all ingredients adding about 1/2 to 3/4 cup to cook coconut. Boil about 20-30 minutes. Stir well and drop by spoonfuls into onto a greased tin sheet.

Yields 12.

GRATER CAKE

To make with granulated sugar use:
2 cups grated coconut
3 cups granulated sugar
1/2 cup water
To make with brown sugar use:
2 cups grated coconut
1 lb brown sugar
1/3 cup water
Also: 1/2 teaspoon ginger and a pinch of salt

Combine all ingredients in a thick saucepan, boil until coconut is cooked and the liquid dries up and the mixture holds together. Remove from heat and beat with wooden spoon two to three minutes. Drop onto a greased tray or mixture can be poured into a square dish 8 x 8 x 2 and pressed with the back of a spoon. Brown sugar can be shaped into balls while still hot and allowed to cool. If poured into square dish, allow to cool before cutting into squares.

GIZZADA

Pastry:
2 cups flour
1/2 tsp salt
2-1/2 oz butter or margarine
1-1/2 oz shortening
1/4 cup iced water

Sift flour and salt. Add butter and shortening, and cut in flour. Pour in ice water a little at a time and make a dry dough. Shape in a ball and wrap in wax paper or plastic and place in refrigerator (not in the freezer) for 30 minutes. Divide pastry in eight pieces, roll each piece into a ball. Use a rolling pin to make a circle three inches by 1/4 inch thick. Pinch edges to form a ridge to hold in coconut and sugar mixture. Put on greased tin sheets and partly bake shells.

Filling: Mix coconut, sugar, nutmeg and water, cook over a low flame for about 20 minutes. Add butter. Fill shells and bake a further 15 to 20 minutes. Yields eight.

ORIGINALLY PUBLISHED JANUARY 1996

Fiona MG'97

From the Caribbean Sea

BARBARA NELSON

Jamaica's coastal waters teem with an abundance of colourful, edible fish. Any fishvendor's cart or tray can reveal rainbow colours of green parrot-fish, yellow hagfish, blue turbot, rosy pink goat-fish and pink and silver snapper fish.

Fish is a popular dish in Jamaica and perhaps because of the innate culinary ability and creativity of our cooks, it is prepared in a variety of ways. It may be steamed, fried, escoveitched (from the Spanish word escabeche meaning, pickle) roasted, baked or cooked down into a creamy 'fish tea'. Whichever way it is done, Jamaica-style fish is something to write home about.

Many Jamaicans make a kind of ritual of drinking a bowl or two of fish tea every Friday night or on Saturday. A ritual. usually practised by imbibers at thousands of taverns across the country. Don't be misled by the name, however, fish tea is a broth, or clear soup served steaming hot. It is made preferably with doctor fish, welchman or turbot, (called turbit locally) highly seasoned with herbs—especially thyme and escallion, with hot 'country' or Scotch Bonnet pepper and pimento seeds. A few vegetables: chocho and Irish potato, diced carrots perhaps, add to the body of the soup, but the real goodness comes from the type of fish used.

Come Friday night fish tea vendors can be seen at certain street corners, in front of some bars and adjacent to bus stops selling paper cups of steaming hot fish tea. It warms the stomach and 'makes the body feel strong'.

Roast fish is another Friday night experience. The fish is prepared in a really rustic fashion. Turbot, a thick-skinned species, is the ideal kind for roasting. The fish is cleaned, seasoned and stuffed with herbs, wrapped in heavy aluminium foil and roasted over hot coals. Although the turbot is not what one would consider an attractive fish, it has a firm flesh and is delicious when roasted.

Snapper, goat, king and jack have been part of the Jamaican diet for always. The latter two are usually sold in slices or steaks. With the rising cost of food and fish in particular, more Jamaicans now opt for what was traditionally considered 'trash fish', the cheapest of the catch. Today however, many of these like grunt and pargie are finding their way to the frying pan!

Snapper is beautiful when served steamed. It must be cleaned, dusted with salt and pepper and steamed in butter or margarine with a tablespoon of water and garnished with escallion, pepper, small tomatoes, thin strips of carrots and chocho. Another method of preparing steamed fish is to stuff the fish with seasoned breadcrumbs, Irish potato, cornmeal or croutons. The steamed fish should be served piping hot.

A really savoury fish dish in Jamaica is escoveitched fish. Kingfish and jack are the ideal ones for this purpose, but other fish are often used. The fish is seasoned and fried in very hot oil, then placed in a container to absorb the juice and flavour of pickled onions, pimento grains and hot Scotch Bonnet pepper. Watch out this can be hot, but don't let that deter you —it is a delicious, finger lickin' dish.

We could not think about fish and not mention the marriage of 'fish and bammy' a very traditional and soon to become national dish.

Fried fish and bammy is synonymous with Old Harbour, Port Royal and a few other spots on our south coast. Medium sized fish and small sprats are usually used. Sprinkled with salt and pepper, fried in hot oil and served with pickles these fish are eaten with bammy—a small flat cassava cake. It's close to addictive. Once you eat this dish, you'll have to come back for more.

A variation on this is 'fish and festival', more readily found on the white sand beaches of Hellshire, across the harbour from Kingston. The fish is prepared in like manner; the festival is flour-cornmeal cake, an elongated roll, deep-fried golden brown in the same oil in which the fish was just done.

From parish to parish, community to community, there are different ways of doing fish. Many methods are inherited and are as old as Jamaicans can remember. Most of these appetising dishes, whatever the recipe, depend a great deal on the high-flavoured Jamaican spices which are now attracting international attention.

ORIGINALLY PUBLISHED AUGUST 1985

OLD HARBOUR FISH TEA

To the uninitiated, a fish tea would seem to be a very strange tea indeed! However, in Jamaica the word "tea" connotes not only the brew from the tea plant but brews from other plants as well. So you will find "mint tea" "cocoa tea" (chocolate) and the many other "bush teas."

Unlike the traditional soups that are one-pot meals and very thick in consistency, the fish tea is thinner and usually served in a cup.

This fish tea recipe was given to me by a fish vendor in the Old Harbour fish market.

INGREDIENTS

8 cups (2 litres) water
4 okras, sliced
2 carrots, sliced
3 Irish potatoes, diced
1/2 cho cho (chayote), diced
1/2 lb pumpkin, diced
2 lbs (1 kg) fish, (shad, maccaback, doctor), scaled and washed
salt and pepper
2 stalks escallion, chopped
sprig of thyme
6 pimento berries
hot pepper

METHOD

In a large pot, pour the water and add all the vegetables cut up or diced. Bring to the boil and cook until all the vegetables are soft. You can either leave them as they are or mash them with a fork. Add salt and pepper to your taste.

Lastly, add the scaled and washed fish, either whole or sliced. Bring to the boil and cook for 5 to 10 minutes. Serve immediately.

Serves 4.

ORIGINALLY PUBLISHED AUGUST 1995

Out to Lunch

ROSEMARY PARKINSON

Being asked to interview Norma Shirley is a trip! Every single time.

This Grande Dame of Caribbean cuisine, 'swathed' in bright colours, head tied with twisted trademark bandana, does not just move around her restaurant—she zooms!

I thought I had run a mile and been to the theatre six times by the time I left Norma's On The Terrace. In and out of the kitchen, checking every table, answering the telephone, ordering wines, "the flowers on that table need changing," discussing the menu for a luncheon, giving instructions to staff, sitting for a moment to sip a glass of water and in the same breath organizing a wedding for three hundred, a dinner for fifty, an embassy gathering of forty—all for the same night!

With an "Excuse me Rosie" into the kitchen she runs. A waiter is stopped in his tracks, "Honey, nothing leaves my kitchen looking like that—no sah! How long have you worked for me? Come along, come along. Do your best, and by the way fix you collar. How you looking so tired this morning—you don't sleep at night?? The people waiting for food." She whizzes past me. "Rosie, you alright dahling? How about a little something to eat? A glass of wine?" Suddenly she spots a diner, "Hello precious, welcome my lovely... come for lunch my sweets? How's the pickney? Where you got that ugly tie from? No! no! I know you have lovely ties at home, go back and start again.... Rosie I made some johnny cakes yesterday — took them up a notch, added a little cheese. We have to go to Coronation Market and let Miss Janet cook us some food—you must go Vegas and see Delius' restaurant..." she pauses a moment and smiles that beaming broad smile, a captivating smile that only Norma has. Her eyes light up and begin to do a waltz. Finally she calms and speaks like only a totally unrepentant proud Caribbean mother can. No one would dare interrupt her now. Delius her one and only son has front, back and centre stage.

Delius Shirley and Cindy Hutson have just opened Ortanique (restaurant) in Las Vegas and by the end of December, Ortanique will also be in Washington—Miami's Ortanique is already an icon for exquisite Caribbean fare. The pride of her son's achievements suddenly becomes the focus of her interview. Every detail of the décor, the menu, the reviews they have received, the success of their establishment backed by Black Entertainment Television (now Viacom) mogul Bob Johnson, the first African American man to be on 'America's Richest List'. She finishes with "Delius says he won't retire me because I wouldn't know what to do with myself. All that time on my hands....Okay so take the photo Rosie. I thought we had finished this interview. What taking so long? I have twenty people coming here any minute....do your best...." And there you sit. Totally in awe, laughing merrily while you savour every mouthful of the absolutely scrumptious Panko Shrimps that have been put before you.

Norma Shirley on the terrace.

This is truly Norma Shirley. Her striking vivaciousness is infectious. When you leave her presence you want to go straight to a market, buy everything there is Jamaican and go home and produce wondrous 'tings'! You want to kiss the soil of the island that made this woman. Mostly you cannot wait to see her again. And as for that food. Well honey there's nothing like it this side of the galaxy!

Norma's On The Terrace nestled at the back of the 19th Century Devon House ('Kingston's Central Park' according to

RED PEPPER BISQUE

INGREDIENTS

8 large red peppers deseeded and cut in large chunks
1 large onion chopped
4oz. butter
2–3 generous sprigs of thyme
1–2 sprigs of parsley
2–3 tablespoon sherry
6 cups vegetable or chicken broth
Salt and pepper to taste

METHOD

In a large saucepan melt butter over medium fire, do not burn. Add onion, thyme and parsley, Saute until onion is transparent then add peppers, vegetable broth. Bring to the boil, cover and simmer for about one hour. Cool red pepper mixture. Blend or process in food processor. Strain through a fine sieve. Season to taste with salt and pepper, add 2-3 tablespoons sherry. Heat to serve in individual soup bowls garnished with chopped parsley or sour cream.

Serves 6-8

CARIBBEAN GARDEN SALAD

INGREDIENTS

4 large cucumbers peeled; using a peeler make ribbons of the cucumber, discarding the seeds
1 large avocado cut in slices
1 large papaya in slices
1 tin heart of palm cut in chunks or julienne
2–3 large tomatoes cut in slices approximately 2–3 slices per person
8 lettuce leaves
1 large mango, julienned
1/2 lb feta cheese

METHOD

Toss all ingredients except feta together. Pipe in individual lettuce leaves. Drizzle vinaigrette over salad and top with crumbled feta cheese.

Serves 6-8

Norma) is a truly magnificent setting for what has to be one of Jamaica's most exquisite restaurants. The décor is elegant Caribbean. The tables set with magnificent style and tropical flair. Dainty flowers, pale green or yellow linen cloths, fresh white napkins, brilliant crockery, greenery everywhere. The larger than life photographs of flowering Jamaican trees by Carlysle Hudson picking up the lights and hues of the garden and courtyard. Add to this stage the greatest players (the waiters choreographed to perfection by 'Miss Shirley') and the theatre opens and the play unfolds. Just sit back and enjoy the show!

Norma Shirley is passionate about food. All good food. But more than any other, she is passionate about Jamaican food. A 'nomad' for almost twenty years in countries within Europe, Asia, the Middle East and America, she certainly left her mark as a restaurateur, caterer, food stylist (worked for famous photographers such as Hiro and Jean Pagliusio), television presenter (*Great Chefs of The World*—on the Discovery Channel) and now has finally come 'home.' Her intention—to prove to the world that Jamaica can be counted as a gourmet destination and to give her Jamaicans a chance to savour the bounty of their country in the way it deserves. The winner of *The Jamaica Observer* newspaper's Table Top Food Awards for 2001, her representing Jamaica at the 'Cuisines of the Sun' held at the Mauna Lani Bay Hotel in Hawaii, being a guest chef at the James Beard Foundation, New York, a feature speaker at the New York City American Institute for Wine and Food's NAFST 1997, her numerous interviews in top international magazines and now her recent appointment to the newly-constituted Caribbean Culinary Federation (CCF) Blue Ribbon Board, all attest to the obvious. This amazing daughter of Jamaica is certainly achieving her goals.

Norma Shirley will soon be opening Norma's at SeaSplash, Negril and is already looking around for other new locations. The interview with me ends in her kitchen where she stops a young trainee and says: "Young man, when you handle the food in my kitchen, I want you to handle it with love—to the last little bean. Just do yourself a favour, and handle it with love." Does this not tell the whole story?

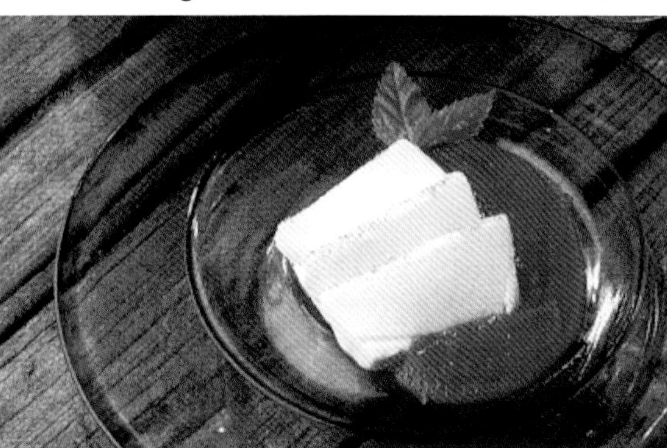

Eating at Norma's On The Terrace is a must but for those of you who most unfortunately have to live 'in foreign, overseas and abroad' places, Norma advises "try these recipes at home and surprise yourself!"

ORIGINALLY PUBLISHED FEBRUARY 2002

PANKO SHRIMP IN PAPAYA BOAT

INGREDIENTS

2 lbs. shrimp
(approximately six per person)
Japanese bread crumbs
(found in Jamaica at JoJo's)
2 eggs – beaten
Salt & pepper to taste
1 onion
1 clove of garlic
2 limes – juiced
Corn oil
3 papaya cut in quarters
(deseeded and peeled)

METHOD

Peel, de-vein shrimp. Remove heads. Wash with lime. Rinse and pat dry. Season shrimp with blended onion and garlic, salt and pepper to taste. Refrigerate covered for about 1 hour.

Dip shrimp one at a time into egg mixture. Place shrimp in Panko (bread crumbs) and repeat. Do this with each shrimp. Place shrimp covered into refrigerator.

Heat a pot with corn oil deep enough for frying. Place shrimps, 12 at a time in deep fat basket. Fry until golden brown.

Place mixed greens on six luncheon plates. Top with halved papaya shells. Fill with six shrimp each. Serve with avocado slices and or citrus segments. Drizzle lettuce with a light vinaigrette and garnish with a sprig of parsley and half of a lime.

Serves 6

TAMARIND MOUSSE

INGREDIENTS

2 cups thick tamarind juice
1 cup 1/2 and 1/2 or heavy cream
1/2 cup condensed milk
lime juice
2 tablespoon white rum
2 packet (envelopes) gelatin dissolved in 1/2 cup warm water freshly ground nutmeg

METHOD

Blend all ingredients. Check for degree of sweetness. To serve, strain in a bowl or individually glasses top with grated nutmeg. Cover and chill. Serve with wild raspberry coulis and any other fruit coulis and mint leaves.

Serves 8

The Real Taste of Jamaica

KEN MAXWELL

Jamaica is full of good food and not all of it is by any means found in hotels and restaurants. Some of the best is in the most unlikely-looking accommodation, little shops and small restaurants by the side of some country road, or in the back streets of the smaller towns. Here you will find the local people, often farmers who stop for a meal and a drink to or from their fields. In the townships, the restaurants are used by small businessmen, merchants, lawyers, and shopkeepers who have a taste for well-cooked Jamaican food.

For the visitor who is willing to try anything once, these roadside eating places offer an opportunity not only to eat food he or she is unlikely to find anywhere else, but also to get to know Jamaicans in their own setting and find out what sort of people we really are. Although some of these eating places look shabby, the truth is that the food is very well cooked and perfectly safe to eat. I have yet to find anyone who was seriously affected as a result of eating it. The one exception I would make to this is the ubiquitous Jamaican patty, which can be delicious though peppery. The pepper can conceal a multitude of sins, and it is unwise to make use of them unless some Jamaican friend recommends a particular shop from personal knowledge.

Probably the safest way to eat if you are on a trip through the countryside and want to stop for a snack or a meal, is to stick to fruit, most of which is hygienically packed by the Almighty. Coconuts, bananas, oranges, pineapples, sweetsops, are all safe to eat off any stall, or fresh from the tree; such fruit as otaheite apples, rose apples, or anything where the skin has to be eaten as well, are best left alone if you are apprehensive about germs or stomach upsets. In any case, it will do most of us no harm to have a meal entirely of fruit and there is such a variety that at any season there is always a wide choice.

In the winter months, oranges and tangerines are at their best and these abound in the parishes of Manchester, Clarendon and St. Ann. Naseberries, which are the fruit of the tree from which chewing gum is made, are often always available along the roads of St. Thomas. A few out-of-season pineapples are to be seen, though here it is wise to buy the conical-shaped variety, Sugar Loaf or Ripley, and avoid small, round fat pineapples which, while they can be eaten quite safely, have nothing of the flavour and can be rough on the plate. Bananas, of course are always bearing, and here it is wisest to choose the dark yellow ones. If you want to be Jamaican, pick one that has a few freckles on it. That is really ripe and has a totally different flavour from the ones that are brightly, unmarked yellow.

The other motto when eating outside of the established hotels and restaurants is, always ask for soup. My own heavily-biased opinion is that the best soup in the world is made in Jamaica, and of them all, the congo (pronounced gungo locally) and the red peas, make the best. You are likely to get a soup that is almost solid, with the pease still in it, and also yam, coco, dumplings that stick in your ribs and anything else that comes to hand, including meat. They are highly flavoured, not only with pepper, but with thyme, escallion, salt and other condiments. They are usually served in to your plate or cup, straight off the stove, so treat them with respect. With a bowl of soup, if you need anything else, a slice or two of hard-dough bread is excellent and tends to sooth the digestive tract after, or with the soup. The hard-dough bread is solid, and a meal of a bowl of soup and one or two slices will certainly keep you going until dinnertime.

So much for the cautions or the traditional, anxious only to stave off the pangs of hunger, or for a chance to talk to some country people. This, by the way, is a good idea, since a full stomach makes friends easily. For those who feel more adventurous, there are other Jamaican dishes which are expertly cooked at almost every little cold supper shop and certainly in every home, however, humble. My favourites are ox-tail and beans, and stewed peas. The difference lies in the meat, for both are made with the red pea, which is in fact a bean, but if you ask for red beans, no one will know what you're talking about. These are examples of the one-pot meals that appeal to us so much, because they are so economical and save fuel and the washing of pots. Both will certainly contain dumplings, so their smaller cousins, spinners, which are not the light fluffy creations of temperate lands, but good, solid mouth-stopping things, made of a mixture of flour, cornmeal and water. The more prosperous the times, the less water, the stiffer the dumplings, hence the old Jamaican saying for hard times as being when "water more than flour"—a thin, characterless dumpling.

Our best known national dish, saltfish and ackee, is now hard to get, for the fish is a special type of highly salted cod that is scarcely made in the Maritime Provinces any more, and which, in any event is no longer the source of low-cost protein that it once was. Saltfish now costs more than some meat and although ackees are still plentiful, they do not bear all year round. However, if you have the chance of sampling saltfish and ackee, try it. The ackee looks, when cooked, very much like scrambled eggs, with a nutty flavour of its own. It is one of the fruit trees brought here by Captain Bligh whose first voyage, in the Bounty, was short-circuited by the famous mutiny.

He made other voyages, however, later in his career and brought us not only the breadfruit, but the ackee and the otaheite apple, which is the shape of a temperate land pear, and a bright red. The flavour is rather scented, but it is sweet and succulent and well worth sampling when available, mostly in the middle of the year, although different parts of Jamaica have crops at different times. The road from the north to the south coast, over Mount Diablo has stalls that seem to sell them year-round. At these stalls, you can get watermelons and roasted corn on the cobs are safe to eat and delicious.

Sooner or later, during your stay in Jamaica, someone is going to offer you curried goat. Personally, unless I'm in a place where I know for certain that it will be good, I always refuse for, "curry goat" as we call it, can be delicious or it can be full of unyielding lumps and spikey bones, greasy and un-appetising. My personal advice is, avoid it, unless you're in the company of a Jamaican friend who knows what he's about; even then, take a small helping and sample it first.

Fried fish, on the other hand, is almost uniformly excellent, and eaten with a slice of hard-dough bread or, better still, bammy, is a gourmet food. The fish is fried with a lot of red pepper, onions, escallion, and vinegar, so beware if you do not like peppery food. It is also full of bones, and the only way to eat it satisfactorily is with the fingers, in some inconspicuous place where you can lick them before using a paper towel. Another seafood delight is shrimp, hot and peppery, readily available in parts of St. Elizabeth, but especially delightful at Middle Quarters.

Bammy is a thick round plate-like object, usually fried, and it is made from the root of the cassava plant. The root is first peeled, then pounded, then squeezed to get rid of the juice. The resultant flour is dried and made into thick, flat cakes which can be kept in a dry place for some time, and cooked when needed. It has a nut-like flavour and is an interesting substitute for bread. It was a favourite food of the Arawaks, and in many places in Jamaica, is still made in a way that differs little from pre-Columbus times. The best place to get bammy is anywhere in the parish of St. Elizabeth, in Jamaica's south-west, roughly on the road from Santa Cruz to Black River or from Black River to Treasure Beach, and from Treasure Beach to Santa Cruz. A look at the map will give you a good idea where the area lies. Don't be surprised if almost everyone to whom you mention this tells you it is nonsense. We all have our own special places where we believe the best food is to be found, it is nevertheless true that most bammies eaten in Jamaica, are made in the region I have just described.

As for drinks, we have an excellent beer, Red Stripe, and, of course, Jamaican rum; the most popular (worldwide, too) is Appleton. Beer, you can drink any time of day, but it is stronger than it seems and tends to make you sleepy in our hot afternoons. The rum is, of course excellent, and comes in bewildering profusion. Many country people drink Wray & Nephew's traditional "whites", the colourless liquid which is how all rum starts life, before it is coloured with burnt sugar. It has a very strong taste and is powerful so don't try the local trick of drinking it at a swallow and then take a chaser. When you're not used to it, the chaser comes too late. By and large, for anyone not used to rum, it is best to avoid it entirely, until the evening. It is potent, and if you are driving yourself, a couple of drinks can straighten out corners and eliminate traffic in a way that is alarming for others not similarly anaesthetised. My advice is to leave it till later, when you're sitting down and haven't far to go to bed.

A delightful thirst-quencher is fresh coconut water, drunk directly from the nut. Stop by one of the many carts you find dotting the cities or towns, or at possible a roadside stall. The vendor will open the nut right before your very eyes, and you can enjoy a drink which, for many, is second to none.

Fresh fruit juices are specialities of the 'house'. At many small eating-places you wait while they squeeze the fresh fruit, and there's glass of juice with no additives. In Clarendon, just beyond May Pen, here is a shop specialising in fresh citrus juice, and you can even take some of the fresh fruits along with you.

And where are most of these delicacies to be found? That is one of the easiest and most difficult questions to answer. The people who own the shops and restaurants and stalls where they are available, are constantly on the move, and most of their places have no names. The stalls on the side of the road are obvious enough, but the shops are not, and the only way to find out is to ask. If you're hungry in a small town, ask a local shopkeeper or someone who sells hardware or cloth, where you can eat; or go into a grocery and ask if you can get a meal. All of them have a room somewhere at the back where food is served, and if it is a small village, you will probably end up eating some of the family's food and that will be excellent. Otherwise, if in doubt, stick to fruit, cheese or bully beef from a tin, and hard-dough bread...there is other bread, by the way, but hard-dough is uniformly good and very filling. You will have some failures, and more successes, and the one thing to remember is that Jamaicans, like people all over the world, if approached with courtesy and friendliness, will go out of their way to help a visitor. If you find us being rude and unhelpful, check your own attitude, and when you have, look out for the miracles.

ORIGINALLY PUBLISHED JULY 1978

Gourmet Delights

BARBARA GLOUDON

I have this fantasy...of a formal dinner party at Faith's Pen, guests in black tie, tuxedo, boutonnieres, cummerbunds, little black dresses appropriately accessoried.

My guests and I would travel to Faith's Pen, that collection of smoke-soaked cook shops nestled in a curve of the St. Ann hills, an oasis in the desert of bauxite soil and asphalt roads. Faith's Pen, where smoke rises like incense from charcoal and wood stoves bringing chicken and fish to golden brown perfection, where corn is roasted and boiled, where mannish water, soup of the gods, is coaxed to its fullness to revive the weary and the worn. Yuh nuh! Give thanks.

But back to the fantasy. I can see us now...my guests and I, descending from air-conditioned coach (with driver in an appropriate livery—definitely no sawed-off pants and mesh merino). Our arrival at Faith's Pen would be greeted with cries of "Rahtid" and "Coo yah," affirming that we are indeed in Jamaica—and "no problem, man."

Having acknowledged the welcome from Miss Rose and other operators of the centre of epicurean delight, we would proceed to dine, moving elegantly from one shop to the next. For an appetiser, some roast salt fish, delicately shredded. A spot of avocado (just plain "pear" to a real Jamaican) and a toops (un soupçon) of chopped onions and the very necessary Scotch Bonnet pepper (whose fame has gone abroad). And of course, Red Stripe in crystal flutes, thoughtfully brought along by the ever-thoughtful hostess. (Nuh true!)

Elegantly, making conversation as we go, ignoring the remarks like "But see yah lawd, a wha dis," we would proceed from appetizer to soup. Mannish water, of course, robustly flavoured with herbs (no, not *that* one!) and spices. The faint of heart would be advised not to squabble about the small bits of entrails trailing through the liquid. It is the broth (not the thought) that counts. And now for the entree. A choice of chicken, seasoned to perfection, grilled in the fresh air (occasionally intruded upon by the exhaust of a passing vehicle but who cares) or perhaps, a spot of fish, tilapia (aka African Perch aka pond fish) from the rivers of our fair isle, or more probably, nurtured in man-made ponds.

Delicately, we proceed to strip the sweet flesh from the bones, our pinkies extended appropriately. On the side, pegs of roasted breadfruit, servings of yam (yellow and powdery) brought to fulfilment over an open fire, too. And perchance, a spot of curry goat, to prove that the mannish water had origin and pedigree in the flesh of some goat which gave its all for our epicurean pleasures.

On the side, if needs be, a spot of rice, if you must, but this is really a night for natural fare, not to be confused with coarse cuisine. As we dine, our laughter tinkles in the St. Ann night air. All along the strip, the glow of light bulbs illuminates our al fresco feast. So what if they think we're mad? Mad yes—over real Jamaican fare, the food of our land.

As we nibble, as we slurp, the gracious hostess will excuse the guests who loosen cummerbunds and belts, undo ties, let what is to hang out...hang. More crystal flutes of The Stripe. this is time "fe pop laugh fe peas soup", a cultural metaphor for enjoyment to the max. And if we pass the cholesterol limits, "better belly buss than good food waste" (another ancestral proverb). We've gone way past that now. Time to cleanse the palate with slices of cold sliced melon, or pegs of juicy oranges or perchance a sweetsop or two. And for dessert...Here the hostess has providentially provided a pudden of sweet pitater (do we really have to translate? Okay. "A pudding of sweet potato" which is not the whole story. The array of flavourings and trimmings which go into a good pudden, make it an essay of its own, but that is for another time. So that is my culinary fantasy. Maybe I will make it real.

Meantime, back at the ranch, have you noticed the proliferation of cooking shows on satellite networks? Everybody is a big cook these days. Okay, I'm ready to join the parade. My show will be called "The Jamaican Roadside Epicure." It will initiate its audience into the delights of out-of-doors dining alfresco by Jamaican highways and byways. My opening show will be on location at West Heroes Circle, formerly known as Race Course, in Kingston (where else).

In case you didn't know, the area is on the map as Manchester Square, but who remembers? (My mother's friend Vera used to live there, but that is a story for yet another time). Corn on the corner has been a way of life there for as long as I can recall. It goes back to the days of kerosene tins, which didn't necessarily contain kerosene. Sometimes cooking oil came in them. Whatever, kerosene tins were treasured, in the age B.P. (Before Plastic). Cleansed of their original contents, they became treasured cooking vessels, placed on an open wood fire. These days, they have been replaced by aluminum pots, another sign of change. Into the water, appropriately salted and sometimes peppered, the ears of corn were placed. The variety of maize which we know here, is nothing like the soft, sugar-sweet variety now imported into supermarkets from Up So (Merica). Jamaican corn is like our people, hardy stuff, requiring much boiling. When the golden yellow grains are brought to some degree of tenderness, they are taken from the steaming tins (or pots) and served, wrapped in the husks saved for that purpose. Woe betide the unsuspecting eater who does not understand the need to drain off the boiling water which dribbles from the corn. Do you see now why the service of a roadside epicure would prove invaluable, especially to a world audience, eager to be in on what's hot?

The real way to serve boiled corn is with a wedge of "dry coconut," on the side. The combination of the cool crispness of the coconut meat with the heat of the hot grains is a gastronomic experience worthy of being shared. And then, besides boil corn, there is roast corn which gives credence to the old-time Jamaican proverb "pay fe roas and bwoil." Being interpreted: "you get it coming and going," or, "if it ain't one thing, it's another." Roas corn ("roasted" to the initiated) can be tricky business. Improperly done, the crunch of the upper layer of the roasted ears can give way to a sullenness underneath (Sullen corn? Yeah. We epicures delight in abstract imagery. Ask Martha Stewart).

A well roasted ear of corn can be an interesting experience, not just for dining but for simpler pleasures of a bygone time, as in "Ship sail, sail fast." Yes children, this is what your ancestors did in the days before electronic games. Grains of roasted corn off the cob were used to play the game. The player would rattle the corn grains in his/her hand like a crap shooter on a roll while calling out "Ship sail, sail fast, how many men on board?" The other player/players were supposed to guess the number of grains in the hand. Win or lose, the round would then continue. Sometimes—more times—the victor would eat some of the grains, for to the victor belong the spoils.

"Roas corn" also stands at the base of another old Jamaican cultural manifestation i.e. the proverb or wise saying which remind us of the value of sacrifice. "Waan roas corn, finger haffe bun." No, bun is not that which we eat at Easter or the American name for a hamburger roll. Bun, my dear friends from Foreign, is "burn." In other words, the price of roasted corn is burnt fingers or to put it another way, if you want the ultimate prize, you must be prepared to make sacrifice.

Now, you see why I have to get this "Epicurean Channel" on the air? And if for some reason, we are unable so to do, then I invite you to go share the experience for yourself. Go see the corn ladies round at Race Course, aka Heroes Circle, ole time Manchester Square. And while you are at it, don't be surprised if you find the corn pots sharing space with large crustaceans—land crabs, claws and all, boiled and ready for feasting. If you want a discourse on that, we're quite prepared to do it another time. Now, you see why we need that Jamaican Roadside Epicurean Show. All offers will be considered very seriously. Meanwhile, ship sail, sail fast.

ORIGINALLY PUBLISHED AUGUST 1999

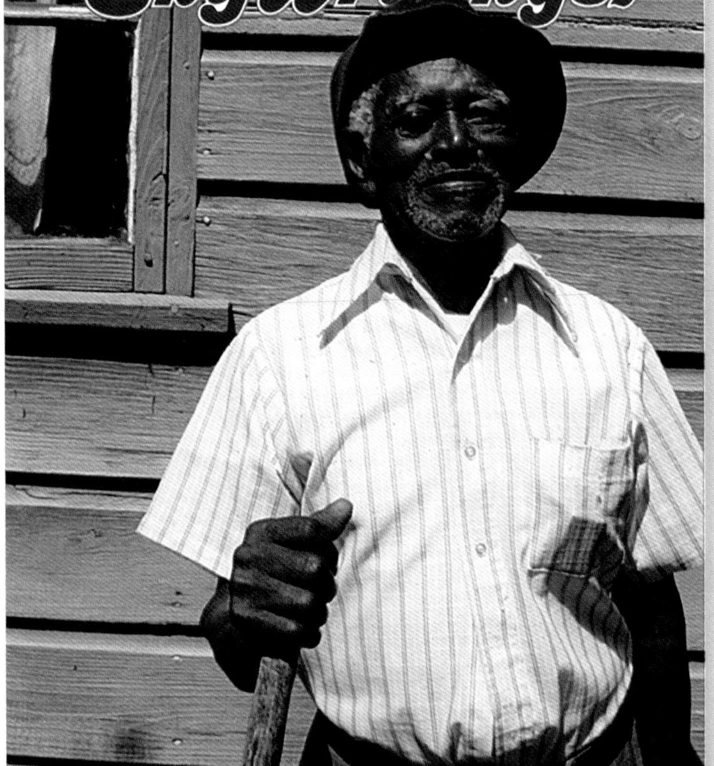

SKYWRITINGS COVER
July 1983
Mr. Bennett of Green Island.

Dance Wi Dance

IVY BAXTER

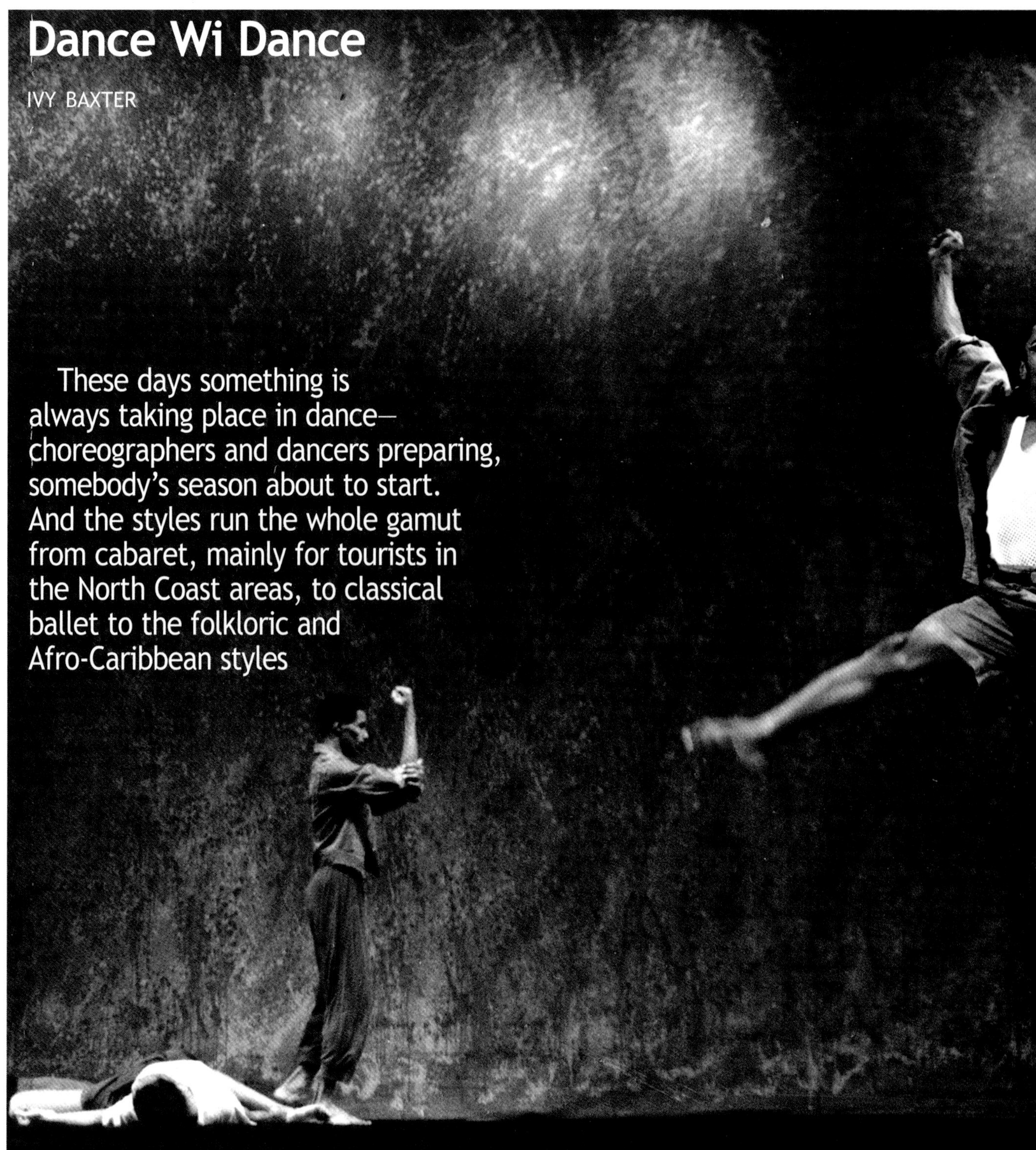

These days something is always taking place in dance—choreographers and dancers preparing, somebody's season about to start. And the styles run the whole gamut from cabaret, mainly for tourists in the North Coast areas, to classical ballet to the folkloric and Afro-Caribbean styles

Today's strong and growing dance theatre is built on the foundation of those early years when few pioneers had visions of what is now taking place—Jamaican dance and dancers accepted and acclaimed at home and internationally.

There is no company that better epitomises the emergence of the Jamaican dance theatre than the National Dance and Theatre Company (NDTC) under its artistic director, Professor Rex Nettleford.

Formed in 1962, the year of Jamaica's independence, its members originally came from the Ivy Baxter, Fay Simpson and Eddie Thomas dance groups and Soohih's Ballet School, some of the groups founded in the 1950s.

Now highly acclaimed for its modern and folkloric dance, the NDTC has performed far and wide, including throughout the Caribbean, North America and Europe, including the Soviet Union.

But the NDTC is only one of the many dance companies and/or schools operating and acclaimed in and outside of Jamaica. Many branches have spread from the same root with many of Jamaica's most prominent dancers, choreographers and dance groups having been a part of this small nucleus.

Institutions—large and small where people can level in Jamaica—are centred mainly in Kingston and St. Andrew. The oldest of them are 30-40 years old. These are the ballet schools of Fay Simpson and the Rowe sisters, who between them, have trained hundreds of dancers.

In the last seven years the ballet classes at

L'Acado, "Llow Mi Nuh! (1986)," choreographer L'Antoinette Stines.

©MONICA DASILVA

©CHARLES ROUSSEAU

Rowe Ballet, "Le Gran Pas de Quatre" (1988), choreographer Punkie Facey.

COURTESY BUDDY POUYATT ©AMADOR PACKER

Ivy Baxter, early 1950's

the Jamaica School of Dance using the Cechetti methods, and Norma Spence's Ballet Dimensions, and Petits Dimensions, who with the Rowe-Spence School, take the examinations of the Royal Academy in England, as well as L'Antoinette Stines' L'Acadco School, give excellent grounding in ballet. However, there is now only one pure ballet company—Ballet Dimensions.

There have been many shows put on by the Rowe sisters, and in the 1960's by the late Madame May Soohih and Anatoly Soohih, her husband, and a short-lived Ballet Guild.

With modern dance the scene is different. The origin of this style in Jamaica began with the visit of two teachers from Canada to the YWCA in Jamaica. After their return, Ivy Baxter was sent to the University of Toronto. Later she went to London to the Sigurd Leeder School of Modern European Ballet.

After teaching at the YWCA in Kingston, she began the Ivy Baxter Dance Group. The style was modern creative dance. It used general and local Jamaican themes. The group attracted many enthusiastic adults and had as its musical stimulus the Mapletoft Poulle Orchestra and the Frats Quintet, a folk-singing group composed of five men who sang Jamaican songs.

The Group existed to develop a Caribbean idiom of dance. It made contact with other dance pioneers in the region, namely, Beryl McBurnie, founder of the Little Carib Theatre in Trinidad, and Lavinia Williams, formerly of the Katherine Dunham Company, whose work in ballet and Haitian folklore is well known. These and other teachers came to Jamaica through the collaboration of the Ivy Baxter Dance Group with the then University College of the West Indies.

The Ivy Baxter Dance Group, as well as having its own school, produced teachers of other schools and groups such as the Alma Mock Yen School, the Eddie Thomas Dance School and Company, and the Jay-Teens directed by Joyce Campbell.

(ABOVE) Three pioneers of dance in the Caribbean, from left Beryl McBurnie (Trinidad), Ivy Baxter (Jamaica), Lavinia Williams (Haiti) along with Rex Nettleford (Jamaica) at the National Dance and Theatre Company's 25th Anniversary Celebrations held in 1987.

(BELOW) Movements Dance Company, "Pressure," choreographer Monica Campbell.

In 1962, the year the island achieved independence, ten members of the Ivy Baxter Dance Group became the basis of the National Dance and Theatre Company of Jamaica—including its Artistic Director, Professor Rex Nettleford, O.J. This Company has performed consistently. It has carried high the name and dance reputation of Jamaica. It has a large repertoire of dances of modern, folkloric and contemporary content and style.

The main school for instruction in dance for recreation, performance and education is the Jamaica School of Dance. This school is part of the Cultural Training Centre where four schools are located on one campus on Tom Redcam Avenue in Kingston—schools of music, drama, art and dance. The director of the School for Dance is Mrs. Sheila Barnett and the Junior School is supervised by Mrs. Barbara Requa. Students can take a teacher's or performer's certificate or diploma. There are regular performances of the senior and junior departments, and a yearly summer school in July/August with local and guest instructors, and attended by local and overseas students.

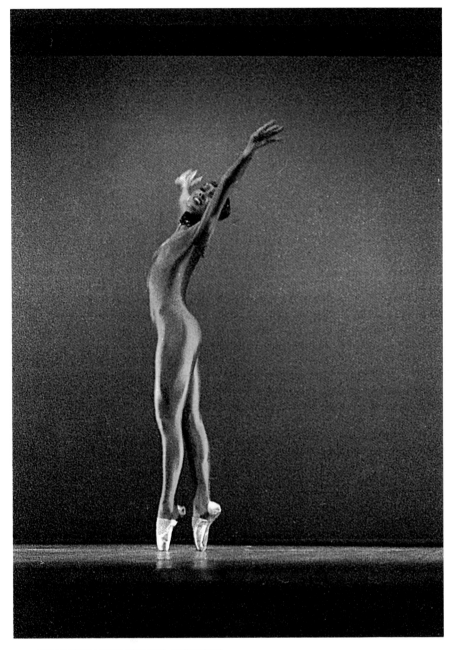

(ABOVE) L'Acadco, "Avia Egyptus," choreographer L'Antoinette Stines

(AT LEFT) "Street Scene," choreographer Ivy Baxter.

The greatest participation in dance activities and events in the island today, however, is generated by the Jamaica Cultural Development Commission's yearly competitions in dance and the other art forms, and the production of shows around the island in July/August when the anniversary of the island's independence is celebrated.

There have been visits for performance by dance companies to Jamaica, often organised by the United States Information Service. Jamaican dance has been displayed at festivals in the Caribbean from the first Caribbean Festival of Arts in Puerto Rico in 1952, where the Ivy Baxter Dance Group represented Jamaica, to the Carifestas in the 1960's and 1970's, as well as Commonwealth festivals held in Britain, and festivals held in South America and Europe. Dance groups from Jamaica have taken part with credit. Exchanges take place through such organisations as Partners of America where students and teachers visit the Jamaica Western New York Partner City—Buffalo, New York.

Dance directors have grown out of the many groups and schools in Jamaica and many are performing overseas with credit to Jamaica. One such is Clive Thompson, himself a performer with Martha Graham and Alvin Ailey. He has a group and school in Staten Island and has taught in Africa and Japan. Another, Garth Fagan directs the Bucket Dance Theatre in Rochester. He was the first university teacher of dance in New York state to receive the Governor's Distinguished Professor's Award in 1985. He has toured Africa and choreographed for the Harlem Ballet. Frank Ashley was chosen from a field of 35 persons to be dancer and group in residence at the Henry Street Playhouse in New York. Vernon Nash, directs a group in Calgary, Alberta, Canada. Tommy Pinnock, a solo dancer in the United States, choreographed the Garvey Musical in June last year in Jamaica. The list could go on to reflect the growing number of Jamaican dancers excelling overseas.

If you are a visitor to the island, the best time to see dance is during the months of July and August. The National Dance Theatre Company, L'Acadco and Movements have their seasons around this time. Competitions in dance and exhibitions of traditional dance, organised by the Jamaica Cultural Development Commission also take place at this time. The Dance Summer School of the Jamaica School of Dance, specializing in Caribbean and modern dance, classes in liturgical dance take place and shows celebrating Independence, are staged during this period.

Other dance activities occur in November and December—a mini season of the National Dance Theatre Company; the Jay-Teens (every other year); and some shows of the ballet groups. So see you at some of these.

ORIGINALLY PUBLISHED JUNE 1988

Ancestral Echoes and Artistic Discovery

REX NETTLEFORD

The National Dance and Theatre Company of Jamaica celebrates its 40th Anniversary.

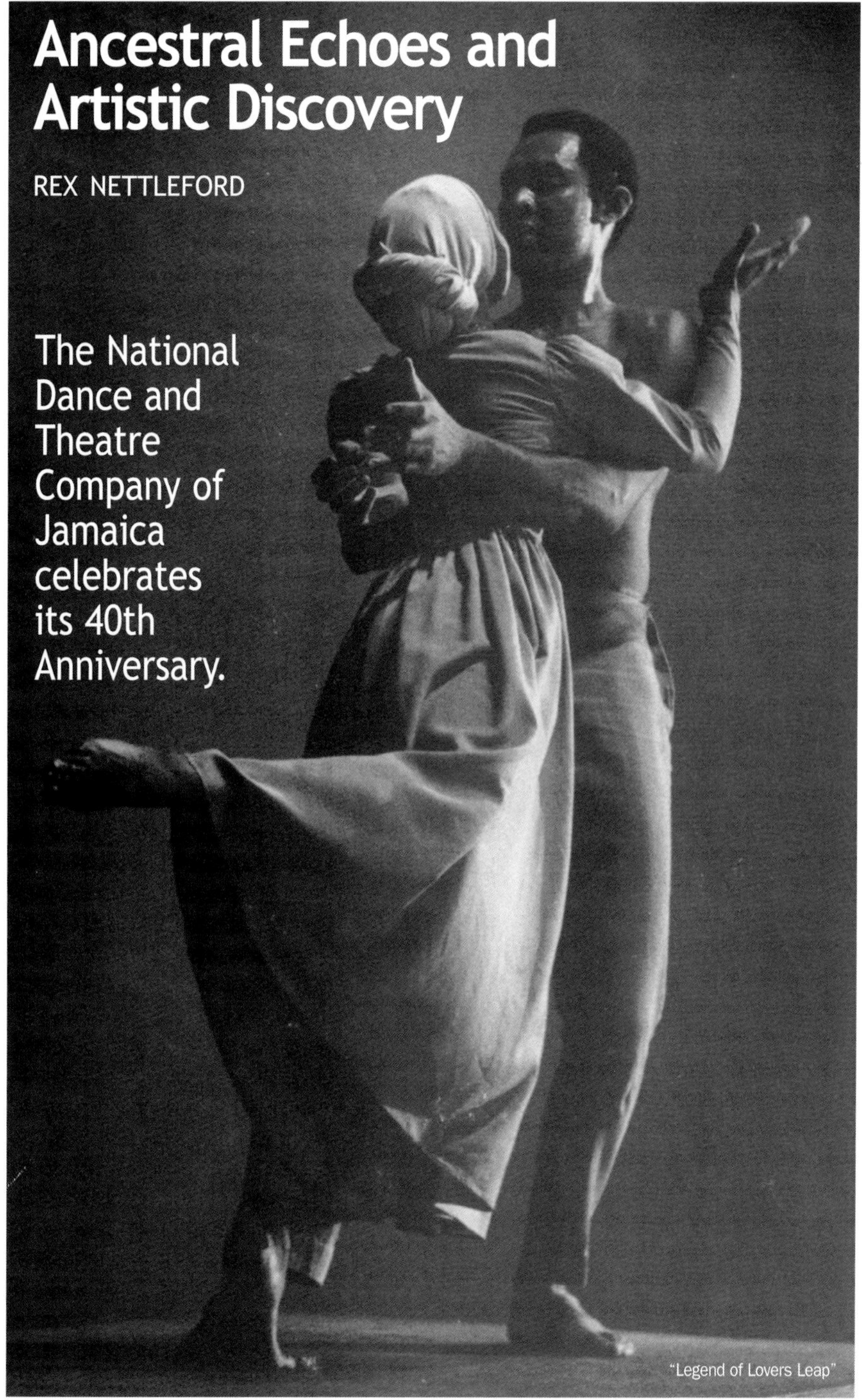

"Legend of Lovers Leap"

"The greatest gift that can be bestowed upon a dance company is to be rooted in a society in which dancing comes as naturally as sitting down or going for a walk. The National Dance Theatre Company (NDTC) of Jamaica are the recipients of just such a gift and have demonstrated once again that their dancing (and their singing too) is a natural disposition and means of expression."

But that "natural means of expression", takes ideal form and greater purpose only through the discipline of continuous training, enduring dedication, aesthetic weight, artistic integrity and cultural certitude. This, the author of the above quote writing in the prestigious United Kingdom magazine *Dancing Times* of November 2001, might have added.

It has taken all of the 40 years of the Jamaican NDTC's existence to display all this as well as to sustain the excellence for which it has won international acclaim and considerable respect in its native Jamaica. In its four decades of experimentation and exploration of the many sources of energy which the ex-slave, ex-colonial, newly-independent Jamaican experience offers this ensemble of dancers, singers, musicians and creative technicians, the NDTC has performed all over the world with Air Jamaica, lest it be forgotten, as 'official carrier' wherever the national airline flies. The NDTC has long become more than just Jamaican. It is a Caribbean entity that plumbs the ancestral depths of Caribbean cultural expressions in search of definition and self-assurance.

The repertoire of dances and music range from those based on religious rituals following on the encounter of Africa and Europe on Caribbean soil, through the pantomimic recreational play consequent on said encounters, to the aspirations, anguish, and promise of redemption shared with all who tenant Plantation America (from Nova Scotia to Uruguay) and the new Caribbean diaspora on both sides of the Atlantic. Corresponding creolised forms emerging through the East Indian-African mix of Guyana and Trinidad are yet to take as central a place in the NDTC repertoire but Jamaican choreographers familiar with the cross-fertilisation of thoughts and beliefs between nineteenth century indentured East Indians and ex-slave black Jamaicans arriving as far back as the 16th century are not unaware of this feature in Caribbean cultural life. Hosay, the Indo-West Indian festival art, is alive in Jamaica and both the 'Indian Spirit' in the 1963 work 'Pocomania' has long acknowledged that presence along with Africa's and Europe's.

But no one can deny the weight of the colliding presence of the last-named two for over three centuries and the NDTC repertoire naturally reflects this, going even further afield to Brazil ("Brazilian Ode"), the United States and the Americas generally ("The Crossing" and a number of pieces danced to jazz music and American Negro spirituals) and South Africa ("Diaspora", and "Praise Songs").

Meanwhile the deeply seated cultural roots serve as wellspring for such works as kumina, based on ancestor worship in the ki-kongo tradition, and pocomania inspired by the syncretised religious worship still extant along with zion revivalism all over Jamaica. Bruckin Party, dinkimini and gerreh drive the singers and the dancers and choreographers to works like 'gerrehbenta' and so on. It is arguably in this regard that the influence and stamp of founder, the current artistic director and principal choreographer Professor Rex Nettleford (now Vice Chancellor of the University of the West Indies) is most felt. His rural upbringing and childhood nurturing in Jamaican traditional life equipped him for seminal work in dance starting in the Ivy Baxter Creative Dance Group the forerunner to the NDTC.

The NDTC Singers

The repertoire of dances and music range from those based on religious rituals following on the encounter of Africa and Europe on Caribbean soil....

"Kumina"

Meanwhile the deeply seated cultural roots serve as wellspring for such works as kumina, based on ancestor worship in the ki-kongo tradition, and pocomania inspired by the syncretised religious worship....

Jamaicans are of this century and also city-bred; so younger-generation members are into the concerns of the times. Monika Lawrence has explored abstract movement in a beautiful work entitled "Identity" while Arlene Richards added an encounter with space ("Cocoon") and the anguish of Siamese twins ("Side By Side") to the repertoire. Sheila Barnett had years before questioned the dominance of technology in her "A Question of Balance" while exploring history and legend ("Ni Woman of Destiny") alongside her pieces on classical literature ("Shadows" inspired by Macbeth). Eddy Thomas, co-director and co-founder had started in 1962 with "Legend of Lover's Leap", a great Jamaican story but was himself concerned from early with the population explosion in his "Omegan Procession". Barbara Requa has tackled cricket, the regional game, in "Caught and Bowled" as well as the travails of the Jamaican woman in "Treadmill". Clive Thompson who once danced with Martha Graham and Alvin Ailey in the USA returned home to the NDTC with offerings utilising jazz and black spirituals (as in "Ancestral Images" and "Of Prophecy and Song"). Bert Rose had long explored the spirituals in his "Glory Road" following Rex Nettleford's "Journeys" but it was he who celebrated the work of Jamaica's cultural icon and animateur Edna Manley in his drama "Edna M". Arsenio Andrade of Cuba has brought to the Company the West Indian Yoruba heritage in his "Congo Laye" following "Sulkari" a dance work by the Cuban-Jamaican Eduardo Rivero his teacher.

The NDTC alumni list is long and impressive. Many have taken the Jamaican dance vision beyond Jamaica's borders. They carry such names as Jackie Guy (UK), Tommy Pinnock and Noel Hall (USA), Derek Williams (Germany) and Gene Carson (Barbados) while at home Tony Wilson, director of the Company Dance Theatre and Monika Lawrence of the Stella Maris Dance Ensemble add to the bevy of dance activity for some time alongside the Jayteens of Joyce Campbell and the work long directed in the tourist industry for the Sandals chain of hotels.

Renowned dance performers nurtured by the NDTC are well enough known. Among them are founding members Sheila Barnett, Barbara Requa and Bert Rose (co-founders along with the NDTC of the Jamaica School of Dance), other founding members like the Casserly sisters (Maureen and Bridget), the Campbell sisters (Joyce and Shirley) Pansy Silvera (later Hassan and balletmistress), Yvonne daCosta, dance diva who dominated the stage in the first decade of the NDTC's life, Audley Butler and the endurable Barry Moncrieffe (now artistic co-ordinator who reigned as the "dancer's dancer" among the males for some three decades). The seventies saw the emergence of Patsy Ricketts who later became with Derek Williams a founding member of the Dance Theatre of Harlem. Melanie Graham emerged a shining star in the eighties and early nineties followed by Arlene Richards, totally trained in the NDTC system and now a triple-threat artist excelling not only in performing but also in costume design and choreography. Ms. Graham returns to the NDTC 40th anniversary celebrations as a guest artist along with Denise Robinson, Sandra Minott, Jacquie Fisher all excellent dancers in their time.

None of these would have found their way without the support of the NDTC Singers who have sung to international acclaim in some of the most prestigious theatres in the world. Originally led by vocal soloist Joyce Lalor, the group is now led by musical director Marjorie Whylie whose compositions and arrangements are pivotal to the development of the NDTC's repertoire. The annual Easter Sunday Morning of Movement and Music gives opportunities for musical experimentation in addition to the annual Seasons and the NDTC Singers have pioneered the staging and presentation of choral theatre in the island evident in the highly acclaimed work of ensembles like the Jamaican Folksingers and the University Singers. The NDTC Orchestra also led by Ms. Whylie rounds off the musical section comprising flautists, trumpeters, guitarists, pianist and congo drummers.

The creative technicians are no less eminent. Veteran lighting designer, George Carter has been supported by Rufus McDonald in lighting the dances. Barbara Kaufman has been in charge of the extensive (and expensive) wardrobe; Tony Locke succeeded Freddie Hickling and Felix Barnett in stage-managing the shows at home and on tours and the sound direction now under Tony Holness was for many years under the charge of Clyde Cunningham following years of service by Baldwin Lennon.

The excellent photographic record in two books about the NDTC and countless promotional photos represent over 35 years of work of Maria LaYacona recently joined by Denis Valentine as company photographer. The interesting thing about all this, is that the members of the NDTC are all voluntary cultural workers in the tradition of voluntarism which has characterised Jamaican social development since the post-Emancipation period.

Where next for this unique and very Jamaican entity? The work never ends and as the saying goes, one is only as good as one's last work. After the fortieth anniversary, insists Director Nettleford, "the work of the NDTC like that of the nation of Jamaica must remain in pursuit of excellence and positive achievement on the basis of hard work, dedicated commitment and an intrinsic faith in the creative potential of the Jamaican people."

ORIGINALLY PUBLISHED AUGUST 2002

Sixty Years of Jamaican Pantomime

BARBARA GLOUDON

Little girls in pretty Christmas outfits, boys with squeaky new shoes. Mothers, fathers and grandparents, while visiting family home, from New York, Toronto and Miami, London and other points, gather in Kingston's Ward Theatre. The Jamaican National Anthem is played, the lights are dimmed. The overture of original music, composed by one or other of the island's pool of talented musicians, begins and the excitement mounts. It is pantomime time again.

Each December, as has been the custom for 60 years, the audience will be treated to a folk spectacle filled with songs, dances, music of the Caribbean, exciting costumes and imaginative set designs.

It was back in 1941 that the first English-style pantomime was introduced to the Jamaican stage. In the convention of those days, there were stock characters like the Dame (a man costumed outrageously in women's clothes) and the leading girl was played by a boy and vice versa. But all of that was soon to change.

The first of the Jamaican pantomimes was "Jack and the Beanstalk," an adaptation of a fairy tale, popular with countless children. Produced by the Little Theatre Movement, an organization of persons who worked for no reward but their love of the stage, the first pantomime paved the way for others to follows.

Persons unfamiliar with this style of theatre often believe that pantomime is a silent art (mime). There is nothing silent about anything in Jamaica, hence our pantomime is a riot of sound, music and snappy dialogue, including the voices of the audience who talk back to the characters onstage, giving advice when they feel it is needed, letting the villains know where to get off, cheering the good people when they triumph.

The history of the Jamaican National Pantomime, as it is now known, holds within it the names of seminal figures in Jamaican theatre development, none more revered than the Hon. Louise Bennett and her onstage partner the late Ranny Williams. The founders of the Little Theatre Movement, Henry Fowler and the late Greta Fowler are also recalled whenever there is research into the roots of modern Jamaican theatre.

Over the years, most of the island's major actors and actresses can boast of doing at least one pantomime season. The LTM in producing the National Pantomime now draws on a talented pool of new actors and actresses organized into the Pantomime Company, who performed not only the annual end of year show but stay together between seasons, producing also a mid-year work focused on some aspect of Jamaica's rich cultural heritage.

ORIGINALLY PUBLISHED DECEMBER 2000

Jamaican Body Moves

Source and continuity of Jamaican movement

CHERYL RYMAN

The Jamaican body moves with a uniqueness of form that belies the many points of common reference to movement in the rest of the African diaspora. The rhythm of movement in the dipping stride of the Jamaican male exudes confidence and a sense of well-being that carries over naturally into the other dance expressions on the island–traditional, popular and theatrical.

Typical S-back kotch.

Dominant images flash across the eye of the local and visiting observer, the bounce being one of the most prominent features. But the whole body moves, with degrees of subtlety and exaggeration depending on the level of involvement and on the context of performance—street, yard, dance hall or stage.

At all times, the Jamaican "body moves" of this era are haunting reminders of another time and place, of a continuing link with the range or "body moves" of our forefathers, as they performed them on the continents of Africa or Europe, and as they transformed them in Jamaica. The dee-jaying sounds of some Jamaican reggae artistes bring into focus some of these transformations:

Shoulder move, shoulder move
an yu get inno de groove.
Yu get inna de groove
an yu do de shoulder move.

The body stands poised, stationary in a kotch—back characteristically S-shaped, the chest leading, the buttocks peacocked, one hand "akimbo" (knuckles of the hand resting on the hip), the other hanging loosely at the side of the body. A typical Jamaican stance.

Yellow Man, D.J. extraordinaire, struts S-backed in a moving kotch across the stage, shoulders rolling, with a bounce at the end of each step; the arm swinging slowly against the steady "ridim" of the shoulder and the feet. An emphatic drop through the knees and one arm shoots up and above the head, the index finger pointed, punctuating the lyrics of his song.

Saturday night. The Red Hills Road strip. Garth Thomas strides confidently down the strip towards his waiting "daughter" (girlfriend), shoulders and ribcage rolling to the front and back alternatively, on top of an almost imperceptible bounce at the end of each step. The arms swing smoothly at a slower counter rhythm to the regular time of the "shoulder move" and step. Abruptly, he checks the regularity of this rhythm to hail his "bredren" across the street. With an obvious drop in the knees, an arm shoots up above the head in salutation.

On stage with the National Dance Theatre Company of Jamaica, the ballet is "Street People". The prostitutes have just completed their seduction dance; stage right, downstage, the ultimate male seducer—the reggae dancer enters. He bounces on stage in "S-90 skank"—feet spread wide with both knees bent; each step an exaggerated bounce through the knees and shoulder. This action simulates the equally stylized antics of the S-90 motorcycle rider who bobs and weaves through the Kingston traffic. Shoulders and ribcage always moving—arching and twisting—the lower torso responding to the bounce which results from the

Revivalist... possession is near.

machine's contact with the rough asphalt.

In a yard of West Kingston, Sister Matthews rocks her body from side to side, forward and backwards, the shoulders leading. Each step is punctuated by a bounce which in turn initiates the next step. The arms swing slowly, loosely around her body as the upper torso shifts forward on the first step and then back on the second step with a bounce. A revivalist sister directly in front of her in the procession suddenly drops through the knees, one arm shoots up in the air, fist clenched above the head...the power descends, possession is near.

Manchioneal, Portland, the signature Bruckin Party bounce of the dancers is heightened by the pounding of the bass drum. Quadrille, French, British, sedate and rigid-backed is transformed. Jamaicanized by the bounce.

And, in the night clubs and at home parties, the dance floor bobs with the incessant bouncing of heads and shoulders with frequent interjections of the "drop" break.

Ghana, West Africa, the asante dancer rises, he steps side to side moving forward, bouncing, one arm swinging loosely around the body, warming up. The adowa dance begins with regular bounce steps - 1, 2, and 1, 2 and, on top of which the hip shifts with unbroken ease from left to right at double time. The tempo of the music changes, a syncopated drop through the knees and in one motion, the dancer flicks the now falling kente cloth up and over the shoulder as a prelude to rapid footwork or a gliding series of spiralling turns, the bounce, though almost imperceptible, nevertheless underlining each step.

The movement principle of the bounce is perhaps the most pervasive characteristic of Jamaican movement, whether it is the man walking down the street or skanking on the S-90; the popular or traditional dancer or on stage, the trained dancer executing a choreographed ballet. Its source resides primarily in an African heritage and in the kinetic memory of the body which carries this heritage.

In technical terms, the knees must be bent, relaxed, in order to facilitate the relaxed-but-controlled stance common to Jamaica and in the rest of the diaspora. The bounce is a natural progression of this aesthetic. It effects a posture of "cool", "equilibrium and balance", "ease and effortlessness", with overtones of virility and strength, all important features of black dance. Similarly, the arms tend to be held close to the body either falling loosely by the body or held at waist level with elbows bent. In the latter position, the hands tend to be held in a loose fist or to hang limply at the wrist.

In some cases, the limp wrist is actually employed as a stylistic feature of a particular dance, like the "rock steady", which preceded reggae.

Not only does the body bounce and the shoulders move, but the whole body moves when "yu get inna de groove". As Jah Thomas reminds us, "Boy, yu wais', it ha fi wine, to de bass line."

And "wine" (wind—undulate and rotate the hip and waist) it does in many of the traditional dances in Jamaica, particularly those which celebrate life in the midst of death, as the "nine-night' or funerary dances of gere and wake do.

This feature, retained from our African ancestors, has surfaced in Jamaican popular dances, from mento to today's reggae, and include the "dry grind" or "rent-a-tile" of the ska and rock steady era and the present day "dub" or "rub-a-dub". And from these sources, it has been taken on stage to be reflected back at both Jamaican and international audiences.

...yu head it ha fi shake,
it ha fi shake...."

The head may be held regally and cool and then, surprisingly, bobbing through the chin, with an exaggerated bounce or simply as a punctuation at the end of a movement phrase as in kumina (traditional African dance ritual still practised in Jamaica) or shaken side to side, at varying speeds.

The memory of the Jamaican body reflects the dance heritage in selective terms. This selection from the vast repertoire of African and European dance makes Jamaican movement unique and distinct while being consistent with the principles of black movement that pre-dominate in the African diaspora.

The Jamaican emphasis is to be seen in the monotony of the bounce; in the moving 'S-back' kotch, one hand akimbo and the other swinging around the body or pinnacled above the head or bent at the elbow with the hands limp wristed; and in the swaying, rotating movements of the Jamaican "wine."

See it on the street, on stage, in the club, in the home, in the yard and in the endless expressions of the Jamaican dance heritage wherever and whenever the body moves.

ORIGINALLY PUBLISHED APRIL 1985

Rub-A-Dub-Dub

'Im gone a groun'

KEN MAXWELL

"Whey Mas Tom?"
"'Im gone a groun' fe look some food."

Simple as that seems, and incomprehensible as it may be to some readers, that brief exchange actually contains a lot of information for those who either speak Jamaican, or who are prepared to learn something about our way of life.

First of all, in reply to the question "Where is Mas Tom?" comes the answer that he has gone to the ground, or his ground, for the missing pronoun can easily be supplied by the imagination of anyone familiar with Jamaican ways. Mas Tom is not hiding, he has gone off to his cultivation, and he is gone to get some food, real food, like yam, potato, dasheen or cocoa, maybe pick some naseberries, a breadfruit or a couple of pears, (avocado pears that is) for we do not know any others.

All that information in a couple of brief half sentences, spoken in a strange manner, a kind of shorthand, assuming a lot of knowledge on the part of both speaker and listener. Rather like the use of a dictionary assumes you can read and have some nodding acquaintance with the language.

Jamaican farming is based on the ground, or groun' as it is pronounced more properly. The groun' is a mixture of almost everything that is cultivated for either home consumption or sale, and one of the difficulties that successive Ministries and Ministers of Agriculture have faced is the one of trying to teach us to grow crops in pure stands, where reaping is simpler and dealing with pests or diseases becomes a feasible matter.

In the groun' you will find fruit trees growing, shading crops like coffee, bananas growing as cover for young annotto plants, breadfruit shading coffee, and orange, and grapefruit growing alongside sugar cane, and under them all will be a few pineapples, some cacao, and some coco plants, the two being entirely different, with pepper trees, a chocho vine, a

passionfruit vine on the fence and all sorts of other goodies.

This is difficult for well-disciplined extension officers, in spite of the fact that they grew up with the system, but have been converted by education and training. Yet it has its advantages. Citrus of any kind, in pure stand orchards, is heir to all kinds of pests, and diseases which the oranges, ortaniques, grapefruit or citrus growing in the groun' never get. Coffee grown by itself gets the coffee borer, bananas get banana disease and leaf spot, they are afflicted by nematodes. Hardly any of these complications affect those same crops in the groun', mainly because there are not enough of any one plant to attract a major infestation. But the lack of disease is at least partly due to the care and attention that the groun' gets from the farmer.

He is in there every day, either to reap or to plant, and the two tasks often go on simultaneously. A man goes in to reap a few pears, trims his banana suckers at the same time, prunes a citrus tree, and before he leaves, trims some young shoots off his grapefruit and picks six chochos for his wife to cook for dinner, with a handful of okras for soup.

Some order!

I must not give you the idea that everything is planted higgledy-piggledy, just because all these plants and vines and trees grow cheek by jowl; there is order in the groun', though it often is not immediately apparent. Crops tend to be grouped in sections so that all the sweet potatoes are in one place, probably with cabbages and red peas planted among them. The yams will certainly have a plot to themselves, but there may still be one or two special ones, rare varieties, or they are being grown to give heads for future crops and so on, scattered in the coffee, or growing beside the bananas.

There will more than likely be some gungo peas growing along the fences, or maybe a good sized patch by itself. This is a kind of pea that grows into a sizeable plant, often six feet high, and its proper name is the congo pea, from its place of origin. Over the years, it has become the gungo pea, and that is how you buy it in a market. You do not plant your gungo peas near the fence of a neighbour you do not trust, because how can you tell which peas are his, and which yours? Hence the expression "Me and him no ha' no gungo a line". The line fence is the boundary fence, so the saying exactly conveys mistrust, but no accusation.

This somewhat casual method of growing crops is becoming less common these days, under pressure from officials who love orderliness and tidiness. But the Jamaican farmer has not survived the attention of generations of colonial officials in order to yield to their Jamaican counterparts, and even the best run and most orderly farms almost always have a groun' as well, away from the prying eyes of extension officers, Ministry of Agriculture officials and foreign consultants. They are kept to supply the house, and also, I suspect, to fill a basic emotional need of all of us for the essential adjunct to life, a hedge against hard times and inflation, and a hobby and healing recreation.

It is just as well, for when a hurricane comes and banana cultivations are blown flat, some survive under the breadfruit and the citrus, and this is why even after the worst hurricanes, at least some of the groun' continue to keep their owners and their friends supplied with food.

It is the possession of the groun', I believe, that gives us our basic independence, and tends to make life hard for those who would dragoon and regiment us. Always at the back of our minds is the feeling that if push comes to shove there is the little piece of land, or the old house somewhere in the country, that we can flee to for sanctuary, and keep body and soul together until times improve. It is this small settler mentality that enables us to treat politicians with the sort of disrespect that we do, and which defies laws and regulations with such apparent casualness. Because we are still a pastoral people, and because the countryside still sets the habits, the atmosphere and the mores of society, we retain that free-booting, disrespectful attitude that we learned under slavery.

We are respectful enough on the surface, because that can be the way to survive physically. But to survive as a people with customs, beliefs, and traditions of our own, melded where it suited us to those of other nations, we needed to have that inner independence that finds a physical counterpart, and source of nourishment, in the groun'.

If anyone wants me, mi will be in mi groun'.

ORIGINALLY PUBLISHED JANUARY 1983

Rolling Calf… And Other "Duppy" Stories

CYNTHIA WILMOT

Any Jamaican ten-year-old can tell you that if you call out "green bush," a wasp won't sting you. If you put three pennies in your pocket on a dark night, and drop two out on the path, a duppy (ghost) won't follow you—he'll stop to search for the third penny of course. But, there is very little you can do to save yourself from Rolling Calf, the monster who wears a clanking chain to scare the wits out of hapless victims, and anybody who walks past a grave yard without removing his cap and saying a polite "good evening" deserves exactly what he gets!

Dismiss them as superstitions if you like—but don't blame us if trouble overtakes you as a result! You're sceptical? Then we won't tell you that the best way to prevent grass-ticks from settling on you is to rub your skin with "crush-up" guava leaves and the only way to stop a jellyfish burn from driving you mad is to "P…" on it. Of course,

Smart, mature adults don't believe in folk remedies and end up bee-stung and tick-bitten as a result. But even adult Jamaicans know that duppies DO exist—because if they themselves haven't seen them, their Cousin Winston's baby-mother's auntie has, and who would call such a nice old lady a "liard"!

Take the Golden Table. Never heard of it? Go back to days of pirates and privateers, when a buccaneer craft flying no colour but the Jolly Roger and carrying a cargo of plundered gold, was put under the command of a mutinous mate while the drunken captain snoozed below.

On deck, as bottles passed from hand to hand, the talk turned to a division of the booty—and a plot was hatched: why not sink the ship, make off with the gold, and live in luxury forever after? The villains waited until dark, then packed the precious cargo in small boats. But one man among the crew was a traitor twice over, and secretly emptied a strange potion into the wine...

Not long after, the ship burst into flames, and a single rowboat could be seen making its way to shore. The details are hazy. But on the shores of the Rio Cobre, out of nowhere, a dour Scottish ship's carpenter suddenly appeared. He lived the life of a hermit, practiced his trade by day and a more secret trade by night, fashioning a magnificent table, the entire top covered with golden doubloons...

Twenty-seven seamen had died at his hand and despite his wealth, heaven had a grim punishment in store for the rascal. Rains fell in torrents, the river behind his humble door was in spate, and the small house disappeared in the rising tide.

The ship's carpenter was never seen again. But on certain nights, when the rains again swell the waters of the River Cobre, the golden table is said to float upwards, reflecting the light of the stars.

Now, obviously clever people don't believe in the Golden Table—and those who have seen it have the good sense to keep it to themselves. So, too, do those who have heard the hoofbeats of the Phantom Rider of Seville, or have encountered the Devil Bull.

The Phantom Rider, a Spanish soldier, took advantage of a simple Arawak maiden, who died of a broken heart. The Arawak gods swore eternal vengeance, and the Phantom Rider is condemned to ride the lonely stretch of coastline near St. Ann's Bay on certain midnights, invisible to human eyes, with only his screams of remorse and the sound of his horse's hoofbeats to announce his presence.

No, of COURSE we don't believe any of this! We heard the sound of hoofbeats, but after all there's a polo ground nearby at Drax Hall (but who plays polo at midnight?)

Then there was a beautiful Arawak princess, Martha Brae, who knew where the gold was hidden. Christopher Columbus searched in vain...but of course she wouldn't tell her secrets to her captors! Instead she led them up a river and then re-directed its flow. They all drowned and she became the ever-flowing Martha Brae River.

If it weren't enough that Jamaica had its own aboriginal ghosts and things-that-go-bump-in-the-night from the days of the Spanish occupation, it seems that every new group of arrivals brought new haunts with them. The wily African spider, Brer' Anancy, who can take human or spider form as suits his fancy, is perhaps the most famous, followed closely by the less endearing Old Hag, a witch worse than any to be found in a northern Hallowe'en. And the Indian plantation workers indentured to replace the labour of the slaves after Emancipation are without doubt responsible for the Devil Bull, Gashanami, who terrorized entire plantation villages until he was outwitted and slaughtered by a brave young lad, Randath, for love of a fair lady. The story goes that Randath tricked the bull by hiding in a guango tree and taunting it to ram its horns in vain against the tree's tough trunk. Finally, as Randath put an end to the animal in true matador style, the dying creature limped off leaving a trail of blood. To this day it is believed that every drop of blood caused a fresh spring of water to burst from the earth on the spot.

But again, utter nonsense! Yes, there ARE strange bellowings at times in the hills, but isn't that the sound of the waterfalls which are always nearby, you say? Well—so you say, but don't blame us for what happens if you walk there alone after dark.

Neither does any sensible person seriously believe that the infamous Annie Palmer, Mistress of Rose Hall Great House, haunts the halls at midnight. True, she tortured her slaves, murdered her lovers, and came herself to a grisly end, but surely those bloody footprints on the stairs (which have never faded) were caused by somebody whose big toe was "jooked by a macca", and the strange sounds of sobbing are really only the echoes of wind in the coconut palms.

Every land on earth seems to have its Lovers' Leap, and Jamaica is no exception. Here, in St. Elizabeth, the star-crossed lovers, as everywhere else, jumped to their death rather than face a life apart. Every land which boasts mineral springs such as our powerful spas at Bath in St. Thomas and Milk River in Clarendon have similar tales of their discovery. In North America, the springs were all discovered by native warriors wounded by army riflemen; in Jamaica the springs were come upon by runaway slaves escaping cruel masters. In every case, the healing waters worked their magic and the victims were miraculously cured.

And this gives us pause for thought. The fact is that mineral springs DO work wonders, and medical science now agrees (a bit reluctantly perhaps) that some of our "bush teas" are better than medicine from a pharmacy. Similarly, most countries have their traditional tales which seem, superficially, to be the stuff of bedtime stories until anthropologists and geologists track down their origins through millenia. For thousands of years, for example, First Nations people of the Pacific Northwest passed on folk tales of a "great monster like a giant white bear" which came down from the mountains to sweep entire tribes into oblivion. Now scientific investigation has identified a huge glacier which aeons ago broke loose from the polar ice and did, indeed, sweep down to wreak such havoc. So too, someday, a scientist with an enquiring mind may find historic justification for the occasional sighting of the alligator in the top hat which walks like a gentleman on the road towards Morant Point.

Meanwhile, being intelligent, sophisticated people, we have no time for such stories.

So why do we carry a rabbit foot key chain, and send opening-night telegrams to theatrical friends urging them to "break-a-leg"?

Don't ask.

Don't ask, either, why a Jamaican house is not considered properly built unless a bottle of white rum has been opened and sprinkled on the foundations. (Not all of it, of course, at today's prices!) Don't wonder why, on some ancient sugar estates, the planting season officially opens with the sacrifice of a fowl to the River Mother, a stern but good spirit who rules the waters that flow to the sea.

Don't be surprised, either, when you see youngsters break into a run when they pass a cotton tree. It is probably quite untrue that these trees are inhabited by duppy-ghosts, and after all, children will believe any foolishness. But it wouldn't hurt to quicken your pace a little—after all, jogging is good for you, isn't it?

ORIGINALLY PUBLISHED SEPTEMBER 1992

Talk Jamaican

TONY HENDRIKS

I think I must have been about seven years old when I realised that I am bilingual. Although not officially so, to all intents and purposes, I am. I speak English and Jamaican.

Now Jamaica is part of the English speaking world. In fact it is commonly known as the capital of the "English speaking Caribbean," a term that creates quite the wrong impression of language in the region.

Our influences are African, English, Spanish, Chinese, East Indian, Middle Eastern and, most recently, North American. It was the English, however, who dominated in the sixteen and seventeen hundreds and passed on their language, laws and bureaucracy. Since then we have perfected the bureaucracy, interpreted the laws and moulded the language into a many splendoured thing. Yeahman!

I have often imagined that somewhere deep in our folklore and mythical history there was an old woman called "Mother Tongue" who lived in the hills in a small shack built with bamboo. Her sole purpose was to invent our patois; words and phrases that come from African, English and Spanish influences such as, attaclapse (calamity) boottoo (an uncouth person of low order) coroaches (personal belongings) dibby dibby (inconsequential).

Now I could go on and on for ever, but we don't have the time or space for a complete dictionary of the Jamaican language. In fact there are some available in stores and of course there is Cassidy's Dictionary of Jamaican English. Suffice it to say that if you are to try to understand "Jamaica Talk" you will need time and patience. The same as learning any language.

So rather than lists let me give you an example of how we use our humour and wit in our language.

One day I was sitting in a favourite hostelry of mine when one of the patrons started to pontificate on the spending and saving habits of our nation. "If people would only save a dollar a day, every day of the year," he said. "At the end of a year how much would we have?"

"Three hundred and sixty five dollars," chimed another patron. "And after ten years?" he asked. "Three thousand six hundred and fifty. With compound interest it would be more though," added one more of our party. Then just as the first man was about to continue the bartender, a man of no small wit, interrupted, "De people too 'fraid a det." Confused I asked him, "Do you mean death or debt?" Quick as a flash he retorted "Boat (both)." Now clearly this must show you that the letter "H" is a very mobile and sometimes redundant letter in Jamaica. One must learn to 'ear with your hears and you must heat your food once it as been 'eated up on de stove.

We change the way a sentence can be constructed, too. I was once told by a friend that after filling out an application form all he needed for completion was a "size passport picture." That is nothing, however. Once you get into patois fully it is another language totally. In the art department of an advertising agency that I worked for, I overheard a young lady enquire; "Da ad deh. A whoofa da deh ad deh fa?" I beg your pardon? I can hear you saying. Well what she meant was: "That ad there. Who's ad is it?"

Our language can often, as with the example I just gave, be a series of short, monosyllabic words sometimes crammed together to create one multisyllabic word that conveys a meaning that only a Jamaican could understand. A visitor to the island could be forgiven for thinking that a conversation between two people was in fact the start of World War Three.

Now imagine two men in conversation. Each says one word to the other. Back and forth they go. It could sound just like this;

Ay! Oo? You! Me? EeHee! Awha? Cooya! Cooweh? Yasso! Wehsso? Yasso! Desso? Eehee! Nahsah! Yesah! Oohsehso? Meesehso! Oohyou? Yehmeesehso! Gweh! Aybwoy! Awha? Nabaddawidat! Cho! Awhoa!

Now all that is being said is that the first person is asking the second to come over to where he is. The second person though, is not particularly interested in joining him. I am sure that you can work out the rest out for yourselves. Yeahman!

To my memory though, when, as a youngster, I was showing any interest in a foreign language or the customs and practices in a land to which I was going to visit, the first thing I wanted to learn were the swear words, profanities and rude gestures applicable to that region.

Now I'm sorry if I got you all excited there but I don't think I would be allowed to teach you those areas of the Jamaican language in this publication. This is a shame because we have by far the most creative and colourful way of cussing that I have come across in any language in the world. Not only is it beautifully inventive but it is so unique that most people who visit would not have a clue what the words mean, and would not even realise that they were being cussed other than the fact that when a Jamaican is cussing you, you know about it.

Slang, buzzwords, fads and newspeak are not unique to Jamaica. One of the best in recent years has become a standard greeting in Jamaica: "Respect!" It has all the class and style of years gone by and is opposed to the "dis" of disrespect. But "Irie" must be one of the best known words recognised as Jamaican by all visitors and natives alike. Meaning so much, it is hard to give one definition of this great Jamaican word. It can be used as a greeting. It can be used as a response to a greeting. It is heard in the hotels as visitors are encouraged to shout this at the top of their voices at every turn they take. "How are you feeling?" "Irie!"

"No problem!" can hardly be claimed as originating in Jamaica but we have taken it and claimed it as our own. "Jamaica! No Problem Mon!"

Our national and now internationally known music form has a title uniquely Jamaican: "Reggae." The dictionary describes the word as a noun. A type of West Indian popular music having four beats to the bar, the upbeat being strongly accented. That rather inadequate definition, although accurate, does less to explain what the word means than just hearing the word itself. Reggae speaks for itself.

Our proverbs are legendary although sometimes inexplicable to the untrained ear if not on the correct wavelength. "Ooman luck deh a dungle heap. Chicken peck it out." Now you try and work that one out. When it comes to the metaphor one of my favourites is:

"Dem two people is like batty and bench." Now you don't get much closer than that do you?

Amongst us we have poets and lyricists, writers and composers. Bob Marley's words "Emancipate yourself from mental slavery, only we can free our minds," remains one of the great messages of our time. But sometimes it seems that us Jamaicans take the language and create new words and meanings. As one man was recently overheard saying: "We can develit up." He meant, we can develop it. We can indeed "develit up."

Rhythm, cadence and melody of our language is similar to some and unlike any. Much joy and pleasure can be derived from listening and learning, hearing and observing. Remember as with many other nations, in Jamaica when we want you to understand what we say, you will. When we don't want you to understand, you haven't got a chance, believe me!

All said and done when any visitor to Jamaica finally leaves our shores they won't go empty handed. For sure you'll be saying, Yeahman, Irie and No Problem Mon, and maybe a few more if you persevere. Nuff respect!

ORIGINALLY PUBLISHED JANUARY 1994

Jamaican Invasion

TONY HENDRIKS

Jerk fish & chips might not be in every chip shop, yet, but it's rare to enter a bakery that doesn't have Jamaican patties jostling for a position alongside Syrian bread, Danish pastries, Swiss rolls and French croissants. That's proof of the pudding of Jamaica's cultural impact on Britain.

Fittingly enough the nation that gave us our mother tongue has been 'bigging up' the Jamaican version of English by adopting phrases like, 'big up.' I'm not sure we'll hear Her Majesty say: "My husband and I would like to big up our breddrin' in the Commonwealth..." in her next Christmas speech, but I bet the Princes' William and Harry have used the buzzwords: "respect", "wicked" and "bonafide," as all youth do in Britain.

Fortnum & Mason's do not offer cerasee for afternoon tea, but I know they sell guava jelly. Boots the Chemist won't fill a prescription for medina but they do sell condoms and they are called 'boots.' If you do want authentic Jamaican supplies like yam, cho cho and plantain you can find bonafide Caribbean markets across the country from Brixton to Birmingham, Bristol to Bradford and shopping at Sainsbury's or Marks & Sparks reveals a source of escoveitch, jerk seasoning and hot pepper sauce.

For decades British TV has had a Caribbean face. Sir Trevor McDonald and Lenny Henry have become British institutions and as much as Lennox Lewis's world title may be in dispute no one can deny his Jamaican roots.

Of course reggae has influenced the world and even Lady Thatcher quoted Bob Marley in a speech when she said: "Get up, stand up, don't give up the fight!" She wasn't talking to striking miners at the time but Jamaicans on a visit to our island. Prime Minister Tony Blair was eager to point out that he listened to reggae and *One Love* by Bob Marley and the Wailers was chosen as the Millennium Song.

Our music has been an integral part of growing up in Britain from the 1950s. Ska, rocksteady and reggae chopped, pumped and skanked their way out of sound systems, bars and nightclubs finally licking the airwaves with *My Boy Lollipop* by Millie Small. Desmond Dekker aced the charts with *Israelites* and Ken Boothe hit Number One with *Everything I Own.* This influence was seen in every little thing the Police did as they spread their unique version of reggae across the globe and although he says *It Wasn't Me,* Shaggy has continued to keep the reggae flame burning brightly.

Jamaicans arrived wholesale on the *Windrush* in the 1950s, landing in droves to help rebuild a nation but the influence was there long before that. West Indian troops fought in WWI and WWII. In the 1700s slave riots in Bristol spurred abolition. British history is peppered with references to Jamaicans. One of King Arthur's Knights was from Yard. Sir Nuff-Gal-A-Had was his name. His horse was called Lexus and he wore gold chain mail. He was known as the late knight but always won at round table dominoes. He cooked wicked jerk dragon but never ate any as he said "it favour croaking lizard too much." It was Nuff-Gal-A-Had who found the Holy Grail. He'd always find a chalice.

Public office is something we've never been shy in taking. We've supplied mayors, councillors and I know at least one of us has held the most famous civic post in Britain, Sheriff of Nottingham. Unfortunately we've supplied a few robbing hoods too.

When Britain experimented with decriminalising marijuana they tested it in Brixton, a testament to Rastafarians who championed the cause for so long that the law has finally listened. Dreadlocks of many colours can be seen all over the country, which is indicative of the impact rasta has had on the outside of people's heads as well.

In sporting Britain where foreign players ply their trade, many English players are second generation West Indians. There was a time when so much Caribbean blood ran through British Olympian's veins only one of their male runners was white, and his name was Black! But when the offspring of cricketing great George Headley plays for England and not for the West Indies I think the argument is done. There's plenty Caribbean influence in England.

What next? I wouldn't be surprised if one of the princes gets involved with a Jamaican girl. The amount of true multi-cultural mixing that goes on these days in Britain is a joy to see. One day we may have a real Caribbean Queen.

ORIGINALLY PUBLISHED DECEMBER 2001

Street Art

CHRISTINE KRISTEN

On a quiet street in Portland, Jamaica a man in a dapper powder-blue suit and matching hat smiles at his girlfriend looking stocious in a floor-length green dress. Nearby a stylishly dressed young couple and a demure woman strike a pose against a backdrop of trees, a lake and cloudy skies. A young Rastafarian with dreadlocks and tam wryly observes them leaning casually against a wall. These are not real people but painted ones which decorate the Eastern Fashion Store one of the many shops, bars, beauty parlours, restaurants and push carts throughout Jamaica which use sign-painting to advertise their wares or services. These signs are usually painted by self-taught artists in a straight forward and what could be called 'intuitive' style. Not only do these painted images indicate what business is being carried on, they also embody various aspects of Jamaican culture including music language food and religion.

While driving along Jamaica's scenic highways you may notice small brightly painted buildings with names like Stanley's Stop Relax Bar, Sunrise and Parke's Love Joint. You are looking at Jamaica's rum bars, local epicenters of social activity and of course drinking. Several varieties of locally produced rum are available from the top of the line Appleton Estate Special to white rum an expensive overproof rum.

At a rum bar you are likely to find a rousing game of dominoes in progress. Jamaicans takes their dominoes quite seriously and delight in slapping down a domino with a resounding smack. You will be able to listen to the latest reggae tunes on the jukebox and you will find

BAR
Roof Club
PARKER
PRODUCTION

this an excellent opportunity to hear local language being spoken.

Another common sight in Jamaica is the humble pushcart careening precariously down a crowded street, bearing a huge load of anything from pineapples to bricks. These are not commonly decorated but occasionally one is treated to the sight of an amusingly painted cart such as the black one proudly bearing the simple name 'Boops' a Jamaican slang term for sugar daddy. "Kisko, Kisko!" is the familiar cry of the sky juice or snow cone vendor can be heard throughout Jamaica but especially in downtown Kingston where the painted carts have become a sort of travelling billboard for the vendor's philosophy. They feature elaborate inscriptions such as "Yes Juicey, I like how the man a fight it. Just try to have a little faith. Sell I a earth juice." One cheerful cart painted a sunny yellow with a silver dragon two dreadlocked drummers and a large Pepsi bottle proclaims, "Cool Runnings! Here comes Mr. Cool. Check him out nuh! Silver Dragon Mr. Cool is the best in the west. Dread at the Controls!" The Blue Fox International entices, "Psst! Hi dear, are you feeling hot or what? Come and have a juice right here!" And on a more serious note, "The Lord is my light and my salvation. Of whom shall I be afraid?" In addition to sky-juice,

some vendors sell coconut water or 'jelly' (young, unripe coconuts full of a refreshing clear liquid very satisfying and very healthy). These jelly carts are often painted with idyllic tropical sunsets and palm trees.

So if you're out walking or on the road make the acquaintance of a friendly juice vendor or take a peek at the wall murals on bars and stores across Jamaica, often humorous in nature they will delight your eyes and give an imaginative look at life on the island.

ORIGINALLY PUBLISHED MAY 1999

The Higgler

JOHN MAXWELL

It is four o'clock in the morning and you are driving down the hills from a very late party and there is nobody else on the road. It is cool, almost cold, there is mist, peaceful and solitary and suddenly there in the road is a woman with a donkey loaded with bananas, yams, oranges and God knows what else in the wicker hampers. She is so unexpected she is almost like an apparition and you wonder where but where can she be going to at this time of the morning and why.

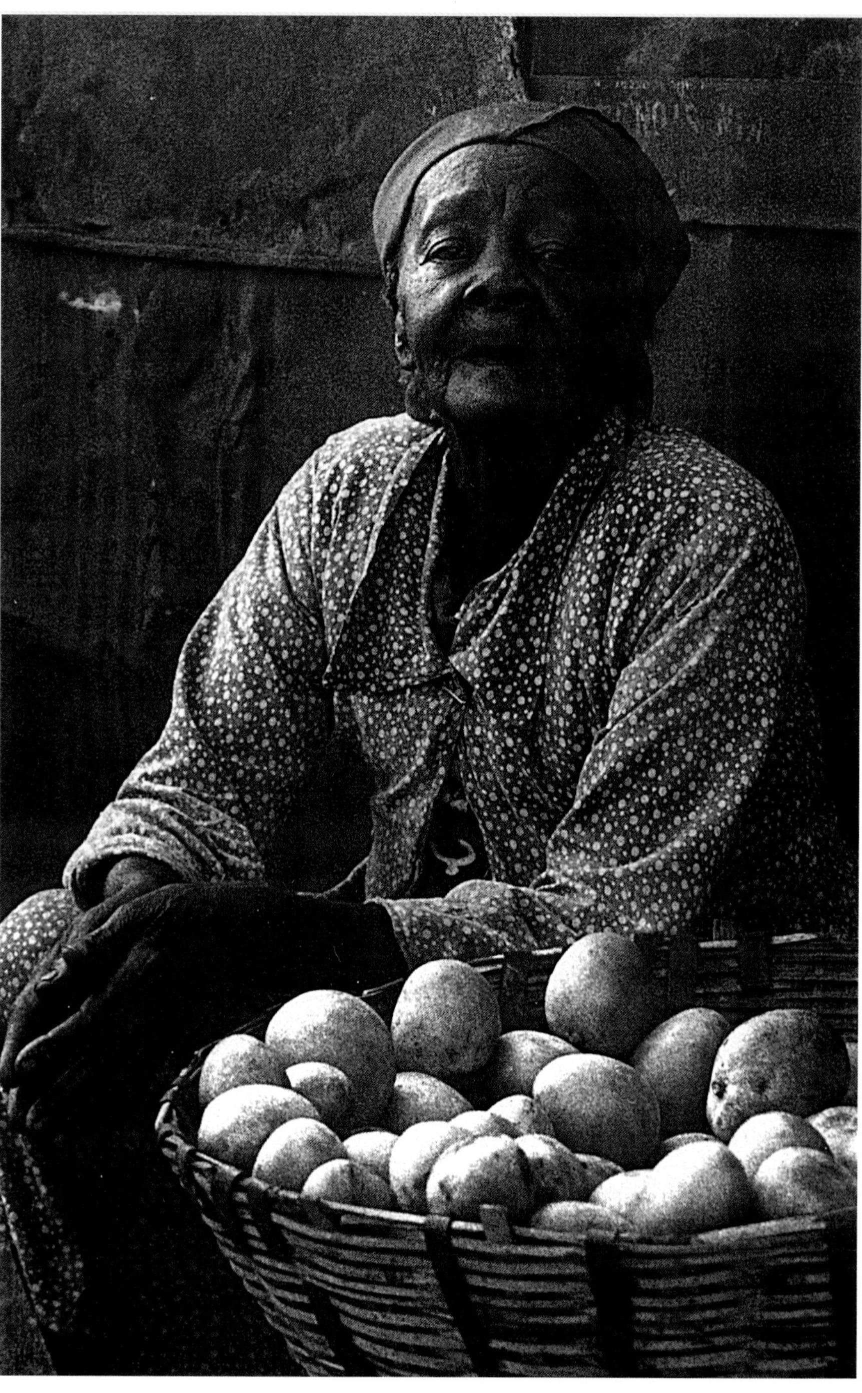

By the time your speculations end you will be at home perhaps, and twenty-four hours later, if you are a typical town-dwelling Jamaican, you yourself, or your wife, or your helper will soon be on the way to the market to buy your supplies for the week.

The woman you passed on the road would have been a higgler and depending where you lived, you (or your wife or help) would meet her at the market.

Higgler is an old English word, and like such, it has survived in Jamaica and one or two other places while it has died out in its native land. It survives in Jamaica because it describes an activity vital to the life of the community which can't quite be described in any other way.

According to the dictionary a higgler is "one who disputes about terms, a huckster or peddler." In Jamaica the term means no more than that. In the days when most black people in Jamaica were slaves, the plantation owners who owned the slaves, were obliged by law to provide a certain minimum sustenance for their slaves, and also, in the late days of slavery, to give each slave family a plot of ground on which they could grow the tubers and vegetables which could not be grown on the estates or imported. Many of these plots provided a surplus which the slaves were allowed to sell or exchange in special markets, on Sundays, markets which gradually became important social centres to the slaves and serious threats, eventually, to the livelihoods of the merchants who considered it was their right to supply the estates.

Even then it was common as it is now, for agreements made among the growers to take it to market to sell their produce and to buy manufactured goods or other produce which they could not produce themselves.

These markets became so important not only to the slaves, but to their masters, that in 1774, the historian Edward Long estimated that one-fifth of the money supply in circulation was in the hands of the slaves in the form of small coins.

After slavery was abolished a great impetus was given to this marketing system, for many thousands of ex-slaves continued to own the grounds they had, or rented parts of the sugar properties which were being progressively abandoned because of a shortage of wage labour.

Today, despite the introduction of a government marketing organisation to handle crops for local consumption, and a proliferation of organisations to handle export crops, the import marketing system in Jamaica is still conducted by people who collect goods from their neighbours and come down to the towns to sell.

The most important reason for this is that when the ex-slaves left the sugar plantations, the only land available to them became progressively more and more inaccessible, as laws were passed to make land-holding on the plains more difficult so that more labour would be available for the surviving sugar estates.

As a result, today, much of the agricultural produce in Jamaica comes from steep hillsides which, ideally, should be forests, but which are planted in vegetables and ground crops such as yams and potatoes. To get to these areas is difficult in any case, but is very often more than uneconomical for a modern distribution system.

Here the higgler comes into her own—and it is mostly her own because the man of the house usually stays at home to mind the cultivation and see after their children.

There are town higglers and country higglers, small higglers and large higglers, higglers who sell only one class of goods and higglers who sell anything available.

Some growers from the rural areas come into town each weekend, give their produce to higglers to sell, and collect their money when they are about to leave the town for home. On the other hand, some people from the country areas come into town and sell their goods themselves. These so-called "country-higglers" are the most important sector of the Jamaican marketing system, because they collect produce from areas where the official marketing organisations are either unwilling or unable to go.

The country higgler usually collects her goods in midweek and then comes to town on a Thursday afternoon or Friday morning. She waits on decrepit buses or trucks which charge a fairly stiff fare for transporting her and her goods and when she comes to town she sells in markets which may sometimes be comfortable but usually are inadequate for the purpose they are intended to fulfill.

The country higgler wants to sell her goods as quickly as she can, naturally, because since she is selling mostly vegetables, the fresher they are the higher the price she will get. Not only that, but she must be ready to go when the truck or the bus is ready to return to her district, because there may be no more trucks or buses going to that area for another twenty-four hours or more.

The higgler's relationship to her customers is complex. She may sell some of her produce to the so-called "town-higgler" who buys wholesale from several higglers and sells in the same markets with some of her suppliers. She has the advantage of living in the town, so she doesn't have to wait on a bus or be worried about getting aboard the last truck home.

If the country higgler prefers to sell her produce herself she very often has a group of valued and constant customers who patronise her for no better reason than that she comes from the area in which they spent their childhood, or because she has a nice smile or whatever. Because although the prices for the same commodities do not vary greatly in any given market, the prices to each class of consumer do certainly vary. The higgler buying her produce will, by mutual agreement, be allowed a certain margin which depends on the generally ruling price. She expects, say, to make six cents on a large bundle of callaloo. If the price goes up because of shortage, a bundle of callaloo will remain the same price but the size of the bundle will go down. A small bundle of callaloo may be sixpence to a poor customer—that is, one in the same economic class as the higgler, but it may be seven cents to the middle class housewife or her help if she is sent to the market, and it may be eight cents to the foreigner. All of these relationships will probably of course change in time but the basic principles remain the same.

Higglers do their own public relations: a good customer will get extra portions consistently, so that a good customer who happens to be a foreigner will by this process pay more or less the same price as the Jamaican middle class lady and sometimes less. And if a certain item is in short supply and you are a regular customer of "Miss Adina" she may refuse to sell what she has until you, her valued customer, arrives.

This accounts for a common libel upon higglers. It used to be said that higglers were idle women who came to town to enjoy themselves and squander their menfolk's money. This was because if you approached a higgler on her way to market and offered to buy something, she might refuse to sell on the ground that she was going to market. It was not that she wanted to go to market, but that she had customers who expected her to be there and who might not be there when she next appeared if she didn't have her regular supplies for them. It is more important to her to sell her goods every week than to make a killing one week and have nothing the next. She does not enjoy most of her coming to market, though she makes a joy of the necessity of sitting on a crowded uncomfortable truck—she can talk to new people—and she accepts without complaint the hard benches she is given as beds in the market and the hard answers from people who do not understand why she is there and why she will not sell them green peppers although it is plain that she has them. She will not save in the conventional way and she is not one of the classic components of a money economy. But in Jamaica she is a most important person.

ORIGINALLY PUBLISHED NOVEMBER 1972

Come We Go Down

BARBARA GLOUDON

"Hey Mammy...step this way nuh and keep yuhself young wid a coconut water. Wash off the heart."

I love markets, Jamaican markets, with their hustle and bustle and an undertone even of adventure. A Jamaican market, with its throng of sellers and buyers, each intent on getting the best of the deal, attracts the good, the bad and sometimes, the ugly. It takes nerve not to panic when, in the middle of a crowded market, a cry goes up of "Hot water... coming through ... hot water." After the initial scare, one turns to find that this is but an attention-getting device of a pushcart man clearing a path through the crowd. When you turn to confirm that you have been duped, he flashes by, laughing, with his load of nothing more threatening than a pile of carrots, escallion and some yams.

Markets are part of the West African legacy which Jamaica has inherited. The pattern of markets, according to one source, goes back to the times of slavery (from the 1600s to the 1800s). The histories remind us that slaves were encouraged to cultivate their plots of land with food crops for sustenance. Eventually, permission was granted for surplus produce to be sold or bartered and so the markets sprang

up, usually in proximity to the sugar cane plantations on which slave labour was employed.

Anthropologists note that it is from those early markets that many words for Jamaican foods came; for instance head sugar, for unrefined sugar boiled and moulded into a block, which one supposes, could be the size of someone's head. It was in those early markets that were sold the original varieties of yams—Afoo and Renta and many other varieties. It must have been from those early times that the ackee made its appearance. Now adopted as the National Fruit of Jamaica, it came to us from West Africa and it is said that Jamaicans may well be one of the few people anywhere who have made a food item of this fruit which is treated, for culinary purposes, as a vegetable.

It is in the markets of old that we found the yabbas, the clay pots fired by methods said to be still known in parts of West Africa. Then there were, and still are, straw baskets called bankra and cutacoo.

The influence of the market made its way as was to be expected into other aspects of Jamaican folk culture. Two of the best known folk songs which play on the market theme are "Carry mi ackee go a Linstead Market" and "Come we go dung (down) a Solas Market." Both songs speak of the buying and selling activity which was a part of rural life with its triumphs and its trials. In Linstead Market, the singer bemoans the slowness of sales: "what a night, not a bite, what a Sattiday night." The anguish is over the fact that he or she took ackees to market and "not a quattie wut sell." The quattie is no longer known in Jamaican currency but in its day was equal to a penny and a half, small change by today's standard but of value in a time past. In contrast to the plaintive tone of "Linstead Market," the song about "Solas" is much more vigorous and is linked to the sale of bananas. "Come we go dung a Solas; fe go buy banana." Solas is one of Kingston's oldest markets.

A Jamaican market, in full swing on Friday and Saturday, is a palette of rich colours; the produce piled high on stalls or on the ground. The scarlet, yellow and black of ackees contrast with the pale to mid-green of breadfruit. Bananas, from green to yellow, stand in contrast to the matted brown of dried coconuts, not far away from the pale green of "water jelly" (young coconuts).

Bright red kidney beans, which all Jamaicans know as red peas, can be found in season next to their pale-skinned cousin the gungo peas which produce their greatest show in the Christmas season. Bright yellow carrots pulled from hillside soil; cucumbers heaped alongside escallion and melon and purple eggplant and hot peppers from yellow to dark red; leafy clumps of dark green calaloo (spinach) and pak choy, introduced from the Orient; mangoes, from the tiny Blackies to the round and robust Tommy Atkins, of recent vintage, a hybrid introduced for the export market.

A Jamaican market in all its fullness is the sum of many parts. Besides the fresh fruits and vegetables, there are meat stalls and, in some, fresh fish can also be found. Before the age of refrigeration, the meat section of markets went into operation mainly on Friday and Saturday, the high days of trading.

Then, from great metal hooks, hung carcasses of cow and goat and pig. In early times, the butcher's weight was influenced by his generosity of spirit. To a regular customer, there was often a "Brawta," that special extra thrown in for good measure. It was the place where one went for "gooseneck" which had nothing to do with goose but everything to do with the richness of Saturday beef soup. In today's market, there is refrigeration and other modern amenities, especially in the urban areas. My favourite butcher, in one of the city markets which I frequent, takes my order by phone and has it packaged when I arrive. At another market which I also frequent, a young butcher there not only sells meat but rents videos, all at the same stall.

A Jamaican market is colourful language, not always appropriate for polite company, yet very often followed by laughter. It is banter and jesting of vendors seeking sale for their produce. "Hey Mammy ... step this way nuh and keep yuhself young wid a coconut water. Wash off the heart ... Hello sweetness, buy some carrot nuh fe mek juice fe yuh man ... gie him strength and stamina." Laughter abounds.

Markets are not only about produce but about clothing, hung on railings blooming like strange fruits; shoes and caps; crockery and enamelware; and sometimes a jumble sale. Jumble sales do well at market but they requires a quick eye and a strong hand on the part of the sellers or the stock might be depleted more rapidly than the returns at the end of the day.

Market is about salvation of souls. Preachers have always been part of the market scene. In a time gone past, it was where you found the "warner," the woman or man dressed in the colourful red, white and blue robes of pocomania, warning about some disaster to come, as foretold in a message from on High. One doesn't see too many "warners" at the market these davs but there is a lot of gospel, retailed through the medium of electronics, for you can just as soon buy cassettes of your favourite gospel singer as buy a handful of chocho from a vegetable stall or bammies, those indomitable cakes of cassava, from a man who prowls the market shrieking "Bamee ... get yuh St. Elizabeth Bamee..."

Market is about colourful dress, of vendors and of buyers. One of the regrets engendered by time's passing is the steady disappearance of the traditional form of dress associated especially with rural women. Chief of these was the head tie, often of crisp bandana plaid, tied around the head, terminating in peaks at the back. Rural women took great pride in their head ties. You can still see them in some markets but not as much as before. One's favourite market lady today might just as well sport a wig or jherri curls, the impact of which would be negated by a head covering. You will still find older market women too with aprons fashioned with deep, deep pockets to contain the day's sales. However, market ladies, like everyone else, have become more security-conscious and the location of the day's sales is less likely to be on obvious view. It can either be concealed in "the sawf" (soft), a wonderfully descriptive term for the depths of a bosom, or in some location of the stall which no prudent vendor would reveal.

The clash of Today and Yesterday is to be found also in the presence of solar calculators with which some market persons (usually younger ones) tot up a sale. Older heads, however, have no difficulty in adding up long columns of figures with astonishing accuracy, confounding those who render judgements about the numeracy and literacy of the Jamaican working class.

There is no telling who you will meet in a Jamaican market. In two markets which I frequent, we have a regular "pack" who exchange views on the week's headlines over the produce. And the last time I saw Bob Marley, it was in a market—Papine Market, where he arrived accompanied by a retinue of assistants. Then, with his mighty lion's mane thrown back, and his fists clutching piles of dollars, he issued commands: "Yam, brethren... green banana... pumpkin... ilaloo... (calaloo).

The market folks were impressed. "Lion man, lion. Is so man fe run tings." So it is, in a Jamaican market where "fe we people" run tings... or to put it another way (if you must), we are in control.

ORIGINALLY PUBLISHED NOVEMBER 1993

Whatever happened to "The Harder They Come"

BARBARA BLAKE

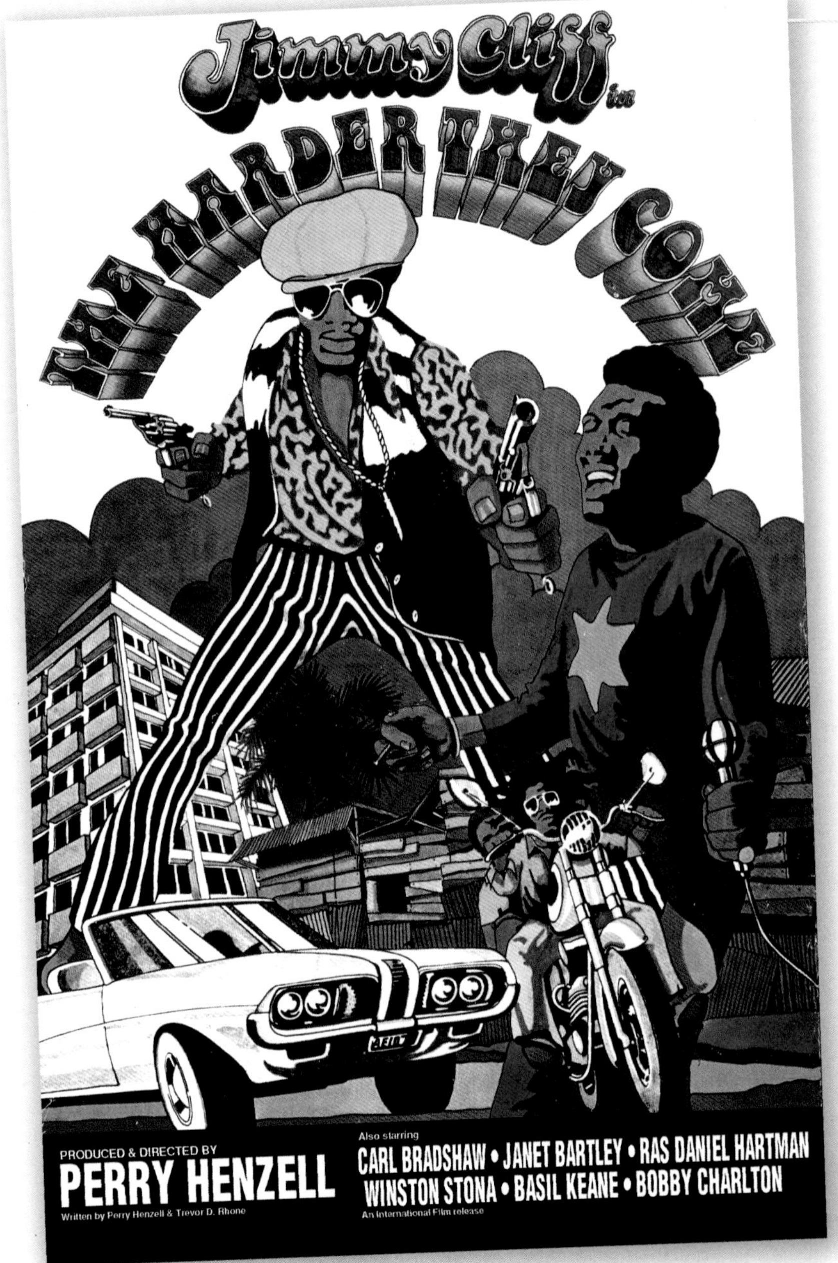

The poster hails Jamaica's first full length film and was used as a *SkyWritings* cover.

The 1972 Cannes Film Festival had been quite an eye-opener, but there was an even greater pleasure awaiting my return to my London base from a filming trip with BBC TV: "Would you like to promote the first-ever Jamaican film?"

I was cautious. The offer came fom Chris Blackwell, Island Records' millionaire boss, a Jamaican. He was financially shrewd, I knew, but also a gambler which is probably why he made so much money. But what sort of film could little Jamaica have produced? Let me see it first, I decided.

The screening was in a private cinema in London's Soho. I was the only Jamaican in a small group of young, long-haired music industry hippies, which made me feel even more apprehensive. I sat nervously, as the first spotty frames of a lurching country bus jiggled erratically onto the screen.

That was the beginning of what became for me, as for many others, one of the most interesting experiences of my life. *"The Harder They Come"*, the most spectacular first hit to come from the Third World to stardom, had started its non-stop journey deep into the consciousness and hearts of its first foreign audience, taking with it the indelible impression of the New Jamaica, the philosophy of Rastafari, and the African rhythm of reggae music.

It was also for me the start of a homecoming, a magical glimpse into the new Jamaica which had smouldered under ten years of Independence, eight of which I had spent in faraway England. Although audience reactions differed (Jamaicans rocked with laughter throughout, while Europeans and Americans sat in stunned silence), the first sight of the Kingston ghetto life and the sub-culture of Rastafari as lived in Jamaica today, were a glimpse into a world at once shocking, yet riveting. It was a place where we all wanted to be, dangers and all, and the music was the magnet.

"The Harder They Come" became a superstar; the music, the actors. the lifestyle, the story, the philosophy and the makers, all rolled into one.

But the journey from unknown to superstar was not without its events, I distinctly remember the response from the English film critics invited to the first press preview. I had created invitation cards using the film poster in miniature, with a written wording on the reverse to 28 persons in all. This departure from what I later learned was usual procedure, caused offence. (Later the invitations became souvenir items.)

Only two critics turned up, and one was a personal girlfriend. I sat in numbed silence throughout the screening, wondering what this cold response would mean.

It was a week in which all the critics had been shown Brando's *"Last Tango in Paris"* and tlne Sunday's columns were tull of praise for this film. The critic who turrned up to our film also praised "Tango" but began his column with the words: "Far and away the best film of the week was *"The Harder They Come"*, the first Jamaican film." We couldn't have begged for more—his column happened to be in the most influential British newspaper, the *Observer*.

I had the satisfaction of a stampede of sheepish critics begging for a look at what they had missed. Film clips appeared on television and to Jimmy Cliff's first ever press interview the leading evening paper gave a double page spread.

The film opened in Brixton, the only cinema which would take it. No one was sure how a black film would go down. The overwhelming West Indian love of the films made them flock to every showing and enjoy every minute. But in Brixton, where few whites live or venture, it was hard to come up with the only criterion distributors would accept for a West End screening—60% white audiences.

Critically, however, the film established itself with ease. It was, quite simply, the most interesting item in town. Cubby Broccoli, the Bond movie mogul, arranged for a special viewing in his plush private screening room, surrounded by a few hushed aides. There was silence through nearly all the film (a phenomenon I was now accustomed to from non-Jamaicans) until the scene where Jimmy Cliff as Ivan hijacks a limousine from a Kingston hotel and drives it away in a lyrical, swirling sashay around some rolling grass lawns. "OmiGad, no," shouted Broccoli, bursting with loud laughter. "I was just getting to like him until he drove over the Liguanea Club golf course," he shouted. I had forgotten that he knew Jamaica, and joined in his laughter. His minions relaxed; the boss loved the movie.

We took the film to the Cork Festival, Ireland, where the only sound in the auditorium was the very loud guffaws of the one Jamaican in our group who hadn't seen the film yet. But once again, film maker Perry Henzell was overwhelmingly congratulated by the audience for having made such a great film, and we became the festival celebrities. By the time we reached Venice's festival, we could relax and see the incredible sights, including the view from our Grand Canal hotel verandah—by then we were simply acquiring prestige.

Nothing, of course beat the night the film opened in Kingston, June 6, 1972. There was never a larger (nor more good-natured) "riot" in Kingston than when almost the entire city's population tried to get in to see themselves on the screen. The film did not let them down. Hardly a word could be heard from the screen, as Jamaicans, three to a chair, hooted, roared, rocked, shouted and cheered what was the greatest experience of entertainment pleasure in their lives—a Jamaican film on the Jamaican screen. Or at least, so I am told. I was one of the thousands marooned outside, clutching an aborted VIP seating plan in my hand.

Since that time *"The Harder They Come"* has done many things, most of them serious and significant. Firstly, it gave prominence and consciousness for the first time to the life of the typical ghetto dweller, and told the story from their side of the fence, thus making it impossible for them and their condition to ever be ignored again.

Then, it popularised and established the brilliant new Jamaican music, reggae, nationally and internationally. The hit sound track (Island Records' Blackwell's shrewd gamble) contained the best of all Jamaican music. Toots and the Maytals' great "Pressure Drop" with its intricate rhythms; Jimmy Cliff's beautiful "Many Rivers To Cross," and the rousing, starry, "The Harder They Come," not forgetting the Rastafari hymn "By the Rivers of Babylon" and so many other beautiful songs.

White America was as eager as the Kingston ghetto to hear and enjoy the music, and the film and music set a trend, which was eventually capped by the superstardom of Bob Marley Jamaica's first acknowledged rasta millionaire.

The film also gave a legitimacy and focus to an indigenous black Third World self awareness which had its roots in Garveyism and Pan-Africanism, and which had strengthened because of happenings in black America and Africa, as well as Cuba.

It also—and this perhaps is what eventually caused it to be a Pied Piper for young white Americans to Jamaica—exposed the philosophy of Rastafari, that curious blend of religion, ganja and reggae which is a vibrant reality in the Jamaica of today, growing as it has out of cultural, political and spiritual realities which the film so carefully observes.

The film has, at the same time, established a standard for Jamaican films which is a merciless measure by which any film made in Jamaica must be judged. Films have been made since— *"Smile Orange"*, the work of Trevor Rhone who, coauthored *"The Harder They Come"*, thoroughly enjoyed by all Jamaicans, especially since Carl Bradshaw, the supporting star of *"Harder"*, also starred in a role that showed off his comic genius.

Another later effort, *"The Marijuana Affair"*, which starred Calvin Lockhart and local actors in a combination of sex and crime in a Jamaican locale, was an embarrassing failure. Surprisingly, and sadly, the film had inspired a great deal of talk, rather than action, on the establishment of machinery to develop an industry based on its success. Even an attempt at an annual film festival has floundered for lack of interest in seeing Jamaica take her rightful place as a centre of film expression, even though the boldness of the film has inspired successful industries in other West Indian islands and produced notable efforts, especially the lyrical *"One People"* from Surinam.

The film's stars still sparkle. Jimmy Cliff, a popular recording artist before the film's success, joined the band of those who "made it", with his portrayal of the handsome, daring revolutionary hero. He parlayed this success as a platform on which to launch himself as a serious singer of songs, and a Muslim convert, although he is more popular in Jamaica as his film persona.

Carl Bradshaw can never be anything in Jamaica's heart than Jose, the badman, even though a role he played in *"Smile Orange"* as Ringo the hustling waiter runs close second in the list of names he is called as he drives happily through Kingston. Carl has played in four of the five Jamaican films made since *"The Harder They Come"* and is never far from the Jamaican stage as one of the island's leading comic and dramatic actors.

But the Jamaican who has been linked witli *"The Harder They Come"* longest has been its producer, director and co-writer Perry Henzell.

It was his dream project that sustained him during the years he made a steady stream of television commercials. *"The Harder They Come"* was two years in the making eventually, filmed on location in West Kingston and in lower St. Andrew at Confidence View Lane. "Everything happened here", Henzell, "from rain to riot".

The film received its fair share of critical recognition but what about its commercial success? That has been the story of Perry Henzell's last seven years except for the period when he launched into unsuccessfully making his second film.

In London it joined the realm of cult movies. In the United States, widely promoted to highlight black exploitation and aimed primarily at black audiences, it attracted little interest.

With Henzell's personal involvement, however, it gained acceptance with college audiences throughout the States, running solidly for four years in one Boston cinema.

When its commercial success seemed to be faltering once more Perry Henzell literally took to the skies again to promote and market it in Japan, India, West Africa. Sweden, France, Switzerland, West Germany and Australia.

His belief in Jamaica and a Jamaican film industry is as strong as ever.

"I feel that culturally Jamaica is absolutely unique," he says, and with much fervour. "It is the only black, Third World country directly plugged into the North American experience. The Jamaican community can go in on one side with the basic African experience and on the other it can be plugged into the North American experience."

"The Harder They Come" lives on.

ORIGINALLY PUBLISHED OCTOBER 1979

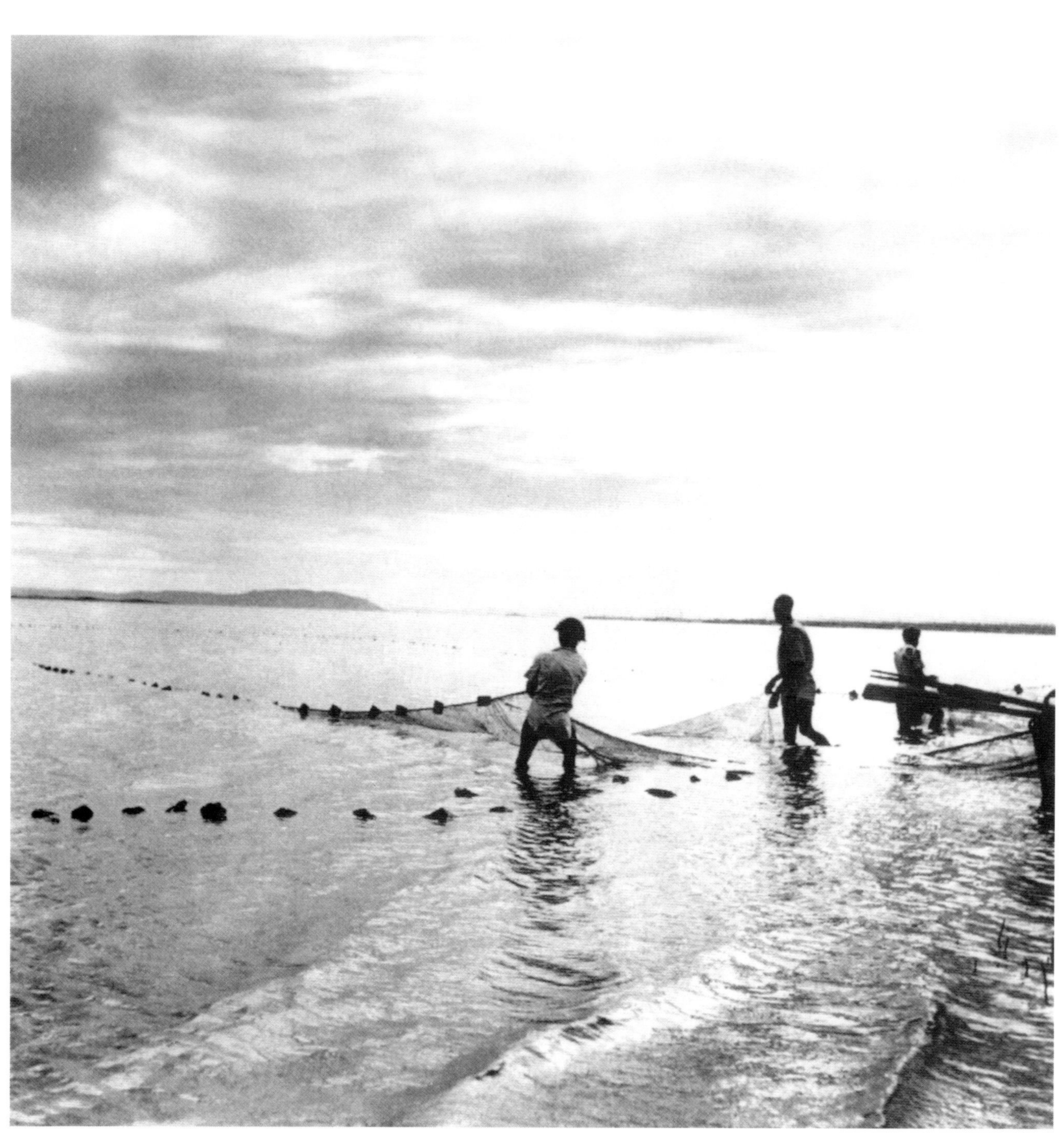

Living with the Sea

HILARY SHERLOCK

Across the sand I saw a black man stride
To fetch his fishing gear and broken things,
He stood beside the old canoe which lay
Upon the beach; swept up within his arms
The broken nets and careless lounged away
Towards his wretched hut beneath the ragged palms
Nor knew how fiercely spoke his body then
Of ancient wealth and freeborn regal men

— PHILIP SHERLOCK

"I was born to fish! From a child I just want to go out with my father—drop a pot—watch the water—get to know the signs—signs of the water, the moon and the wind."

Our sea surrounds us, like our mountains it forms part of our very being. Never far from sight the sea both feeds and renews. For some of our people though—it becomes more—it is their livelihood. Each fisherman has an abiding love, a deep respect, and a feeling of direct ownership in the life the sea contains. Man and the sea, with its creatures and plants alive within it read each other with a knowledge born of experience.

Driving along the coastline in the mornings you may see the canoes coming in—some with engines, some paddled. If you look closely on a calm day you may also see "spearmen" in action. Relying on their lungs alone they dive sometimes to considerable depths. Fishing in whatever form whether in a high powered boat of the first world or in yesterdays wooden canoe demands a love of chosen craft.

Over the past two years I have been living and working with fishermen in Annotto Bay and Robins Bay. I've come to know more of the sea and the men who daily commune with its forces. To know their skills, independence, choice of craft, vulnerability, suspicion of one another, but above all their pride in themselves as "men who go to sea." These are the true fishermen, not those who choose to crew a boat because they have nothing else to do. It is estimated that there are about 16,000 fishermen in Jamaica.

I keep referring to fishermen in the masculine because I am yet to encounter a woman fisherman. Women may own a boat or sell the fish when it is caught, but we don't seem to go to sea. Each fisherman has his own particular speciality. Harry is a hook and line man, he will also do some spearfishing. Trawling with Harry is serious business—certainly not the relaxed early morning outing I had imagined. No gentle rocking of the boat with a line dangling over the side in the clear water while watching the sun rise red over the low eastern hills. It was rather more like a cross country race, outside the reef, cutting through the surf, lines held firm—and not a fish biting. "Fish not biting today!" says Harry and that's that. Back we go to the small cove where five or six boats are anchored.

Harry's boat is fiberglass as are most of the newer boats. Some traditional canoes carved from cotton trees remain, used mainly by older men who keep close to the shore, often catching bait. There must still be an added magic in a canoe made from a living tree with all the appropriate rituals along its path of transformation. Making such canoes however is becoming a dying art. The depletion of the fishing stock on the narrow coastal shelf particularly on Jamaica's north shore now calls for bigger boats with powerful engines which can go further out to sea.

Walter favours fishpots. Each year at a particular time he and others invest in building very large fishpots made from mesh wire and sticks to "ketch de run"—in our area "the run" is jack fish. Frank, on the other hand, has beautifully constructed nets—he is a netman.

There is something always very satisfying in even just watching the nets being cast and pulled in, maybe it's the biblical allusions. Once caught, fish are divided into "dinner fish" and "trash fish" (used for making fish tea). Fish tea is not a tea at all, but a soup varying from a strong clear broth to one strengthened with okra and banana.

Each fisherman defends his method and blames any destruction or decline in the numbers and size of fish on the users of the other methods. In particular many point a finger at the spearmen who seem to be the cowboys of the sea free-ranging beneath the waves. Whatever the cause—"moon nu mek like before," "de fish smaller dan before and not so plenty,""de runs change up—yu cyan count on dem again" or "de fish dem smarter dan dey use to be"—it is a fact that the catch is often small. More effort is being put out for less fish.

The men are right in that, for whatever reason, fewer and smaller fish are being caught. Other forms of marine life are also noticeably affected. The authorities' explanations are many and all are probably contributory factors—overfishing, pollution, destruction of reefs and breeding grounds including mangrove swamps, the noticeable changes in rainfall and wind patterns.

Efforts are being made to respond and prevent further deterioration. Fishpots are required to be built with one-and-a-half or two inch meshwire, so that immature fish may escape; it is illegal to catch lobster during the breeding season between April 1 and June 30.

Over the years many groups of fishermen have come together for cooperative management of their common resource. They will purchase supplies at the Jamaica Cooperative Union outlet and sell to members of local cooperative groups as well as lobby with a united voice for individually felt concerns. As with so many other aspects of Jamaica's traditional culture it is hard not feel that the way of life of these fisherman is threatened.

Can we imagine not seeing the small canoes come in early in the morning or not witnessing nets pulled in on a small, black sand beach? It is equally hard to come to terms with balancing the need for an economically viable way of life—a love for a craft—and to take the measures which may seem individually restrictive to preserve the gifts of the ocean and its life. But the way must be found.

ORIGINALLY PUBLISHED MARCH 1992

Kumina
Old Traditions in the New World

LAURA TANNA

Few facets of Jamaican heritage are more controversial than kumina. "Devil worship!" detractors cry. Others point to its origins in authentic African religious beliefs, but all agree that the ritual drumming, dancing and singing form one of the country's more colourful cultural practices.

Kumina is practised primarily in the eastern parishes of St. Thomas and Portland, although isolated adherents of the cult live in Kingston, St. Catherine and St. Mary as well.

A kumina ceremony may be held to mourn a loved one's death, and/or (later) to cement over the grave in a "tombing" ceremony. The ceremony may celebrate a birth, give thanks, solicit healing or ask for help in more mundane matters.

In short, all the critical human needs or rites of passage for which members of any organized religion seek assistance from their god or church are covered by various kumina rituals.

The controversial aspect of kumina arises because a ceremony involves contacting the ancestral dead. Kumina adherents believe that spirits live on after physical death in an extended form of life. Kumina ceremonies provide continuity between the living and the ancestors, restoring or maintaining harmony between individuals and the nation of "African" people as a whole.

Kumina groups, known as "bands", have a male or female leader who serves the spirit world by interpreting the wishes of the spirits to the living and by observing certain rituals to honour the spirits, thus reinforcing the influence of the ancestors.

A yard where a kumina ceremony is to be held will display a pole which acts as the central focus to attract the ancestral spirits. Participants will wear colours appropriate to the occasion, for instance black and white for a mourning dance but green and white for thanksgiving. During the ceremony both men and women are free to join the dancing and singing. Primarily men lead the all important drumming which is the essential means of summoning ancestral spirits, although women may play the accompanying percussion—graters, shakas and "katta" sticks.

The spirits speak through the drums and direct the dancers and so the kumina leader begins the ceremony by making a gesture of deference, (a curtsy) to the drums, as a sign of reverence to the spirits.

Two kinds of drums are played. The kbandu, a relatively large, low-toned instrument keeps a steady beat. The playing cast, although smaller, controls the rhythm of the music. Rarely is either drum more than a foot in diameter or two feet in length, and both are covered by goat skin.

The drummer sits astride his instrument, pressing his heel against the bottom of the playing surface to vary the tone. Another person beats on the wooden side or back of the drum with a short "katta" stick. The rhythm of the drums changes throughout the night because different spirits respond to different rhythms.

The evening begins with "bailo" songs, mainly in Jamaican creole, to which the dancers move with erect backs, gyrating their hips as their feet inch along the ground, dancing in a circle around the musicians and centre pole.

This is the preliminary stage of invoking the spirits. Later "country" songs are sung in the Kikoongo language of the African ancestors, any of whom are free to enjoy themselves by dancing within the bodies of the living. Once a dancer is possessed—"in the spirit"—he or she may move uncontrollably, sometimes thrown to the ground, in what becomes the most dramatic aspect of the evening for those who are not themselves participating in the ceremony.

Kumina leader, Cyrus Wallace, remembers once when the spirits of Manoka Mvula and the great departed drum player, Matthias, were present at a ceremony and Wallace saw a drum play without anyone playing it.

"I see it with my eyes!" he maintains.

Occasionally a certain type of spirit may be too violent or possess a dancer for so long it could endanger the dancer's health. So the kumina leader sprays a mouthful of white rum upon the possessed person as a form of offering to the spirit. Or, the lyrics of a "country" song and a change in drum rhythm may persuade the spirit to leave.

By allowing the ancestors to enjoy themselves in these festivities, it is hoped they will then help the living to achieve whatever is being sought.

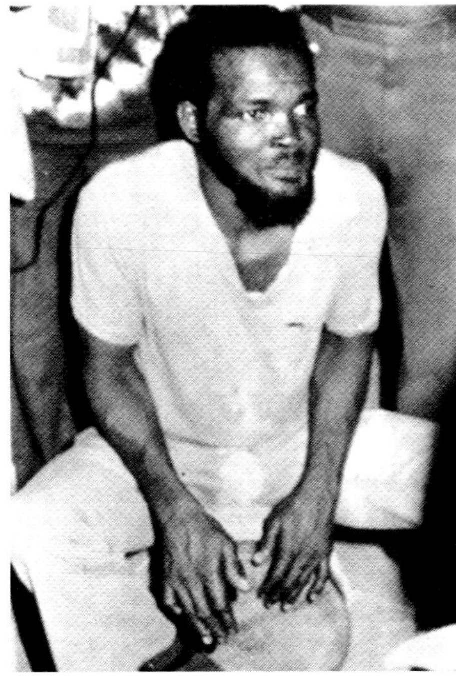

Food and drink are offered to the ancestral spirits.

Libations of white rum are poured in each corner of the compound so that the entire spirit world is embraced. For small ceremonies, white rum alone may be a sufficient offering, but in larger gatherings chickens are beheaded and, in the most elaborate rituals, a male goat is killed with one stroke of a machete.

These birds or animals are symbolic carriers of sin and the sacrifice restores spiritual harmony between the living and the ancestors.

Dancing stops only when curried goat and rice are ready to be eaten. Both the living and the ancestors share in the feast. The spirit food is left unsalted and offered to the ancestors by being placed before the drums, accompanied by an African prayer. Later it is buried.

The dancing and drumming then continue through the night until dawn.

Jamaica's Prime Minister, Edward Seaga, as a young sociologist in the fifties, was one of the first to describe the kumina cult and tape selections of its music which are available on phonograph records (*Folk Music of Jamaica*, Ethnic Folkways Library Album No. FE 4453, Folkways Records & Service Corp. NYC, 1956). By lending his considerable influence to educating other Jamaicans to the genuinely religious nature of kumina, Mr. Seaga has tried to dispel the antagonism some Christian Jamaicans feel towards the African tradition.

There can be no doubt that kumina is derived from authentic African roots. Because of the assumed predominance of the Akan people from Ghana in the 17th and 18th centuries, the tradition has arisen that Akan culture, as evidenced among the Maroons, is today the major remaining African culture in Jamaica. What has been largely ignored, however, is the influx of over 8,000 Yoruba and Central African (the latter largely Bakongo) immigrants who came as indentured labourers to Jamaica between 1841-1865, particularly after the emancipation of slaves in 1834. Dr. Monica Schuler, a Guyanese historian, through careful research in various libraries and archives in England, the United States, Sierra Leone and Jamaica, as well as from oral sources in Jamaica, was able to piece together a fascinating mosaic of cultural history which takes the Central African contribution into account (*"Alas, Alas, Kongo"*. Baltimore and London: The Johns Hopkins University Press, 1980).

Schuler and Maureen Warner-Lewis conducted a significant interview with kumina Queen, Imogene Kennedy (Lewis, *The Nkuyu Spirit Messengers of the Kumina*. Kingston: Savacou Pub. Ltd., 1977). This interview was further examined by poet/historian Eddie Kamau Braithwaite who enlisted the aid of Congolese anthropologist Fu-Kiau Kia Bunseki-Lumanisa, to interpret the material ("Kumina - The Spirit of African Survival In Jamaica", *Jamaica Journal* No. 42, Sept. 1978).

The Congolese found the Jamaican Imogene Kennedy to be speaking in the Kiombe dialect and that her experiences and knowledge indicated she was a remarkable priestess.

More recently, Bunseki-Lumanisa has collaborated with American anthropologist, Kenneth Bilby, to produce a comprehensive study showing the direct bonds between Congolese traditions and Jamaican Kumina (*"Kumina: A Kongo-Based Tradition In The New World"*, unpublished manuscript available at the African-Caribbean Institute, Jamaica).

One of Mr. Seaga's informants years ago, kumina leader Cyrus, "Baba C" Wallace, independently adds another confirmation to the Congolese origins of kumina. He knows that his great grandfather came from Africa and explains: "My great granfada... he was a Kongo...I don't know im, but this Mother Bartlett represent him to me."

Seventy-five-year-old Baba C was just a child of ten when Mother Bartlett was an old woman instructing him. She had been "a young gal" when Baba C's grandfather "was a big ole man". Which means the knowledge Baba C gained goes back at least 120 years.

She said to Baba C: "Me gwine teach you de language. Your granfada language a Kongo language. My language a Mumbaka language." She knew of 42 different tribes, but the most prominent were the Kongo Muyanji, Munchundi and the Mumbaka who all spoke related dialects. Modern Kikoongo words such as ngoma for drum, Ndzaambi Amphuungu for God, muuntu for person and many others are still used by Jamaicans who keep up the kumina tradition.

Baba C remembers Mother Bartlett saying: "Your parents is dead and gawn—fwiidiko—a Kongo, but me talk to you now de Kongo language. Every nation pray to dem God in dere own language. Well we de African, we say:

Kwali kwali non den den de
Beli gunuma kisamaya
Pan lakaya
Len legele
Luwi zakwe n'de
Ye kutabele mpe
Kuta m'baambe

Baba C cannot give a translation for this Kikoongo prayer but he swears that: "If you back against the wall and you say the prayer, you get free."

As with the cultures of many other non-English speaking Jamaicans, only fragments of the Kikoongo language and ancestral customs have survived. Just as many Jamaican Indians adopted the Christian religion of their British rulers but still participate in the Moslem Hosay festival or the Hindu Diwali observance, so too have Afro-Jamaicans adopted Christianity while still believing in the religious practices of their ancestors.

Afro-Christian revivalism and kumina share some of the same songs and superficial practices but kumina remains a basically non-Christian, African religion.

ORIGINALLY PUBLISHED MAY 1994

Peace and Love

HEATHER ROYES

"The rastaman is dealing with life," Samuel Clayton makes an exclamation mark in the air with his bamboo flute. "Love. Our doctrine is based on love, because love is the cohesive force that binds all events to make life purposeful and to keep on living. And because of this, we see life through love."

Samuel Clayton goes back to his flute, blowing a few trills as we contemplate his words leaning against the wall outside of the MRR (Mystic Revelation of Rastafari) Community Centre at the foot of the Wareika Hills. He's a musician with the MRR, plays the drums and has been with them for some 17 years.

The rasta drums are very symbolic. There are three kinds: the repeater, the funde and the bass. The funde holds the rhythm, the repeater kind of chatters and the bass gives that deep, background grumble. To a rasta, the drums symbolise togetherness, and playing the drums hour after hour with other members of the 'Brethren' is an important ritual.

As a musician, he feels that music is a means of educating people, of "edifying them" ... because we have seen a lot of change through the state of consciousness right here in Jamaica," he explains. "There was a time in Jamaica that when you play the drums, police would come and mash it up! And that was because they were not informed, because just a few years ago nobody knew anything about Africa right here in Jamaica ..."

As we talk, children run around the yard and adults trickle in. The greeting everywhere is 'Love, Brother' and 'Irie'. The signboard says that there are all sorts of classes and activities held in the centre.

The atmosphere is friendly and there is a peaceful feeling about this community centre similar to the atmosphere of many Rastafari gatherings throughout Jamaica.

The Rastafari movement is one of the most popular religious cults in Jamaica today. But it is not only a religion—it is a way of life. They make up a significant percentage of the population under 25 and their symbols: the beard, uncut hair (dreadlocks), the colours of red, gold and green on caps, belts, carts, trucks, flags flying on long bamboo poles; are seen all over Jamaica.

Words from the rasta vernacular have become part of everyday life in the island: peace and love (greeting), I-man (I in the rasta concept of the first person), Ja (God from the biblical reference Jaweh), queen (woman), herbs (ganja, marijuana), i-tal (according to orthodox rasta customs).

The rastaman is usually self-employed, plying his fruits, vegetables, brooms, art objects and goods from door to door. The Rastafari way of life is based on communal living. There are camps out in the country, some of which do not admit women because of the celibacy of their members, and there are yards which house families. The real rasta is strict about his diet, eating no pork, no fertilized foods and some are vegetarians.

The Rastafari movement is based on two beliefs; that Haile Selassie is the Living Messiah who was prophesied to return and that every black man outside of Africa must seek repatriation, his return to Africa, since he is merely living in bondage as the children of Israel were in bondage in Egypt. They support their belief by detailed references to the Bible, especially to the Books of Genesis, Jessie and David, as well as with historical facts about Africa and especially about Ethiopia. Many rastamen can outquote you when it comes to the Bible and to African history.

The Rastafari movement started in the 1930's and was one of the direct results of the political and social awakening of the Jamaican people. At that time, Jamaica was a British colony (and remained one until 1962), but a whole new concept of what Jamaica was all about began to spring up.

For the first time, Jamaicans looked into their history and recognised their African origins (80% of the population is of African or partially African descent) as a thing of pride rather than of shame.

Two things happened at around that time which were to stimulate the Rastafari movement. Marcus Garvey, a Jamaican, went to New York and began a movement among black Americans which was to become the nucleus of the Black Awareness movement today.

The other thing was the emergence of the late Haile Selassie as a world leader. In the early 1930's, he was crowned Emperor of Ethiopia. He was also one of the founding members of the League of Nations and the founder of the Organisation for African Unity.

Selassie's royal and biblical lineage made him the greatest on earth to the Rastafari who claimed that he was the Living God.

An important part of the Rastafari culture is the use of ganja (marijuana). This "herb" to them is one of the natural fruits of the earth and is to be used by man as part of religious worship: to increase awareness of self, and to allow one to discuss freely and constructively with the Brethren.

But ganja is illegal in Jamaica where you can get an 18-month prison sentence for smoking or being in possession of one cigarette.

Despite this, the rasta who smokes ganja (not all Rastafari smoke) will either do it alone to help him meditate or will smoke it with his brothers so that they can hold a "reasoning" (discussion usually of a philosophical nature). Besides the usual "joint", there is also the "chalice" which is a pipe made of cow or goat horn or bamboo.

The ritual of preparing the pipe with water, mixing the tobacco with "herbs" and lighting the pipe is a sacred one which is accompanied by the recitation of prayers, psalms and benedictions—each section of the ceremony symbolising something. For example, the lighting of the pipe is the act of Creation combining earth, water, fire and air.

Roderick Ebanks, a university graduate and an assistant curator at the Institute of Jamaica, is a Rastafari. Speaking about the recent popularity of ganja as a drug among the middle class, he says many use it as an escape from reality.

"Now I-and-I regard ganja as another plant out there. Just as how you have carrots and pumpkins for your eyes, and you have cerassee for your blood and you have these other things which they say is good for different parts of your structure, so I-and-I see ganja as a brain food. I really don't know how scientifically it works, but it makes you much more aware of reality. I think it has something to do with the physical reaction it triggers."

Born in England, of an English mother and Jamaican father, Roderick Ebanks was educated in Jamaica at Jamaica College and the University of the West Indies, which makes a very middle class education.

What attracts boys from this kind of background to the Rastafari? He feels that, aside from ganja which attracts the fringe element, it is the idealism of the movement which draws such recruits.

"Because of the idealism of youth and the words and life of rasta, youth naturally gravitate towards rasta. This was the only group that expressed the kind of idealism youth wanted."

But the majority of the converts to Rastafari are from the lower socio-economic groups in Jamaica and their reasons for conversion are quite different. Take Ras Shaggy Berry of Bull Bay, for example.

"Why I turn rasta?" He pauses, looks at the ground and spits. We wait for his reply. "I was born in a very decadent situation in Jones Pen. Now I watch my mother work for capitalist all her years—for about 25 of those—as a woman that her eyes roll over when she sick, her heart is in problems. You hear? And when she come out of that she like a lion with pain!"

"Seven of us to feed and couldn't stop. As she get up, she gone. Understand that we had to roam the Trench Pen and shoot bird in a grave. Yes. You see falling grave with skull and bone? You just take your sling-shot and bop down a dove and take him and pick him.

"You don't have a condensed pan with oil, you know? You wash out the first one you see and put him in there to fry in his own fat. You know what with? A piece of paper when you find out you light it. Sometimes we work miracles with hot stones and make the paper to light. We don't have any matches, you hear. That is how come I am involved with the Roots as I am so born!"

"That is who we are," he continues, "and we shall fight to the end to perform the works of God—from here to eternity, anyplace we be. Believe that too. We do not know how to lose, that is why we survive."

Sociologists who have studied the Rastafari report that one of the major reasons for its attraction to the people of Jamaica is the sense of identity it gives its members, a sense of knowing exactly who you are and how you fit into the whole scheme of things in the world's history.

The result is that the Rastafari have produced a great flow of cultural activity.

Paintings, carvings, pieces of handmade clothing and leather goods, music, songs, dances—all celebrating the beliefs, colour and the drama of the Rastafari existence. Today, the rasta is prominent in every aspect of cultural life. In painting—Ras Dizzy and Ras Daniel Hartman; in music—Count Ossie and the Mystic Revelation of Rastafari; and Bob Marley and the Wailers; in writing and poetry—Frank Hasfal.

Frank Hasfal lives on the grounds of the Harambe Theatre which is the cultural showcase of the Rastafari. Frank Hasfal and Hortense and their two children live there, in a comfortable house behind a shop which they operate.

He smiles a lot as he describes his life. First, working with the Post Office and the Department of Statistics. Then in the insurance field and later producing textbooks for the Literacy Board when it first started. He used to attend the Jamaica School of Art and did courses in ceramics, sculpture and commercial art.

On the subject of expressing the Rastafari message through the arts, he says,"You find that now not everybody can listen to you because you get a new concept, a new way of life different from the general thing the average person is used to. For instance, I couldn't go back to those places where I used to work and sit down with this kind of reasoning, because it would come indirectly square to them. They just could not understand what I am trying to say.

"So if you can sit down and write something and you hope that what you write can be published that who are interested can read and understand. That is fine. Or whatever you can draw, you can get across to people."

He shows me his scrapbook which has photos of *Groundations*, a show he helped to produce which starred Count Ossie and the Mystic Revelation of Rastafari, and of *Black Destiny*, a play which he wrote and was put on at the Harambe. Some of his poems are in an impressive book of rasta writings called *One Love*, published by Bogle Ouverture of London. But today he says, "things stiff that you can't achieve anything through writing."

His relation with Hortense and the children are obviously very important to his life and his philosophy. I ask his wife what it is like living with a rasta. "Just normal, as any other woman would live with a man." She shifts the child which she is carrying on her hip and thinks again. "It would be unusual if I wasn't a rasta. Then you would have conflict, thinking something else than he is thinking."

Frank reads me the poem which he wrote to open *Black Destiny*. Characteristically, it is about the rasta woman.

"I-and-I African daughter, black culture
a-dawn Natural beauty,
Ancient reality.
I-and-I Ethiopian daughter have all the
quality.
Up-full trodding, no imitating,
Real Sister Love, the apple of creation.
Come stand by us in this Black
liberation..."

ORIGINALLY PUBLISHED SEPTEMBER 1975

All Jah's Children

BARRY CHEVANNES

In travelling to the four corners of the earth, Rastafari has accumulated a global community of followers and its traditional Afro-centric identity is being redefined as a means to encompass the diversity of its 21st Century membership.

The VIIth Meeting of the Society for Caribbean Research took place in Vienna early in July 2001. The theme being "Caribbean Critical Cultures," the conference organisers invited Mutabaruka and Barbara Blake-Hannah, two articulate members of the Rastafari community in Jamaica, and several scholars from the Caribbean who had done work on Caribbean religions, including of course the Rastafari movement. Muta and Barbara were not the only rastas present, however. We were quite surprised to find three white female students bedecked in Rastafari attire—long white skirts, hair turbaned, red-gold-green shawls, waist bands and jewellry. They sat together throughout the three days, a small community of believers. Also present were three white male Rastafari, one of them a "bald head", and another a student, who wore a multi-coloured tam. None of them had yet been to Jamaica.

At one of the sessions devoted to the issue of reparation, the well-known slogan "Repatriation is a must!" was heard repeatedly from among them. Leonard Howell, the first preacher to declare that Ras Tafari, the Emperor of Ethiopia, was the true and living God, the returned Messiah, come to redeem black people from their bondage and take them home to Africa, could never in his wildest dreams have imagined that the doctrine for which he had more than once been declared a lunatic, would one day boast adherents from among the very people who enslaved black people.

A remarkable achievement this—from Leonard Howell, through Claudius Henry, a treason felon for allegedly seeking the overthrow of Her Majesty's Government in 1960, Prince Imannuel Edwards, founder of the Bobo mansion within the movement, and Mortimo Planno, the Nyabinghi Elder who made the first link with the University College of the West Indies, to Robert Nesta Marley, the international superstar, as popular an icon in death as he was in life. And all in less than fifty years.

Indeed, it could be argued that the Rastafari movement really took off in the 1960s, the result of two developments in Jamaica. One was the respectability it began to receive, once children of the black and brown middle class began identifying with it. Intellectually, this identification was made possible by the seriousness with which the University, led by Sir Arthur Lewis, had taken the movement in commissioning the study requested by Mortimo Planno (*The Rastafari Movement in Kingston, Jamaica*, by M.G. Smith, Roy Augier and Rex Nettleford). Politically, it was made possible by the bridge forged by the brilliant lecturer, Walter Rodney (*Grounding with My Brothers*), whose "groundings" with the Rastafari earned him the wrath of a paranoid government which expelled him from Jamaica.

But more far-reaching was the attraction of the urban youth of the 1960s. Young men like Bob Marley, Dennis Brown and Alton Ellis found in the Rastafari a vision of hope in the face of an oppressive and confining system, and in return gave to it the rich legacy of a new song. In the voices of the youth reggae music became a perfect vehicle for Rastafari critique, so that by the end of the formative decade of the 1960s virtually every serious artiste and composer was a dreadlocks Rastafari. Most, like the Wailers, were already hitting the charts before being swept up in the Rastafari tide. The lyrical content of their songs became harder-hitting and more deeply religious. They popularised Rastafari concepts, like Babylon, sang the praises of His Imperial Majesty, Haile Selassie I, and elevated Africa to a place of spiritual meaning.

These were the new missionaries—the reggae artistes touring the world. Rastafari must be the only religion to have spread its influence more by the power of the performing arts than by the power of the evangelising word. The first point of contact with Rastafari by people in West Africa, Southern Africa, Europe, North America, New Zealand, Brazil and other countries was the reggae artiste and his music. In a typical Rastafari play on words, this was a "heartical" movement (where "heart" is pronounced the same as "art", without the "h"), not a "wordical" one—art touching heart, 'eart touching 'eart.

Two things about Rastafari that touch the heart more than any words can are its counter-cultural critique and its Afrocentrism. The religion emerged as a folk response to hegemonic ideas about race, but in the course of its evolution it developed a way of life that presented itself as an alternative to the prevailing ethos. Rastafari replace the superficiality of "style and fashion," of formalism and societal rituals with an authenticity that makes the outward show a sign of an inward state. The greeting "Perfect love!" is not to be taken the same way one says "Good morning"—a polite but insincere ritual, but a genuine prayer instead, derived from the rasta's inner conviction of the power of Jah's love.

Rastafari counter the artificiality of modern life with a signature preference of natural life and ways. Their ital foodways have crept quietly into the consciousness of many people, finding affinity with growing concerns the world over with what and how we eat. Fresh vegetables and fruits, groundnuts, starches from the field, grown without artificial fertilisers, are preferred over chemically processed and tinned foods; herbal brews over bottled drinks; rain and spring water over tap; calabash and earthen vessels over aluminum; the ackee pod over artificial soaps; natural over conditioned air; herbal remedies over pills and chemicals.

But it is their Afrocentric iconography that identifies the Rastafari in an age signed by a "race contract" (to paraphrase Charles Mills's book of that title) against black people. The central icon is the Rastafari himself/herself, the dreadlocks a riveting symbol of *the power of the margin*—all Jah's prophets come from the margin. And this persona is attired in iconic regalia—tam or head-tie, waistband or belt, stole, scarf, buttons and medals of coconut shell, pendants, all depicting Africa, the original home of mankind, or His Majesty, or the Lion of Judah, in the combined red-gold-green-black colours of the Ethiopian flag and Marcus Garvey's Universal Negro Improvement Association. And in his hand a rod or a staff, symbol of authority.

The Rastafari-inspired reggae artiste has been a bearer of this tradition. His lyrics, his performance prayer and affirmation, the designs of his albums and CDs, all serve to introduce the Rastafari, living icons of an alternative vision to a world without 'eart/art.

ORIGINALLY PUBLISHED DECEMBER 2001

On The Move
A Rasta's Pilgrimage, Ethiopian Faces and Places

ASHLEY GAMBRILL

"My book is like 'Ethiopia 101 by Neville,'" jokes Jamaican photographer, filmmaker and writer, Neville Garrick, of his recently published book of photographs and accompanying text, *A Rasta's Pilgrimage, Ethiopian Faces and Places,* Pomegranate Communications, Inc. However on its review, the book reveals itself to be more than that of course: it is the embodiment of Neville's life-long journey to the spiritual sanctuary of his Rastafarian faith; it is the witness of Neville's personal soul-searching at a point of cross-roads in his life; and, perhaps most important of all, it is the gift of a new perspective on the history and culture of a country often ignored, or even forgotten.

With this book Neville has set out to re-orientate his readers from thinking of Ethiopia only in terms of the stereotypical image of sunken-eyed starving children from the wartorn north to a country rich in beauty and historical significance—or, as Neville writes in the chapter on Lalibela, "To a Rastafarian proud of Africa's greatness, standing here in Lalibela was a testimony to the truth of our contribution to world cultural history, often forgotten in the West." And so Neville's 118 colour photographs (he shot a total of 70 rolls of film) feature such awe-inspiring images as the castles of Gondar ("They are Ethiopia's Camelot"); the magical double rainbows of the majestic Tissisat Falls ("They make Niagara Falls look like somebody taking a pee"); the second largest lake in Africa and the source of the Blue Nile, Lake Tana; and the celebration of Maskal or "Finding of the True Cross," a religious festival in which a 100 foot pyramid of leaves and branches topped by a cross is set alight to the chant of thousands of onlookers and clergymen.

Neville admits that growing up in colonial Jamaica he, himself, was not exposed to African, and certainly not Ethiopian history, until as a young man he was drawn to the Rastafarian religion. As a result of this encounter he became a self-taught student of his African heritage and was drawn to two persons who have left an indelible mark on his life and on this book: National Hero, Marcus Garvey, and the great Bob Marley. Neville says, "Quoting from Garvey, 'A people without the knowledge of this past history, origin, and culture is like a tree without roots' and (from Marley), 'Emancipate yourself from mental slavery, none but ourselves shall free our minds—those are the driving mission statements in my book and that's all I am trying to do."

Although Neville's aim is to expose all people to the Ethiopia he found—"a place where God lives"—there is one group of persons to whom the book is specifically directed: fellow Rastafarians. He explains, "Let's face it, most rastas in Jamaica have a dreamland vision of Ethiopia and one of the reasons for really doing this book was to give them a better grip on the reality—at least it been seen through someone like them...this is one of us returning and saying 'Brethren, this is what Zion look like, here's a rasta's pilgrimage.'" And although Neville says he was never disappointed in his pilgrimage, he does admit to being overwhelmed by the humility of such a Christian and ancient nation of people: "Begging is a tradition (in Ethiopia) and it is done with humility. You want to give. The praise they shower upon you to get ten cents, whereas here a man would stone you back with the money...I learnt humility. I have been among some of the poorest of the poor but they are not angry because they believe in God and so this is for a time."

Neville was also struck by the willingness of the people to take him as one of their own which could only have been amplified by the presence of his long-time friend from the University of California at Los Angeles, former Ethiopian soccer star, Shoa Agonafir who also acted as guide and translator. In even the most remote places on their three-month trip, Neville, Shoa and Jamaican artists, Jimmy Smith, would be hailed with greetings such as "Hey, brother," "Jamaican," "Bob Marley" or "Rastafari." To Neville, who at the time of the trip back in 1996 had just resigned as executive director of the Bob Marley Foundation, this synchronicity was further encouragement that he should take his life work to another level. "My own take on this is listen, I have been known and associated with Bob Marley all this time. I have done the most that I can in enhancing and promoting Bob and so the only way I could take it to a new level and to at the same time satisfy my soul was to help put a finger on where Bob was pointing to; 'cause it wasn't about him, it was about Ethiopia. So the only way that I could carry that on was to introduce Ethiopia to people...that's what the journey, and maybe the rest of my life, is about; exposing Ethiopia to the rest of the world, the history that they didn't know."

This combination—of student and teacher, Marley and Ethiopia, writer and artist—is now leading Neville in many directions as he divides his time between Los Angeles and Jamaica. Among the projects that he is currently involved in are: the making of the first feature-length movie on Bob Marley's life; and the writing of a new book to be called *Dreadlocks: Origin and History.* But perhaps what is the most unconventional and certainly most exciting of Neville's projects is his dream to one day build a golf course among the castle ruins of Gondar where, he says, players would "ride camels from hole to hole instead of golf carts and I would get Michael Jordan and Tiger Woods to open it." As Neville sums it up, "That is the way I think. Remember I know I can make it happen; that is where I am in my head—I now can afford to have those dreams."

ORIGINALLY PUBLISHED JUNE 1999

FASHION

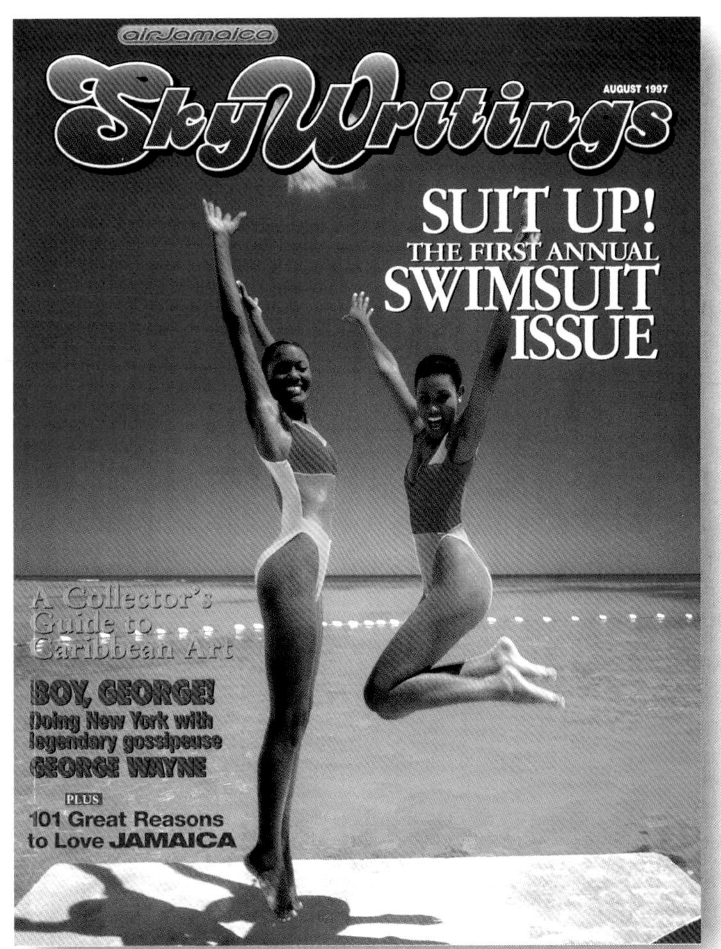

SKYWRITINGS COVER
August 1997
Models Michelle Small and Kenisha Gooden get ready for a hot summer wearing the Air Jamaica "Lovebird" colours.

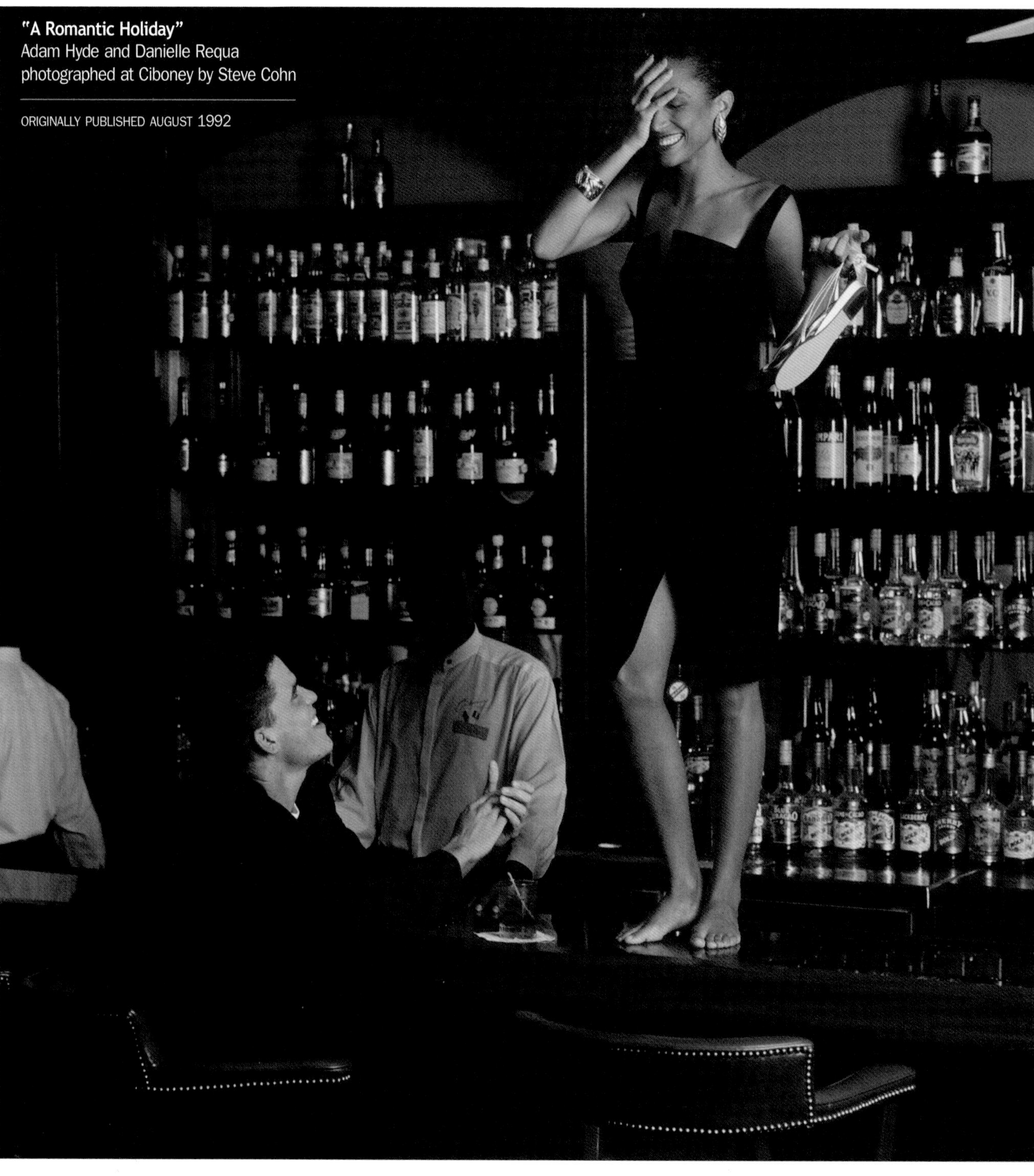

"A Romantic Holiday"
Adam Hyde and Danielle Requa
photographed at Ciboney by Steve Cohn

ORIGINALLY PUBLISHED AUGUST 1992

"Sunshine and Coolshade"
Judy Roman photographed at High Hope
by Peter Ferguson

ORIGINALLY PUBLISHED JANUARY 1995

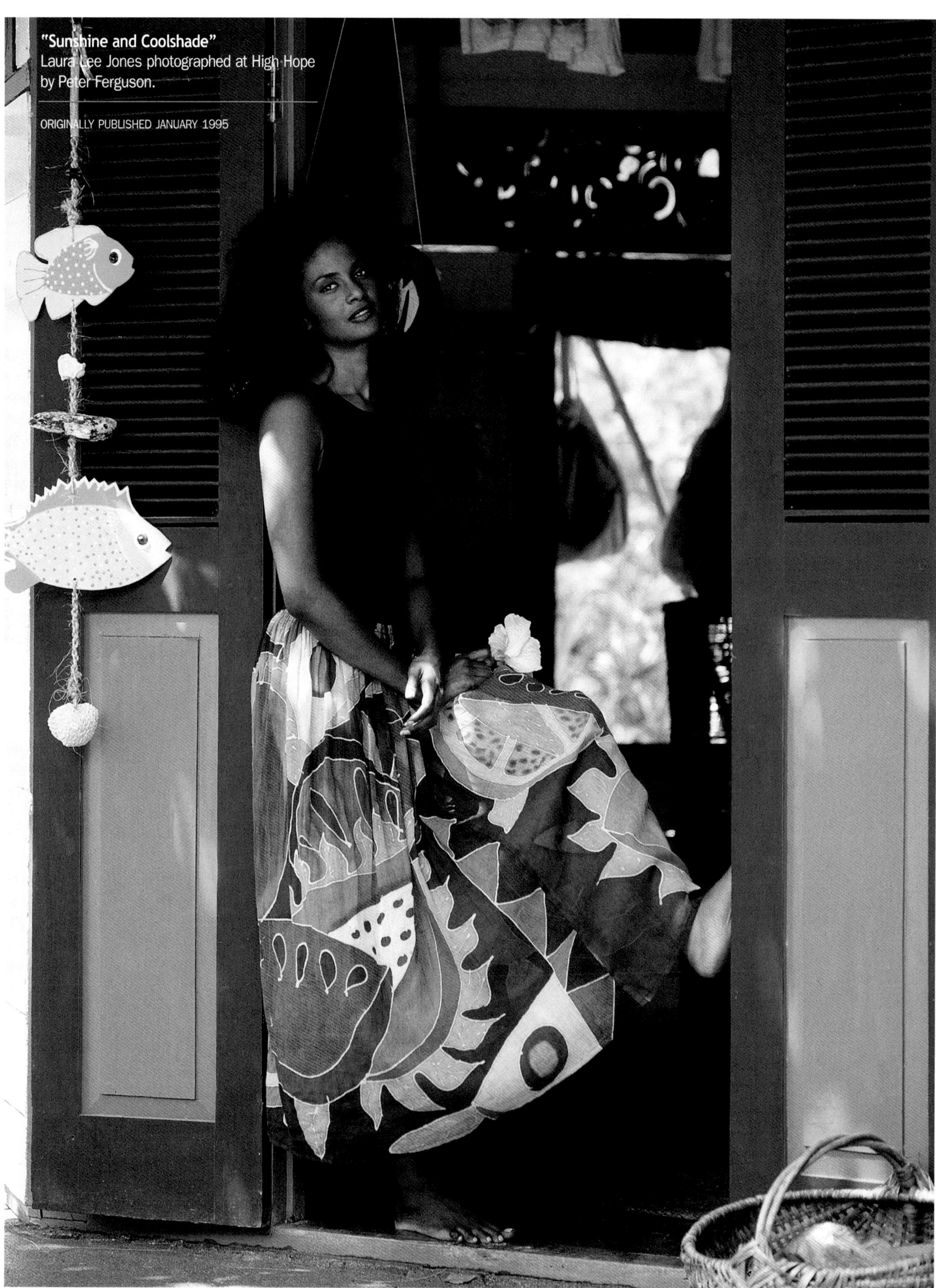

"Sunshine and Coolshade"
Laura Lee Jones photographed at High Hope by Peter Ferguson.

ORIGINALLY PUBLISHED JANUARY 1995

"**Body and Soul**"
Katrina Irons photographed at Braco Village
by Steve Cohn

ORIGINALLY PUBLISHED DECEMBER 1996

"Body and Soul"
Katrina Irons photographed at Braco Village
by Steve Cohn

ORIGINALLY PUBLISHED DECEMBER 1996

"Body and Soul"
Katrina Irons photographed at Braco Village
by Steve Cohn

ORIGINALLY PUBLISHED DECEMBER 1996

"Suit Up"
Paula King photographed at Scotch on the Rocks by Ian Cumming.

ORIGINALLY PUBLISHED AUGUST 1997

"Suit Up"
Paula King photographed at Scotch on the Rocks by Ian Cumming.

ORIGINALLY PUBLISHED AUGUST 1997

"Suit Up"
Keneisha Gooden photographed at Scotch on the Rocks by Ian Cumming.

ORIGINALLY PUBLISHED AUGUST 1997

"Absolutely Fabulous"
Janine Henry photographed
at Swept Away by Franz Marzouca

ORIGINALLY PUBLISHED AUGUST 1998

"Absolutely Fabulous"
Karen Walton photographed at Swept Away
by Franz Marzouca

ORIGINALLY PUBLISHED AUGUST 1998

"Too Darn Hot"
Ahsaki Clennon photographed at Jake's Place Treasure Beach by Franz Marzouca

ORIGINALLY PUBLISHED AUGUST 1999

"Too Darn Hot"
Ahsaki Clennon photographed at Jake's Place Treasure Beach by Franz Marzouca.

ORIGINALLY PUBLISHED AUGUST 1999

"Too Darn Hot"
Ahsaki Clennon photographed at Jake's Place Treasure Beach by Mark Steven Weinberger.

ORIGINALLY PUBLISHED AUGUST 1999

"Zen and Now"
Carla Campbell photographed in the hills of St Andrew by Paul Stoppi.

ORIGINALLY PUBLISHED JUNE 2002

"Zen and Now"
Carla Campbell photographed in the hills of St Andrew by Paul Stoppi.

ORIGINALLY PUBLISHED JUNE 2002

"Hide and Chic"
Carla Campbell photographed in the hills of St Andrew by Paul Stoppi.

ORIGINALLY PUBLISHED AUGUST 2002

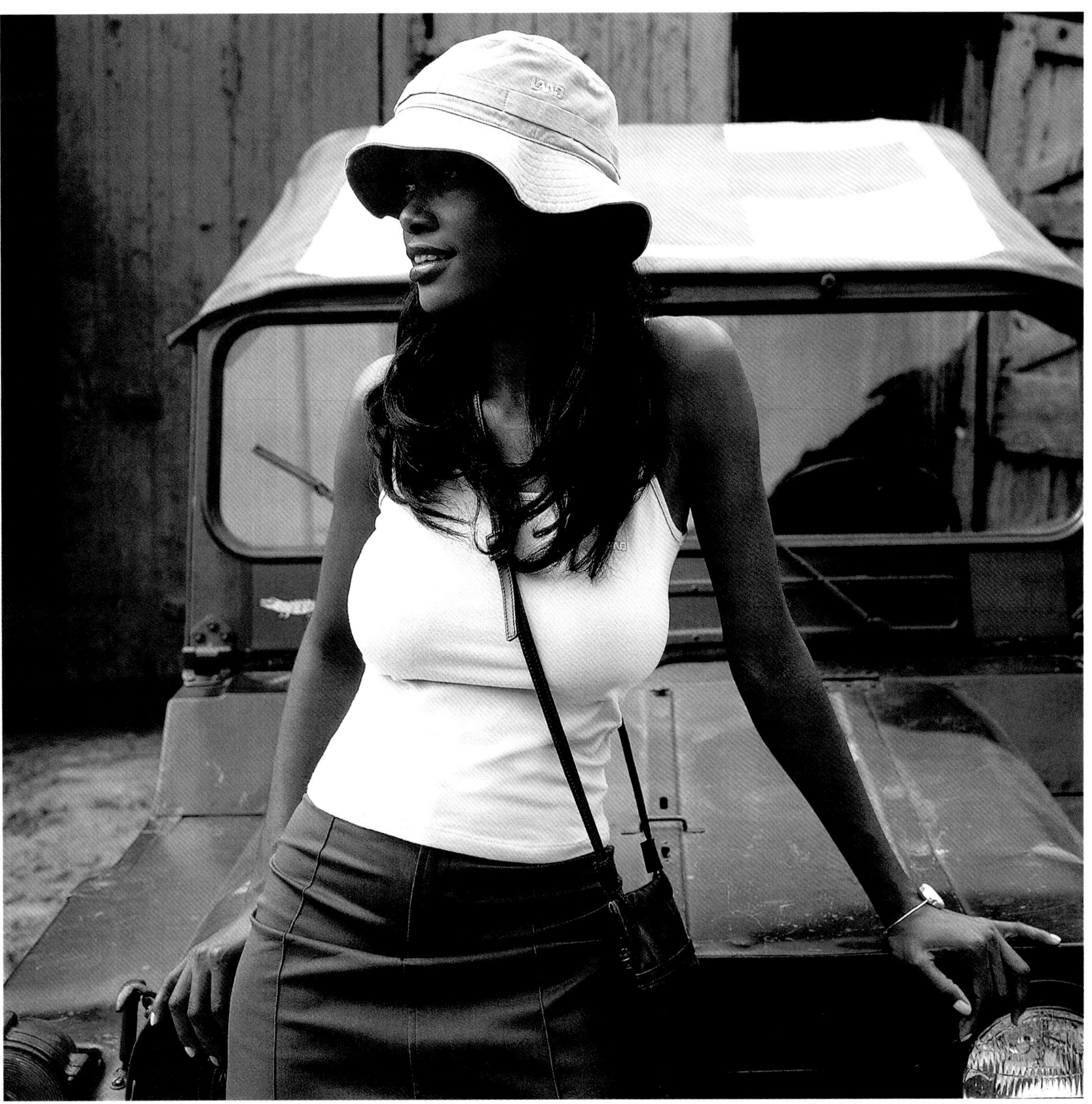

"Hide and Chic" Carla Cambell photographed in the hills of St Andrew by Paul Stoppi ORIGINALLY PUBLISHED AUGUST 2002

SKYWRITINGS COVER
December 2001
United States Secretary of State
Colin Powell

The Lighter Side of **Bustamante**

WENTY BOWEN

Sir Alexander Bustamante, Prime Minister of Jamaica, National Hero, labour leader, was, despite the prominence he gained nationally and internationally, a most human, down-to-earth person, with a strong sense of humour which was one of his endearing qualities.

His famous chuckle—"heh, heh"—was known and loved throughout Jamaica long before he rose to local leadership. His love of jest and his penchant for clowning, his sharp wit and his gift of the felicitous phrase—all contributed to the lighter side of this unforgettable man who made such an impact on Jamaica.

One of the most amusing stories told of him is his encounter with an English journalist in which his remarkable facility for repartee was displayed at its finest. It was during his visit to London for the pre-independence talks in 1962. He was with a group of newspapermen, telling them, with typical Bustamante flamboyance, about his ancestry.

"I am 50 per cent Irish, 25 per cent Spanish, 25 per cent Negro and 25 per cent Arawak," he declared drawing himself up to his full 6-foot-plus height.

"But, sir," interjected the bright reporter, no doubt thinking to catch him out, "that adds up to 125 per cent!"

"Aha", replied Busta, not stopping in his hyperbolic stride, "that is why I am 25 per cent better than other men!"

Other men might have been nonplussed or caught off guard. Not Bustamante.

His love of a jest and his tendency for clowning were well known—and experienced—by those who were close to him. B. St. J. Hamilton, his biographer and one-time personal assistant, gives many glimpses of the lighter side of the great man with whom he worked as permanent secretary when Sir Alexander was prime minister in the first government of independent Jamaica.

One very typical episode is recorded by Hamilton in his book *Bustamante, Anthology of a Hero.*

During an election campaign, Busta heard that his equally famous cousin, the Right Excellent Norman Manley, National Hero, was going to hold a meeting in a certain country town. He himself happened to be in the town on the day of the meeting and was leaving that night.

Before leaving, he called together some of the people. Pointing to a heap of stones by the side of the road, he told them. "You see those stones? When I return, I wish to see every one as I left it".

Later, he confided, with a mischievous twinkle in his eye, that on his return the next day there was not a stone there! Which was, of course, what he had anticipated.

Political meetings were very "stony" affairs in those days.

Another story tells of his adventure with an orthopaedic bicycle, a gift from an overseas group of businessmen. It was installed in his office and he would occasionally mount it, more for the purpose of clowning than for exercise.

On one occasion members of the donor group visited him and, during their discussion, asked him how useful he was finding the bicycle. Ever ready for a bit of pleasantry, he invited them to come and see.

By the time he had mounted, they were all in laughter, as his long legs came way up to his chest.

"So you say ten minutes of this is good exercise for a man who sits in an office," quizzed Sir Alex.

"Yes, yes," the businessmen replied in chorus.

"And you say it will reduce you, will take off flesh?" Busta asked slyly.

"Yes, yes," was the reply, again in chorus.

"Same damn thing!" explained Busta, pulling up his sleeves to reveal his slender arms. "Here am I trying to put on flesh and you have given me something to take it off!"

There is, indeed, a fund of stories about Sir Alex. There is the somewhat apocryphal one in which he is said to have told an enquirer that if he had sired a child, as had been rumoured, it must have been with his nose!

There is also the tale that Busta, no great scholar, once spelled the word bread 'b-r-e-d' while addressing a group of workers.

"No, Chief", whispered an aide. "It has an 'a.'"

"Alright", replied Busta—who was called "the Chief" by his followers—and he proceeded to spell 'b-r-e-d-a'.

Since this is an anecdotal piece, perhaps the writer may be permitted a personal memoir. I was a young reporter with the *Daily Gleaner* in Kingston when Busta was starting out on his trade union/political career back in the 1940s.

One night, he spoke at a public meeting in the city, which I was assigned to cover. It was at a street corner, and I stood in the crowd listening to him, not taking notes.

When the meeting ended, I went back to the Gleaner office and wrote an account of it, reporting what Busta had said, complete with direct quotes.

Next morning, Busta strode into the office, as was his wont every now and then. He expressed surprise at the report as he had seen no reporter there. When he was told that I was the reporter, he gave one of his famous chuckles.

"The reporter who writes in the dark!" he exclaimed.

Every time we met subsequently, he would call me by that fond title.

But perhaps the best Bustamante story is one told by the Hon. Robert Lightbourne, former cabinet minister, who was one of the great man's close associates.

As Bob Lightbourne tells it, he and Busta went during election time to a little country village named Welcome, so remote and isolated that the people there hardly knew anything that was happening in the island.

As the two men arrived at the centre of the village, after a laborious climb on foot up the steep track that led to it, a small group of villagers gathered around them.

One of the number, a little old man, obviously the village wiseacre, came up to Busta, whose lanky brown frame towered above him, dwarfing him.

"But ah dis ah de Busta?" asked the little old man, more to himself than to anyone else. "Me did hear 'bout him. But me did tink him did black!"

For once, Busta didn't know what to say!

But never the one to take umbrage or to bear malice, he took the incident in good humour. And, true to a promise he made that day, the village had a proper road after the election had been held and his Jamaica Labour Party had become the government.

Very warm, very human, that was Bustamante. And so it is in no spirit of *lèse majesté* that I end this piece with what is, for me, the crowning story of this most remarkable man.

Busta was attending a reception in London, given by Her Majesty, Queen Elizabeth II, for Commonwealth Heads of Government. He was in conversation with Jawaharlal Nehru, India's great leader, when the Queen came up behind him.

Turning suddenly and seeing her, he extended his arms and said, in that soft, light voice of his, "Hi, honey!"

And Elizabeth of England, a happy, smiling young woman, moved into his arms—a spontaneous response to a reflex expression of unaffected endearment.

There was only one Busta!

ORIGINALLY PUBLISHED 1979

The Lighter Side of Norman Manley

CALVIN BOWEN

In the consciousness of Jamaicans, Norman Manley is associated with the quest for excellence in a number of areas of national life. Returning from study and war service in England to Jamaica in 1922 as a lawyer, he soon established himself as Jamaica's and the West Indies' leading advocate, brilliant in cross-examination and with an excellence of oratory that was wed to a simplicity of language.

In 1938 he agreed to lead what was to become the first of the two enduring political parties in the island, the Peoples National Party, giving it its two major objectives—the winning of universal adult suffrage for all Jamaicans, and the achievement of Jamaican nationhood. He struggled unceasingly for both these objectives, though ironically when each was realized, it was his cousin and rival Alexander Bustamante, the leader of Jamaica's other great political party, the Jamaica Labour Party, who reached the tape first; winning the first election under universal adult suffrage in 1944; and becoming the first prime minister of independent Jamaica in 1962.

It is politics and law that encompassed most of Norman Manley's public life. But he was interested in many other things besides. A phenomenal athlete in his youth, and the first Jamaican schoolboy athlete to take training seriously, he ran the hundred yards in ten seconds in 1911, a record that stood for 30 years until equalled by his son, Douglas, in 1941. But he was also a demon medium fast bowler, a rugged football player and a marksman with the rifle, all while at school.

Years later, his continuing love of sports led him in 1929 to form the Jamaica Boxing Board of Control, and he drafted its constitution and became its first president. The following year, 1930, he organised the Jamaica Olympic Association, and also helped to draft its constitution.

In brief outline, those are just a few of the public activities which led his countrymen to elevate him posthumously to the status of a National Hero in 1969, the same year he died. But what was Manley really like as a man? Did he have a lighter side? And what was this lighter side like?

Those who were in close contact with him, either as relatives or political, governmental or legal associates, all say that there was indeed another Manley, quite separate and apart, though not completely different, from the public figure. A man of whom, had he lived in an earlier age, it might have been said that the "humours" were so uniquely mixed, that here was the noblest Jamaican of them all.

"If you don't understand it, at least try to look intelligent."

It's difficult to know where to begin really. He was a curious mixture. He had a wicked sense of humour. His grand-daughter Rachel Manley recalls that "he used to share the most appalling jokes with his friend and personal physician, Dr. Ludlow Moody." Sir Florizel Glasspole, now Jamaica's Governor General, but one of the foundation members of the PNP, recalls that once they visited an art show together, and he was puzzling over the meaning of one of the painting when Norman came up beside him and asked: "Glasspole, what are you doing?"

When the latter replied that he was "trying to decipher what the artist was saying", Manley replied, "Well, if you don't understand it, at least try to look intelligent."

Another time they had gone together up to Manley's house at Mavis Bank in the Blue Mountains, and Manley's driving around the dangerous bends had been so hair-raising that Glasspole remonstrated and asked him to slow down. On the drive back down, Manley drove at a snail's pace, and again Glasspole interjected, and asked why was he now driving so slowly. Manley's reply was: "Oh, this isn't me driving, this is Glasspole driving. "

His furious driving is of course legendary. He drove like Jehu, those who know him said. He often exceeded speeds of a hundred miles per hour on the Washington Boulevard when he was in his seventies, and in fact his driving skills approached the sort of scientific precision that Formula One drivers bring to their profession. An example of his approach was recounted some year ago by fellow barrister V.O. Abendana, who recalled "many years ago he drove me in his car —I think it was a Buick at that time—from Kingston to Hope Bay one Monday morning to do a civil case in which I was instructing him. We met with a slight accident at the top of Stony Hill, a cart and mules were involved and the side of the gas tank was punctured. He measured the flow of the gasolene with a quick mathematical eye, asked me how many miles we had to go, and when I replied 'about forty' he said, 'hurry up, jump in, the gas should last for about an hour and we should make it by then. 'He made it averaging about 40 m.p.h. over the Junction Road which in those days was not as good as it is today."

If he had a marvellous sense of humour and sense of fun, he was also very short tempered and prone to what, since Nixon and the White House tapes, are euphemistically referred to as "expletives deleted."

Alluding to his temper Glasspole recalls that when after the bus strike of 1947 trade union leader Thossy Kelly was charged with sedition and Glasspole himself had been charged for an offense a little less than sedition, Manley was defending them and had them in his chambers the morning of the trial cross-examining them about the facts.

On the way to the courts, Kelly suddenly turned to Glasspole and said: "You know Glasspole, Mr. Manley I believe is missing one of the important points in this case, and I think I should have a word with him."

Glasspole, knowing Manley much better than Kelly did, and aware of his irritability where his legal practice was concerned, tried to give a word of advice to Kelly.

"Look, Kelly," he said, "if you have any knowledge about the man you wouldn't approach him at all about that."

Kelly stuck to his guns. "I'm convinced Mr. Manley has not seen the point."

A determined union leader is difficult to restrain, so Glasspole resigned himself. "I can't stop you," he told Kelly, "But I'll stay at a safe distance when you approach him."

As Manley came up the steps at the Sutton Street court and walked up the passage to the courtroom, Kelly ambushed him.

"You know sir," he blurted out, "I think that there is a point that you are missing."

Manley paused momentarily, and then the explosion came. He was carrying some law books in his hand. Without hesitation, he took them and smashed them to the ground and turned to Kelly.

"What the hell do you think people pay me high fees to do?" he demanded!

Glasspole says that Kelly, who was a big man weighing something like 200 pounds, seemed to wither and shrink under Manley's rebuke into a 97-pound-weakling.

Ken Hill, who as a court reporter for the *"Gleaner"* in the late thirties often travelled with Manley and saw him in action. As one of the earliest members of the PNP, Hill recalls that Manley was very arrogant "perhaps with good reason" about his legal knowledge, and was besides a very aggressive person.

No doubt the aggression was a necessary concommitant of his profession as a lawyer. It is interesting then to know that Manley himself had grave doubts about whether he should indeed have studied law, and said in an interview with Corinna Meeks that if he had not chosen law, he would instead have pursued his great interest. "What was that?" He asked the question of himself and answered: "forestry."

Indeed, Theodore Sealy, former *Gleaner* reporter and editor, recalls that: "he was a man of the hills" who planted a grove of forest trees up around his Guava Ridge mountain retreat, Nomdimi.

"I used to visit him climbing the mountains," Sealy recalls. "He had to walk some two miles to get to his place, and he was very cross that the public road and motoring and electric light had reached up to his mountain resort."

Says Sealy: "He loved the loneliness of the mountains."

He was also fond of physical activity. "He genuinely loved to work on his own little farm up in the hills," son and former Prime Minister Michael Manley recalls. "And he never wanted anybody to chop a tree down. If it had to be chopped down, he'd chop it down. He was a great axe man. He'd grown up on a property as a boy (in St. Catherine) and he had this love of doing things with his hands." This love also extended to making furniture and carpentry. Up at Nomdimi he'd make chairs and benches, and bookcases.

Whilst he was a man of great physical strength, he also seemed preoccupied about his health. Rachel Manley, who lived for many years with him and her grand-mother Edna at Drumblair, recalls that he was always on some sort of diet, and was also prone to self-medication in the form of pills of one sort or another.

Rachel, who called her grandfather "Paddy" and her grandmother "Maddie", says he would take an aspirin and she'd say "Paddy, have you got a headache?"

And he'd say: "No. But I don't want to get one and I'm making damned sure I don't."

He was also a great holiday man. Whenever he could, he would escape to the seaside or to the mountains, and he loved having his family around him on such occasions.

He had a great appreciation of classical music, so much so that he was once the *Gleaner*'s music critic. But though he was knowledgeable about music he was not publicly known to be a performer on any musical instrument. Except to his family, for he was on the mouth-organ.

His son, Douglas, recalls that he was quite a performer on this instrument, "And he had quite a large repertoire of Jamaican folk songs and popular songs of various sorts, which were performed at great length; very often when we went to the country on weekends. After supper he'd get it out and the rest of us would clap and sing and we'd have a sort of jam-session on the mouth organ, largely doing out Jamaican folk music of one kind or another."

It's quite an image to contemplate really, the great Norman Manley, legal luminary and political trailblazer playing the mouth-organ while his family is gathered around him singing.

Was there a lighter side to Norman Manley? There most assuredly was!

ORIGINALLY PUBLISHED 1979

Abe Issa
Father of Jamaican Tourism

JEAN MIRANDA

He was running out of time. This was an interview once already postponed because of a power outage in the city.

Today was his regular monthly luncheon with the Kingston Cricket Club. He remarked, with a tinge of regret, that it was an all-male affair. We would have to continue our talk sometime soon. His suggestion—over morning coffee at the nearby Pegasus Hotel.

We never got to talking over coffee. Abe Issa, dean of Jamaican tourism, businessman. hotelier, philanthropist and Jamaican extraordinaire, died before that meeting.

What was amazing and a matter of secret pride with most people he had contact with was, every conversation with Abe Issa seemed a continuance of the last.

Once we reminisced on the golden years of tourism in Montego Bay, another time it was Jamaica becoming a year-round tourism destination. He later spoke of his company's acquisition of the Terra Nova Hotel, which was once a stately private home, turning it into a businessman's hotel. Always coming through was his love of life, people and Jamaica.

It didn't seem odd that this conversation began with the entry of the Issa family into tourism in 1943... the war years. That year United Fruit Company of Boston instructed their local office to sell the Myrtle Bank Hotel, the 'grand dame' fronting the Kingston Harbour in downtown Kingston, at 'whatever price'. The Issa family bought it for £35,000.

"Even if the hotel proved a failure, the real estate was worth five times more", Abe said.

This was a Jamaican. Born in 1905, Abe was educated locally and in Massachusetts where he majored in Spanish and graduated with honours. Secretly he nurtured hopes of becoming a teacher. But he entered his father's dry goods business in 1930 and in a very short while he established himself as a leading member of the commercial community.

Under his astute leadership the family business of E.A. Issa & Bros. expanded into a multi-interest complex, embracing several retail stores, importing and distributing agencies and then hotels.

As Abe Issa talked of Myrtle Bank and its success, he also spoke of the barriers he broke down. Everyone was welcome at Myrtle Bank as long as they 'behaved well'. A significant trade was built up among Jamaicans and with that they were able to keep 'body and soul' together until the war was over. Tourists were few then, but after the war the Myrtle Bank Hotel gained a foreign clientele and made back costs in the first post-war year of operation.

Soon after Abe Issa's brightest idea was born—the Tower Isle Hotel. It came from the need to satisfy guests from Myrtle Bank who wanted to stay in a resort area.

"Shouldn't we build a north coast hotel so

(ABOVE) A high point for Jamaica at the opening session of the ASTA convention in Havana was the meeting between Prime Minister Fidel Castro of Cuba and Abe Issa, representing Jamaica as president of the Caribbean Tourist Association and chairman of the Jamaica Tourist Board. (BELOW LEFT) The Hon. Abe Issa, OJ, CBE, recipient of the 1984 Norman Manley Award for Excellence in the field of tourism, poses proudly with the award after it was presented to him by the Hon. Edna Manley, OM. (BELOW RIGHT) Abe Issa with jazz musician and singer Louis Armstrong at the Myrtle Bank.

we can send our visitors there?" he had asked himself. Tower Isle soon became the first resort hotel in Jamaica to open all year round.

Abe Issa enjoyed a full and active career. He served his country publicly as a member of the Senate, the 'Upper House' of Parliament and was chairman of the first-ever Jamaica Tourist Board. Privately he has served education, health and welfare.

The island's present and only race track—Caymanas Park—is a monument to the enterprise and energy of the man. There followed another first for him—his pioneering drive and ambition led to the establishment of the now vibrant commercial complex in uptown Kingston, known as New Kingston, and formerly the site of Knutsford Park race track. The Abe Issa flair for doing new and different things also led to Jamaicans having their first supermarket and first uptown shopping complex.

But, it was in tourism that he played his greatest role. This was where he excelled (never mind he was a director of 36 companies), was a brilliant speaker and always in demand. He had a remarkable memory for names, and this helped to endear him to his colleagues and friends.

As we talked tourism, this father of Jamaica's modern tourism industry recounted the beginnings at Tower Isle. The area was all bush when construction began. His friends and others said it was a project doomed to failure. The one international airport was in Kingston and Tower Isle was mid-way between Kingston and the north coast. For Abe Issa this was a plus factor—this was a halfway point. He finished his hotel and it brought about a change in the industry.

When the second international airport was built in Montego Bay many felt for sure that Tower Isle was now doomed. They didn't know the grit and determination of the man Abe, who later became known worldwide as "Mr. Jamaica". At the expense of his time and his money he promoted Tower Isle and Jamaica across North America—a labour of love. Guests came there to share the entertainment spotlight with the staff and to enjoy Ocho Rios.

Abe Issa confided: "I'm convinced that if Tower Isle wasn't built, Ocho Rios would still be a fishing village".

The problems of the Jamaican tourism industry in those days was the paucity of rooms and the minimal funds available for promotion. He became chairman of the Jamaica Tourist Board in 1955 and remained in the post until 1962. It was a non-paying job, but Abe Issa was always at his best selling Jamaica, at whatever the cost. Those earnings he loved best—visitors coming, leaving satisfied.

To hear him tell of the difficulties he encountered with the political directorate trying to convince them that tourism could be big business, was testimony of his sincerity.

"They were ever convinced that at best tourism could only be small fry".

Wills O. Isaacs, a government minister then was swayed by Abe into believing that "tourism earns money and sells nothing".

"People don't take away the sun, and the sand and the sea."

Mr. Isaacs, he said, persuaded the late Norman Manley, National Hero, then premier and then minister of finance, Noel Nethersole, founding father of the Bank of Jamaica who all became believers.

It was an unpaid chairman and an unpaid board but they set about selling Jamaica as a year-round destination with zeal. It was the first time this was being done, and at the same time they stimulated both foreign and local investment in tourism facilities.

In 1948 Sunset Lodge was built. Tower Isle was built in 1949 and it grew to become the most successful hotel in Jamaica's history. Others came on the scene later—the Arawak, Half Moon and Bay Roc and all were the products of private investment. Only during the last decade did government begin building hotel rooms Mr. Issa said.

There was one thing Abe Issa was always willing to do—stick his neck out and say that tourism could be the biggest industry in Jamaica. He estimated that it could earn for the island US$600 million annually. Today, he remarked, Jamaica was playing host to some 750,000 visitors annually, including cruise ship passengers. Consider this against the performance of the resort islands of the Bahamas and Puerto Rico which hosted four million in 1983. Hawaii, with no casino gambling, hosted just as many visitors. The story was the same in cruise ship passengers, we were far below our potential.

"We've been scratching the surface for far too long". The basic requirements for the industry as he saw them were to recognise and appreciate its potential as a top contributor to our economic wealth and to have it gain the full support at official and individual levels.

His prescription for a turnaround: high-powered publicity and promotion, more airlines and encouraging more international hotel chains to become involved in Jamaica. Added to all this should be improved tourist shopping, more sightseeing tours and more activities for visitors.

Abe Issa said passionately that tourism needed more vibrancy, more innovation and more professionalism to go with Jamaica's natural and man-made attractions.

Admittedly, tourism was Abe Issa's second love. It ranked next to his wife and family. It was something for which he had a passionate, attachment.

Change was something this dean of Jamaica's tourism never resisted. In 1976-77 business slowed at Tower Isle mainly because most of their clientele was repeat business. "The repeaters were getting old, less came so business went down". Then and there the Club Med-type vacation was conceived for Jamaica—an adult holiday, for couples, with everything provided.

Reflecting, Abe said that when Couples was established for the first few months they wondered whether they had made the right decision. But came September 1978 and it took off in a most extraordinary way, with occupancy running in the high nineties. Tower Isle (now Couples) had become the symbol of stability and endurance in the ever-changing world of tourism.

They were again to demonstrate the Club Med style, and successfully, at Negril Beach Village, and after a break are again operating this property as Hedonism II.

Abe Issa was the personification of the new citizen that had come forward to inhabit the Jamaica of the last quarter century. He was hardworking—his day began at 8:00 a.m. and ended anytime. He was the sportsman, philanthropist, businessman, industrialist, family man, world traveller and gracious host always. He said he was a moderately good Catholic who had faith, and it had helped turn his dreams into reality.

In 1960, Queen Elizabeth II awarded him the honour, Commander of the Most Excellent Order of the British Empire (CBE), for services to his country, particularly tourism. He received the Jamaican honour, Order of Jamaica in 1980 for his work in tourism development.

But the award which seemed to humble yet honour Abe Issa most was the Norman Manley Award for Excellence in 1984. He admitted to being overwhelmed...excellence was something he had always aspired towards, and "perhaps I have attained it to some degree for I note that this word 'excellence' is associated with this signal honour". Abe Issa told his admirers that it was an evening that would take its proud place among the memorable events of his life.

It was his last public and major award. But his monument in Jamaica will always be the Jamaican industry, an industry with which he had had a passionate love affair for more than four decades.

ORIGINALLY PUBLISHED AUGUST 1985

Remembering Tower Isle

PAUL ISSA

In the late forties when my father Abe Issa began building a luxury hotel near a little fishing village called Ocho Rios, the idea was so preposterous that many people actually thought that he had lost his mind. "Oh, here comes Abe Issa driving down King Street," they would say. "Look at him, waving and smiling. Totally mad."

Tower Isle became one of the most famous hotels in the world, and in the fifties was a favourite of all sorts of celebrities and aristocrats.

I remember sitting on Debbie Reynolds' lap, telling Linda Darnell I didn't want her autograph, being scared by Vincent Price in the buffet line, asking Sarah Vaughan to sing. I remember Errol Flynn trying to flirt with my mother, much to my father's discomfort.

Like Flynn, there were many North Coast notables who made Tower Isle their headquarters in those early days: Lord Ronald Graham, Sir Harold and Lady Mitchell, Major Vaughan, Walter Delisser and Roy Lindo were all regulars. Noel Coward, who lived in Port Maria, often stopped by on his way to Montego Bay. I remember hearing about Noel Coward and the great Lord Beaverbrook stopping for breakfast on the way back to Coward's house "Firefly". When Coward placed his order, the waiter became visibly upset.

"Mr. Coward," he pleaded. "You not going to drink champagne for breakfast, sir?"

"Of course, dear boy," Coward replied. "Doesn't everyone?"

Going to Tower Isle as a small boy in the fifties was always like entering a magic place. There was a crispness and a feeling of excitement that permeated the atmosphere. And for me there was, of course, the personal dimension. Every detail, every corner showed the relentless perfectionism of my father; every piece of furnishings reflected my mother's good taste. (I was born the month Tower Isle opened; my mother, Lorraine, very pregnant with me, pounded the pavements of New York choosing all the original furniture for the hotel.)

I remember the days, sunny and breezy and always filled with music. There was racy calypso and mento played by a wandering trio called the Ticklers, and the hot Afro-Cuban rhythms of the mambo and cha-cha played by the resident band at lunch—incredible buffets concocted by a troop of Swiss chefs. At nights, an elegantly dressed crowd would dance under the stars to the exotic strains of the rumba and foxtrot. The band would always begin each night with the hotel's theme song, appropriately titled "Tower Island Magic." A Nat King Cole-like ballad, its closing lines, romantically crooned by the lead singer, were:

Tower Island Magic will capture your soul from the start.

Tower Island Magic will capture your love and your heart!

A hotel that lasts for forty-four years must go through several metamorphoses if it is to survive, and Tower Isle was no exception. In the late seventies, Tower Isle was transformed into Couples, the first fully all-inclusive hotel for couples only.

It's a different kind of tourism, to be sure, but the guests still carry on their love affair with the hotel, returning year after year. And while the atmosphere has a more barefoot type of elegance than in the past, the place is as romantic as ever, still capturing souls and hearts.

The best-selling American humorist Max Shulman expressed the nature of the love affair beautifully in the dedication of one of his novels, *"I was a Teenage Dwarf"*, published in 1959:

Some men love women, some love other men, some love dogs and horses, and occasionally you find one who loves his raincoat.

Me, I love a hotel.

It is near Ocho Rios on the north coast of the island of Jamaica, and it is called the Tower Isle Hotel. It is spacious and serene and impeccably run and situated on a warm white beach on the warm blue Caribbean.

Here, in this blessed haven, I put this book together. Here, if luck is with me, I will soon return.

ORIGINALLY PUBLISHED MAY 1993

Abe Issa (rght) with actress Eva Gabor and guest at Tower Isle

The Art of the Deal

Behind the scenes with Butch Stewart

MARC GOODMAN

Gordon "Butch" Stewart

There was a problem at Sandals. The hotel, newly purchased by Butch Stewart, had one of the best beaches in Jamaica but was directly across the street from Montego Bay's airport. Day and night the planes screamed in overhead like something out of an old World War II movie. And, Stewart notes grimly, "When we opened (in 1981), airplanes were a lot louder." It was the hotel's director of entertainment, Basil Cahusac, who came up with the improbably simple solution—staff would encourage guests to wave good-bye to other departing guests on the planes. Sixteen years later, Stewart smiles, "I don't remember ever losing a guest because of the plane noise. We've had a lot of guests make fun of it, in the guest shows—saying the airport's going to ask for its hangar back, and so on..."

The story is typical of the fly-by-the-seat-of-your-pants ingenuity that has characterized the dizzying rise of Stewart and his Appliance Traders Group, 20 companies that make up Jamaica's largest private corporation. Another: A few years ago, the freely-floating Jamaican dollar went into a sudden tailspin. With Sandals, ATL Group had by now grown into a Jamaican colossus and it was clear to all that, what was good for Jamaica was good for Stewart, and the other way around. And certainly, good business sense happened here to mesh perfectly with Stewart's plucky patriotism. Buying $1 million worth of US dollars a week at six dollars below market price, his companies took a modest financial loss to provide the shaken local business fraternity with an invaluable gesture of confidence in the economy. The dollar dipped again, then stabilized, for a long time.

With the success of Sandals Resorts, Appliance Traders Limited, The *Jamaica Observer*, ATL Automotive, ATL Motors, and, recently, the remarkable makeover of the airline you're travelling on, it's no wonder not a few people in Jamaica are clamouring in the op-ed pages for a Stewart run in politics. In his de luxe, well-appointed Kingston office, Stewart leans back in a couch and looks at the St. Andrew foothills, over which a light rain has begin to fall. He shakes his head and smiles. "I don't think that because people have been a little successful in business that they would necessarily make good politicians. I've been in the public arena—I've been president of the Jamaica Hotel & Tourist Association, and I've been president of the Private Sector Association of Jamaica—but at the association level, not the political one. Still, having politicians with business experience, so they can relate to business, I think is very good." He adds, slyly, "The other thing is, I live a good life, happily, and I don't need to change it."

Any big-city North American resident has probably been made aware of the Sandals marketing monolith by the splashy billboards, oozing bubblegum colours, that loom over freeways and around buildings selling the all-inclusive couples-only resort chain. Amazingly, the Sandals empire might just as easily have never been. Stewart, after all, is in the appliance business, importing and distributing air conditioners, water heaters and the like for office and home. "We went into the hotel business because in the 70s with the import permits and the shortage of hard currency we wanted to earn our own hard currency in order to pay for the commercial goods we were importing. So we bought an old hotel and fixed it up. We lost a lot of money for about two and a half years, but little by little we learnt the business, and started to get our strategies and philosophies right." Sandals is now a Caribbean powerhouse, with properties in Jamaica, Antigua, St.Lucia, the Bahamas, the Turks and Caicos.

In what must be his most daring venture yet, Stewart risked his reputation and a not inconsequential sum of money in the volatile airline business. And yet Air Jamaica has amazed the most hardened sceptics. There's the vibrant staff, a cheerful redesign that screams "Caribbean!," new aircraft, and a general sense of joie de vivre and efficiency that has endeared the national carrier to its countrymen in a way not seen since the elegant 1960s infancy of the airline. A major Kingston travel agent told me of customers that regularly postpone travel plans, rather than fly a rival, until seats open up on Air Jamaica. Stewart couldn't be prouder. "We've brought back a lot of excitement. You should have seen the Jamaicans that turned out at the airport when we arrived in London for the first time in 12 years. We've had tremendous support from the communities we fly to."

Stewart's PR staff wouldn't be able to compete with him once the topic of the airline is brought up. His blue eyes brightening, he gestures enthusiastically with the look of a man who is talking about his baby. "Air Jamaica right now is flying one of the world's best airlines, the services being delivered can be compared with the best in the world. We have the newest fleet in this part of the world and as new a fleet as any airline anywhere. Anyone who steps onto that red carpet is royalty. The champagne, the service, the world's only flying chef.... overall the airline is now just a very sound, good, reliable, on-time, no-line airline."

"Airplanes are all quite the same," he explains. "It's either Boeing or Airbus or Douglas. It's a question of the people behind it, and I think the people that make up Air Jamaica have shown a professionalism and a determination to provide so much to be proud of. Air Jamaica on the ground and in the air has really become a special airline."

Stewart's position in the high reaches of the local business community is an impressive leap from the fairly modest circumstances of his youth. He was born in 1941 and grew up in Ocho Rios. After high school and further education in England, he returned to Jamaica at 21 to take a sales position at a Dutch company that sold everything from TVs to pharmaceuticals. For his first entrepreneurial outing six years later, Stewart showed the same daring and risk that would characterize all his later ventures, plunging into an air-conditioning market locked up by some of the most venerable and trusted names in Jamaican distributorship.

"When I first started out with air conditioners people said, 'Man,(the established firms) are going to put you out of business overnight.' But I really didn't have much of a business to lose." Stewart courted architects and businesses, cajoling them into carrying his brand Fedder with a charm he wielded like a cudgel and that would later become his trademark and the scourge of female travel agents worldwide. He admits, "I think a lot of people bought air conditioners from me as much for my own enthusiasm as for the service they knew I'd deliver." He also beat out the big guys with something that has always spelled success in Jamaica: service. Stewart promised installation within five hours of a sale, and more often than not he would come along to supervise. In a country with a decidedly laid-back attitude towards efficiency, this went over like gangbusters. "What I found was that there's enormous room for small companies that can move quickly, that are nimble, that can provide personalized services. I think there's room for everybody, and anyone who starts a business and tries to develop it sensibly and with a lot of energy, I think people respect that."

Within a year Fedder was the number one brand of air conditioner in Jamaica and ATL had won the Amana distributorship and was selling refrigerators and other appliances as well. By 1973 government policies favouring local manufacturing over importing encouraged ATL to develop new businesses. When the company was contracted to supply appliances to a new style all-inclusive hotel (à la Club Med) in Ocho Rios, Stewart visited and was impressed by the concept. In 1981 the Bay Roc, in Montego Bay, went up for sale. Former director of tourism Adrian Robinson suggested a name, and seven months and a US$4 million renovation later, Sandals Montego Bay opened for business.

Never allowing himself to slip into debt, Stewart waited five years before opening the second Sandals, Sandals Royal Caribbean. Then other properties started appearing, every two years or so apart. They had caught on with honeymooners, and Stewart's community-minded inclinations didn't hurt either, with the chain offering $1 million in free rooms to Gulf War veterans in one memorable promotion.

It was also flying needy Jamaican kids to Miami for surgery unavailable locally, giving to clinics, homes, drug abuse centres and to charities large and small. But Stewart rejects calls for a universal private-sector panacea for the island's challenges. "A large activity of Sandals is working within the community: in all sports; with the hospitals, police stations; we maintain the fountain in the centre of Montego Bay... but there's a point at which you have to draw the line. It's for government to regulate development, it's for government to deal with law and order. Governments have their roles. You can contribute and help, but...."

Realizing too many hotels in Jamaica would only cause Sandals to start competing against itself, Stewart now expanded into other Caribbean islands. There is now a new wave of all-inclusives—Beaches, which adds family and singles options to the couples-only Sandals. "We have an enormous family of repeat guests who said, 'Look, we know single parents and families who want to go to hotel with the standards and quality of Sandals.'"

With all this feverish expansion is there a limit, environmentally speaking, to tourism development in the region? Stewart moves to the edge of the couch to answer. "Well, look at Orlando, perhaps the biggest bedroom city in the world. But all of the hotels are developed with a purpose, with the environment in mind, and the communities do better as a result; you end up having better services and the surrounding vegetation improves because people cater to it rather than ignoring it or abusing it."

"Generally, I think Jamaica has come leaps and bounds in terms of respect for the environment. I think Jamaica is a greener island and a healthier island than it was ten years ago. Fifteen years ago when we started, the environment as it is discussed today was not a major issue. Still, we were environmentally-correct before it became fashionable. Take our gardens for example: one of our main features are the beautifully manicured gardens at Sandals, but we also have sewage plants that recycle water to irrigate these gardens."

The rain has stopped, and shadows deepen over Newcastle, high in the Blue Mountains. Most of Kingston has gone home, but at ATL there are only small signs of work slowing down. Now asked if there exists a grand Butch Stewart vision for Jamaica, Stewart pleads a modest emphasis on only what he does best. "I don't try to make too many rules. We have a vision for the product we've developed—Sandals, Air Jamaica. Air Jamaica's new Montego Bay hub is very much part of that vision. And the partnership we've put together with Delta Airlines will make us a global airline. The bigger the opportunities for Air Jamaica, the bigger the opportunities for Jamaica—we view Air Jamaica and the hub as a catalyst."

Perhaps Stewart's greatest ongoing contribution to the island is his unyieldingly sunny outlook. Returning, he adds, "I think Jamaica probably has the biggest potential for tourism that any sun/sand destination can have. We've come a long way in raising the standard of the overall hotel product we have. I think there's plenty of room for all different categories of hotel. We certainly have an enormous wealth of attractions, whether it be great houses, rivers, falls—it's non-ending. In poker you make the most of the hand that's dealt to you. I think we ought to start feeling better with the hand that we're dealt. I think The Man Above dealt Jamaica the most potent hand possible. All we need to do is to use it a lot better."

So what does it take to be successful in our often maddeningly idiosyncratic island? "I think it's much the same as anywhere in the world—think smart and move fast."

And who or what inspires the man? Stewart is clearly more eager to stay on work-related topics, but before the subject is changed he allows, "Churchill."

He's certainly known for workaholic tendencies which, combined with the energy of a teenager, leaves colleagues crumpled in defeat in his wake. But he gives a laugh of mock protest when confronted with the accusation, then thinks. "I play a little tennis, sometimes. I fish when I get a chance—I'm going fishing for two days next week. I enjoy people, playing a little dominoes, that type of thing." He warns with twinkling eye, "There're some people that need so much downtime that work is in the way, too." What's next for the peripatetic tycoon? "I don't know, but a man once said we'd be in the motorcar business and I said 'you're crazy'. We're in the motorcar business. In 1977 a friend of mine said, "There's this hotel in Runaway Bay; why don't you take it over?." I said, "The hotel business? You're mad!" We're in the hotel business. I never dreamt for one minute that we'd be involved in a newspaper and worst of all—I mean, I would have considered the airline business the maddest thing of all. So never say never— just keep trying to do the best you can."

ORIGINALLY PUBLISHED FEBRUARY 1998

Chris Blackwell's Island

MAUREEN SHERIDAN

Chris Blackwell built Island Records on reggae music. It was Blackwell who guided Bob Marley from reggae rebel to international pop stardom; and it was Blackwell who took reggae from a local rhythm to a world music.

The story of Chris Blackwell began in London in 1937. Brought to Jamaica by his parents while still an infant, Blackwell considers himself Jamaican. His interest in Jamaican music started in the fifties when, as an atypical white teenager, he hung out at sound systems, the travelling discos that were the forerunners of today's dancehall (or D.J.) craze. "Middle class Jamaicans didn't go there and white people certainly didn't" he says. "It was just a Jamaican street thing."

> *"Chris never travels with any clothes. Once, in Cannes at the Film Festival, we were invited to a gala performance. We had jackets and bow ties but no shirts, and shoes (sneakers) but no socks. We clipped the bow ties to our T-shirts, put our jackets and shoes on and went to the gala." — Dickie Jobson, Director, "Countryman."*

But the street is where trends start, and Blackwell was savvy enough to spot—and mine—the potential in the Jamaican music scene. The sound systems were highly competitive—having the hottest records offered an important edge. Noting the need for exclusive product, Blackwell began commuting to New York where he'd buy records for under a dollar, scratch off the label to prevent identification and resell them (sometimes for as much as $50.00) in Jamaica.

Blackwell's next step was to produce "blank label" records in Jamaica. Sally Henzell, who with husband, Perry (director of *"The Harder They Come"*) met Blackwell as teenagers, remembers Blackwell "doing everything...producing the records, getting them pressed, designing the album jackets and even gluing them together. He used to drive around to sessions selling them out of the back of his van. He had a great time."

His first three records for this market went to number one in Jamaica.

"This is easy" Blackwell thought to himself. But it wasn't quite as simple as that. As Blackwell's producing technique got better (he learned as he went along), he began to lose his street touch and sales dropped. And his competition (including Edward Seaga whose interest in music preceded his political career), he recalls, got "very stiff". But as Blackwell's sales declined in Jamaica, they increased in England, a market he had begun to tap. Shrewdly approaching his major competitors and sewing up their UK distribution rights, he decided to start a company in England.

The story of Island Records begins in London in 1962. Specializing in ska (reggae's predecessor), Island's first pressing—Owen Gray's *"Darling Patricia"*—sold out the first day from the trunk of Blackwell's Mini Cooper. As he had done in Jamaica, Blackwell personally drove his product to the marketplace (which in London was record shops). With a unique guarantee—if the records didn't sell, Blackwell exchanged them—and a proven "feel" for what the public wanted, he soon built a good and credible reputation with his customers.

> *"Chris came to my restaurant in New York's Greenwich Village with Grace Jones. I used to play Bob Marley tapes all the time and Chris asked why I was playing that music. 'Because I love it', I told him. Chris liked the idea that he could come to my place and get Italian food and listen to reggae. Eventually he asked me if I would like to come to Jamaica and open this restaurant. Chris gives people a chance the thing I like about him most is that he's genuine. ...in fact, he's almost naïve." — Nuccio, Of Nuccio's Restaurant, Ocho Rios.*

In the spring of 1964, a song by Jamaica's Millie Small, *"My Boy Lollipop,"* gave Chris Blackwell his first big international hit. *"My Boy Lollipop"* sold six million. "With this record" Blackwell says, "Jamaican music was now becoming a worldwide phenomenon."

At the same time that Blackwell started making international headway with Jamaican music, English rock, until then a poor cousin of its U.S. counterpart, was suddenly taken seriously by the music world and Blackwell got caught up in the energy. Signing artists like the Spencer Davis Group and John Martyn, he diverted his Jamaican artists to Trojan Records, a label Island had acquired in a merger, and spent the next few years immersed in rock. Not that he intentionally left ska... "Rock was the growth side of the company" he says "(it) took me rather than me driving it... if you're successful in something people shower you with opportunities. "

> *"It is an understatement to say that Chris Blackwell is a shrewd businessman." — Neville Garrick, Bob Marley's art director.*

The Harder They Come, Perry Henzell's seminal reggae film brought Blackwell back to reggae. Produced in 1972, with Jimmy Cliff cast as Rygin, an infamous Kingston gangster, *The Harder They Come* became an instant cult hit. And the film brought reggae out of Trench Town, the Kingston ghetto of its birth, and introduced it to the world. "The early seventies" Blackwell says "was one of (Jamaican music's) most creative periods". That it was, for Bob Marley and the Wailers were a product of this period.

"Chris Blackwell is a musical prophet"
—Sly and Robbie

Bob Marley, Peter Tosh and Bunny Wailer, a.k.a. the Wailers, came to Chris Blackwell's attention at the time that Jimmy Cliff left Island for EMI (believing that Island hadn't promoted him enough). Chris Blackwell was actively looking for a replacement and when he spotted the Wailers he knew he wanted them. Already signed to CBS, Blackwell bought out that contract and gave the group £4,000 to produce an album. The result: *Catch A Fire*, an album Blackwell believes to be "one of the best records we've ever put out."

"Chris Blackwell genuinely loves reggae...Chris has a winner's streak. His father gambled heavily and he inherited that." — Dermot Hussey, writer and broadcaster.

The price of Island Records' interest in the Wailers was the dissolution of the group. Tosh and "Whitewell" (as Tosh called Blackwell) didn't get along and Bunny Wailer didn't want to tour, so Blackwell concentrated on Marley to the exclusion of the other two. Asked whether he intended to break reggae music as a big new sound (in an interview with Ted Fox in *Audio* magazine,) Blackwell answered "No, it was my intention to break Bob Marley initially...I don't think people will buy a sound in general. I think they will buy an act, and if that act has a different sound they will look for other acts that have that sound." Blackwell did sign other reggae acts—like Third World—but his concentration on Marley led to accusations that the music of his other reggae artists was left sitting on Island shelves.

"Chris Blackwell is the driver of the reggae bus" —Cat Coore, Third World.

Reggae broke internationally in 1977 when, following a sold-out world tour, Marley's *Rastaman Vibration* climbed to 8 on the U.S. pop charts and hit in parts of Europe. Marley's popularity was enormous and his musical potential, because of the universality of his message, seemed limitless. But then he died.

So synonymous was Marley with reggae that his death from cancer in 1981 almost killed off the "riddim" he'd ridden to international fame, and, after a bad experience with Black Uhuru (who chose breakup over breakthrough), Blackwell again shifted his attention from reggae to rock. He worked on acts like Steve Winwood, Robert Palmer and U2, and, through his Compass Point Studios which he had built in Nassau in the seventies, began to experiment with Compass All Stars, a houseband that included "rhythm twins" Sly and Robbie, and new avant garde acts like Grace Jones whom he met in New York's Russian Tea Room. He also started Island Pictures.

What happened to Robert Palmer, Steve Winwood, Grace Jones, and the great Irish rock group U2, is now history, and Sly and Robbie have moved out from their backing positions to become one of reggae's most important acts. Island Pictures has had success (*"Choose Me"* and *"She's Gotta Have It"*) and failure (*"Good to Go"*), but as with all Blackwell's ventures, he's in it for the long term. "If you're in music, you need to be in films, because they're now very much one business."

"Chris is a great gambler...one of the few left who have the balls to be in the music game." —Perry Henzell, director, The Harder They Come, author of Power Game.

In 1987, with the promise of a reggae revival in the air, Blackwell signed a couple of new Jamaican reggae acts—Foundation and Donovan. A third is in negotiation. The new Island artists are scheduled to tour Europe with Sly and Robbie this summer. Other current interests in Jamaica ("my spiritual home") include Nuccio's restaurant in Ocho Rios; "Golden Eye" (Ian Fleming's house in Oracabessa); Island Bees Ltd., (take a guess); and real estate projects in Irish Town and on the north coast. But music, especially Jamaican music, remains his first love.

"Chris is nice to work for, not easy, but nice. He jumps from one thing to another and he's very hard to keep up with." —Deniece Mills, Island Records representative in Jamaica.

To Chris Blackwell, "the great labels are the ones with an identity of style, like (Ahmet Ertegun's) Atlantic... and (Berry Gordy's) Motown. That's what I've always wanted to have." Blackwell has what he wants. Like Ertegun's Atlantic and Gordy's Motown, it's Blackwell's Island.

ORIGINALLY PUBLISHED AUGUST 1988

High Society Josef Forstmayr Inn Keeper for the Rich and Famous

MARC GOODMAN

Josef Forstmayr, the man at the helm of Round Hill—one of Jamaica's legendary resorts—talks to Marc Goodman about being innkeeper to the rich and famous.

2:00 PM

Round Hill's cottages are like every villa James Bond walked into in *Dr. No* —that is, if those villas had had their toiletries provided by Crabtree and Evelyn and their furniture by Ralph Lauren. It's the kind of place where guests arrive by private plane and are whisked to the property in the hotel's Cadillacs, where beautiful children take sailing lessons watched by svelte women wearing Céline scarves as sarongs, where the fellow on the next court over might well be investment banking titan Michel David Weill.

The bookcase in Cottage 10 contains a copy of Black's *Tales of Old Jamaica*, next to the *Social Register*. It's an apt pairing, for it is Old Jamaica indeed that's being sold at the hotel—open verandahs caressed by sultry tropical breezes, wood floors, bamboo armchairs, sisal mats, fans turning slowly overhead, massive carved mahogany beds. And the combination of this upscale colonial fantasy aesthetic with a dream clientele of Establishment WASPs, Hollywood types and Euro-tycoons makes for a potent mix, all overseen with flair by manager and managing director Josef Forstmayr.

4:00 PM

"We learned guerrilla tactics. We parachuted, ran around painted black, dug foxholes—it was a lot of fun." Thousands of miles from Austria, Forstmayr leans forward in his seat in Round Hill's modest manager's office, recounting youthful exploits in equal parts irreverent and nostalgic. After 17 years in

Jamaica, Forstmayr is as energetic as the day he arrived as a 20 year-old tourist and never left. After university and compulsory military service in Austria, Forstmayr went to Cornell University, home of America's most prestigious hotel management programme. When December rolled around, he fled upstate New York's frigid weather for a holiday at Negril's Coconut Cove Hotel. Forstmayr became friends with the hotel's owners but had a habit of pointing out little improvements he thought they could make to the hotel. "They finally said, 'Well, why don't you stay and help us run it?'" With the prospect of a bitter winter ahead, Forstmayr agreed. "I stayed on for cigarette money. I loved every minute of it."

Nevertheless, Forstmayr moved on, in September 1980 signing on as general manager at Trident Villas in Port Antonio in what must be surely one of the more dramatic introductions to any job—with Hurricane Allen bearing down on the town.

"Four days after I arrived there was no hotel. All my life I'd lived out of three suitcases—at boarding school, college, the army, whatever—but this time even those three suitcases were washed away. All I had left was one pair of jeans. I was actually lucky to escape with my life." After nine years and another hurricane, Forstmayr came to Round Hill, perhaps Jamaica's most legendary luxury resort.

4:40 PM

On the patio overlooking Round Hill's golden beach, a strong wind whips the pages of the *Ocean Drive* magazines Forstmayr is holding. He shows me several full-page ads from the hotel's recent campaign, featuring photographs from the hotel's archives. One shows Grace Kelly waist-deep in the water off the property, wearing a mask and snorkel, another Alfred Hitchcock with a female admirer in the bar. A third shows a Hawaiian-shirted John F. Kennedy talking with his sister-in-law, Princess Lee Radziwill, on the sun-dappled verandah of a Round Hill cottage.

"John Pringle opened Round Hill in 1952 while he was still in his twenties. There are many great properties in the Caribbean right now, but Round Hill was the first luxury hotel here and they all copied us." Noel Coward had his first Jamaican house here, Cottage 3, until it became too social for him. Photos hanging in Round Hill's bar attest to the clientele in those heady days. Astors. Vanderbilts. Cole Porter. Lauren Bacall and Clark Gable. Bob Hope. A fashion show has models sporting bathing suits with mink stoles. In the 90s, Forstmayr says, ownership took on a decidedly international—as opposed to primarily American—flavour, with cottages now owned by Argentinians, French, English, Italians and Jamaicans (sprinting superstar Merlene Ottey is one owner). "Many of the cottages are in their third generation of ownership. The present Viscount Rothermere [of London's *Daily Mail*] is the grandson of the first owner of his cottage."

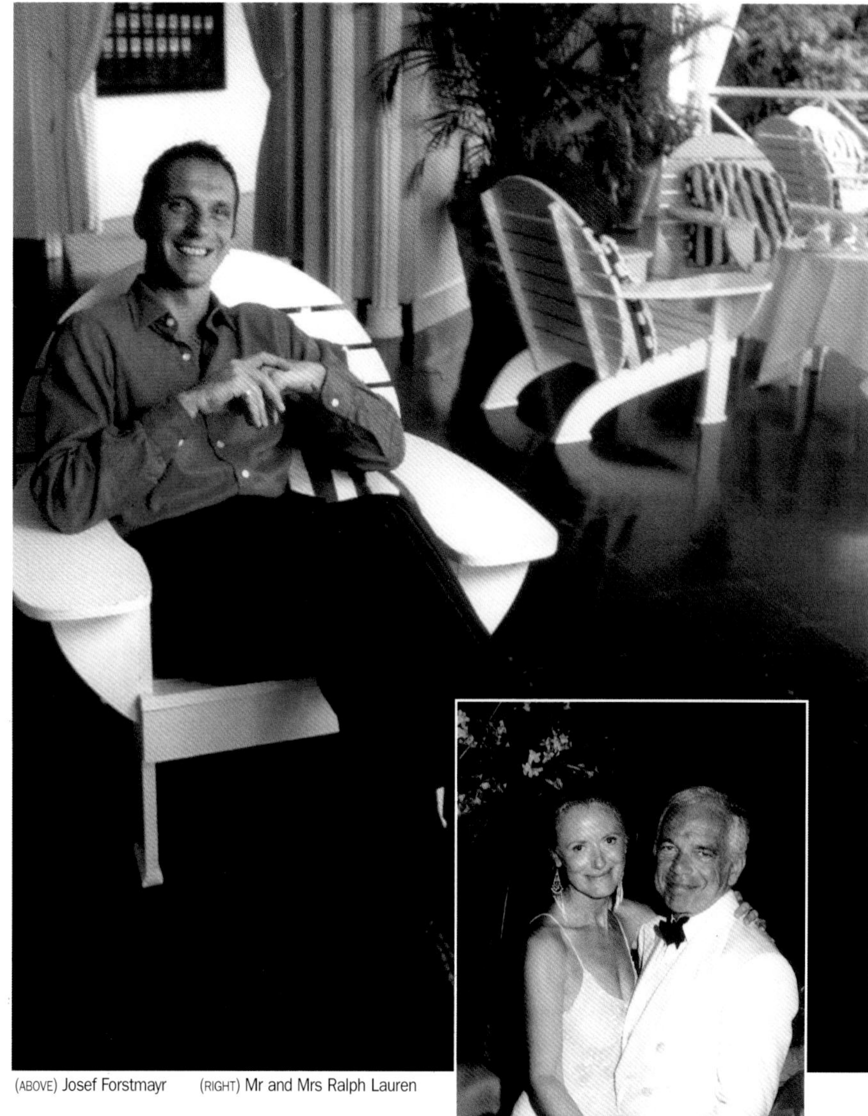

(ABOVE) Josef Forstmayr (RIGHT) Mr and Mrs Ralph Lauren

The bar we're sitting by is a testament to Round Hill's staying power with the glitterati—it was redesigned by cottage owner Ralph Lauren with broad striped sofas, a restored sisal and mahogany bar with a dramatic banana leaf arrangement behind the bottles and a proper brass rail to put your foot up on. The walls are hung with original photographs by Herb Ritts, Annie Leibovitz and Robert Mapplethorpe.

Regular visitors to Round Hill now include an even broader spectrum of the Hollywood and media elite, including Bruce Willis and Demi Moore, Kurt Russell and Goldie Hawn, Mike Nichols and Diane Sawyer, Blake Edwards, Harrison Ford, producer Joel Silver and Condé Nast owner S.I. Newhouse. Then there is the annual Sugar Cane Carnival charity ball, which benefits local charities and brings down New York society fixtures such as the Newhouses, the Gutfreunds, *Vogue* editor Anna Wintour, *Allure* editor Polly Mellen, *Time* editor and publisher Henry Grunwald and financier Steve Schwartzman. The hotel's star-pulling power was once again in the headlines two years ago when, from his poolside perch at Round Hill, cottage owner and *Forrest Gump* director Bob Zemeckis brought Steven Spielberg, David Geffen and Jeffery Katzenberg together to form entertainment giant Dreamworks SKG.

Round Hill oldtimers might be able to tell you about Cottage 12 owner Oscar Hammerstein II's 1952 meeting with Maria von Trapp, from whence sprang *The Sound of Music*. Or about when CBS' Bill Paley, determined to blast out a rock formation to better place Cottage 26 on the water, wrapped the entire hotel in mattresses to cushion the explosions. Two Christmases ago Round Hill simultaneously

entertained Paul McCartney, Julian Lennon, the Rolling Stones' Ron Wood and Bianca Jagger, leading to all-star jam sessions in the bar led by McCartney on piano. With the perpetual atmosphere of whimsy that tends to acompany the international jet set, what's the most bizarre request Forstmayr's ever fielded? He grins. " 'I want a villa at Christmas.' It's really almost impossible, because everyone immediately puts down money for the next year's stay while they're here."

Jamaica's size and cosmopolitanism is clearly a draw for the worldly Austrian. "The proof is, I'm not an 'island' person at all. We're really a country here. We have a culture, a mind of our own. There's a tremendous pride and an independent spirit in Jamaicans, a knowledge of where they come from. And I don't know many places that would have given a foreigner the chance I've gotten. You really have the opportunity in Jamaica to get involved, get elected to things, to do things."

Forstmayr's contagious enthusiasm was recognized by the Jamaica Hotel and Tourism Association in 1993 with its Hotelier of the Year award. "I act like I run a small hotel, getting out and dealing with the guests, because that's the fun of the business in my eyes—not being in an office making the 'big decisions.'"

How does managing Round Hill differ from managing, say, the George V in Paris? "One rule applies to hotels everywhere: develop what you have. Here, we should be trying to be the most Jamaican of the two-star hotels, or of the three-star hotels, and so on. You have to get the visitors excited about where they are. I mean, Jamaica's a fantastic country. I've been here 17 years and I wouldn't want to be anywhere else."

He waves a hand around the shaded patios. "I didn't try to re-invent the wheel here. I just looked at John Pringle's philosophy and just built on it. We sell tremendous style and Jamaican elegance. Jamaica should be sold with its excitement. We're about a certain sense of adventure and an exotic ambience."

While Round Hill caters to the elite, a populist spirit prevails in its office. Each year's Christmas card showcases not a sunset or a coconut tree but a different member of staff. "We have a great relationship here. We really try to make our staff happy. We've instituted a profit-sharing scheme where 15 percent of our total profits goes to the staff equally. So they feel that this is their place, a place they have an interest in. Yes, we have a union—but they can help you solve problems as well."

7:20 PM

Before dinner, I look up Jackie Onassis' home address in the *Register*. Down at the beach, guests in blazers and bare feet are already milling around at the pre-beach dinner rum punch party. As waiters light torches and the tide eddies around the buffet tables, a mento trio plucks out a perfect rendition of "Come Back Liza". It's Old School Jamaican hoteliering at its best. Later, a real calypso band, with steel pans and electric instruments, will play as guests gather on the sloping lawn under a near-full moon. Forstmayr looks around at the big almond trees, the groups of suntanned kids, the lights of Tryall in the distance. "I have so many more things to do here at Round Hill, in Montego Bay, in tourism in general. I'm very ambitious, but I've never had a Five Year Plan...." He pauses to ask a passing guest about a trip he's recently taken. He returns, his eyes still on the waiters setting up. "I want to be happy and I don't want to be bored. Right now I'm not bored and I'm happy, so if you ask me what's next I'd probably say more of the same." And he walks down the steps to his beach, to another beach dinner, to greet the guests.

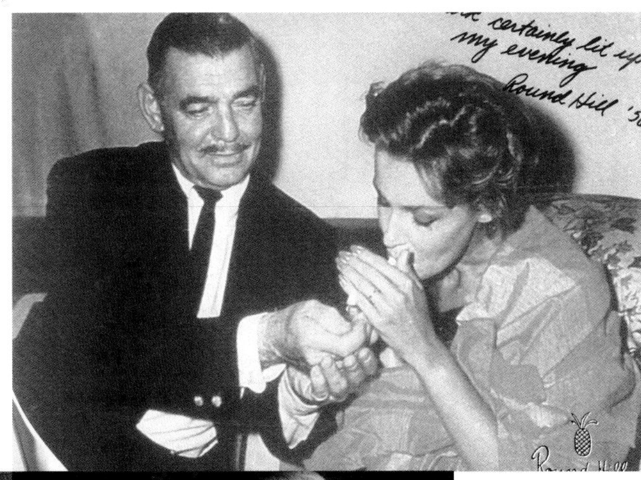

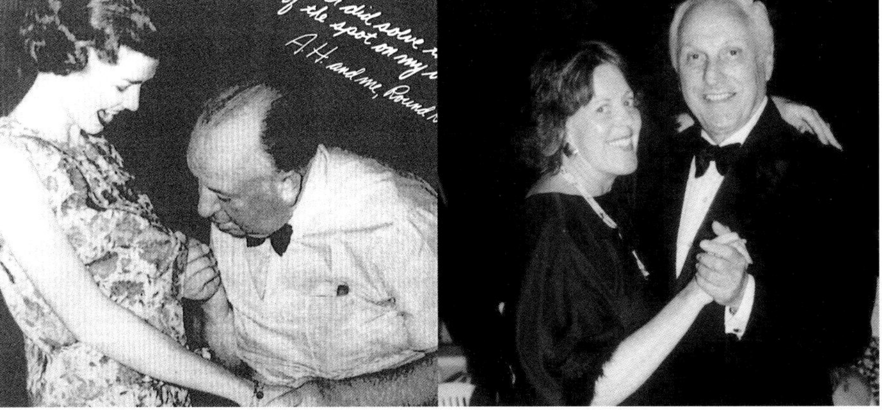

(FROM THE TOP)

HM Queen Sonia (2ND LEFT) with Billy Craig, Forstmayr, and Yvonne Sternerson.

Clark Gable lights up Lauren Bacall.

Alfred Hitchcock delves into the mystery of a spot on a blouse.

Rhode Island Governor Bruce Sandlum and Mrs. Sandlum at the Round Hill Annual Sugar Cane Ball.

ORIGINALLY PUBLISHED APRIL 1997

Colin Powell
The Son of Jamaican Immigrants at the Centre of World Power

BEN BARBER

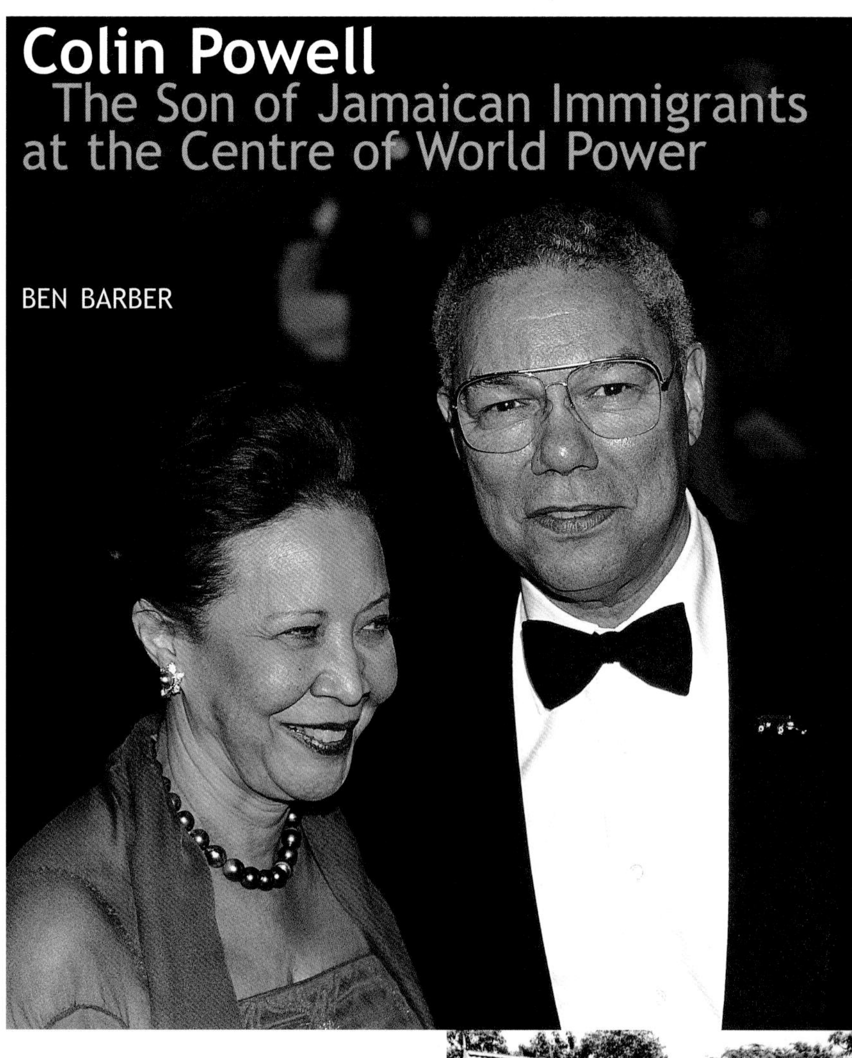

At the center of world power, directing the worldwide struggle against terrorism and controlling U.S. foreign policy, stands the son of Jamaican immigrants Colin L. Powell. Even before the events of Sept. 11, Powell was a potent symbol of the links between Jamaica and the United States. As the head of the U.S. armed forces under the first President Bush he led the coalition of 28 countries to liberate Kuwait in Desert Storm in 1991. He served as the national security advisor and this year became President George W. Bush's secretary of state. Some even said he could have become president—either party would have given him the nomination—but he chose not to run for political office.

As I have traveled with Powell around the world, stuck in the back of his official plane with a dozen other reporters, I saw a man who was determined to show a human face, no matter what the traumas he dealt with and what pressures he faced. As he wrote in his best-selling biography *"My American Journey,"* Powell seemed determined to enjoy life and to have others around him enjoy it as well. Even while commanding tens of thousands of nuclear-armed U.S. troops in Europe during the Cold War, Powell said he wanted people around him and under him to have fun at whatever they did. In case anyone imagined that meant his foreign trips would be leisurely jaunts to places with fine beaches or high cuisine, his first trip abroad was a dash to a half dozen Arab states and Israel made in three or four days of nearly sleepless travel and meetings. By the time Powell headed off to Africa in May, to deal with the HIV/AIDS pandemic and regional wars in Sierra Leone, Congo and Sudan, we were thankful that the schedule allowed two nights in the same country.

Hard driving, clear and motivated, Colin Powell has shown especially since the terrorist attacks of Sept. 11, a steely resolve to resort to the ultimate use of all out military might once a decision has been made. But typical of his style was his plan following the terror attacks to build a coalition of Middle East countries that back the United States—just as it was the key to success in the Gulf War against Iraq's Saddam Hussein. If Muslim countries and troops fight alongside Americans, it makes the United States immune to attempts by terrorists to claim they are victims of an anti-Muslim campaign by the West. Without huge public fanfare, buried inside one of his short press conferences in the wake of the attacks on the Pentagon and World Trade Center, Powell said he was calling up foreign ministers, kings and presidents of Egypt, Saudi Arabia, Morocco, Tunisia, Algeria and other Arab states. The message in public was that Powell sought their cooperation in a long, deep and costly global war against terrorism. Behind the scenes, a Powell subordinate told us that he was reading them the riot act. "Either they are with us or with them—the terrorists," said the aide to Powell. Within hours, Middle East countries that for years had shed crocodile tears at terrorist attacks in the United States, Israel, Europe and Africa, climbed on board Powell's armada.

Powell, born to Jamaican immigrants Luther and Maud "Arie" Powell in New York City on April 5, 1937, was raised in the South Bronx. A "C" student at City College he excelled at military classes with the Reserve Officer Training Corps and joined the army where he would remain for 35 years, rising to become the first black

THIS PAGE U.S. General Colin Powell with his wife Alma. The old house at Top Hill, where Secretary Powell's father, Luther, lived with members of his family. U.S. Secretary Powell decending the stairs at Kings House, Kingston Jamaica, with Sir Howard Cooke, Governor General of Jamaica. Prime Minister P.J. Patterson, Alma Powell and Lady Cooke just behind them. OPPOSITE President George W Bush, Secretary of State Colin Powell and Vice President Dick Cheney

chairman of the Joint Chiefs of Staff. After leaving the army, Powell toured the United States as an inspirational speaker and was chairman of America's Promise, a nonprofit organization dedicated to building the character and competence of young people. Powell still wears on his lapel a little red wagon pin symbolizing the group. Powell married Alma Vivian Johnson of Birmingham, Alabama and they have a son Michael; daughters Linda and Anne; daughter-in-law Jane; and grandsons Jeffrey and Bryan. His Jamaican ancestry has been a great influence on his life even though it is not immediately apparent. Powell presents an austere, almost military, dignified, appearance, and he speaks with crisp, clear standard American pronunciation. But he often says the influence of his family culture and values is the driving force in his life. One sign of Jamaica's influence is that his autobiography begins with his visit to the island in 1992 after an invitation by then Prime Minister Michael Manley to "Come home, even if only for a few days." He described his trip to Top Hill where he visited the house his father was born in in 1898 and met relatives and many local people who revelled in the rise of one of their own to become a world figure. However, like many first generation Americans, Powell's ancestral culture was largely experienced in his home. "As a kid, I did not understand the lyrics of the calypso songs I heard at family gatherings," writes Powell in his biography. "But as I grew older I started to decode the sly double entendres." His favourite singer was Slinger Francisco of Trinidad known as "The Mighty Sparrow" and Mr. Powell delighted in playing calypso tapes in his office when he was chairman of the Joint Chiefs of Staff at the Pentagon. "You don't hear much calypso music in the Pentagon's E-ring," he wrote. Powell says that his relatives and friends at home in the Bronx when he was a child would often speak about "going home" to Jamaica—either for visits or to return for the rest of their lives. Like many other immigrant groups, few ever did return home since they and especially their children had become too American to switch back easily.

Powell's family was hard working in America—his father pushing carts loaded with dresses and suits around the crowded streets of America's fashion capital, the garment district in Manhattan, and later becoming head of shipping for his company. That provided a decent, lower middle class U.S. lifestyle with a house, medical care, schools for the children and plenty of opportunity to advance—as Powell has demonstrated. Perhaps the greatest element of Powell's character and style has been the man's essentially reasonable approach to people and things. Without a hint of arrogance, the man who has commanded millions of troops and sent armies into battle speaks in a simple, direct manner that is refreshing among the diplomats and bureaucrats of world affairs. Typical of Powell's inspirational attitude was advice he gave to children recently at the State Department, telling them: " Look in a mirror, look at yourself, look deep in your own heart and make a choice, a choice that says: I'm going to be a success . . . because God has given me a strong body and given me a healthy mind and given me the ability to make choices." Powell also referred to his race. "When I was a kid, a black kid living in a slum area in New York City, they said, 'You're black and you're a second class citizen. No, worse than that. You're a tenth class citizen. Because you're black you can't go to that school. Because you're black we're not going to let you go to that restaurant.'" Powell gave a huge boost to morale at State when he arrived and hailed U.S. diplomats as the first line of defense. He began using desk officers for briefings and said he would not insert a slew of political appointees but use the experienced officers from within the headquarters at Foggy Bottom.

Much has been written about the balance of power in the Bush administration and some write that Powell, seen as a moderate by conservatives, has been pushed aside by hard-line conservatives such as Defense Secretary Donald Rumsfeld, Vice President Dick Cheney, his deputy Paul Wolfowitz and others. Critics on the right say Powell at first opposed using U.S. force in Kuwait and later in Bosnia and Kosovo. Since he became secretary of state he's clashed with conservatives on a number of issues. Powell, for example, at first said that he would continue Clinton administration policies of dialogue with North Korea, only to have to reverse direction when Bush suspended the talks. The administration also dropped cooperation on the Kyoto environment treaty without consulting Powell. He also has criticized Israel's targeted killings of suspected Palestinian terrorists only to find Cheney and Rumsfeld saying those are justified as self-defense. But Powell and his aides simply say they expect to have differences and they know how to work together as a team and resolve them. "These guys are adults," said one aide. And now that the United States has been attacked as never before, killing thousands in the heart of New York and at the Pentagon, Powell's voice and image has been enormously reassuring. He now faces his greatest challenge—steering U.S. foreign policy into a long battle to seek out terrorist networks that have taken root—according to a recent Congressional Research Service report—in more than 30 countries including the United States.

ORIGINALLY PUBLISHED DECEMBER 2001

Father Richard HoLung
Profile of a Ghetto Priest

CECILLE DALEY

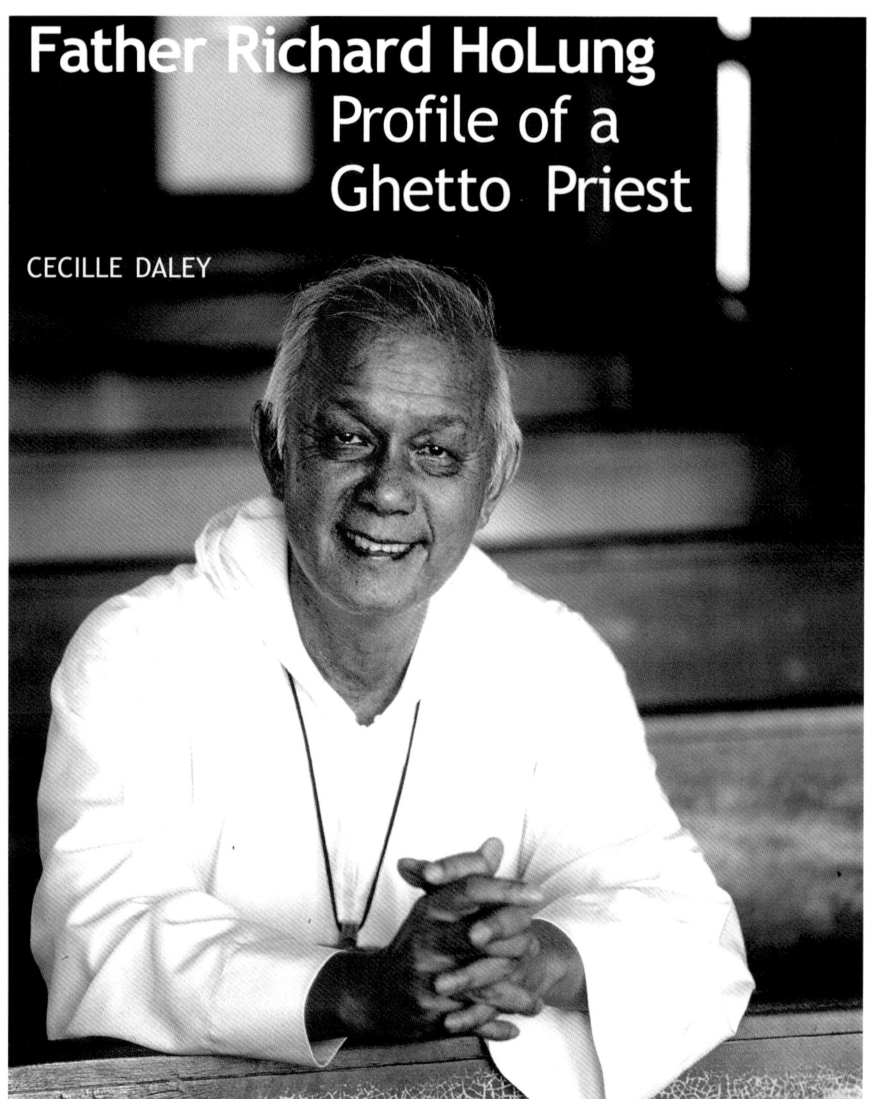

This man is a paradox. A highly educated intellectual whose beliefs defy logic, he is a gentle nature-lover who lives and works in some of the most turbulent sections of downtown Kingston. A simple Catholic priest who has given up personal possessions yet whose influence touches people in every sector of society, Jamaica's Father HoLung is a compelling and much-loved personality.

The first thing Father HoLung did when we met for our interview was offer me a fruit bar. "Try it, it's good", he urged in an almost, well, father-like way. "It's made with real mango, all natural". Not the way one usually greets a total stranger, but as it turned out, second nature to the man renowned for his unhesitating generosity.

It is 9:30 a.m., a time when Father HoLung is usually busy with the demands of his work as head of Missionaries of the Poor. For now, however, he is happy to take a break. Sitting on the verandah of the North Street headquarters of the Missionaries, the 59-year-old priest seems to be quietly enjoying the extraordinary turns his life has taken.

It was in the early 70's that he decided to devote himself completely to the church. "At the time, there was great turmoil in Jamaica and because I loved my country I wanted to make more of a contribution. More than that, I was teaching at the time and wanted to inspire my students, by my example, to live their lives for Christ. Most importantly, I wanted to live the life that Jesus lived." A big step to take, but Father HoLung is not into half-measures.

While still in his teens, he realised he wanted to live a life of service to God and set out to do just that. At 18 he joined the Jesuits and later, went to the US to further his studies in the faith. With characteristic thoroughness, he earned three Masters degrees in Philosophy, English Literature and Theology at Boston College in Massachusetts and a PhD. in Humanities from Syracuse University in New York.

For six years after receiving his Ph.D. he lectured in English at the University of the West Indies and worked as an assistant priest at Aquinas Centre in Kingston. It was during this time that he began to feel that God was calling him to do more. "I felt that everything that I had done up until that time had been somehow hypocritical. I was preaching God's word but not really living it." Although he felt God's call, he was not quite ready to take the next step. Until one fateful night in downtown Kingston.

"I finally took the decision to begin working full-time with the poor after I was held up by a gun-man", he says calmly, enjoying his fruit-bar. Smiling at the memory and my expression, he explains. "One night, I was walking through an area quite near to here (the downtown location of the Missionaries of the Poor headquarters) when a man robbed me at gun-point. I decided then and there that this was the place where my work would begin: the place where the need for love was greatest".

Together with Fathers Hayden Augustine and Brian Kerr, Father HoLung took the first steps towards full-time ministry to the poor in the slums of downtown Kingston. Today, the path he took is marked with remarkable accomplishments.

Missionaries of the Poor made history last year when it became the first male religious community in the English-speaking Caribbean to be elevated as a Religious Institute of Diocesan Right. There are now missions in Haiti, India and the Phillipines.

In Jamaica, the order has been joined by over 100 Brothers from the Caribbean, North America and the Far East. They now have four homes in Kingston where some 400 destitute and handicapped men, women and children are cared for. Over the years, the work of Missionaries of the Poor has transformed sections of the inner-city, creating much-needed shelters where the most destitute can find love and care.

To the homes, Father HoLung has tried to bring the spirit of family he experienced as a child growing up in a poor but loving family in Richmond, St. Mary. "Even more than food, shelter and clothing, people need love. We encourage the people we care for to take care of each other. There is a real community and family spirit at the homes now".

A passionate defender of "the poorest of the poor" and unafraid of controversy, Father HoLung's outspokenness has often drawn criticism from political quarters, but has more often brought about changes in the treatment of society's most helpless members.

Perhaps even more importantly, his work has served to raise the awareness of ordinary Jamaicans. "Because of his efforts, the consciousness of many Jamaicans has changed", says Maggie Lyn, a close friend, "People look at the homeless and the destitute differently. They automatically think of him when someone is in need and has nowhere to go."

Although he laughingly admits that he "can't play a single instrument", Father HoLung has written hundreds of religious songs which have been published and recorded and are sung in churches here and overseas. He has also directed over 10 musical productions, works which have been staged to raise funds for the ministry of Missionaries of the Poor. The productions of Father HoLung and Friends, are now eagerly anticipated events on the entertainment calendar.

He loves to write and for years has been bringing Jamaica face-to-face with life in the ghetto through his newspaper column, "Diary of a Ghetto Priest." Plans are underway to have a collection of his columns published.

For someone who has seen more sadness and desperation than most, his work and music reflects both joy and hope. Typically, he gives God full credit for the happiness he feels and expresses in the midst of the most desperate poverty. " In my life, I have known nothing but the love of God", he said during a Mass to celebrate his twenty-fifth anniversary of ordination to the priesthood two years ago. "The love I have known is all that I seem to remember."

If there is any dissatisfaction, it is because he feels he has not done enough of God's work. "I think of the years I spent doing just part of God's will", he reflects. " There is so much more I could have done." That's why he is restlessly looking to the future, to doing even more to spread God's word. Missionaries of the Poor recently saw the establishing of a Sister branch headed by Sister Joan Clare. He feels that the new mission, now one year old, will grow even more rapidly than the mission of the Brothers has.

For the Brothers of the Poor, he wants to further growth overseas and locally. "I'd like to see more missions in China and Africa. I'd also like to begin working with the mentally handicapped and to create special homes where they can be cared for."

Despite the difficulties and the challenges, he continues to look ahead. "We are taking this forward, we have a lot more to do to bring God to others."

ORIGINALLY PUBLISHED JUNE 1999

Powerpuff Girls
Jamaican Women in Science

DIANA THORBURN

With uncanny smarts and driving ambition three young Jamaican women are smashing the glass ceiling and taking a firm hold on the tower of knowledge.

Karen Nelson

When they say "Jamaican gone abroad" it means that a local has made it big in "foreign," usually meaning North America or Britain. Karen Nelson, Ph.D, has not only turned up as one of the brightest young minds in the cutting edge field of microbiology research, she has also created multiple firsts in being very young (late twenties early thirties—she refuses to tell),

Jamaican, a woman, and very important in the US where she is based, black.

Her field of research can be overwhelming if you think about it enough, though Karen herself is very relaxed, almost blasé, about leading a team of scientists investigating an unusual organism that grows at the bottom of the ocean called thermatoga, which has been recognized as one of the earliest forms of life on this planet. Working on a project funded by the Department of Energy in Washington D.C., Karen has been researching how thermatoga, which grows in boiling water, can be exploited for industrial applications—for which it has enormous potential—and how it can give us answers to questions about the origins of life on this planet.

The focus of a four-part PBS series on revolutions in microbiology, *Intimate Strangers: Unseen Life on Earth*, Karen and her work were featured in one installment entitled, *"The Tree of Life"*, parts of which were filmed in Jamaica, USA, Germany and Italy. Besides the fascinating aspects of microbiology and the revolutionary implications of the newfound ability to look inside of genes, the show also sought to uncover a little bit about Karen herself: how does a young Jamaican woman end up sequencing the DNA material in one of the most pathfinding fields, dominated by old, white men?

Not too many years ago, Karen specialized in animal science in the Faculty of Agriculture at the University of the West Indies St. Augustine campus in Trinidad, because she wanted to be a vet. But when she won a scholarship to the University of Florida to do a Master's in animal science, her interest was captured by the bacteria in animal intestines, which eventually led to a Ph.D at Cornell looking mainly at unusual microbes. Upon finishing her Ph.D, amidst a wealth of job offers, Karen found the thermatoga project at the forefront, and she plans to stay there for a good while, though the thought of "giving something back" to the Caribbean is also a goal.

Will it be a Jamaican who tells us how it really all began? It's shaping up to look that way!

Alison Gajadhar-Plummer

You know when you go to get an MRI scan and they inject some stuff in your veins and then you can see your organs on the screen? Well the "stuff" is chelates and what it does is bind to the hydrogen atoms in the water molecules in your body and so gives a different image of diseased tissue from non-diseased tissue. Amazing, isn't it? Well it's actually not that great, at least not from the perspective of the inorganic chemist: it's inefficient and has a higher than ideal level of toxicity. But you will be relieved to know that there is someone working on a way to make chelates less toxic and more efficient, so you can have your MRI scans with less worry.

It should happen in about two more years (don't need an MRI before that!) when Alison Gajadhar-Plummer completes her Ph.D in inorganic chemistry at the University of the West Indies Mona campus in Jamaica. Born and raised in St. Lucia—and bonded by her government to return there upon completion of her studies—Alison "always loved chemistry". The enthusiasm with which she talks about the periodic table of elements and the laser chemistry machines with which she can observe the photophysical behaviour of metal irons would lead you to know this even if she hadn't said it herself.

Alison's work area, in the inorganic and environmental research laboratory in the chemistry department at UWI, is covered with your stereotypical scientist "stuff"—test tubes and beakers with different coloured liquids and a big fat lab book where everything gets written down. Alison's main area of work is with rare earth metal irons, which are those elements such as manganese and lanchanities that occur in the soil in small quantities..

Specifically, Alison aims to design a better chelate, which binds the metal irons, to transmit more metal irons in a more efficient manner to diseased tissues, so that in the MRI the diseased tissue will still show up purple, but the process of getting it purple will be faster and less harmful to the rest of your body. Her work will not end there; designing good chelates has further implications for extractive metallurgy, so that more valuable metals can be extracted, for example, from the bauxite waste mud.

When she goes back to St. Lucia, Alison will be the only Ph.D. chemist in the island. Though there is not a great deal of inorganic chemistry research going on there, a chemist is on the priority list of human capital needs in the island of some 120,000 people, and Alison is not worried about being away from the challenging environment of research. Before that, however, there's just a little problem with MRI scans that needs to be taken care of.

Paula Tennant

Tucked away in a corner, through the winding maze of corridors, laboratories and doors in the biotechnology centre at the University of the West Indies, Mona, you'll find a young woman in a lab coat sterilizing green paw paws (papayas) in order to put them into a tissue culture for analysis.

That young woman is Dr. Paula Tennant, who has spent the last six years at Cornell University formulating a strain of the paw paw that is resistant to the ringspot virus which has had a deleterious effect on the crop since the late 1980s. She recently returned as a research fellow to the Biotechnology Centre at UWI, where she continues developing this new breed of paw paw, a process which should take another three to four years. This is a major project, because the paw paw has enormous export potential for Jamaica, and a strain resistant to the ringspot virus could mean a boom for the island's export industry.

Since her undergraduate studies in biochemistry and botany at UWI, Paula developed on her interest in plants, with a focus on plant pathogens and diseases. Supported by the Jamaica Agricultural Development Foundation, she decided to focus on the paw paw because many farmers stopped growing the crop despite its promising commercial value. She began doctoral studies in plant pathology at Cornell in 1991, where, until 1996, she experimented with taking a gene from the virus itself and transferring it to the paw paw, somehow rendering it resistant. From 1996 to 1997 she did a post-doctoral greenhouse analysis, where she observed the plant inoculated with the virus in simulated conditions.

The next phase of the project is put the new paw paw out in the field to see how it does in the natural environment.

When this project is over, Paula hopes to work with other strains of paw paw, then with other fruits and vegetables and the pathogens that affect their development. She also has an interest in working with plants with medicinal properties.

The future is bright for the paw paw, and for Paula! ⓢ

ORIGINALLY PUBLISHED OCTOBER 1999

Professor Lawson Douglas

A Quiet Hero

TARA ABRAHAMS

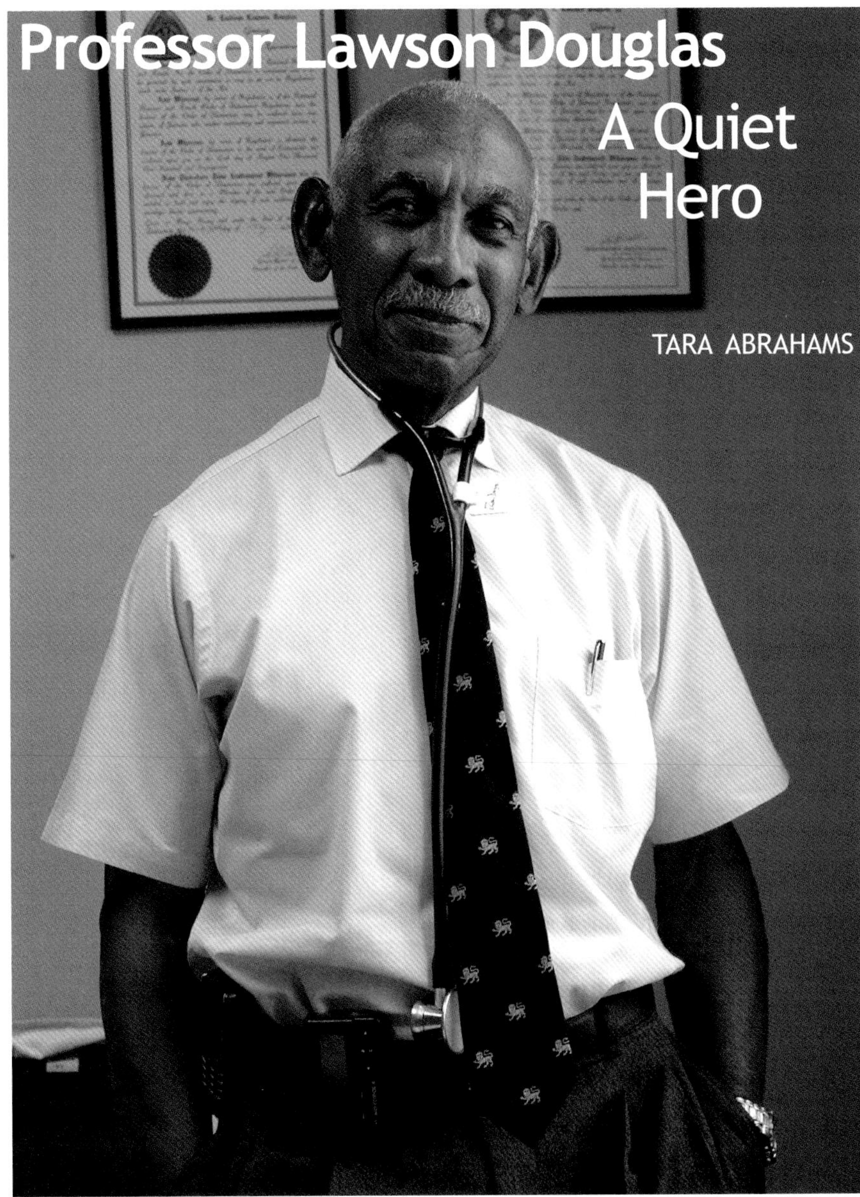

As a writer I have the unique opportunity to meet many people, all of whom have some kind of story. Recently, I was asked to interview one of Jamaica's foremost surgeons, Prof. Lawson Douglas, a gentleman of the old school who knows his field thoroughly; the kind of man who could easily intimidate you with his long list of achievements. With all this in mind and very little knowledge of renal failure, I nervously knocked on his door.

Once inside, a quick glance around the office and I see awards, certificates, commendations and other accolades including Jamaica's highest national honors: the Order of Distinction and the Order of Jamaica.

Professor Lawson Douglas spoke with me, with great detail on the function of the kidney and the causes and symptoms of renal failure. He spelt out every medical term with great patience. He went through the theories and dispelled the myths, all in an effort to educate me and hopefully through my article, others. Professor Lawson Douglas spoke humbly about himself, when I asked about his wall of fame, he simply replied that when you have been around as long as he you pick up these things.

Professor Douglas began his career training to be a plastic surgeon until he saw a medical journal announcement for a well-paying fellowship in urology at the University of Ottawa and decided to apply. His application was accepted and he became a urologist and transplant surgeon and started transplanting organs in Jamaica, in 1970. Professor Douglas pointedly avoided all of my prompts for self-assessment and only came close by attributing his drive to his father who was a Baptist minister who decided to study medicine at age 40, went to Edinburgh and graduated "with prizes."

What Douglas does not avoid is talk of what motivates him: saving lives. "You don't want to watch people dying, it is not nice." Professor Douglas' words bear a heavy load. His eyes are tired for an instant, and I understood what pushes this self-proclaimed "old man" to fight for his cause like a bold stallion who would literally walk across the island to save another life.

"It hurts me to see people dying from a treatable disease." As he speaks, it becomes clear that the killer is not the condition but simply the cost of treatment. Patients who face kidney failure will pay J$8000 for each dialysis treatment; with ideally three treatments each week, a number that will be reduced to two per week in an attempt to care for more persons. A transplant costs J$300,000 with a follow up cost of J$30,000 per month for the drugs that prevent rejection. If there are complications from the transplant the required medication costs J$80,000 per dose.

Presently, Professor Douglas has stopped all transplants until he can be sure that patients will be able to afford the follow-up drugs to prevent rejection to the new kidney. He says that all too often recipients of transplants return to him with symptoms of rejection and upon investigation there is not enough money to pay for the requisite drugs. However, Professor Douglas is attempting to raise these funds himself. His goal was to raise J$1.5 million by walking around the island. He began his walk at a busy intersection in Kingston last spring, and along with Tracey Rattray-Neil, Dr. Mark Cadogan and Duncan Young, he ended that islandwide trek in the fall. Each Saturday morning the group would begin walking from the point where they ended the previous Saturday. They visited hundreds of small towns, passionate about raising awareness on kidney disease and on organ donation. They inched towards the target of J$1.5 million dollars with the help of "small Jamaicans" who would come out of their homes and give $100 here, $50 there. Professor Douglas was obviously touched by the generosity of these ordinary and less impressed by the response of corporate Jamaica.

While Professor Douglas watches people wage the battle against renal failure, he lives with a calculation he says he gives at every opportunity: if just one third of the population or one million people gave only $20 each, the lives of 100 more patients could be saved. Professor Douglas simply rejects the "times are hard" argument.

Douglas remains undaunted by his mammoth goal to ensure recovery for all Jamaicans with renal failure. He and his Kidney Support Committee will next walk across Jamaica by way of the interior. While the trek may be small steps for Douglas and his team, it's a great stride for Jamaican healthcare.

ORIGINALLY PUBLISHED OCTOBER 2001

Our Films Their Films

Film Maker Natalie Thompson

DANIELLE GOODMAN

As line producer on most of the top studio films shot in Jamaica for the last 15 years, from *Cocktail* to *Cool Runnings* to *When Stella Got her Groove Back*, Natalie Thompson has helped to put Jamaica on thousands of screens.

But she's still waiting for a viable challenge to Hollywood's picture-perfect image of the island. "You see, Hollywood has a conveniently commercial, shorthand version of Jamaica, while we have a complex, inconvenient, non-commercial version of ourselves. As long as we're not making films, we can't dictate how others portray us. *Cool Runnings* was itself a Jamaican story. It made you stop and say, 'Why didn't we get together and make this—and make it real!'" Thompson's aim is to get the complexities of that view onto the screen.

Director Chris Browne, for whose *Third World Cop* Thompson was line producer and production manager, says that the filmmaker "understands the restrictions of filmmaking in Jamaica very well, and adapts to that. She knows her craft, and that inspires confidence." It's a craft that has been honed over more than 20 years. Explains Thompson," I've tried to understand every step of the business. I've dealt with writers in development, I've worked in pre-production, I've been a producer, and I've worked in postproduction. I worked on a couple of visiting productions as a production consultant in the early '80s, and very quickly learned what feature production is all about. I continued to study and amass quite a library on production techniques and procedures, which taught me the way Hollywood works."

Thompson's work in all aspects of the business gives her an overview that specialists can't have. Recently, she's been researching co-production treaties, encouraging the Jamaican government to follow the lead of other small filmmaking countries. "I'm writing a paper for the Minister of Entertainment to explain what a co-production treaty is. It's a baby of mine I've been trying to give birth to. They make such a difference. Senegal and Canada signed one—and you know what? There were eight co-productions in Senegal last year!"

"There's no money for film production here, and up to now, film has been a money-intensive industry. On the other hand, it's getting cheaper because of the ease of digital filmmaking, production and editing. On local TV, showing local product is not a priority. There's a lack of respect for copyright, so pirating people's work is the norm. Everybody feels they should view and enjoy it for nothing: for example, *Third World Cop* was shown by a pirate cable operator while it was still in the cinema, and *Laugh Jamaica* [a hugely popular comedy revue] was broadcast on cable within a week of its release," laments Thompson.

Does she ever fantasize about leaving Jamaica for Hollywood? "No, but recently, I have thought about just writing. It is where everything is born." But the lack of control over what gets written scares her: " I know what happens to it once it leaves your hands." It is here that Thompson zooms in on one of the limitations of the medium. As an art form it is semi-transparent, like the celluloid on which it's printed. We see the world it presents on the surface, but there's always the subtle surrounding reality glimpsed through it, the reality we think we own. When what's on the surface jars too much with our version of reality, conflicts and contrasts of sensibility are set up—sometimes to Thompson's great amusement.

"I run into a funny example of that over and over. One of the first things visiting film crews remark on when we're taking them on a location scout is the goats roaming the streets. They can't get over it: "Are they holy? Whereas to a Jamaican, what we see is curry goat!" Then there's the perennial translation bugbear of the 'm' word: 'man', also known as 'mon'. It's the biggest stumbling block for any dialogue coach working with a visiting actor playing Jamaican. Says Thompson, "Most Americans can't hear the difference between a fake and a real West

Indian accent. And of course, we're hypersensitive to it. I remember a dialogue coach working with an actor to get him to hear the difference between what he said and 'man'. "We don't say 'mon', we say man!" Replies frustrated actor: 'You just said 'mon'!"

The problem of translation goes both ways. Thompson is aware of the local desire for authenticity, but also of the resistance to portraying the grittier aspects of the Jamaican reality. Browne's *Third World Cop* (1998) "looked at a Jamaican situation—one that maybe most people wouldn't want to see, because it portrayed violent inner city problems—from a Jamaican point of view, which was different from what people come in and shoot." As a production milestone, *Third World Cop* is the most successful Jamaican film to date, having made back its budget from Caribbean theatre receipts alone: a first. But, thematically speaking, Thompson says, "It was not a comfortable film. Because we're a small island, we think that if one negative aspect of us is seen, then people abroad might think that's the whole of Jamaica." In a useful contrast to *Cop*, "the 1992 season of Lorimar Productions' *Going To Extremes* did show a different Jamaica visually—a rarely-seen rural Jamaica—in their production." Then again, the show was critiqued for its generic, idealized Caribbean atmosphere. How will we get it right?

Thompson thinks it will be through our stories. "Stories to write... I would try to cross over. I would deal with layers: somebody from outside coming in and recognizing these layers. Sees a cliché, digs a little deeper and finds out that's not the way it is. So we can get into another level of understanding, and gain perspective." Thompson's analysis is penetrating: "It's something unique about us: the different layers of society have a lot in common with each other, while being wrenched apart by complex class distinctions held over from British colonialism. The stories that communicate our culture better will be stories written by us that represent the many different layers of society and their interaction. That is where there is conflict. That is where there is drama." Our films would offer a sensitivity to these nuances that American films just don't have."

"You know, sometimes I wonder if I'm a control freak." One doubts it: she is manifestly healthy and uncrabbed. On her office wall looms a poster listing the Creed of the Sociopathic Obsessive-Compulsive: "If anything can go wrong, fix it. If you can't beat them, join them, Then beat them. 'No' simply means 'begin again at one level higher'."

This provides a clue to Thompson's customary state of mind and to her basic production techniques, namely calm and good humour. It is this quality of competent good humour that has gained admiration for Thompson from her peers—and from many in the business that she's mentored. Young producer, Sarah Manley, one of her protégées, cites Thompson's legendary calm: "What impressed me most about Natalie was her ability to handle any crisis in exactly the same way. Whether it is a major catastrophe or the simplest thing, her reaction is the same: we can handle it."

Thompson's version? "I make sure everyone on my sets behave themselves." As for the high-tech requirements, "you have to know how Hollywood works. The studios require a lot of daily paperwork, which is very specific." As a production manager on *Cocktail* (Touchstone, 1988), *Prelude to a Kiss* (Fox, 1991), *Milk and Honey* (Cineflics, 1987), and *Popcorn* (Movie Partners, 1989), she was responsible for getting all the documentation to the suits back in Hollywood. "All those forms serve a purpose: you have to know where every cent is, every minute. The studios exercise a tight rein . And one mistake, they're not hiring you again. You have to 'get it'."

"You want the dirt?" purrs comedian Tony 'Paleface' Hendriks. "Sorry, you won't get it from me." In a competitive industry, Thompson is notoriously highly regarded, recently winning a lifetime peer award in advertising for the over 250 commercials she's directed since starting Cinecom Productions in 1973. Some of the most-recognised and well-loved commercials over that period, like Cable and Wireless' "Let's Keep in Touch" and Red Stripe Beer's "Night Rider" have been made by Thompson. "I describe her as the dean of the film industry in Jamaica," says Maxine Walters, another leading Jamaican line producer and with Thompson, co-founder of the local chapter of Women in Film and Television. "For me she's been an amazing resource—well, not just for myself, but for everyone in the industry in Jamaica. She has always shared her knowledge willingly and generously."

Thompson's hopes are high for the Jamaican chapter of Women in Film, intending it to be a springboard to encourage training and film production in Jamaica. "If we don't motivate it now, it'll die. I think WIFT will play a very important part in getting it going."

Maxine Walters agrees. "Film, for an island like Jamaica, is an incredibly beneficial industry. Foreigners bring in all kinds of resources and equipment—and the only thing they take out is a roll of film."

Hendriks, too, is enthusiastic about Thompson's commitment to film in Jamaica: "She's always had the same belief in the local film industry that by developing people's skills and knowledge we will ultimately have more of a human resource base of talent, from the writers and actors through to the technical crews." Thompson also sees a future in local investigative programming to examine documentary subjects. "There are stories taking place now that we should be examining—otherwise, our history is not being recorded." Thompson tells her own history with characteristic wry humour: the high school student in the science stream, with every intention of doing medicine. "Then the drama teacher cast me as the (unwilling) lead in a pantomime of Mother Goose. After that, I decided I wanted to do something in the creative arts all my life." At 17, she went to Cincinnati, Ohio to study acting, and in her very first year performed in the professional theatre, both on and off campus. "It amazed me. But then my parents decided I should transfer schools, as I was turning into a hippie freak and attending antiwar demonstrations." From there to the University of Windsor went Thompson the actress, until insecurity set in: "It became very obvious how competitive the professional acting world is and in any case there were not many roles for black women. I decided to share my major with communication arts, and learned directing." Her first commercial was shot on black and white film 29 years ago. "There was no question about coming back to Jamaica. I felt this was where I was meant to be to work and to live. Life in Jamaica was pleasant enough. I could be a part of this burgeoning new industry. I came this close to working for an advertising company, and instead (a commercials director) Paul Noble matched their price. I've never done anything else. I like that I get to work with very talented people from here and abroad in front of and behind the camera—and Jamaica looks great through the camera lens!" Translating the smooth shiny high concepts of Hollywood production to the nuts, bolts and snags of Jamaican filmmaking, Natalie Thompson talks LA lingo with Jamaican understanding. Says Hendriks, "Natalie's bilingual: she speaks Panavision patois."

ORIGINALLY PUBLISHED DECEMBER 2001

Coffee Commodore
Keble Munn

SUZANNE FRANCIS-BROWN

Blue Mountain coffee is a symbol of Jamaican excellence, and Keble Munn is the standard bearer. From his Mavis Bank Central Factory, Munn presides over one of the island's largest coffee enterprises. It's a business that he grew up in—a 1923 photo shows him as a three year old toddler, helping to turn the coffee on a barbecue at his grandfather's Strawberry Hill estate.

Between then and now, he has been Jamaica's first coffee cup tester and grading officer, working with the Coffee and Cocoa Clearing House (CCCH) which pre-existed the current Coffee Industry Board (much later, he would chair that Board); he has been heavily engaged in the Jamaica Agricultural Society (JAS), lobbying heavily for the coffee industry, especially in the Blue Mountains; and he has been an active politician, first in municipal government, then a Member of Parliament and minister of government.

But Munn's first love is coffee and not even his strongest critics could deny that he knows his trade. Keble Munn has had his opponents, among them those who disagree with his promulgating—as Minister of Agriculture—the geographical boundaries within which coffee can be categorized as Blue Mountain coffee. Everything outside those boundaries is classed as high or low mountain coffee, even if it is grown within the general Blue Mountain area which covers much of the eastern end of the island. Since only certified Blue Mountain coffee attracts the premium price, locally and on the export market, critics have castigated him for decreasing the earning potential of Jamaican coffee.

His response: Of course he is interested in earning money. But he wants to be in business over the long term. He notes that the best coffee is all grown at high altitudes. Other elements contributing to an excellent cherry berry, as the ripe fruit is called, include soil type, weather and sun-shade ratio. These he says, are found in the defined area, and premium quality can be maintained as long as the coffee is grown in this recognized area and delivered to the few, officially recognized pulperies. Correct processing is vital to creating a product which has the rich aroma, good background taste and smoothness of premium coffee.

As he speaks, Munn is standing in the Gallery, a mini museum with a range of coffee machines as well as sample beans, framed photographs, and a brief history of coffee in Jamaica and especially at Mavis Bank. The gallery runs the length of the office building at Munn's Mavis Bank Central factory, high in the Blue Mountains, only a few hundred yards from his elegant two storey wooden home. The office, a recently rebuilt wooden building, was originally a family home.

He is usually in his office by 7:30 each weekday morning, dressed in shirt jacket and khaki long shorts, black shoes laced up about his ankles. He chuckles, recalling that the workers told him they always know when he has meetings in Kingston, because he comes to work in trousers.

Once a fiery red, his hair and mustache are now quite gray. But at age 75, he remains as active and unconventional as he was as a young man. At 20 years old, this scion of a middle class Jamaican family joined the Canadian army to fight in the Second World War. The tattoo on his right forearm is of that vintage. He would serve four years in the Canadian army, including seven and a half months as a prisoner of war outside Dunkirk.

Keble Munn returned from his army experience in September 1945, far more broad-minded than he went into it: "In the army, I was dealing with everybody, of all shapes and descriptions. Before that, I was in my own little world. So I came back with a totally independent spirit and a quite different social outlook."

Keble Munn's return to Jamaica marked his real entry into the family's coffee tradition. The

Munn's had been in the coffee business since Cecil Augustus Munn, originally from Kent, England, settled in Jamaica in 1885. He bought the Strawberry Hill plantation at Westphalia, 4,000 feet up in the Blue Mountain.

But Strawberry Hill, then accessible only by mule as was much of the Blue Mountain area, lacked the consistent sunshine needed to move the crop speedily through its processing stages. So, in 1919, Cecil's son Victor bought five acres at Mavis Bank.

"Mavis Bank faces east in the morning, west in the afternoon, so we could have a long run of sun" Munn explains. Erection of the original Mavis Bank factory started in 1921, and it opened for business in 1923.

So when Keble Munn came home to Mavis Bank, it was to join his uncle—who was, by then, also his stepfather—in business. "I started here at the very bottom level, knowing next to nothing about coffee" Munn recalls. "I had great help from an excellent headman, Adolphus Davis. I also got a boost from Richard Youngman, then head of Thomson Hankey & Co. Jamaica Limited. He called and said, 'You know nothing of the business, but if you'll show that you're capable of handling it, we'll finance you."

Another layer of experience was added to Munn's business life when he was offered the opportunity to become Jamaica's first coffee cup taster, working with the Coffee & Cocoa Clearing House."

Munn, then a young man of 26 years, was sent to C.A. McKay of Wall Street, New York for training. He was certified as a cup tester six weeks later, and returned to the CCCH as cup taster and grading officer. Tastings are events steeped in tradition, similar to the practice used in grading fine wines, with cup testers looking at the product's appearance, aroma, flavour, body and taste.

"Imagine me, a youngster, certified as a cup tester and having to deal with coffee from large houses. I was dealing with people long in the business and very unwilling to change," he says. But testing at the CCCH, was now the required means of establishing quality, and thereby price; and change they had, by the time Munn left the CCCH four years later.

By then, he had also become heavily involved in the Jamaica Agricultural Society though, as he notes, "at that time, it was totally unknown for people of my social type to move around in agricultural meetings." After a period in which he was involved in every aspect of the JAS work, he focused on the industry of which he was already a part. "I've virtually done that for the rest of my life," he says. "I've encouraged coffee growing, especially in the Blue Mountains."

He recalls that in the forties and early fifties, Blue Mountain growers were hampered by negative attitudes. "There was a government report which said the only remedy for soil erosion in the area was to move the coffee people and reforest the entire Blue Mountain area. "It was only in the mid-fifties that the attitude began to change, and Blue Mountain coffee stared moving again."

By then, Munn had decided that the JAS wasn't proving as effective a vehicle for change as he had originally anticipated, and that a move into the political arena might be more productive. He joined the People's National Party (PNP) and, in 1956, was elected a councillor in the Kingston and St. Andrew Corporation which ran the city of Kingston and its environs, including the hill country. In 1957 he was named deputy mayor. In the 1959 general elections, he became a Member of Parliament and served as Minister of Agriculture from 1959-62.

Then, the PNP lost the 1962 elections and remained in Opposition for ten years. After the PNP returned to govern in 1972, he served another two years as Minister of Agriculture, then as Minister of National Security and later as Minister of Parliamentary Affairs before retiring to the back benches and finally from the party.

"I enjoyed the political years," Munn says. "I really did. But after 25 years I figured that the time had come to look after the family. The truth is that I'd learned by then as well that politics does a terrible thing. It removes you from our family, unless you're very careful. And I was a very active politician."

Munn's first wife, Lilian, died fairly early in his political life, and he had married Yvonne Murray with whom he has three children, Gordon, Jodie and Lisa. He also has a daughter, Gwyneth, from his first marriage.

Keble Munn's political years saw vast changes in the Blue Mountains. Many of the old estates which had stopped operation by the mid fifties, were sub-divided and rented to farmers. Road building began and, by 1959, there were roads reaching into all areas. The negative side of that development, says Munn, was the rapid disappearance of the pack animals, which not only carried supplies and coffee but also provided manure. There have also been changes in the way farmers grew and fertilized their coffee trees.

The interest of the Japanese was another important input. They bought their first barrel of Blue Mountain coffee in 1953, and began boosting interest in this premium product at home. They also paid Jamaica a far better price for the commodity than the United Kingdom had been paying over the years.

As the fortunes of Blue Mountain coffee have waxed, so too have those of Mavis Bank Central and its processing partner Jablum Jamaica Limited. "In the forties, when I came back, there were virtually no big estates left," Munn recalls. "There were about 14 places buying or collecting Blue Mountain coffee for sale. None were that big. So the coffee was barely going along. In a good year, you would have gotten about 180,000 pounds of good, exportable Blue Mountain coffee. Today, some 2,700 farmers supply ripe coffee to Mavis Bank Central, the berries coming in by the bag or the truckload.

The small, three storey cedar building, powered by a water wheel, which was the first Mavis Bank factory, has long been eclipsed by a new, larger factory and warehouse buildings. The business, once a seasonal one, now proceeds virtually all year, though things slow down in midsummer, in December and January.

The Mavis Bank factory takes in the cherry berry, floats it to get rid of light, below standard fruit, then pulps it to remove the outer skin, bringing it to the wet parchment stage. It is then fermented, dried on the barbecue or in hot air dryers, and rested for six weeks. Hulling then removes the parchment skin from what is now green bean coffee and the beans are polished and graded. The best coffee is handpicked before being packed into wooden barrels for export.

All Jamaican coffee must be tested by the Coffee Industry Board before export, and Mavis Bank also does its own testing. Jablum Jamaica has a roasting plant at Mavis Bank, where coffee is roasted and packed for sale locally and overseas.

Keble Munn is openly proud of what his family has achieved in the industry. And the tradition continues. His wife has her own property, at Cedar Valley in St. Thomas, which supplies cherry berry to Mavis Bank. She also, in partnership with one daughter, is in business selling coffee. Their other daughter is at the University of Georgia studying agriculture and son Gordon helps supervise Mavis Bank Central.

And Keble Munn? "I have become what could be classed as a relic in the hills," he says. But he seems to have envisioned another mission, beyond that of continuing the champion Blue Mountain coffee as the best in the world. "There's a whole raft of incorrect history floating around. It's important to write things down. And I have picked up all sorts of knowledge along the way. I'd like to share it."

ORIGINALLY PUBLISHED JULY 1995

Dr. T.P. Lecky An Inspiration to Youth

VIN LUMSDEN

Jamaica is blest with four of the finest tropically adapted breeds of cattle in the world—one dairy breed, the Jamaica Hope and three beef breeds, the Jamaica Red Poll, the Jamaica Brahman and the Jamaica Black.

This is internationally accepted and must be recognised as no mean feat for an island with a land area of only 4,400 square miles and a population of over 2.3 million persons.

For this, Jamaica, owes a debt of gratitude to one of its most famous sons in the field of agricultural science, Thomas Phillip Lecky, Doctor of Philosophy, animal geneticist and farmer.

(ABOVE) The Hon. Dr. Thomas P. Lecky, OM., 1987 recipient of the Mutual Security Bank Foundation Outstanding Achievement Award enjoys a light moment with his niece, Dr. Hazel Bennett, senior lecturer of the department of library studies at the University of the West Indies, Mona, during the annual awards ceremony at King's House in 1988. (OPPOSITE PAGE) Dr. Lecky has a pat for a favourite in the herd, a supreme champion when she was younger.

It was his dedication; love of livestock; brilliance as a scientist; and, intuition that pioneered the work which changed the course of livestock breeding in Jamaica and indeed the tropical world.

It was therefore a fitting tribute that, when the first presentation of the Norman Manley Award for Excellence was held in 1970, it should be in the field of agriculture which had brought international recognition to Jamaica over the centuries and that the award should go to Dr. T. P. Lecky, Ph.D., O.M., O.B.E.

(The O.M., Order of Merit, is Jamaica's third highest national award. The O.B.E., Order of the British Empire).

"T. P.," as he is popularly known throughout Jamaica, recalls that occasion as his proudest moment. As he said, in his slow drawling voice, reminiscent of the movement of the animals he so loves: "It was for excellence among my peers and for having served my country."

Dr. Lecky's story is one of which every Jamaican can be proud and one which could serve as an inspiration to the country's youth.

The boy from Swift River, one of the many scenic valleys in the foothills of the majestic Blue Mountains in Portland, was born on the very last day of 1904.

He was born into farming even as his father was before him and grew up on the family farm of some 40 acres on which mixed farming was conducted.

His early preference for livestock was dictated by the traumatic experience of seeing his father's banana cultivation wiped out three years in succession by hurricanes, This was during the years of the First World War. Livestock was clearly a more bankable proposition—a belief shared by thousands of small farmers up to the present day.

"T.P." attended elementary school, as it was then called and then went to "Farm School", the Jamaica School of Agriculture, in suburban Kingston on a scholarship. On graduation he went to work with the government herd at Hope in 1925, then under the directorship of H.H. Cousins whom Lecky recalls as "one of the best Englishmen ever to come to Jamaica."

One can understand his appreciation of Cousins because it was he who started the work at Hope Farm, importing and testing, in a detailed manner, a number of European breeds of cattle for adaptation to the tropical environment. Indeed breed records embracing the performance of Ayrshires, Brown Swiss, Guernseys, Holstein Friesians, Jerseys, Shorthorns, South Devons, Zebus and Grade Native cover a period from 1910, when the work started, to 1931, all under the direction of H.H. Cousins.

Young Lecky worked closely with Cousins but found time to do night studies so as to equip himself to enter University. This he did in 1930.

He went to McGill University, completed the diploma course in agriculture and went on to Ontario Agricultural College, Guelph, where he obtained his B.Sc. in animal husbandry.

At Guelph, Lecky reviewed the work being done with cross-breeding to acclimatise the European breeds to the tropical conditions of Jamaica and came to the conclusion that the wrong approach was being taken. What was needed, he thought, was not an acclimatised European breed, rather a tropically adapted Jamaican breed. And the pattern of cross-breeding attempted in Jamaica was not likely to succeed, since this had already failed in work done in India using the Sahiwal (Zebu) and the Ayrshlre (a European breed).

"Pure intuition, not brilliance" Lecky says modestly, "since I did not have enough data to back my conclusions mathematically."

He decided that he would attempt line-breeding instead of crossbreeding to produce a breed and then select from among the highest producing animals for upgrading performance.

T.P. Lecky returned to Jamaica in 1935 and devoted himself to research work, testing the ideas at which he had arrived.

Perhaps he was fortunate in that Cousins' work had thrown up two lines with which he could make comparisons. One was a Jersey x Sahiwal cross and the other was a Holstein x Sahiwal cross.

Lecky noticed that in the Holstein x Sahiwal cross, an increase in the amount of Holstein blood generally led to a decrease in production. The same was true for the Jersey x Sahiwal cross. He therefore concluded that selection for production was in fact selection for adaptation to the tropical environment.

He went on to select from the best producing cows irrespective of the amount of Jersey or Sahiwal blood. If a particular cross produced most, her son was used as the bull for breeding. It was the pursuance of this line of work that led to the development of the Jamaica Hope.

In 1949 Lecky took all the data available to him from his work in Jamaica and went to the University of Edinburgh where he analysed the material and submitted his findings in his thesis "Genetic improvement in dairy cattle in the tropics" for the degree of Doctor of Philosophy. His conclusions in his thesis led to the discontinuation of the work with the Grade Holsteins and an intensification of the work with the Grade Jerseys.

In 1952 the herd of Grade Jerseys was closed to the introduction of new blood and Jamaica had its first breed of tropically adapted cattle—the Jamaica Hope—and a provisional Herd Book was started.

The work on the Jamaica Hope led to the development of the Jamaica Red Poll, the Jamaica Black and the Jamaica Brahman—all outstanding tropically adapted beef breeds.

Unknown to Dr. Lecky, his work prior to submitting his thesis for his doctorate had already caught the attention of the United Nations and the publication of his doctoral thesis brought him international acclaim.

The impact of his work was felt throughout the livestock areas of the tropical world because the development of a number of tropical breeds, including the Australian Milking Zebu and the Israeli Holstein were patterned upon the work of the Jamaican, Dr. T. P. Lecky.

He has been called upon to present papers at international forums. In 1958 he prepared a paper on the breed development work for the Tenth International Congress on Genetics. In 1962 he presented a paper at a United Nations Conference on the Application of Science and Technology for the benefit of less developed areas.

Dr. Lecky retired from the Jamaica Government service in December 1964 but made his services available for consultancy to the livestock industry up to the present time. Indeed at the age of 75 he was called upon by the Government to rescue a dairy project at Shettlewood in the western end of the island. By bringing his dedication and experience to bear he has transformed this project into a viable commercial operation.

More recently at the age of 78 Dr. Lecky has again been called upon to assist in halting the deterioration at the Bodles Experimental Farm, home of the national herd of Jamaica Hope which he created. To this exercise he currently devotes his energies.

Reflecting upon his achievements, Dr. Lecky paid tribute to the farmers with whom he has been associated over the years and without whose contribution during the developmental years he felt he could not have succeeded.

Questioned about the state of the dairy industry despite the presence of the Jamaica Hope, "T.P." ruefully shook his mane of white hair.

"There is nothing wrong with the breed, there is a lot wrong with the industry. When you can have a 14 year old cow producing over 25,500 lbs of milk in 10 months there can't be anything wrong with the breed."

He blames the present state of the industry upon the introduction of subsidised skimmed milk powder.

"No fresh milk industry can compete with that. We have to decide whether to use skimmed milk powder to build the industry or destroy it and the present minister seems to be interested in building the industry."

"T.P." also maintains that successful dairying can be built on a small farm basis but this cannot be done without training and technology.

"We seem to be training people for jobs not for farming."

Jamaica can well be proud of Dr. T. P. Lecky, a man who started from relatively obscure origins in rural Jamaica and rose to leave his mark upon the development of cattle breeds throughout the tropical world. Jamaica's four breeds, the Jamaica Hope, the Jamaica Red Poll, the Jamaica Black and the Jamaica Brahman are a fitting monument to his life's work.

Dr. Lecky's life and work is indeed an inspiration to young Jamaicans.

ORIGINALLY PUBLISHED APRIL 1984

Dr. Olive Lewin— Jamaica's First Lady of Folk Music

BRIAN HEAP

Dr. Olive Lewin interviewing Imogene "Queenie" Kennedy.

To be given the chance to meet Dr. Olive Lewin is to encounter a Jamaica very different from the one characterized by its rapidly developing industrial and commercial sectors, or even ultra-modern tourist resorts. Dr. Lewin's Jamaica is an altogether gentler, less complicated place, one which, far from being a thing of the past, still continues its quiet existence in certain parts of the island.

Best known by many people in Jamaica as a distinguished folk researcher and ethnomusicologist, Dr. Olive Lewin is also the founder/artistic director of the internationally acclaimed Jamaican Folk Singers, and a former director of art and culture in the Office of the Prime Minister. As she herself says, with more than a touch of that dry sense of humour which is one of her trade marks, "How people see me depends on their age. Some would still remember me mainly as a pianist." Certainly it was her outstanding musical ability which enabled the young Olive Lewin to take up a Royal Academy of Music scholarship just after the Second World War.

While opportunities for her to study drama and dance outside the Academy also presented themselves, (she even played piano for dance classes as she herself states, "all for the experience") music remained Olive Lewin's first love. Courses with such daunting titles as "Harmony, Counterpoint and Composition" led her to the startling realization that the composers which she revered were products of their societies. "It meant," she says, "that we Jamaicans could never really contribute significantly to the world of art music until we knew our own musical styles and forms and respected them."

As the children of teachers, Olive and her two sisters enjoyed the stability of a rural upbringing in the parish of Clarendon, surrounded by the music of the folk. "Christmas wasn't Christmas without the burru masquerade; Sunday not the same without the sound of revival drums. If someone died, not only was there a funeral, but also a wake, and work songs came to us on the breeze."

It wasn't until her years of secondary education at Hampton, that Olive began to understand that not everyone in Jamaica grew up with this kind of exposure to the folk music and traditions of the island. Many people were born and grew up in Jamaica, yet had no idea of the names or musical styles of these forms. Despite being offered a sub-professorship by the Royal Academy at the end of her studies there, Olive resolved to return home to Jamaica to the source of her own musical inspiration.

If Olive Lewin encountered any resistance at all to her efforts to document the folk music of Jamaica, it was overcome by her understanding that on a purely musical level, Jamaica's contribution to a world picture of music would have to be a contribution of Jamaican styles and forms. She also began to see that, in order to do justice to the music, there was also a need to know something of its background and context, to develop an understanding of "not just the music, but the beliefs and social mores which surrounded and supported the music."

In this she was supported by contacts she made with other scholars conducting similar research across the face of the globe. Connections were made with African, Asian, American and European ethnomusicologists and researchers, people whose work has largely contributed to the present decade's unprecedented interests in "New Age" and "World" music.

In the case of Jamaican popular music, Dr. Lewin has no hesitation in acknowledging the enormous debt which reggae, ska and dancehall music owe to Jamaica's folk musicians. She expresses her concern however, that "we have been inclined to stop too near the surface to look for the roots of pop in secular music. Often we are not seeing the spiritual dimension of a given form, but only the physical in, say, the hip movement of a particular ritual dance."

Olive Lewin has learned from long years of work in the field, waiting for months on end for a few bars of a previously uncollected song, not to rush recklessly to conclusions about the music's origins, but to compare notes with colleagues and be guided by their experiences sometimes on different continents. She speaks of an African colleague identifying an African retention in Jamaica in the style of tuning a drum. "We have to go back to the drums," she says. "Not just how the drum looks, but how the drum sounds. For its sound is more than just sound. It is a psychic force."

In this way Dr. Lewin has been able to trace lines of development to the popular Jamaican forms directly from the roots of Jamaican folk music. Her eyes light up as she recalls fond memories of the late, great Count Ossie from whom she learned, among other things, that the drums used in Rastafarian drumming, had come from the burru tradition of her native Clarendon. "Ska came straight out of revival. The song "If I Had The Wings of a Dove" illustrates just one of its obvious links, because the music of revival was what was most familiar to many of the young musicians who contributed to the development of ska music. They made use of what they knew."

A tremendous source of pride for Olive Lewin is the fact that Jamaica, "which is so small on the world map," should have had such an impact on world culture. "Bob Marley was able to reach people worldwide, not because they always necessarily understood what he was singing about, but through the way in which he communicated." And, in her opinion, it continues today in the dancehall culture. "The basic rhythm of dancehall is the same as that heard in mento, Jamaica's indigenous folk dance. Yet this is not necessarily a conscious adaptation of the folk rhythm to the contemporary urban culture. Much of it is instinctive. The links are often subconscious. But these things at least allow us to realize that we are a people with our own roots and traditions, and not just imitators."

Dr. Lewin finds the basic confidence in people which she sees growing out of this realization exciting, albeit that she may have reservations about their taking things too far. "Education is the important factor in cultural development. I certainly hope that we will take the trouble to let our children know their traditions and their heritage, because that is the way for them to grow in self-esteem and in commitment to home and to establishing a centre within themselves, which will enable them to build up a confidence, a certainty as to who they are and what they are."

Dr. Lewin taking a break with members of the Jamaican Folk Singers at a presentation in Washington D.C.

But the real teaching resources are dying out fast, which is one of the reasons why Dr. Lewin has put so much of her energy over the years into the development of the Jamaica Memory Bank, a national repository for the oral history, folk wisdom, musical and literary traditions of hundreds of ordinary Jamaicans who have made their contributions to it over the years. Prejudice against oral wisdom is often openly displayed, perhaps because people know about rumour and hearsay, so that the true significance of this invaluable collection many not be fully realised for many years to come.

Another way in which the collected traditions have been given a continued existence is through the work of the Jamaican Folk Singers. Started twenty-five years ago with encouragement from the late Jamaican dance pioneer Ivy Baxter, the group's first performances at the tiny Barn Theatre were greeted with such great enthusiasm that they were forced to seek out a larger performance venue. The Jamaican Folk Singers season became a regular feature at the Little Theatre for many years thereafter, but as the expenses became greater the group came to the uneasy realisation that the very people from whom these traditions had been collected were no longer able to afford to come to the performances.

The Singers together took a group decision to take their performances out into the open, to work alongside traditional peoples and seek out a target audience of visitors and young persons whose minds were fresh and who could become excited about Jamaican traditions. Such were the beginnings of the Jamaican Folk Singers "Pepperpot" Old Time Fairs, for which the audiences and enthusiasm have grown steadily. They have featured Maroon folkways, traditional candy-making, bammy making, dinky-mini, mento bands, and quadrille dancing among other fascinating folkways.

The Jamaican Folk Singers continue to take traditional Jamaican culture to other countries, most recently to Washington D.C. in the United States, and the Cayman Islands, but wherever they go there are always workshops and performances for the children, whether in schools or hospitals—anywhere.

The Singers have even put a selection of their works together on videotape for Jamaicans living abroad, or to be enjoyed by visitors to the island long after they have returned to their home. As Dr. Lewin says, "Technology is not a threat. It's how it's used that's important." And certainly in the Jamaica Memory Bank, or the audio and video recordings or the Jamaican Folk Singers, technology has been placed first and foremost at the service and preservation of tradition.

Turning once again to the subject of the island to which she has devoted her life, Olive Lewin reflects, "We probably have more creativity per square yard here than in most other places in the world. But we have to learn how to harness it. We are all part of one world, but if we don't develop the assuredness within ourselves, our children are not going to inherit the earth."

But somehow the look of determination which Olive Lewin holds in her expression as she says these words leads one to believe that nothing quite so negative will be allowed to happen if she and others like her have anything at all to do with it.

ORIGINALLY PUBLISHED JULY 1993

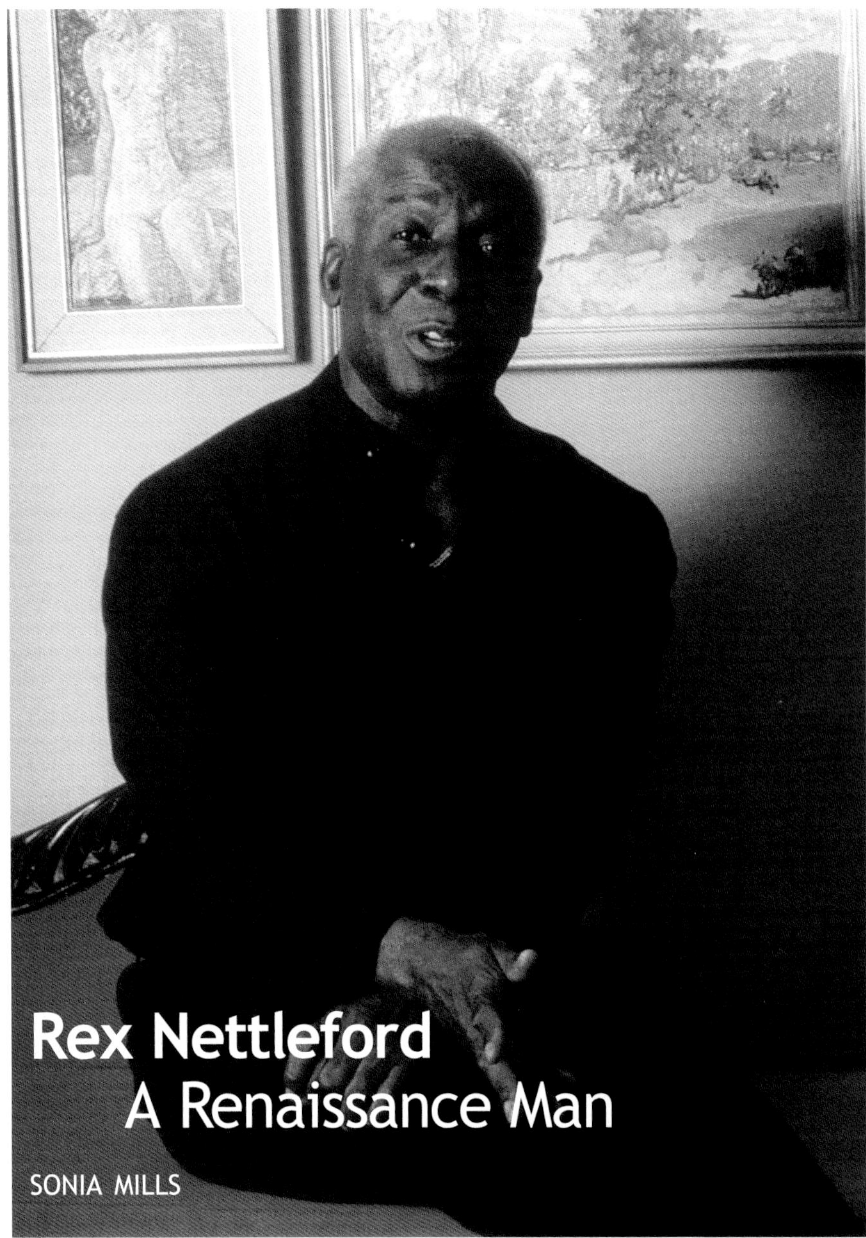

Rex Nettleford
A Renaissance Man

SONIA MILLS

I have taken all knowledge to be my province. With that statement, the great seventeenth century English philosopher Sir Francis Bacon encapsulated, for all time, the concept of the Renaissance man: inquisitive, reflective, eclectic, committed to the world's welfare. Within the twentieth century, the Honourable Rex Nettleford has earned the appellation for he is, at once, author, artist, editor, cultural historian, and, above all, educator, not only in the formal sense but as a mentor to the nation.

–Excerpt from the conferral of the Degree of Doctor of Letters on Rex Nettleford, Office of the President, St. John's University, New York.

Educated at schools in his native Jamaica and then as a Rhodes Scholar at Oxford University, Rex Nettleford currently holds the titles of Professor of Continuing Studies, head of the Trade Union Education Institute, and Pro Vice-Chancellor (now Deputy Vice-Chancellor) at the University of the West Indies. He is also the founder, artistic director, principal choreographer and a former lead dancer of the National Dance Theatre Company of Jamaica, now in its 35th year. Indeed, his native land is the love of his life; he writes, speaks about and advocates its indigenous national culture. That culture has been the subject of innumerable books and scholarly articles, all of which contribute to the definition of a Caribbean world view and identity, born of the experience of its peoples and suffused with their dignity and creativity, their struggle for intellectual and cultural as well as political independence. In short, Rex Nettleford's master project, as one scholar has put it, is the "decolonization of the Caribbean spirit."

His compatriots have honoured him with the Order of Merit; the university he serves has recognized his extraordinary talent by presenting him with its coveted Pelican Award; the Institute of Jamaica has named him a Fellow, only the fourth time it has awarded this honour in its more than 100 year history. The international community has both commended him and called upon him for counsel.

Sonia Mills: *You are often referred to as a Renaissance man. Who, or what, is a "Renaissance man" in the 21st century Caribbean?*

Rex Nettleford: One of my central concerns is of course redefinition. And naturally, the most central of all concerns is getting out of Europe's definition of us and defining ourselves for ourselves. We're not at the margins; we must place ourselves at the centre. When we talk, for example, of entering the mainstream, our responsibility is to determine the mainstream, not to enter it.

SM: *If I may quote from the citation from St. John's University: "Rex Nettleford's master project....is the 'decolonization of the Caribbean spirit.'"*

RN: Transforming non-peopleness into people-hood.

SM: *A year ago, the University of the West Indies convened a major conference on Caribbean culture, in your honour. It seemed as if just about every scholar in Caribbean studies anywhere in the world responded to the call for papers. That is quite a tribute. How did it come about?*

RN: My colleagues in the Faculty of Social Sciences came up with the idea because of my own intellectual and academic interest which has become very central to discourse in the academy. In fact, I have been lecturing all over the world exploring culture in development and using Jamaica and the Caribbean social phenomena as grist for the mill. There were just under 500 registered participants and over 100 papers from scholars from universities all over the world, as far away as New Zealand.

SM: *I am sure it is because (to use another definition from another culture) you are regarded as a cultural icon.*

RN: I thought I was regarded as an iconoclast. Which doesn't bother me at all. It comes with the territory. Of course being regarded as an image in a gilded frame is not necessarily how I would wish to be considered.

SM: *"Kumina", one of the major dances of the repertoire of the National Dance Theatre Company, is an icon in today's spirit—a multi-media celebration of a spiritual/religious form.* Mirror Mirror *(Nettleford's seminal essays on identity and race in Jamaica and the Caribbean, first published in 1971) is also regarded as a cultural icon. So, in addition to being yourself an icon, you are also iconoclast and iconographer.*

RN: I would be reluctant to accept those particular categorizations, but I would accept a definition that describes me as non-monodimensional human being. Both culture and development speak to a totality of human experience and the panoply of expression of the creative imagination.

SM: *And who are your icons?*

RN: I would say my teachers. All of them. Miss Bernard at infant school; Mr. Clifford Francis at primary school, in my village, Bunkers Hill; Rupert Miller and Philip Wright at Cornwall College; Elsa Goveia and Roy Augier at the University College of the West Indies; Isaiah Berlin at Oxford. And to this day, Sir Philip Sherlock. You know of course, he has been described by those who feel he has betrayed his class as "an irresponsible radical!" Can you believe it? At age 95!

SM: *There is your major involvement not just in the NDTC, but in dance and the development of a Caribbean vocabulary of dance, in the annual pantomime, in Festival of the Arts, etc. All this while being recognized as one of the foremost scholars and thinkers of the Caribbean. I believe four universities have awarded you hounorary doctorates, and you have also received the Presidential Medal from Brooklyn College, New York.*

RN: I give credit to our university for enabling the work. And the work continues; and bears fruit. At present, in addition to the School of Continuing Studies and the Trade Union Education Institute, my intellectual responsibility at UWI is to spearhead the university's Cultural Studies Initiative. The purpose is to make the UWI outreach programme more central to the university's work, and to bring all those current, daily expressions of the creative imagination of the Caribbean people, into the academy. So that our living, breathing culture can inform development. And intellectual pursuits. The initiative will radiate out of the graduate studies programme focusing on research to capture what is out there and bring it into the academy, while serving as yeast for the dough in both undergraduate studies and outreach work.

SM: *This concept of cross-fertilization is always very present in your thinking and your expression.*

RN: I say it often, that we in the Caribbean have always lived in a global village. We are products of globalization —an aspect of cross-fertilization.

Take the name Nettleford. I believe it is a Cornish name. (Cornwall, England of course.) I was born in Falmouth, the capital of Trelawny which is in the county of Cornwall, Jamaica. I sometimes make a joke that one of my ancestors must have seen the name on a zinc pan, liked it and took it! It sounds good after all.

SM: *Since we are in the process of redefinition, what about the most central redefinition of all: self.*

RN: I consider myself part African, part European, part Asian, part Native American and totally Caribbean—I am a creature of all the cultures that have shaped this Caribbean region.

SM: *In your closing address to the conference last year you say that "learning to live together is the essence of the creative diversity which characterizes Caribbean existence, and is about to overtake the entire world."*

RN: Ethnicity, or more narrowly, race, has been one of the major and unresolved issues of the "modern" (post-Renaissance) world. To be specific, Europeans have used white and black to polarize the human race and to dehumanize "black" people.

SM: *Is it possible to redefine the issue in our own terms?*

RN: By all means! It has to do less with how much melanin you have in your skin than in your capacity to relate. There are questions and issues which may not be "burning" at this particular time, but they are always present.

SM: *For half a millennium, at least, black has been dehumanized and devalued. "Jim Crow" and apartheid in the 20th century, following centuries of African slavery and colonization cemented the dehumanizing process. Has black self-esteem grown strong enough to allow Caribbean people to redefine themselves for themselves?*

RN: You know, the Caribbean is a living laboratory. And we are living our own redefinition. The idea of a Caribbean people is an idea whose time has come. An idea whose time has come out of the living of it. I am not alone—many Caribbean scholars have verbalized the idea in many ways. To use Edouard Glissant's words: "Our myth is less a myth of origin, but more a myth of relations."

SM: *Would I be correct in saying to you that in the definitions that we have been used to, "blackness" does not fully describe Rex Nettleford? In the fifties and sixties when racism was rampant in the United Kingdom and became a topic for conversation and action, black scholars and students would vie for the descriptive word to emphasize the utterness of their black identity....playing around with definitions of "how black"— utterly, unalterably, indubitably, hopelessly. Have we moved beyond "hopelessly black"?*

RN: Well of course, I am "hopelessly black". But race is a European political construct. And, culturally, black is not all that I am. We are creatures of all our ancestors. Even in my colonial conditioning there was much to be gained; if only to give me the opportunity to transform liability to advantage.

SM: *What about "the diaspora"?*

RN: I think I have contributed considerably to discourse on and in the diaspora. I have found myself operating in concentric circles, spiraling outwards, but nevertheless deeply rooted in my immediate society. Jamaica, out into the Caribbean, the Americas, the African diaspora, the world. That's what the diaspora means to me.

SM: *Let me quote you again, from the same closing address: "Caribbean educators need to take a look at the long haul of human history and locate the region where it appropriately belongs—that is on the trajectory of human "becoming" via that process of cross-fertilization which enriched ancient Egypt, ancient Greece, Renaissance Europe, Iberian Spain during the times leading up to 1492, the Americas of modern times as well as Europe of the future, which promises that promontory of Asia a challenging dose of multiracial multi-culturalism." So, the Caribbean person is the precursor of the 21st century person?*

RN: Culturally, yes. But there is more. The 21st century citizen will be a highly textured person with a cross-roads sensibility, eyes in the middle, back and front of one's head.

SM: *Looking for what?*

RN: All human impulses. The totality of human experience. 21st century human will reclaim our heritage. All of it.

ORIGINALLY PUBLISHED OCTOBER 1997

Orlando Patterson

DIANA THORBURN

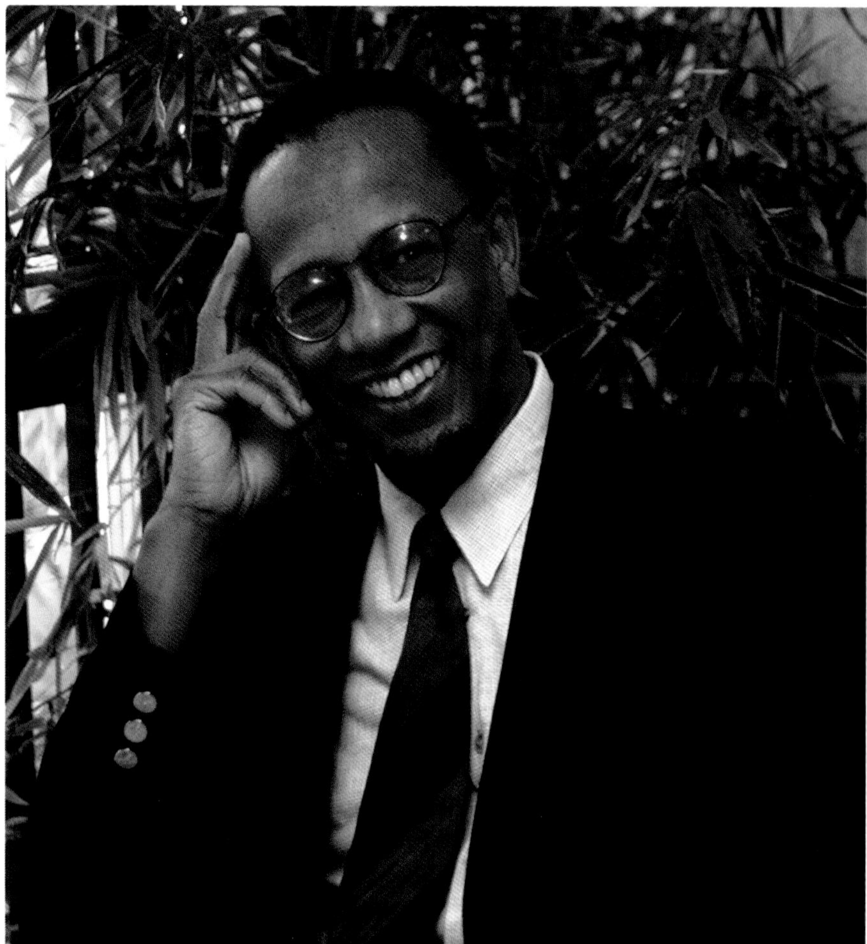

He is what they call a public intellectual, sharing his thoughts on national issues with the entire population through books, articles, or op-ed columns. So what? Well, the issues he thinks, writes and opines on are only centred around what has been called America's biggest problem, and the media through which he speaks his mind only happens to be the *New York Times*, books publicized around the entire continental United States, and US national radio.

This is Professor Orlando Patterson, the maverick of the US intelligentsia on race and race relations in the US and original yardie hailing, yes, from the Rock. "Caribbean people are the smartest people in the world," says he, "unabashedly, and *that* is what is going to carry us through, if we are to make it all, into the current global phase."

It has been a busy morning for the Senior Professor in Sociology at Harvard University. He appeared on a radio show in New York over the telephone, then was in studio for another radio show in Boston, then had to prepare and present his lecture on the Afro-Caribbean oral tradition and literature at noon for the course he teaches on Caribbean culture—where he also conveys his opinion of the inherent wealth of intelligence and creativity found in the region. As he walks into his office his assistant informs him that *Newsweek* has been calling every hour on the hour to set up a photo shoot for that day or the next. He gave a commentary on slavery for a *Newsweek* feature on Steven Spielberg's brilliant epic *Amistad*. He says he can do it at noon the next day, before he leaves for New York where he is a panelist at a Caribbean writers forum.

The radio shows, and the book tours he embarks on almost every weekend, surround his latest and very well received (despite its controversial thesis) book, *The Ordeal of Integration: Progress and Resentment in America's "Racial" Crisis*. First, in this work, as in others, Patterson puts race in inverted commas: he does not believe race really exists. Second, unlike many of the other opinions on the issue, Patterson sees that race relations—that is, relations between whites and blacks—in the US are improving, and provides many convincing arguments to support his position. He is one of the few positive voices on the issue, though he does recognise that there is still a long way to go. Again he is the maverick—he can't be placed in any one position—he is left on some issues, right on others: he thinks government must intervene to address poverty, but there must also be some action taken for black people to address their family patterns. One of the solutions he advocates to the race problem is for the races to intermarry. Criticism follows closely behind him, as does praise, from all sides of the debate.

Ordeal is the first book out of the new publishing house, Civitas, headed up by Harvard star and guru on all things African-American, Henry Louis Gates, Jr. It is also the first of a trilogy, all looking at race and class in America, and how they affect national life, policy and culture. Civitas is the first press dedicated to quality African American scholarship, and when Gates became aware of *Ordeal* he insisted that it be the first to headline Civitas's debut. And it has been quite a debut. Not only have the major critics passed an enthusiastic thumbs up, but the readings around the country have been well attended. He was the subject of a feature story for the trendsetting *New Yorker* magazine, and major publications across the US are seeking his opinion on just about anything race-related, as in the *Newsweek* story.

This is not his first book on the US—in 1994 he won the top book honour in the US with the National Book Award prize for *Freedom in the Making of Western Culture*. In this work he asks the question, How did the West become so preoccupied with freedom? Why is freedom such an important part of Western thinking and culture? It is not a feature of non-

Western cultures. The answer he came up with is striking, troubling and most of all, brilliant: that the recognition of freedom as valuable came when freedom was lost—that freedom and the quest to attain it arose with its loss, that is, with slavery. So that one of the most significant features of western culture is tied to one of its darkest truths. An unusual idea, yes, but challenging and carefully arrived at.

The second volume in the American Trilogy, *Rituals of Blood: God, Sex and "Race" in American Culture*—which argues that American culture is really a product of what Patterson calls the violent embrace of Africa and Europe—is on press for a 1998 release. Third volume *Ecumenical America* which examines how American culture affects the rest of the world, with a case study of the Caribbean, is now in progress. However, Patterson's interests have returned to fiction. As soon as the trilogy is "out of his system," as well as the follow up volume of *Freedom* gets off the back burner, he'll put on paper the novel that is already written in his head. The novel is set in 1940s Jamaica and has cricket as a theme.

Orlando Patterson, who was born and grew up in Jamaica, accredits his background for his insight into the US race situation: "Bringing a Jamaican perspective—or certainly a foreign perspective—to what is usually a very parochial discussion is often what people find refreshing about my views." It is, perhaps, this distance from his subject that affords him greater objectivity and clarity. His early works, however, both academic and fictional, were primarily based in Jamaica. His landmark work, *The Sociology of Slavery*, considered a seminal text in the study of slavery and slave society dealt with the New World in general. His most famous novel (and a core literature text for Caribbean students), *The Children of Sisyphus*, is set in a Kingston ghetto and gives a vivid and sobering, if somewhat explicit, account of the more unpleasant circumstances which the legacies of slavery and colonialism have left us. Then, as now, he doesn't mince words: "I find that both African Americans and European Americans are obsessed with race, and it diverts attention from real issues, and I don't have any hesitation in saying so. I think the greatest paradox in America today is that the most segregated part of America is its churches, and its most integrated part is its armies—yet the army is the instrument of destruction, and the church, supposedly, the instrument of love and peace. It's disgraceful."

Patterson's shift to the U.S. as a focus of his analysis was a matter of natural progression, though for him it's not so much a shift as an expansion of his scope. As he puts it: "Since the 1980s I've become more involved with policy issues and problems, problems of poverty, having to do with race and class... these were issues I was always concerned with in Jamaica too, I've just sort of extended them to America. My own vision of the Caribbean now is that it is now part of what I call the West Atlantic system. I see Jamaica and the Caribbean as part of an emerging global culture, one region of the global culture, and we're moving towards a post-national age, in which the nation-states really mean less and less."

In academia Patterson has made a name for himself in the Caribbean, and is hailed as a Jamaican scholar who has excelled internationally. After completing his B.Sc. at the then University College of the West Indies in economics, he went on to do a Ph.D. in sociology at the London School of Economics—the breeding ground for the likes of Forbes Burnham, Michael Manley and Errol Barrow. This is the period he calls his "literary phase," which saw the publication of *Sisyphus* as well as another novel, *Ruins*. He stayed on as a faculty member at LSE for two years, but broke his contract to come back home, where he joined the UWI faculty and taught sociology from 1967 to 1969. In 1969 he took sabbatical and went to Harvard for a year. Today, 28 years later, he is still in Cambridge, now as senior professor, previously as chair of the graduate programme and before that as head of the department of sociology. Yet despite his primary role now as a commentator on US affairs, in speaking about the Caribbean he never fails to use "we" and "us".

Certainly his first decade in Cambridge did not stop him from being integrally involved in Jamaican politics in the exciting and turbulent "socialist experiment" of the 1970s. He was then special adviser to Prime Minister Michael Manley for eight years, with an office in Jamaica House, at the same time as he was lecturing America's brightest at Harvard. He lived, effectively, in both countries, going back and forth between semester breaks. As the specialist on social policy, it was his idea, for example, to set up the Basic Shops, which were meant to provide the basic goods a person needs for survival within reach of every Jamaican. These were among the first projects the IMF got rid of when it came in towards the end of the seventies.

The seventies. That time in Jamaica's history that is like a not-properly-healed wound: fine to look at, but don't touch because it's still a bit too sensitive. But Patterson speaks openly about it: "We tried to do too much, we were ideologically naive, and we were not sufficiently sensitive to the fears of the middle class. We lost our managerial class. You can't run a country without that. Add to that the U.S's negative hysterical reactions at the height of the Cold War." But he is also cognisant of the positives of the seventies; he speaks, for example, of the agricultural programmes that were then a significant achievement. Most important was the huge success of cultural transformation, where Rastafari, reggae and the voices of ordinary people were heard for the first time.

And now? Whither Jamaica, whither the Caribbean? Though not as directly involved now as then—who wins what elections really doesn't matter to him; he maintains a great interest but nothing more—issues of economic and social development still concern him, and still comprise his academic and intellectual work. "I take a global perspective on things, and I think the Caribbean had better do that too. It's quite clear that the Caribbean has to move to the stage where they emphasize their own human resources far more, because we don't have many natural resources. If we're not going to sink, we have to learn to leapfrog into the post-industrial age. I think we've missed the boat in terms of producing pots and pans, and exporting them to America, there are other countries that can do that cheaper, faster and in greater volumes than we can. We have to survive by our wits and it seems to me that we have to emphasize overwhelmingly an economy which is going to take advantage of its proximity to America, take advantage of the fact that we are an English speaking country, take advantage of the fact that we are some of the smartest people in the world... and live by our wits."

Jamaica still sees Orlando Patterson, usually about twice a year, when he comes back to "crash" and see family. But home is definitely Harvard—"heaven for a scholar"—and, increasingly, extended research and lecture trips around the world, most recently to South Africa and Sweden. And, contrary to what one might imagine of an old, traditional Ivy League like Harvard, they love what he's doing. They want their professors to be famous, and, in turn, being a Harvard professor does help. "The university is only as good as its people; I have helped to define what this place is. Remember we Jamaicans are feisty, when we are somewhere we make sure we belong!"

ORIGINALLY PUBLISHED JUNE 1998

La Numero Una

MARC GOODMAN

Jamaican-born New York politico **Una Clarke** goes for the big time.

Una Clarke with grandsons Kari and Khalil on her birthday

After nine years representing Brooklyn District 40 in the City Council, Democrat Una Clarke is beginning what promises to be one of November's more bitterly-contested Congressional races. Her opponent, Major Owens, is a nine-term incumbent and has won at least 89 percent of the vote in each of his elections. The two are former good friends: Owens attended Clarke's son's wedding. The two families have spent a lot of time together. In *The New York Times*, a hurt Owens described her as his former "protegé." This does not seem to matter anymore. Tucking into her usual grits with scrambled eggs and bacon at a greasy spoon teeming with lobbyists one cold spring morning, Clarke says merrily about the primary election, "Once I win in September he can kiss it goodbye."

Another reason the race is contentious is that it crystallizes the sometimes uneasy political relationship in her district between African-Americans and newer arrivals from points south. "I think that many African-Americans feel that Caribbean-Americans come better-educated and more prepared to take on positions of responsibility. They think the one bastion that should be left for them is politics. So they will say in their private moments that we've come, we own real estate, we own businesses, our children go to the best schools, and we hold down big jobs, and therefore they should be allowed to do the politics. You see, the only way to protect what you get in education or what you own in property is to be in politics, because that's where your tax dollars get divvied up and the resources get returned to your community. But it's counterproductive. The sanitation department doesn't ask whose garbage they're picking up as they come down the block."

"Many don't mind my being in the City Council, but a move to Congress, for them, is just too big. In many ways I'm facing the same struggles that Shirley Chisholm faced, being a descendant of Barbadians. Although people didn't say outright, 'We're against you, because your roots are in Barbados and because you talk about the Caribbean too much,' the men just didn't want her to be the person on top to decide what happened in the community. But I have almost nine years in the city council of demonstrated leadership, so being a woman doesn't negate my strength and ability as a leader."

Clarke swept her last election with a 96 percent majority. A signal accomplishment, the legalization of gypsy van drivers who ply Flatbush Avenue, kept or created 500 jobs while preserving local public transportation jobs. She partnered with Magic Johnson to build one of his movie theatres in her district, and made sure incentives were in place to attract an enormous supermarket to Flatbush Center. True to her background as an educator, she created a programme at the local college to help her immigrant constituents with the transition to the American educational system. She's built labs in high schools and hooked the schools in her district up to the Internet.

But this morning her thoughts are on the incendiary topic of the month, the police shooting of Patrick Dorismond, an unarmed man from her district. The case, in the wake of several other highly-publicized incidents of alleged excessive police force, has brought mounting criticism to Republican Mayor Rudy Giuliani's office. Clarke arrives dressed in all black, save a Kente cloth wrap, for the pre-funeral events later tonight. After 41 years in New York, she has not lost her Jamaican accent. "I'm sorry I'm late. I was out at an Eastern Caribbean event last night, and when they start fête-ing, honey, they don't stop."

En route to breakfast, she says gravely, "This is the fourth case I've had to go through: first with Jamaican van driver Carlton Brown, who had his back and neck broken in the 63rd Precinct. Then there was a young man shot on Church Avenue by the name of Osmond Watson, an African-American of Jamaican parentage. With him it was 18 bullets. Following that was the Abner Louima case..." (which Clarke first helped publicize). The councilwoman has been named in a lawsuit brought by the police officers from that precinct, who were transferred on her urging. "My district is reflective of the pattern of policing—when they police an immigrant community where they feel people are powerless, some just do as they please."

Her convictions aside, Clarke has a sense of the compromise politics demands. Where Giuliani is perceived in some quarters as being insufficiently sensitive to minority concerns, "Most people see me as having close ties to the mayor—that I'm probably one of the few blacks that he respects." As it turns out, Clarke's fence-mending moderation is pragmatic. "I've been able to access and receive the kind of services that my community needs and deserves, and I think it's because I don't engage in the racial rhetoric."

Needless to say, Clarke will support Hillary Clinton this November. "She'll have to work hard. She's not a native New Yorker like I am," she laughs wickedly. "She's going to have to understand the many interests and needs of the people that live here, and stay away from the personal stuff."

Clarke was born in Thornton, near Maggoty in St. Elizabeth. "My father is from Lacovia, and was a cane farmer. My mother was born in Accompong, and is a Maroon (direct descendants of escaped slaves who successfully defied British military rule). She's 100 and she's still in St. Elizabeth. I'm a part of the Rowe clan. Meredith Rowe, the last Maroon Colonel, is my relative."

Clarke went to Buxton High School and then on to Kingston Technical. Her husband, now an engineer at the Port Authority of New York and New Jersey, was a big cricketer and football player at Excelsior. Manhatttan's stone canyons were an eye-opening change for the young immigrant. "Coming from the countryside, where everybody owns a house, I remember thinking, 'Where do all the people live?' " After courses at the New York Business School, Clarke did her undergrad at Long Island University. Then came an N.Y.U. M.Ed, and a Revson Fellowship at Columbia, which she used for doctoral studies around education and non-profit management. Clarke is just short her dissertation. She's unsure whether she'll complete it, but is planning an autobiography focusing on her life in New York.

Clarke's work week can be seven days long, a day perhaps taking her from reading to children at the Brooklyn Public Library to attending a West Indian festival to doing interviews on radio shows to standing with the mayor at a press conference to publicize a green card lottery. Now, Clarke's daughter Yvette is being talked about as a successor for Clarke's seat. Clarke is circumspect. "There is no set decision that she'll run for my seat. I'm mindful of the demands of public life on anyone and their family life..."

Clarke tries to put her finger on the successful New York political character. "You have to be interested in everybody, irrespective of their race or status. I describe myself as one as good in the streets as I am in the suites. I travel very easily. I have no problem with race or ethnicity and I think that is one of the great virtues of being Jamaican. We've been able to go to school with Chinese, Indians, whites and blacks, and it's never a thought that we should undermine each other based on our ethnicity

...opening the Imagination Playground in Brooklyn's Prospect Park, a $3 million project funded by her.

...with First Lady Hillary Clinton

...with Jamaica's Counsel General Dr. Basil Bryan

...with her priest, Father Andrea Duvert, St Gabriel's Episcopal Church

...with James Garnor, Mayor of Hemstead; PJ Patterson Prime Minister of Jamaica; Patrick Williams, Nassau Co. Rep; Dr Basil Bryan, Jamaican Counsel General.

...with Fernando Ferrer, Bronx Borough President.

...with Jamaica's Governor General Sir Howard Cooke, at his residence in Kingston, Jamaica

...with Mrs Marie Dorismond, mother of Patrick Dorismond, who was slain by the New York City Police Department.

...with Prime Minister PJ Patterson

...with Reggae Artist Freddie McGregor

because we come from a nation that belongs to all of us. And I feel that every Jamaican feels they have a stake in the country."

Later at City Hall, someone makes light of Clarke's constant high-wire act between this Jamaican identity, which is also so useful politically, and her commitment to her new constituency. Clarke is cheerfully unrepentant. "If you had dual citizenship you'd know how to use it for you!" She points admiringly to the example of the Jewish community of New York as a role model for her definition of an engaged expatriate community. "They are always travelling back and forth to Israel, to help secure the borders of their country and promote it as the Middle Eastern democracy. Patriotism doesn't end when you leave a place. I would encourage nationals abroad doing well to contribute, and for both political parties to harness the wealth of Jamaicans abroad for the development of the country. Many have been disappointed in their overtures to Jamaica, feeling that government has not been receptive to their ideas."

Clarke acknowledges the challenges facing the island: drug transshipment, crime, housing. "I think Jamaica needs a complete strategic plan for its development. The empowerment of women in particular as a resource for the nation has to become a centerpiece. Jamaica can take a leadership role in being a center of information for the region."

"I always tell people, if you think you're going to die, and you didn't do right and you won't see paradise, you should go to Jamaica. Of course, once Cuba opens up we're going to have to compete for tourist dollars even more. But there are still a lot of untapped resources for tourism. Jamaica should challenge itself to rebuild its history in a way that's alive. A lot of people like sightseeing over the beach—I'm one of them. We should go back to the time of the Spaniards, and develop all of our historic sites so they become new channels to tourism."

The breakfast crowd in the diner has now decamped, and the waitress is absently flipping through a magazine in the back of the room. There is no one left for Clarke to schmooze but her interviewer. "So—where do you live? Are you going to do a house party for me?" There is some protest, at this. "No conflict of interest! No conflict of interest. I need your card because I'm going to have Jean Garvey call you—the wife of Marcus Garvey, Jr. She's helping to coordinate my fundraising, and she'll ask you for a date." She had been told earlier that her interviewer attended acting school, and now

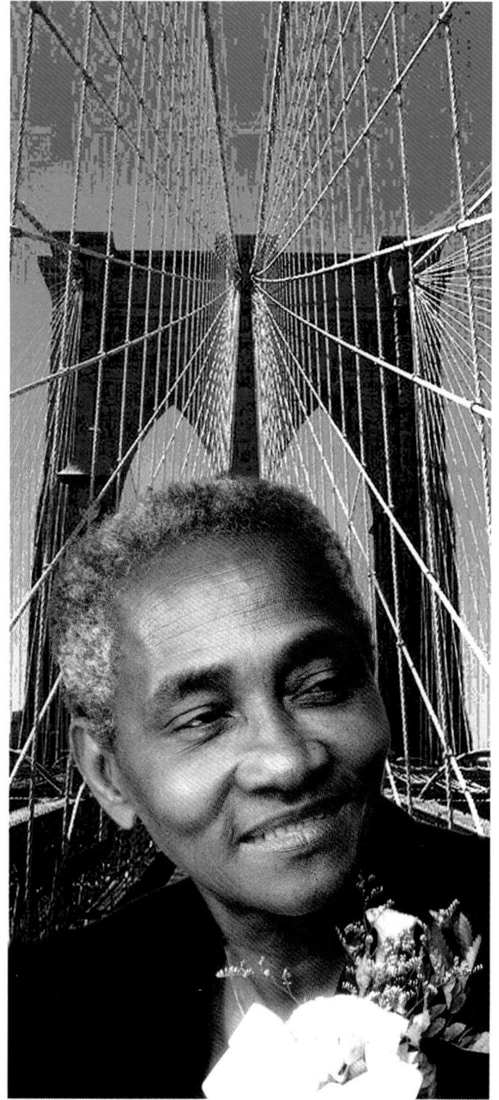

she smiles. "I will tell them that you're doing it because you're a movie star—you're not doing it because you're a Jamaican, but you're doing it for your star quality. And that's what I'll tell Butch—I'll say, "Look, Butch, he's a movie star, and I tapped him for his handsomeness." She laughs.

We continue on to City Hall to take a few photos. By chance, we bump into Deputy Mayor Rudy Washington. There is talk of a vote they'd prefer Clarke to miss, which would sustain one of the mayor's vetos. Washington's aide suggests an alibi, "You just say you had an emergency in your district you had to attend to."

With a glint in her eye, Clarke now remembers Dorismond. "I was just telling him he better bring his ass there, to that 'emergency in my district I have to attend to' ! Who is coming out to this young man's funeral?" Clarke torments the deputy mayor with some amusement. "I have to find out what I'm getting for all of this argument you a go gi' me ya now!" She exacts her price: "You're going to go to (Dorismund's mother's) house with me if it's the last thing you do, with your damned black face!" Washington smiles wearily and agrees.

Inside the beautiful Federal-era structure, the scene is classic local politics, all bad haircuts and cheap suits. The entrance halls are thronged with lobbyists and staff. Clarke is in her element—glad-handing, back slapping, catching up—all the way to the Barbadian cleaning lady who greets her like a sister.

In front of the stairs of the beautiful rotunda—a smaller version of the one in the Capitol in Washington that Clarke hopes to work in come January—we come upon the council's whip gossiping with toothy, grinning, high-ranking Irish and Italian cops in their formal uniforms, their chests ablaze with 'fruit salad', or badges of service. It's City Hall as drawn in *Dick Tracy.* Clarke is greeted as an old friend. She introduces her guest as "my *landsman*", the Yiddish word for someone from your country. The whip points out that Clarke has not put the correct city council license plates on the front of her car. "Una, you're a lawmaker, not a lawbreaker." He says to one of the policemen: "Arrest her!" The cop recoils in mock-terror: "Like hell I will!" Clarke replies triumphantly, "He knows who to fight with and who not to fight with!" Light is made of her careful dress—indeed, Clarke is already known affectionately in some corners of City Hall as 'The Black Bella Abzug', after the famous local pol known for her extravagant taste in headwear.

There is an ease about Clarke here, as with people who show you around their old college campus, but it's almost too familiar—Clarke has outgrown the council, and small-time politics. It's on to the hustings of the summer, and the reggae tribute at the Brooklyn Academy of Music with Glen Washington, Half Pint, Mighty Sparrow, and "...how come I'm forgetting my sweetheart's name? Freddy McGregor, my sweetheart! If he knows I'm having trouble remembering his name I'm in a lot of trouble."

We walk out into a prematurely summery day, past the illicit Ford Explorer. Article II of the Constitution, limiting the Presidency to natural-born citizens, casts the only shadow, it seems.

"I can't be President," Clarke says with a sly smile. "But I'm going to be a Congresswoman."

ORIGINALLY PUBLISHED AUGUST 2000

The Timeless Trevor Rhone

DIANA THORBURN

Trevor Rhone's mastery as a playwright and producer is unsurpassed in the Jamaican theatre. His plays are timeless, thought provoking, entertaining, revealing and often funny. But they also speak to serious, sometimes painful issues, and in unveiled terms.

DIANA THORBURN: *How do you see the theatre in Jamaica now?*

TREVOR RHONE: It's going through a sort of crisis. In the fifties there were little theatre groups who would put on a play once or twice a year, for two weekends or so. These plays were like therapy—a way of organizing, communicating, interacting with people.

Then in the seventies the theatre started to blossom. It became a source of income for people; it became a discipline. One of the things that delighted me was how the theatre helped to reverse how people saw the products of their creative life energy. Many took great pride in taking their American friends to the theatre. In the sixties the upper class troupes would do Shakespeare and Molière, or versions of the Broadway play. All of that went and people reaffirmed their faith in their own creative energies. The Jamaican play became The Thing. People felt that this was something of which they could be proud.

Then in the eighties there was a growth of theatre and cultural activity that was quite mind boggling, both in terms of quantity and quality. *Smile Orange, School's Out*, the *8 O'clock Jamaica Time* revues, *The Rapist, Operation P* were some of the productions of that period. The essential thing was that they were well steeped in thought, well-written, well-produced, well-managed theatrical fare.

Then came stuff that just made you laugh. For me it was a real denial of my training. I spent four years in England studying the theatre. There was a callousness about detail, and the plays reflected, for me, this kind of thinking. The theatre had become simply a source for a laugh. That sort of theatre has its place, but when you regard everything else as nonsense, or not worthy of a visit, then one becomes wary. Ours is a profession which dates back hundreds of years, that has produced wonderful writers, wonderful ideas, wonderful reflections on life. To see it sort of dissed...I find it a little bit upsetting. Every so often there are people like Basil Dawkins and young playwrights who are making their mark, and people aren't going to see their plays. That distresses me.

DT: *What does it take to write a play?*

TR: It takes a tremendous amount of concentration. There is a great deal of technical skill in creating a story, to make story interesting. One deals with things like dramatic structure, not just the beginning, middle and end. There are characters who drive the story, and time. You start out with an idea, a tiny idea. Then it has to grow and develop and take shape and form. The average time to write a play for me is almost two years. Some people do it quicker than that. It's very time consuming, but it's a wonderful process in a way. It's amazing how much you discover about yourself, about people, and about your society. In many ways, writing plays has been my education. It is discovery. I never tire of it, no matter how long I spend on it. It's pursuit of excellence. Hopefully when I'm finished with it, it will last for along time, like a document.

DT: *Like Old Story time?*

TR: Yes, like *Old Story Time*. In fact *Smile Orange* is about 25 years old.

DT: *I saw Smile Orange about two years ago and it was still relevant. Tell me about your* *characters. Do you research your characters or do you know them already?*

TR: Usually one researches. One goes out, talks with people who are similar to the character. Usually I get some sort of basic information that I can build on. Plus, there is the whole power and process of observation.

Dear Counsellor is about a "browning". Everybody tends to hide race relations in this country, right? It's swept under the carpet. It's not as overt as one would find in Europe or North America where the divisions or separations between the races are obvious. Here, the separation is within the race. There's "browning" and there's "black".

This play is based on a story I heard about a young black woman who used some sort of chemical to get her face brown. Her response when she was asked why she had done this was, "Browning run 'tings." Now, there is a whole scenario involved there. Why would she want to do this? What are the advantages to be gained? Social, economic? The story is loosely based on that—that was the thought, the seed, the idea that was sown.

What it is, at heart, is a love story between a browning and a black man, and the journey they both have to take to have this reconciliation, and for their love to grow, to blossom, and to bear fruit.

***DT:** How did you do the research for this play?*

TR: I chatted with some "brownings"; researched my own life, my own responses. One listens to stories. One gathers information. I am a constant gatherer of information. I hear things and I record them, without actually writing them down. Things I hear today will peak in my memory in ten years, and then I will give that idea some form.

***DT:** Do you often look at your own life?*

TR: That's the major resource.

***DT:** Have you written love stories before?*

***TR:** Two Can Play* was a love story, except the couple had been married for 20 years and then discovered that, in fact, they do need each other.

***DT:** Race has always been a central issue...*

TR: ...in all my plays.

***DT:** You're still writing about it now. Have the dynamics of the issue changed since way back then?*

TR: There isn't too much difference. I think the traditional thinking remains within the mind and psyche of the people. It's not an overt problem, but for me it's there—in how people react and respond to each other.

In Old Story Time there's the character Margaret, who is a "browning". One could take a long jump across the divide, and this could be the exploration of her story.

***DT:** Do you see this issue ever being resolved? Can it be resolved?*

TR: It needs to be resolved. For a girl to actually go to that extreme length to make herself attractive... it's an extreme measure, I find. The play is about two people of the same race for whom race is an obstacle.

***DT:** You recently won the Norman Washington Manley Foundation's Award for Excellence in the field of dramatic arts. Your plays are on the literature curriculum in high schools over the Caribbean. How do you feel about being an institution?*

TR: It drives me to do the best possible job. I will turn every stone to make the piece as fulfilling as possible for myself, and for an audience. Even with a great amount of experience, one is often aware why a play is not working. That which will make it work is the greater difficulty.

I went to America two years ago to the National Black Theatre Festival. All the black stars of great fame were there. At the opening ceremony I was quite happily going off to my seat in the audience, when one of the organizers informed me I was one of the honoured guests. That evening I was named a Living Legend. I was quietly delighted that I was outside of my own environs, outside of my own country, knowing that my name and my work had gone beyond these shores with a source of positive influence and had given cheer to the universal community. It was sort of nice, actually.

ORIGINALLY PUBLISHED FEBRUARY 1997

(W)Uman Tong(ue)

ODETTE DIXON-NEATH

It's Friday and Carolyn Cooper has made one man angry. Very angry. So angry that he has written a biting letter to the editor of the *Jamaica Observer*, the paper that publishes her weekly column "(W)Uman Tong(ue)." Among other things he says that any fourth former could do a better job at writing English than Carolyn (Dr. Cooper, if you please). The trouble though is that Carolyn is not writing English. She writes in Jamaican—patois to some, Creole to others—and with each column on everything from sex to politics, she gives the "other" language a legitimacy that has escaped it for centuries.

A striking woman, Carolyn's closely shaven head works much like a magnet, pulling the eyes of anyone meeting her directly to her face. Her voice is almost velvety, coating each word with the expected style of academia and belying the status of evil queen of "bad language" which has been accorded to her by critics. Carolyn is an Associate Professor of English at the University of the West Indies where she says she is "trying to make a contribution to debates about culture. What I have to share is an expression of not only all the experiences I have had as an individual, but also as a black person in a post-colonial society."

Her parents were pious Seventh Day Adventists, her father a tailor and her mother a school teacher. "I was born in 1950, the middle of the century, on Constitution Day," she says, pausing to search for the significance of her birthday. "We felt that we were part of the new Jamaica, we had benefited from all of the opportunities fought for by our parents. We grew up in a home where education was valued, and the discipline of going to church was important. I knew I was growing up in a society where blackness had been devalued and I had to use any competitive advantage to get ahead, and in my case I thought of that advantage as brains." And so, she put her brain to work, leading to a Ph.D. in English.

Her two year-old newspaper column has made her subject of both admiration and ire. The column started out of work she had been doing with noted Jamaican poet Mutabaruka, translating the news from English into Jamaican for his radio show. "The editor of the *Jamaica Observer* asked me to write the column. I got the paper to agree to a bilingual column with both English and Jamaican. People were very upset, because I used the Cassidy system; a specialist writing system for Jamaican which looks difficult at first. The problem is that people do not write the language, we don't think the language is serious enough to have a writing system," she says. Since its inauguration the column has been the subject of an assault in which she has been charged with among other things: "ignorance;" "irresponsibility;" and "taking the whole society backward." To temper all the carping, the paper tried to encourage her to write three weeks of each month solely in English, the other in Jamaican, but she held out—no Jamaican, no column. For the most part, Carolyn is unmoved by all the flak. "The reason I am stirring up controversy is because it has touched people in a very core

Carolyn Cooper

the time we were asked to look at the way a university functions as part of the whole colonial establishment. It was there to perpetuate certain values, so that radical intellectuals—people like Rodney—could not readily be accommodated into the system.

In contrast to her university rebel days, today she says she is "... not interested in change in a political sense. I believe that you have to change people's values, it is the things that people believe in an motivate them that really matter." Her own values revolve around what she calls the culture of African peoples in the diaspora. "The history and culture of African people is important to me. This does not mean sentimental idealization of Africa. I have been to Africa, and everybody knows the problems of underdevelopment there. But for example, I know so many of the young, black women on campus see themselves as ugly. You must look at yourself in a positive light. What I want is an affirmative way of seeing black people's culture."

Carolyn believes that the strength of Caribbean intellectual life does not take place in the formal school system but is instead entrenched in popular culture. "The University has a major role in developing ideas and passing them on and hoping that they will circulate through society. Some cynical university people see the every day existence of people as anti-intellectual, and they believe that it is only at the University that culture and sophisticated thought is generated. I believe that ordinary people have a lot of value, that the creativity of ordinary people is important."

Outside of the classroom Carolyn herself has been a kind of cultural icon; the rebel with a cause. Aside from her work to legitimise Jamaican, hers is a voice above the din on myriad issues. "I am interested in things like heritage and cultural tourism; the music industry; marketing our culture efficiently so that when tourists come they are not just exposed to stereotypical 'island' stuff, but to authentic Caribbean culture," she says. "By staying in the University I can function as a kind of bridge between, for example, tourism, and music industry and academia, even though people might think that I, as literature teacher, should have nothing to do with all of this."

Carolyn has recently published *Noises in the Blood; Orality, Gender and the "Vulgar" Body of Jamaican Popular Culture* (Macmillian, Duke University Press) a collection of essays on the oral tradition in Jamaican culture. Among other subjects, the book deals with the works of Louise Bennett-Coverly, Jamaica's foremost folklorist and poet; Perry Henzell's cult classic film *The Harder They Come*; the Sistren Theatre Collective, a women's group with working class roots; the classic reggae of Bob Marley; and the new wave of the dancehall culture. She describes dancehall music; often dismissed as "noise" as reflecting revolutionary ethos, "Not revolutionary in the Bob Marley sense of equal rights and justice, but revolutionary in the sense of an affirmation of our culture identity which could be seen as counter to the eurocentric model," she says.

Carolyn is particularly vocal in her support for dancehall music. She has been instrumental in setting up the International Reggae Studies Centre at the University of the West Indies and is a popular speaker on the international lecture circuit. "Dancehall is one of the spaces in which people are expressing culture and values. Traditionally, dancehall has been working class, but we have had middle class incursion. The issue is now accommodation, middle class people taking on the values of dancehall, while working class people are moving up."

With her book receiving adulatory reviews in England and the United States, she should feel pretty wonderful now, right? But she has one regret that is a throwback to her Adventist roots: Not keeping the sabbath. "Not necessarily going to church, but I have to find a way now to start keeping the sabbath, where one day a week me don't do nothing, except just relax," she says, for the first time speaking in Jamaican.

way, and people don't quarrel about things that don't bother them."

At the University her classes are not purely about literature. They are more a mélange of social and sexual politics, cultural history and in-your-face self-awareness. At the end of the semester it is not uncommon to see a couple of her female students being inspired to emulate Carolyn's own signature style of shaven head and African prints. Is this kind of influence a burden? "In my role as a teacher, I realize that I am functioning more than as an academic mentor. I try to be sensitive to that instead of making it a burden to myself; I try not to have to meet people's expectations. I do my best to be a positive person and people feel that energy, but other than that I am not going to let people's perception of me determine what I do."

One of her influences was Walter Rodney, a university lecturer and the centre of 1960s campus protest on issues of Black Power. "At

ORIGINALLY PUBLISHED NOVEMBER 1995

She is known as the Bird Lady of Anchovy

MICHAEL RECKORD

What's a 13-letter word for one who studies birds?

You don't know? Well, I'll give you a hint—Lisa Salmon is one. Though, to be fair to Lisa Salmon, and to the 13-letter word, Lisa Salmon is a lot of other things as well.

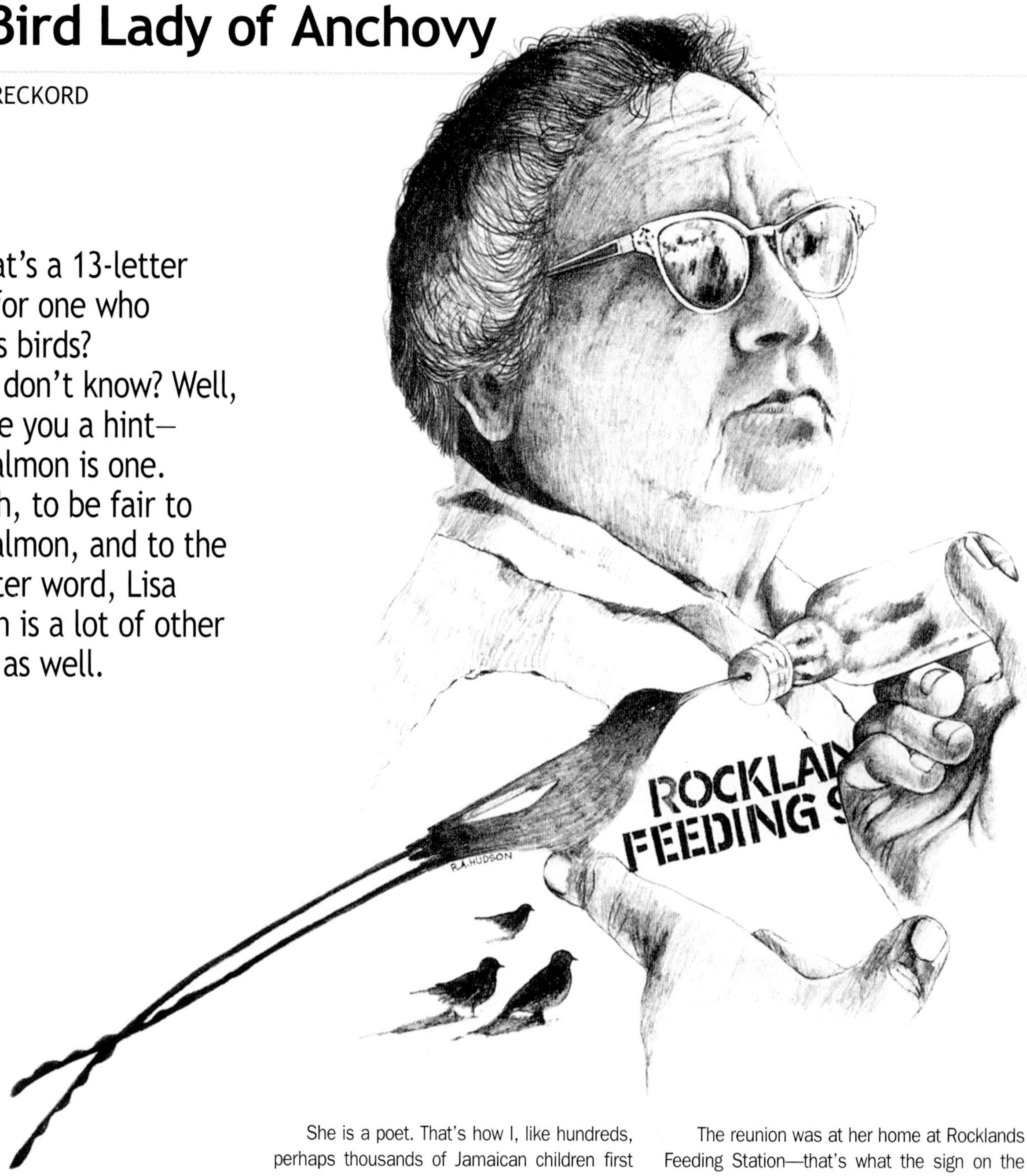

She is a poet. That's how I, like hundreds, perhaps thousands of Jamaican children first met her—through her poetry. That was some... let's see...twenty years ago; and I now have only the memory of the memory of having to learn one of her poems about animals—she was always writing about animals—one about Lena Lizard.

You'd like to get the book with the poem? Sorry, it's out of print; and the publishers, Pioneer Press, are now defunct. Twenty years is a long time. In fact, I am able to quote these names only because I recently had a reunion—for me—with Lisa Salmon, and she reminded me of them.

The reunion was at her home at Rocklands Feeding Station—that's what the sign on the poinciana tree at the gate says—about eight miles from Montego Bay, just outside the village of Anchovy. And I'll give you another hint: she is known as the Bird Lady of Anchovy.

Bird-lover? That doesn't have 13 letters... though she is a bird-lover. But as I said, she is a lot of things.

Physically, she is just the opposite of what I imagined her to be when I first started reading her poetry. I had pictured a tall, thin, angular woman; she is actually short, plump and round. I was right about her wearing glasses, though.

When I met her the other day, she was

wearing a white blouse, faded blue jeans and slippers. She had been working all morning, she told me. I later found out that she works practically all the time; loving birds is an arduous business.

Among the things she had been doing that morning was overseeing the construction of two two-room flats for bird watchers. She has done a lot of that work, for there has been a lot of construction done at Rocklands since she first moved there in 1952 and set up her bird sanctuary. The construction included the building of large birdhouses, small bird-cages, the patio and a lot of other buildings between.

In the patio where we sat was a host of feeding bottles for feeding the humming birds, feeding trays for other types of birds, and lizards, bamboo bird houses and what appeared to be dozens of pots for a variety of plants. She also loves plants.

She is, to my mind, the perfect woman to be a conservationist (no that's not the word, either), a view evidently shared by the Minister of Mines and Natural Resources, who recently appointed her a member of the wildlife protection and conservation committee, the island's governmental conservation committee.

There are many things that Lisa Salmon wants to conserve. She has been trying for years to get the area within a five mile radius around her house declared an official sanctuary for birds; she wants to prevent the extermination of certain Jamaican birds whose numbers have been dwindling over the years; she wants, especially, sanctuary and protection given to the Tryall coot. The latter is a New World bird which was discovered in Jamaica on the Tryall golf course ponds two years ago. It is presumed to be a hybrid between the American coot and the Caribbean coot. A pair of these have nested, she told me, and produced young —a rare thing as everybody knows for hybrids to do.

It has been proving very difficult, she said, to get these birds protection. And it will no doubt prove extremely difficult for her to get a lot of other things she wants—things that have little to do with birds. She wants something done, for example, about the emissions from the hundreds of motor vehicles in Montego Bay that are fouling up the atmosphere. For years she has been watching the town from her hilltop residence, and the view has been gradually getting more and more obscured because of the smog.

She wants the St. James Court House moved from its present site across the road from the St. James Parish Library. On court days, especially traffic court days, the yard outside the court is jam-packed with vehicles, and they overflow onto the lawns of the library; with the result that the library's grounds are now in a very sorry condition.

Still, Montegonians are lucky that the library has any grounds at all, lucky to have Lisa Salmon, that is, for it was she, the originator of the library's garden committee, that managed to prevent the grounds be taken away by some developer or other some years ago.

She also wants Jamaicans to stop being rude to tourists and driving them from our shores; and she frequently gives impromptu lectures on the values of tourism to persons she hears being rude.

She might not get all she wants right away, if ever—just as she could not persuade a shopkeeper, a woman she told me, who never smiles, to have her little boy catch cockroaches for some of the Rocklands' birds—but she has a lot of patience. And with patience, she may get what she wants in the end.

It took years of patience, she told me, to domesticate literally hundreds of birds to such an extent that many will feed from her, or a visitor's finger. A brochure that Lisa Salmon has compiled reveals that "in January 1965, after years of patience and perseverance, the red-billed streamertail hummingbird (the "Doctor Bird"—Jamaica's National Bird) was persuaded to perch on her finger to drink sugar-and-water from a feeder. Next to perch was the Jamaican mango hummingbird.

The brochure continues: "Other birds that can be seen eating offered food are—white-chinned thrush (hopping dick); orangequit (long mouth blue quit); Jamaican euphon (short mouth blue quit); northern mockingbird (nightingale); whitebellied dove; white-winged dove (lapwing); common grounddove; saffron finch (wild canary); yellow faced grass-quit, black-faced grassquit; bananaquit , the "Yellow Bird" of the song.

Altogether, about 116 different species of birds have been listed as having been seen at Rocklands and environs, and some 31 different species have eaten offered food. The feeding of the grounddoves is one of the main attractions for the hundreds of visitors who go to Rocklands because every afternoon, at about 3:30 o'clock, some 600 of these bird fly in to be fed. It's quite a sight. (You're darn right, she has quite a food bill. She uses about a 100-lb sack of grain each week, as well as a good supply of cheese, raisins and fruits.)

And she not only feeds birds; she also tends to their illnesses, and the wounds many suffer from the gunshots of careless hunters every hunting season. She also paints them—yes, she' a painter, too; and photographs them —yes, also a photographer.

Though she loves all her birds, she has her favourites. One cannot help making favourites of some of the 'characters' among the birds. There is, for example, the hummingbird that has taken the patio for himself, and will only occasionally allow other birds to perch there.

Her favourite character, Lisa Salmon told me, was one hummingbird she called "The Bather". He evidently had not read the books which state that hummingbirds only bathe in spray or dew, and "The Bather" would actually jump into a shallow dish of water for a bath. This unorthodox bird also proved to her that birds have a sense of taste, and he would not drink a C grade brown sugar mixture, only a mixture of granulated sugar and water.

Lisa Salmon is also a professional hostess. Circumstances have forced this job upon her, for hundreds of visitors come each month to her bird sanctuary.

And many of these visitors are not just the common or garden variety. She has had the Queen of Denmark and her husband to Rocklands; Prince Rainier and his children have been there; and so have several dukes, earls, lords and ladies of title.

But I have digressed, and while I was digressing you probably looked in your thesaurus and found that original 13-letter word I asked about. So, I needn't tell you what it is. But I repeat, Lisa Salmon, the very remarkable Bird Lady of Anchovy, is that 13-letter word... and much more.

ORIGINALLY PUBLISHED DECEMBER 1972

George Wayne—Maverick with a Mission

MARC GOODMAN

Contributing editor to *Vanity Fair* and publisher of the avant-garde celebrity quarterly *R.O.M.E.*

MONDAY

The phone rings at 8:10 am. "Huh-hello?" "It's George Wayne. I just got back from Jamaica last night. I saw your other article—yes, well, I had to see if you could write before I approved you! Well, it's Fashion Week, of course. I'll take you to a show, then the *R.O.M.E.* party is on Friday. How about Isaac Mizrahi on Thursday? ...well, Wednesday night is great; we'll have the Mercedes limo. What about Anna Sui? Anna Sui will be perfect. Alright: meet me...here. No! Nobody comes to my house...I'll call you back."

And we're off. George Wayne's Magical Mystery Tour, or How New York Was Done In A Night, With Particulars Concerning Who Did What To Whom and Which Parties They Did It At (Did They Look Good Doing It?). The thirty-something Mandeville native is famous for changing the way thousands of people read *Vanity Fair* magazine—starting in the middle, with his naughty celebrity interview. But now it is indeed Fashion Week, with every American designer from Ralph to Calvin to Todd to Mary showing their Fall '97 *schmattes* under or around the tents in Bryant Park on 40th Street. Wayne has been given the new Mercedes model with chauffeur to show off for the week. G.W., as he often refers to himself, is in his element, since all the elements of spontaneous gossip combustion are in place as at no other time: haughty teen-aged models and their rock star boyfriends, hangers-on, egomaniacal magazine editors, bouncers and bodyguards, photographer's exhibition openings and after-parties. It's glamour overload. One invitee asks, finally, exhausted: "Aren't you glad it's over!! Escape and celebrate the end of Fashion Week at...".

But it's not to be. George turns in early on Wednesday night.

FRIDAY

In an article, Wayne is quoted: "I want to create the George Wayne Haute Institute of Millennial Studies to conduct serious research on superficiality, scandal, glamour, and of course, sex. The Institute's main goal would be to usher in a Golden Age of Decadence in 21st century society."

The new issue of *R.O.M.E.*, Wayne's gossip magazine, is out and its party is at V.I.P.'s, a strip club. George Wayne steps out of the chauffeured Mercedes-Benz with model and New York Party Girl Bijou Philips and her publicist, Lara. The venue ties in nicely with *R.O.M.E.*'s risque and very camp image. An even better reason is soon revealed. "This is Doug, he's my Larry Flynt," introduces Wayne, once we've climbed to a roped-off section overlooking the stage. Doug and a couple of other partners, as it turned out are the publishers of *R.O.M.E.*

Below us, the main floor looks like a well-attend Roman orgy. It's packed. Doug jerks a finger at the seething mass of people and says eagerly, "We get stars in here; the Rangers, the Mets, they all come in here. Other clubs publicize who comes in, but we don't. We are the V.I.P. club. Everyone's a V.I.P. here." Wayne is perfectly turned out as always, in a pinstriped jacket of French cut. It's held together by a large safety pin. "It's his trademark," confirms Lara.

THURSDAY

Wayne makes a grand entrance half an hour late at a seminar on entertainment journalism. "I'm sorry. You know how hard it is to get a cab in the rain in New York. At rush hour!"

A producer from *Entertainment Tonight* is here, *Access Hollywood*, *Entertainment Weekly*, *The New York Times*'s Arts and Leisure section. They're talking about the business in serious tones. Wayne quickly wins over the crowd with catty remarks about stars and an appealing self-depreciation. "I'm just a little boy from

Jamaica," he pleads. He reveals that his Q&A column in *Vanity Fair* has one requirement: interviewees must do the photo shoot before the interview. On occasion, subjects get so riled by Wayne's questions that they refuse to do pictures afterwards, as was the case recently with a certain diminutive East Coast rocker. Wayne spills more industry tattle, announcing, "With (legendary agent) Mike Ovitz gone, (legendary PR person) Pat Kingsley is the most powerful person—and definitely the most powerful woman—in Hollywood. She knows where all the bones are buried." The eyes roll theatrically. "The fake marriage she'd orchestrated!" The crowd, mostly people trying to get in the gossip industry, titters nervously.

Afterwards, enroute to Fred's, the restaurant in chi-chi department store Barneys, Wayne stops to admire the Gucci window display. "Tom Ford designs for me!," he says. "Especially since I've lost this weight recently."

Spreading out his napkin, Wayne orders the lobster bisque and reminisces about school days at tony Munro College in St. Elizabeth. "I loved it and I hated it. The eight years I spent in prison—excuse me, boarding school—couldn't have prepared me better for living in Manhattan: the cubby hole of a room, the cold water every day, the awful food. Once you've survived the jungles of Malvern you survive anything." Wayne—full name Gary George Wayne Prendergast—had a Scottish great-grandfather and only dropped the last name after one person too many misspelled it.

He was first journalistically inspired at Munro. "In that environment, it was like...manna from heaven." A further taste of the glamorous life came when Munroe won local television's *School's Challenge Quiz* with Wayne on board. "We won a trip to Toronto. We became superstars at Munro. It was the first time I felt truly famous, and I loved every moment of it." During Wayne's journalism school days at the University of Georgia, the college town of Athens was a pretty hip place. Rock intellectuals R.E.M. were getting their start there, as were the B-52s. "That bohemian, artistic spirit would make a great training ground for Manhattan." One weekend during school, Wayne went up to New York and found himself at the old Mudd Club. "It was the first club I went to here and I was amazed—I knew I had to come to New York."

He moved to the city in 1988. Wayne quickly tired of the nine-to-five and decided to devote himself to writing. He was spending a lot of time at the clubs, especially Palladium, but glamorous writing assignments were unforthcoming at first.

He finally got work with a small West Indian paper, and also began his "Resident Alien" gossip column for the *Daily Gleaner* brought him notice in Jamaica. Wayne puts it like this: "I truly believe that the column revolutionized entertainment journalism in not only Jamaica. but the West Indies. I'm not bragging, Jamaica had never seen a style of journalism like what I brought to the table—and so neither, apparently, the rest of the world." But he longed for the fast times of the U.S. magazine market.

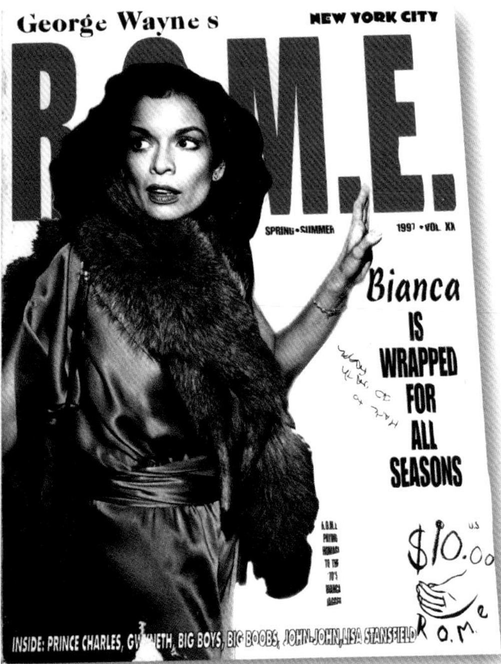

He needed some entrée, some attention-getter that would turn the heads of world-weary Gotham editors.

What he came up with was a magazine, *R.O.M.E.*, a brazen concoction of cheerfully admitted fake quotes, biting skinny on the New York jet set he observed out at the clubs, and reviews of everything from architecture to Gwyneth Paltrow's cigarette manner. The first issue was 50 copies that Wayne had snuck into a former employer's to photocopy and cajoled the owner of a grungy but trendy East Village shop into selling for him.

About this time, Wayne was developing into a certain type of New York fixture, a dandified party-hopper with a burning need to mix with the glitterati and the outrageous self-confidence to make it happen—the type to go, as he did year after year, to the Paris fashion shows without an invite. And, predictably, pretty soon it looked to everyone as though he belonged there. Wayne had become famous for being famous. A future editor of his observed, "He's one of those self-invented people that New York is for."

Liberally sprinkled with exclamation points and capital letters, *R.O.M.E.*'s fanzine/ransom note look has the feel of samizdat from behind society's Iron Curtain, and is admirably suited to its purpose of suggesting illicit urgency. Indeed, it carries the whiff of the perpetual threat of the obscenity ordinance. Inside, the dirt is dished with such swagger it's hard not to love it. Wayne walks the gossip's tightrope of both eating from and biting the hand that feeds him. In an otherwise sycophantic piece about some swell's elegant but cold modernist mansion, Wayne can't resist a snide handwritten annotation in the margin: "Can you imagine living in something like this?!" Scathing annotations to Wayne's backstage snapshots at the Grammys are elbow to elbow with a breathy tribute to Wayne's editor at *Vanity Fair.*

After seeing *R.O.M.E.*, editor Michael Hershkovits of downtowny *Paper* magazine gave Wayne a column. He went from there to Interview, and then to a Condé Nast startup, *Allure*. Nothing, he has said, has brought him more happiness than the breaching of Condé Nast's impenetrable and impossibly hip walls. Today, of course, Wayne is famous for his scabrous *Vanity Fair* interviews, where he asks male celebrities about the size of their appendages and women about their romantic liaisons. Those who play along escape unharmed; woe to the thin-skinned star who gets indignant at Wayne's queries. Lest anyone be deceived, Wayne is the true star of Wayne's columns, and always comes off well.

He leans forward. "I'm the only monthly column in *Vanity Fair,* and that's a major achievement." Wayne's V.F. colleague, Fashion Director Elizabeth Saltzman, explains the success of his column: "He asks the questions you want to know. He's unafraid. He's one of the few originals—hard to be in this age of the know-it-alls and do-it-alls. He's so perfect at his job." Roshumba, the model, once found this enterprising charm the difference between life and death. "We had both arrived at the Chateau Marmont Hotel in L.A. on the day in 1992 that the riots began. We were stuck in a suite for a week together with a few other people. George

(ABOVE LEFT) G.W. with his "sista" Naomi Campbell, at the trendy New York City boîte, Café Tabac.
(ABOVE RIGHT) G.W. with Boy George in London.
(AT RIGHT) G.W. on the town with New York socialite and TV hostess Nina Griscom.

was absolutely entertaining, and got people to do things that they would never do—for example, when the food ran out, getting the room service guys to give us their own private stash of wine."

And then there's *R.O.M.E.* which doesn't actually stand for anything; Wayne liked the glamour the word seemed to connote. "I dreamed about doing something like this as a kid. It's not filling a niche—it's creating one; it's not a magazine: it's a period piece about popular culture, a collector's item that you get four times a year and save." Wayne swabs at a saucer of olive oil with a piece of bread. "It's an elitist rag for the media-savvy intelligentsia—do you know how to spell that word?"

He continues airily, "I was inspired by Warhol's Interview. I want it to cover a range. You should be able to see a piece in there that could just as well be in (right-wing political journal) *The National Review* as well as in a gossip column. It has a scent and sensibility like no other publication that has ever existed!" Wayne's team hopes to break even with this first issue of the magazine in its new glossy format. "That's unheard of for a new magazine." The issue does sport some impressive advertising, from Stolichnaya to hip New York photographer's studios to Ian Schrager's trendy hotels. "My ultimate dream is for (Condé Nast owner) Si Newhouse to buy me out and for us to be part of Condé Nast. It's time for *R.O.M.E.* to make the millions I deserve. These are the worst waiters in the world. They just walk right by and see your empty plate and don't pick it up."

Wayne's contract with *Vanity Fair* prevents him from writing for anyone else, but he does have a column, previously arranged, in Miami's *Ocean Drive* magazine. He's also occasionally syndicated in magazines abroad such as Australian *Elle* and London's *Don't Tell It.* But even with the proliferation of gossip shows and magazines Wayne doubts that this is the golden age of the form. "Walter Winchell had his time. Hedda Hopper had her time. As long as there's music film, celebrities and popular culture to digest there'll be gossip. Long live gossip!" He sets out the prerequisites for the job. "You have to have an inherent love for this shallow business called celebrity. You have to be a writer, a man of letters who can present it with clarity, wit and a sense of accessibility to the world being covered. I want people to feel like they're standing right there beside me. I prefer to witness things myself, but a good source might be an astute waiter in a fancy restaurant, or assistants on talk shows."

R.O.M.E. gained particular notoriety in 1992 when Wayne published photos of model Claudia Schiffer topless backstage at a fashion show. Schiffer was unamused and sued. About l' affaire Schiffer, Wayne says carefully, "At the time it was really scary. I was sued for $30 million. It was scandalous but ridiculous. Here was a supermodel making $30,000 a day suing a pauperized journalist who put out 2000 copies of a photocopies magazine." In a piece entitled "Storm In a C-cup", London's *Sunday Times* agreed that "...indignation by Schiffer is hard to understand; she had already been photographed in underwear, revealing dresses and, for a particularly saucy calendar, cavorting in wet scanties...£17 million for damage for her reputation for inadvertently being caught topless might seem rather steep..." It didn't hurt, either, that Wayne retained Raoul Felder, one of the U.S.'s most famous celebrity lawyers. "We settled out of court. I agreed not to put any more pictures of her in *R.O.M.E.* and gave her the negatives. But," he points out, "It helped both of us. It made headlines all over the world. But at the time I was shaking in my boots." Wayne remembers fondly, "I saw her the next season in Paris backstage at the Chanel show. She thought I'd be blackballed. She nearly fell off her chair in shock to see me exchange double kisses with Karl Lagerfeld. Lagerfeld loved it, of course. No," he holds the rest of his wine in the air. "I have nothing to say to Fräulein Schiffer."

Wayne lives in Greenwich Village in an apartment he says is "...tinier than a shoebox", in a building formerly inhabited by writers such as Susan Sontag and *Native Son* author Richard Wright. "Maybe their karma will rub off on G.W.," he muses. He goes back to Jamaica constantly. "The greatest thing my Jamaican heritage has given me is a sense of humour. Jamaicans are the funniest people in the world. It's just a look when someone kisses their teeth, the way they might raise an eyebrow. They see right through the bull. It's really helped my career."

"I love Ocho Rios. It was always a great thrill for a Mandeville boy to drive over the mountains on the big holiday weekend and go to the old Jamaica Hilton. Now I love staying at Sans Souci Grand Lido." Ominously, he adds, "I want to start hanging out in Kingston and getting a fix on the whole Kingston scene."

Well, then, who does George Wayne think is the hippest Jamaican? With a bit of prodding, he says, "I think in terms of influence and power, Island Records' Chris Blackwell. I just wish he'd produce *The Harder They Come Part II* and give me a million dollars to write it—then he'd really be hip!" But what about legendary disco-era nightcrawler and diva, Grace Jones? Wayne laughs. "Grace Jones is a Jamaican mess," —a trademark Wayne phrase—"...in fact she's an international mess, but we love her. She can rest on her laurels. After her remake of "Send In the Clowns" she doesn't need to do another song. Grace is forever in."

The food is gone, the waiters in the background quietly preparing for the main dinner rush. Asked about the future, Wayne clasps his hands together and wrinkles his brow. "I don't know what I'll be doing in ten years. Hopefully my guardian angel will still be over me. I'd like to build a dream home for my parents in Oracabessa, a townhouse in Kingston and a New York pied-à-terre." He has a pleading look. "But you know, I'm on TV all the time in that CK One commercial, and I'm soon playing myself in a cameo in a Scott Rubin (*Ransom*, *The First Wives Club*)-produced movie, starring Matt Dillon and Kevin Kline called *In and Out*. I'd like to do more TV and film, it all synergizes with what I do, anyway." He looks at his watch. G.W. has a dinner appointment.

Wayne slips on his baby knapsack and Discman headphones. "I always have my music," he declares. "Every day I do the catwalk—the New York catwalk!" In the player: Pet Shop Boys' newest, *Bilingual*. He walks out with his peculiarly good posture, past the Barneys personal shoppers. "I always listen to Pet Shop Boys. They write for me." Outside, a light drizzle washes the perpetual grey, glamorous twilight of Madison Avenue. The store's doorman, in a long charcoal duster, whistles at the canary-coloured taxis stuck in traffic. "You know that lyric:

Arriving at my hotel there
are faxes greeting me,
Staying in a junior suite so
there's room to meet and greet...
In Brussels Bonn or Barcelona
I'm in demand and quite at home there...

That's so me! I love it!"

ORIGINALLY PUBLISHED AUGUST 1997

THE LAST PAGE OF VANITY FAIR *ASSIGNS CELEBRITIES MARCEL PROUST'S FAMOUS QUESTIONNAIRE ABOUT LIFE, LOVE AND SEEMINGLY EVERYTHING ELSE. IT SEEMED ONLY FAIR THAT GEORGE WAYNE FILLED ONE OUT.*

WHAT DO YOU CONSIDER YOUR GREATEST ACHIEVEMENT?

I have yet to have my greatest achievement, or orgasm for that matter. But certainly seeing the fruition of *R.O.M.E.* as a gorgeous glossy—sold across the globe. I guess my greatest achievement will come when the magazine mogul billionaire owner of Condé Nast Publications—Si Newhouse—offers to snap up *R.O.M.E.* for $40 million ($10 million per letter).

WHAT IS YOUR CURRENT STATE OF MIND?

Quite mixed emotions. Moments of exhilarating highs. Moments of great joy and excitement. These are the most exciting times for G.W. But then he quickly realizes that there is so much more to be done, and then he has to get off his lazy ass, and get back to work!

WHEN AND WHERE WERE YOU HAPPIEST?

Moscow, Russia, 1992. Sitting and jotting in the little black-book by the Pushkin statue on the Tverskaya. and looking up to see the most gorgeous Russian beauty fixing intrigue on G.W. Needless to say, G.W. spent the next seven ravishing days exploring all the beauty of Mother Russia.

WHAT IS YOUR IDEA OF PERFECT HAPPINESS?

I don't think there exists perfect happiness. But I'm waiting to be proven wrong.

WHAT IS YOUR GREATEST FEAR?

G.W. often rushes in where even angels fear to tread.

WHAT IS YOUR FAVOURITE JOURNEY?

After saying my prayers at night and thanking the Lord for G.W.'s guardian angels, and for his small mercies. And then cruising into the R.E.M. phase, then sleeping queeniously for the next seven hours, having the most gorgeous dreams and inspirations. Definitely my favourite journey.

WHAT ARE YOUR FAVOURITE NAMES?

When my fashion designer friend Isaac Mizrahi calls me 'Georgina.'

WHICH WORDS OR PHRASES DO YOU MOST OVERUSE?

Fabulous!

WHAT DO YOU MOST DISLIKE ABOUT YOUR APPEARANCE?

My double chin.

WHAT IS YOUR MOST TREASURED POSSESSION?

My health.

WHERE WOULD YOU LIKE TO LIVE?

Two months in the hills of upper Ocho Rios. Nine months in Manhattan. One month in South Beach.

WHAT IS YOUR MOST MARKED CHARACTERISTIC?

Telling it like it ought to be told.

WHAT DO YOU MOST VALUE IN YOUR FRIENDS?

Being the complete confidant. And always there.

WHAT IS THE QUALITY YOU MOST LIKE IN A MAN?

Beautiful, beautiful, extremely beautiful feet.

WHAT IS THE QUALITY YOU MOST LIKE IN A WOMAN?

Perky——.

ON WHAT OCCASION DO YOU LIE?

Silly question.

WHO ARE YOUR HEROES IN REAL LIFE?

Any researcher trying to decipher cures to all the infectious diseases that exist on this planet.

WHAT OR WHO IS THE GREATEST LOVE OF YOUR LIFE?

That is a secret.

WHICH HISTORICAL FIGURE DO YOU MOST IDENTIFY WITH?

Sidney Poitier.

WHICH LIVING PERSON FIGURE DO YOU MOST IDENTIFY WITH?

Princess Diana.

HOW WOULD YOU LIKE TO DIE?

I will never like to die.

IF YOU WERE TO DIE AND CAME BACK AS A PERSON OR THING, WHAT DO YOU THINK THAT WOULD BE?

A Ming vase.

IF YOU COULD CHOOSE WHAT TO COME BACK AS, WHAT WOULD IT BE?

Tina Turner.

WHAT IS YOUR MOTTO?

There is only one motto—Be Prepared.

Garth Fagan—
All The Right Moves

MARC GOODMAN

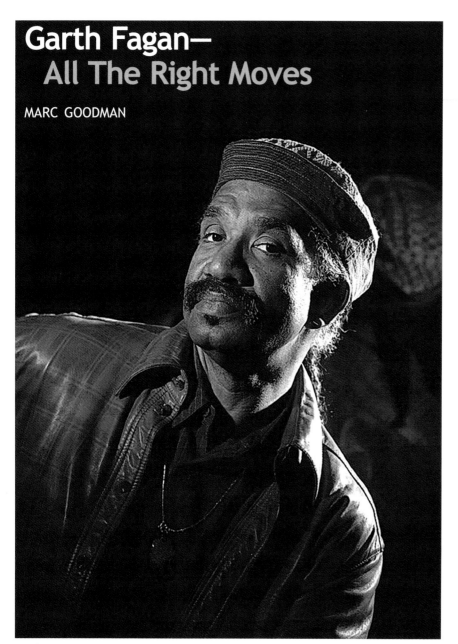

New Yorkers have a tender place in their hearts for the charms of 42nd Street.

Standing on the corner of say, Eighth Avenue, they'll tear up at the sound of sirens wailing or at the sight of a nimble suspect outrunning a passel of portly, gasping cops. Grit is good. So it was with no small apprehension that they greeted the Walt Disney Company's new investment in the area, which brought stores, lights and a new stage version of *The Lion King* to Forty-Deuce. After all, this area was more for adult entertainment, not sappy kid's shows. But what resulted surprised even the most hardened cynics: a delicious concoction of a musical, for anyone of any age. Stuffed with mature delights and the occasional bit of humour that a child could never understand, it was transformed from its movie persona by a director steeped in world puppetry traditions and a Jamaican choreographer, Garth Fagan.

As soon as the curtain rises on a lone South African singer, you get the feeling this is a dramatic experience like none you have ever seen. And indeed, what unfolds is perhaps the most extraordinary opening sequence in theatre: as a huge mylar sun grows against the endless African veldt, a parade of animals (actually magnificent puppets)—ponderous elephants, lanky giraffes, flitty birds—stream down the aisles to the chants of a South African chorus. Chokes are heard from an audience that often finds itself, as with this reviewer, thoroughly moved by the emotion of the piece, teary-eyed with the puppetmakers's art, transported by the uninhibited joy of the performers and the sheer child-like pleasure of each theatrical moment.

And while a movie that had earned $765 million in theatres, that was the biggest home video of all time and had attracted 50 million viewers when shown on television was probably a safe financial bet, no-one expected the critical woo the new Broadway version of *The Lion King* was thrown. It was another emblem of the revived New York, buoyant with the end-of-century, Guiliani-ized brio that the papers had been marvelling at recently. *The New York Times* said "You will gasp again and again at the inventive visual majesty of this show" and spoke of its "...instances of breathtaking beauty and scenic ingenuity." "Even the exquisitely restored New Amsterdam Theatre, a former Ziegfeld palace" said its chief critic Ben Brantley, "...disappears before the spectacle within it." *New York* magazine's authoritative curmudgeon John Simon, a man truly despised by much of the New York theatre community for his perceived mean-spiritedness, could only enthuse: "a cornucopia of dazzlements...the spectacle rightfully earns that most abused of epithets: magical. You will be bombarded by some of the most beautiful and spectacular sights theatre can offer from before and behind, so eyes in the back of the head will come in handy...the animals, re-created with unparalleled imagination... keep you

marvelling... Garth Fagan's choreography becomes an integral sharer in this convocation of the arts..."

Eight shows a week, Fagan's dancers indeed spark Director/Designer Julie Taymor's amazing creations into life. They were both sure of one thing, he says: "She never wanted the same old thing and neither did I. We're both known for taking risks in our work and we see a lot of things alike, multi-culturally." There are tangos. There is a meerkat's charleston. In an elegant, graceful swaying, 20 dancers become a perfect, fully-formed grassland (trust me). There is a hyena *corps de ballet* that jumps into hip-hop combinations worthy of the latest Puff Daddy video, and a warthog's soft-shoe that gives new meaning to Gregory Hines's "Ethiopian shim-sham" from *History Of the World, Part I.* "I've worked with the best: Merce Cunningham; Joe Papp; George Wolfe; so I have high standards. But I just saw it again for the first time in five weeks, and I cried like a baby. Julie Taymor is absolutely brilliant. She had thought out her concepts very well and I could tell this would be something extraordinary," says Fagan. "The cast is absolutely amazing. I auditioned 400 people to choose 14."

Circle of Life from Disney's "The Lion King."

As he describes it, the production has ended up as being sort of all in the West Indian family "Lana Gordon, who plays the cheetah—her father is Jamaican. There's a Barbadian in the cast, and Heather Headley, the adult Nala, is from Trinidad." For lead drummer, Fagan championed a linchpin of New York dance and music, Jamaican percussionist Junior "Gabu" Wedderburn.

"I insisted on Junior. He knows my language. When I'm stuck I can always say 'Give me something, Junior,' and I can rely on him to feed me with something inspiring. It was a real comfort having him there. He's even got a little Jamaican flag up there with him in the box!"

Fagan's father was a Jamaican Minister of Education whose idea of a respectable career did not seem to include dancing. Fagan has said he hated him as a teenager. Despite his father's discouragement, Fagan studied with Jamaican dance legend Ivy Baxter, touring Latin America and performing with the famed National Dance Theatre Company at Fidel Castro's inauguration. After Wayne State University, where he was a psychology major, and a postgraduate spell in Detroit, it was finally off to Rochester, New York in 1970 to found Garth Fagan Dance.

With his company, Fagan gained renown for the idiosyncratic mix of ballet and modern techniques practised by his dancers—the so-called "Fagan Technique"—and above all for his striking, often post-modern work (one piece, incorporated Culture, Wynton Marsalis, Brahms, modernist composer John Cage in one dizzying mixture). His fame reached an apogee of sorts in 1994 with "Griot New York," a collaboration with Wynton Marsalis and sculptor Martin Puryear. The piece prompted the *New York Times* to say that Fagan, whose choreography had "...acquired a cult following in recent years..." and who had "... built a reputation for work that is virtuosic in its physicality and unpredictable in its blend of ethnic and modern style and rhythms," had here created "...a suite of ensemble dances or love duets of such natural purity that the audience is moved to roars, or simply moved."

For a choreographer known for rigorous works that play to dance audiences, what

compromises now had to be made for such a commercial, mass-appeal show as *The Lion King*? Fagan admits, "It was a delicate balance. In the end, I think I succeeded." Paradoxically, this was by not making it too accessible. "For Broadway dancing, it's actually very sophisticated. In the wildebeests' stampede, for example," (a breathtakingly staged sequence with rows of mechanical animals criss-crossed by terrified gazelles, much more affecting than the movie version) "there are 11 rhythms. It's quite complex. There is, of course, some traditional Broadway-style dancing, such as with Timon and Pumbaa. And I harked back to my ancestral African roots by including some elements inspired by the war dances I've seen in Africa."

His eponymous technique, he says, is "...based on people dancing, people who happen to be brothers and sisters and aunts and uncles, whatever, dancing. As opposed to people pretending to be these people. It's subtle but it's very effective. It's freeness and openness, as opposed to being stiff and turned out. It's not pretending to be a prince, even when you're not playing one, that 'I'm-a-dancer' attitude. But the dancers can do it all. This is a more humanistic and open approach but not a lack of technique. It's dancing from the inside out. It's like the Africans—they dance for themselves, and if you want to watch, fine."

So what does this look like on stage? "My dancers have strong, supple backs, use of true poly-rhythms, and the speed and ballon [how one stays up in the air] of ballet. They also have a virile grace —my women really move with authority and elegance; they jump and turn with the best of the men. My men have sensitivity—they are strong and virile, but there's none of that macho b.s."

West Indians of any background will most probably find the African imagery of *The Lion King* almost overwhelmingly powerful. The wondrous clicks and pops of the Xhosa language are joyously recreated. An oasis lake dries up with frightening and beautifully simple suggestion, as a shimmering blue-cloth circle slowly drawn into its centre from below the stage. Above all, Rafiki, as the "wise old woman" character, with an infectious teasing humour, will spark a sort of instant, nostalgia-inducing communal recognition of for urban West Indians—for visiting a grandmother in the country, and for the old, rural character of the region in general, a world gone in a haze of traffic jams and Monday Night Football.

Fagan was himself deeply affected by the African elements of the show. "The primary reason for the success of *The Lion King* besides Julie and myself is (South African composer and performer) Lebo M, and all of the African choral work. The African singer Tsidii Le Loka gives "Circle of Life" a completely different spin than in the movie. The six South Africans in the cast are invaluable—the beauty of their spirits and their pride in their culture..." At the same time, he says, "I wanted not just a specifically African feel but to celebrate the Caribbean too. I wanted it to be accessible to all the children who came, whether they had studied ballet, modern, African, or—as with the carefree tumbling around in "I Just Can't Wait To Be King"—nothing at all. But the African rhythm is always there, even under the ballet. That pride, that African underpinning, fills me with a great pride and joy because...that's our cultural background."

He says wistfully, "I get back (to Jamaica) as often as I can. Alas, because of my growing schedule it's not as often as I'd like. In the last two years I've been back four times: once to accept an award from the NDTC for their 35th anniversary, once to dance at the Ward Theatre...The minute I get there I feel myself relaxing from the pressure we have up here. It's the beauty of the island and of the people. A real beauty, not something from some tourist PR thing, a light in the eyes, a sincere congrats, a smile. And the ocean really revitalises me. As a young man, it was summers in Ocho Rios. I try not to miss a trip to Port Antonio because it's so lush and beautiful. Absolutely Port Antonio, absolutely Ocho Rios, and if I can get up to the Blue Mountains, that too." He thinks back for a moment. "Having roast yam and fish at Mount Diablo on the way to the beach evokes the same thrill and emotion with me as going to the best restaurants in New York or France."

Fagan remains a keen observer of the Jamaican arts scene. "I'm glad to see the arts continuing and surviving considering the lack of funding. It's a real testament to the country. The NDTC was in fine fettle when I saw them last year. I was especially pleased to see the younger dancers, awesome young ladies and young men. It gave me great hope for the future. As terrific as the founding members are, the future obviously lies in the young dancers, and I really saw some brilliant young people." He shakes his head. "I'm very proud an island as small as ours makes such a contribution to the world in every way—sports, politics, education. I can't think of a place we've toured where people haven't come up to tell me how much they love reggae."

Scott Irby-Ranniar as young Simba and John Vickery as Scar from Disney's "The Lion King."

He laughs. "And then there's Rex (Nettleford, National Dance Theatre Company founder and University of the West Indies professor). If there's a committee on Mars, Rex is on it! He's so well respected all around the world."

In 1996 Fagan was himself named a Fulbright Foundation 50th Anniversary Distinguished Fellow—among 50 renowned scholars such as political scientist Ronald Steel, sociologist Nathan Glazer, English and Black Studies Professor Houston Baker and historian John Gaddis—chosen to teach in countries vying for their favour. Fagan returned to a favourite tour destination, Australia and New Zealand, to conduct workshops on modern American dance and to judge the Kiwis' national dance competition. These days, Fagan's company is continuing its gruelling touring schedule: across the U.S. now, with a European tour after that and a return trip to Egypt promised for sometime else in '98.

With the biggest show on Broadway under his belt, Fagan's current personal project has nonetheless brought him back home to a more rarefied world of rigorous, non-musical theatre. "I'm choreographing an interesting play called *Famous Orpheus*, by Oyamo, an African-American playwright. It's set in the Caribbean, a contemporary updating of the Orpheus and Eurydice legend, to be performed in May at GEVA in Rochester. Then we'll be touring it." But *The Lion King* does not mark Garth Fagan's last venture into the world of Broadway mega-shows. "There are other big shows in the works, but I can't speak about them yet. I'm very superstitious about mentioning things before they happen."

Reflecting on the journey from Kingston to Broadway, Fagan thinks back on being taught by the doyenne of modern dance, Martha Graham. "My Lord, when you stopped shaking...you could start dancing. Even when you just saw her walking across campus with her red umbrella..." "Once, she asked us to just do a simple, unadorned walk across the floor. People kept dropping out. Finally, after 13 rounds, I was the only one left. She said "You're going to go places." He laughs, then thinks for a moment. "You know, I think my first dance teacher, Ivy Baxter, would love *The Lion King*."

ORIGINALLY PUBLISHED JUNE 1998

Willard White and the Power of Music

BERNARD BURRELL

Willard White is Jamaica's most celebrated classical musician, a bass-baritone known in opera houses throughout the world. He has sung leading roles at the Paris Opera, in San Francisco and Los Angeles, at London's Royal Opera House, Covent Garden, and at the English National Opera—and at exclusive, glitzy Glyndebourne, the opera dimension of Britain's summer social season—and an honour roll of Europe's leading opera houses: Munich, Geneva, Hamburg, Madrid and Amsterdam.

Based in London, his repertoire stretches from some of the earliest operas still performed, by Monteverdi and Handel, to Mozart, Rossini, Verdi and Wagner, Puccini—that romantic favourite, *La Boheme*—to some of the most modern established works. He has appeared in Stravinsky's *The Rake's Progress* and *Oedipus Rex* and works by Shostakovich and Prokofiev.

And Gershwin—a definitive "Porgy" in the American master's *Porgy and Bess*, both for Glyndebourne and filmed for television. A great opera singer is also an actor; almost uniquely, White clinched his mastery of both dramatic disciplined by appearing with the Royal Shakespeare Company in 1989 in a much acclaimed performance of *Othello*.

Speaking with Bernard Burrell in the Royal Retiring Room at the English National Opera House, White shares some of his earliest memories of Jamaica: "My first recollection is from when I was about three, walking under the guango trees of my father's little farm, having just picked some coconuts, some bananas and so on, walking back then to the house to prepare some of what we had just picked for dinner."

"I liked to tease people a lot. And, even then, I liked to sing and to imitate the sounds of the animals, the sounds of nature and in particular just enjoy the warm sunshine. I think my experience in the countryside led me to appreciate a certain openness and freedom of expression, which you need to have with farm life—the feeling of not being attached to a particular outcome, for you never know exactly how the crop will bear."

BERNARD BURRELL: *Make hay while the sun shines?*

WILLARD WHITE: Pick the peas before the rain comes!

BB: *When did music first come in?*

WW: It was certainly on the radio. But I also remember my father whistling. Then, church—my first experience was in Ewarton, but close on the heels of that came Kingston, where I moved when I was four years old.

My first church was Kingston Parish Church and shortly after that St. George's Church in East Street and I certainly remember singing hymns out of the fullness of my heart. I never did join the choir as it required a schedule and a commitment which I did not aspire to at that time.

BB: *What other sort of music was around?*

WW: The burgeoning popularity of the time, the precursor of reggae, was ska. The foreign influences in the popular area were the Drifters and the Platters and later on there were the Four Tops and groups like that. In the ballad areas you'd have people like Dean Martin and Pat Boone.

BB: *You went to school at Excelsior?*

WW: But one very important thing before that was that the power of music revealed itself to me. In the morning, as I prepared myself for school, I would sing. It lifted my spirit, allowed me to forget or to deal with whatever pain might be in my life at that moment, to turn it into positive energy.

Singing is a very potent driving force, as the slaves found, to make one's work easier, or seem to be easier. The same for the work-gangs in Jamaica with those songs like "Woman A Heavy Load." Songs with a strong rhythm—just like ska and reggae. As a child, I could sing, relieving wholly any emotional blockage—I remember very clearly my being aware of this power.

Later, out of my education, out of my experience in music and of being moved by music—written or sung by black people or white people—has come my belief that in music there is a universal energy, an energy for change. I have learnt in every sense to stand up and sing my song or speak what I have to say.

BB: *How did this develop in your school days?*

WW: Well, I didn't have any educated awareness of my voice—only that it could make people jump! And I do remember my first day of registration at Excelsior School, when I stood up to give my name there was a lot of laughter. I only found out later this was because of the low tone of my voice. I was given a lot of labels at school because of this. Bigga, Thunder, Old-Man Grumble, Rumbler, Frog were just a few of them!

Now, at this time I just felt that singing was not something for me—there weren't at the time many pop singers with a low voice, and I didn't want to have just a one-hit. So, schoolboy-like, I rather saw other music as, well, that sissy stuff! Oh, yes, I would stand on the desks in school at break-time doing my Elvis Prestley imitation or whatever.

But then one day I was singled out in the music class because I was singing out loud and not recognising the distinct quality of my voice. The singing teacher noticed it. And at the end of the class she said: "Come here Willard...you have a beautiful voice and I want you to sing this song in the school's eisteddfod."

I remember this feeling I had, of being very, very proud that I was singled out—but also feeling that I must give the impression that I didn't want to do it (for the benefit of my friends!). So, many afternoons I would be in, after school, learning this song.

BB: *What was it?*

WW: Valentine's aria from Gounod's *Faust*. The next year I entered the competition, I earned a first prize and it was suggested that I be given a scholarship to the Jamaica School of Music, a nice accolade. Well, I decided just to dabble with this thing, because there was the urgency of making a career, making a life, a family—you don't do that through music, I then thought, at the age of 17 or so.

But I started singing in earnest at school. I was also an athlete, but I played the bass drum in the cadet corps band and the tuba in the school band.

And then many things led to a decision to explore singing as my future. Mainly it was the frustration of working in an office, which I did after school for a while, and then full-time for a year with Grace Kennedy. But my mind was elsewhere. I realised that I wanted to sing, really, and so I finally made the decision to go and study in America at the Julliard School in New York. Meanwhile, I joined the amateur operatic society, did Gilbert and Sullivan, and was in the annual pantomime, with Louise Bennett and Ranny Williams. It was called *Ananci and Pandora* and I was the young prince!

I remember taking off from Jamaica on the 31st of August 1968. For the first time I realised how beautiful that island was. Tears filled my eyes, because, all this was there and I never saw it...certainly not from that angle.

BB: *How did your career take shape? Where is it now?*

WW: When I first began I was advised by many people that I was being foolhardy—there weren't many black men singing classical music, certainly not opera—because there is this whole desire of a certain sector of the society to maintain a certain historical integrity (he laughs) about operatic presentations and so you wouldn't have black people doing certain roles. But the fact is, though I have encountered resistance, I'm around! Maybe withstanding the test of times.

BB: *You made your debut with New York City Opera. In which roles?*

WW: Major roles! My first was Colline, the bass role in *La Boheme*—a significant role. Then the bass in *I Puritani* by Bellini. Now, I could have started with Porgy, which would have killed me. Many bass roles need a certain amount of maturity. It was one of the things which was dangled in front of me to do because of the timbre of my voice and because I was black. I knew at the time that if I did Porgy it would be to satisfy some entrepreneur, some opera company's whim to fill a bill. And, maybe I'd spend the rest of my life being Porgy!

BB: *You have played a great variety of roles since then. Are there any you particularly identify with?*

WW: All the roles are somewhat like that, for I am the one who is doing them and I have my beliefs.

BB: *What of your present connection with Jamaica?*

WW: I go back to Jamaica because I had the fortunate experience of being born there. There is tremendous energy in the island. Now, some of it is very often driven in a negative direction. But a lot of it is also driven in a positive direction. And my dream is that this energy will continue to live and the potency of the negative will give rise to a very strong positive, because without that negative element the positive won't be as strong.

I think that is what the universe it made up of—take a man like Bob Marley, who did just that, using his music to speak out against certain aspects of society and to be able to affect a change in other people's attitudes. I think we need to be able to listen more to one another, and not be judgmental.

One Love! ☻

Against Time and Tide

ROBERT EDISON SANDIFORD

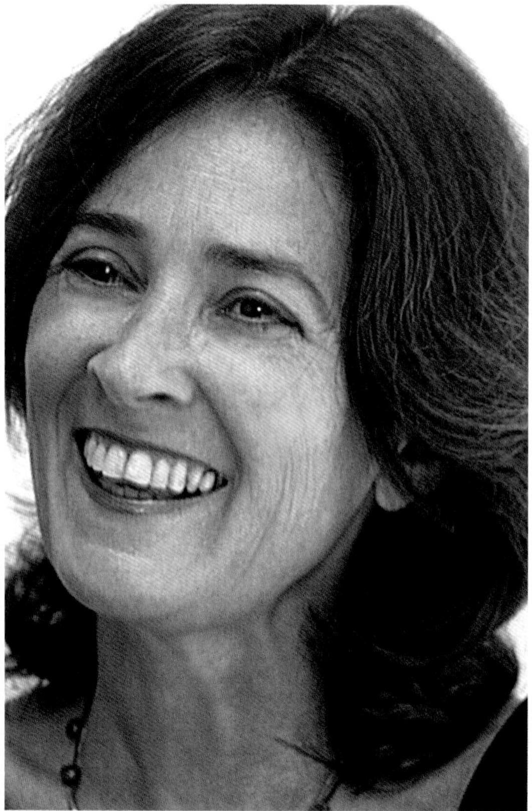

Rachel Manley sits overlooking the sea at Hastings in Christ Church, squinting against the glare of the early setting sun. She sips her tea and talks. She sounds older than she is, she's had an active life; three marriages, two children, many homes yet very solicitous, like a kindly Jamaican aunt.

Her small talk is about family, politics, and beaches, the writing life is anything but. In Barbados to promote her latest book, *Slipstream: A Daughter Remembers*, Manley seems like a woman who is now very much at ease with herself and others. Her brown hair is wispy free; her enquiring eyes roam, haunted and haunting. She apologises: "All Manleys are longwinded."

But a more just statement is that they are genuinely gregarious, interested in people. There's something wholly sympathetic about her. It may be her grief talking. Manley wasn't always so diplomatic. How much of her character is indebted to her father, Michael Manley, is made clear in her carefully observed memoir about his life and, especially, death.

"From grief," she confesses, slowly, almost solemnly. That's why she wrote the book. "The last few pages were written at my father's bedside while he was dying." Manley, a published poet ("I fled to prose"), had always wanted to write about her family. She first wrote *Drumblair*, which won the 1997 Governor General's Award for Non-fiction in Canada, where she lives when away from Jamaica. That book was about her grandfather Pardi, Norman Manley, Jamaica's first premier and architect of its 1962 independence, and about growing up in his house, from which the book takes its title.

Next, she would write about her grandmother Mardi, Edna Manley, arguably Jamaica's best known artist, who loved horses and mountains and wood. Finally, she would deal with her father, who twice led Pardi's People's National Party to victory: in 1972, holding on to power for two terrific, turbulent terms, and again in 1989, at the age of 64. But then he was diagnosed with cancer.

Manley thought she would have more time. "Because, to me, daddy was eternal," she recalls. But she didn't; he wasn't. Within three years, he had left politics; by 1997, not long after *Drumblair* came out, he was dead. His story urgently became the second book in her proposed trilogy. "I think I wrote the book because I couldn't help it," she says. In other words, it would have been harder not to write it. Yet Manley is quick to add: "All books, for me, are difficult to write in that they're work."

Like (Michael Manley)—Jamaica, its people and their family increasingly found themselves caught in the slipstream of the book's title, fighting wildly, powerfully divergent post-colonial currents.

The title of this one refers to the destructive currents created by two large engines: those would be her father's and her country's. For *Slipstream*, on another level, is the story of post-colonial Jamaica. Although, in Manley's opinion, her father "nearly but didn't destroy himself" in working against time and tide, he did succeed in destroying Jamaicans' inferiority complex. "Of all the Caribbean people, we are most definitely who we are, I think, defined," she says with bitter satisfaction.

Slipstream came out in Canada around the time of the death of Pierre Elliott Trudeau, one of that country's most daring prime ministers. Like Trudeau, who was friends with her father (and godfather, the late, great Barbadian prime minister Errol Barrow; Manley also lived and worked in Barbados at the Caribbean Broadcasting Corporation during the '80s), she says her father gave his people a sense of themselves and their place in the world that was undeniable.

Then she makes an odd admission, particularly for a memoirist; or maybe she makes it because she is one: "I have a very bad memory for things that don't interest me, but when something catches my memory, I hold onto it." Those times stuck. She has no doubt, for instance, the Caribbean would be "further along" if it had persevered with the West Indies Federation in which her father and grandfather believed. Nor does she question "that it is right and good", and inevitable.

Slipstream was actually a bigger book. There was more politics to it; her editor cut about 200 pages from the over 500-page manuscript. The excised material was researched rather than first-hand accounts. Manley's satisfied with what was left in, though. She still cries when she reads it and hopes readers aren't put off by any excess of sentiment. "The emotion just throws you apart...there is no coherence to the universe when you have lost a father or anyone you have loved dearly," she says, humbly. "But I hope it's forgivable, in the context of what he meant to me."

ORIGINALLY PUBLISHED FEBRUARY 2001

ART

SKYWRITINGS COVER
September 1975
"Malachi–The Prophet," The Boswell Trust Collection.

"But the trees still stand together like they're shouting over Jordan"

HILARY SHERLOCK

Over the past year I have been enjoying long conversations with my father, Philip Sherlock. When he has had enough of my questioning he says very gently, but firmly—in the manner so characteristic of him—"Hilly, your line of questioning is very gentle, but this is enough for now."

He looks back in order to encourage us to look within ourselves for strength to face the future.

Daley was a plumber
Served his time to Hard Up
Hungry Belly walked beside him
Never left him quiet,
Through the slum he had for home
From door to door he asked
If anybody wanted toilets fixed
And they laughed because the
toilet wasn't theirs anyway...

I (Philip Sherlock) was born two years after the beginning of the twentieth century and am still around. As I think about it the past sometimes looks like a funny thing—100-120 years, that's not a long time, but so much has changed. I can see my own movement—I used to see my experiences and my perceptions of the world through English eyes to an affirmation of my West Indian eyes.

What was so different about the 1920s and 1930s here is the burst of creativity we enjoyed then, as soon as we felt or sensed that colonialism was no longer acceptable. This was the period when the people who had been born here began to say "who are we?" We didn't do

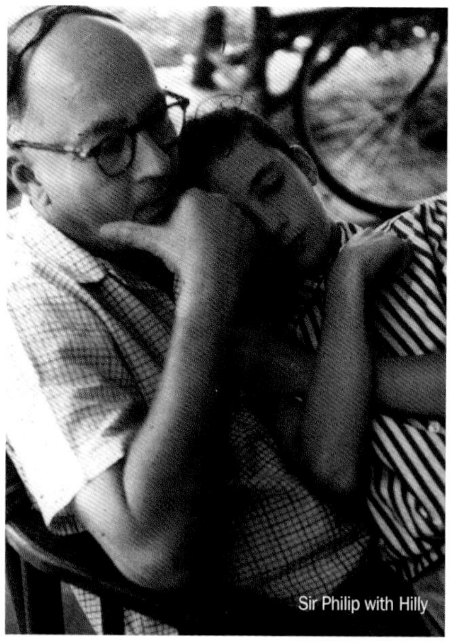
Sir Philip with Hilly

it because some one else did it or told us to do it, we were finding ourselves throughout the Caribbean.

The period before had been caught up with war and killing—a European War with which we identified—Armageddon I remember so well reading the *Gleaner* headlines. Coming out of the war there was the tremendous excitement of the Garvey Movement, with its encouragement of all forms of cultural development, of us as black people who could be a proud people, proud about our accomplishments.

Our new task found expression in many aspects of cultural development. Making a beginning was important, we knew we might make mistakes. But once we knew what our goal were—the immediate task was to begin to think about it as ours, we never really began to move until we began to change our minds. The 1930s—you might call the second phase of liberation, the first phase was the freedom which came with Emancipation, the second phase was the creativity which comes from freedom.

Creativity was what we needed—the intellectual discipline of a society concerned with thinking—an unfolding of an almost spiritual freedom to believe in our own experience as a people and to find strength and positive purpose within our history.

Henry Daley was one of the artists who found something within himself which I think really was a connection with the real mother country—Africa. It was a reflection of what the Africans brought with them, nothing really material, but creativity and spirituality.

Daley printed and he was an odd kind of chap, he liked to do things his way. He painted as he lived in his own way, some thought he was crazy, he even spent time in Bellevue. I remember one Saturday morning he came to see us at home. He was smiling all over, telling how he had been put in a room at Bellevue, inmates went on strike and either were released or released themselves. He was very pleased with himself because instead of going on the street with the others he had gone back to 'let out the women'.

...Hungry Belly restless talked
When he saw his Daley buy
Paint and Canvas for a picture
For a picture when a plumber
had to live...

...But the painter was a seeking
For the something he couldn't talk about
That he knew inside himself that he
couldn't tell about
That he knew inside himself he
must search and search and find...

John Dunkley (1891–1947), also reflected

The Petitioner
(Self Portrait) Henry Daley, 1945

himself in his paintings, chopped off branches, roads that didn't arrive anywhere. I think he pictured himself as if all his hopes ended like the branches, asking himself what have I done? What have I achieved? I liked him very much, in a different way I think he knew that he had achieved something through his paintings.

Albert Huie just painted, I don't think anyone taught him. I remember him going to the Institute to see Molesworth. Molesworth who was the Secretary of the Institute helped him. Molesworth gave Edna Manley (1900–1987) one of the first 'heads' Huie did, it was a self portrait, a kind of self discovery. Edna encouraged him a lot. Edna was an exciting kind of person and once she saw a gift in you she helped others to see it.

Girl in Pink Dress, Albert Huie, 1945.

When Daley died I wrote a poem and sent her a copy, she replied and I think the spirit of the letter reflects very much the spirit of these years.

> *Dear Philip,*
>
> *I couldn't send my letter because it was on dirty studio paper, but this is what I feel about the poem.*
>
> *It had a sort of terribleness of truth—and re-reading through it—a serene goodness of value...because of the truth of it, which people should know.*
>
> *It made me cry. I remember getting to the hospital, just five minutes after he died, even that was so typical of his life...also it gives one a sense of urgent responsibility.*

So the explosion at the time was not just with art, but we were beginning to write and to support each other along our individual paths of search. To find strength within people who were previously often just seen as property to be owned and later often only as labourers, yard boys—sometimes laughed at by those who had money and professions.

Take the life and work of Roger Mais, (I knew Roger very well indeed because he was interested in reading and in writing and I shared those interests). I can almost see him in front of me—he was particularly interested in the poor and those who had no opportunity, but are remarkable in their character and it all comes out in *Brother Man*. It is a very remarkable book. It helped to open our West Indian eyes. Norman Manley told how it opened his eyes to the sensitivity among talented, but relatively formally uneducated people. Roger helped to teach us about sense of community, of belonging together—a basic response to hardship and oppression. The strength of character in *Brother Man* the same generosity when you had very little, the same striving after ideas that you believe in—it was all there.

It was the same creativity that Edna Manley saw in her wonderful carving "the Negro Aroused." Our history of this time is a story of the unfolding of the inner capacity of a people, the spiritual as well as the physical needs. Because of this unique past we understand, if we choose to connect with this inner understanding what creativity means, what living in a multi-racial community means we have much to offer in the new age, but it is a choice we make through a rejection of violence and a dependence on economic or political control which excludes the value of all life.

THE POEM QUOTED IN THE STORY WAS WRITTEN BY SIR PHILIP SHERLOCK AFTER HEARING OF HENRY DALEY'S DEATH.

ORIGINALLY PUBLISHED DECEMBER 1999

SUZANNE FRANCIS-BROWN

Albert Huie is an artist in love with his work.

"It sounds like an affectation, but I have a romance with art" he said, sitting behind a wooden desk in the front room of his Kingston studio—several landscapes and figure studies hanging on walls or perched on tables around. Through a door, a table with a still life arrangement on it, stands in a splash of sunlight streaming through an open window.

"It's as if you go through a new lover every day" he said. "So things never really seem stale because you are sustained by this romance which starts afresh every time you look at something or someone."

"You look out there." He gestured out the window at the yard with its fruit trees and flower beds. Look at the different times of the day. You see what is happening at the different times of the day, and there is something so human

Drumblair home of Norman and Edna Manley, and Huie was often invited there. Through the game of badminton, he met the young Michael Manley—later to be Jamaica's Prime Minister. In 1937, through Molesworth, he sold his first painting, 'The Lace Girl', to the Manley family. By 1938—a turbulent year in Jamaican political and cultural history—he had met Edna Manley who was to become Huie's great friend.

Looking back at the early years and his early work, he comments: "It was a lot of foolhardiness, because you listen to what people say, and then you contradict them with all the vehemence at your control.

"I am lucky that I have never been affected in my work by what people said" he adds. Yet he recalls very vividly some of the harsh criticism that was his lot:

"When I was very young and I was the lone voice in the wilderness in the early 40s. I remember I gave an exhibition. It was the first exhibition I gave and it was at the YWCA on North Street. There was a man around here, his

(PRIOR PAGE) *Still Life Roses*. The Fong Tom Collection.

Huie's First Landscape, 1938. The Wallace Campbell Collection.

Head of a Boy, 1971. The Fong Tom Collection.

about a day. It seems to go through all the processes of a human being—from the early stage which is like youth, to the middle stage and old age. It seems to happen every day; and it's like rejuvenation every day."

Whether or not some spill-over from rejuvenation has played a part, Huie remains a strong painter—one whose name has long since found its way into the annals of Jamaican art history, and who is considered by many as the Grand Old Man of the local art scene.

"Yet I am not the oldest" he is quick to point out. "There are others much older. And even so, outside of Edna Manley and John Dunkley and, of course, Koren Der Harootian who was my teacher—we were the sort of lone voices in the wilderness for the longest time."

Huie's own rites of passage began early in his life. Born in the parish of Westmoreland, on Jamaica's western coast, Huie recalls that the walls of his grandmother's house were his earliest painting surfaces—and that old lady his earliest and most faithful fan. In his teens, he moved east to the capital city of Kingston, where he found work painting short-lived decorations onto china and tableware.

He worked for various periods with the biggest names in local merchandising at the time—the Issas whom, he recalls, had a china shop on Peters Lane, behind King Street in the heart of downtown Kingston; the Taylors who had stores on Princess Street, West Queen Street and Heywood Street—all in the vicinity of the city centre, and another on Spanish Town Road, not far away; and the Karaams.

"We had an influx of country people into Kingston at the time, and it satisfied the country people more if their plates and glasses were decorated" he said. "And I was one of the people who used to decorate those plates. I wasn't too happy with doing it, because it lacked permanence. There was no way of baking or firing them at the time. We just did it for quicker sales. And I could do it so quickly—I did four gross a day."

He was still painting on china when in 1937, at age 17 years, he met the then Secretary of the Institute of Jamaica, Mr. H.D. Molesworth. It was Molesworth—later a Curator of the Victoria & Albert Museum in London—who arranged for the young Huie to start twice-weekly lessons with Koren Der Harootian.

"Molesworth was the first person who encouraged me to be a full-time painter, even against the will of my relatives" Huie says. "As a matter of fact, he met with my uncle, because I lived with my uncle at East Street. He met with my uncle and told him—'Leave the young man alone, that's his calling.' And I remember him saying to my uncle, who was a sort of rabid nationalist: 'If you really believe what you are saying, you will realize that art is really a very important part of the national struggle'. Those were his exact words."

Molesworth's influence went even further. He lived at Cassia Grove, a property near to the

name was Street; he used to be critic for the afternoon paper and for a monthly journal—the *West Indian Review*... He said that what I was doing at the time was a betrayal of our technical accomplishment."

In fact, Huie recalls, some of those pieces sold to people overseas and one piece received considerable critical acclaim in London. And, he adds with a certain dry relish: "Of course a lot of those people who were saying such dreadful things about me—afterwards they came and tried to buy some of those same pieces. Of course they weren't available for sale."

Huie added that with that sort of background, when people talk about his work today "it either means something or nothing". And he commented that young artists today make too much of the critics and what they say.

Banana Boy, 1969. Fong Tom Collection.
The Poinciana Tree, 1990. Mr and Mrs Vincent Hill
The History Lesson, 1943. Judy Ann MacMillan.

"You look out there." He gestured out the window at the yard with its fruit trees and flower beds. "Look at the different times of the day. You see what is happening at the different times of the day, and there is something so human about a day."

"I think they worry too much about the critics" he said. "After all, it is better to be criticized than not to be criticized at all, even if it is bad."

Looking back now, Huie sees his early work as having been full of vitality: "as the expression of young people usually is. There's a tremendous vitality there; vitality which didn't necessarily have the finest vehicle of expression.

"You get more polished in your technique and you say things with greater refinement; and things that, in the truest sense of the word, have international appeal."

But the artist adds that the technique must always be saying something. "When you look at something, when you look at somebody, if you look at even a still life composition and people love it—they are not just seeing a still life composition. They're seeing a still life composition refined by the spirit. There are few occasions when one is just saying something without saying something. As a matter of fact I'm not sure there's any such time. It may be difficult for people to recognize it at the time—at the place where it is said."

Returning to his favourite subject, Huie commented on the overwhelming versatility of the Jamaican countryside with its geographical variety and its moods. But it is figures, he said, that are his greatest love.

"A piece of figure composition," he said, "is almost like a stage where lots of things happen at a time. You have the actors, you have lights, you have backdrops. And it's very important because all these things are inter-playing."

Huie works regularly between Jamaica and New York, with frequent summer excursions into the Canadian provinces of Ontario and Quebec. He exhibits, but rarely, finding this activity to be "an unnecessary encroachment on working time, because you cannot separate yourself from what is happening. Worse still," he says, "when the artist completes the exhibition pieces, he is empty—almost to the point of feeling suicidal."

Now well known, in more than one country, Huie can concentrate on immersing himself in his work, knowing that people will come to share in the magic of his creations. His approach is very pragmatic: "Work is the most important thing, and next to work is survival" he said. "The business of survival is very materialistic and quite often one gets so absorbed in what you are doing that you neglect the importance of survival. It may seem a bit unnecessary to some artists but it's not unnecessary. You have to live somewhere and most of all you need the material to go on working. And there's only one way of getting that—and that's the business of doing and at the same time dispensing of some of what you're doing so that you can keep on doing."

He added: "Usually I get my head in the clouds when I get involved in my work. But I find that it always is important to come back to earth."

ORIGINALLY PUBLISHED JUNE 1988

PAINTINGS: ***ALBERT HUIE—FATHER OF JAMAICAN PAINTING;***
EDWARD LUCIE-SMITH; ©IAN RANDLE PUBLISHERS

Mama Lou

SUZANNE FRANCIS-BROWN

The scene is a yard on Featherbed Lane, some miles outside the old Jamaican capital of Spanish Town, St. Catherine which borders Kingston. In the centre of the yard is a tree. Beneath it, taking advantage of its shade, is a weather-beaten wooden seat with room enough for three.

One woman sits beneath the tree on the bench. A strong, squarely built woman; her back straight, despite her sixty-seven years; her hands capable. She is working on a piece of red clay, moulding it first, then shaping it, smoothing and then ornamenting.

This woman is "Mama Lou". Her real name is Louisa Jones. She's making clay pots. She has been doing so for more than half-a-century.

Her pots are made and fired by a traditional method which is reminiscent of West Africa. Some local experts in the art of pottery have pinpointed her style of work, more specifically, as being indigenous to the Shoir Hills in Ghana.

West Africa, and particularly the area then known as the Gold Coast, was the major source for slaves whose descendants form some 70 percent of the Jamaican population. These slaves could bring nothing material with them from their homes. But they held on to their memories and they had their skills. Some of these skills have been passed down from generation to generation; some in their purest form; others have been adulterated.

Mama Lou's skill is a microcosm of this process. She began making clay pots when she was only eight years old, imitating her mother, uncle, aunts and all the villagers who lived in close proximity in the Winters Pen district, near Spanish Town.

She remembers that the making of clay pots was very much a part of the life of her small community.

Sunday evening was the time for digging the clay, which was later chopped up with some water. On Monday sand was sought, and a section of the yard was swept clean so that the sand could be sifted.

A pot rejected from precious makings, was then filled with water, and the tools of the trade were placed inside—a pot spoon made from a gourd, and used to 'belly' or scoop out the inside of the pot, a 'smoothing stick' to give the outside of the pot a smooth, clean feel, and a 'mouth cloth' to give the top edge of the pot an even finish.

When one pot was completed, the potter would put his or her mark on it, place it on the ground to dry, then start another. Mama Lou, now down to making about six pots per day, remembers that as a strong, skillful young potter she could make two or three dozen pieces in a day.

The drying process takes about two weeks, after which the item would be coloured (if the potter so desired) with a dye made from iron-rich red earth and water. This would be smoothed on before the firing.

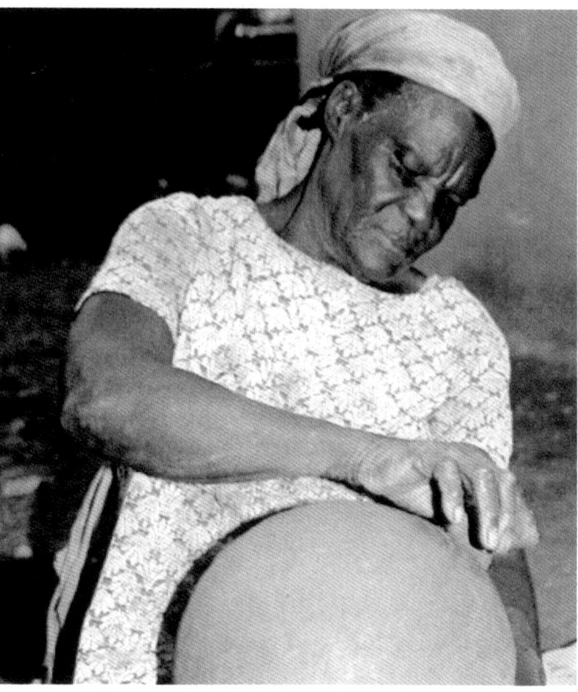

Firing, a job for Friday or Saturday, involved the laying down of a wide bed of wood on which the pots would be packed in rows, steadied by chips of old, broken pots. Five or six rows of larger pots would form the bottom layer, with smaller and smaller layers on top, giving the whole construction a dome shape.

The largest, widest pots, 'yabbas', used by some Jamaicans for mixing puddings and cakes were leaned against the sides of the pile, strips of wood about a yard-and-a-half in length were then packed around the outside of the stack until the pots were invisible. Wooden chips at the edges of the heap were used to start the fire, and then dried grass was thrown on top to fuel the blaze.

Mama Lou remembers watching the blaze as a child—from the first hot, furious burning as the wood caught fire, to the gradual cooling of the ashes some two hours later and the careful removal of the pots.

This traditional timetable which she learnt so easily as a child is one she still follows today, some sixty years later. She worked as a potter from childhood until she was twenty years old; she was to become disillusioned with the trade because of its lack of profitability.

For several years she worked at a variety of other jobs, only to be drawn back to pottery, it is this trade together with the raising of some chickens which has provided her with a livelihood.

There is variety to her output. Mama Lou makes the wide-mouthed yabbas, cooking pots of all shapes and sizes, flower pots, and the occasional monkey jar, traditionally used for storing water.

She never takes her wares to market. There's no need to. Most of her customers, and they have been increasing in number over recent months, come to her home and choose their pots from a pile of finished goods stored in a small, wire-sided shed.

Some market people buy her pots for re-sale. However, her major exhibit area is the small museum in Spanish Town where the pots are on show and where they can be purchased. They do reasonably well there.

Mama Lou's work has formed part of the National Exhibition, an annual showcase of the visual arts in Jamaica.

As she gets older and her strength diminishes, and with her body more susceptible to cold from working with the clay and the heat of the fire, Mama Lou becomes increasingly concerned for the future of her craft.

"I knew 'nuf clay pot people, but plenty of them died out" she said. "I'm trying to gather in some."

Three of Mama Lou's four daughters have learnt from her the traditional art of making the pots, just as she did as a child from watching her elders. But, they are dissatisfied with the slow pace of the process.

"You know what happen to the young people" and Mama Lou analyses... "if they make the pot this week, they want to fire it Friday, and they want their money same time.

"Sometimes you burn it and nobody come buy it. But they want money quick, they are living by it, you understand? So that's the reason they don't interested."

She added, "One of my daughters make it down the road here. She not so interested, but I encourage her, you know, to start. Because the people they want a lot of pots."

ORIGINALLY PUBLISHED JULY 1983

Kapo Jamaican Artist and Spiritual Leader

VEERLE POUPEYE-RAMMELAERE

One of Jamaica's foremost artists died February 24, 1989, at the age of 78.

An internationally renowned sculptor and painter, revivalist bishop and community leader, Mallica Reynolds, or "Kapo" as he was better known, made a lasting contribution to Jamaica's cultural development.

As one of Jamaica's foremost artists, "Kapo" belongs to the "Intuitive" stream, as Jamaica prefers to call its "primitive" artists and his often visionary work draws heavily on his revivalist background. Through his work, on the other hand, "Kapo" also contributed greatly to the recognition of revivalism as a major part of Jamaica's cultural heritage.

Revivalism, the generic term for a group of traditional Afro-Christian cults, has long been controversial in Jamaica. The association with obeah, Jamaica's outlawed counterpart of Haiti's voodoo, is one major reason, and on several occasions in his life Kapo was accused of practising obeah. The African element in revivalism and its popularity with the poorer classes also made it difficult for colonial Jamaica to appreciate its importance. A lot has changed since, and Kapo's revivalism-inspired work has become the object of national pride and international recognition.

This tremendous change in socio-cultural attitudes can be attributed to the coming of age of modern, independent Jamaica, as well as to the contributions of concerned individuals. The present Leader of the Opposition, Edward

Kapo had his first exhibition in 1959 at the Juster Galleries in New York and his first Jamaican exhibition in 1962 at Hills Galleries in Kingston. Since then Kapo has had numerous exhibitions in Jamaica and abroad, and has received a most impressive number of honours and awards. He was one of the revelations of "Jamaican Art 1922-1982", a major exhibition of Jamaican art organized by the National Gallery of Jamaica and the Smithsonian Institution, which travelled in the United States, Canada and Haiti.

His work is represented in many private and public collections in Jamaica and overseas

Seaga, for instance, who was trained as an anthropologist, developed a scholarly interest in revivalism and became one of Kapo's earliest local supporters, while Kapo's personal contribution in this field is not to be underestimated.

Kapo was born in 1911 in Byndloss, St. Catherine in rural Jamaica. He received only a basic education and was entirely self-taught as an artist. Early in his life, he claimed at the age of 12, he received the Spirit of Conversion and became a revivalist preacher. After a period of travelling in the rural areas of Jamaica, he came to Kingston in 1931 and settled down in the ghetto area of West Kingston, which was at that crucial time in Jamaica's history a centre of social and cultural ferment.

Kapo started his career in the late 1930's, after receiving divine instruction to start carving in stone and wood. His early works were met with apprehension by his environment and he was even arrested on charges of preaching obeah. In the 1940's he also started painting. By that time, the interest in his work started to grow, although most of Kapo's early works have left the island, because he sold mainly to tourists and foreign collectors. Where this early international interest in his work is concerned, Kapo undoubtedly benefitted from the publicity surrounding Haitian art at the time. American art critic and connoisseur of Haitian art, Selden Rodman, for instance, developed a keen interest in Kapo and described his paintings as comparable in quality to those of the great Haitian painter and voodoo priest, Hector Hippolyte.

including the Stedelijk Museum in Amsterdam, the Museum of Modern Art of Latin America in Washington and, of course, the National Gallery of Jamaica. In 1981, a work by Kapo, "A New Spring" was selected as a wedding gift by the government and people of Jamaica to Prince Charles and Princess Diana.

One of the highlights of the permanent collection of the National Gallery of Jamaica is the Larry Wirth Collection, a unique and consistent group of 65 carvings and paintings by Kapo, spanning the period from 1949 to 1975. The collection was in 1982 acquired for the National Gallery of Jamaica from the heirs of Larry Wirth, the American owner of the Stony Hill Hotel in St. Andrew, Jamaica, and an early patron of Kapo. The Larry Wirth Collection, the most important collection of Kapo's works in Jamaica, contains a number of Kapo's masterpieces, such as the carvings "Paul Bogle" (1952), "The Angel (Winged Moon Man)" (1963), "Obedience Covers All" (c. 1965) and the "Royal Rooster" (c. 1967) and the paintings "Revivalists Going To Heaven" (1968), "Be Still" (1970), "Kubalee" (1972), and "There She Go, Satan" (1974).

The best works in the Larry Wirth collection illustrate the visionary side of Kapo's work: a symbolic homage to Jamaican National Hero Paul Bogle, an intense evocation of the spiritual realm in the "Winged Moon Man" or spirit possession and exorcism in "Be Still" and "There She Go, Satan". The category of work is most obviously linked to Kapo's revivalist background although every work Kapo has ever produced is in essence an expression of his world view. His portraits, whether realistic or visionary, represent people from his environment or revivalist personalities, depicted with humouristic sympathy, as in "Miss Spindle Leg" (1962), or with awe for their spiritual power, as in "The Flame" (1971). His landscapes and even his occasional erotic works, exemplify his fundamental respect for the natural order of things, a firm belief in the goodness of creation.

As a carver, Kapo's favourite medium is wood—especially lignumvitae, Jamaica's national tree—which he worked with extraordinary sensitivity and intuition, both where craftsmanship and understanding of the ancestral, spiritual connotations of the material are concerned. As a painter, he immediately captures the viewer's attention through the apparent simplicity and immediacy of his designs: the frequent use of (symbolic) primary colours, the bold, graphic outlines, the pattern-like compositions, the occasional use of impasto.

In recent years Kapo had stopped carving. He claimed that working with the heavy logs of wood resting on his legs was responsible for the circulation problems that finally led to the amputation of his legs, although his diabetic condition at least compounded the problem. Despite the serious health problems he experienced in recent years, he remained in the forefront of Jamaican art, as a prolific painter and through his outspoken commitment to the development of Jamaican art and the recognition of the Intuitive stream in particular.

One American critic, Benjamin Folgery, writing for the Washington Post in 1983 in a review of "Jamaican Art 1922-1982", saw Kapo's sculpture as the answer to pioneer Jamaican artist Edna Manley's call for an art that would be an "expression of the deep-rooted, hidden pulse of the country" in 1934. His work indeed touches on the very essence of the Jamaican cultural heritage. This together with the purely artistic merits of his paintings and carvings, makes his oeuvre one of Jamaica's national treasures and secures him a place among the ranks of Jamaica's greatest artists and spiritual leaders.

ORIGINALLY PUBLISHED JUNE 1989

Barrington Watson Portrait of an Artist

IAN BOYNE

Barrington (Barry) Watson is a study in determination and discipline. His story proves that obstacles, hindrances and opposition need not deter the truly ambitious from the path of fulfilment.

For a young man to say he wanted to become an artist several decades ago was to invite rebuke and scorn from his parents; especially if those parents had high hopes for him. Such was the case with the Watson family.

The "old man" wanted Barry to become a lawyer and to add prestige to the family, but young Barry had an unquenchable fascination with drawing. To make matters worse, Barry was not doing well academically at high school (during his first term at Kingston College, he came last out of a class of 31 boys). He was doing so badly that he was asked to leave the school. When his father begged for him to be given another chance, the young Watson finally realised that he had to do some trade off. The very next term he came first in the class; one of the first lessons he gave in determination.

Whatever Barry Watson puts his mind to he achieves. Small wonder that he was the first black man to enter the Royal College of Art in England—and that after he graduated with high honours—he won scholarships to study in Italy, France, Holland and Spain. Small wonder, too, that today he is one of the leading artists in Jamaica and the country's premier portraitist.

"I am very conscious of the need for technical training. I don't hold the view that only the intuitive is important. Talent is important but so is training. The Caribbean people need to get into art with solid foundations."

Asked whether Caribbean peoples should emphasise largely African art as opposed to European art, Watson shouts, "Hell no!" "We are part European and part African. You can't put down Europe. I mean, why are we talking English? We are not complete Africans. I believe that we in the Caribbean have the unique opportunity of producing art that embodies world culture as we are a mix of many races and nations. Every culture—be it Aztec, Oriental, North American, European, African—has found its way into the Caribbean. We can produce an art that is unique to the world. I would love to see people from England, Holland, Spain coming to the region to see what we have."

Barry says it was his intense desire from he was young to study the great artists and to go to Europe to learn as much as he could from the Europeans.

But he was to get no encouragement from his father who told him he would live to see him push a handcart—the lowliest of occupations in Jamaica. "I was determined to prove him wrong." Barry says he told his father: "If I succeed, you can be proud. If I fail you can say I told you so."

He was about fourteen and he had made some Christmas cards which his father sold in his drug store. The Christmas cards he drew did very well and were normally sold for one penny. But there was this particular one he had done for Mom, which he never intended to be sold. His father, however, got a hold of it and sold it—for five shilling. It was that striking. Barry cried endlessly—or so it seemed. While Dad had felt that "Barry could draw another one," Barry had special sentiments for that card and hated the idea that money should come before anything else. Barry did remake that card—as well as stop making cards commercially for his father.

But the experience also taught him that money could be made from art. His passion for art was so strong that to learn that he could actually make a living from it thrilled him. He remembers seeing an advertisement in the local newspaper for a book published in America called *It's Fun to Draw.* He immediately sent for it. Problem was, the book contained nude prints and the school authorities confiscated it as a porno book! "I cried every day over it and begged for it to be returned," he relates.

After school he got a job at the General Post Office, in a clerical position, but, as expected, it failed to excite his imagination. "I couldn't stand the thought of just wasting away in a civil service office and waiting for fifty years to become postmaster general," he says, a faint smile gliding across his bearded face.

Barry Watson then decided he would go to England to study. He had no relatives or close friends there (he was the first member of his family to travel) but that would not deter him.

With fifty pounds in hand, nowhere to stay and with no certainty as to where he would study or work, he left on a boat for England. He knew of one person in England who was supposed to meet him on his arrival. But when he arrived in England, he got a letter saying the person had died.

There he was, completely alone in the "Mother Country", without mother and without country. But that was not enough to deter Barry Watson. He wanted to become an artist and to learn all that he could and that was what he was going to do, despite the difficulties.

He scurried around and found some Jamaicans who decided to help him out with lodgings. He had brought a lot of foodstuff from Jamaica and fifty pounds. Soon the food was devoured by his new-found "friends" and after a touching "hard-luck" story, the fifty pounds were gone too. Barry was broke and without any food.

He decided to take some odd jobs—as street cleaner, barber, bartender, painter, rubber moulder for aircraft parts—just about anything he could lay his hands on. "I decided I would take two years to check out the scene in Britain. I was just looking at life."

After his two years of checking out life he applied to the London School of Printing and Graphic Arts. His work regime was rigorous. He went to school from nine in the morning until eight at night. Then he would go to work at nights from nine until seven in the morning—believe it or not. Here's how this ingenious young man did it. He would use his one-hour lunch time to catch some sleep. Then he had a break from classes between four to six, so he would catch some more sleep. He would also sleep on the train to work and school.

"I would train myself to sleep for exactly the time it would take to come off at my train stop. I would tell my mind to sleep for a certain time and just as I reached my stop my eyes would open. This happened without fail."

I asked him whether he ever experienced prejudice and discrimination while in Britain. He laughs loudly and brushes the matter aside, saying, of course he had, but he never let that bother him. He says he learnt the sarcastic diplomacy of the British quite well and was able to use it back on them!

The fact that he was never hypersensitive also stood him in good stead while working and studying in England. He recounts one incident while at college in England. A leading professor there asked him to clean off his car, a normally objectionable thing as that was well outside the curriculum requirements. But Barry did it without questioning him. After he had finished, the man then asked him to polish it off. "The other black students laughed at me and said that was an expression of the man's racism. I could have cursed the man and told him where to get off. Instead, I just did it. It turned out that the man and I became very close and I subsequently learnt a great deal from him. He was just testing to see what I was made of. I don't think it was a racist thing."

Barry also remembers playing football as the only black member of the team in England and hearing white people scream, "Go on darkie, keep it up, blackie." He says he was never disturbed.

Vayden McMorris, avid art collector and a well-known Kingston architect and personal friend of Barry's for many years, says he knows of no one like Barry Watson who shows the kind of dedication and devotion to work. McMorris, who bought his first Watson painting in 1957, remembers periods when Barry's productivity was prodigious and staggering. "He would just shut himself away in that studio and work and work and work for many hours a day, producing some of the finest stuff. At first his

work and his colours were largely Dutch but gradually he has become more Caribbean and Jamaican. When Jamaica became independent in 1962 he painted something authentically Jamaican and it was fantastic. Barry is now into a lot of water colours. He has a great colour sense and, of course, he draws beautifully Speaking of Barry's nudes, McMorris says he has captured them superbly—"You can almost feel the flesh."

McMorris says Barry deeply respects professionalism and excellence and he spends the necessary time to develop his art. "He is always improving." Barry tells me that he sees art just as he sees life: "You have to take it to a point where you can't improve it any further; in that sense no art is ever complete." There is this passion for perfection that is evident in Barry's art.

Barry brings to his work a willpower made of steel. "When some years ago a stroke laid him up, he went straight ahead painting and pushing on with his productions," comments artist and art critic Gloria Escoffery. Escoffery says she admires his determination and courage.

Barry says that while he has the prerequisites of being an accomplished artist—such as vision, a sense of perception and hand-and-eye coordination, these are not the most important elements in being successful in the field. In fact, he says it is not the technical competence which is the most critical factor in any field of endeavour. "It is your will or determination (there's that word again) to succeed that is the most crucial element. You have to have the confidence that you can do it. I had the self-confidence from early to know that if I applied myself to my work I could succeed and could do as well as anybody else, once given the opportunity."

His drive for excellence has helped him pile accomplishment upon accomplishment. He has given lectures at the prestigious Harvard University and, was visiting professor of art at Spellman College in Atlanta Georgia. His murals include the "Out of Many One People" at the Lyndon B. Johnson Memorial Library in Austin, Texas. He has done special portrait commissions for Jamaican National Heroes Alexander Bustamante and Norman Washington Manley, as well as Dr. Martin Luther King and all of Jamaica's Prime Ministers. His paintings hang in over 1,000 private collections the world over.

He has won coveted international awards for his work as well as local awards, including the Prime Minster's Award for Excellence and the Commander of the Order of Distinction (C.D.).

Barry Watson has also contributed significantly to art education in Jamaica and was Director of Studies at the Jamaica School of Art between 1962-1966.

ORANGE PARK (ABOVE AND AT RIGHT) is the near-fulfillment of Barrington Watson's vision for the Contemporary Jamaican Artists Association, which he founded in 1964 and the Jamaica Art Foundation which he founded some 20 years later.
"All cultures of the world meet here—in the Caribbean. Its equidistance between north, south, east and west and influences from all the cultures create a type of art that is unique to the area." In 1994, title for 6.5 acres of Orange Park was accepted by the Government of Jamaica on behalf of the nation to be used as a public facility for the advancement of the Jamaican/Caribbean artistic movement. Architectural plans have been laid for a centre for the arts at Orange Park—a naturally inspirational environment where research; studio, exhibition and performing arts; and art education from resident artists can take place. And, in addition to the main house with Barrington's personal art and antiques collection, it will house a museum of Jamaican and Caribbean art.
Ironically, this bequest to the nation comes from someone who nearly 50 years earlier refused a benefactor's largesse on the grounds that if he accepted he "would never know if I made it on my own." So very typical of a gentleman's style. —TAMARA WILLIAMS

But perhaps the most gratifying and pleasantly surprising news for patriotic Jamaicans to hear, was the announcement this year that he had donated his massive collection of paintings and his beautiful rural mansion, a former Great House, Orange Park in St. Thomas, to the country. A trust has been established to handle his art estate.

Barry is still producing at a feverish pace. After his two-and-a-half mile walk in the morning he goes to his studio to paint, breaking at about 1:30 p.m. At about 2:30 he resumes and works until 4:30 when he gets in a couple of hours of tennis. His evenings are usually dedicated to work, television or conversation. Barrington Watson is an individual without whom the art world would be much poorer.

ORIGINALLY PUBLISHED JANUARY 1992

Gonzalez A Jamaican Artist

DENNIS SCOTT

Gonzalez lives here. Small, sculpted pieces of wood and metal rest like visitors in the garden. The rooms of the house are richly hung with his work. Mingus is playing piano on some unfamiliar record —quiet and surprising. It's hot and quick, outside in Kingston. But in the artist's home time moves with a cooler swing, the paintings say there's no hurry, talk easy, this is a calm place. We drink tea. He sits on a stool in the studio and waits for me to be comfortable.

Christopher Gonzalez: Jamaican. He is thirty-three. His wife is an anthropologist. Their small daughter's name is Nigerian: Chinyere. It means "God-given." Everybody says he looks like a saint or a mystic. Everybody's right.

He is patient, but amused by the reminder. Gonzalez is eminently practical, a man who works with his hands. Except—"I suppose you could say that in my work I'm in pursuit of an extended reality. Of silence, I suppose." The paintings themselves are full of silence. The faces there, and in the sculpted pieces, seem all turned towards a distant vision. The figures are caught in the act of journeying to a moment of perfection. I say, "Remember Dag Hammerskjold? 'The longest journey is the journey inwards?'" He smiles, accepting the statement.

His own travels and exhibitions have taken him east to Europe, north to Massachusetts, to Canada, west as far as California. Gonzalez graduated with his Bachelors from the Jamaica School of Art in 1963.

"That next year was the most terrible time of my life, I think." A poor artist, in a poor country, virtually unknown. The frustration of not being able to create—materials cost money. At that time "painting for me was only a pastime," he says. What he really wanted to do was sculpt. The Art School had marked him as a very promising talent.

Gradually, things began to fall into place. One semester as Visiting Artist at Spellman College, in Georgia. And in 1965 he went to Denmark as a guest artist at the Herning Folk High School. "That was a good time. I could work really hard, I mean all your material needs were taken care of, and there was all the stimulation of the place." Back home afterwards, refreshed and excited, his name beginning to be recognised in his own country.

"Though the influence of being abroad was very strong, of course; a lot of my work for a long time was very clearly affected by those tremendous works I saw." Like the sculpture in the Gustav Wegland Museum in Oslo.

Then acceptance at the California College of Arts and Crafts. "I guess that experience had the most lasting effect on me", he says. It was there that for the first time really he connected with the beauty of African art, and began to explore its principles in his own work.

"I had a fair amount of teacher-student friction. The faculty said I wasn't responding to the environment." He grins without malice. "My work was 'too African!'" But by 1972 he was Master of Fine Arts, and choosing his own path with total assurance.

There in California he began to feel more Jamaican than ever before, and to be inspired by the traditions of African art. But it was an important time for another reason—he discovered his love for paint. Today he is as much a painter as a sculptor. I prod him for an answer: "What's your favourite medium, though?" It is clay, he admits.

And goes to change the record. I half expect reggae, or maybe something "classical"—he likes Beethoven very much. But the mood is lighter than either: acid rock, turned down low.

I've been looking at some of the work In progress. The sketches are full of great rocks that could be faces, or faces that seem half-hidden in stone. And several views of a very beautiful black woman.

"There's a small place in the country, by a river," he says. "It's very peaceful. I may paint her there." The drawings fascinate me. "You know ... I'm experimenting, just that, now. See? Different textures, here, and here, these are just sketches, trying out the idea, most of these I probably won't keep, that one, maybe..." He goes to answer the telephone. I want to walk around the house again.

The work is full of shapes like icons. There are constant images—of woman and man together, of horizons, of snakes, of circles, of the moon. I get a sense of forces held in tension, of balance. When he comes back we talk about that for a little.

Yes, the sexuality is there, he observes. In a way the paintings, like the sculptures, are about man in quest of perfection, searching for an inner rest. Sometimes the man in the picture is supported by the female principle, love, intuition. Sometimes the woman is a symbol of lust, physicality, material appetites; that can hold a man back, instead of helping him to develop. But generally the image is of a man striving to become a whole person, energy and gentleness combined; body and spirit in harmony. The end of the quest is completeness, and the discovery of oneself.

There is enormous control in his use of line and colour, I think.

"Well, I try to teach my students about stillness," he says hesitantly. "You have to conserve what you have. And what you use to create." Gonzalez enjoys teaching. Understandably he is a strong influence on the work of the students at the Jamaica School of Art now, and in the teacher training colleges and high schools where he encourages new talent. And naturally too, his reputation goes before him: he was awarded Jamaica's Silver Musgrave Medal in 1975 for outstanding creative work.

"No, I don't think there's a kind of Jamaica 'stamp' on my work, that a tourist can pick out and say 'yes, that's Jamaican art.' But even though there's very little physical representation of Jamaica, the vibrations, the sensations of the island are very much there." I think of the monuments he recently completed for the tomb of Norman Manley, National Hero of Jamaica, and father of the prime minister. And of the crucifix he created for St. Jude's Church in the Stony Hill district above Kingston. The Christ figure is a poor black man....

"I want art to heal people's inner life. It's got to work for their development—for the dormant life that's inside us... I'd like my work to move beyond an appeal to any one nation, or type of person...."

The house is quiet around us. 

ORIGINALLY PUBLISHED FEBRUARY 1977

(AT TOP) A lithographed drawing of the 2nd of August Celebrations to mark the total abolition of slavery in 1838.

From the series the Daguerrian Excursions in Jamaica, (AT LEFT) Ferry Inn and (ABOVE) the Coke Chapel.

(AT RIGHT) A carte de visite of George William Gordon, a Jamaican National Hero, c.1860.

The Duperlys
Early Photographers of Jamaica

DAVID BOXER

Adolphe Duperly, a young Frenchman who had traveled to the West Indies to teach lithography in Haiti, first visited Jamaica in 1824. Enamored with the country, the 23 year old decided to settle in the island's busiest town, Kingston. Ten years later he married Louise Desnoes, a young Haitian Creole of Eastern Caribbean origins and began to raise a family. Four sons were born to the Duperlys: Armand in 1834; Adolphe Jr., in 1835; Theophile, in 1839; and Henri Louis, in 1841.

During these early years Duperly eked out a living primarily as a printer operating his own lithography press. He is known to have drawn and published lithographic prints, which were usually hand-coloured. Few of these prints have survived today.

In 1834, Duperly announced a grand scheme, a projected series of 48 lithographic prints of Jamaican "views" and "occurrences." Lack of subscriber interest however, caused the series delay and Duperly got involved in other projects such as his collaboration in 1837 printing the well known second folio of Belisario's Sketches of Character. The Scottish painter J.B. Kidd arrived that same year and launched his own extensive project of 50 views of Jamaica. The release of Kidd's first prints must have put a damper on Duperly's project as not only were Kidd's prints much larger than those so far produced by Duperly, but the Scotsman's superior skills in drawing would have been painfully evident.

Lower King Street, c.1895, Albumen print mounted on display card. PRIVATE COLLECTION

In 1838, Duperly drew and lithographed one of his best-known works. It depicts the celebrations held in Kingston on the 2nd of August, to mark the total abolition of slavery. The illustration is an exuberant work: fireworks and a bonfire brighten the night sky while countless figures join in the festivities. But technically there are problems.

Duperly was a careful, but not a technically advanced draftsman, and he clearly had difficulties in working out the perspectives of scenes, so when the news of the invention of the daguerreotype, the earliest form of photography, reached him, he was quick to embrace the new technology as a drawing aide. In doing so, he became the first known daguerreotypist in Jamaica and in the early 1840's opened a daguerreotype studio in Kingston.

DAGUERRIAN EXCURSIONS IN JAMAICA

In the early forties Duperly revised his 1834 scheme and began taking daguerreotype views in Kingston and around the island. These were later transformed into lithographs in Paris and published in Kingston. In doing so Duperly gained his place in history. *The Daguerrian Excursions in Jamaica*, as he titled the work, was the first such photographically derived work in Jamaica and one of the earliest such series in the New World.

One wonders why the plates were lithographed in Paris when we know of Duperly's own competence as a lithographer. The suggestion is that he wished the series published quickly and that the laborious task of copying and adding figures could be shared by contributing artists in Paris. The truth may be that Duperly himself recognized that he was not up to the task. Tracing or copying the daguerreotyped scene was one thing but the "realist" settings that the daguerreotypes provided required special skills when it came to integrating the human figures, horses, carriages etc. that were required to animate the scenes. (It must be remembered that at this time, the camera's shutter speed would have been too slow to record figures unless they remained perfectly still). Further, announcing that they had been lithographed in Paris, and that they were based on daguerreotypes was to proclaim their modernity, that they were in vogue.

Duperly had projected a series of 48 prints, however, only 24 were actually published. The series begins with nine views of Kingston, four concentrating on important buildings, including the Coke Chapel illustrated, surrounding the large central "Parade" of the city. The remaining 15 works offer a variety of views from around the island.

Save for *The Daguerrian Excursions*,

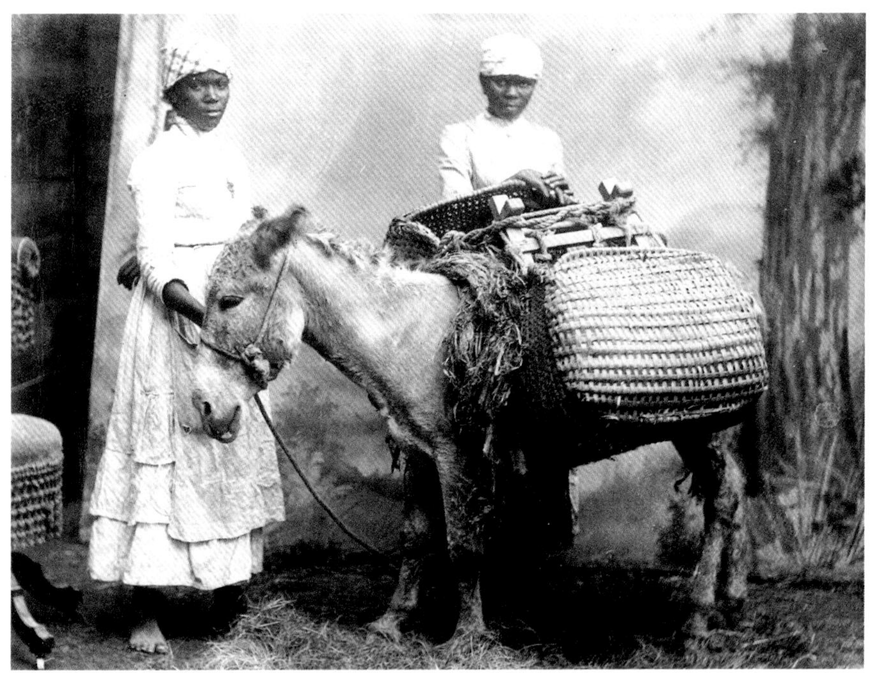

(ABOVE) Two market vendors, c.1870, albumen print.
(BOTTOM) Resting after a days work in the banana fields, c.1900, silver gelatin print. PRIVATE COLLECTIONS

records of Duperly's activities as a photographer are scarce. We know that he took portraits, but in daguerreotypy, no negative exists, so that the image produced was unique and very few of these appear to have survived. Occasionally, however, where reproductions were required, the daguerreotype would be copied by hand and multiple prints reproduced by a lithographer. We know for instance that a lithograph of Hector Mitchell, Custos and for a time mayor, of Kingston, was lithographed by A. Maurin in 1848 and published on the occasion of a special address to the electors of Kingston. The lithograph was copied from a daguerreotype by Adolphe Duperly.

Duperly's penchant for the recording of current events, or as he would put it "occurrences" continued as is attached by *The Daily Advertiser, Kingston*, April 22, 1856:

"We have seen an excellent drawing of the burning of the steamship Osprey executed in coloured crayon by Mr. Duperly, artist of this city. It was first taken in daguerreotype and afterwards copied in crayon. At the time we saw it, it was not quite completed, but nevertheless the skill of the artist was well shown in the faithful delineation... which was given the sad scene." Neither daguerreotype nor drawing have yet surfaced.

The report is important for another reason, it informs us that in 1856 Duperly was still using the daguerreotype method of photography. He appears to be lagging somewhat behind in the advances in the profession. By 1856 the daguerreotype was on its way out. In major centres like London and Paris it was virtually obsolete. The advances since the discovery of the "wet collodion" process had made the production of glass negatives and albumen paper prints virtually standard by that date.

ADOLPHE DUPERLY AND SONS

Certainly by 1860 Adolphe Duperly's studio would have been totally converted to the "wet collodion" process and the production of albumen prints. Two of his surviving sons (Theophile died in 1858) Armand the eldest and Henri the youngest, had joined their father in the business, which in the early sixties operated from a Harbour Street address, in Kingston. By 1860, the firm, which had been known simply as Adolphe Duperly, had been incorporated as A. Duperly and Sons.

In the 1860's portrait photography was the mainstay of the firm and in the 1860's portrait photography meant the production of the immensely popular carte de visite. The Duperlys quickly adapted to the new technologies that could produce these little visiting-card-size pictures which were now within the reach of all but the very poor. An example, which is the most famous of all Jamaican cartes de visite, was produced sometime in the early 1860's of George William Gordon, a victim of Governor Eyre's hangings in the wake of the Morant Bay Rebellion, now celebrated as a National Hero of Jamaica.

Adolphe Duperly died in 1864 and his two sons continued the firm under the new name Duperly Brothers. The brothers seemed ideally matched. Henri was particularly interested in portrait photography while Armand's interest was in "view photography" which continued the tradition of Adolphe's Daguerrian Excursions. The firm from around 1860 had begun to build up an inventory of full plate "views" of Jamaica to supplement their activities as portrait photographers and after their father's death this aspect of their work greatly developed.

After four or five years of operations as Duperly Brothers they separated. There then seems to have been something of a tussle over the name Duperly Brothers until two separate studios were established, each identified by the brothers names: H.L. Duperly and Armand

Duperly. Presumably after H.L's departure from Jamaica in the mid 1880's (he settled in Colombia where he established a firm Duperly and Son) Armand reclaimed the name A. Duperly and Sons, thus restoring the firm's link to his father.

The views created by A. Duperly and Sons, for local consumption and for travelers, would serve the burgeoning tourist industry in the last decades of the nineteenth and first decades of the twentieth century. Duperly views and the popular "environmental portraits" were sold as original prints and after the mid 1890's were reproduced in the many tourist guides that were published using the new half-tone invention. After 1900, a succession of postcard series reproducing "translations" of their photographs (often introducing artificial colour) would dominate that part of the industry and by 1908 the first of several editions of their popular *Picturesque Jamaica* was published. After a modest initial edition, the several later editions of this picture book were modeled after the earlier (1903) publication by Dr. James Johnstone, *Jamaica: The New Riviera* and shared honours with Johnstone's book well in to the 1920's as the most substantial publication of Jamaica views.

In the 1890's Armand's own two sons, Armand Jr. and Theophile had been active members of the firm along with another Duperly, Henry Sylvester who was most likely Armand's nephew, a son of Adolphe Jr. Armand Jr. died in 1903, at which time Armand Sr. (who died in 1909) turned over control of the firm to Theophile his younger son. It was probably around this time that Henry Sylvester left the firm and established his own firm of H.S. Duperly.

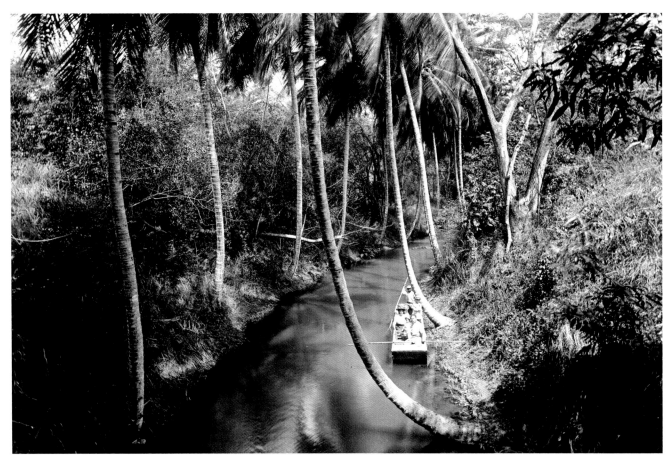

(ABOVE) Boating on a canal near Spanish Town, c.1900, silver gelatin print. PRIVATE COLLECTION

(BELOW) Mrs. Rachel Arnold, c.1910, cabinet card: silver gelatin print. COURTESY MRS IRENE MCFARLANE

A. Duperly and Sons continued to operate right up until the death of Theophile Duperly, in a motorcar accident in 1933. For the final two decades of the firm's operation the portrait studio had once again become central to their activities although now they faced severe competition from other studios notably that of Cleary and Elliott. A. Duperly and Sons continued to publish their old photographs in editions of *Picturesque Jamaica* and they produced new series of postcards, but most of the new photographs created by the firm were studio portraits such as the fine dignified image of a Jamaican matron which is simply signed, Duperly.

The work of Adolphe Duperly and of his sons and grandsons, is the subject of a special exhibition being staged by the National Gallery of Jamaica to mark the bicentenary of the birth of Adolphe Duperly.

ORIGINALLY PUBLISHED OCTOBER 2001

Jack Tyndale-Biscoe

Capturing Jamaica From Above

SONIA GORDON

Jack Tyndale-Biscoe is a tall, soft-spoken man with a matter-of-fact, yet precise way of expressing himself, and a permanent twinkle in his eyes. His relaxed manner and self-deprecating humour belie a love of challenges, of adventure, and a refusal to accept that he cannot accomplish anything he sets his mind to.

Most of us know of him through his outstanding aerial photographs. There is hardly a local magazine, newspaper or brochure with a bird's eye view photograph, which does not carry his by-line. Most property developers would be lost without his services; many would have lost considerable sums of money were it not for his meticulous photography. For almost 40 years he has recorded Jamaica on film, from one end to the other, flying the plane himself and taking the photographs. You could say he has put his stamp on the country, literally.

But he did not set out to be a photographer. He wanted to be—and became—a mechanic. Aerial photography came later, as a result of his having learned to fly. His 60-year love affair with aeroplanes and flying began with what he considers one of his biggest thrills—flying solo in a glider at the tender age of 14.

Now in his early seventies, he talked with me at his home in Kingston about his career from apprentice mechanic, to licensed aircraft & engine (A&E) maintenance engineer, to pilot with his own air charter service, to Jamaica's premier aerial photographer. Along the way, we touched on some well-known Jamaican personalities and landmarks, as well as a glimpse of the country as it was in the 30's and 40's.

Tyndale-Biscoe senior had been a surveyor and he wanted to teach young Jack surveying, but there were a couple of snags. "I had to pass trigonometry in Junior Cambridge but I couldn't add two and two and get four regularly... I didn't want to do that (surveying) anyway; it didn't appeal to me.

"I wanted to be a mechanic; I'd always known I wanted to be a mechanic. So, after I left school, my father sent me to England, to Guildford Technical School... and I worked with Dennis Bros. (Guildford) too as an apprentice mechanic. Dennis Bros. made trucks and buses and so on... but Lord, boy! The place cold you see!"

The cold drove him back home to Jamaica. "There was not much scope for progress," he said of his first job, so he joined J.S. Webster & Sons who were just getting into the air-conditioning business which was relatively new to Jamaica then; Webster's also owned a shipping line.

"Carl Webster employed me with the thought of making me a ship's officer. But he didn't tell me that. Not that I would have minded... that would have been alright too! But they'd just started this air-conditioning business and they put me to work with their engineer until they made other arrangements."

He was a quick student and "pretty soon learned what the air-conditioning business was all about." The job of ship's officer never materialised, however, because in 1937, work was started on the Carib Theatre and Jack was made foreman in charge of installing the air-conditioning, a job which took a year. When it was finished, the management of Carib offered him £4.10/- to stay on and run the air-conditioning unit and work in the projection room. This was a princely sum to a youngster earning £1.10/- a week, out of which he paid £1.00 for board and lodging! "In those days things were cheap, though," he said. "I wore shoes that I paid 2/11 d. a pair for! I used to wear white trousers made out of a fabric that was called coconut drill, and the longer you wore them, the longer they got, so they were always under the heel of your shoes! Anyway...I went to Mr. Webster and told him about the offer and asked him what did he think I should do. 'Well,' he said, 'I don't think we'll ever be able to pay you that, so you'd better take the job."'

The years spent working at the Carib Theatre were fun ones too. In his spare time he played stand-up bass in an orchestra which played every Tuesday night at the old Myrtle Bank Hotel in downtown Kingston. It was the era of the Big Band sound: Count Basie, Duke Ellington, Glenn Miller, Tommy Dorsey, and in those days Myrtle Bank was the hotel in metropolitan Kingston. Tennis dances were also a popular social event and Hugh Cox's Orchestra played them all, from Port Maria to Montego Bay.

Then came World War II and Jamaica geared up to play its part. An American army base was constructed at Vernam Field, and J.S. Webster opened a plant to bottle Coca-Cola and Canada Dry. They invited Jack to run the plant. "Boy, it was dreadful," he recalled. "The American army couldn't possibly fight without Coca-Cola and our plant was never designed to supply an entire army base. We ran some terrible hours...used to start at midnight Sunday and shut down at 6 p.m. Tuesday!" He soon recognised that this job, too, was all sweat and no future and he became restless.

Despite the terrible hours and his involvement with the orchestra, he found time to do a course in aviation through the International Correspondence School. On the strength of his successful completion of this course, he applied for and got a job with Pan American Clipper Service, as the airline was then called, in October 1944. "By then they'd discovered it was cheaper to hire people locally than to send Americans down the line." He spent a year training with Pan Am in Miami, along with about seventy others from all over the Caribbean and Central America, at the end of which time he had acquired the first of two licences, his aircraft mechanic's licence. This was no small feat, because, as he explained, trainees normally were not allowed to sit for the exams before a year and a half. He went on to become a fully-fledged aircraft and engine (A&E) mechanic. "They eventually changed the 'E' to 'P' for power plants (with the advent of the jet aircraft) and you were known as an A&P mechanic...a bit like the stores!" he added with a chuckle. "Of course, I worked in the early days of aviation; they had flying boats which used to land in the sea when I started. Every time they got a more advanced aeroplane, we'd either go for training in Miami or we'd get a course and study here. We worked on everything—DC4's, Convairs, DC6's. It wasn't until 1959 that the jets started coming here. That was a big change."

Working on the 'planes was not enough for Jack, however. He wanted to learn to fly, and the story of how he achieved this illustrates his persistence and determination in achieving his objectives.

"There was a chap, Earl Gardener, a Seventh Day Adventist. He had come out here (from the States) to teach at the Seventh Day Adventist College in Mandeville and he'd brought a small aeroplane. I remember they had to pass a special law so that he could operate his American registered craft and operate with an American licence. Well, I struck a deal with him: I'd maintain the aeroplane if he would teach me how to fly. Although I could maintain the aeroplane, he'd never taught anybody to fly and all he did was sit beside me and let me try, you see. At the last moment, when I was going to crash, he'd take over! It was only perhaps once a month that he wanted the plane serviced, then he'd give me an hour and just sit there while I tried. So, for a whole year I maintained his plane and I was still not able to fly. It wasn't that I couldn't fly—I could take off and I could fly, but I couldn't land and Gardener couldn't tell me what the devil I was doing wrong—that's where the trouble came in!" He laughed fondly at the recollection. "He was quite a guy though —I liked old Gardener..."

It was not left entirely up to Earl Gardener, however. He managed to get lessons from other people that he knew, striking similar deals, and in late '48/49, he got his private license. In 1951, together with a friend, Tony Kelly, he started a flying club which attracted other members. "Eli Matalon was the chief flying instructor; John Harrison, Garth Drew and quite a few others were instructors. There are lots of fellows flying for Air Jamaica who were first taught to fly by those fellows (from the flying club). That club carried on until about 1970. By then there were quite a few private aeroplanes around and I was operating a maintenance business on the side. I was still with Pan Am, but I had a couple of mechanics working for me and we did the maintenance on all the light aeroplanes in the island.

"Marjorie (his wife, whom he married in 1942) didn't like flying at all so that's why I started taking photos to show her what it was like. I've been taking photos from the air from the early 50's. I wasn't getting very good results to begin with, I'll admit... it took a long time before I discovered how to do it properly."

In 1963 he quit his job with Pan Am. "I've never regretted it for two consecutive seconds, though they did give me a nice award the other day that I was very pleased to get." The award, prominently displayed on the wall behind him, reads: "For dedicated service to Pan American and the development of international air transportation."

By now he had his own aeroplane and eventually bought four or five more. Together with his partners they started their own air charter service, Airways, based at Palisadoes. Lack of security and a high rate of theft forced them to move their base of operations to an airstrip above the golf course at Caymanas Park in 1969. This location, however, eventually proved worse than Palisadoes as, again, they were plagued by theft and a lack of security. "The airfield was supposed to be fenced off, but they stole the barbed wire... they stole the posts... there were cows all over the airstrip half the time." They moved once more, in 1987, to Tinson Pen aerodrome.

Despite the problems, he recalls that business was brisk and things were going very well in the early 60's and 70's, and they did a lot of intra-island flying, particularly of visitors to the resort areas. Errol Flynn was one of the personalities he recalls flying, although that was back in the 50's. "When he bought Boston (in Portland) he brought two aeroplanes with him—a Sea-Bee and a Navian, and he needed someone to look after the planes. I took on the job on the understanding that I would fly them as well, because an aeroplane sitting on the ground soon goes to hell—it's got to be flown! Well, I recall one time Errol and his wife arrived and wanted me to fly them to Boston in the Navian... they put up a devil of an argument but I said 'no way, boy!' I don't want to see the headlines 'Jack Biscoe kills Errol Flynn!' I wouldn't take them, because the landing strip that they had built at Boston not only sloped down—it turned the corner and went round the hill! And it was all wet grass, you know. I landed there subsequently many times, but at that time there was no way I was going to fly an aeroplane in there. Flynn was really quite a character. I suppose you could say he was a hippie, although they didn't have any in those days."

He talked fondly about his family: his marriage to Marjorie, "one of the high points of my life," their two daughters and four grandchildren. It is Marjorie who keeps Jack—and his photographs—organised. The family had a reunion earlier this year and there is a proud twinkle in his eyes as he reminisces. One gets the distinct impression that Jack Tyndale-

Biscoe feels he has been a lucky man who not only counts, but is thankful for his many blessings.

I asked him how he got into aerial photography professionally. "I bought a surplus camera and went down to the Survey Department to get work. Because I wasn't an Englishman or a Canadian it took them forever to agree... well, I tried with that. "Not that it was even worthwhile," he added wryly, "because I got so little work from them, it's a laugh."

The majority of his work comes from property developers who require progress photography. He explains why. "People are renting equipment, for instance, and they are paying by the month or whatever, and that equipment is supposed to be on the site. They use my photographs to check. Before now, I've been hired to take photograph every three days because (the client) was pretty sure they were paying for something that wasn't there. Furthermore, no one is going to do these developments with their own money. They have to borrow it and they have to be able to show what stage they are at the end of every month. So something like that is actually vital to a construction project, to show at a certain date just what stage the work had reached." He paused, then added, "You have a lot of variables with aerial photography, but the main thing is to be able to fly well enough that the whole thing becomes automatic. I don't have to stop and think 'how should I do this, or what do I do next." Any near misses? Ever run out of gas or had the engine conk out? "I've had the engine quit on me, in very heavy rain, but it always came back. I've scared myself a couple of times too. Anyone who tells you that they've never been scared is not telling the truth!" he laughs.

He has a solid library of every square inch of Jamaica it seems. "The last time I counted - which was over a year ago—we had 62,000 negatives listed and cross-referenced, dating back to the 50's. I do all the development myself. Survey work is all black & white, you see. I just give out the colour stuff."

In his spare time, he plays the organ for recreation, and he reads a lot. He has also written a book, a work of fiction, "which I haven't done anything about getting it published yet, but..." Does he consider himself semi-retired, or is he still fully active? He laughs and says "I'm still fully active—I'm a workaholic, you see!"

ORIGINALLY PUBLISHED MARCH 1993

Maria LaYacona's 25 Year Love Affair

ANTHONY GAMBRILL

Can a big girl working for a famous magazine find happiness on a small Caribbean Island? Cleveland-born Maria LaYacona, formerly of *Life* magazine, did indeed and,

25 years later, doesn't regret for a minute the decision she took to make a career and live out her life in Jamaica as a citizen of Jamaica.

Market lady at Papine (1955)

Ladies in church, Port Royal (1986)

Cricket first bought her to the island when she came on a freelance assignment from *Sports Illustrated* to cover the historic inaugural Caribbean encounter between West Indies and Australia in 1955. For six weeks she shot literally hundreds of transparencies of the Test series (from which only one was eventually used!). Although she had lived and worked in New York, Houston and San Francisco and travelled all over the world with Lowell Thomas, the legendary writer-traveller, Maria put her roots down in Kingston.

Maria LaYacona was born into a photographic family, learning her darkroom and photo-taking skills from her father who had first been a shoemaker in his native Italy and, for a time, a Pennsylvania coalminer.

She remembers him vividly as a hardworking perfectionist who taught her his trade well from when she first began taking pictures with a Box Brownie at the age of 12. At high school she processed friends' films for a profitable 19 cents per 8-print black-and-white roll of film.

After graduating, she was offered a scholarship to the School of Art in Cleveland but turned it down because she had to contribute to the family finances. So, she went to work in the photo department at Westinghouse.

A year later she was accepted at a professional photographers' school and after completing a 12-month course her career was launched. She went to work for a nationally recognised commercial photographer, Paul Dorsey, in Houston, Texas.

The stint with the Life organisation followed soon after, beginning in 1951 and ending five years later.

Mount Diablo children (1962)

"Don't think it was all glamorous stuff," she recalls, "I put in years keeping files and developing other people's stuff before I actually got paid for taking a photograph".

She admits that by being "an eager little girl", working long hours and being willing to do any job requested of her she was able to get ahead.

After the honeymoon of "getting the feel of Jamaica" and setting into an airy duplex in the Matilda's Corner area of Kingston, Maria employed her boundless enthusiasm and determination to break into commercial photography.

Using photographs in press advertising in the fifties in Jamaica was a breakthrough for her and other photographers. She quickly earned a local reputation for the high calibre of her technical skill as well as the creative content of her work. Today, Maria LaYacona is a name that comes immediately to mind when Jamaican advertising agencies, art studios and printers need photography. Her colour photography has been used on everything from resort brochures to annual reports, from canned food labels to calendars.

As much as she enjoys the very demanding commercial work, she gets great fun out of doing class photos for a number of city schools. Each year she reckons to photograph 10-15,000 school children... which takes her back to where she started in photography in Ohio at school!

Perhaps her most outstanding contribution to the photographic field in Jamaica—aside from the countless awards she has won in national competitions—has been her coverage of the National Dance Theatre Company.

Michael Manley (1972)

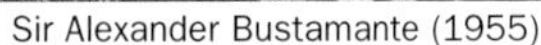
Sir Alexander Bustamante (1955)

Edna Manley (1969)

For the past 17 years she has been the publicity photographer, travelling companion, working patron and photographic chronicler of "the Company". Her first—and only—show featured black-and-white blowups and was staged at the National Gallery. Although she worked on the show for eight months she gave the entire proceeds of the sale to the NDTC whom, at the time, were raising funds to tour Britain.

She also collaborated with Artistic Director Rex Nettleford on *Roots and Rhythms*, a book published by Andre Deutsch on dance.

Maria LaYacona has always been a one-woman organization, processing all her own black-and-white photographs and taking on as much work as she wants to handle in any one week.

She considers herself a hard worker and an eye for perfection as her father did. Over the past decade she has accepted two "apprentices" each of whom have spent a little less than two years with her. Cecil Ward who is currently farming, has done a brilliant study of the ecologically fascinating Hellshire Hills west of Kingston. The other, Cookie Kinkead, is making a name for herself in New York and will shortly be completing a book on doorways and entrances around the world. Unfortunately, Maria says, the kind of dedication and sacrifice that has to accompany such an apprenticeship in photography is a rare commodity in the eighties.

When she is not at work Maria can usually be found at her mountain hideaway, a small country house at Green Hill in Portland which she bought to restore several years ago. When the renovators got to work, they discovered that virtually the whole of the woodwork was termite-ridden and the building had to be scrapped. The rebuilding exercise taught her a lot about the construction business, says Maria, as she became her own contractor.

Back in the city she has been known to prepare and serve with ethnic gusto some memorable Italian food. And on other evenings she can be observed playing a keen game of poker.

There are two ambitions she might—or, then again, she might not—fulfill over the next few years. The first is a book on Jamaica as seen through her lens taken from fifty or sixty thousand negatives she has accumulated in 25 years.

"Everything from polo at King's House to Michael Manley on the campaign trail in 1972 to racehorses at pasture in St. Elizabeth."

The other project could be her second-ever show of her work. But her idea of a show is not "just taking a lot of pictures and mounting them."

"If I'm going to do a show the stuff has got to be very good. And I don't think I'm good enough to meet my standard yet," she says.

When Maria says something she means it. Tough, pragmatic, but always genial, Maria LaYacona has richly rewarded Jamaica with her talent as a photographer over two and a half decades.

TEXT ORIGINALLY PUBLISHED OCTOBER 1983

PHOTOGRAPHS FROM: *JAMAICA PORTRAITS 1955-1993*
ORIGINALLY PUBLISHED MAY 1993

Newcastle lady (1971)

Ray Chen One Picture Is Worth a Thousand Words

SONIA GORDON

Photographer Ray Chen was recently asked on a radio interview what would have been his second choice for a career, had he been faced with such a choice. There was a long pause before he replied, "I can't think of anything else I would like to do...I can't picture myself (no fun intended!) doing anything else," he laughed. Few people are fortunate enough to make a successful career working at something they love as much as Ray loves photography.

The irony of it is that when he left school it never occurred to him to try photography. "It never crossed my mind," he said, and added that he got into photography "just by chance".

Ray grew up like most children of mercantile families, helping out in the family business after school and at weekends. When he left Wolmers Boys School, he continued helping his mother run the grocery store, looking no further down the road into his future.

He and his wife, Linette, married at a very young age. "If my daughter today tells me she wants to get married at 23, I'd say 'you'd better think again!" But at that time all my peers were getting married at twenty-one, twenty-two, twenty-three, and a lot of us went into it not knowing what marriage was all about!" Ray and Lin have survived the early start and are still happily married. "Lin is my rock," he says simply. "She holds the family together."

"Well, anyway, after I got married and my son was on the way, it dawned on me that: Hey! This thing ain't no joke, Chen!" His two brothers were already in Canada (another is in England) and a friend was about to migrate there, so Ray decided to try his luck and migrate as well. But he needed a skill. It was brother Roger who suggested that he try photography. "So I said alright—let me look into it. Lascelles Chin and I were close friends—still are—and I asked him to lend me his camera for a weekend and let me just see what it's all about. Well, I never put down the camera after that. I just fell in love with the whole thing from day one."

A correspondence course in photography left him dissatisfied, so he saved up and enrolled in the prestigious New York Institute of Photography in 1964. A year later, his immigration papers for Canada came through and he migrated with Lin and their young son, Roderick. "We chose Montreal because my brothers were at McGill. But when I got to Montreal they left!" he said laughing, "and I wasn't prepared to pull up roots and go anywhere else." Montreal became home to the Chens for the next 18 or so years, and it was there that Ray honed and polished his craft.

"One of the first things I did when I got to Canada, I said to Lin, "I'm going to buy a car...boasy now, you know!' He laughed, "I said I'm going to buy a car because I really want to know this city we've adopted. There was a used Chevrolet dealer that I'd met who said he had

one for $150, a 1957 Chevy. I bought it! How can you go wrong with $150! It had four tires, it moved and it had a nice radio! So Lin, Roderick and I used to pick up every Saturday and go driving. We drove everywhere...we drove to Toronto, to Vermont, Plattsburg, N.Y.... all over the place. We were brave you know, brave like hell!"

Over the next ten years he held a series of jobs: at a lab, processing the film of other photographers; as a technician; and as a second photographer, learning all the time, his mind absorbing everything like a sponge. It was while working as second photographer for a graphic house "doing the small jobs here and there" that he met another photographer out of New York and a designer from France, and had the opportunity to work closely with these two men. "That, I would say, moulded me in a very special way. I was exposed to the technology and to the European eye. Working with that French designer and observing his eye for things —the lighting, perspective, details—influenced me a great deal." It was the Frenchman, he says, who gave his confidence the biggest boost. "You can do it, Ray, he'd tell me. I was in the right place at the right time," he says of those days citing some of the breaks he had when he first went out on his own. Like the landlord, Mr. Feldman, who rented him his first studio and who said, "here is your key, Ray. Pay me when you have the money". Like his friend and fellow photographer, Bob Fisher, who had the studio downstairs from Ray's. "My studio was empty—I had one so-so 35mm camera—and Bob had his equipment, but he said 'Ray, when you get a job, we'll move the equipment upstairs and when you're finished we'll move it back down,' and that's how we started." He laughs uproariously now, but it meant a lot to him then, and he's never forgotten it.

"I didn't develop my own style until the late 70s, early 80s, during the anti-Vietnam war protests. That's when I really started to gel in my own particular way." That style has won him a number of awards from such prestigious organizations as the Graphic Club, the Art Directors Club of Toronto, and the Publicité Club de Montreal. His work has appeared in several influential publications such as the *Art Directors Index to Photographers* (Rotovision, Switzerland), *Creative Source* (Wilcord Publications, Canada), *Chatelaine* and *Nous* magazines. He has undertaken major assignments throughout the world for Canada's largest corporations and government agencies: the Government of Quebec, Ontario's Department of Tourism, Air Canada, Alcan, Master Card, Bell Canada, Grand Marnier, Hilton Canada, Imperial Tobacco and the Royal Bank of Canada are among many in his impressive portfolio.

But his most important personal project to date, and probably the most emotionally satisfying, has been his two books on Jamaica. In three years of travelling around the island, criss-crossing it in every mode of transportation, he achieved the fulfilment of a lifelong dream. *Jamaica – The Land & the People* was photographed and published by Ray in 1984. "I wanted to show the world that there is more than white sandy beaches and palm trees to Jamaica. I wanted these photos to project the natural beauty of the land and the warm hospitality of its people. This is the true Jamaica," he insists. One book could not encompass all the diversity of this ever-changing island and its people, however, So on March 18, 1993, his second photographic essay, *Jamaica – the Beauty & the Soul of the Land We Love* was launched at the Contemporary Arts Centre, Liguanea.

An emotional man who is reticent about himself, Ray is quite open about his passionate love for his country. "I wanted to give something back to the island that first gave me the inspiration to become a photographer," he said. "And this was the only way I knew how to express my feelings about my country.

Anyone who has seen either of these books will easily recognise the beauty, pride, warmth and love inherent in his personal tributes. Sir Philip Sherlock said it best in his message to Ray at the launching of the second in the Jamaica series. "Unabashed, unashamed, unhesitatingly, unequivocally and all the other words signifying certainty and spontaneous enthusiasm stand with me when I say 'this is the best picture book that I have seen or known of."

So what's next? "I would love to do other countries, but I want my Jamaican operation to run smoothly first. I have to be here to guide it and make sure it runs well, then from there I can venture out". The Jamaican operation to which he refers is the publishing company he set up to publish his *Jamaica* books, as well as postcards and posters of his work. Called Periwinkle Publishers (Ja.) Ltd., it was established in May 1986, and, as well as Ray's work, they produce brochures and material of other organizations. Ray commutes between Jamaica and Canada, where there is a subsidiary company, Periwinkle Inc. He's an artist, a businessman and a perfectionist; a man with a thousand items on his agenda, and he's seldom still. "It's not only me who does this commuting bit you know; a lot of Jamaicans do it—to Toronto, to Washington, Atlanta, New York, Miami...Lin is always asking me 'when are you going to stop, Ray? When are you going to stop?'" Does she want you to retire? Deep sigh. "No—she wants me to come home (Toronto)...to come a yard," he says.

His heart is in Toronto where his family lives and Ray's "rock" and lifelong mate, Lin. His heart is also deeply attached to his country, Jamaica. And then there are all those other places he wants to photograph. It could be a while before Ray Chen stops running.

ORIGINALLY PUBLISHED JULY 1993

NOTICE
DONT WALK HERE
A RASSCLOTH
COWS • DONKEYS
GOATS AND OTHER
ANIMALS WILL BE SHOT

Walter Chin
Still Waiting For His Big Break

MARC GOODMAN

There's a Yiddish word, haimish, that means unpretentious, warm, friendly—someone you can let your hair down around. It's easily applied to fashion photographer Walter Chin. It is a quality that came in particularly handy at his circumcision a few years ago. Chin, a Chinese Jamaican, had based himself in Toronto and married a Jewish woman. He set about converting to Judaism, with its years of study of Hebrew and the religion. Then, one day, came the circumcision.

"I was in my 20s. It was done in a hospital, with local anesthetic. I had, like three rabbis there. It was embarrassing." He pauses, and amends that. "It was really weird." Now three smaller Chins go to Hebrew school three times a week. "Sometimes they ask, 'Why are we Jewish?' I say, 'Go ask your mother.' I tell them I'll make it easier for them—I'll join a Reform synagogue, so they'll only go two times a week," he laughs.

This haimischer mensch (nice guy), now living in the leafy New York suburb of Scarsdale, has the rarest of reputations: as a man of humour and informality in the high fashion world of oversize egos and politicking divas. Another photographer notes, "Big fashion photographers make tons of money and are surrounded by stunning models who will do anything to get in these magazines. They have heads bigger then this room. Walter's just a normal and incredibly unique guy." A magazine editor concurs, "Working with Walter—it's just a Zen-like experience."

Indeed, even in Manhattan's bustle, Chin seems like he's never been off the island. "Cho, man, I'm too old for this fly-and-shoot thing," he kisses his teeth-referring to a trek to Paris to photograph Hugh Grant for *Vogue Homme*. "Who is Hugh Grant?!" he demands in mock complaint to Ernesto, his assistant of six years. We are sitting at a fashionably stainless-steel table in Studio 5 of Industria, the hottest of New York photo studios. A block away, jowly Teamsters are ripping up the jammed West Side Highway with jackhammers, but you'd never know it looking out over this tranquil, three-lined Greenwich Village street. Tomorrow Chin and his team jet to Paris to shoot übermodel Eva Herzigova for *French Vogue* during the photo frenzy surrounding the spring fashion shows, but today as a favour he's photographing a 'makeover' segment of *Allure*. He is waiting for the stylists to finish up on the amateur 'models' who have come to New York from around the country to be given a little big-city glamour. The only sounds are the bossa nova that seeps from JBL speakers hug on the high white walls and the click-click of Kelli, a willowy *Allure* assistant editor, walking around the cavernous room like a languid giraffe in clingy grey cashmere. Ernesto fields a constant stream of calls from magazine editors and Chin's Paris agent.

Occasionally he will pass the phone to Chin, who will look at him with a pained expression. "Do I have to? Talk to them nuh!"

Chin—who looks twenty years younger than his 41 years—grew up in Montego Bay and went to Cornwall College. ("I love shooting in MoBay. I stay at Round Hill and photograph in that area, because it's beautiful and I know if well.") After O-Levels he headed to Toronto, ultimately studying photography and film at Ryerson University. At first, like most budding photographers, he served an apprenticeship. One day, Chin met legendary photographer Richard Avedon. "I said, 'I'm going to be like you." He said, 'Great.'" Chin laughs. When Chin's mentor balked at photographing a part of a campaign for the hometown baseball Blue Jays, Chin stepped in—and into his first break.

In three years he was at the peak of Canadian commercial photography, which is why his wife then insisted they leave. "Well, you can't go straight to New York. So we went to Paris." In the French capital, also the home of Jamaican art photographer Nigel Scott, Walter Chin found himself starting from scratch. "I didn't get work for a whole year. I really bonded with my wife and child then." However, Chin became fast friends with Fouli Elia, French Elle's famed creative director. In the tradition of Broadway stars who let their understudies go on for them to give them their break, Elia pretended to be sick for one job. "I was nervous as hell," remembers Chin. "But they loved my stuff."

In the go-go '80s *French Elle* was at the top of its game, magically breaking all the major new modelling talent from Stephanie Seymour to Claudia Schiffer. "I did Claudia's first pictures. It was a lingerie shoot, she was 14!" He had known Linda Evangelista at 17 in Canada, and Naomi Campbell at 14, and before long he was shooting everyone from Gerard Depardieu to Christopher Lambert as well. "Back then, the last '80s, was the greatest time. They used to fly me to New York just for the day on the Concorde. People don't have that kind of money anymore," he sighs wistfully. But after three years at fever pitch, the Chins had had enough. Also, Chin adds, "We felt that there was anti-Semitism in France. When my landlord came up I had to hide the menorah and everything else!" Besides, there was bigger photography fish to fry—in New York.

Today Walter Chin has photographed for every major fashion magazine in the world, as well as for publications like *Vanity Fair, GQ, Details* and *Interview*. He had a one-man show at a Dusseldorf gallery last year. His subjects include Maya Angelou, Annie Lennox, Susan Sarandon, Jeff Goldblum, Demi Moore, Sugar Ray Leonard, Aidan Quinn, Glenn Close and "Sandra...what's her name?" (An assistant helps: "Bullock.") Brooke Shields appears in *Vanity Fair* in character as a 1940s Vassar co-ed. Matthew Modine, in what looks like a leopard skin boa, has a crazed look and the scuff of a homeless person in a *Vogue L'Uomo* spread. Chin has done at least 35 of the very lucrative ad campaigns photographers salivate after, for everyone from Donna Karan to Absolut Vodka to Neiman Marcus to Tiffany to Valentino. "I do editorial work (the less-money-making magazine photo spreads) to keep my name out there. I really love doing the ad series. "Chanel was won over when, at a shoot, Chin walked in on the wife of one of the company's directors in a dressing room. "She was trying clothes on, and she was just stunning. I said, 'Are you the model?' Next week I was booked! That's how I bought my house." Chanel's luxe image, Chin remarks, runs rather true to life within its own company. "We were staying at a place in Cap D'Antibes in the South of France that starts at about $1000 a night. One day, the Chanel director told the chauffeur to wash the Mercedes—and pointed the guy to the case of Evian in the trunk."

What are those incredible superwhatevers like in person, anyway? Chin says, "They're nice to us. I really love Christy Turlington; she's such a nice person. The younger ones are different," he says, pointing in a magazine spread of pale, emaciated, strung-out girls. "They're into being hip, getting noticed, taking drugs. They're making $10,000 a day. They come on the set stoned but it doesn't matter because that's the look. Some of them do it to get that look, which is sick." Chin flips quickly through an *Allure*. "But the magazines are going back to a fresh, clean look now because people don't buy that s—t."

Near the dressing area Chin's bear-like agent Marek watches a Dallas management consultant get made up for her fifteen minutes of fame in *Allure*. He points out, "Walter has an incredible ability to work with problems and with people. Look at this job," he gestures. "It's not glamourous. Everyone can shoot an easy subject. It takes an artist to shoot a beautiful picture of something that's hard to photograph."

Chin crosses a taupe, narrow-trousered leg and tries to explain his meteoric rise. "People said 'You won't make it. You won't be like Avedon or the others.' I just said. 'I'm going to do this.' I had tunnel vision. I always thought: 'I can do better'." He hints at the attitude that's earned him the reputation as fashion's most stand-up guy. "I'm just not in competition with anyone, except myself. The biggest photographers are mostly very competitive. You're not allowed to watch them work because they think you'll steal their techniques. But technique is nothing. It's how you deal with people, and the content of your pictures. We all photograph the same subjects. Avedon told me, 'Get inspiration from others—and then do what you believe. Do your own thing'." However, don't believe the restless Chin doesn't feel the competition keenly. "This business is transient, trendy, for young people. If you relax, you're finished," he worries. "The big guys—(fashion photographers) Patrick Demarchelier, Arthur Elgort—they were working while I was in school." In a remark that would make many a struggling shooter choke on her cat food dinner, Chin insists, "I'm still waiting to get my big break."

The agreeable Walter Chin certainly has no illusions about the nature of the business. "People don't care—they're only interested in what you can produce for them." The point was driven home recently when, in a freak storm, a tree fell on Chin in his car in the driveway, knocking him unconscious. "They were calling me in the hospital: 'Hey, man, where are you? When are you coming to do this job?" Chin says his family has been the most important reality check in the fickle world of fashion. "Everyone else lives in this world—after the shoot they party with the same people, talk about business... I have to have more dimensions to my life. When I was younger I'd get really stressed out working. Now all I think about is going home, and cycling. Having my family is the best thing that ever happened to me." Chin's status in the industry gives him a little more leeway to decide the shape of his life. "You want me for a job? You come here to New York.' My kids are seven, eight—in a couple of years, they won't want to hang out with me any more. This is the nurturing time." Chin indeed cycles 50 miles each morning, and when the weather gets cold, he heads to the knee-deep powder snow of Utah to ski. "My agent gets mad at me," he allows. The boyish Chin wags a finger after a departing visitor, smiling mischievously. "You're young," he grins. "But life is short, man."

ORIGINALLY PUBLISHED FEBRUARY 1997

Amador Packer
A Man of Vision

ASHLEY GAMBRILL

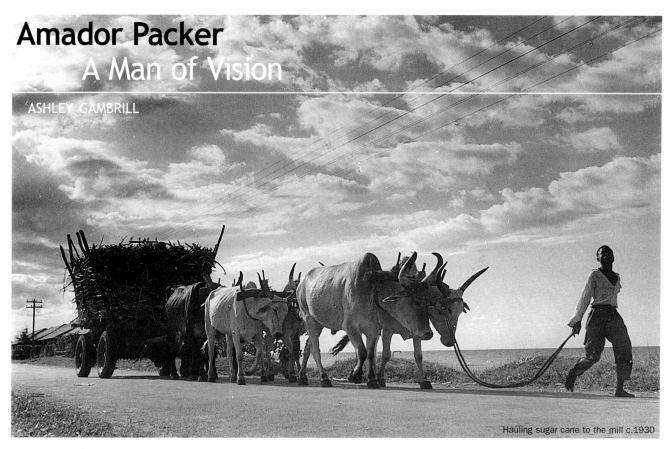

Hauling sugar cane to the mill c.1930

On a desolate country road, a lone herd of Indian cattle, Mysore, pull a ladened sugar-cane cart while up ahead walks a young disenchanted boy, 'the leading cow-head,' the lowest form of labour; behind a veil of trees, an old cut-stone bridge spans a quiet river, its ornate iron lamp-posts, symmetrically placed, have lit the way for many a passing traveller for over a hundred years; a bird's-eye view of a picturesque rural settlement, a place called Amen Corner, which boasts three small churches clustered together....

Scenes of Jamaica that pass unnoticed before us, which have been captured on film by the master of photography, Amador Packer. His portfolio is as varied as it is impressive. Recording images for over fifty years, each is a glimpse of everyday life, whether it be a scenic landscape, still-life or an informal portrait.

Now, 84 years old, he is retired from a profession he truly loved and one that taught him a lot: "I learnt about people in all their vanities," he says, reflecting over the many years, and the many faces that have been before his camera. Amador, a tall imposing man, sits at ease on his patio and lights up a long cigar. Pausing for thought he begins his story. He talks about the early days, the war years, the bustle of downtown Kingston. He recalls the names of giants in their field—skilled surgeons, brilliant intellectuals, powerful politicians, foreign dignitaries, assorted socialities and generations of long-standing Jamaican families. He talks about a way of life in Jamaica, a bygone era, events that made history. Amador is a marvellous story-teller. He likes to tell a story, not explain it. "That's why I like talking to old people," he says, "they know about these things."

Amador's photography career started somewhat late in life. After spending several years in Cuba as a young man, he returned to Jamaica and did "all sorts of things", before eventually settling down as a dry goods salesman. His photography started with snap-shots. His interest grew and he found himself reading everything he could on the subject, and experimenting. One of the first things he discovered was that a lot of people liked photography, but photography didn't like a lot of people. Photography liked Amador, and the people liked his work even more. This prompted him to open his first studio. In a building on the corner of Harbour Street and King Street, in the heart of downtown Kingston, he set up business. Many questioned his timing, some

Mysore cattle

End of the rafting day on the Rio Grande

even discouraged him. These were the war years, the economy was slow; "times hard" were the words on everybody's lips. But Amador was not daunted: "Anytime is the right time" was his motto. "As a young man I used to wonder how one could ever get started in life. But what I came to realize was that there is always space for you. It's a progression—the giants get older and the young ones come up and take their place."

Every photo studio in the 40's had at least two or three retouchers. The camera couldn't lie, but the hands of a skillful retoucher could. "People wanted to see their faces smooth and nice with all the lines and warts removed." So, it was unusual one day when a mother walked into the studio with her 20 year-old son. "No retouching," she firmly instructed. She was sending him off to war, and faced with the reality that he may never return, she wanted to remember him just the way he was. Amador dealt with many personalities, who after a while he came to recognise instantly and he quickly learned how to handle them with finesse. Among them were the 'doting mothers', who would come in and fuss around their children before the camera. "One young man, also going off to war, came in with his mother to have his portrait taken. The mother fussed around straightening his tie, combing his hair, brushing his jacket. Then suddenly she stopped and ordered, "Wait. I soon come." She dashed out of the studio to Times Store across the road, and returned minutes later with a jar of pomade and proceeded to slick down her son's hair. The boy was as mad as hell. He was a real "mama's boy"—he must have been glad he was going off to war," says Amador with a half-smile.

Photography has, over the decades, made many technical advances. In the early years photographers used cumbersome, large-format cameras and heavy tripods. You stood up by a wooden chair and the photographer instructed "Don't move! Don't move!" You froze for a second or two, staring wide-eyed at the camera. Lenses were slow, film even slower. When it was all over, you felt as though a pair of invisible clamps had been removed from behind your head. These were the rules of the game, but Amador always looked for something different. He shot more with artistic intention and a keen graphic sense for composition. He tried to break away from the rigid guidelines imposed by the limits of film. The work that emerged bore his stamp of originality. On a family portrait assignment he would urge 'Let the children play'. Oblivious to the camera, he would capture their innocence. "Don't bother to dress up the boys," he advised mothers, "just comb their hair." Little boys always feel unhappy when you bathe and dress them up. The girls, on the other hand loved to dress up. They loved the frilly dresses and the ribbons."

His assignments were many, some highly unusual. "One woman wanted me to photograph her dead husband. In all their years together she never had a photograph of him. I was just learning photography, and like a damned fool went to photograph the corpse. I had no flash. It was a disaster. I never got paid for the job. Ever since then I have refused such requests. I tell people they should remember loved ones as they were when they were alive."

Amador has photographed hundreds of weddings. "I enjoyed weddings. Lots of good champagne, although the speeches are always long," he says jokingly. "There was one I'll never forget," he laughs out loud at the memory. "It was nearly fifty years ago. I went up to the bride's house and did the usual pre-wedding photographs—the bridesmaids fixing the veil, the bride's mother fussing around...then I jumped on a tram and made my way to the St. Andrew Parish Church for the wedding ceremony. In those days you couldn't take pictures in the church—these days photographers are all on the altar. Anyway, when I arrived there was neither bride, nor groom. The bride had driven up, but the groom had not yet arrived, so she was told to drive around town with the hope that he would eventually show up

Edna Manley with sculpture

"Granny" from above Hermitage

at the church. Well, she went to Hope Gardens, and probably out to Rockfort. Another wedding was scheduled, so we all waited outside the church. After a very long time the groom and his best man arrived, both completely drunk. It was hilarious. The wedding still took place. It was the best."

He has photographed many an important man, but Amador has his own views: "It is said that no man is a hero to his valet; well no man is a hero to me!" He has photographed the good, and the bad. The pompous, downright obnoxious "clothed in a little authority"; and the civil and obliging. "I always felt that public figures owe it to the public to have a good photograph—but there are those who are not photography-oriented. Sometimes you felt you were bothering them, they were too busy. You had to rush in, get on with it, and tip-toe out. They were flash-bulb formal shots, you did the best you could."

Other assignments really roused his interest, and he had a strong liking for the medical photography. "I used to take photographs of major operations for medical records. Whether it was heart surgery or a complete lung resection—you had better be good the first time, there were no second chances. I would prepare myself before the operation. The day before I would familiarise myself with the operating theatre—check lighting, angles and where I would stand. You couldn't walk and jump around like at a wedding." Amador describes the operations with a doctor's clinical detachment. As a layman it did not bother him—"I was there to do a job. I had no time to become emotionally involved." These assignments were often very long, sometimes lasting for eight hours.

Sir Alexander Bustamante

Most of Amador's work has been in startling black and white. When the novelty of colour came after the war, the floodgates opened for photographers. Amador branched out into photography for advertising and fashion and travel magazines, locally and overseas.

Today, as he looks on his profession he muses: "People no longer dress up and go take pictures on a Sunday afternoon. And anyone with a camera around his neck will call himself a photographer. But ask him about 'hypo' (a technical process all film has to go through), or ask him to go make a print..." He laughs at the thought. "In the early days we had just the bare-bone camera and lens, and it was the ingenuity of the photographer that made a good picture, not the sophistication of the equipment. Nowadays you even have 'talking cameras'—it will tell you "too dark" if there is not enough light, or "load camera—no film"—how can you go wrong?" he asks. But there is a subtle difference between the amateur and the professional that puts them poles apart. Amador sums it up: "The professional takes pictures with his eye; the amateur with his camera."

ORIGINALLY PUBLISHED NOVEMBER 1991

SKYWRITINGS COVER
November 1993
A proud Merlene Ottey after winning the 200m Women Finals at the World Track and Field Championships in Stuttgart Germany, August 1993.

Glory Days at Sabina Park

RAYMOND SHARPE

Brisbane has its "Gabba," where Australia and the West Indies starred in Test cricket's first tie over 30 years ago. London boasts of the stately Lord's in St. John's Wood, the accepted headquarters of cricket where the late George Headley, a Jamaican, recorded an unprecedented century in each innings for the West Indies against England in 1939.

Christchurch in New Zealand prides itself in Lancaster Park, its oldest Test centre, dating back to New Zealand's inaugural Test against England in 1930. And in St. John's, Antigua, the Recreation Ground provides an experience of a lifetime with every break during a Test match providing the cue for pulsating rhythms for Chickie's Hi-Fi and those hilarious moments from Antigua's two cricket's clowns, Gravy and Mayfield.

And wherever Test cricket is played, be it in Melbourne, Australia where a record 90,000 watched one day's play during the fifth and final Test of the 1960-61 Australia-West Indies rubber, or Eden Gardens in Calcutta or the Dacca Stadium in Pakistan, there is always some event to remember.

Kingston's equivalent to these celebrated and distinguished cricket venues is Sabina Park or plain "Bina," the home of Jamaica's international cricket, where a local idol Collie Smith scored a first appearance Test century in a short-lived career; where another West Indian legend Sir Garfield Sobers accumulated Test cricket's highest score of 365 not out; and where Australia played their first Test match on West Indian soil in 1955.

Present generation cricket fans will recall that it was here that Michael Holding, the Rolls Royce of fast bowlers, almost single-handedly scared the daylights out of Bishen Bedi's Indian cricketers in 1976 as they surrendered to the mighty West Indies.

Cricket historians will remember it as the venue of the timeless Test, the first Test played there and fourth of England's inaugural tour of the Caribbean in 1930. It was abandoned as a draw after seven days' action and two days' washout and brought the following comment from cricket's authoritative *Wisden*: "This timeless Test was abandoned as a draw when rain prevented play on the last two days before England's voyage home. It set records, all subsequently beaten, for the longest match, highest total, highest individual score and the highest individual match aggregate. West Indies appointed their fourth captain of the rubber. England's Andy Sandham, 39 years old, batted 10 hours for the highest score of his career (325). George Headley (223) in West Indies second innings, was the youngest player to score a double century in Tests until Pakistan's Javed Miandad did so at the age of 19 years and 141 days."

But Sabina Park has not always hosted cricket and its illustrious playmakers who paraded their skills. It is a cricket ground first and foremost, but there were times when Sabina Park was a place for all seasons and for various types of events. It has been home for the game with that little red ball and bats—and wickets, slips and gullies and silly points in the vernacular of cricket.

It has been the major playing venue for the bigger ball (football) and it has accommodated a variety of events, from rodeos to big-time boxing to jazz concerts and basketball exhibitions. World boxing champions have squared off in its rings and Olympic champions have powered their way on its grass track. Some of the island's political and business giants have played ball or run around its tracks. They include former premier and National Hero Norman Manley who, as a Jamaica College student in 1911, ran a record 10 seconds flat 100 metres at the Inter-Secondary Schools Championship, a mark which was to remain on the books for 40 years.

Sabina Park ranks among the smallest of the world's cricket centres, with the Blue Mountain range standing handsomely tall to the northeast and the glistening waters carving an arc on the south from the causeway through Kingston Harbour to Port Royal and the Palisadoes. The cream of the cricketing talent from England, Australia, Pakistan, India, New Zealand and more recently South Africa, has been paraded within its boundaries.

In its earliest years the layout was consistent with most West Indian cricket grounds, the entire playing area surrounded by stands. Today the sprawling George Headley Stand to the south, with its executive and private boxes on the upper level, reserved and unreserved seats on the lower levels, has replaced most of the original seating areas. There remains the uncovered stand to the east, providing a kaleidoscope of umbrellas to offset the sweltering sun rays. And to the north are those two notorious bounds (terraces) with their popular and most critical and authoritative observers.

Before the construction of the National Stadium in 1962, Sabina Park was the only real sports centre in Jamaica, and indeed the English-speaking Caribbean to accommodate night-time sports. For many years the tall metal pylons holding the flood-lights at the four corners of the ground provided a landmark as air travellers began their descent into the Palisadoes Airport, as it was then, or the Norman Manley International Airport, as it is known today.

Those giant pylons are no more, having been transferred to a new location, Jarrett Park in the tourist mecca of Montego Bay; and major sporting events have found a new city base at the National Stadium.

(OPPOSITE PAGE) James Adams at a match against India in 1994. (ABOVE) Brian Lara. (BOTTOM LEFT) An anxious fan waiting for Brian Lara to look his way.

Sabina Park is the home of the Kingston Cricket Club, one of the oldest sports clubs on the island and one which has turned out more West Indian cricketers than any other Jamaican club. Numbered among them are a former captain, Franz Alexander, and a former president of the West Indies Cricket Board of Control, Allan Rae.

Cricket at Sabina Park, or anywhere else, lacks the trappings and "colour support" of say the NFL Superbowl, with its marching bands and platoons of cheering belles.

But cricket and other popular sporting events at Sabina Park were not without their characters and personalities in years gone by. A day at Sabina Park would never be complete without Lennie and his one-man act. A natural mimic, he used the breaks to imitate the best of the time, from cricket's Garfield Sobers, to boxing's Muhammad Ali, football's immortal Pele, faxing dismissals, shifting punches and landing kayos, scoring the most spectacular of goals, and missing the simplest of ones. At times the joke was on him, like when he got "bowled" by a full toss, or conceded a penalty while halting an opponent's run towards the goal.

And Sabina Park was not just cricket and boxing and football and track and field. During the 1950s and onwards when promoters like Lucien Chen were helping to establish Kingston as one of the hemisphere's popular fight centres, international cards with former world champions, world raters and the cream of the crop were monthly features at Sabina. Chen recalls the legendary world heavyweight champion Joe Louis "coming here in the forties for a Stephen Hill-promoted exhibition and knocking out a policeman by the name of Haughton."

There was even a rodeo at Sabina Park with its kicking horses and "wild bulls," one of which "Big Sid" was tamed by a buxom Jamaican woman and was later bought by a former prime minister and National Hero, Sir Alexander Bustamante.

The original Harlem Globetrotters, with the incredible Goose Tatum played basketball there and unloaded their bag of tricks, while jazz legends Dave Brutbeck and Paul Desmond performed under the stars at the peak of their careers.

But, despite its colourful past as an arena of colourful entertainment and sporting spectacles, Sabina Park today is best known as the home of Jamaican cricket and one of the Caribbean's foremost international cricketing venues.

ORIGINALLY PUBLISHED MARCH 1993

Michael Holding First Class Cricketer

SUZANNE FRANCIS-BROWN

In his cricketing heyday, the media often tagged fast bowler Michael Holding 'the world's speediest....' Holding's response: "What you have to pay attention to is what you go out on the field and do is your own performance. You don't think about the labels other people give you."

Underscoring the point, he recalls a time in the late 1970s when there was some discussion as to whether Holding himself, or Jeff Thompson of Australia, was the world's fastest bowler.

"During the Kerry Packer era, we were playing a match, he for Australia, I for the West Indies and I went out there this particular day and said I was going to show them who is faster. I didn't bowl well; I was trying to bowl too fast. That's when I said to myself—forget that! You're supposed to be doing your best for the West Indies."

Holding's best was very good indeed, contributing significantly to the pre-eminence enjoyed internationally by the West Indies cricket team and playing his part both nationally—with the Jamaican team and in the English country competition where he represents Derbyshire.

Born in Kingston, the last of four children, Holding's was a close and sport-oriented family. The young Michael developed an early love of sport.

He remembers his first representative game: "I was nine or ten, and we played this cricket match at Red Hills Oval, behind Dunrobin, where I lived. The youths in the area, we had a team. I don't think we had a name for the team. But we used to play against other teams in the area. They still have a team down there."

Following in his father's footsteps, he joined Melbourne Club in the days when it was changing from a football to a mainly cricket club.

At school—Kingston College—he balanced a love of mathematics with a total enthusiasm for almost any sport: basketball, table tennis, athletics, cricket and football.

"I represented the school at cricket and football; and after a while, just found myself doing more cricket," he says. The change taking place at Melbourne supported this inclination, and he was soon representing the club at country matches.

"At that stage I was doing reasonably well", he say. "Nothing to say that in the days to come I would play with the West Indies; but I was pleased with what I was doing at the time, so I just continued to play more cricket. For me it was always bowling, but not fast bowling," he adds.

"I started off trying to bowl off-breaks; then I did a bit more fast bowling—not really fast at the stage. You take a long run and try and bowl fast. Then, eventually, I was bowling fast."

He characterizes his move towards regional representation as a step-by-step process—playing for Kingston College, then youth cricket for Jamaica, then Shell Shield, and then on to the West Indies team.

"Even when I was going through the process I still really didn't assume that I would be playing with the West Indies team. I played cricket because I loved it," Holding says. " I never ever saw myself becoming a professional cricketer."

What he saw himself doing was something involving mathematics a subject he loved at school. Indeed, his first job was in the then Barclays Bank Computer Centre; and it was only after the Kerry Packer era of 1977–1980 made professional cricket lucrative, that he left computer programming behind.

It was the year 1975, and Holding was 21 years old, when the selectors called him to West Indies team for the first time.

"When I first got selected for the West Indies, it was a great feeling," he recalls. "As a youth my parents loved cricket. They don't just love it because I play it—because they have loved it before I even thought of playing cricket. I used to try and sit up with them to listen when the West Indies was playing cricket in Australia and so on.

"When I realized that I was going to be a part of all that, it was great because I never knew that I would play cricket with people like Lance Gibbs, Keith Boyce, Clive Lloyd, and Garfield Sobers. Those are great names that you hear people talk about but never think of yourself in that sort of atmosphere. So it was great when I first started."

His first series was in Australia: "It was a disastrous tour; we got beaten 5–1", he says. "I don't think Australia is the best place to start your career," he adds, reflectively. "It's a very hard place when it comes to cricket. The Australians can be friendly off the field, but out on the cricket field, it's like war."

Looking back on his first-class career, which spans some 13 years—eight of them as a full time, professional cricketer, Holding muses over a question as to which series was his best.

"I can't really name one and say it was the best", he says. "I've had some series when I have been very successful, like 1981-82 versus Australia in Australia. I got 24 wickets in three Test matches—an average of eight per Test. It's not every day that sort of thing happens. But we drew the series, one all.

"I like to think of a series when the West Indies has done well; not just myself. I think one series where that is concerned was the 1976 tour of England when the West Indies beat England 3-0 and I got 28 wickets in the series. I missed one Test match, played four, and got 28.

"The other series was in 1979-80 against Australia in Australia—the very first time a West Indies team had ever been to Australia and

beaten Australia. Every time the West Indies had ever been to Australia we'd come back with our tails between our legs. This time we beat them 2-0 in a three-match series. It was great. I think it was the very first time I ever lost my senses drinking champagne."

Holding left the West Indies team in February 1987. He had actually wanted to quit after the 1984 series against England, in which he played four Test matches, got 15 wickets and was not bowling as he wished because he could not maintain his fitness.

"With the itinerary the West Indies has, it is difficult to find time to train properly—weight training, a lot of running. It's that sort of extensive thing over two to three months that you need because you have to be able to bowl those overs when the captain wants you to."

Asked by the West Indies Board to stay on, after a tour off to get back in training, Holding played two or three more series before announcing his retirement from the team.

He has also forecast the end of his first class career: September 1989; after a last season representing Jamaica in regional competition, and a final year with Derbyshire.

"February '89 I'm 35 and I don't see myself trying to go much past that," he says." Fast bowling is a very tedious thing—very strenuous; and I don't think people should try to prolong their careers too much, as fast bowlers. It can get embarrassing at times."

He will, of course, continue to play cricket. A member of Melbourne Cricket Club for some 27 years, Holding expects to be active there. But his main concentration, for the time being, will be on going into business for himself.

Depending on his level of success there, he may be able to pursue a long-time wish to do some umpiring—starting with schoolboy cricket and moving up to the top grade—and also get into cricket administration.

"I want to settle down, have a successful business—bring up a family the way I would like to bring them up—and help as many youngsters in Jamaica, or wherever, as I can."

He underlines the importance of involving as many people as possible, in sport—noting that it helps to provide alternative opportunities for youth who have not had a lot of academic success.

"Cricket—because it's the only thing we do together in the Caribbean—has got the farthest. Everybody knows about the West Indies team, the best in the world for umpteen years, and a lot of young men have achieved a lot out of life because of it.

"I think the more people get involved in cricket, and sport in general, the better. Because if you have young men active—using energy to play cricket or other sport—it might stop a few people going the wrong way.

ORIGINALLY PUBLISHED FEBRUARY 1989

Welcome to "Cuddy" Country

A grateful nation celebrates Courtney Walsh's wicket record

BARBARA GLOUDON

Dear Cousin in Foreign:

Chile—watta Jubilee! Whatta excitement! You remember when the Reggae Boyz made it to the World Cup in France? You forget how you nearly mash up the line between Foreign and JA. with your screaming and hollering? And do you recall how your neighbour threatened to turn you in to Immigration because you were adding insult to injury by yelling through the window "Jamdown a de bess to fowl foot."

Apparently you've chosen to forget but I haven't, which is why I didn't call the other day when the whole of the Rock was skanking to the Cuddy Beat. Who is Cuddy? You see that ... you been living abroad too long, chile. Cuddy, for the information of you and others who've been away too long, is none other His Excellency the Honourable Courtney Andrew Walsh, O.J. Ambassador Extraordinaire, taker of 435 Test wickets, entrant in the Guinness Book of Records, artical master and hero of a grateful Jamaican people, long in need of some good news, hungry for happiness.

Now, the story of said Courtney aka Cuddy, is no simple tale of bat and ball. Indeed, nothing about cricket is simple, especially in recent times when the West Indies seemed fated to be beaten by every team in the whole wide world. When I consider some of the teams that beat us over the past year, I have to agree with Uncle Joe: "Ashes cold, dawg sleep in deh," which being translated for the benefit of your stoosh dawtas who claim sey dem don't understand Jamaican talk: "In adversity, liberty will be taken."

Anyway, just when it seemed that we'd been down so long that it was beginning to look like Up, along came Mr. Walsh and a new-spirited West Indies team, led by another son of JA. Mr. James "Jimmy" Adams. Some will tell you that Zimbabwe, the team which we beat, was not exactly Goliath to our David. Nuh mind that, chile, we beat them all the same, from Queens Park in Port of Spain to Sabina Park in Kingston. Two Tests two victory for West Indies.

But the sweetest part of all was the "Cuddy" story. You see, an Indian bowler name Kapil Dev set world record, taking 434 Test wickets. Our Mr. Walsh set out to break that record. Now, you have to understand that Mr. "Cuddy" did not have it easy. Would you believe that at one time, the man reached the level of captain of the West Indies and when he hit a slump, they (or Dem, as Uncle Joe would say) chase him from the work? Another time, he was unceremoniously dropped, even while he was the top wicket taker.

Did he proclaim "smaddy set sinting pon me?" (as in "I have been cursed"). Did he say "bad luck worse than obeah?" ("Perchance the gods have turned against me"). No Cousin. No way. Cuddy put his head down, endured the slings and arrows of outrageous fortune, shape up and come back to bowl out dem blouse. Little by little he moved towards Kapil Dev's record, one wicket at a time. And so it came to pass that on the green field of Sabina Park, on a sunny March day (while you Up So were fighting cabin fever) the one Mr. Walsh not only equalled Mr. Kapil Dev's record, he surpassed it. Four hundred and thirty five in the eye.

Chile party time! Even Clarice whose face, most times, is in a permanent screw (as Bredda Bob Marley used to sing)...even she was seen laughing and dropping a foot. The excitement at Sabina was one thing. The "ring ackee" come when the whole town turn out for a motorcade which swept through Kingston streets. School children, reprieved from class for the day, joined in joyous jubilee, with bicycle man leading the way. Gray head and bald head and locks head and extension-weavey head danced in the sunlight while Mr. Walsh and his captain Mr. Adams, rode on like conquerors, but not too proud to bend down and share their fame with big and small. A grateful nation showered our man Cuddy with gifts and more gifts and even land to build his dream house. Guinness added his name to the Book of Records and we all felt good.

It's not just because our man broke the wickets record why we celebrate. It's not even because the West Indies won at last. It is because in "Cuddy" Walsh, people saw the embodiment of persistence, of integrity, of decency. Not to mention humility. In all the excitement, in all the honour and the tributes, the Hon. Mr. Walsh stood, cool, calm and collected, visiting his old schools (Melrose All-Age, Excelsior High), showing respect to his mother (Ms. Joan Wollaston) and sharing the limelight with teammates. Man in the streets accorded him the highest accolade the real people can give. De man nuh skin up. De man nuh boasie. Respect!

And guess what? Would you believe that Courtney Andrew Walsh was born in 1962 the year Jamaica took on Independence? According to Cousin Esmie, "If that is not a sign I don't know what is." Mr. Walsh is on record as taking the matter seriously too.

Wish you were here, chile. Next time when you come to visit, please remember that this is "Cuddy Country." Hail the man!

Yours very sincerely,
COUSIN B.
BACK A YARD

ORIGINALLY PUBLISHED JUNE 2000

Atlas

Excerpted from *A History of West Indies Cricket*

MICHAEL MANLEY

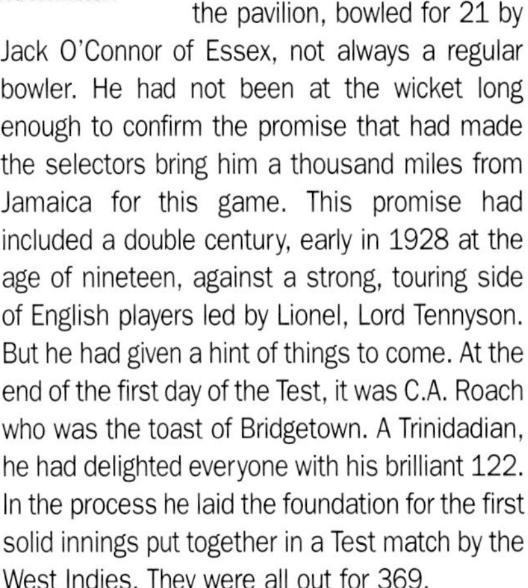

Excerpted from *A History of West Indies Cricket.*
Michael Manley

The West Indies have become a major cricketing power. But as with most other success stories, it had a beginning that was in marked contrast to the triumphs that were ahead.

The earliest West Indies Test teams were hardly equal to the challenge of the two giants of Test cricket—England and Australia.

Indeed, the West Indies had first played England in an official Test series in 1928 in England. They were not beaten so much as overwhelmed, losing all three games disastrously.

In 1929-1930, England made their first visit to the Caribbean to play the West Indies in four Test matches. The following excerpt describes the encounter and the first appearance of the young player who was to become one of the giants of the sport.

He was a compact man of barely medium height. He had the sloping shoulders often associated with boxers who can punch. He was neat, almost dapper, a somehow self-contained human being. On the cricket field his movements were precise and economical. Like many great performers, he had one feature that tended to set him apart. It was not so much as eccentricity as an idiosyncrasy. Whether batting, bowling or fielding, he always wore his sleeves buttoned at the wrist. Together with his cap at just enough of an angle to suggest a confident nature fully conscious of itself and its environment, the long sleeves completed a picture that invited attention without the slightest departure from good taste. He was black and four months short of his twenty-first birthday. His name was George Alphonso Headley.

The 1929-30 series, the second between the West Indies and England, was a close affair. The first Test was played at Kensington Oval, Bridgetown, Barbados between January 11 and 17. The West Indies won the toss and were off to a good start with 369, C.A. Roach making the first ever century for the West Indies in a Test match, 122. England replied strongly with 467. In the West Indies second innings, the hosts hit back with 384, including a superb 176 by George Headley, then the youngest player ever to score a Test century in his maiden appearance. In their second innings England were 167 for 3 at the close of play. This was the West Indies' first Test draw.

The second Test was played between February 1 and 6, at Queen's Park Oval, Port-of-Spain, Trinidad. England made 208 in their first innings with Hendren contributing 77. The West Indies replied with 254. In the second innings England made 485 for 8 declared. Thereupon, the West Indies struggled to 212, losing by 167 runs.

The third Test was played at Bourda, Georgetown, British Guiana between February 21 and 26. West Indies made 471 in their first innings, including a fine double century by Roach and 114 run out by young Headley in their first innings with Constantine and Francis bowling magnificently to take four wickets each.

In the second innings the West Indies made 290, with a second century by Headley of 112. With this century Headley became both the youngest player to score a century in each innings of a Test and to score three centuries in Test cricket. England fought back in their second innings but were eventually all out for 327 to lose by 259 runs. Constantine brought his total for the match to 9 wickets when he took 5 for 87 and was largely responsible for bowling the West Indies to their first-ever Test victory.

The fourth and final Test was played at Sabina Park, Kingston, Jamaica on April 3 and 10. This match was filled with improbabilities. England began with 849 runs in their first innings, including 325 by Andy Sandham and 149 by Leslie Ames. The West Indies' cause seemed hopeless when they replied with 286. Incredibly, England batted a second time, making 272 for 9 declared. Hendren completed a fantastic series for him with 61 in the first innings and 55 in the second. The West Indies' second innings had reached 438 for 5 when the match was abandoned because the English side had to catch the boat home. The architect of this great recovery was George Headley with 223. The series had been drawn.

The 1929-30 encounter was significant for more than the even outcome. Its place in history is assured by the deeds of George Headley. Not more than half of the Test side which had been so soundly beaten in England a few months earlier were in the team which won the toss and elected to bat at the Kensington Oval. It was the first Test match to be played in the West Indies. By lunchtime on the first day, young Headley was back in the pavilion, bowled for 21 by Jack O'Connor of Essex, not always a regular bowler. He had not been at the wicket long enough to confirm the promise that had made the selectors bring him a thousand miles from Jamaica for this game. This promise had included a double century, early in 1928 at the age of nineteen, against a strong, touring side of English players led by Lionel, Lord Tennyson. But he had given a hint of things to come. At the end of the first day of the Test, it was C.A. Roach who was the toast of Bridgetown. A Trinidadian, he had delighted everyone with his brilliant 122. In the process he laid the foundation for the first solid innings put together in a Test match by the West Indies. They were all out for 369.

Not to be outdone, the English hit back with 467, 152 of which came from the Surrey opening bat, Andy Sandham, And so the West Indies prepared to bat again. In the very first over the West Indies' E.L.G. Hoad was out, as the record shows, caught Astill bowled Calthorpe. Headley, for not the last time in his career, was promptly required to play the part of an opening bat. When he was finally out half way through the fifth day of the match, he had ignited the imagination of the entire island of Barbados not so much because he compiled a massive score, not only because he was the youngest batsman to score a Test century, but more by the manner of his doing it.

Those who saw that innings will tell you that it was a thing a joy to behold. The lightning quick footwork provided the foundation for square-cutting and hooking of the utmost authority; the deft late cut revealed the sense of timing which sets the masters apart. The drives, particularly on the off side of the wicket, which penetrated by placement rather than power, served notice that here was no mere "basher" of the ball.

Barbadians know their cricket. They were witnessing the first major statement of a genius and they responded in kind.

Headley went on to Trinidad where his scores were modest. Then at the Bourda ground in British Guiana, he became the youngest player to score a century in each innings, of a Test. Those who performed this feat are usually dubbed "immortal", a title which reflects the difficulty of the task and the likelihood that it will be remembered. Roach had made a double century in the first innings at Bourda. It was the first of its kind for the West Indies. But Headley's feat made the greater impact. Roach's runs were accumulated in dashing style. The flashing strokes outside the off-stump made him both attractive and typical. They also suggested to the knowledgeable that he benefited not a little from luck. By contrast Headley's runs seemed inevitable.

George Headley returned home at the beginning of April already a star. By April 10 he had become a hero. His 223 in the second innings saved the match for the West Indies who, by drawing the match, saved the series and earned their first draw with England, one victory each with two matches drawn. And again Headley's innings was the innings of a master.

Thus it was that before his twenty-first birthday, George Headley, born in Panama of West Indian parents away from home, became a Caribbean hero. It is true he entered the international arena against an England side below full strength. Harold Larwood had not made the tour. Neither had Maurice Tate, his partner and foil who was both fast and a master of swerve; nor Wally Hammond, who could be disconcertingly quick for an over or two. Despite these absent giants and the problems they might have posed, Headley scored his runs in a manner that set him apart. He became a symbol and was to be both the cause of hope and, at least in part, its answer.

ORIGINALLY PUBLISHED APRIL 1988

Understanding the origins of afternoon tea or... A Beginners Guide to Cricket

LINDY DELAPENHA

If you are English, then you have probably timed your Caribbean trip to coincide with the visit of the Marylebone Cricket Club, which tours the West Indies from late January to April. Marylebone is a district in London and, historically "the M.C.C." has been the ruling body of British cricket. When it plays against the West Indies the M.C.C. is called 'England', when the M.C.C. plays against Jamaica it retains is own name, Complicated? That's cricket!

However, you may be from the American continent or Europe where the word "cricket" means an insect which will make a scratchy, irritating sound as the sun goes down.

England taught the West Indies the game, but over the last two years the pupils have taught the teachers a thing or two, both on and off the field.

The West Indians' cavalier and more "showy" approach has transformed a staid Saturday afternoon village green game into a dynamic stroke-making holiday atmosphere. I believe that a mixture of English and West Indian flavours has helped to produce some very exciting fixtures. Depending on your point of view.

An English supporter will not relish boisterous and over enthusiastic crowds when his side is facing a total of 695 and in reply his side is 87 with four wickets down.

West Indian crowds are always noisy and the reaction of their opponents will entirely depend on the state of the game. As a completely neutral individual you can absorb the situation and not care one way or the other.

If you are a lover of sports then your interest will be aroused by any form of activity which brings together teams in exciting competition. If length of play counts, cricket must give you more for your money than any sport but round-the-world yacht racing. In the past it has lasted eight days, but most matched are now played from one to five days.

And many times the match ends without a result.

This attempted introduction to the game is directed at the uninitiated and if by chance you have not heard of a game which can have a team with two short legs, short fine legs or even a square leg, then your curiosity should be aroused.

The only game that one can liken it to—from an American point of view—is baseball, and even then the likeness stops at a bat, ball and players.

The rules are numerous and complex and would certainly call for several hours of flying time to explain fully.

In order to decide which side will bat first, a coin is spun which has always been thought the fairest way.

The teams wear cream flannels and white or cream shirts and white boots with spikes. It is not true that the players run for cover when it rains because they don't wish to get their cream 'togs' dirty. They just prefer to stay dry.

Each team consists of 11 players and unlike baseball two members of the batting side (usually the team winning the toss) occupy the crease of the wicket or batting strip at one time.

Batsmen can be out by being caught, bowled, leg before wicket (L.B.W.), cap falling on wicket, stumped, run out or just plain having a wicket knocked out by a well-bowled ball.

A side is out when 10 of the players have suffered any of the above fates.

Oh, I forgot to mention. There are two umpires also dressed in white apparel and who will also run for cover if it rains.

Only one of the fielding side, strangely enough, is allowed to wear gloves but definitely not for defending himself against attack from the opposing side. He is known as the wicket-keeper or stumper.

A pitch is 22 yards long, and the batsmen bat at each end with the wicket-keeper at the opposite end to the bowler. The batsmen have an area in which they should remain, whilst the ball is in play, otherwise they can be stumped or run out.

A team can decide to end its batting innings at any time by "declaring". A declaration usually comes at a total thought by the captain to be beyond the capabilities of the opponents. Each team should have two innings, but a team making a big score (maybe over 500) can force their opponents to bat twice and lose by an innings if they don't pass the score. This is known as following on. This is very strange because batting is the much nicer part of the game and you'd imagine any captain would be anxious to bat as often as he could. However, although not necessarily an English philosophy, winning seems to be more important.

There are various field placements which are standard, though having variations, such as short leg (closest to the bat on the leg side). A variation could be forward or backward short leg. There are slips, mid-ons, mid-offs, square and fine legs. In fact, if you are uninitiated, as I imagine you are, a fielding side could sound like refugees from trench warfare. Fine legs, square legs, short legs, long legs with gully and slips added for good measure.

The batsmen wear pads which protect their legs. However, as the years went by, the pads became protectors of the wickets as well as the legs. "Leg before wicket" is one way of getting out but the ball must be pitched in a certain position and must be thought in the umpire's opinion to be going to hit the wicket. The wickets or stumps, I forget to mention, are the wooden sticks sticking out of the ground, three at each end.

Incidentally, one of the main aims of the bowler (the fellow who runs up and throws the ball)—I beg your pardon—"bowls" the ball is to try and hit the stumps, thus dislodging the bails (the little tings on top of the stumps).

It is an unpardonable sin to throw the ball at the batsmen as in baseball. If it is done the umpire will call "no ball" if he sees it.

Having read this far, your appetite must be whetted by now.

Speaking of appetites, because the game is of such lengthy duration, naturally, the players will need sustenance of some kind.

For this a tea and lunch break are provided each day, making the days play - 11:00 a.m. to 1:00 p.m. (lunch), 1:40 p.m. - 3:40 p.m. (tea), 4:00 p.m. - 5:30 p.m. There are some complicated rulings about the end of the play on the last day, but to avoid "boggling" your brain further, the simplest advise I can offer you is to leave the ground when everyone else does.

Quite naturally if the players have a break for refreshments, the spectators are also entitled to one.

Your choice of menu is entirely up to you, and watching sport can work up a healthy appetite and thirst. Of course, the game is very closely associated with the English and any excuse for tea is always welcome. As a matter of fact, it is sometimes said that the English invented the game as an excuse to have tea. However, the choice of liquid refreshments is entirely yours and in Jamaica there are many substitutes for tea.

One needn't eat or drink at the intervals of course and one pastime is a quiet saunter to the wicket. This is permitted providing your intentions are not hostile. Another way to spend the break, particularly for the uninitiated, is to listen to the discussions and arguments which will inevitably take place. If the cricket is dull, this is sure to liven up your day. You will learn a lot, but not necessarily about the game. Other known pastimes are reading, just plain meditating or knitting (for the ladies of course).

Cricket can be as exciting as it can be dull, but then travelling several thousand miles to take off your clothes and roll about in the sun and sand can also be considered strange to certain people. Whichever your choice, watching a cricket match for the first time will, if nothing else, prove a fascinating experience.

ORIGINALLY PUBLISHED JANUARY 1974

Winning with the Reggae Boyz

NAZMA MULLER

For all great moments in history, there's that instant of "Where were you when it happened?" For Americans it's when JFK was shot; for Trinis, it's when the Mulimeen coup took place; and for Jamaicans it was Sunday, September 14, 1997.

Some might say there's no comparison between the tragedy of the young president's killing, or the bedlam that broke out in Port of Spain, and a measly football match.

But what a match! Lawd 'ave mercy! Every ticket was sold out as 35,000 Jamaicans—including busloads from as far as Montego Bay, and a few with Yankee accents—packed into the National Stadium in Kingston to back the Reggae Boyz in a World Cup qualifier against Costa Rica.

Who didn't hotfoot it to the Stadium from 8 o'clock in the morning (the match started at 3 p.m., eh), by bus, taxi, truck, bicycle, minibus or as one-tenth the passenger load in a car, was plastered to their TV screens by the time the show kicked off.

And I do mean *show.* Every entertainer who woulda charge an arm, a leg, and your house just to wave at a football match was there to put in their songs. From Beenie Man to Bounty Killa to Red Rat, Goofy and Hawkeye. The remixes came fast, furious and clever.

Rev. Al Miller set the crowd roaring when even he picked up the dancehall vibes and punctuated his prayers with his version of the Scare Dem Crew's tag line: "How many goals Jamaica going to score today? Many many!" The final blessing rocked the Stadium: "If Jah is on our side, why should we be afraid?" MC Jerry D had already gotten the usually Too-Cool-To-Do-Waves Jamaican crowd to do just that. Twice. It was incredible, watching section after section of the Stadium rise and fall, the ripple perfectly timed. Boy, patriotism is a hell of a thing.

Now, I've never been very impressed with Jamaica's national anthem; but when Ian Andrews belted out that baby, fists clenched over hearts and every Jamaican stood erect, heads held high as dark clouds rolled overhead.

"Jamaica, land we love..." The notes just soared in the air, creating some serious vibrations.

"Jamaica...!"

And the Stadium responded with a deep, guttural "Hurugh!"

"Jamaica...!"

"Hurugh!"

My goosepimples goosepimpled.

"Jamaica, land we love...!"

The sky shook. The cheers were deafening.

"Jah Rastafari!...Selassie I send them!" The disco stepped in with razor-precise timing and Beenie's "Foundation."

The Reggae Girlz were dancing up a storm, go-go wining to the left, and to the right while the Costa Rican media men of Deportes Reloj and Radio Monumental sat tight-lipped, stoically transmitting back home the overwhelming reggae vibes the rhumba boys had to battle. To their right, though, a Latino fan was blissfully jamming to the music, waving the Costa Rican flag to the beat.

And then the whistle blew.

The next 45 minutes were a blur of bungled passes and fumbling shots. Both teams were under tremendous pressure from the must-win situation. The roars of appreciation at the contact of a Jamaican boot on ball subsided, and beads of sweat popped plentifully on Costa Rican brows. Photographers half-heartedly raised cameras as strikers closed in on the 18-yard boxes; inevitably lowering them in disappointment.

Standing behind the Costa Rican goal, I

started to reminisce. Just two weeks before the Reggae Boyz had beaten my Trini Soca Boys 6-1 and sent them home in shame. I came back to reality to see the ball bouncing into the goal.

The screams and cheers crashed down on my ears. The stadium was in an uproar, flags flying in a frenzy. One soldier flung his beret in the air.

The Reggae Boyz were hugging each other on the field, while photographers went shutter-crazy, trying to snap them and the wildly cheering crowd at the same time. Prime Minister PJ Patterson was beaming from left to right. The Costa Ricans looked as if their grandmothers had died.

I smiled. Reaching into my back pocket I pulled out a small Jamaican flag someone had given me outside. I began to wave it. They weren't my Trini Soca Boys, but what the hell, a Caribbean team was finally on its way to the World Cup finals.

It's just as well I jumped on the bandwagon while it was at the crossroads, cuz the Reggae Boyz went to Washington and showed those Yankees a goal (not two, unfortunately) on their own stomping ground.

Flag fly all over Jamaica that Friday. Bare green and yellow man ah wear that day. Who didn't have a flag in their back pocket, or tie round their head, put one on their car—one man even wrap up the whole car in flags.

Man, all the Jamaicans (and quite a few Trinis) who live in Brooklyn, Queens, Miami, Atlanta, all of them drove up to the RFK Stadium to meet half of the Jamaicans who live in Jamaica who come up on about 25 different charter flights. And is so they make noise when the referee give USA a penalty (outside the damn box! they swear).

Bredren, bedlam bruck out when Deon Burton slam the ball in dey goal less than a minute later. Hear nuh, man break desk and send chair flying with joy. Red Stripe run in bar like somebody win Lotto.

The match ended 1-1 though. No more goals were scored but the draw made the Americans' chances of qualifying that much slimmer, and left us (that's right, us) with just two points to make in the final two matches.

Yuh think de Reggae Boyz easy? Cho, I done book my ticket to France already.

ORIGINALLY PUBLISHED JULY 1997

Dominoes

FRANKLYN McKNIGHT

"Cho! A play you a play? Play domino, man. (Bam)! How much card you have?" —ERNIE SMITH (JAMAICAN SONGWRITER)

He jumped up, almost overturning the table. Benjie, the man in front of him, steadied it to prevent the dominoes from falling off. He placed his right foot on the chair, held out the two dominoes in his left hand for all to see and quickly slammed them, one after the other, onto the table.

A chorus went up: "Six Love!" Benjie smiled and slapped his partner on the back. The losers rose dejectedly from their chairs around the table over which the dominoes were scattered.

"Six Love!" someone else said. "(Bring) Forward the beer," Benjie shouted, rubbing his protruding belly. The girl skillfully brought over six beers. Benjie pulled two with his teeth and gave one to his partner. He downed half with one gulp and belched. "Next pair," he said, though two men were already sitting there ready to engage them. The police siren wailed past on this busy neck of West Kingston. The men shuffled the dominoes. A new game of six was starting...

"Bring over the lamp here!" Sweet Mouth shouted to the shopkeeper who took the kerosene oil lamp from the shop counter, over to the domino table on the piazza. The men had been seeing very well with the silver light from the full moon in the sky over the Blue Mountains but Sweet Mouth, a lover of theatrics, still asked for the lamp. "Look!" he shouted to none of the five people watching or the three others at the table in particular. "Look how man play domino!". Silence hugged the piazza of the shop, the only one in this district two thousand feet up the Blue Mountains. Sweet Mouth and Killer whose real names no one remembered were leading five games to nil, if they won this one it would be a shameful defeat—like a six love in tennis. Sweet Mouth looked at the faces of the men, seemed uncertain, hissed his teeth and played. Killer, winced, as if a ripe mango had fallen from his hand, and turned away. The man next to him played his last card. Sweet Mouth and Killer had lost the game. Some one marked 5:1 on the board. Sweet Mouth got up from the table. He wanted no further part in the game.

"Come finish your six. Come take your beating," the teenager who had won the game said. Sweet Mouth turned. "I give yuh one game for encouragement and yuh showing off? If you win one more I buy everybody in the bar a drink. Come, pardi!" he called to Killer, pulling him to the chair....

Domino is a widely accepted table game in Jamaica played in almost every physical setting: in the living room, on the construction site, by the river on a stone, in the kitchen at a party, at the church picnic on the beach.... Though men are most commonly seen playing the game, women play it well too. Among the best players are policemen, firemen and soldiers who have a lot of time on their hands while at work.

Hardly any one knows when the game started in Jamaica or where it came from. Some believe it may have been a corruption of the Chinese game Mah Jong and was played here by British Soldiers. Who cares? We play it well and more people perhaps play domino and know to play it than any other game in Jamaica. Yet you wouldn't call it a national game. There is no declared national champion. Which is perhaps why everyone wants to prove he is indeed the champion and everyone else wants to prove him wrong.

The game is played any time of day and there are many neighbourhoods where people are kept awake late into the night by the banging of dominoes and the fevered laughter or shouts of players and spectators alike. A lot of drama is involved, much poking of fun takes place and people do much to prove themselves good at it. There is even a story of a man who, having a hard time on his honeymoon, went out, bought a pack of dominoes, came back and threw them out on the bed and said to his new bride: "Ah! Now beat me at this!"

It is a simple game of 28 cards, normally made of wood or fibre glass (bone) or imitation ivory. Each 'card'—with a line running across the middle, making two squares has little black groves or eyes on one side of the card, in the two squares. Only one card has no eye at all, it is called the "double blank." There are six other doubles (equal number of eyes in the squares) from one to six. There are seven of each (numbered) card from blank to six. The doubles are very important yet can be damning. If the six other cards are played out the double is useless. But it is very valuable if it is double blank and the game is blocked, meaning that not all the cards are played out and cannot be, whence the eyes of the remaining cards are counted. The lowest total count wins the game.

Don't believe though that this is a drab, difficult mathematical game. And it is not only the fact that drink and food is generally available that creates an atmosphere of fun wherever the game is played. Players drink anything from lemonade, to orange juice, coconut water, scotch, rum, beer and stouts. A brand of the latter (Guinness) is associated with club tournaments in domino. In such tournaments a team has twelve members. They occupy six tables and play to ten games. Some of the better known clubs are Dragon Star, Jay Hawkers, Guinness All Star, Fats 'D' and Milwaukee—the latter is the reigning champion in Jamaica. There are many greats, most known by nick names, Blacka, (many think he is the best) Peas Head, Niah, Laker, Great Teacher, Bwoy Blue and Shaggy—the names are part of the aura that goes with the game.

In tournament as in other games one will notice players pouring over the dominoes examining them, sometimes unconsciously handling them, as if to hear them reveal a great secret. And often the player is trying to detect a great secret—who has a particular card—"the key card." Knowledge of that is the basis on which he will make his play so that either he or his partner will play out their card first. And win!

Jamaicans hate to lose. And so sometimes there is a cheating or what is euphemistically called "coding." A man might repeatedly scratch his nose to indicate to his partner that he has four pieces of six or he might rub his palms together to indicate he has only doubles and cannot win. There is a pair of players in Montego Bay who have a whole lexicon for the game. If Shot Gun (famous for the speed with which he plays the game) begins to tell a story, his partner can know all the cards he has. If he speaks about the big breasted woman, he has sixes, if he says her lips are very thin he has blanks and so on. That sort of person is difficult to beat and their pair will reign for a long time.

Play domino!

ORIGINALLY PUBLISHED AUGUST 1986

D.Q.
The Fastest Man in the World

JIMMY CARNEGIE

He's a small man, only 5'8" tall, and weighing 155 lbs. But he's very well-built, with enormously strong thighs; when he runs, his knees are right up at the end of a race, and his head does not swing. A twenty-one year old student in California, U.S.A., he's quiet and gentlemanly; the word 'handsome' might not be out of place except for a crucial missing tooth. His name is Donald Quarrie, known to the cognoscenti of the world of track and field as "Don", or, simply, "D.Q."

He just may be the fastest man alive.

That label usually goes to the record holder for the 100 yards, or more accurately, the Olympic distance of 100 metres. In the last two years Don Quarrie has won the 100 metres title at the 1970 British Commonwealth Games (Edinburgh, Scotland), the 1971 Pan American Games (California, Colombia), and the Central American and Caribbean Athletics Championships (Kingston, Jamaica); in fact, all the leading international competitions for which he was eligible. The final challenge will face him this year in August and September at the Olympic Games in Munich.

Yet his strongest claim to the title doesn't really lie in the times he's chalked up over the 100 metres. His fastest "legal" time (that is without substantial wind assistance) is "only 10.2 secs., a whole point three of a second outside the world's record of 9.9 secs. What's more, he was beaten into third place last year in the U.S. Amateur Athletic Union's 100 yard final, and placed only fourth in the 100 metres in the U.S. vs. Russia vs World All Star meet in California earlier this year.

His strong claim lies rather in his performances over the longer distance of 200 metres, (where he has only suffered one defeat in two years in an early season race this year), and over which distance last year he equalled the world record at the Pan Am Games to earn himself the Clark Flores Trophy and his Gold Medal—the outstanding sportsman at the Games. It was particularly impressive for two reasons. First, simple arithmetic tells us that 19.8 seconds for 200 metres is equivalent to 9.0 seconds for two successive 100 metres—the Olympic record. Secondly, Don equalled the world record set by Tommie Smith at high altitude during the Mexico Olympics of 1968. You'll remember Smith's particular celebrity at those games, earned by the "Black Power" salute he gave along with his compatriot John Charles at the victory ceremony.

Now Tommie Smith's politics may be controversial, but there's no question about his athletics talent: he is universally regarded as possibly among the three greatest all-round sprinters of all time, in the 100, 200 and 400 metres. The other two are Henry Carr of Detroit, Michigan, U.S.A., and Herb McKenley of Clarendon, Jamaica.

Rivals for the title? There seem to be only two, Valeriy Borzov of the Soviet Union, and a fellow student of Don, the unpronounceable Jean Louis Revelomantsoa of the Malagasy Republic. Both were unbeaten in their short-distance races in 1971. That year *Track and Field News,* the "Bible of the Sport", named Don fifth in their list of athletes of the year, one place behind Borzov. What's more, Don was the only one of the three to have equalled a world's record (for the 200 metres), in addition to setting a new indoor world record earlier in the year—100 yards in 9.3 seconds.

A few miles from Palisadoes International Airport, Jamaica, going towards Kingston, is Harbour View, the housing scheme where Don lived with his family. In fact, much of his early training was accomplished in the hills around

Harbour View. Don's coach at school, Mr. Harold Scott, found him a receptive and faithful student. Perhaps he got his patience from his mother, reputedly an accomplished seamstress. His father, Mr. Wilfred Quarrie, a non-commissioned police officer, is said to be an extraordinarily determined man. Obviously this quality has been passed on.

Jamaica's leading sports journalist, Foggy Burroughs, a senior official of the Jamaica Amateur Athletic Association, his also noted two things in Don's training. No sprinter can train harder than Don does, says Foggy; and he takes a long time to complete the assigned programme of work at training sessions. This probably explains his very high "pain quotient". His extraordinary self-discipline, that high knee-lift, the fact that he has never been discouraged by illness or injury—these too are factors that have contributed to the development of his championship calibre, as well as the stiff competition that surrounded him during his school days.

Despite Don's quiet and introspective nature he was a popular student leader at Camperdown High School in Kingston, one of the leading co-educational schools in Jamaica. It has less than 300 boys, but it's produced several fine athletes. The list includes Godfrey Murray, for example, well-known collegiate hurdler in the U.S., and medallist at the 1970 Commonwealth and 1971 C.A.C. high hurdles. One of Don's own brothers, Eric, was the Senior Class 200 metres champion at the Jamaica Inter Secondary Schools Athletic Championships ("Champs") in 1971. Local experts feel that he has the potential to represent Jamaica.

Understandably, Don's schoolboy record of triumphs, which began at Champs when he was thirteen, has set a standard by which both past and future performers are judged. In spite of frequent injuries it has been consistently good. Even before he left school in 1969 he had proved his quality as a track star. That June, representing Jamaica at the U.S. A.A.U. in Miami, Florida, he failed by the narrowest of margins to reach the final, being beaten by the defending A.A.U. champion Charlie Greene of the University of Nebraska. Greene had won a bronze in the 100 metres at Mexico City, and a gold on the sprint relay, and is still a co-record holder at both the 100 yards and 100 metres.

Don's performance was doubly impressive because he had edged Greene in the first round, and Greene went on to take third place in the final. The performance guaranteed Don his athletics scholarship to the University of Nebraska; later he was to transfer to the warmer latitudes of the University of Southern California.

Meanwhile, in 1970, running at Edinburgh in the Commonwealth Games, he won the 100 from Miller, who has started training very late; he took the 200 metres from Edwin Roberts of Trinidad, who had been third in this event at Tokyo and fourth in Mexico; and he beat the Mexico Silver Medallist, Australian Peter Norman. Don then crowned the triple by leading

the Jamaican team to a comfortable victory in the sprint replay. At age nineteen he had emerged internationally and at the end of the year was rated fourth in the 200-metres by *Track and Field News.*

Now in 1972 at the time of writing (near the end of May), Don has shown somewhat mixed form, considering his own high standards. This is not surprising, however, since he has already announced his intention of a slow build-up for the Olympics in late August. His running was, and remains, characteristic: a slow start; smooth, beautiful development and an almost blinding acceleration at the end.

He has equalled his own indoor record for the 100 yards, but had little luck at the shorter 60 yards, failing to make the N.C.A.A. indoor finals in Detroit. He has been defeated at both 100 and 200 yards by an eighteen year-old sensation named Steve Williams of the University of Texas, at El Paso. Williams, with times of 9.3, 20.3 and 45.7 at 440 yards, who shows promise of developing into another really great all-round sprinter.

To counteract these defeats, though, Don has been running some tremendous relay legs for U.S.C., beating 20 seconds on more than one occasion for their 220 yards team. That team has already twice beaten the world's best time (without official recognition, since international rules now state that all runners on relay teams must come from the same country for world record purposes).

Don has a dilemma, however, and sports fans in Jamaica and outside, as well as all his fellow sprinters, are wondering what he'll decide. Should he attempt the 100 metres as well as the 200 and of course the relay? The physical load would be well within his capacity—a possible eleven races in ten days. He's done this (and more) with less rest between races than he will have at Munich, ever since his school days. Repeatedly. But the nervous energy expended at the Olympic Games, particularly by favourites like Donald, is something else again.

If he does run the 100 and wins, the psychological lift may make a victory in the 200 that much more certain. On the other hand, if he loses the 100, his confidence for the 200 may suffer a crippling blow and the relay too may be affected.

History seems to warn against the attempt. Since Jesse Owens' unbelievable four gold medals in 1936, which included the long jump and the relay as well as the 100 and 200 metres, only one other man—Bobby Morrow of the U.S.,—has ever taken the sprint double (Melbourne in 1956). Few great sprinters, including favourites like Don, for both races, even attempt it.

But only he will be able to decide. And whatever the results, there can be no doubt that as of mid-1972 Don Quarrie, Jamaican, has as good a claim as any on the planet to be called "the fastest man in the world."

ORIGINALLY PUBLISHED SEPTEMBER 1972

50 Years of Sporting Success

JIMMY CARNEGIE

Honoured by the Black Athletes Hall of Fame in 1975, (LEFT TO RIGHT) Arthur Wint; a representative of the Black Hall of Fame; George Headley; David Coore, representing the Prime Minister; Herb McKenley; Lindy Delapenha, Jamaica's first national footballer.

Jamaica's first sporting superstar, George Headley, very fittingly for the neo-colonial 1930's, made an international impact in the oh-so English sport of cricket.

Born in the Panama Canal Zone of a Barbadian father and a Jamaican mother, he himself also almost migrated to the United States. Headley's achievements are legion. But among those which particularly stand out are the following: he is the only man to make two Test centuries (100 runs) in the same match at Lord's in England—the "shrine" of the game. He played in international Test cricket series for 24 years, starting in 1930—one of the three longest such spans in the sport. His Test batting average of 60.37 is the third highest among all batsmen. He averaged one Test hundred for every four innings played—the second highest such ratio. He made 10 Test centuries for the West Indies between 1930 and 1939. It was not until 1948 that any other West Indian batsman made more than two. He and C.C. Passailaigue also still hold the oldest partnership record in first-class cricket, this set in 1932. Headley died three years ago and is regarded as one of the two best batsmen that the game has ever produced.

It took 20 years after Headley's emergence before Jamaica produced a cricketer of comparable stature, Alfred Valentine. Prior to his appearance on the sporting scene, however, there were to be three quarter-milers of great note. The first was Herb McKenley. He was a pioneer in more than one way. He was, for example, probably the first notable athlete from outside the U.S. to receive an athletic scholarship to a U.S. institution (Boston College and then Illinois University). Hundreds of others, particularly from the Caribbean and Africa, had followed him in athletics, basketball and soccer. More importantly, he was the first athlete from the English-speaking Caribbean to set a world record in the time-measured sport. He set four world records over the quarter-mile and its metric equivalent, the 400 metres, between June, 1947 and July, 1948, before any other athlete from the area was to achieve even one. The most important of these was when he ran 46 seconds flat for the quarter-mile (a time thought to be a "barrier", somewhat like the four-minute mile) on June 5, 1948. This confirmed him as the overwhelming favourite for the 400 metres event at the first post-war Olympic Games which took place in London that summer. On this occasion, Jamaica entered a team for the first time.

However, he was beaten by a fellow-countryman, Arthur Wint. Wint had set the example for McKenley when he won the 800 metres at the Central American and Caribbean Games in 1938 as a schoolboy. (They both went to the same school—Calabar High.) Wint in fact won the first Jamaican Olympic medal when he took the silver in the 800 which had been thought to be his stronger event. McKenley, meanwhile, had finished fourth in the 200 metres. When both met in the 400, Wint noticed McKenley tiring towards the end of the race and overtook him, equalling the Olympic record of 46.2. Also on the Jamaican team was a third outstanding runner, George Rhoden.

The next year Rhoden went off to college in the U.S., and by 1950 he had reached the same level as Wint and McKenley, giving the country a great trio over the same distance when he beat McKenley's 400 metres world record in Sweden with a time of 45.8.

In the same year the second world-beating Jamaican cricketer came along. Alf Valentine, only 20 and like his Trinidadian "twin", Sonny Ramadhin, had played only two first-class matches when they were selected to tour England for the West Indies. They took a big hand in the West Indies' first ever Test series victory in England. Over the next four years, Valentine was to become the world's best left-handed spin bowler, reaching his 200 wickets in Test cricket (the first West Indian to do so) in only three and a half years.

Before he had reached this target, however, McKenley, Wint and Rhoden and a fourth athlete, Les Laing, who had finished sixth in the London 200, had brought Jamaica perhaps its greatest ever sporting glory at the 1952 Helsinki Olympics. McKenley just missed winning the 100 metres which he had entered primarily to sharpen up. His silver medal meant, though, that he was and still is—the only man in the entire history of the Olympics to reach the finals of the 100, 200 and 400 metres events. Finishing second again—this time to George Rhoden—in the 400 metres, Wint came second again in the 800 metres.

The three then combined with Laing to win the 4 x 400 metres relay in a world record time of 3.02.9 seconds. The same four had been well on the way to at least the silver medal in 1948 when Wint had pulled up lame. This time they made no mistake when they inflicted the only defeat that a full strength U.S. team has ever suffered in this event since the event was introduced at the 1912 Olympics. McKenley ran the third leg, and closed a gap of 12 to 15 yards in 44.6 seconds, the fastest ever leg to date.

That moment has perhaps never been surpassed, although several other Jamaicans have followed in their distinguished footsteps. In athletics the hurdler Keith Gardner and the 400-800 runner George Kerr stood out in the decade before independence in 1962—both being on a West Indies team which won the bronze medal in the 1600 relay at Rome in 1960—when Kerr was also third in the 800 metres. During this period the batsman J.K. Holt Jnr., all-rounder Collie Smith (tragically killed in a car accident at an early age), the fast bowler Roy Gilchrist and, especially wicket-keepers Gerry Alexander and Jackie Hendriks, also distinguished themselves in cricket. Over a slightly linger period going into the mid-sixties, three boxers—Gerald Gray, Bunny Grant and the late Percy Hayles—earned world ranking with the last two fighting for world titles.

The last two decades have seen several great track athletes including two women, superb cricketers, and two world champion boxers. In 1968 and 1972 with silver and bronze medals in the Olympic 100 metres, Lennox Miller became the second of only three men to win two medals in the event at the Olympic Games. He also anchored a Jamaican sprint relay team at the 1968 Games which first equalled and them broke the world record on the same day. The record this team had broken had been one set by a University of Southern California team also anchored by Miller—a team which also includes the famous football running back O.J. Simpson. He was followed in both the Jamaican and USC teams by Donald Quarrie.

ARTHUR WINT

'DQ' became the first Jamaican man to get on the individual world record lists since 1950 when he equalled the world record for the 200 metres in 1971 at the Pan Am Games. In 1976 he became the first Jamaican Olympic gold medallist since 1952 when he won the same event at the Montreal Olympics and the third Jamaican after McKenley and Miller to win the silver medal in the 100 metres. Having been in Mexico in 1968 as a 17-year old schoolboy when injury prevented him from competing, he made Olympic history in 1976 (his third Games), in 1980 (his fourth) when he won the bronze in the 200 metres, and in 1984 (his fifth) when at 33 he won a sprint relay silver medal, as the first male sprinter ever to win medals in his third, fourth and fifth Games. DQ is the first male sprinter ever to have earned a place on five Olympic teams.

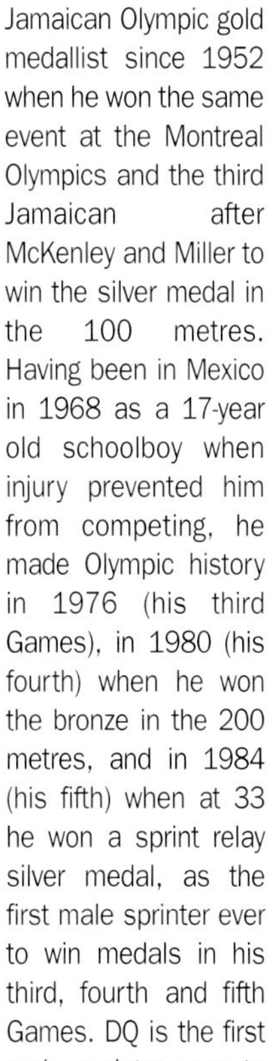

ALFRED VALENTINE

Marilyn Neufville, Jamaican-born but British-raised, decided to represent Jamaica at the Commonwealth Games in 1970. There she became the first Jamaican to both set a world record and win a major championship when she took the women's 400 metres in 51 seconds even. Next year she repeated half the success, winning the event at the Pan Am Games. But in 1972 a serious tendon injury tragically prevented her from competing and she was

MICHAEL HOLDING

MERLENE OTTEY

never the same athlete again.

The seventies witnessed the rise of two great cricketers. Lawrence Rowe created a world record by scoring a double century and a single century in his first Test match against New Zealand in 1972. Two years later he made 302 against England. Michael Holding joined him in the West Indies team in 1975 and in 1976 became the highest ever wicket-taker in a single Test for the West Indies setting a world record for fast bowlers with 14 wickets against England. Holding has now become the second highest wicket-taker amongst West Indians with 249 Test wickets and is the only Jamaican to take more than 150 wickets in Test cricket. He has also played more Test matches, 59, than any other Jamaican. At one stage, he was thought to be the fastest bowler in the world and is certainly the best stylist.

Jamaica now supplies the West Indies wicket-keeper, Jeff Dujon, who may already have achieved greatness, as well as fast bowlers Patrick Patterson and Courtney Walsh who are probably not far from it.

Finally, in the 1980's Jamaica has seen four boxing world champions—the first West Indian territory to have more than one. Trevor Berbick, who is also a Canadian citizen, was until recently the World Boxing Council's heavyweight champion. Michael McCallum, Jamaica's outstanding amateur boxer, has remained undefeated professionally as a junior middleweight, with 24 knockouts in 27 fights, and was the first and only West Indian fighter to win a world championship in the home of professional boxing, Madison Square Garden. McCallum has defended his title three times, all three fights within the prescribed distance. British-based Lloyd Honeyghan is the undisputed world welterweight champion. And our first "home-grown" champion, Richard "Shrimpy" Clarke walked away with the World Boxing Council's Junior Flyweight belt earlier this year.

In the present decade the outstanding male track athlete has been Bert Cameron. He took up the mantle of McKenley, Wint and Rhoden by winning the 400 metres in the First World Athletic Championships in the Helsinki Games in 1983. There have also been two women. Merlene Ottey-Page (the first and only woman from the English-speaking Caribbean to win an Olympic medal—bronzes in the 200 metres at the 1980 and 1984 Games and a bronze in the 100 metres in 1984). A holder of several indoor world best medals, she is also one of only a handful of women to beat both 11 seconds for the 100 metres and 22 seconds for the 200 metres, being the Commonwealth record holder in both events. Recently Grace Jackson has been approaching her level and is one of few women ever to run in four Olympic finals at the same games, including the 100, 200 and both relays at the 1984 Olympic. She has also recently extended her range by beating Marilyn Neufville's Jamaican record in the 400 metres.

Jamaican-born youngsters whose parent have emigrated add another colourful spectrum of sporting achievement to the country's record books. Patrick Ewing, captain of the gold medal-winning 1984 U.S. Olympic basketball team, and now with the New York Nicks; San Francisco Giants outfielder All-Star Chili Davis; Oakland Raiders defensive player Sean Jones; currently the fastest sprinter in the world, Ben Johnson, representing Canada along with Angela Taylor and Atlee Mahorn; Britain's astonishing Olympic titleist Tessa Sanborn, sprinter Linford Christie, weightlifter Louis Martin, World Cup soccer representative John Barnes and his team-mate Luther Blissett, the first Jamaican-born player to represent England.

From George Headley to "Shrimpy" Clarke in a little over 50 years, Jamaica has managed to produce an enviable record of sporting success that is not only significant in its own right but also exciting for the promise it indicates for the next half century.

ORIGINALLY PUBLISHED AUGUST 1987

Michael McCallum— A Dream Comes True

Jamaica's First Boxing World Champion

CLAIRE FORRESTER

> "Jamaica never had a world champion before me, this is the first time and I wanted to win the title for Jamaica!"

So declared Michael McCallum as he savoured his momentous victory over Sean Mannion on October 1984 by claiming the WBA junior middleweight crown. Being the first Jamaican world champion is a truly notable accomplishment. His statement was not brash nor boastful. It reflected the determination, dedication, and self-confidence that were as much McCallum's style as his vaunted body punches, hooks and uppercuts.

"My title has come as a mission accomplished...a dream come true, I have been on the road for a long time. I have been abused and misused, but I hung in there, and today I am the champion of the world."

All who have followed McCallum's uphill battles to the WBA junior middleweight title will endorse that assertion which the new champ made to his MoBay fans at a massive welcome home reception.

Born in Kingston, December 7, 1956, McCallum began boxing in 1972 at the age of 16. He trained at the Dragon Gym and was influenced by his outstanding predecessors, lightweights Bunny Grant and Percy Hayles.

Within a year, the young pugilist was selected to represent Jamaica as a welterweight in the Central American and Caribbean Boxing Championships, heralding an impressive amateur career by any standards which climaxed on October 19, with the junior middleweight crown under the lights of Madison Square Gardens.

Throughout his celebrated amateur career, McCallum secured numerous medals and titles on the Central American, Caribbean and North American circuits. His amateur career came to the fore when he represented Jamaica at the 1976 Montreal Olympics.

At those Olympics it seemed as if Jamaica might have earned its first ever medal in a sport other than track and field athletics. In an unforgettable display of boxing skills, the Jamaican, from all accounts, had the best of his West German opponent. Indeed, when the final bell sounded, tears of joy trickled down the faces of the Jamaicans present.

"We were crying for joy in anticipation of McCallum's announced victory and a first ever Olympic boxing medal for Jamaica," explained official Mike Fennell on his return to Jamaica. "Our tears however turned to tears of disbelief and frustration when the decision, against McCallum, was announced."

It was a decision which McCallum will never forget. "I just couldn't believe it," he said much later. It was little compensation when the judges concerned were disqualified from doing further duties following a protest lodged by the Jamaican team.

That experience would have discouraged many, but McCallum went on from strength to strength as an amateur.

Among his prolific haul were gold medals at the Central American and Caribbean Championships and the prestigious US National Golden Gloves and Amateur Athletic Union Championships. By 1977 he had beaten the best Cubans and Americans, the countries then most dominant in amateur boxing, and appeared poised on the threshold of greatness.

In the process and with the scarcity of competition in Jamaica, McCallum accumulated experience by boxing in international tournaments that were held primarily in the United States. He made New York City his permanent residence in 1981, the same year he began his pro career.

McCallum delayed becoming pro until then in a bid to win the elusive Olympic gold medal but fate was again cruel to him. On the eve of the 1980 Moscow Olympics, he appeared a virtual certainty for the gold medal when he was floored by appendicitis.

That effectively closed the chapter on his amateur crusade and in February 1981, at the ripe age of 24, McCallum launched what was to become a glittering professional career.

Headlining several prestigious Madison Square Garden Felt Forum shows in 1982, he registered knockouts over Greg Young, Reggie Ford and Carlos Betencourt, all world rated boxers. In November of that same year, his managers secured a contest against former WBA Champion Ayub Kalule. In the memorable display, McCallum shut out Kalule, stopping in the seventh round of their nationally televised contest in Atlantic City. It was a victory that forced the world of boxing to stand up and take notice. More importantly, it was a fight which earned him a shot at the world title.

Enriched and emboldened by subsequent training experiences with superstars Thomas Hearns and Milton McCrory, McCallum developed into a class boxer.

Indeed, in 1983, a former trainer in describing his ability said, "I think he's the best technical fighter in the world today, pound for pound."

He was to improve even further when in 1983 he switched training camps, joining ranks with the Detroit Kronk wizard, Emanuel Steward, and promoter, Dan Dura. Armed with this new expertise he improved in sparring sessions with Hearns, McCrory and several other Kronk fighters. His colleagues gave him two nicknames, "Mr. Smooth," because of his fluid movement and combination punching, and "The Body Snatcher," because of the way he drills hooks and right hands to the midsection.

When his chance came for a shot at Duran's WBA title in 1984, Duran opted to fight Hearns for a more lucrative purse. With his 'never say die' commitment, however, McCallum hung in there and went on to fulfil his early dreams on that celebrated Friday night, of October 19, 1984, when he battered the WBA number two contender, Ireland's Sean Mannion, in winning the WBA middleweight championship belt. Since then, he has begun to speak of greater things, such as dethroning the seemingly invincible Thomas 'Hitman' Hearns, and so unify the junior middleweight titles.

McCallum promises to be a great champion and has made an impressive start, improving his record to 23-0, on December 1, when he stopped the Italian Lulgi Manchillo by a TKO in 14 rounds.

It has been a long trek to the top for McCallum and having made it, promises that there is more to come. On his triumphant return to Jamaica he reminded his fans, "I promised you I would win for you all, didn't I!"

Whether or not he goes on to achieve true greatness as promised, remains to be seen. One thing is certain. In winning the world title, he has elevated Jamaica in the ranks of international boxing, but no means the end of his mission, but definitely made a dream come true.

ORIGINALLY PUBLISHED AUGUST 1985

Lennox Lewis
Lord of the Ring

BERNARD BURRELL

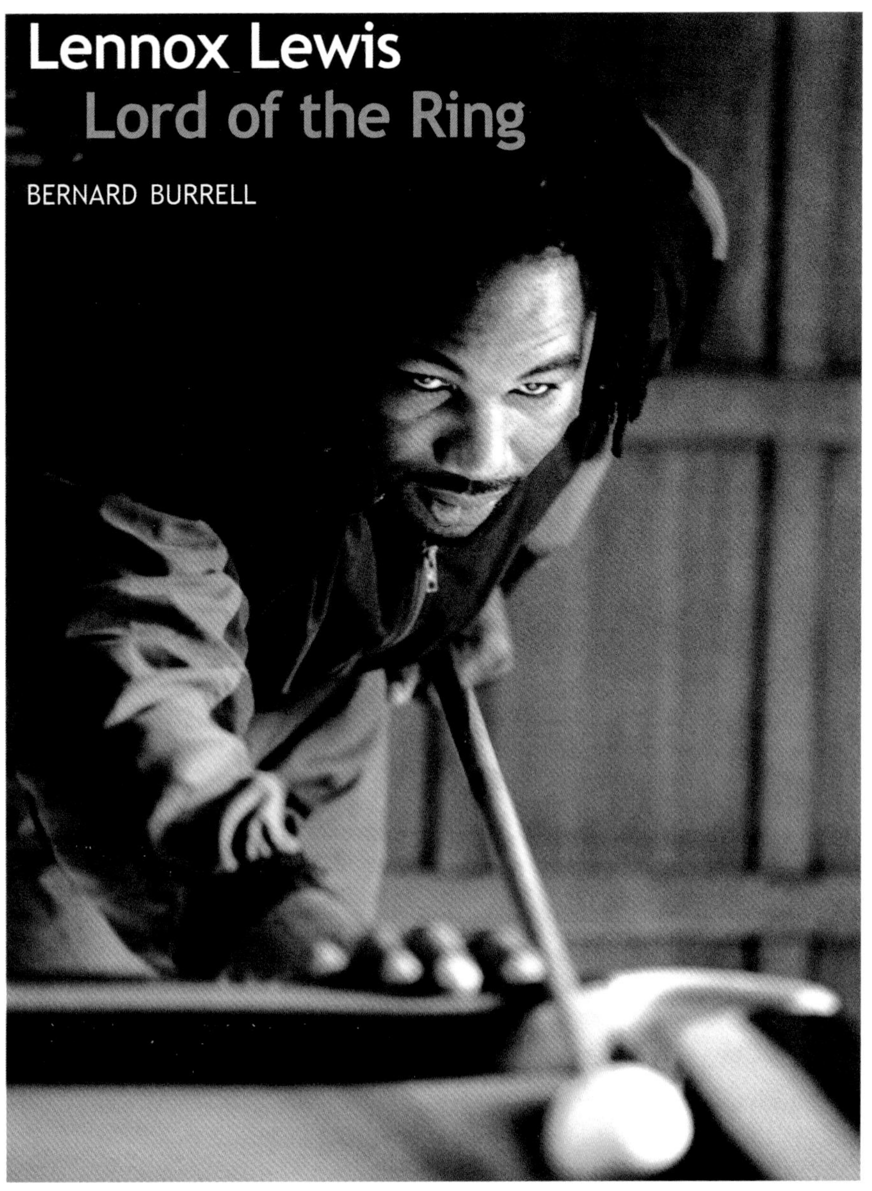

After interviewing WBC Champion Lennox Lewis, I came away basking in the knowledge that I just sat in the home of one of the world's most successful, handsome, wealthy and recognisable sports stars. Lewis has many loves—his stately Enfield home on the outskirts of London, a few prized luxury cars, his love affair with Jamaica—its sunshine, reggae music and ital food and his unselfish support for various youth and community projects. But as I discovered, none can compare to the love and respect he has for his Jamaican mother, Violet.

For the young lady who feels she could easily end the bachelor days of this 31 year old boxing giant, she must first be able to pass several prenuptial tests, including: having the looks of singer Toni Braxton, the body of supermodel Naomi Campbell, the cultural and spiritual awareness of Maya Angelou and definitely the ability to cook like Lennox's mum.

Bernard Burrell: Do you enjoy talking about yourself and how much would you reveal?

Lennox Lewis: Yes, to some degree I do enjoy talking about myself, but I don't like going in-depth although people always seem to want to know every little detail about me. I often wonder why. If I am going to talk about myself openly, then I'm leaving my life open to many different things out there. However, there are certain things and situations, like a funny personal experience that I would talk about, but if it involves something I don't want people to know about, I will not talk about it.

BB: You were born in Britain, raised in Canada and frequent Jamaica—this has raised questions in the boxing fraternity and sports media about your allegiance. Where do you really belong?

LL: My life's journey speaks for itself, because although I was born in the east end of London, I moved to Canada at age 12 to join my mother—a boy has to be with his mother you know—and Canada was where my budding interest in boxing started to take shape. But although I was moving from one country to another, it was in Canada that I became really exposed to my Jamaican heritage, mixing with Jamaican friends of my mother (who is from Port Antonio in Jamaica). So when people question my allegiance I find it amusing because they obviously don't know where I am from or anything about my roots.

BB: Your love affair with Jamaica—what is that all about?

LL: When I am in Jamaica, I feel totally relaxed and at home. I love to feast on the variety of fresh food, vegetables and fruits that abound in Jamaica. I am also a sun person, I love the sunshine and in Jamaica, the sun shines like no other place I've experienced. I have been to other Caribbean islands, but none seem to captivate or fascinate me like Jamaica. There is something about Jamaica that almost defies description. It's a country that can be raw and refined at the same time. Jamaicans are also fascinating and puzzling. But in all of these contrasts, Jamaica has a certain kind of spirituality that appeals to me deeply. When I visit—as I often do several times a year—I'm always surprised by something new and interesting. It's like one is on a journey within a journey. The variations in Jamaica's landscapes and people are a wonderful reflection of the lifestyles, struggles, drive and dedication which characterize the society.

BB: Your mother seems to be the main lady in your life—how important is she to you?

LL: I would say very important because she's been my mother and father and has given me stability when I was growing up as a young athlete who could easily have become victim to my success, money or other vices. If I'm doing something wrong, my mother is always there to guide me as her son and not Lennox Lewis, the world boxing champion.

BB: Outside the ring, you always appear cool, focused and a keen observer—have you always been like this?

LL: When I was young, I was very hyper and aggressive but I have learned to control that side of me. Furthermore, I'm in a sport where control of violence can bring certain advantages and qualities, and being the person I am—easy going, peaceful and observant—I'd like to think I am also focused some of the time. I also know when to turn on and off and I'm not the kind of boxer who likes to rant and run up his mouth in and out of the ring.

There are certain things I do not believe in getting worked up or upset about because they are often a waste of time and energy. My approach is generally to run things through my mind and try and predict the outcomes without always having to go through the motions.

BB: Do you apply the same approach to your professional boxing matches?

LL: I have won 30 out of my 31 professional title fights, including my recent World Boxing Council Championship over Oliver McCall. This was one title which was denied me by Don King for a long time, forcing me to take him to court for the fight to take place. It was a vacant title, given up by Mike Tyson because he didn't want to fight with me. Suddenly McCall became number one and I was number two. I was determined to get back my world ranking position which I did when we fought last February. It was a lucky punch from me which made him panic, leaving the ring crying after 55 seconds. But although his abrupt departure from the ring overshadowed the event, at the end of the day, I fought for the title.

BB: Is the multi-million dollars in prize money the most attractive feature in your fights?

LL: I don't really look at the money aspect because the way my mother brought me up, I've always learned to live within my means. But of course the size of the prize money comes with the kind of title fight—the bigger the fight, the richer the purse. Plus for me, if the purse fight is really big, it's a good incentive to win. You have to understand that boxing is a sport in which anyone can jump in the ring—and usually there's no way out and nowhere to run—therefore, it helps to separate the men from the boys. But for me, the trick is more mental than physical.

BB: You have been described as Britain's second most charitable millionaire—even though you're reported to be worth only £20 million. How important is your support for youth and community projects?

LL: Very important, because I ensure that anything that I get involved in and that carries my name, is worthwhile and done effectively. The only drawback is I don't always have enough time to get personally involved in the daily activities of things like the Lennox Lewis College in London. I decided to fund the college not because I was feeling generous, but because I firmly believe that there's a need for such a college. You see so many black youngsters being expelled from mainstream schools with nowhere to go The college acts as a safety net for them. The emphasis at the college is to get the best from each student, irrespective if they come in as problem youngsters.

The college aims to equip youngsters with necessary skills and qualifications to meet the demand of the information technology and science workplace. Who knows what Lennox Lewis would have turned out to be if my boxing career had not worked out well.

BB: How business minded are you and do you gamble on the stock exchange?

LL: No man, black people nuh bet pon stock exchange (laughter). My brother Dennis is my business manager which is very important for me having family involvement in my business. I am a natural competitor who is always prepared to give any venture my best shot. My main business venture is the CSI Modeling Agency. I realised the struggles black models have trying to get breaks. White model agencies still perpetuate the myth that their clients prefer white models to promote their products. When I am on the beaches in Jamaica I see so many beautiful girls with potential—all they need is the right break. CSI has started to address that imbalance.

BB: With so many millions to your name, what do you spend your money on?

LL: Let me see, I would say lending money to friends. I have a particular weakness in this area which works to my disadvantage. People, even so-called friends, are always looking to take advantage of my generosity but with the help of my mother and Dennis, I am learning to grow and become more astute because life can be very fast and complex.

I also buy lots of music recordings. I am really into reggae and I get most of my reggae music raw from dancehall sessions in Jamaica.

BB: Do you find women are attracted to you because of your fame and status?

LL: It is a life skill, something that I have learned to "suss out." That's why it's good to have my mother because she's always there as guiding force to say "Bwoy Lennox, dat woman is really nat fee yuh, be careful." That motherly advice and intuition is always valuable.

BB: Your home is in a very expensive and exclusive area of London with all the comforts and charm to match—is it necessary to have a woman to make it homey?

LL: If a woman is around, she can add that extra touch and make a difference. My home reflects security, warmth, strong African and Caribbean influences with modern art decor and good quality music system and recreational addictions like my snooker room and tennis court.

BB: How do you relax and where do you hang out?

LL: Music helps me to relax, also hanging out with friends and playing other sports like chess or reading. There is no one particular place that I hang out.

I like to make my movements unpredictable so I pop up just about anywhere. It's the same when I am in Jamaica, I travel all over because every place in Jamaica is unique and has its own attraction and appeal.

BB: Who do you admire in the boxing profession, and what is the true status of your relationship with fellow Jamaican-born boxer, Frank Bruno?

LL: People like Don King, Mike Tyson, Evander Holyfield—they're admirable characters. As for Frank Bruno, ours is not a relationship where we feel comfortable speaking to each other. A lot of public animosity has gone on between us. He would speak to me, but I know he doesn't like me and if I speak to him, I'm not gonna skin-teeth and pretend to be friendly—I don't believe in that, but Bruno does.

He has a different code of ethics to me, which is fair enough. There are things he would do to make white British people like him which I wouldn't do. Not everyone has to like each other but we are both in the same sport and both have a Jamaican background. Its big time envy on Bruno's part, it feels like crab mentality sometimes. I am now coming back as a champion boxer, I'm out there winning important title fights. But Bruno's reaction is—who do I think I am coming to take his glory. I don't live like that because I don't envy no one.

BB: Where would you most like to retire after your boxing career?

LL: Most definitely Jamaica. As I said before, I am a sun person and when I am in Jamaica, I synchronise my waking with the rise of the sun. During those early morning hours, everyone and everything is busy; but by mid-day, everything slows down. I like that, its a spiritual and therapeutic feeling and experience that I get only in Jamaica.

ORIGINALLY PUBLISHED JUNE 1997

The 800 Mile Dash
Miami-Montego Bay Yacht Race

FRANK MCMANUS

Resort towns are capricious by nature and Montego Bay is kookier than most. That's why it never fails to amaze that every two years, come what may, "the Republic" stages a major international sports event with all the aplomb of a Grand Prix fixture.

This is the Miami-Montego Bay Yacht Race, an 800-mile dash down the Caribbean for rum and glory. Since its inception in 1961, it has become part of the World Championship of Ocean Racing and now ranks with such famous sailing tests as the Fastnet, Bermuda, Sydney-Hobart and Transpac races.

In any other month of the year it is almost impossible to get anything done in the normal way in Mo Bay the whole place is kind of fun-schizo....But come every other March, Montegonians come rushing out of the woodwork like termites on holiday in their eagerness to join a race committee at the Montego Bay Yacht Club.

Ted Turner's *'Lightnin'*

Down in Kingston, where they have more good sailors than you can shake a martini at, they have been desperately trying to get their hands on this event for years. To no avail. Montego's got 'The Race' and all those hairy old salts in Kingston can go scratch.

One of the big problems now with the Miami-Montego is its popularity. What started with a dozen boats in 1961 is now limited to 50. Anchorage beginning to look like Hong Kong. If you think 50 isn't much, then multiply this number by an average crew of eight young men per boat which gives 400. Then, add lots of girls, mistresses and an occasional wife down for the mad party whirl which lasts longer than the race. Now you know what gay old Montego Bay is all about.

The action centers at the Yacht Club which never seems to close, and it spins off in all directions to the hotels, supper clubs and discotheques, the beach and private homes. Like Carnival in Trinidad.

When the crews get into Montego tired, scruffy and possessed of deep thirst, there is a round of social wingdingers that requires more endurance than that week before the mast. These can get quite hilarious like the time the crew of 'Windward Passage' turned loose a greased pig in the midst of a tightly-packed cocktail party at the old yacht club on Fort Street. Or the naked lady who found herself in a basket atop a mast at dawn at the new yacht club. Or the Wall Street bunch who sail for their own trophy—a pair of lace panties (specially acquired each race) which the winner flies proudly from his masthead.

The crews of these magnificent sailing machines fall into two lots—the seasoned professionals who compete on every major ocean and the amateurs who are mainly young, strong and adventurous. And all looking for a good time. Most are college lads out on holiday or young middle-agers out to recapture the thrill and tang of yester-year.

Manning a big racing yacht whose skipper is pushing it to the limit to extract that extra knot of speed in heavy seas and darkened night is not for the faint of heart. An ocean voyage of 800 miles threading through some tricky island navigation and roaring trade winds that can send a big boat booming along on a Nantucket sleigh ride takes skill, strength and courage. All at the mercy of the wind—no engine, man.

The race, which is a classic beat, a reach and a run (in that order) can vary tremendously in elapsed time. In 1971, big 'Windward Passage' caught the winds round-the-clock and made the run in an incredible three days and three hours. This year many of the competitors were out there on a generally windless, salt-caked seven-day voyage. In all fairness, 1973 was a most unusual year, weatherwise and otherwise

In preceding years, the whole fleet went over the starting line together off Miami. This year the slide rule boys determined that if the smaller (30-foot) boats started one day, medium class the next and the big, fast 70-footers the third day, then ideally all would finish together like a handicap horse race. It didn't happen.

What did happen, unfortunately, was that the small boats off the first day caught good wind and took it with them leaving the big fellas to wallow along behind in light airs. It could have worked the other way with the wind dying farther down the course. But, it didn't and the five or six big boats that refused to participate in a staggered start were vindicated. In 1975, it should be back to the 'all over the line at the same time', boys, and may the luckiest bloke win(d).

The 1973 winner was a cocky, young chap name of Ted Turner from Atlanta, Georgia. He also won in 1967 with another small boat, 'Vamoose', which didn't endear him to the veterans. The Miami-Montego trophy is the Governor-General's Cup, more commonly known as the 'Silver Pineapple'. A number of really first-class skippers like Huey Long have been trying to win it every year since 1961. Huey has won just about every other major sailing race in the world, but this one.

Ted Turner receiving the Pineapple Cup.

Turner is typical of the new breed in ocean racing. He believes in piling on every scrap of canvas until the whole yacht is humming with tension like something from outer space. He has snapped more masts and spars than he would like to remember the cost of.

Incidentally, costs are the first consideration in this business. Many of these racing yachts get up into the $100,000 or more figure, so it helps to be a millionaire. You don't have to be one to participate, but you sure as hell have to be one to own, maintain and operate one of these money burners. But Lord, are they pretty!

ORIGINALLY PUBLISHED JUNE 1973

For Love of the Game

MIRAH LIM

Jamaica's national netball team proves they can stand head to head with the world's best.

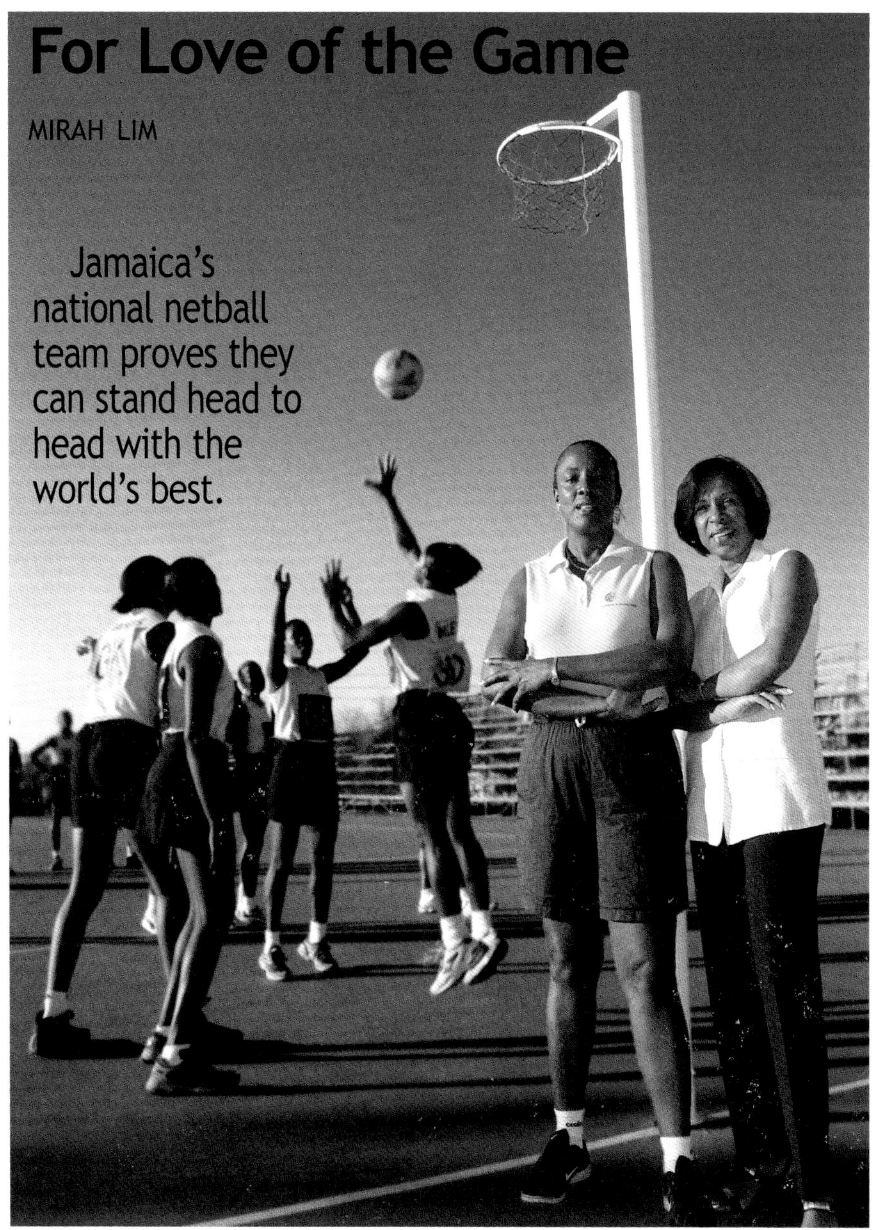

Over the years, Jamaica has gained a reputation for producing some of the finest athletes in the world. From bringing in the gold in several track and field events at the Olympics, to success in arenas such as swimming, football and bobsleighing, our athletes are consistently beating the odds.

One such testament is the little-known story of our Jamaican netball team, which is ranked fourth out of the 67 countries competing worldwide. In fact above all other sport, netball has been the highest world-ranked Jamaican team for over a decade, holding a spot in the top six of the International Netball Federation ranking. In 1991 alone, they were the number three team bettered only by Australia and New Zealand. This record has made Jamaica's senior squad one of the best netball teams in the world, and has earned them the respect and admiration of the entire international sports arena.

Standing alone, these accomplishments are certainly impressive. Yet, even more remarkable is that the national netball team has thrived and prospered solely on the dedication of the people involved—a combination of cash (through donations made by Jamaican companies) and kind (in the form of professionals who volunteer their time). Molly Rhone, president of the Jamaica Netball Association, is one such volunteer who finds time outside her responsibilities as director of information and technology services at Air Jamaica to manage the team. Head coach Maureen Hall is another who currently volunteers to train and travel with the team while working as the general manager of Allied Insurance Brokers and studying for her MBA at the University of Manchester.

"When you look at how much time the players dedicate to training and competing you have to admire netball because it's the only sport that's still amateur," says Molly. "What can I say—like the girls, I enjoy what I do, otherwise I wouldn't be doing it. It helps me feel in touch with my country. My reward is working with these young girls, helping to mold their lives, teaching them to have confidence in themselves." With many of the players coming from inner-city communities, Molly says that her satisfaction also comes from knowing that she's helping to "get the girls out of that (inner city) environment and excel through netball. It helps them get jobs, travel, even sometimes, to go away and study... It's definitely frustrating at times, and a lot of work, but then again there is always a success story to hold on to."

Looking at the team of players who are essentially still juggling school and work and have found success in netball, the stories of triumph are evident. Oberon Pitterson, the team's captain who was recruited at 16 to play for the national team, is a good example. Through her participation in the sport, she received a scholarship to play basketball at a junior college in Texas and then went to Western Illinois University. Currently, she plays professional basketball in Turkey but returns every year to play on the national squad. Leading goal-shoot, Elaine Davis is another. Last year, a team from New Zealand recruited her to play in their semi-professional league. Elaine says that while she was in New Zealand she was "treated like a celebrity. Everywhere I went people wanted autographs." Elaine is currently finishing her degree at the University of Technology, in Jamaica.

"It's the ultimate feeling to hear the national anthem being played on the court and know that it's being played for you,"says Oberon. "Through netball I've gone to places I never thought I would ever go," adds Elaine. "I like that I can be a role model for other young girls in the community," states Simone Forbes, the upcoming star player who won a scholarship to GC Foster College in Jamaica to study physical education because now she, in turn, wants to become a coach.

And yet, despite these rewards, when asked why they play, the girls respond naturally and without hesitation, "For love of the game, of course."

ORIGINALLY PUBLISHED APRIL 2002

The Big Catch

GUY C.M.HARVEY

All three lines got a bite as Herman drove the canoe around the edge of the school of feeding skipjack tuna. He slowed the craft and worked on his fish, handlining the struggling tuna toward the canoe as did his two other crew. Bertie got his in first, then Jocelyn, both fish of about eight pounds. Herman's was bigger and was fighting him below the canoe, when out of nowhere, moving with lightning speed, a blue marlin inhaled the tuna. The marlin was "lit up", electric blue bill, pectoral fins, and tail, stripes on its back glowing vividly. Herman gave the huge fish time to swallow the big tuna bait, before recovering slack line and striking the fish.

The reaction was instantaneous as the the marlin powered its way into the sky, angrily shaking its head, water pouring off its flanks. The fish grey-hounded away, completing a series of jumps and contortions. The line sizzled out through Herman's hands. He was careful not to let it burn him and made sure the line fed smoothly from the line ball in the bottom of the canoe. Bertie took over driving and turned the canoe to chase the rampaging marlin. Herman stood up and worked the line as the canoe gradually overtook the fish. Herman was careful to set the line in the bottom of the canoe, so in another rush by the fish, he could let go line and not have it snag on a seat, fish basket or on his foot.

The great fish sounded and the boat stopped some 200 yards above the fish. The marlin began circling deep down but, with years of experience and hands of iron, Herman started inching the fish toward the surface. In half an hour, the exhausted marlin was in sight, as Jocelyn got ready with the gaff. Bertie manoeuvred the canoe as the marlin made a last rush along the surface. The fish was beside the canoe, rolling in the swells, blue and bronze, as Herman maintained the pressure and pulled the fish closer. Jocelyn sank the gaff and Herman grabbed the marlin's bill. Bertie slammed the club down on the fish's head. All three men rolled the marlin into the boat, along with a lot of water. They were elated. The fish would weigh more than 300lbs, and would fetch $35/lb at the market in Whitehouse.

Blue marlin are caught by artisanal canoe fisherman all year round in Jamaica, along the north coast and south east and south west coasts. But they are only targeted by fisherman on the north coast out of beaches such as Lances Bay, Whitehouse, Oracabessa, Port Maria, Port Antonio and Manchioneal.

The best time to catch blue marlin is in the autumn, from August-October, and during this time blue marlin tournaments are held out of Montego Bay, Falmouth, Ocho Rios and Port Antonio. In May 1984, Bobby Marsh and the Ocho Rios Angling Association added another category to the tournament scene by creating a day for local canoe fishermen. Marsh said, "the Ocho Rios Anglers Association conceived of the competition as a chance for professional fishermen from the area of the north coast to show their skills, and as a mark of appreciation for the knowledge they have passed on over the years about big game fish.".

Canoe tournaments have been held every year subsequently, and still continue in Montego Bay and Port Antonio, during which time, sponsorship and participation have grown steadily, with substantial prizes, such as outboard motors being donated for the heaviest marlin caught. The best result was in the 1993 Port Antonio canoe event, when seven blue marlin were caught. The biggest marlin caught in a canoe tournament, was by Captain Trevor Nichols on "RULER," with a fine fish of 255lbs in the 1991 Port Antonio event.

Much larger fish have been caught on hand lines by canoe fishermen, largest on record is a 726lbs marlin caught off Lucea, after a battle that lasted more than 12 hours, in the late 1970s. In 1982, a sport-fishing boat, "BALAO 11," captain by Reuben "Skippy" Bajjo, (now of "Screaming Eagle" fame) assisted a canoe to fight and boat a marlin in excess of 700lbs, also off Lucea.

Historically, most large marlin were caught drifting a whole dead fish bait, in the way described by Ernest Hemingway, in his famous story of *The Old Man and the Sea*. However, in recent times, the method of trolling artificial baits or dead fish has resulted in good catches. This technique also allows canoe fishermen to target tuna, dolphin fish and wahoo, while looking for a billfish, and greater area is covered in the hunt. The fishermen all stand in the canoe, as they troll along at about eight-ten knots. They look for signs of fish, birds feeding, fish jumping and floating objects such as driftwood, mats of Sargassum weed which harbour baitfish, under which the large predators are found. Normally two or three lines are used. The two outside lines are attached to rubber shock absorbers on the end of bamboo out-riggers. This keeps the lines separated and prevents tangling when the canoe makes a turn. It also allows a "drop back"; a short period of time for the marlin to turn and swallow the bait before the line becomes tight against the clenched fist of the fisherman, or the reel of line.

Artificial lures are used primarily in the recreational sport-fishery, as this method takes advantage of the marlin's speed and natural aggression and allows a boat to cover a wide area in the days' pursuit of the elusive billfish. The canoe fishermen, catching other species, such as tuna around the numerous banks, can have hooked fish overtaken and swallowed by a cruising marlin, as described in the opening paragraphs of this article. Live baiting is a common technique used by fishermen who work the banks off Westmoreland or St. Thomas and is seldom used in recreational fishery, due to the lack of expertise in this very productive and exciting way of fishing for marlin.

On a general note, the current exploitation of billfish stocks in Jamaica's 200 mile E.E.Z., by artisanal canoe fishermen and the recreational fishery, has had little negative impact on the resource, compared to commercial longline fishing. Socio-economic studies analysing the economic benefits of recreational game fishing, specifically tournament events, have clearly indicated the huge value of billfish as a recreational resource. In the 1993 Port Antonio tournament, anglers spent JA$75,000 for each marlin landed, whereas the commercial value of the same fish as meat, is only JA$3,000. It is my opinion that in developing new policies regarding exploitation of this resource, the Jamaican government cannot allow shore-based longlining activity or licence foreign, off-shore long-line activity to deplete the resource as has happened in many other Caribbean and Central American countries. Jamaican canoe fishing activity is considered artisanal and uses low technology while employing a large number of people, without harming the resource. The same can be said for sportfishing, but the operating costs are much greater. To allow commercial, industrial longlining for billfish and tuna in our waters will deprive both artisanal and recreational interests of the use of the resource and bring about the collapse of billfish stocks, as has been seen in so many neighbouring countries.

ORIGINALLY PUBLISHED SEPTEMBER 1994

David Lee
Deep Sea Diver

DANIELLE GOODMAN

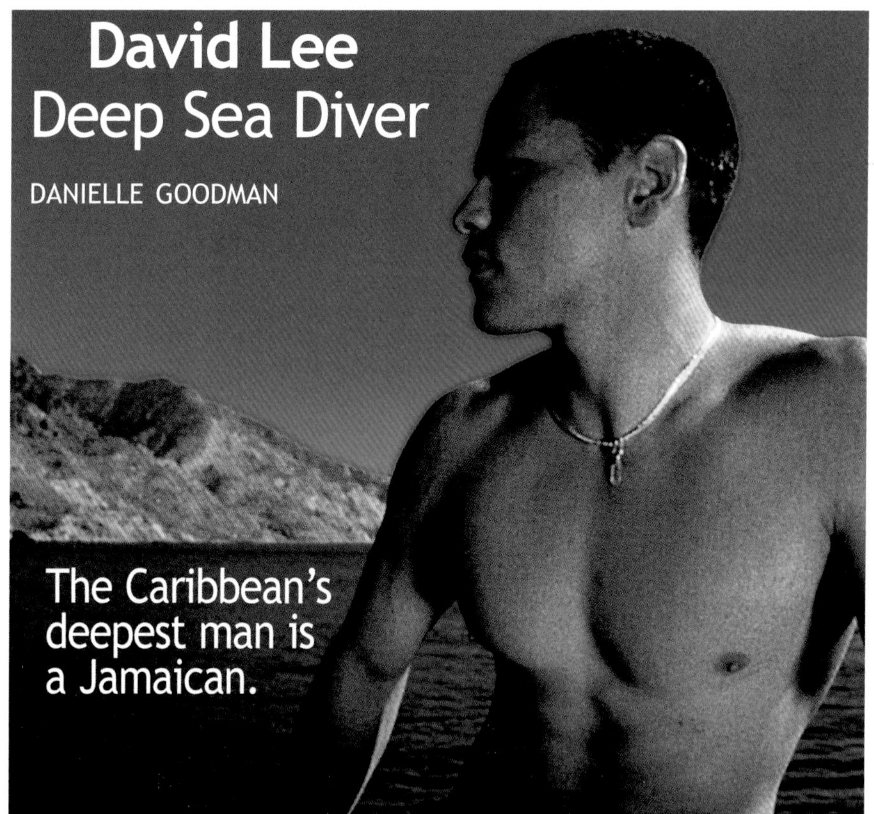

The Caribbean's deepest man is a Jamaican.

Since his childhood, David Lee has swum, dived, and surfed the dark blue waters of Port Antonio, Jamaica.

In April, 2001, he reached the bottom of the "bottomless" Blue Lagoon, setting the world record in freediving—diving 45 meters underwater and back in 1 minute, 40 seconds without oxygen tanks or fins. He broke it again in October, 2001, in Greece, reaching an actual depth of 48.9 meters in 1 minute 49 seconds.

David Lee is the world record holder in unassisted constant ballast diving, but he lives a thousand miles from the nearest sea. "For a freediver, it's pretty strange." In Tulsa, Oklahoma, he settles for a pool instead, training up and down the lengths hours a day after work as network engineer for a medical electronics company. It's a strictly disciplined regime, for food, for work, for life. "I'm always in training," he says. Growing up by Port Antonio's dark blue waters, around his mother's dive shop, Lee, 26, lived for the sea. "I used to take off from school at Titchfield and go surfing...but I still got good enough grades to go to university." It brought him to Tulsa, about as far from diving and Port Antonio as you can possibly be. Three years after graduating, "I'm still here. As long as I can get to go home three times a year or more."

In December last year, Lee came home to Port Antonio for a visit and left with a new world record in freediving, set in the "bottomless" depths of the Blue Lagoon. He practices the purest form, in which the diver uses "no weights, no fins, no nothing. You just breaststroke down and back." What does it feel like to reach those depths? "The only thing I focus on is the rope, so I go straight down. There's so much adrenaline you don't hear anything except the divers giving the signals. They bang aluminium poles together about every 15 meters down. In Blue Lagoon it's a small hole. The difference in light is drastic because of all the overhanging trees. All of a sudden at 120 feet it gets pitch black and you hear the second to last signal. Everything happens so quick. You see this very faint light and go towards it straight down the rope. At the bottom, you see just enough to pick up the tag and go. When you take one minute to go from the surface and one minute back, you don't have time for your eyes to adjust. It's like somebody put a flashlight on in front of your eyes and took it away.

"You get to the surface and you're still holding your breath. The trainer is there on top shouting at you, reminding you to 'Breathe!' You take three small breaths and then you start to breathe [normally]. If you took one big breath after you came up, that amount of oxygen coming in on the high carbon dioxide could make you pass out."

The pressure is inside as well as outside, in the nervousness before the start and in the crushingly deep water. The way Lee handles it is counterintuitive: "You have to *not* follow your natural instinct."

"When you're diving for a world record you don't listen to your body, because your body was never designed to go that deep." Although he's made and broken records, Lee is not motivated by external achievement. He measures himself against his own extreme baseline. "I've always wondered, how much weight can I lift? How fast can I run? How far can I push it before my body breaks down? This was a way to do it. It's a matter of finding out how deep I can go." After a time, Lee found that even he would only go so far. It took his trainer to push him out of his comfort zone and towards the world record.

"When I was freediving just for fun, you'd always listen to that little voice in your head that said "Come back up now, you're running out of air." Then I met my trainer, Rudi Castineyra. He said, "From now on you're not going to listen to that little voice anymore." The advice breaks with conventional wisdom, but it has provided Lee with the training to withstand the deep dives' extraordinary shock to the system. "It was very hard at first. I'm always used to doing what feels right. That was difficult for me to overcome. At a certain point in record freediving, you start to feel strange. If you feel that, you go anyway. You force yourself to do it. With the training, you keep experiencing all these changes over and over—for example, you have involuntary contractions—so that later on when you're diving and you experience them, you keep calm."

The calm has to last. Under the surface, time stretches out into another element. "The first dive took a minute and 50 seconds. This one took two minutes. A dive that takes two minutes feels like five."

Diving to more than 45 meters underwater on one lungful of air is a mysterious experience. "The one thing on my mind is to get the tag without losing consciousness. I can't explain what it is that makes me do it. It's almost like someone else takes over. You're not fully aware of what's going on. Something mental happens. Half the time when I get back to the surface I can't tell what I did and where I was." Deep.

ORIGINALLY PUBLISHED APRIL 2002

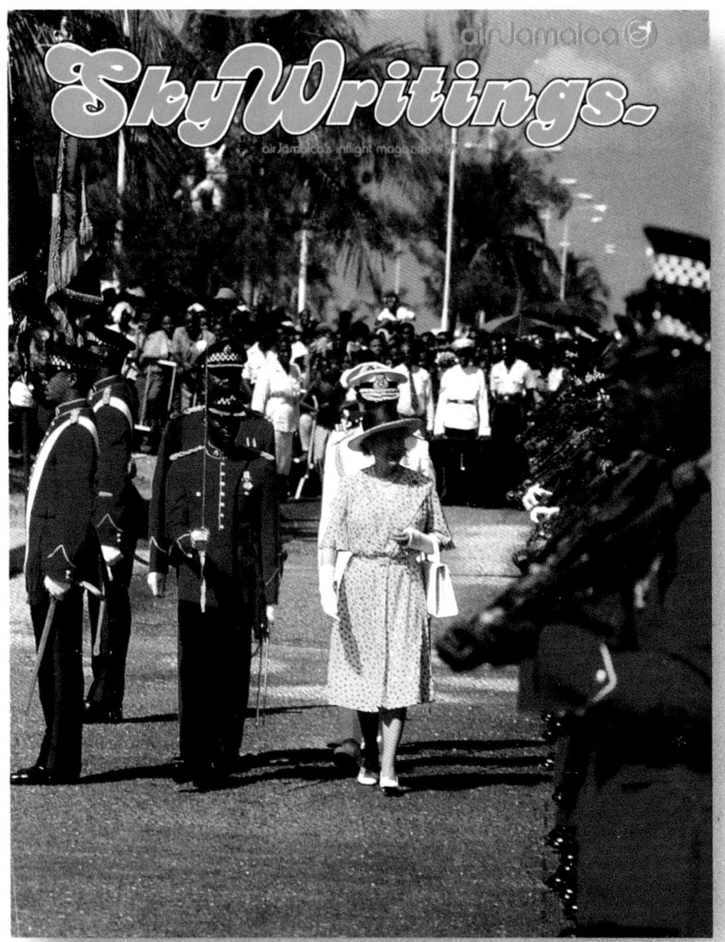

HISTORY

SKYWRITINGS COVER
May 1994
Her Majesty Queen Elizabeth II inspects the Guard of Honour, the 1st Battalion The Jamaica Regiment.

©PHILLIP LYNCH

The Arawaks Arrived Before Columbus

PHILIP SHERLOCK

American Indians called "Arawaks" discovered and settled in Jamaica before Columbus arrived. They were six or seven centuries ahead of "the Discoverer."

The Arawaks migrated in waves from their homes in Eastern Venezuela and the basin of the Orinoco. To this day Arawak-speaking Indians live in that region.

From giant trees in the forest, working patiently with fire and stone-axes, they fashioned great dug-outs, some so large that they would hold forty or fifty men. They propelled them only with oars, for they did not know how to harness wind power with sails.

Slowly, generation after generation, they and their kinsmen, the fierce man-eating Caribs made their way through the Caribbean archipelago, settling or moving on as they thought fit.

They travelled light, for they wore few garments if any. They travelled with what they needed to survive: batatas (sweet potatoes), cassava bread (the Jamaica bammy) and the cassava plant, a store of maize, grinding stones for crushing the grains, and their sacred tobacco. The plant was called "cohiba." It was the pipe used for smoking it that was called "tabaco." Smoking set them dreaming of "Coyaba", their paradise.

The Arawaks also took with them their "zemes"—images in stone and wood—spirits that they worshipped. The name was given also to anything that had magical powers.

Finally the Arawaks came to the Greater Antilles, the four large islands of Puerto Rico, Haiti "land of mountains", Jamaica "land of springs", Cuba, as well as to the Bahamas.

The Arawaks were the first dwellers in Jamaica of whom we have record. The description that Columbus gave of the Arawaks whom he met first in the Bahamas holds true in general for those whom he met in the other islands. As Columbus himself wrote:

"All that I saw were young men, none of them more than thirty years old, very well made, of very handsome bodies and very good faces; the hair they wear over their eyebrows, except for a hank behind that they wear long and never cut. Some of them paint themselves black (and they are of the colour of the Canary Islanders, neither black nor white), and some paint themselves white, and others red, and others with what they have. Some paint their faces, others the whole body, others the eyes only, others only the nose."

They had a liking for finery and ceremony, and showed great respect to their chiefs, whom they called caciques. In each island, caciques, assisted by village headmen and sub-chiefs, exercised authority and enjoyed certain privileges and special favours. For example, caciques were allowed several wives whereas other males were allowed only one each. The best of the cassavas, sweet potatoes and maize went to them, the best of the wild coneys and iguanas caught in the forests, the best of the harvest yielded by the sea. The cacique's house was larger than the others and contained revered idols.

But there was one special favour that would not seem to us as desirable as the others. This was that if a cacique were ill or dying he would be strangled. This was not as cruel as it seems for other people who were ill were usually abandoned in the bush with some cassava and water.

There may have been as many as 100,000 Arawaks in Jamaica when Columbus arrived in 1494. Being coastland people rather than forest or mountain people, they built their villages on high ground overlooking the sea or river estuaries, within easy reach of the inshore waters which they harvested for the shell-fish, the mussels and chip-chip that they loved. The shells they threw on the village middens or scrap-heaps, providing in this way the abundance of shells by which we identify the sites of their villages.

The settlements were scattered at points along the north coast from Priestman's River, just east of Port Antonio through to a populous village they called Maima at New Seville near St. Ann's Bay, and on to Rio Bueno and Montego Bay. They settled along the south coast also, at Savanna-la-mar, Bluefields, Cow Bay at Portland Bight, at White Marl on the Kingston-Spanish Town highway, on Jacks Hill overlooking Kingston harbour, and at some points inland such as Ewarton and Moneague.

The houses were small and round, with a cone-shaped roof of thatch. The circular wall of wild reeds tied together with vines or withes was supported by posts which were driven into the ground, with a strong centre-pole to hold the structure together. Some settlements consisted of only a few households while others had as many as forty or fifty.

The Caribs, according to Columbus' account, built better houses and were more skilled than the Arawaks. He reported that "they appeared to be more civilized than those that we had hitherto seen, for although all the Indians have houses of straw, yet the houses of these people are constructed in a much superior fashion, are better stocked with provisions and exhibit more evidence of industry, both on the part of the men and the women. They had a considerable quantity of cotton, both spun and prepared for spinning and many cotton sheets so well woven as to be no way inferior to those of our country."

Within easy reach of their settlements the Arawaks made clearings in the forest for their food-gardens or "conucos", no easy task because in those days primeval forest extended, on the north side, from the topmost mountain ridges to the coast. Streams were plentiful and ran sparkling to the sea. In the forest they hunted the coney (utia) and the iguana, the only wild animals in the island.

Their tools and implements were simple, for they were stone-age people and had no knowledge of iron. With stone-axes and pointed sticks and fire they cleared and prepared the ground, and planted their staples, sweet potatoes, maize, cassava. These, with fish and shell-fish, were their mainstay.

The larder was a limited one, lacking in high-energy foods. They had no domestic animals, neither cattle nor sheep nor swine, no horses, no mules, no asses; only a sort of small dog that never barked. Sometimes Jamaicans, deafened at night by the barking of their dogs, wish that the Arawak dogs were still around.

Limited though the larder was the Arawaks delighted in festive occasions when they dressed themselves up in red, painting faces and bodies yellow, black and red and wearing cloaks and head-dresses of bright feathers. They wore on arms and legs ornaments of shells which rattled as they moved. Usually there was a parade led by the cacique who beat a wooden gong. Singing and dancing followed, with offerings of cassava bread to the zeme. The priests then broke the holy bread in pieces which they distributed to the people who kept them as charms for protection against disasters. Most fearful of these was the onslaught of the god Huracan, who brought storms in the summer, whipped the sea to fury, drove mountains of water against the land and uprooted the trees that sheltered their conucos.

After the distribution of the sanctified cassava came the drinking of fermented juice made from crushed maize and the smoking of tobacco, either as crudely made cigars or with pipes. Generally the pipe was a tube shaped like a 'Y'. The two branches were put into the nostrils, and the smoke inhaled in deep breaths. The smoker was soon knocked out.

This love of ceremony and their delight in bright colours comes out in the description left by Andres Bernaldez, of a meeting between Columbus and an Arawak cacique on the south coast of Jamaica, at Portland Bight. Bernaldez was not an eyewitness but he probably heard the account from Columbus himself. He told how a fleet of canoes approached Columbus' ship. In one of the canoes, very large, painted throughout, "came the cacique with his wife and two daughters, one about 18 years old, very beautiful, entirely naked as is the custom and very modest... There were two sons and five brothers and others who must all have been his servants and vassals; he brought in his canoe a man acting as an ensign who stood alone in the stern, with a cloak of coloured feathers...and on his head a large plume and he bore in his hand a white banner." With him were "two or three men, their faces painted in similar colours...each with a large plume arranged like a helmet...and these men had in their hands a kind of musical instrument which they plucked..."

The cacique wore around his neck a very delicate ornament of copper, so delicate that it looked like eight-carat gold. It was suspended from a string of thick beads of marble stone "on which they set great value here", and on his head a large wreath of small green and coloured stones.

But there was no dressing up for death. We know that they sometimes buried their dead in caves, and that they sometimes put the head and certain bones in a bowl of clay, for that is where some of the best preserved Arawak skulls and finest examples of their pottery have been found.

After death the soul went to a happy land called Coyaba, a place of perpetual feasting and dancing.

On the morning of 12 October 1492, the old world of Europe collided with the old world of the Americas.

Columbus, in command of a little fleet of three ships, had set out from the port of Palos, near Cadiz, to sail westwards across the Atlantic in order to reach India. He stopped briefly at the Canary Islands, then on September 8 began his history-making trans-Atlantic voyage.

Thirty-two days later, at about two o'clock on the morning of October 12, the lookout on one of the ships saw land and shouted "Tierra, tierra!"

The ships lowered sails and jogged off-shore. At daybreak Columbus and his men saw before them a little island in the Bahamas that the Arawaks called Guanahani and Columbus named San Salvador, Holy Saviour.

That morning Columbus went ashore in the armed boat, with him his captains and with the Royal Standard of Spain and the banner of the expedition, "and said that they should bear witness and testimony how he before them all took possession of the island...for the King and Queen, his sovereigns."

Columbus' first act, then, was to dispossess those who first discovered and settled the island and who had lived in it for generations.

The Arawaks gathered around the strangers in friendly fashion. Columbus said of them, "They bear no arms nor know thereof, for I showed them swords and they grasped them by the blade and cut themselves through ignorance." The blood-shedding, accidental though it was, foreshadowed the future. A century later there were few Arawaks left.

The third sign foreshadowed slavery: "They should be good servants and of quick intelligence and I believe that they would easily be made Christians..."

Enforced slavery, cruelty and imported diseases wiped out the Arawaks of the islands in a century and a half.

The tragic story of the genocide of the Arawaks and of the indigenous people throughout the Americas justifies our applying to them the words of a distant kinsman, Seattle, chief of the Dwarmish and allied tribes of Puget Sound, spoken in 1855 as he thought of the collision of Europe with the old world of the Americas: "My people are few. They resemble the scattering trees of a storm-swept plain. There was a time when our people covered the land as the waves of a wind-ruffled sea covers its shell-paved floor, but that time long since passed away with the greatness of tribes that are now but a mournful memory."

ORIGINALLY PUBLISHED MAY 1992

Columbus Marooned in Jamaica

PHILIP SHERLOCK

Columbus spent longer in Jamaica than in any other Caribbean island save Hispaniola. He was compelled to do so by mischance. While exploring the western limits of the Caribbean, searching for a strait, he was buffeted by storms. He had only two ships left, La Capitana and Santiago, and these were in bad shape, leaking badly. After a brief stop in Cuba he decided to try to get to Hispaniola.

Pugna inter Columbum & Franciscum Poresium. XIIII.

QVARTA nauigatione Hispaniolam portus aditu prohibitus Columbus à Bombadilla, Iamaicam insulam tenuit. Ibi Franciscus Poresius vnius Carauellæ Prætor cum fratre & maxima militum parte seditionem in eum commouet, & contractis aliquot Indorum lintribus in Hispaniolam profugere conatur. Sed quum tam exiguis lintribus impetum maris superare frustra tentasset, regressus est. Audito eius aduentu, Columbus cum fratre suos in aciem educit: ventum est ad manus: cadunt nonnulli: multi vtrinque saucij: Franciscus Poresius cum fratre capitur.

The winds, however, were unfavourable. On the night of the 22nd and on the 23rd June the water flooded the deck of the Capitana, causing "universal anguish" amongst the crew. The crippled vessels continued east, past Discovery Bay, or Puerto Seco, to St. Ann's Bay, Santa Gloria.

"With all rigging gone," Columbus wrote, "the ships more perforated with worms than a honeycomb, the men dejected and downcast... the bad weather pushed me back again; and after eight days I took to the road again and arrived in Jamaica at the end of June always with headwinds and the ships more worse than ever; with three pumps, tubs and boilers, the whole crew could not conquer the water which came into the ship, nor is there any other cure for shipworm... The other ship ran into port almost submerged and our Lord brought me to land by a miracle."

Among those who were with Columbus on that voyage was the courageous, loyal Diego Mendez. Columbus was the positive, obsessive kind of personality that evokes extraordinary loyalty or deep animosity. Diego Mendez was the loyal follower, while the Porras brothers, whom we shall meet shortly, were the disloyal ones.

Diego, in his journal, described vividly the broken night of anxiety and fear. "We drove the ships on shore;" he wrote, "and made on them two cabins thatched with straw, in which we took up our dwelling, not however without considerable danger from the natives, who were not yet subdued, and who might easily set fire to our habitation in the night, in spite of the greatest watchfulness. It was there that I gave out the last ration of biscuit and wine..."

The location where the ships were beached has been identified, with assistance from the United States. It is at Seville, near the site of the first Spanish capital of Jamaica, and efforts are under way to bring the ships to light. It is not an easy task for the former coastline now lies some distance inland.

Food and security were the major concerns. Again Diego showed his mettle. Sword in hand, with only three of the crew accompanying him, he set out to find both food and a reliable source of supply.

Fortune favoured him: "It pleased God that I found some people who were very gently and did us no harm, but received us cheerfully and gave us food with hearty good will. I then made a stipulation with the Indians who lived in a village called Aguacadiba, and with their cacique, that they should hunt and fish to supply the Admiral every day with a sufficient quantity of provisions, which they were to bring to the ships, where I promised there should be a person ready to pay them in blue beads, combs and knives, hawk-bells and fish hooks, and other such articles."

Columbus chafed at the enforced idleness. He was desperately anxious also, for he knew that his enemies in Santo Domingo would be happy if he were marooned in Jamaica forever. The only remedy was to send someone he could trust to Santo Domingo to seek help. But who would set out on so perilous a mission, for it meant going by canoe; and, as Diego told him, to cross with so small a craft a gulf of forty leagues of a sea that was always tempestuous and never at rest was impossible.

Columbus had no one else on whom he could depend. He knew that if he sent the Porras brothers they would, in all probability, never return with help. If Diego undertook the mission he would not give up until it was accomplished. Diego pointed out that some of the crew were jealous of him: "there have not been wanting murmerers who have said that your Lordship entrusts every honourable undertaking to me while there are others amongst them who would perform them as well." Finally Columbus agreed to ask for volunteers, and Diego agreed to go if none came forward.

On the following day Columbus called the men together, described the mission and asked for volunteers. No one offered. It was impossible, they said, in so small a craft to cross a boisterous and perilous gulf of forty leagues. Many strong vessels had been lost in those seas, through the fury and force of the currents.

At this point Diego rose and said, "My Lord, I have but one life and I am willing to hazard it in the service of your lordship and for the welfare of all those who are here with us; for I trust in God... He will give me deliverance."

It was an emotional moment. The Admiral embraced Diego, kissed him on both cheeks and said, "Well did I know that there was no one here but yourself who would dare to undertake this enterprise. I trust in God our Lord that you will come out of it victoriously."

The very next morning Diego made ready. Drawing his canoe up on shore he fixed a false keel on it, pitched and greased it, nailed some boards on the poop and prow to keep the sea out, fitted it with mast and sail, put in the necessary provision for himself, one other Spaniard and six Indians, eight being as many as the boat could hold. All the preparations having been completed he bade farewell to the Admiral and the others and set out toward the eastern end of Jamaica. From there he planned to turn toward the north east, in the direction of Santo Domingo.

Then disaster overtook him. First he was taken prisoner by some Indian pirates from whom he escaped. He and his men reached the eastern end of Jamaica and camped there, waited for calmer seas; but the natives collected together, planning to kill him and seize the contents of the canoe.

"As soon as I became aware of their project," he wrote, "I betook myself secretly to my canoe which I had left at three leagues distance from where I was and set sail for the spot where the Admiral was staying and reached it after an interval of fifteen days from my departure."

A lesser man would have given up the mission after this setback but not Diego Mendez. The one condition he laid down was that Columbus should arrange for a party of men to go with him to the eastern end of Jamaica and to stay with him until he could set out for Santo Domingo. Columbus assigned seventy men to accompany him and to remain at the place of departure for three days after he set off.

This time things went well. They reached the eastern end of Jamaica without incident, waited for four days until the sea grew calm, and then, wrote Diego, "I parted from the rest of the men with much mutual sorrow; I then commended myself to God and our Lady of Antigua, and was at sea five days and four nights without laying down my oar from my hand, but continued steering the boat while my companions rowed. It pleased God that at the end of five days I reached the island of Hispaniola at Cape San Miguel, having been two days without eating or drinking for our provisions were exhausted." It was a remarkable, unforgettable experience—one that Diego sought to immortalise by leaving instructions in his will that on his tomb should be engraved a ship with the inscription CANOA beneath it.

The long weeks passed and the men at Santa Gloria grew tense and restless with uncertainty. The Porras brothers and a group of followers rebelled against Columbus, moved away from Santa Gloria and settled at the neighbouring Arawak village of Miami. After a series of futile negotiations Columbus' brother Bartholomew and a small group of loyalists put down the rising. The rebels begged for pardon, which the Admiral granted.

But drama continued to attend the Admiral. He knew how important it was to retain Indian help. The honeymoon period, however, had ended. Relationships had soured and the uprising which the Arawaks had witnessed lowered the esteem in which they held the Spaniards. On their first arrival at San Salvador the Indians had greeted them as men come from heaven. Now, at Santa Gloria, enduring the discourtesy and cruelty of the Spaniards, they lost their respect for them. The supplies of food fell off. For Columbus to seize supplies by force from Miami would only make matters worse.

Columbus gives a vivid account of the way in which he regained the respect of the Arawak and reasserted his authority over them. An almanac that he had with him told him that an eclipse of the moon was due. It gave him the date of the eclipse. He summoned a number of the caciques to the Capitana, and through an Indian interpreter told him that, by reducing their supplies of food they had offended the Christian God who ruled over all things. God would put a sign on his anger in the sky. The moon would become inflamed and angry. Some of the Indians grew fearful but others mocked at Columbus.

There followed an extraordinary confrontation between 14th century European scientific knowledge and stone-age innocence. When night fell, and the eclipse began, panic spread amongst the Arawaks. Columbus withdrew to his quarters and remained silent until the eclipse reached its peak. He then spoke through the interpreter to the Indians, telling them that God would take away his anger from the sky if they promised to be obedient and to continue to supply the Spaniards with food. Panic-stricken, they promised. Gradually the eclipse passed. The next morning the Arawaks began to supply food once more.

After twelve long months help came from Santo Domingo. The ever-faithful Diego Mendez had triumphed over all obstacles. But Columbus was no longer in favour. His royal protector, Queen Isabella, was dead. His days as an explorer and navigator were over. Bobadilla, who had been sent out to Hispaniola to enquire into complaints against him and to take over from him, put him in prison and then sent him to Spain in irons. Columbus' sovereign restored his titles and property and treated him with all courtesy, but never again was he allowed to exercise his office of Viceroy or to interfere in the government of the island of Hispaniola.

Time, however, enlarged Columbus' achievement. To say that he discovered America is a misuse of words. He established contact between two worlds, both already old. He did so at a time when European technology was good enough to maintain that contact by regular voyages. By his voyages he doubled the size of the known world and shifted its centre from the Mediterranean to the Atlantic.

ORIGINALLY PUBLISHED NOVEMBER 1992

Columbus' Gold Mine

ED KRITZLER

The search for a secret treasure reveals some surprising 21st century connections.

I didn't shout "Eureka," but I could have—before me lay a centuries old map of the alleged gold mine of Columbus. I was in the archival vault of the Spanish Town Record Office, a cavernous, dimly lit room, full floor to ceiling with leather bound volumes of Jamaica's historic documents.

For 20 years I have been researching the history of Jewish pioneers in the New World, principally those in Jamaica. The story of Columbus' legendary mine was a part of it. In 1623, with the threat of the Inquisition weighing on them, Jamaica's covert Jews contacted England's Duke of Buckingham, and enticed him to invade by offering to disclose the site of the "secret mine."

This was a time when Jews in the Spanish empire were burned at the stake by the Holy Inquisition. Until then, Jamaica had been an exception. Jamaica was Columbus' island. It had been discovered by him in 1494, and he was marooned here in 1503. In 1509, the island was settled by his son, and in 1536, Jamaica was deeded to his family. It was the one Spanish colony in the New World the Crown agreed his heirs could own, and not coincidentally, it was the only place the Inquisition was not allowed to operate.

From the start, conversos (converted Jews) called Portugals were welcome by the Columbus family. Since the family owned all of the land, few Spaniards other than Jewish merchants, were interested in settling Jamaica. During the 16th century, the island's Portugals lived peacefully and profitably. In partnership with the family, they transformed the island into a major, albeit illegal, transshipment port.

This was revealed in 1568 when current heir, Luis Colon, was charged with importing more goods to Jamaica than the island could consume and exporting the surplus to the Spanish Main. This violated the cardinal rule of the mercantile system that stipulated "first profits to the homeland." All goods to and from the New World had to first go through Seville. Although the charges were later dropped, they disclosed the state of the island.

In part to protect the Portugals, the Columbus family kept the Inquisition away. But this was not to last. By the second decade of the 17th century, the Spanish ranchers grew restive. They had grown rich supplying passing ships with cow and pig fat from Bahia de Manteca, (Montego Bay, the Bay of Lard), but wanted more, specifically title to their land. This, they decided, could be accomplished by having the Crown reclaim Jamaica. To justify the Crown's action, they charged the island was riddled with heresy, engineered an ecclesiastical coup and invited Inquisitors to Jamaica.

Alarmed by this development which threatened to expose them as "false conversos" (i.e. heretics), the Portugals got word to the Duke of Buckingham. In return for a British invasion and their liberation, they would reveal the site of Columbus' "secret gold mine which hath not been opened by the King of Spain, or by any other...The earth is black. Rivulets discover the source." It was a secret they had been privy to since their ancestors were marooned with Columbus and had defended him when half his crew mutinied. Passed down the generations, the secret was a safeguard, only to be revealed if and when their covert lives as Jews was threatened. The Duke, together with Sweden's King Gustav Adolphus, was set to lead an armada across the Ocean Sea to capture Jamaica and seize the mine, when he was assassinated.

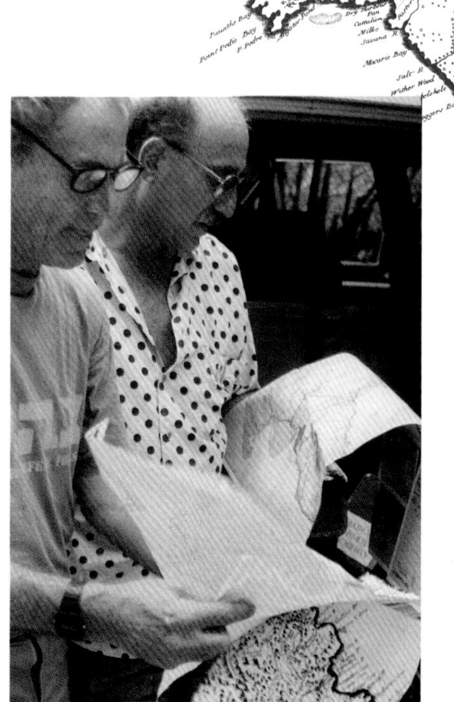

Was there a mine? Everyone then believed so. The 17th century was a time when New World legends were indistinguishable from fact. As was the case with Eldorado and the Fountain of Youth, finding the Lost Gold Mine of Columbus had long been a dream of the royals, who were the only ones who could afford to entertain such fantastic ambitions.

In 1655, the English under Oliver Cromwell conquered Jamaica. Afterwards a former Spanish governor of the island lamented:

(ABOVE) Christopher Columbus painted by Sebastiano del Piombo; A Spanish map of Jamaica; Ed Kritzler (FOREGROUND) and Eran Spiro examining old world and modern day maps of Jamaica. (OPPOSITE PAGE) Jamaica Arawak Gold Disc found near site of Columbus' maroonment. Volumes of Jamaican history inside the archive vault; where Ed Kritzler and Ainsley Henriques study a contract between the brothers Henriques (decendants of Ainsley) and King Charles II of England regarding the division of Columbus' gold.

"There are many gold mines (in Jamaica). Although it is not known now where they are, it is nevertheless an established fact that when his Excellency, the first Admiral of the Indies (Columbus) discovered this island, he extracted much and of high karat, and some old pits of that gold are still there. Today on the island there are still some old jewels made from that gold.

Seven years later, in 1662, Charles II was restored as England's king, how much the tale of Columbus' mine played in his royal fantasies is not known, but the first foreign mission he initiated was to contract two Dutch Jews to lead a royal expedition to find and develop the legendary mine. Charles was so taken with the fantasy of finding the mine that he removed his gold necklace and placed it over the head of the son of one of the Jews "as a mark of Royal favour." When the so-called "gold finding Jews" arrived in Jamaica, the harbour master, noted in his diary:

"Six Jews (with a rich cargo), who pretended they came to discover a gold mine, known to them in the Spaniards government, but disused, for fear it might bring enemies on a place so weakly manned as Jamaica was in the Spaniards time. But this was barely a pretence, for their design was only to insinuate themselves into the country for the sake of trade."

A year later when no mine had been found, the king banished the Jews from Jamaica and demanded the return of his necklace. The project was declared a hoax. Over the ensuing centuries no gold was discovered in Jamaica. The harbour master's early judgement became the historical truth, and today talk of the gold mine is greeted with derisive laughter. No gold now, means no gold then. Or does it?

Before my archival finds, I treated the gold mine story as a scam extraordinaire, of conniving Jews spellbinding a king with a promise of fantasy fulfillment. But gold was recently discovered in Jamaica, and the cynical harbour master, Col. Beeston who went on to become governor, was a rival merchant and no friend of the Jews; Beeston had said they came "for the sake of a trade," specifically pimento, but a reading of the contract negates this. Rather it stipulates that the Jews had the right to export "all hollow pepper (pimento)...only in the event of the discovery...finding and working of the mine." Most convincing is the evidence found in the documents which suggest that the only hoax the "gold finding Jews" perpetrated was pretending that they had not found the mine.

The land deed and map from 1670 show that the expedition's leader Abraham Cohen secretly returned to Jamaica and took possession of an isolated river valley in the island's mountainous interior. Why would Cohen, then in his 60s, and living with his second wife and family in Amsterdam, and wealthy beyond need, hazard a two-month ocean voyage to an island he had been banished from in order to secure land in a heretofore undeveloped part of Jamaica? To me, the answer was obvious—he had returned for the gold. Apparently not satisfied with the royal contract that awarded him one third of the mine's ore, Cohen had returned to grab the whole.

Minutes after I found his land deed, I came across a second document that provided the answer why Cohen never developed the land. If before I was ready to shout eureka, I was now too stunned to do more than look again and again at the crumbling document, and stare away in amazement. The 1675 document, headed "Cohen vs. Cohen," was a settlement to a lawsuit between two extraordinary Jewish pioneers who after a lifetime of fighting the Inquisition, were for the first time revealed to be brothers. Abraham Cohen, international merchant, and brilliant negotiator for the rights of his people, was in this document identified as the brother of the Jewish pirate Moses Cohen Henriques. Apparently the pirate was trying to horn in on his brother's deal, because a few weeks after their settlement, a third document revealed that the land had been sold. Today, more than three centuries later the valley is still isolated, and the land largely undeveloped.

That the two were brothers was startling enough, but what sent chills up my spine was the fact that their current descendant is Ainsley Henriques, the leader of Jamaica's Jewish community. As chairman of Jamaica's National Heritage Trust, Ainsley was sponsoring my research—and if the gold hunt proved successful, is a rightful claimant to Columbus' mine.

A year before, I off-handedly told Ainsley about the fantastic deeds of the Jewish pirate Moses Cohen Henriques. A 1636 Inquisition document in the Seville archives accuses him of masterminding the 1628 seizure of the Spanish silver fleet, a billion dollar haul, the largest in history. When Ainsley said that he too was a Cohen Henriques, I thought it possible that in his later years Moses may have had something to do with turning Jamaica into the pirate capital of the New World. Later, I found evidence of this, including his citizenship papers signed by famed buccaneer Sir Henry Morgan.

However, there was no way of knowing Ainsley was related to the other brother Abraham Cohen, because Cohen never used his Spanish name. A sworn enemy of Spain, he had forsaken Henriques, his "oppressor" name. Even in the document he is identified simply as "Abraham Cohen, brother of Moses Cohen Henriques..." Only here is his full identity revealed; only in a legal dispute with his brother would it have been required.

Ainsley's 17th century uncles were giants in an era when Jews were outlawed in most of Europe and the Spanish Empire. Only in Amsterdam where the brothers came of age in the early 1600s, could Jews safely call themselves such. World trade had become the major source of world revenue, and seeking to become the trade mart of Europe, it welcomed the People of the Book. Scattered worldwide by their ancestors' expulsion from the peninsula, the exiles settled everywhere they were permitted and many places they weren't. In Spain and Portugal, Jews had been compelled by circumstance to learn the "secrets" of the business entrepreneur. By the 1600s, they formed a global tribe of inside traders, bonded by heritage, language and a hatred for Spain.

Before his last hurrah took him to Jamaica, Cohen was an international merchant in the Dutch colony in Brazil. Nothing of consequence happened in Recife without him knowing and abating. For two decades (1630-1654) he dealt in sugar and diamonds, was the Governor's buying agent, and set up a global trade network. His fealty to Judaism was such that he often signed his name in Hebrew. In 1654, when Portugal reconquered Brazil, he returned to Amsterdam where he used his economic muscle to establish Jewish settlement in the West Indies, and in collusion with his son Jacob, secured Jewish rights in New Amsterdam, soon to be New York.

After the capture of the silver fleet, Moses led a company of Dutch Jews in the invasion of Brazil; he then settled in Recife and embarked on a piracy career that spanned a half-century, during which he owned his own pirate island, donated three percent of his booty to the synagogue, and wound up in Jamaica as an advisor to the buccaneer leader Sir Henry Morgan.

Surrounded by enemies, the Henriques brothers grew up strong and free in Amsterdam, a city known in the diaspora world as New Jerusalem. Although few in number, they and their comrades over the course of a half century of leadership (1623-75) invaded the New World, settled openly in Brazil, helped conquer Jamaica, negotiated the return of Jews to England, pioneered Caribbean settlement, and when "a new nation conceived in liberty" was being born, Cohen sent his son ahead to secure settlement rights for his people.

Ainsley's ancestors were not gonifs (Yiddish for con men) hustling a king, but freedom fighters who battled the forces of the Inquisition orchestrated their people's freedom, and made themselves rich in the process. Although it was reported their search for Columbus' mine was not successful, my discovery of Cohen's map convinces me otherwise. At the very least, his journeying to a forbidden island to obtain land he did not need, is persuasive that he believed he had indeed found the site of the "secret gold mine unopened by the King of Spain or any other." Other evidence I have accumulated also points to the valley as the likely site. I have been there and scooped up handfuls of river sand. No luck yet. But the valley is large, and the vein of gold is reportedly but "two inches wide." When Ainsley and I interest a documentary maker, we will return with metal detector to find if where "the earth is black. Rivulets discover the source of the mine."...If we find even one nugget, we are going straight to Spielberg.

ORIGINALLY PUBLISHED APRIL 2000

Early Maps of Jamaica

DAVID BUISSERET

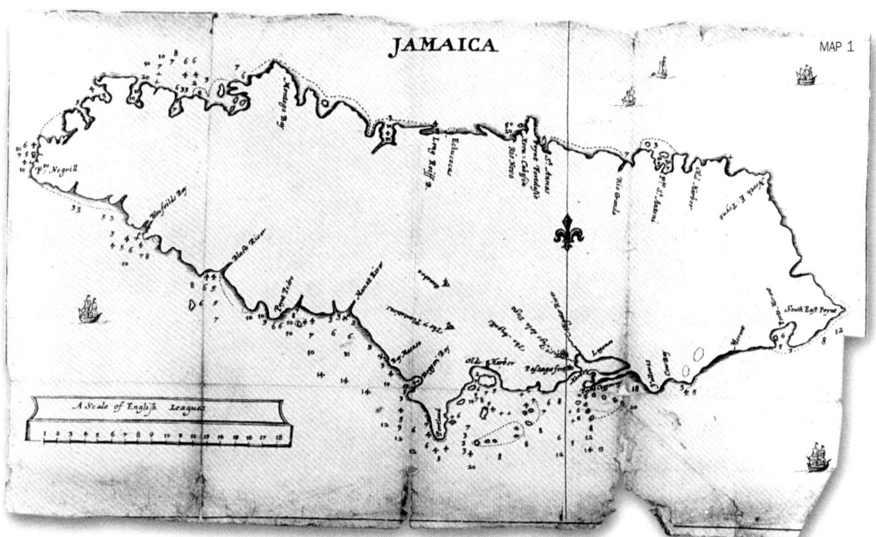

The Spaniards settled in Jamaica from the beginning of the 16th century but, their maps of the island long remained very approximate.

The first printed English version (map 1) is a good deal better as far as the general shape goes, and quite interesting when you can analyze the place-names. Captain Edmund Hickeringill, who drew it, evidently know much more about the coast than about the interior, except in Saint Catherine and Saint Andrew, which the English were holding quite strongly. He was also well-informed about the best anchorages, setting out their depths with some care (in fathoms?). If we look around the coast, we come to a good many places that we recognize. Port Royal is 'Poynt Caggoway', as the English called it for some years after 1655. 'Legonee' is of course the plain on which Kingston now stands, and 'Yallowes' is Yallahs, named after the Spanish Ayala who had a ranch there. 'Morant' is Morant Bay, and 'porto Morant' is nearly the same; we now call 'South East Poynt' Morant Point.

Up on the north-east coast is 'Old Harbour', which is hard to place, but it was a little east of 'Pto St Antoni', evidently Port Antonio. 'Rio Grande' is easy, but Port Maria seems to be marked 'St. Annas'. On the other hand, 'Rio Novo' (Rio Nuevo) is correct; after all, the English had just won a decisive victory over the Spaniards there in 1658. Working along to the west, we easily recognize 'Morant Bay' and 'Pto grill' On the south coast, too, the names are mostly easy: 'Blufeilds Bay', 'Black River' and 'Poynt Pedro' are all in the right place. 'Marat River' is puzzling, but 'Bay Macase' is Macary Bay, a name known locally until quite recent times. 'Doggeri Bay' is a fine name for the anchorage by what is now Rocky Point, and then we come round to what are still called Portland (where did that name come from?) and Old Harbour.

Inland, the settlement at 'Gonaboa' is Guanaboa Vale, just below the hills where Juan de Bolas had been operating; 'The 7 Plantations' are of course Sevens, up the Rio Minho valley. Notice finally 'The Angells', which comes from the Spanish and still marks a northern suburb of Spanish Town. Considering how difficult it must have been to map the interior of a country as mountainous as Jamaica, particularly when the mountains sheltered guerillas, this first English map was a commendable effort.

Alas, the same cannot be said for its successor, which came out in 1671. Originally drawn by John Ogilby, this map was copied by other cartographers including John Seller, whose version we show (map 2). Whereas Hickeringill had got the general shape nearly right, Ogilby squashed the island right up, greatly exaggerating the thickness of the eastern end. In other respects, though, his map and Sellers' give us new and useful information. We see for instance that the parish structure has begun to take shape, even though there are 11 parishes (actually called 'precincts') instead of the present 14. Three of Sellers' parishes have disappeared, and six others have emerged. The vanished ones are St. John's (in the middle, based on Guanaboa Vale), St. David's (with the capital at Yallahs) and St. George's (whose centre was at Buff Bay). Of course, the word "parish" has become an anachronism, now designating a civil administrative unit. But, in these early days each parish had a church at its head and was an ecclesiastical division, just as it was in contemporary England.

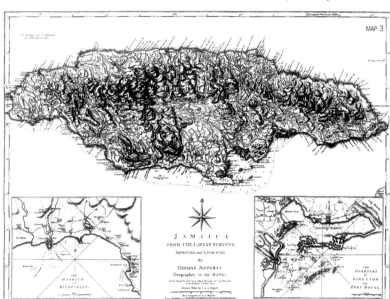

MAP 3

JAMAICA FROM THE LATEST SURVEYS; IMPROVED and ENGRAVED By THOMAS JEFFERYS Geographer to the KING.

Sellers' map has other points of interest. The interior is quite fully described, at any rate where the English were most thickly settled, and the table below gives some indication of the names of the early settlers: 'Coll. Freeman's stores', 'Robert Bagnall's farm', 'Juan de Bola polink' and so on. Indeed, we can build up quite a good idea of the social structure of these early parishes, by following these names through in the wills and other documents at the Archives in Spanish Town. The coat of arms is also interesting, because at that time it had been newly composed. It is still Jamaica's badge, except that the Latin tag at the bottom has been replaced by the motto 'out of many, one people'.

Of course, there was no guarantee that once a more accurate map had been produced, its features would necessarily be retained. This was demonstrated by a map (not shown here), produced about 1688 by 'John Taylor, Gent.', and preserved in the Taylor Manuscript at the Institute of Jamaica. Taylor must have been shown Slaney's map of 1678, but he chooses to revert to the earlier, chunky, view of Jamaica adding certain fantasies of his own. His version of the island's mountain-chains is totally false, with 'Mons Diaboli' (Mount Diablo) far over in the west; indeed, the best thing about this map is the ships at sea, charming little sketches of small merchant-vessels, with a substantial man-of-war anchored off the south-east coast.

Well into the 18th century the erroneous outline of 1671 continued to be used for maps of Jamaica. The next considerable improvement came in 1774, when Thomas Jefferys published his Jamaica from the latest surveys (map 3). This is a fine piece of work, which shows the coastline very much as it is. The place-names are nearly all those in use at the present day, and the delineation of the mountains is quite faithful. After more than a hundred years of occupation, the English now had a map whose main features were reasonably accurate. Notice, in the small inserted map called 'The harbour of Bluefields', how well and carefully the hills are shown; it has hardly been possible to do better than this, down to the present day.

ORIGINALLY PUBLISHED JULY 1979

Port Royal

TONY AARONS

Fort Charles

Port Royal of 1655 was a careening cay for the Spanish, Admiral Penn and General Venables discovered as they landed in Jamaica with an English expedition. For them, the strategic importance of capturing the island was that of having a harbour that could safely anchor "over 500 ships." That harbour was Port Royal.

A True and Perfect Relation of that most Sad and Terrible
EARTHQUAKE, at Port-Royal in JAMAICA,
Which happened on Tuesday the 7th. of June, 1692.

The earthquake of 1692

England's first task then was to build defences to protect this harbour. This began in the 1650's. The first fort to be constructed was Fort Charles. Described as an octagon-polygon, it commanded the whole channel and flanked the entry to the harbour. Two hundred paces north of this, at Bonham's Point, Roger Pemberton began building Fort James, a hexagonal structure mounting 26 guns.

To the east of Fort James was Fort Carlisle, the work of none other than Sir Henry Morgan, buccaneer and later Governor; and so, too was Fort Rupert. The other defence was Fort Walker with 18 guns. These made Port Royal almost impregnable for an enemy ship attempting to enter the harbour had to contend with all these forts.

Buildings of prominence during the seventeenth century included St. Paul's Church, the Audencia, the King's House and Governor's House. St. Paul's, an Anglican Church was built from bricks with battlements of stone. The Audencia was the courthouse, and at the timber King's house the governor held the Court of Chancery, while he lived at the palatial Governor's House.

Two prisons—Bridewell and Marshallsea—were built to house the more unruly elements.

On the north side of the port a strong wharf was constructed to anchor ships of up to 1,000 tons. Private merchant warehouses as well as the King's warehouses were also located there. Near Fort Carlisle the waters were shallow and lighters would load and unload cargo here for the more than 100 sloops that took goods around the island.

England in the meantime had discovered that the buccaneers could assist in resolving her long-standing feud with Spain. Henry Morgan, having legal standing with England, raided many Spanish ships and colonies and brought the booty to Port Royal. This added to the wealth of the newly-found port. The Treaty of Madrid in 1670 ended the war between England and Spain. With the English promise to no longer sanction privateering, Morgan, on being knighted and made lieutenant governor, returned to Port Royal and immediately began to suppress buccaneering.

But the suppression of buccaneering had little effect on Port Royal as a trade centre. Her name was already established, and in the Caribbean she had no peer. Daily, shipments arrived from England, Ireland, and America and along with the African slave trade, the town flourished.

Port Royal was the centre for the exchange of wines, linen, silks, fruits, ironwork, naval stores, dairy products and fresh and salted meats. Spanish gold and silver was the trade coinage. Departing vessels took supplies of sugar, indigo, cocoa, cotton, ginger, logwood, rum, hides and tallow.

With any other European trading town, Port Royal was comparable in size. There were three local markets daily. One was at High Street for fruits; the second was the western end for fresh meats and the third was for fish and was located on the wharf.

A count in 1688 showed Port Royal as having about 8,000 inhabitants. They were of English, Scot, Irish and Jewish descent, with a few Spanish and the rest being African slaves. There was toleration of all religions, including Anglicans, Jews, Presbyterians, Quakers and Baptists.

The several thousands inhabitants occupied some 2,000 houses divided almost evenly between brick and wooden structures. The brick houses were up to four storeys high, having ample storerooms and were for the most

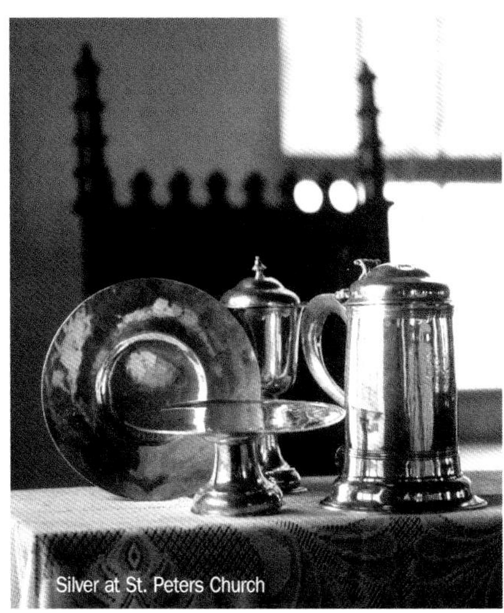
Silver at St. Peters Church

richly furnished and boasting "a fine cupboard of plates." Rents were as high as contemporary London.

In these houses all the trades were represented. English smiths, carpenters, bricklayers, cabinetmakers, wig makers, tailors and painters were all to be found in Port Royal. Three good doctors kept the population healthy.

The merchants and gentry lived well, enjoying the best in food and drink and they followed the latest London fashions. For diversion they would seek out the taverns, gaming houses, billiard rooms and brothels, or watch cock fighting or engage in target shooting. These were also pursuits of buccaneers and visiting sailors.

A regiment of 2,500 men, trained and disciplined, protected the town day and night. Loose living and rowdiness seemed to prevail despite all these.

On June 7, 1692 tragedy struck, Port Royal, described as "the wickedest city on earth" was disastrously shattered by an earthquake. The town rested on sand and silt, built upon the sides of limestone. About 90% of the land area slid into the sea and approximately 2,000 people perished in the quake which was followed by a tidal wave.

Forts James and Carlisle rested under 25 feet of water and were covered by sand; Fort Morgan was seriously damaged and Fort Rupert sank 12 feet into what is now a lagoon. Throughout the town there was looting, profiteering, sickness and religious fanaticism.

In less than a decade Port Royal began to rise again. The forts were repaired and Fort William was erected to replace Fort Rupert. Trade was slowly revived. But, in 1703 disaster visited again. A fire abruptly halted the reconstruction; almost immediately the shift across the harbour to Kingston began. While most of the seamen preferred Port Royal, the merchants favoured Kingston.

The eighteenth and nineteenth centuries were times of a steady decline for Port Royal. The British Naval Squadron brought some measure of prosperity for a while. Such famous British naval leaders as Admirals Benbow and Rodney and Vernon all commanded here at one time. In 1799 Nelson was in charge of Fort Charles.

A portrait purported to be of Morgan

By 1884 there was only about 200 houses left in the town. In 1905 the dockyards closed and a garrison manned the artillery units until the 1950's. Disaster again overtook the town in 1951 when Hurricane Charlie struck. Subsequently a new town was rebuilt.

ORIGINALLY PUBLISHED OCTOBER 1979

The Giddy House

Sojourn 1789

DOUGLAS HALL

I boarded the "Westmoreland," Captain Brown, at Gravesend on Tuesday the 14th of August, 1789, bound for Kingston and Savanna-la-mar in the island of Jamaica. Although excited by the prospect of visiting that island of which I had read many accounts of its great natural beauty, I was also not a little apprehensive that our voyage might end disastrously at sea, for the months July to September are counted the seasons of violent tropical hurricanes; moreover, though by God's will we might escape that danger, I might later fall prey to some tropical disease such as yellow fever.

The voyage, however, proved uneventful, and now that I have been ashore and well for several days my fear of fevers and other perilous ailments are less considered. I am, indeed, enjoying my visit, and Jamaica, certainly that part of it which I have seen, is even more beautiful than the books describe.

On the morning of Monday, the 5th of November, I disembarked at Savanna-la-mar, the capital of the parish of Westmoreland in the county of Cornwall. The town itself is still recovering from destruction wreaked by a terrible hurricane in the year 1780 and several less destructive in the six years following. A wide main street leads down from the open savannas to the wharves and the fort at the water's edge.

I dined at Mrs. Mary Pinkney's Tavern, the "Free and Easy." Much company was there, for the white population here seems very fond of convivial parties and tavern dinners. These are held on every excusable occasion. On this day the officers of the Militia were celebrating, and though the cause of the celebration was not notable, they dined and drank exceedingly and expensively.

Dinner in Jamaica is taken in the mid-afternoon following what is called the "second breakfast" which is also a substantial meal in the mid-morning. People here rise early and the first breakfast, like "supper" taken at night, is a light repast. At Mary Pinkney's Tavern the food was well prepared and served, though Mrs. Pinkney spoke of better days in the past when she was supplied with fresh fruits, vegetables, kitchen herbs, fish and mutton by a Mr. Thistlewood, a noted gardener nearby, who died about three years ago.

My host in Savanna-la-mar is Mr. George Haughton with whom I am to undertake a journey to Montego Bay, and by his kindness I am enabled to go tomorrow to witness the procedures of a slave court, and, in the afternoon, to attend the horse-races.

There were two cases tried in the Court. The first was that of a black man belonging to the Hope Estate who was accused of sheep-stealing. He stoutly denied the charge, but on the word of the overseer, who gave him a bad character, he was found guilty and sentenced to be transported. He will be put on board a ship, probably sailing for Georgia in North America, and there sold again into slavery. The second was a young mulatto girl of fifteen accused of attempting to poison her master. Being a house-slave she had access to the medicine chest and she acknowledged that she had put a powder into her master's drink, but said she had been ordered to do so by her mother who is a fieldworker on the same estate. She was not, however, exonerated and was sentenced to be hanged the next day. She heard the sentence calmly and expressed no regret for her actions.

The cases were heard by three magistrates on the bench and a jury of nine—all white people—and although they appeared to hear the charges and to act judiciously, I could not avoid feeling that in the first case, at least, they had lacked clear proof of guilt. The white people here, almost without exception, seem constantly to be on guard against acts of resistance by the slaves.

From the courthouse I rode directly to New Market, the chief centre of horse-racing near Savanna-la-mar. There were to be half a dozen contests between the horses of well-known planters. A vast throng of people of all shades of colour and all class of society were there. Some of the black and coloured ladies on horseback whom I mistook for free people, were, I was informed, slaves from neighbouring estates who were favoured by their owners or overseers.

The entire scene was one of great colour, movement, and noise. Fashions of every description, a constant thronging of people between the gambling booths, the race track, the drinking and the dancing tents and rooms; the coming and going of horses and carriages of all descriptions; the lively concatenation of cheers, jeers, blares, snortings and rattlings; and the noisy stamp and swirl to fife and drum all assailed the eye and ear. After a couple of hours of this and the loss of seven shillings, mistakenly placed on a handsome but unlively mare, I was happy to return to what I expected would be a quiet hour and then dinner at the table of my host. I was mistaken, but not unhappily so.

At Mr. Haughton's I found a convivial party already gathered. He invited several of the neighbouring planters and attorneys to join us at dinner and already the liquor had begun to flow. It was a sumptuous meal: roast beef, green peas, asparagus, roast-duck, broiled fish, stewed crab and shrimps, pudding, cheese, fruits of several kinds, rum-punch, strong ale, claret and brandy. The others went for home at about 6 p.m. They were merry enough, and so was I, for I cannot recall having supped that night.

Nonetheless, before daybreak I was roused by Psyche, a graceful pretty girl sent by her master to call me. Indeed, I had been made to understand that Psyche was to be mine for all purposes for all the days and nights of my visit; but whilst I had been eager to enjoy such tempting company, I had observed a sulleness in sweet Psyche's eyes, and fearing that an unwelcome advance might lead to both my death and hers, I had treated her only with an admiration which she did not deign to acknowledge.

My host and I set out at half past eight in the morning on horse-back, attended by Mr. Haughton's personal slave, a young powerful-looking black man of about 25 years. (I was later to learn that Psyche was his "wife" and so complimented myself on the previous restraint). My host had altered his plan. Instead of riding by New Hope, Retreat, Negril, Long Bay, through Green Island to Lucea and Montego Bay, he had decided to take a more inland route to Green Island in order, as he explained, to allow me views both of the mountainous interior and the coastal strip.

We rode very leisurely into Little London and then turned through Masemure, Morgan's Bridge, and Kendal, and so down to the coast at Green Island. The visitor from northern climes can only marvel at the variety of scenery.

An endless diversity of hills, valleys, woodlands, mountains and narrow passes, wide fields of cane, pastures shaded by huge trees, plaintain-walks which provide a main staple of the slaves' diet, and here and there the overgrowth of a ruinate estate. In the distance, loftier mountains and narrow valleys precipitating into the coastal plains beneath; and the morning mist here thick, there fading before the sunrise. Then, after some hours of slow travel, down into Green Island where we were glad to stop for rest and refreshment for us and our horses. From there to the town of Lucea, the capital of the parish of Hanover, would be another dozen miles of easier, but hotter, riding along the coastline.

We left the pleasant little tavern at Green Island just before 2 p.m. thus avoiding the hottest hours of the day and about an hour later came to Davis Cove where there is a battery of guns. There was some excitement here earlier this year when a Dutch vessel carrying contraband from Curacao was seized offshore by the revenue officer and soldiers from Lucea. She was said to have had over a hundred cases of gin aboard.

An hour-and-a-half later we came to Orange Cove, beautiful beyond description, though there are several other lovely little coves along this coast. We were now in "Haughton" territory. The Haughton family were owners of Haughton Towers, Haughton Court, and another of more ribald name, Fat Hog Quarter, near Lucea; but much of the property had passed by marriage, out of their hands.

Miss Ann Haughton, heiress of Philip Haughton, had married Sir Simon Clarke, who died in 1777. (I was later to be shown the mural tablet and floor slab in the parish church in Lucea marking his death). Another Miss Haughton, Elizabeth, had married Sir John Taylor, the brother of Mr. Simon Taylor who is reputedly one of the wealthiest men in Jamaica,

Savanna-la-mar

owning, or attorney for, cattle pens and sugar estates in three parishes, including Haughton Court, through which we were now riding.

In addition to his cattle and sugar properties Mr. Taylor also owns Prospect Pen, a residential establishment, in the parish of St. Andrew and spends much of his time there.

Lucea is a pretty little town on the edge of a lovely bay. Fort Charlotte stands in protection just west of the town centre where the parish church has only this year been supplied with a clock with three dial faces installed in the tower. Near the fort is a school established by the endowment of a Mr. Martin Rusea who died some 25 years ago. There were, however, many years of delay before the school came into existence.

In Lucea there are several Jewish merchant families who conduct an import and export trade especially with the new Republic in North America. Mr. Haughton tells me that this is also true of Savanna-la-mar and Kingston, And speaking of North America, Mr. Haughton remarked that Mr. Alexander Hamilton has now been appointed in the British colony of Nevis in the Leeward Islands.

We spent the night in a very comfortable boarding house belonging to a Mrs. Agatha Redwing and excellently managed by herself and her daughter. Mr. Haughton whispered that the "Mrs." is merely an "honourable title" and that the good lady is indeed Miss Redwing the mistress of a local planter, now deceased, the father of the younger lady.

The entire day following, Thursday the 8th of November, was spent in the company of Mr. Haughton while he conducted the business which had brought him to Lucea, the purchase of slaves. There was a Guinea ship in the harbour and a sale of newly-arrived Africans was to be conducted by Mr. Cuthbert, the local agent. Mr. Haughton explained that he would be very careful in his choice. He wanted young people—"men-boys" and "girls" under 18 years old—well-formed, neither fat nor thin, with full, dark lips and clear whites in their eyes. He would be especially watchful against closely shaven and well-oiled people since those were means by which the dealers tried to conceal age and some physical defects.

The sale was well-attended by planters and others from estates in Hanover, Westmoreland and St. James, some of whom seemed to have placed their orders previously with the agent. In consequence, though we were early on board, Mr. Haughton failed to obtain all that he wanted, purchasing only twelve, of whom two were labelled "privileged Negroes" which meant "prime cargo" selling at higher prices. For all of these—eight "men-boys and four "girls", including two "privileged"—he paid eight hundred and twenty five pounds, local currency. In order to allow us to proceed to Montego Bay, Mr. Haughton arranged for his new slaves to be housed and fed, until our return two days hence.

Next morning we set out before daybreak. This was a most pleasant ride along the coastline with alternating views of high cliffs and rocks and the smash of waves into mists of spray, peaceful little coves and inlets, and stretches of white sand and blue sea—tempting in the morning sun. Landwards, the road seemed, for long stretches, to be cut out of the mountainside, and in others it rolled like a crumpled, dusty carpet over green pastureland.

As we rode, Mr. Haughton pointed out to me the boundaries and houses of estates visible from wayside: Maggotty, Blue Hole, Tryall, Orchard and Round Hill, until we crossed the Great River which separates the parishes of Hanover and St. James. Three miles beyond the river we came to Reading Wharf where there is a warehouse belonging to a large inland sugar-estate, Montpelier, and soon after, across the Montego River through another large estate of sugarcane into the town itself.

Montego Bay is the largest Jamaican town I have yet visited—I shall see Spanish Town and Kingston on my journey home. There are about 200 houses in the town and nearly 30 capital stores and warehouses, clearly flourishing and opulent. In the roadstead I could count half-a-dozen merchantmen and two of His Majesty's ships. The market-place thronged with people—slaves, free people of colour, whites, all busily engaged either in displaying or examining the vast variety of produce. Fruit of every description—pineapples, tamarinds, cashews, custard-apples, oranges, grapes, melons, figs, pomegranates; vegetables known to European tables such as lettuces, tomatoes, asparagus, green peas and artichokes, and others strange to us—ochras, lima beans, callaloo and cho-chos; and the starchy staples of the country—plantains, yams, eddoes, cassava, and sweet potatoes.

We looked, and tried a small sketch or two, but we purchased nothing. We were bound for the boarding-house and tavern of Miss Judy James, and Mr. Haughton declared that nowhere might we be better fed and housed. He was right, and it was with relief, after the long journey, that I bathed, slept, and awoke to a bounteous dinner served at 6 p.m.

After we had eaten well and drunk of porter and brandy, Miss James summoned Beneba, her cook, a large black woman of about fifty years, a slave, purchased from a Guinea ship by Miss James' mother nearly forty years ago. On Miss James' invitation, and with increasing enthusiasm, Beneba regaled us for nigh on two hours with Ananci stories—tales of West African origin dealing with the sly exploits of Ananci, the spider. And then to bed.

Once more we took to the road before daybreak and re-traced our way to Lucea. In view of the next day's march back to Savanna-la-mar with Mr. Haughton's new slaves, another early bedtime seemed desirable; but then we received an invitation I did not wish to refuse.

Mrs., or Miss, Redwing informed us that her coachman, Hampstead, was intending to go that evening to a place on the outskirts of town where the slaves would be holding a dance. If we wished, he had offered to escort us as sightseers. Mr. Haughton declines, saying he had seen enough of that on his own property, but I readily accepted.

Leaving the tavern, we walked to a small piece of open land just east of the town where the "play" or dancing was to be held. The Negroes hold a variety of "plays" to mark births, deaths, housewarmings, crop-over, and other important events, but this, I was told, was simply an entertainment of no special significance. Nonetheless, I had never seen anything like it.

The music was odd to European ears and the movements of the dancers exceedingly and excitingly lascivious. The main instruments were a sort of drum, a banjo, and a kind of flute together with various sticks and boards beaten together. Hampstead named them as the Gumbay, the Merry-wang, the Coromante-flute, and the cotta sticks. The slaves from each African nation had their special dances which they performed. Generally, the music was lively and with a pronounced beat to which the dancers moved. The women were easy and languishing in their motions, with wondrous movements of their hips; the men vigorous and active and full of boastful gestures. I came away wondering how the Vicar of Wakefield would have reacted to such a display.

Tomorrow comes the long journey back to Savanna-la-mar, then a day of rest before I begin a voyage in an open boat to Kingston; but already Mr. Haughton is persuading me that after this night's entertainment I should counteract the African influence. There is, he says, a group of travelling players now in Savanna-la-mar, and he intends to take me to watch their performance of Arthur Murphy's play "The Way To Keep Him", advertised as a lesson to wives and husbands, which I think may not be useful in this island.

ORIGINALLY PUBLISHED SEPTEMBER 1991

The Barbadian-born Soldier Who Defeated Yellow Fever

ANTHONY GAMBRILL

William Maynard Gomm, the eldest son of Colonel William Gomm of the 55th Regiment, was born to May Alleyne, daughter of Joseph Maynard Esq. in Barbados in 1784. His long and illustrious military career began at age 10 and ended 71 years later when he retired as a field-marshall, the highest rank in the British Army. During that time he fought in the Napoleonic Wars, governed Mauritius, commanded the British troops in India and received honorary degrees from both Oxford and Cambridge. But in Jamaica he is remembered as the man who defeated yellow fever.

Major-General Sir William Gomm arrived in Jamaica in January 1840 and by April had already witnessed the devastating impact of yellow fever on his troops. At the time one in four died of the disease and a posting to the West Indies was considered a virtual sentence to death. He began a relentless campaign aimed at the island's Governor and the military authorities in England to allow him to remove the bulk of his forces from the plains and build a camp in the higher elevations of the mountains overlooking the capital Kingston.

In this salubrious climate he calculated that the mosquitoes which caused the fever would be less prevalent. The November seasonal rains in 1840 were accompanied by a virulent outbreak of this dreaded disease and gave even greater urgency to his plea. By this time he had identified a site at Newcastle "at an elevation of 4,000 feet, in the Port Royal Mountains, thermometer standing at 63 degrees, while mounting to 83 and 84 degrees in the plain" where he wanted to build an experimental barracks.

Early in 1841 he went ahead ordering the 82nd Regiment to start building quarters for 100 men. Ironically, this regiment was recalled to England in June having lost its colonel, four other officers, nine sergeants, 149 foot soldiers, 17 wives and 22 children, all recorded victims of yellow fever.

It was the men of the 3rd West Indian Regiment that completed the task. These soldiers, recruited out of slavery, went on to serve with distinction in Britain's colonial wars in West Africa. The first regiment to occupy the site were the Royal Americans (later renamed the King's Royal Rifle Corps) and was originally raised amongst Swiss and German settlers in America to fight the rebellious colonials in the American War of Independence.

A young officer wrote: "We encamped on the Newcastle Estate Government Plantation, some 4000 feet above sea level, and out of the range of yellow fever. By degrees the men constructed log huts thatched with long grass and wattle and mud walls but the officers were for a long period under canvas; shingle roofed houses were by degrees constructed by the authorities.

Humming birds built their nests in coffee trees. Rook-pigeons were abundant, also ground grouse ran about the roads and ravines, whilst strawberries grew on the higher hills called St. Catherine. The coffee trees were cropped twice a year, in April and October. The flowers were white and fragrant. Orange trees were on the hills and produced fruit in abundance. Transport for all provisions were on pack mules..."

The mountains proved a godsend in many ways of which the dramatic improvement in mens' health was the most beneficial. In 1842, 24 out of 197 troops died of disease, by 1847 only seven out of 583 perished and six years after that just two men were laid to rest in the Newcastle cemetery. Below the parade ground on the southern slope of the camp dozens of gravestones bear silent witness to the finality of yellow fever now long banished from the island of Jamaica. Seldom were those who died older than their early twenties.

Sir William Gomm did not stay in Jamaica long enough to see the results of his foresight and determination although before he left he wrote to Lord Fitzroy Somerset, Military Secretary at the Horse Guards exclaiming, "we have carried the hill," an expression more commonly used to acknowledge a victory on the field of battle.

Today visitors can drive up to the Jamaica Defence Force training camp at Newcastle, enjoy the spectacular view of Kingston from the parade ground and feel for themselves the temperature difference that defied mosquitoes. If time allows nearby Hollywell Park is a tranquil forest reserve and the Gap Café offers a pleasant opportunity for a lunch or snack. For the even more adventurous a drive down the newly rehabilitated road to Buff Bay on the north coast will prove especially rewarding.

ORIGINALLY PUBLISHED FEBRUARY 2001

The Maroons
Masters of their own Destiny

CAREY ROBINSON

Maroons in ambush on Dromity estate, Trelawny 1796

Columbus arrived in Jamaica in 1494 and came again in 1503. Shortly after his death, his son, Diego, newly-appointed governor of the Indies, gave instructions for a colony to be set up in Jamaica. The Spaniards took over the country and forced the Arawaks (the original inhabitants) to work for them. The depressed Arawaks soon died out, and, to replenish the labour force, Africans were brought in to work as slaves. The first batch arrived between 1513 and 1517, probably from Upper Guinea in Africa.

The Spaniards found no gold in Jamaica so the island soon ceased to attract settlers. But livestock, brought by them multiplied tremendously. Good export markets opened up for hides and fats, and ranching and hunting developed as the main activities.

With the rapid disappearance of the Arawaks, the Africans became increasingly more important. They functioned mostly as cowboys and hunters, using bow and arrows, lances and firearms. They lived a semi-free life, roaming the plains, forests and mountains, and becoming, in the process, very familiar with the terrain.

The position of the Africans was further strengthened by the fact that the island was frequently attacked by pirates and raiders. Every able-bodied man, free or otherwise, was needed for military service. The Africans soon became an invaluable part of the defence force.

Recognizing their importance, the Spaniards began to treat them like their own children, with affection and even respect.

When the British invaders arrived in 1655, the Spanish government surrendered almost at once. But a hard core of hunters, ranchers and other hardy folk, who regarded Jamaica as their home, decided to fight. They were led by Jamaican-born Arnaldo Ysassi, whose great-grandfather is said to have come to Jamaica as a settler.

One of the terms of surrender drawn-up by the British required "all Slaves and Negroes" to appear on the open ground near the town of Villa de la Vega (now called Spanish Town) to be informed of "the favours and acts of grace concerning their freedom to be granted to them." The majority of the Africans ignored this command and marched off with the Spanish resistance force.

It was a time of crisis, of radical change. A new life was about to begin, and among the Africans an idea was taking root, which challenged them to control their own destiny. They had earned a unique position in the Spanish colony and were not going to take a backward step. The British appeared to be offering some kind of freedom, but, at that moment, the Africans were not prepared to put their fate into the hands of an aggressor.

A five-year war began. From the outset the Africans were in the forefront. They ambushed soldiers on the march and attacked detachments in search of food. One night they even penetrated into the British headquarters in Spanish Town.

The British had never before encountered such a swift moving, relentless enemy, who might turn up anywhere, and to whom no successful appeal could be made. They were at a loss as to how to deal with them, but knew they had to make every effort to win their support. They put up notices on trees, written in Spanish, promising freedom and land to any who would join them.

Meanwhile, the Spanish cause was being undermined by internal squabbles and rivalries. In a display of independence the Africans separated themselves and set up their own camps under their own chosen leaders. The most influential of these leaders were Juan Lubolo (later called Juan de Bolas) and Juan de Serras.

The Spaniards were badly defeated in two major battles: at Los Chorreras (near Ocho Rios) and Rio Nuevo, both in today's parish of St. Mary. After the crushing Rio Nuevo defeat, Juan de Bolas secretly agreed to join the British with his large community. In return, he was to be made colonel of a black regiment with the powers of a magistrate. His people were to receive land and settler privileges, provided they gave loyal service and learned the English language.

Juan de Bolas knew all the trails used by the Spanish force, and all their camps and hide-outs. His desertion was a mortal blow to the Spanish cause. Before the others were aware that he had switched sides he attacked the settlement of de Serras and he led the British to Ysassi's main camp.

When Ysassi realized that Bolas had turned against him he lost all hope of recovering the island. On May 9th 1660, he packed most of the survivors of his force into two hastily-built canoes and set off for Cuba. He never returned, and according to legend, died in a monastery in Spain.

De Serras and his people stayed on in Jamaica and continued to defy the British. Offers of freedom and land meant nothing to them for they had already declared their freedom, and had allocated to themselves all the land they needed for hunting, farming and living.

When all attempts to bring them into submission failed, the British sent Juan de Bolas to exterminate them. But Bolas fell into an ambush. His force was cut to pieces and he was slain. De Serras and his people remained at large, free and independent: "Masters of their destiny, subject only to the voice of their own spirit, neither bowing knee nor head, nor standing in the shadow of any." They were the first Maroons of Jamaica.

When the British discovered that sugar was becoming enormously profitable they set up large estates and brought in more Africans to work as slaves. Some of them broke away into the woods and mountains, despite the terrible punishments for rebellion. At first the British simply referred to them as rebel slaves.

Most of the rebellions were led by West Coast Africans, who were called Coromantins by the British and other Europeans. They were described as fierce, bold, proud and courageous; possessing "an elevation of soul which prompts them to enterprises of difficulty and danger, and enables them to meet death in its most horrible shape, with fortitude or indifference."

One of the first, big revolts under the British took place in 1678, and was followed by several others. In 1690, two years before the earthquake which destroyed Port Royal, a very dangerous rebellion erupted on Colonel Sutton's estate in Clarendon. Many of the rebels were killed or captured, but a few escaped. Among them were three boys who were brothers. Their names were Cudjoe, Accompong and Johnny.

They grew up in the Clarendon hills, probably in the company of older runaways, who were operating in gangs. Cudjoe had natural qualities of leadership and, as a young man, became a gang chief. He soon acquired a formidable reputation as a daring raider.

The British grew increasingly alarmed by the success of the rebels, and launched an all-out offensive, beefing-up their "local" military with dogs, Mosquito Indians, regular troops from Gibraltar, and sailors and marines from the warships.

To meet this onslaught the rebel gangs in western and central Jamaica joined forces and chose Cudjoe to lead them.

In the east, rebels gathered under the leadership of a powerful "high priestess" called Nanny. Their foremost war chief was a man call Quao.

The fighting reached desperate proportions in the 1730s. Whole parishes became desolate "no man's lands", traveling was unsafe, plantations were thrown-up and abandoned, and valuable tracts of land could not be cultivated. Neither side gave any quarter. It was during this grim period that the British applied the name Maroons to the relentless rebels.

The Maroons camouflaged themselves with leaves and twigs, ambushed the troops in the tremendously rugged countryside, and despite the loss of some of their towns, were never decisively beaten. Time after time they sent the British assault parties reeling back to their bases in defeat. They communicated with each other rapidly and over long distances by means of an alphabet of notes, blown on their cow horns which were called abengs. Their women and children suffered greatly from hunger and exposure wherever their settlements were destroyed, but surrender was entirely out of the question.

A scene from present day Maroons

When all the British colonists' best efforts failed, they asked their governor, Edward Trelawny, to make peace with the Maroons. The peace treaty with Cudjoe was signed on March 1st, 1739 and the peace with the eastern Maroons (the Windwards) was signed with Quao on June 23th, 1739. The treaties guaranteed the freedom of the Maroons, gave them ownership of lands in St. Elizabeth, Trelawny (then part of St. James), St. Mary and Portland, and ensured a certain amount of independence and autonomy. In return they were obliged, among other things, to help to maintain the peace and security of the country, especially in connection with slave rebellions.

In 1795, fifty-six years after the peace treaties were signed, the Trelawny Maroons, descendants of the community over which Cudjoe himself had presided, went to war with the colony when they perceived that their rights, dignity and statues were being infringed. Two of their members who were accused of stealing pigs, were found guilty and whipped at the tail of a cart by a runaway, in the presence of slaves in the common workhouse. This sparked the war.

Twenty actions were fought during a terrific struggle in the rugged Cockpit Country, which lasted about four and a half months. Nearly five thousand regular troops, militia and Accompong Maroons, supported by Mosquito Indians and Cuban Chasseurs with savage hunting dogs, were assembled to overcome less than three hundred Trelawny Maroon fighters.

In the end, the Trelawnys were persuaded to make peace and lay down their arms, on the clear understanding that they would not be exiled from Jamaica. But as soon as they disarmed themselves they were shipped away into exile, first to Nova Scotia in Canada, then to Sierra Leone in Africa.

The main contribution of the Maroons to Jamaican culture was in their total rejection of servitude, and the determination to control their own destiny. They relied upon themselves, made maximum use of natural resources and converted a rough countryside into an impregnable fortress and refuge. Their confident bearing was a phenomenon wonderful to behold, at a time when the self-esteem of others was being crushed.

The Maroon heritage is a constant reminder that a people, small in number but great in spirit, making creative use of their environment and believing whole-heartedly in themselves, can achieve tremendous things.

Out of all the many heroic Maroons, Nanny of the Windwards was chosen to be one of the National Heroes of independent Jamaica.

There is much more justice in this choice than many realize; for Nanny symbolized not just the fight for freedom, but human dignity, self-esteem, self-discipline and supreme courage and endurance.

ORIGINALLY PUBLISHED NOVEMBER 1993

Sam Sharpe
From Slave to National Hero

SUZANNE FRANCIS-BROWN

It is May 23, 1832. Montego Bay, capital of St. James, lies limp in the heat. But, the town square hums with excitement as a black man of medium height, dressed in a new white suit, walks to a well-used gibbet.

As he stands beneath the waiting rope, he tells the crowd: "I am going to die because I thought I had a right to be free."

Minutes later, Samuel Sharpe was hanging from the rope – a statistic of a Court Martial for the record books – one of 312 slaves executed during the first half of 1832 for participating in the last slave rebellion in Jamaican history.

Samuel Sharpe's contribution transcended his death. The rebellion he helped plan was a factor in hurrying along the process which led to the emancipation of slaves in Jamaica and other British colonies. The month Sharpe died and nearly four months after the rebellion, the British House of Commons adopted a motion "that a Select Committee be appointed for the purpose of effecting the extinction of slavery throughout the British Dominions." By August 1833 the Emancipation Bill, long supported by politicians such as William Wilberforce, and Thomas Burchell, was passed. In August 1834, it was all over.

Sharpe and his fellow slaves are remembered for more than their timely intervention in the affairs of the colony of Jamaica and by extension, in the affairs of the British Empire.

Although their revolt became an armed rebellion with widespread destruction of property, and with 14 "free" people and an estimated 200 slaves killed in action between December 27, 1831 and January 7, 1832, Sharpe's original plan was for the slaves to initiate a strike. A Baptist deacon, Sharpe took the biblical injunction that "No man can serve two masters" as the rationale for his plan—that

on December 28, slaves in large sections of the western parishes of St. James, Trelawny, Hanover, Westmoreland and St. Elizabeth, should refuse to work without wages. They were to maintain this position regardless of the inevitable violent reaction of the ruling plantocracy.

The plan also had its own military aspect in the form of a black regiment, believed to have had some 50 guns, and which was led by two other slaves who were also leaders in the Baptist church—Thomas Dove it is thought came from the Belvedere Estate, and Robert Gardiner from Greenwich Estate. It remains controversial whether Sharpe was actively involved with the martial aspect of the rebellion, or whether he was an idealist whose plan for non-violent strike action was overcome by a general feeling of excitement when the long suffering slaves saw their chance to strike back.

Who, then, was Samuel Sharpe?

He was born a slave, in Jamaica, around the turn of the century. In the hierarchy of slavery, Sharpe was one of the lucky ones, being assigned to serve in the household rather than the fields.

His surname, Sharpe, was the same as that of his master—a custom in many slave-owning societies. Documents identify his master as Samuel Sharpe, a Montego Bay lawyer, with a small estate outside the town; there is another reference to him as Charles Sharpe.

Sharpe, the slave, became a senior and trusted member of his master's household, well-treated and evidently well-liked—so much so that the women of the families made him the white suit he wore for his execution.

The church was an important outlet for Sharpe, as for many other slaves. In the Burchell Baptist Church he rose to the position of deacon and there were the less formal 'native Baptist' groups which developed, mingling Christianity with traditional African religious forms.

Between church and home, Sharpe learned to read. Lessons which enabled him to read his bible were applied to English and Jamaican newspapers so, he must have become aware of the opposition to slavery which gradually grew in England, especially in the 1820's, and of the Jamaican planters' adamant opposition to any change in their status quo.

The matter was of more than academic or spiritual interest to Sharpe when, in 1828, his master purchased a pen in Cambridge—some miles outside of the town—and made him caretaker of the jobbing gangs there.

Sam Sharpe saw at first hand the conditions in which other slaves lived... and by 1831 he seemed convinced that Jamaican slaves must take action on their own if their lifestyle was to change.

A Methodist missionary, Henry Bleby, who knew Sharpe and was impressed by him, said in a memoir, 'The Death Struggles of Slavery', he was "of middle size, his fine sinewy frame and handsomely moulded, and his skin as perfect as jet as can well be imagined.

"His forehead was high and broad, while his nose and lips exhibited the usual characteristics of the Negro race. He had teeth whose regularity and pearly whiteness a court beauty might have envied, and an eye whose brilliancy was almost dazzling."

Of his mental prowess Bleby wrote: "He had intellectual and oratorical powers above the common order; and this was the secret of the extensive influence which he exercised."

When Sharpe decided that the slaves had to act on their own behalf, he formed a secret society of conspirators. Unlike others he could move around fairly freely.

By October 1831, he had began outlining his plans for strike action to aides, using nightly 'native Baptist' prayer meetings to spread the word and he swore the people to secrecy by asking them to 'kiss the Book'.

These aides in turn enlisted other slaves, using the same oath of secrecy, and all under cover of darkness on states in western Jamaica.

But word got to the planters. Troops were sent into St. James in case of trouble, and warships anchored in Montego Bay, and at Black River, on the southwest coast, with their guns trained on the towns.

On Tuesday, December 27, the last day of the Christmas holidays, fear of a rebellion sent the occupants of Kensington Great House into Montego Bay, and members of the St. James Militia apparently marched on the estate, seemingly to ensure that the slaves did return to work.

The slaves reacted to the militia's presence. Kensington was fired that night—a rebellion had begun.

The fires, and, inevitably, the fighting, spread from estate to estate: Roehampton, Lethe, Friendship, Retrieve, Harmony Hall, Tryall, Golden Grove, Friendship Grove.

Martial law was declared as the fires and the revolt spread and regular English troops were brought in to supplement the local St. James militia. Violent repression halted the revolt in the first week of January 1832.

The missionaries, often the slaves' only champions in the white community, suffered some repercussions. Knibb and two other Baptist missionaries suspect of involvement in the revolt, were arrested in Falmouth, capital town of Trelawny on January 3 and taken to Montego Bay where they were reportedly treated insultingly. Burchell, who was holidaying in England since June 1831, was arrested on January 7, on returning to Montego Bay.

Slaves connected with the revolt were rounded up and tried. Some, like Dove and Gardiner, and later Sam Sharpe, gave themselves up to the authorities.

Sharpe's surrender is said to have been influenced by the plight of the missionaries.

Sharpe's trial was convened on April 19, 1832, in the Montego Bay Court House, before three Justices of the Peace—John Coates, Robert Downer and Henry Plummer. The charges: administering unlawful oaths, convening unlawful night meetings and rebellion.

Eleven witnesses were called by the Crown, two by the defence, but Sharpe never denied involvement in the rebellion. What he did was testify to the innocence of the missionaries, and said that the destruction of life and property was not part of his plan.

The case closed that same day, with the twelve jurors bringing a verdict of guilty. Sharpe was to be hanged.

While he remained nearly a month in prison before his trial, the courts and the executioners were busy.

Bleby describing the days in his memoir said. "The Gibbet erected in the public square, in the centre of the town was seldom without occupants during the day, for many weeks. Generally four, seldom less than three, were hanged at once."

Sam Sharpe went to his execution on May 23, 1832 having told Bleby in conversation: "I would rather die upon yonder gallows than live in slavery."

As was the custom for criminals, he was buried in the sands beside Montego Bay harbour. His friends later recovered his bones and put them in a mahogany coffin. It is said that they were buried under the pulpit of the Burchell Baptist Church.

Sam Sharpe has not been forgotten. In 1975 he was named a National Hero of Jamaica and later, the town square of Montego Bay was renamed Sam Sharpe Square. There's also a plaque honouring his memory at the Cage, built in 1806 to imprison slaves, and still standing in the square.

ORIGINALLY PUBLISHED APRIL 1982

There'll Nearly Always Be An England

H.P. JACOBS

There is a place called Chippenham Park in Jamaica, and there is a place called Chippenham Park in England. It is natural to suppose that the Jamaican place was named after its counterpart in England. But the opposite is the case. Chippenham Park in St. Ann was named after Chippenham in England. Then a Jamaican from Chippenham Park built Chippenham Park in England (not at Chippenham!).

Nearly all the great admirals of English history, from Queen Anne's time to George III, have been connected with Jamaica. Admiral Benbow is buried in the Kingston Parish Church; there is a statue of Rodney at Spanish Town; at Fort Charles in Port Royal Horatio Nelson is commemorated by an inscription "In this place dwelt Horatio Nelson. You who tread his footprints remember his glory." (Curiously it is not known who wrote this memorable inscription, nor when it was put up.)

From 1872 to 1889, Rodney's statue was in Kingston at the foot of King Street. When it was taken back to Spanish Town, the pedestal was left empty until a statue of Queen Victoria was acquired for Kingston in 1898 following her Diamond Jubilee. Her statue was placed on Lord Metcalfe's pedestal on the Kingston Parade looking down King Street and Metcalfe was moved to where Admiral Rodney had stood. Rodney's was the only Kingston statue not affected by the 1907 earthquake which inelegantly spun Queen Victoria around 360 degrees.

In the church at Stratford-on-Avon is a monument to a man whom a 17th century writer calls "an old rich usurer", John Combes (pronounced Coombs), for the writer quotes some lines on him by Shakespeare, who survived him; and these lines end -

"If anyone asks who lies in this tomb,
"Hah!" quoth the Devil, "Tis my
John a Combe."

In Jamaica, the term 'a greedy Coombs" is still used—and a magistrate heard the expression actually applied to a usurer. It is also applied to great eaters, or to people (and animals) who will eat anything going. A lady who lived as a girl at the present tourist resort of Ocho Rios on the north side of the island remembers that there was a man there whom others called John Coombs, though neither name properly belonged to him. This man would complain that he could not eat more than one hand (or bunch) of plantains at a sitting.

In the 18th and l9th century, almost everyone in England who was of any importance had some connection with Jamaica. Lord Byron, the poet, illustrates this very well. His friend R. C. Dallas, who publicised a book about him, came from a Jamaican family, whilst a son of his taught in a Kingston school and died in the city. "Monk" Lewis—Matthew Gregory Lewis who owned great estates in Jamaica was a friend of Lord Byron; it was of him that Byron wrote:

"I would give many a sugar-cane
Matt Lewis were alive again."

Lewis was anxious to see how his estates were being managed and how his slaves were being treated, so he came twice to Jamaica and

died on the way home after his second visit—hence Byron's lines.

Another literary figure historically associated with Jamaica was Anthony Trollope, the novelist who visited the island in 1858 to re-organize the post office and published an account of his Caribbean travels.

There is a Malvern in Jamaica, named by a landowner born in the Malvern Hills of England. Curiously, he gave the name to the Jamaican Malvern just about the time that the town of Malvern in England was coming into prominence as a health resort through the work of Dr. Gully,

a Jamaican, son of a coffee planter. Gully's own son became a Speaker of the House of Commons and later the first Viscount Selby. Gully was at Malvern for about 30 years (roughly 1842-72). His professional reputation was ruined by the infamous "Bravo Case", which at every point is connected with Jamaica. In 1876, Charles Bravo, stepson of Joseph Bravo, a rich London merchant born in Jamaica, died mysteriously of poisoning, and suspicion fell on his widow and on her companion, a Mrs. Cox from Jamaica. The matter was never cleared up, but in the course of the enquiries Dr. Gully admitted that he had had improper relations with Mrs. Charles Bravo (before her marriage to Charles). Books are still being written on this sensational case.

The British Museum has several odd connections with Jamaica. The most significant of these is the fact that the nucleus of the museum was provided from natural history the collection of Sir Hans Sloane.

There are several places called "Lilliput" in Jamaica. But very likely they are not derived from "Gulliver's Travels", but from an old London street name, from which Dean Swift may have taken his Lilliput. Similarly there is a Pickwick in the Jamaican parish of Manchester —but it does not come from the "Pickwick Papers", for it is an older derivation.

Because of their tremendous wealth Jamaican planters could finance explorers, exploiters and egomaniacs. "Jamaica" Dawkins, a Jamaican estate owner, was a supporter of Bonnie Prince Charles but when he decided that the Scots prince was played out, the Jacobite movement virtually came to an end in Britain.

Strawberries are grown in the mountains above Kingston but it seems that Strawberry Hill on the road to Newcastle in the Blue Mountains almost certainly takes its name from Horace Walpole's house in England.

Lady Holland, who died in 1845, was the most famous London society hostess of her time. She was born in Jamaica; her maiden name was Vassall, and her second husband, Lord Holland, to whom she brought great estates in eastern Jamaica. He gallantly assumed the name of Vassall before his surname, Fox, although he was more likely to be known as "Holland".

In England, one hears of the lord lieutenant of a county, but never of a custos rotulorum, or keeper of the rolls. In fact most people know of such an official only through a joke in Shakespeare. In Jamaica, however, each parish has a custos rotulorum, who is head of the lay magistracy. The office did not exist in any other part of the British Empire, except at one time in the Cayman Islands, which took it from Jamaica, of which they were a dependency. In England, the lord-lieutenant absorbed the office of custos —the same person holds both position. Yet in Jamaica the custos took over functions which resembled those of a lord-lieutenant.

ORIGINALLY PUBLISHED JUNE 1974

R. SIMKIN.

A Flash of Colour

The Zouave Military Uniform

COL. ALLAN DOUGLAS

There are some curious subjects which have become old-fashioned—-which have drifted, by degrees, so far outside the necessities of ordinary educations and occupations, that most of us grow up and live and die with but a faint perception that they exist at all, and with the incompletest notion of their details. If accident should bring any of them under our observation, we look at them with more or less indifference, according to our particular proclivities; but, as we get on very well without them, as they have nothing to-do with money-making, or athletic sports, or ritualism, or novels, or last night's ball, or the state of the crops, or the few remaining social strata, we never think of going out of our way to make an explanation of them. And yet, however superannuated they may be, they are seldom altogether stupid; they all contain some sort of teaching; they may even occasionally be enlivening...

FREDRIC MARSHALL, *INTERNATIONAL VANITIES*, 1875.

Fredric Marshall's nineteenth century quotation can, perhaps with good reason, fall within the ambit of an article on the uniform of the Jamaican Military Band. But an article about the Zouave uniform without at least a historical trace to the units with which it has been associated, would be incomplete.

The Jamaica Military Band has direct descent from the first of the old West India Regiments, which was formed in 1795 in the Windward Islands of the Eastern Caribbean. One of two units drafted into this regiment was the Black Carolina Corps, the remnant of a British loyalist regiment in the aftermath of the American War of Independence.

By 1799 there were twelve single-battalion West India Regiments, some of which were involved in the fierce West Indies actions of the Napoleonic Wars, and a few in the later Ashanti Wars in West Africa. From early in the nineteenth century they had been reduced in numbers until 1888 when there was but a single regiment. In 1892, a Jamaican, Lance Corporal (later Sergeant) William James Gordon of the West India Regiment received Britain's highest, and very rarely awarded gallantry decoration, the Victoria Cross.

Throughout much of the nineteenth century, what is now the Jamaican Military Band was the band of that original and last surviving regiment.

The transformation into the Jamaica Military Band is in itself noteworthy. As the band of the West India Regiment, it gave its final performance at a reception at Trafalgar House in Kingston in early 1927, before Their Royal Highnesses the Duke and Duchess of York (Later King George VI and Queen Elizabeth, the present Queen Mother). The bandsmen turned in their instruments after the performance, but fortunately sentiment prevailed and the band was revived on February 27, 1927 as the Jamaica Military Band.

Looking at the uniform of the Jamaica Military Band, one is immediately struck with its unusual design and picturesque appearance that it invokes dialogue on its origins. Thanks to the Zouave (a body of French light infantry of North African origin) whose uniform so impressed Queen Victoria (who saw them at a review of French colonial troops), that she insisted on introducing it into her army. History states that in 1856 the brilliant ceremonial Zouave uniform was therefore allotted to the 2nd Battalion of the West India Regiment, the only regular British colonial regiment in existence at that time.

The Zouave uniform continued to be worn by the West India Regiment from that time until 1926 when the regiment was disbanded. The disbandment of the regiment did not cast the uniform into oblivion, as the band of the regiment remained to become the Jamaica Military Band, whose members today continue to wear this historic uniform with pride.

The composition of the uniform is somewhat intriguing because of its Moorish background, making it unique in the Western World. The headdress is a turban made up of four parts viz. A fez, which is dark red in colour (similar to that worn in Nigeria, though not as high because it is turned up at the side) with a yellow tassel hanging from the back. The white material around the fez is approximately 84 by 48 inches of poplin or calico rolled from one corner and is to this day still done by four persons—three holding whilst one rolls diagonally. When the rolling is complete, a common pin is used to fasten the loose end; a yellow braid is then wrapped around the white and technically placed around the fez in a special way allowing the two ends to meet in front of the face overlapping to form a 'V'. The ends are then tucked into the fez.

The waistcoat which is red and trimmed with yellow braid is worn over the jacket, which is white or cream-flannel trimmed with yellow piping and fitted with specially made buttons. This unusual fitting of the waistcoat and jacket has been a source of interest and speculation, if not amusement.

The trousers are dark blue with yellow stripes and are worn with suspenders (braces) because they are loosely fitted; reaching the ankles, the legs are then turned under and tied below the knees, then bagged. White stockings, gaiters (spats) and black shoes, complete the outfit.

Except for the addition of a card case (pouch), now made of plastic and worn on ceremonial parades by members of the band below the rank of sergeant and the drummers, a change in the texture of the material (because of climatic conditions) of the uniform has maintained its original look over the years and no doubt will remain the same for a very long time to come.

The Zouave uniform has survived and indeed flourishes. It has an enduring appeal added to which is the fact that it is worn by the Jamaica Military Band; a band that has soothed many a troubled heart and has provided for Jamaica, in one of Churchill's memorable phrases, "a flash of colour on the hard road we have to travel."

ORIGINALLY PUBLISHED DECEMBER 2001

350 Years of Military Tradition

FRED WILMOT

When the smartly turned-out Jamaica Defence Force solemnly Troops the Colour on state occasions, it reflects a tradition 352 years in the making. In 1662, five regiments of foot and a troop of horses, was raised by British governor, Lord Windsor, as the Jamaica Militia. Arriving with the proclamation giving Jamaicans full rights as British subjects, he became commander of the Militia's Port Royal Regiment and himself paid the troop of horse from his own pocket.

The force was blooded in 1694. Over five days, at Carlisle Bay, it defeated a pillaging French force commanded by French Admiral DuCasse from Saint Domingue (Hispaniola). It was granted blue facings on its uniform by grateful rulers William and Mary for success in battle.

From the early 1700s troops from England garrisoned the island. Frequent alarms and threats of invasion reflected the wars in Europe. Despite the rout of the French, the militia was not believed adequate to the island's defence. Spain, France, Britain, Denmark and the Netherlands fought for territory in the Caribbean. Jamaica was constantly threatened.

With the British Imperial Army busy in Europe, the West Indian Regiment was formed in 1795 to protect Britain's Caribbean possessions. It wrote bold pages in the empire's and Jamaica's military history. Over more than a century it assisted expansion and protection of the Empire. Because of recruiting difficulty, African slaves, destined for servitude in America's south were offered "the King's shilling" to serve in the Regiment, a practice continued through the 1800s. A W.I.R. detachment was on par to the British force defeated by the Americans at the Battle of New Orleans. Praised for valor by British General Jackson, they returned to garrison the British Caribbean islands.

There were 426 slaves in the regiment by 1837. Under European officers, black and coloured troops served to the level of sergeant. They fought with distinction in Martinique and Guadeloupe, and in other engagements in many places for the rest of the century.

The first black soldier to be awarded Britain's highest military honour was a Jamaican. Sergeant William James Gordon was gravely wounded in Gambia protecting his commander from being killed during an assault. In addition to the Cross, Queen Victoria decreed he should never face a court martial, regardless of the offence. He was presented to the Queen during Jubilee celebrations and was one of two West Indians to earn the "V.C."

A rifle corps was created in 1906, supported by the Kingston Artillery and the St. Ann troop of the Jamaican Mounted Scouts. In 1907, a disastrous earthquake shattered Jamaica's capital. Fire swept the ruins and chaos reigned. The corps helped West Indian Regiment troops to fight the fire, guard shops and warehouses, and maintain public order. The Kingston Infantry Volunteer replaced the corps in 1914.

In 1927 the West Indian Regiment was disbanded after 127 years. The band, retaining the colourful Zouave uniform adopted in 1858, became the Jamaica Military Band. The band earned international repute and today performs on important state occasions. Its march, "North Carolina", recalls that it was part of Britain's North American command from 18th century colonial times.

The Kingston Infantry Volunteers became the Jamaica Infantry Volunteers in 1939, in a precedent in the Empire were granted colour, and with the outbreak of World War II were mobilized for the defence of the island. They were renamed the Jamaica Battalion in 1944 and the Jamaica Regiment in 1955.

The Jamaica Regiment was absorbed into the revived West Indian Regiment as its First Battalion with the birth of the short-lived West Indies Federation in 1959. Two years later the Jamaica National Reserve was created, and within a year and 300 years after the formation of its first militia, the Jamaica Defence Force was born. Despite bewildering changes in name and role, Jamaica has enjoyed a proud national and regional military history that is being proudly carried forward by the Jamaica Defence Force.

ORIGINALLY PUBLISHED NOVEMBER 1992

August Morning Come Again

BARBARA GLOUDON

Dear Cousin:

So you're coming home in time for "Fuss-a-Augus" and Independence. I hope you've not forgotten how we talk. "Fuss-a-Augus" is our way of saying First of August, the date of Emancipation, the day when, according to we old time ginneration (generation) Queen Victoria set we free. Of course, is not so it go. Queen Victoria wasn't there when Emancipation papers sign but for some reason, our ole folks firmly believed that it was the goodly Queen V. who gie we free paper. Be that as it may, when our ancestors sing of freedom, they used to proclaim:

Jubilee, Jubilee,
This is the year of Jubilee
August morning come again
This is the year of Jubilee.

Our ancestors used to love to sing bout the Queen. You ever been to a bruckins party? No? When you reach home, we should go over to a village celebration (most likely in Portland), where they are performing bruckins. In a pinda shell, this is a dance in which the people divide themselves into two courts; the Red Court and the Blue Court. Each Court has a King and a Queen and attending courtiers. They are richly dressed in satin and fake jewels and the men carry impressive swords (silver paper and cardboard), as they dance to rich drumming and singing of a tune "De Queen a come in."

Cousin, you have to come and see for yourself, how the dancers bow and weave and kutchie (curtsy) inna beautiful style. And you know of course that behind it all, our ancestors were getting back at those who enslaved them in the only way they could, by tekking bad sinting mek laugh, or as Miss Lou would say "Tek kin teet kibber bun heart." All of which added up means, we had to find a way to laugh through our pain.

There are a whole lot of songs and dances and rituals associated with Emancipation, all of them honouring the spirit of our people, how we fight through the hardship and come out victorious. So, that is what we celebrating, the cultural heritage, Cousin, along with serious reflection on what it means to come from slavery to freedom. Serious ting.

When we moved on to Independence in 1962, some people say we should have kept Fuss-a-Augus as our Independence Day but with one thing and another, August 6 was the date we chose. Still and all, nuff people never forget Fuss-a-Augus. So, in the fullness of time as Grandpa would say, as you come home this year, we will celebrate Emancipation and Independence.

Cousin, me love me Jamaica can't done. I know it full a problems. Some days it give so much trouble that I want to weep but you know they say there is bad and there is good. I cling to what is good. Let me tell you, nothing in the whole world give my weary soul a lift than when I am up in the Love Bird like you and we're coming in to land. When I see the sea in all its colours and shades, I just start to smile. And as for the mountains, with the dip and fall back of the hills, with a zillion trees and more, with rivers winding though the valleys and the dwelling places looking like dolly-house from the distance way up above. Chile, me heart full so tell and I say to myself "This is Jamaica, my Jamaica."

Hear me now, nothing in the world can bring a smile to my face like the sight of a good Jamaican yellow poui tree in full bloom or a bank of shaded bougainvillea dripping blossoms to the ground, or banana leaves in moonlight or a hedge of croton of every imaginable pattern and shade. That is what you call environment.

Look around you when you come home and see for yourself. Forget your diet. Come celebrate with the bite of the jerk on the tongue. Sip the sweet coconut water to cool it off. Renew your faith in miracles and feast like the multitude on bammy and fried fish. Eat the mangoes so till the juice flows golden and triumphant down your chin. Leave aside your power suit and the laptop. Rest the internet. Let it all hang out and surf the wave of love and "pop laugh fe peas soup." Welcome home to Jamrock.

The conversation is going to be lively and noisy. Play some domino. Enjoy a little village cricket. Renew memories of the good old days. Try to deal with the challenge of the new times. How we wish that all was perfect, but alas, it is not so. Still and all, give thanks. Sprinkle a little whites on the ground in tribute to the Ancestors. Bear with Uncle Felix as he tells you his secret of longevity: a wine glass of the whites in the morning and one at evening—"for the stomach's sake," he says, quoting no less an authority than St. Paul, although I don't think the Apostle had made the acquaintance of overproof rum. And that's another thing. We can quote Scripture for we still love go church. You will find many more churches than when you left, two and three on the same corner and evangelistic tents galore. We never do things in half measure, mi chile.

Put on your dancing shoes and rock steady to the latest beat at oldies sessions—we have them all lined up for you. Relax and kick back for you are home, and there's no place like it. The land of the Black, Green and Gold.

So welcome home. To borrow from Miss Lou again: "Rain mighta fall and dutty tough, pot mighta boil but food nuh nuff.." still and all, I will always love this place. I believe you love it too. After all, we navel string bury here, don't it?

Your Cousin, Bee 

ORIGINALLY PUBLISHED AUGUST 1997

The Vision of Marcus Garvey

BEVERLY HAMILTON

My Trip To The West Indies

My Trip to West Indies has proved a boon;

I hope to make the trip again quite soon.

I met there men and women, children, too,

Whose hearts rang out with joys and grace quite true.

I ne'er shall joys of such a kind forget,

As coming from those friends out there I met.

MARCUS GARVEY, 1937

Today, many people have caught the vision of Marcus Garvey and benefited from it. But in his day he was seen by many as a visionary, a man who dreamed dreams but who had no method. But as Martin Luther King was to say decades later, dreams are very important and he too had a dream. And as the Scriptures say, without vision the people perish. Garvey was to go about seeing that his people did not perish.

It is the vision of Garvey that we celebrate in his centenary year—it is the daring of a man only 5' 4" tall but who had a 360° range of intellectual foresight; this larger than life figure who looms at times with god-like qualities in the psyche of many Jamaicans.

Garvey's entry into this world was quite inauspicious. Born in St. Ann's Bay (nestled on Jamaica's north coast), of peasant background, his father was a competent stonemason. Thus young Marcus was a little better off than many other peasants.

His father, though a man of limited means, kept an extensive library and spending time there seems to have been Marcus's greatest joy. Marcus was to inherit this trait of his father for the rest of his life. He was able to supplement his education by this means since like most others at the time he had to leave school by age 14 as secondary education was not available to the majority of the people. He then became apprenticed to his godfather, one Mr. Burrowes, a printer who was said to be from a family of printers originally from Britain.

His stay there was successful and he soon moved on to Kingston in search of a better job and wider horizons. Kingston proved a bustling place of activities for the rural youngster but one which he enjoyed thoroughly. He soon became a part of this moving mosaic. He joined the National Club, a political organization which advocated self-government and so got his first taste of political organizing. It is important to remember that this period—the first decade of the twentieth century coincided with the height of the British Empire.

He participated in a general printers' strike in 1908, the year after the great earthquake had devastated Kingston; and was the only foreman to do so. For his effort he lost his job and was blacklisted among private firms. He eventually secured another job at the Government Printing Office. During this time he systematically developed his oratorical skill, a skill which was to help him tremendously in organizing in later years; and he started his journalistic activities working on the paper of the National Club *Our Own* and later editing his own paper, the *Watchman*.

Garvey's vision of equality also started during this period. He soon left Jamaica for Central and South America to raise money to carry on his projects. But this experience was to leave him saddened and downhearted—

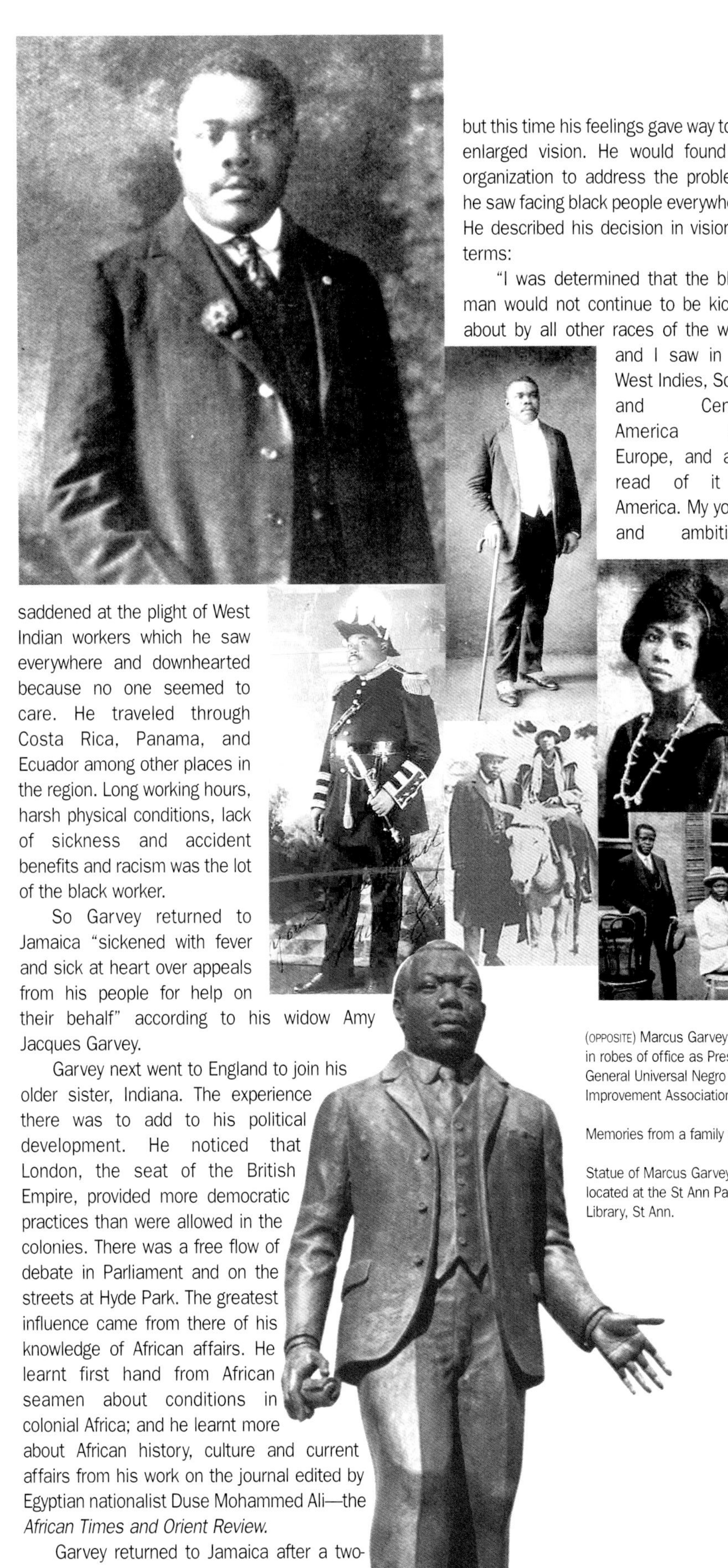

saddened at the plight of West Indian workers which he saw everywhere and downhearted because no one seemed to care. He traveled through Costa Rica, Panama, and Ecuador among other places in the region. Long working hours, harsh physical conditions, lack of sickness and accident benefits and racism was the lot of the black worker.

So Garvey returned to Jamaica "sickened with fever and sick at heart over appeals from his people for help on their behalf" according to his widow Amy Jacques Garvey.

Garvey next went to England to join his older sister, Indiana. The experience there was to add to his political development. He noticed that London, the seat of the British Empire, provided more democratic practices than were allowed in the colonies. There was a free flow of debate in Parliament and on the streets at Hyde Park. The greatest influence came from there of his knowledge of African affairs. He learnt first hand from African seamen about conditions in colonial Africa; and he learnt more about African history, culture and current affairs from his work on the journal edited by Egyptian nationalist Duse Mohammed Ali—the *African Times and Orient Review.*

Garvey returned to Jamaica after a two-year sojourn. Once again he was distressed—but this time his feelings gave way to an enlarged vision. He would found an organization to address the problems he saw facing black people everywhere. He described his decision in visionary terms:

"I was determined that the black man would not continue to be kicked about by all other races of the world and I saw in the West Indies, South and Central America and Europe, and as I read of it in America. My young and ambitious mind let me into flights of great imagination. I saw before me then, even as I do now, a new world of blackmen, not peons, serfs, dogs and slaves, but a nation of sturdy men making their impression upon civilization and causing a new light to dawn upon the human race." (*Philosophy and Opinions of Marcus Garvey*).

(OPPOSITE) Marcus Garvey D.C.L., in robes of office as President, General Universal Negro Improvement Association.

Memories from a family album

Statue of Marcus Garvey located at the St Ann Parish Library, St Ann.

So the Universal Negro Improvement Association and African Communities League which was to have a profound effect on the colonial world. was born in Jamaica in 1914.

The UNIA at first proposed a fairly modest programme with the accent on social and self-improvement. Garvey was then under the influence of noted black American leader, Booker T. Washington who advocated industrial improvement to the detriment of political rights. Garvey hoped that the educated middle classes would provide the leadership for his organization—but they rejected this role.

Garvey decided to go to the U.S. to seek help to set up an industrial school similar to Booker T. Washington's model at Tuskegee. The decision was one of the most important ever made in his life; for there he found a more receptive audience to his message. And also there he saw that the Washington model could not work in the current scheme of things. He soon rejected this model and instead radicalized his message, adding political demands as an important component and using a mass base for organizing. His vision now encompassed a free Africa; he thundered against colonial rule. How dare the white man deny the democratic right of millions of Africans? How dare he to think that the sun would never set on his empire?

His motto now became "Africa for the Africans, those at home and those abroad." To the masses his message was one of hope and deliverance. Whatever man has accomplished, man can do. Blacks were once a great people, founders of great civilizations; slavery and the resulting disabilities—racism, loss of culture, segregation, unemployment, colonialism—these were just temporary measures that could be overcome. "Up you mighty race! You can accomplish what you will!" he exhorted. And the people responded. Within three years after his arrival in the U.S. he was the most important black leader there. By 1921 he became the leader of the largest Pan African organization ever seen, with membership running into the millions, in about 90 countries.

To carry out his work certain structures and programmes were put in place. The UNIA became a nation, albeit an embryonic one, as a way of demonstrating how things should be done. Certain posts corresponded to national ones—e.g. a president-general, ministers with portfolios (labour and education were the most important ones), there was a civil service, police and fire department. There was a judicial service with a counsel general; there was an auditor general. The UNIA had its own propaganda arm in the *Negro World* which soon became the largest black weekly in the U.S. and was distributed all over the world—provoking such responses as outright banning and curtailment with prison terms for those caught with copies in some countries.

The UNIA also had its economic arm—the Negro Factories Corporation which ran a number of cooperative businesses—laundries, grocery shops, a doll factory, a millinery and a printing plant among others. The UNIA even attempted to get into high financial business with the launching of the Black Star Line which eventually bought three ships, a move which astounded sceptics. This venture ended disastrously for many reasons among them mismanagement, sabotage, internal dishonesty and external racist pressure. But the Black Star Line, while it lasted, proved a great psychological boost to the people, however, and thousands greeted the ships wherever they went. These became almost a symbol of the black man's hope.

The UNIA had its own flag and anthem. The one thing it lacked was a land base—and this it attempted to rectify by negotiation with the independent government of Liberia for settlement of people from the west there. The idea was that if blacks could have their own nation developed for their own benefit this would be the best answer to racism and the best fulfillment of black people everywhere.

"We organized a plan for building four model cities in the Republic of Liberia as the first concentration centers for the Negroes of the West Indies and America to link up their intelligence with the native of Africa in a scheme of nation building." Garvey wrote in 1932 in the *New Jamaican*. But the plan collapsed. The Liberian government had first granted lands to the UNIA but went back on the promise and expelled its members, the main reason being pressure from the colonial powers of Britain and France which had colonies bordering that country.

The ending of that dream was one of the biggest blows to the Garvey movement; it meant the end of the political programme for nation building as well as great financial losses. The UNIA sought to obtain land in South-West Africa's Namibia—and twice protested South Africa's mandate to that Territory to the League of Nations. This was also not successful.

Garvey's vision provided a great psychological uplift to the ordinary black people; but it was a nightmare to the U.S. government and colonial authorities. Fairly soon after his entry into American life, he came under surveillance, with no less a person than J. Edgar Hoover (later of FBI fame) being given special responsibilities. He was harassed through the courts and informers were placed inside the organization. He was eventually arrested for "using the mail to defraud" in connection with public shares sold for the Black Star Line.

The trial of Marcus Garvey remains to date one of the great dramas of human history. The political nature was evident to all, most of all to Garvey himself. He used the courtroom as his stage to make a stirring plea for the cause of his people and their right to seek their own liberty. But the judge asked the jury, "Gentlemen will you let the tiger loose?" The jury responded accordingly—they caged the tiger, relying for evidence on an empty envelope in which a circular encouraging purchase of Black Star Line shares was supposed to have been sent.

For that Garvey received a prison sentence of five years. It was eventually commuted, due partly to the great outcry at the severity and injustice of the trial. He was then deported to Jamaica never to set foot on U.S. soil again.

Garvey's return to Jamaica did not lessen his dream in any way, although a new dimension was created. He was still an international figure and he still held hopes of building a nation on Pan African concepts; but local aspiration now was incorporated into his vision. He now had a vision of a new Jamaica and the editorial of the first edition of his second Jamaican daily explained it:

"We shall do everything in our power to help the government bring about a better order of things: considering that it is not only Government's duty to initiate relief for its citizens; but inform the Government of their needs. In this latter respect we shall not fail to do our duty. No Government anywhere is perfect. We can only get the best out of Government everywhere and anywhere when the citizens of themselves are sufficiently alert as to force their needs upon Government, and in a constitutional way see that they are attended to.

"Jamaica is a fine country from a natural view point. It is a terrible country from economic observations. When one considers how the bulk of the people of Jamaica live, it makes one wonder if we use or have any system of economics. We shall endeavour to enlighten the country on the possibility of creating a better order of things for everybody through a system of education in economics—a thing not generally known or taught in Jamaica." (July 9, 1931).

The most comprehensive plan for his vision of a new Jamaica had been his 1929 election manifesto presented during the campaign to the Legislative Council. The manifesto addressed itself to practical things—industry, labour, health, education, culture, legal reform among others. It called for a minimum wage, sickness and accident benefits for workers; the use of idle lands for agricultural projects to alleviate chronic unemployment; urban upgrading; low-income housing for the peasantry; prison reform; free secondary education, a visiting nursing system; land reform; legal aid system and the establishment of a performing arts centre among others.

Garvey was unsuccessful in his bid for election to the Legislative Council mainly because the majority of the people did not have a vote. He was however elected to the Kingston and St. Andrew Corporation where he continued to push for the programmes outlined in the manifesto.

He set up the Jamaica Worker and Labourers Association to encourage workers to organize among themselves. And his headquarters at Edelweiss became a training ground and showcase for some of the best creative talent in Jamaica—in music, drama, elocution and dance.

He practiced a vigorous brand of journalism starting two papers, the *Blackman* and the *New Jamaican*, where national issues could be discussed form the point of view of the ordinary black man.

But harassment continued and colonial authorities were successful in weakening links with the outside world, an important aspect for any internationalist. The courts again were used against Garvey. He soon turned his eyes overseas and in 1935 moved the headquarters of his organization to London. He tried to re-organize the UNIA and paid particular attention to training a cadre of leaders through his School of African Philosophy.

He used his magazine to write about the impending World War II, and to rail against Nazi and Fascist doctrines. When the workers in Jamaica, and indeed the entire Caribbean, rose up in rebellion in the 1937-38 period, he wrote in support of their efforts. He never gave up on the hope that one day the black man would be in control of his own life, of his own destiny.

Garvey died in London in 1940, after suffering two strokes. But the vision he helped to fashion, of independent, free, black nations, remains alive today wherever and whenever equality and justice is sought.

ORIGINALLY PUBLISHED AUGUST 1987

Jamaica The New Riviera

CYNTHIA WILMOT

"In cities on both sides of the Atlantic there are professional and businessmen who are worn out with working at the high pressure that modern life seems to demand, until what would under normal conditions be accepted as matter of course becomes a perpetual worry and irritation... so that the wearied and jaded worker feels that his life is little better than that of one doing time on a treadmill..."

No, dear reader, these words are not a description of life in the 1980's. They were written at the turn of the century by Dr. James Johnson, a British medical man of Brown's Town, St. Ann, in a rare book titled "Jamaica: the New Riviera." With true missionary zeal, the good doctor wrote this book about his adopted country ("blue sky over blue sea, luxurious vegetation and lovely scenery, fragrant with the odour of spice and flowers, refreshed by an invigorating sea breeze....") in order to persuade the tired businessmen of his time to seek a physical and spiritual renewal in the island, and also to publicize, the country's incredible powers of healing the ill.

"There is a still more numerous class among dwellers in temperate climes ...who, either by inheritance or otherwise, have acquired a physically delicate constitution and are unable to resist the rigours of a northern winter, to whom the cold, bleak winds...aggravate the natural susceptibility to pulmonary trouble, bronchitis, rheumatism or allied infections. To both classes (the wornout from work *and* the infirm) I say most emphatically—Jamaica is the place for you!"

The doctor's own story was a case in point:

"Lest the reader may be tempted to criticize the extravagant language I use in describing either the scenery or climate of Jamaica. I give briefly a bit of my own experience. In 1874, while still a young man in college in London, I contacted a severe case of pneumonia, followed by pulmonary symptoms of very grave character... Jonathan Hutchinson, one of England's most famous specialists on the lungs, limited my prospects of life to six months...after six months (in Jamaica) my temperature was normal and my cough had entirely left me. My weight when I left England was less than 130 pounds... I present my photograph lest anyone should be inclined to commiserate with me for being compelled to reside for so long in the tropics."

And, indeed, Doctor Johnson's photograph (below) shows a most handsome, husky young gentleman, twinkle in eye and hat jauntily at an angle, resplendent with gold watch chain and silver-headed cane—clearly the picture of radiant health!

Of course, Dr. Johnson's recovery might have been a one-time miracle. Yet if we look for other examples, they are easily found.

In 1902, Dr. Benjamin Lee, Secretary of the State Board of Health in Pennsylvania reported similar cases and suggested that the hilly towns of Jamaica would be ideal for locating health resorts. A Dr. Clarke, resident of Santa Cruz in St. Elizabeth, had declared even earlier, "rarely do Europeans suffer from disease of any kind in our mountains." Dr. Robb, practicing in Kingston in 1883, declared that residence in Jamaica was the best insurance for longevity, and remarked that on his visiting list were "nine patients whose combined ages amount to 751 years"—at a time when life expectancy hovered in the fifties. Dr. Clarke was later to declare that "if there is one ailment above all others for which this climate is especially adapted it is incipient phthisis (tuberculosis) or pulmonary trouble of any kind... and observations of medical men in Jamaica's Dry Harbour Mountains prove that Bright's Disease is by no means the dangerous malady it is supposed to be."

Dr. James Johnson author of "Jamaica: The New Riviera."

One of the most famous stories of recovery reached England via the banana boats which carried Jamaica's "green gold" to England and to America to lay the foundation for the island's tourist trade more than a quarter century before a gangly young man named Charles Lindbergh piloted the first commercial overseas flight to Kingston in the remarkable time of ten hours. On one of the banana boats travelled a pale, debilitated young man named E.B. Hopkins, who had "never known a day's good health." His friends had bid him farewell without hope of seeing him alive again. Yet on arrival in Jamaica he went to work with the famous old sea captain, Lorenzo Dow Baker, who was busy establishing what would later become part of the vast United Fruit Company. Full of enthusiasm, young Hopkins decided to spend his last few days helping Baker build the business, so that he could die content. Instead, he gained weight, his cheeks grew pink and he lived to a ripe old age, eventually using his hard-earned fortune for philanthropic work in gratitude for his "rebirth".

The fame of the new nirvana spread. American poetess Ella Wheeler Wilcox chided her readers: "What are you thinking about, you northern men and women, who rush to Florida or Bermuda or Europe in search of a winter resort .... Why do you not know of this lost Garden of Eden, a combination of American comfort, English cleanliness, and Italian climate? Such opulence of Nature's best gifts. As I write the majestic Blue Mountains are back of me. ..the temperature marks 84 in my room, but a delicious cool breeze blows in from the hills...Americans can no longer be blind to the wonderful advantages offered by this beautiful spot."

And so they came. They sat in their deck chairs aboard their steamers, day by day feeling the winds grow warmer as they approached Jamaica. Some were adventurers, like the unconventional Mrs. Wilcox, appreciating the "cachet" of discovering a new destination. Montego Bay was still a village, with no large hotels and only a few boarding houses kept by respectable ladies. Ocho Rios was a sleepy spot on the north coast inhabited only by fisherfolk. "Real" tourism existed in the hills of Malvern, in Constant Spring, in Kingston, and in Port Antonio, where THE place to go was the Titchfield Hotel, the most elaborate and imposing establishment in the entire Caribbean, three storeys high, with 400 rooms, and an Italian orchestra playing in the dining-room. The upper floors were particularly lavish, served by elevators and hot and cold running water, and wired for electric light. Such opulence attracted the rich and famous, so that a young J.P. Morgan Jr., would later remark on the Titchfield verandah, "Christopher Columbus discovered this? How did he ever leave!"

But in the early days, a large majority of the visitors had been dispatched to the Caribbean by their doctors in Boston or London to recuperate from lingering illnesses: phthisis, phlebitis, rheumatism, anaemia. Some suffered from less exact maladies—"nervous disposition", "insomnia", "weakness of the blood" which had confounded the medical men. Perhaps their doctors were skeptical of Jamaica's healing power in such cases, but if Jamaica did not cure at least it would clear the hypochondriacs out of their consultoria. Even so, to the believers and the non-believers alike, the facts spoke for themselves: Jamaica was "the doctor". Ailments that had persisted through London fogs and New England snows seemed to disappear by magic. Gentlemen suffering from gout or tired livers soon found themselves on horseback before breakfast (a breakfast downed without fear of indigestion at that) and languorous ladies put away their smelling salts and took up binoculars for bird-watching or sketchbooks for their pastels and took to the woods.

So many documented cases of recovery exist that it is impossible to dismiss them as coincidental or improbable. But how did it happen? Obviously, fresh air is an excellent physician—but there was more than this to the mystery. For one thing, many visitors of a century ago made fast for the mineral spas at Bath of the Apostle in St. Thomas or Milk River in Clarendon. As early as the seventeenth century Bath in St. Thomas had cured ailing soldiers and sailors of everything from dyspepsia to venereal disease. By the eighteenth century Milk River had become a popular spot for members of the plantocracy suffering from the results of high living, who drank the waters for their livers or bathed in them for gout. One well documented case concerned a British surveyor who arrived at Milk River comatose and left on horseback.

Modern medical science provides two other clues to the mystery. Today, Vitamin C is considered by many nutritionists to be important in the treating of coughs and colds and in speeding up the healing process. For this reason, many of us drink our orange juice daily, which provides 50 milligrams of Vitamin C for each 100 grams of liquid. Yet it was the custom in Jamaica, a century ago, for boarding-house keepers to serve their guests a refreshing drink of the juice of West Indian cherries; 100 grams of this magic elixir contains no less than 1,790 milligrams of Vitamin C.

Similarly, visitors with digestive problems were urged by local doctors to eat pawpaw (papaya) for breakfast along with sliced bananas. Now we know that pawpaw contains valuable enzymes which aid digestion, and our nutritionists suspect something that Jamaican doctors knew many years ago—pawpaw, eaten alone on an empty stomach has such strong digestive powers that it might "digest the walls of the stomach". Jamaican housewives, long before the advent of today's food tenderizers, wrapped paw-paw leaves around tough meat overtight. So powerful were the leaves, the legend goes, that once a pirate, weary of plundering, lay down to rest among some pawpaw trees, pulling the leaves over him for shade while he slept. He never awakened, the tale goes: when his friends came to look for him they found only his cutlass and his breeches buttons!

And finally, there was another factor—often overlooked—which aided recovery. The very condition of the Jamaican roads, and the lack of high speed transportation, made inland travel strenuous, thus invalids who wanted to see more of the "unbelievable paradise" than they could glimpse through jalousied bedroom windows were forced into strenuous exercise. Today's travellers, whisked to ultra-modern hotels in air-conditioned limousines would seem wickedly indolent to those travellers of yore. In Dr. Johnson's day, ladies in skirts below their ankles, hats and veils and gentlemen in three piece suits and solar toupees were undaunted by "tour suggestions" such as these from a turn-of-the-century guidebook:

"Drive by buggy to Gordon Town, and proceed at horseback at an easy pace through the bush to the first buildings of Newcastle, and a superb view of Kingston".

Or: "Hire a buggy for six shillings at the Rio Cobre Hotel, head for the hills, or travel by punt up the canal for two hours then back to Spanish Town by buggy in time for the 5.32 train to Kingston."

Visitors with more time to spare were advised to climb the Blue Mountains, carrying all of their provisions and blankets. "There is scenery of incomparable beauty as you approach Whitfield Hall at an altitude of 4,000 feet. At 6,000 feet you enter the forest primeval.... another hour and you reach the Summit, with the whole fair isle of Jamaica spread out at your feet... In the morning, bestir betimes and see a sunrise which will amply repay you for the fatigues of the journey...."

A popular jaunt for convalescents was to Cane River Gorge, near Kingston. This entailed a buggy ride and a stroll of a mile and a half through mountains, across a river bed, into a ravine. "How delightful the breeze that blows softly down the canyon," says the author—and in those days before wash and wear fabrics, we can well believe it!

So the recipe for recovery, then as now, apparently contained these ingredients: fresh clean air, a dry, balmy clime, good natural food, out-door exercise.

"Jamaica is a perfect paradise," wrote Dr. Johnson. "I have met people in robust health who left Britain without a hope of recovery. Were I required, as a medical man, to give an unbiased opinion as to what parts of Jamaica would be the most favourable, I would unhesitatingly advise Browns Town in the Dry Harbour Mountains and Malvern in the Santa Cruz Mountains...Some may say I have a 'bee in my bonnet' and that my mental abberation takes the form of extragant adulation of Jamaica, and Browns Town in particular. Well, everyone is said to be 'a button short' somewhere."

Maybe so, but the eminent British author, Gervaise Mason, describing a drive along Jamaica's north coast, in St. Ann, wrote: "It is only those who have witnessed these manifold glories, become entranced by the thousand and one perfect pictures by Nature's most delicate brush, and felt the refreshing influences of her climate, who can credit the enticing tales that must forever be crossing from the little Colony to the Motherland. Drive through the finest picture gallery in the world, where no catalogue is necessary, the quaint bridges crossing the innumerable streams...if anyone could wish for anything more majestic in adornment, sweetly accidental in design, refreshing in every momentary and undulating change, then indeed he must be hard to please!"

Apparently, every visitor to Jamaica had a "bee in the bonnet" about this favoured isle. But let us give the final word to Dr. James Johnson himself—physician, lecturer, and author of "Jamaica—The New Riviera".

"Here is a veritable Mecca for the invalid, for what pilgrimage could hold out a greater reward than restored health? What Jamaica has done for me I feel certain it will do for others, if they will only give it a chance."

ORIGINALLY PUBLISHED FEBRUARY 1988

Mandeville Hotel, Built in 1898

Old Hotels

LORRAINE DEEKS

Over the past two hundred years Jamaica has had many visitors, several of whom have left written accounts of their impressions:

"...the Dunghill of the Universe, the Refuse of the whole of creation...the Nursery of Heavens Judgement, where the Malignant seeds of all Pestilence were first gather'd and scatter'd thro' the Regions of the Earth, to punish mankind for their offences...subject to Tornadoes, Hurricanes and Earthquakes, as if the island, like the people, were troubled with the Dry Belly-Ache."

— A TRIP TO JAMAICA, EDWARD WARD 1698.

Montego Bay Hotel

Others had a more favourable opinion:

"I travelled over the greater part of the island, and was very much pleased with it. The drawbacks on such a tour are the expensiveness of locomotion, the want of hotels, the badness of the roads. As to cost, the tourist always consoles himself by reflecting that he is going to take the expensive journey once, and only once. The badness of the roads form an additional excitement; and the want of hotel is cured, as it probably has been caused, by the hospitality of the gentry." Anthony Trollope, 1859

Providing accommodation was a problem until the late 19th century, prior to this there were a few inns and lodging houses, such as Ferry Inn on Spanish Town Road, and Couba

Titchfield Hotel, 1905

Gall's Myrtle Bank Hotel

Cornwall is where Nelson stayed in Port Royal, but these places were not really geared to take care of visitors. By 1888 three hotels were established, these were the largest in Jamaica at that time, and included Myrtle Bank, Titchfield and the Constant Spring Hotel.

The Myrtle Bank Hotel which was located on Harbour Street in Kingston, was made famous in more than one generation. The first hotel was constructed in 1870, on the site of an old 'watering yard', where ships obtained drinking water supplies. It was the home of James Gall, a waspish Scotsman. A journalist by profession, Gall was a 'Jack of all trades', who advertised his home as a sanitarium in his newspaper, offering personal advice on health matters. Mrs. Gall ran the lodging house at a modest fee of ten shillings per day. In addition, stables and a coach house were provided for the guests horses and buggies, free of charge.

In 1875 Christmas Bazaars were introduced, usually lasting for ten days over the festive season, offering adults and children a variety of attractions, food, drinks, games, raffles, exhibitions, and mechanical toys. A music stand was erected in the garden, and the fine band of the West India Regiment played twice a week. Such events drew large crowds, and Gall's Myrtle Bank soon became the chief recreational and social centre of Kingston.

An agreement was also made with the United States Signal Service to hoist a hurricane signal flag on a high mast whenever there was reason to believe a storm was brewing, but being unskilled in the use of a barometer Gall gave many false alarms, and was requested to discontinue this work.

The hotel consisted of a central building with out-lying cottages, a "capacious court", circulating library, and a shop "specializing in valentines, fans," and other objects listed as "aids to the art of Flirtation".

In 1891 the Kingston Hotels Company purchased Gall's property and constructed a new building, this was one of the two hotels erected in Kingston as a result of the 1890 Hotel Law. At the turn of the century it was leased to the Elder Dempster Steamship Company, which was being subsidized to run ships between England and Jamaica to attract tourists and develop the economy of the island.

An earthquake struck in 1907 completely destroying Myrtle Bank, and a third hotel was built on the site, which was subsequently sold to the United Fruit Company. In 1943 the hotel was acquired by Issa interests, and its importance grew rapidly during the 1950's. Several years later closure became imminent, due to a decline in business, despite desperate efforts by a committee of businessmen to raise £500,000 to purchase the hotel. In 1964 a landmark in Jamaica's tourist trade passed into history.

The Titchfield Hotel was built in 1897 by the Boston Fruit Company, following the opening of a shipping route between Port Antonio and Boston. In addition to exporting bananas to the United States, the company also offered vacation packages to Jamaica:

"15 Day Tours,
Jamaica, British West Indies,
$200.00 including all expenses,
Every week in the year".

The steam ships came direct to Port Antonio, making their first stop at the private wharf in front of the Titchfield Hotel, to off-load passengers.

The hotel consisted of several cottages, one group for sleeping rooms, and a separate building for the dining room, kitchen and laundry. A central building contained the parlour, reading room and baths. In 1901 one writer noted that alcohol could not be obtained there "except by favour, and more or less surreptitiously".

In 1905 a new magnificant Titchfield Hotel was declared open. It was considered a "triumph of architectural skill" having taken only five months to build, at a cost of 65,000 pounds. This building was completely destroyed in the Port Antonio Fire in 1910. Three years later the hotel was reopened with "six hundred feet of Piazza" and "many rooms with private baths". It became known as "the most commodious hotel in the south seas".

The Constant Spring Hotel in Kingston was another grand attempt at hotel building, it was a "palatial stone mansion" on sixty acres of land, consisting of one hundred rooms. It was constructed in 1888, three years before the Jamaican Colonial Exhibition, which was organised to attract visitors to the island. It was taken over by the government several years later, and leased to an American hotelier. Shortly after the hotel was destroyed by fire, and in 1940 the property was purchased by the Catholic Church to be used as a school.

These three large hotels were managed by men, and it was noted that "nearly all the smaller hotels were managed by women, and most successfully managed some of them were, too". Such an example was Brooks House which consisted of 17 rooms, and was under the management of Miss Jane Brooks. Mandeville was always a favourite resort area, owing to the "salubrity of the climate", and Brooks House, built in 1898, was one of the earlier and better known hotels in that area. It later became known as the Mandeville Hotel.

During the 18th and 19th century the sugar and rum industry in Jamaica prospered, and many fine great houses were built on numerous estates. By the early 20th century most of these mansions were converted into guest houses, and later became hotels. Mona Hotel, which has been remodelled, was once the residence of the owner of the famous Mona Sugar Estate, on a part of which the University of the West Indies is built. Fairfield in Montego Bay was another 18th century great house, which was turned into a hotel, and has since been converted into a health clinic.

The Shaw Park Estate in the parish of St. Ann, is said to be where Christopher Columbus encamped when he arrived in Jamaica. Rumour has it that the Spanish hid a large quantity of treasure on the grounds, which has never been discovered. In In 1962 the original Shaw Park Hotel was completely demolished, and a new hotel was erected. Other great house hotels include Eaton Hall in Runaway Bay, and Tryall and Richmond Hill Inn in Montego Bay. Many other hotels were built as a result of the 1890 Hotel Law incentives. The Rio Cobre in Spanish Town was built by the St. Catherine Hotels Company, and was named after the river that ran through the grounds. It was a two storey building with 27 rooms, and had a high reputation for creole cooking. Rates were set at six shillings and sixpence per day for "man and wife", and carriages and horses could be "procured from the hotel for excursions" at a moderate fee. One of the entertainment highlights was punting trips on the irrigation canal.

Moneague Hotel was built on part of the Rose Hall property in St. Ann, and was owned by a company of citizens. It consisted of 14 rooms, and was converted into a teacher training college in 1956.

Queens Hotel located in Kingston, was one of the most successful, erected for the purpose of housing the working classes at the time of the Jamaican Exposition in 1891. In the years following it was largely patronized as a lodging house by market women, who were compelled to remain in town overnight.

Burkes Grand Hotel was located on the corner of North Parade and Upper King Street. It was a two storey "much jalousied green wooden building" and had many famous guests, including one of Jamaica's National Heroes, George William Gordon. It is now used as the headquarters for the Salvation Army.

Many of the early Jamaican hotels and guests houses have lost their importance, fading into history. Some have been completely demolished, while others still standing, are now abandoned ruins bearing no semblance to their colourful past. Yet memories of them live on. Who will ever forget Myrtle Bank?

ORIGINALLY PUBLISHED JANUARY 1980

Aviation in Jamaica

BARBARA NELSON

BSAA York "Star Dale" at Palisadoes Airport 1946. Note the flags flying from the cockpit.

In 1999 Air Jamaica celebrated its 30th birthday. The national airline is one of several scheduled carriers that operate in Jamaica today. As far as aviation goes, we have come a long way.

The very first time a plane was flown in Jamaica was on December 21, 1911, by an American aviator called Jesse Seligman. This was particularly significant because until the 1940s almost all aircraft flying into the island were sea planes.

Jamaicans may be surprised to know that commercial aviation routes developed in the Caribbean in the late 1920s but it was Pan American Airways that brought Jamaica into the age of commercial aviation in 1930.

The 1930s were exciting years for aviation in Jamaica as the pioneers made their mark. Captain Charles Lindbergh, the world famous aviator who had made a solo nonstop crossing of the Atlantic in 1927, brought the inaugural Pan Am Clipper flight to Jamaica in 1931. He was making the first half of a survey flight for the airline. Lindbergh, who was called the "Lone Eagle" landed a four-engined Sikorsky S40 on the Kingston harbour to the delight of many spectators. On leaving Jamaica he flew some 600 miles to Panama thus completing the route inaugurated by Pan American Airways: Miami-Cienfuegos (Cuba)-Kingston-Panama. Lindbergh and another aviator, an Australian—Bert Hinkler—are attributed with landing planes in Jamaica in the 1930s.

"I think we can pinpoint the first ever commercial passenger service into Jamaica as Pan Am Clipper Service Sikorsky-40 to Harbour head in 1931," says Pat Simmons, the past company secretary at Air Jamaica. "It landed near Bournemouth. They started the flying boat service from Miami and the boats continued right through the war years. People used the service to go anywhere from Jamaica through Miami. The flying boats were discontinued when Pan Am started a land-plane service into Palisadoes when it opened up in 1944."

The registration in 1931 of the first aircraft in Jamaica was a milestone in local aviation history. A DeHavilland Moth seaplane with a 100 horsepower Gypsy engine, it was registered VP-JAA. It was owned and operated by Caribbean Airways, the first locally owned carrier and had a mail franchise. The airline also established a service between Kingston and Santiago de Cuba in 1931.

In 1935, a Jamaican, Rowley Horne encouraged by Roy Munoz of New York, went to Roosevelt Field, Long Island, USA, to learn how to fly. Horne bought a three-seater single engine F2-WACO biplane, 210 hp with continental radial engines, registered NC 12447. It had a range of 350 miles with a cruise speed of 135 miles per hour.

On December 12, 1936, Horne who was employed as a Morse Code operator at the Pan Am seaplane base at Harbour Head, (accompanied by a friend, Dale Scott) began a journey in the "WACO" from Pt. Washington in Long Island heading for Jamaica. Horne had to make many stops along the Atlantic coast of the United States and in Cuba. The journey ended in Jamaica on Christmas Eve, December 24, 1936.

The next decade saw rapid development in Jamaica's aviation industry. In 1940 the British Admiralty built the Royal Navy Air Station at Palisadoes. In early 1944 the facility was handed over to the Jamaican government for public use, signaling the end of the Pan Am (seaplane) Clipper service and the beginning of scheduled commercial land-plane service into Palisadoes. Links to all of South America and the eastern Caribbean were quickly established.

A KLM Lockheed Hudson aircraft which flew three or four times per week between Curacao, Aruba, Kingston and on to Miami via Camaguey, Cuba, provided the first land plane service into the Palisadoes airport in early 1944. It carried ten passengers.

Soon after, in 1944, Pan Am began daily DC3 21-seater flights into Palisadoes on the route between Miami, Camaguey, Kingston and Barranquilla, Colombia.

Pan American also operated the Palisadoes control tower until the Civil Aviation Department took over in 1947. As a matter of interest, the Morse Code room was situated right beside the tower at Palisadoes. Up till the 1950s the only contact between commercial scheduled airlines from wherever they were coming, was by Morse Code, a code in which letters are represented by combinations of long and short, light or sound signals and was named after it's inventor an American electrician, S.F.B. Morse. The operating crew had a radio operator on board and regular messages were sent from check points all along the route. Voice communication was possible only when the plane was ten to fifteen minutes away from its destination.

"Yes, 1944 was a very important year for aviation in Jamaica," Pat Simmons recalled. "It was the first year of commercial land plane service in Jamaica. British West Indian Airways, owned by the British, started passenger service from Trinidad via umpteen islands to Jamaica on December 15, 1944."

On that day a blue and white Lockheed Hudson plane bearing the symbol of a flying horse arrived from Port-of-Spain. The last stop for BWIA was the Dominican Republic because of the range of the aircraft.

Simmons himself "got into the business" when he started to work for Pan American Airways in 1945.

In 1946 a company called Jamaica Air Transport Ltd. started regular service between Kingston and Montego Bay using a Vickers flying boat.

Under banner headlines an article in the *Gleaner* of January 15, 1947 reported "Jamaica to be big air trunk junction". British South American Airways announced that from January 18, the island would become an important air trunk junction for South American and Caribbean passengers. It was the first company to fly 'same plane airplanes' from London to Jamaica. The complete route was London—Azores—Bermuda (alternating with Nassau)—Jamaica—Caracas. On the first fortnightly services BSAA used reconverted 13-seater Lancaster and 22-seater York bombers. Pat Simmons who worked with BWIA at that time described the aircraft as not only antiquated, but quite uncomfortable.

Soon after the services were increased to weekly in each direction, but at the start Jamaica was served only on the southbound journey.

The airline moved quickly to improve the level of comfort and speed and in 1947 introduced the first of the British postwar airliners, the Avro-Tudor plane. Built as a transport plane, able to seat 32 passengers, it cruised between 250 and 300 miles per hour at up to 25,000 feet. It was much more suitable for the trans-Atlantic flight.

But there was a problem, Pat Simmons recalls, "The planes developed a habit of disappearing into thin air and in two consecutive years, January 1948 and January 1949 two of them, the *"Star Tiger"* and the *"Star Ariel"* disappeared on their way to Jamaica in the infamous Bermuda triangle. To this day it still a mystery. There is no confirmed evidence of any wreckage or debris found that could relate to their disappearance."

Simmons personally took part in the search for the second plane which was on its way from Bermuda to London. "I had just started working with BWIA," he said, "and the morning after the plane disappeared we went out and flew up and down at about 500 feet over the Turks and Caicos islands looking for debris or any evidence. The plane had taken off at 7:30 from Bermuda to Kingston in broad daylight with 13 passengers and seven crew. There were at least three Jamaican among them. The flight used to go on to South America all the way down to Santiago, Chile, and then come back up the same route. It radioed in from Bermuda about an hour after it took off saying it was in good weather, on course, on schedule for arrival in Jamaica and it was changing over to the Jamaican radio frequency. That's the last word they ever heard of it."

The same experience was recorded with the *"Star Tiger"* almost to the day. The plane took off at night from the Azores. Its last contact was only about 300 miles north of Bermuda saying it was "a clear night, beautiful weather ...see you soon."

The first recorded disappearance of a United States ship in the Bermuda triangle occurred in March 1918, when the U.S.S. Cyclops vanished. On December 5, 1945, a squadron of five U.S. bombers disappeared, and a seaplane vanished while searching for the aircraft.

Change was, however, in the air and in 1947 commercial aviation got a boost with the opening of the aerodrome at Montego Bay (later renamed the Sangster International Airport). In his book "Reflections on Jamaica's Tourism" L. Emile Martin says it was thanks to the vision and efforts of the late Hon. Walter Fletcher, CBE, (a former custos of St. James and businessman) that Montego Bay's direct air link with the outside world emerged when Pan Am's seaplane service terminated just offshore the Doctor's Cave beach and Casa Blanca hotel.

The service proved popular enough to highlight the need for a land-based modern airport that could accommodate a larger passenger-carrying aircraft.

The Montego Bay site was identified as early as 1936 for an airfield, and a runway was, in fact, constructed there, remaining alone until the 1940s when a decision was taken to construct an aerodrome beside it. The aerodrome had a longer runway than Palisadoes airport in Kingston, therefore altering the route structure of many airlines. The inauguration of the Montego Bay airport was celebrated in January 1947 with Pan American World Airways initiating regular flights to and from Miami. The first of these flights were regarded officially as charters since flight licenses had not been issued to Pan Am. The licenses were issued later when the airstrip's radio transmitters were strengthened.

Pat Simmons, who went to Montego Bay as station manager for BWIA and BOAC in 1958, explains, "The popular BOAC double-decker Stratocruisers, for example, that carried about 50 people from London to Montego Bay, most of whom wanted to land in Kingston, were obliged to turn around at Montego Bay. The BWIA 28-seater two engine Vikings that did daily service from Miami to Montego Bay and on to Kingston introduced a shuttle service for both incoming and outgoing passengers. The service continued until 1959."

Simmons recalls that the shuttle system which went on for at least five years "was a miserable operation. Sometimes, because of the number of people going on to Kingston from Montego Bay there had to be two shuttles, but there was only one plane. People would try a bribe to get on the first shuttle. Sometimes they got on but left their bags behind."

From 1947 to September 1949 Pan Am operated the Montego Bay aerodrome under Jamaican government supervision until the Civil Aviation Department took over in 1949. The facility underwent constant structural upgrading after 1949, but the steady increase in air traffic indicated that a major expansion was necessary. The second Jamaican airline—British Caribbean Airways, was registered in March 1947. This was the first totally local-owned transport land plane. Its 14-seater Lockheed Lodestar registered VP–JAN was owned by the Cox brothers. BCA started a route from Kingston to Belize and later to Miami. It was later bought by BSAA. Pat Simmons recalls that in mid 1948 Chicago & Southern Airlines of New Orleans, later renamed Delta, started service to the island and by the end of the year Trans-Canada Airlines, later called Air Canada, inaugurated service from Toronto to Jamaica with the fully pressurized 'North Star', a plane with four Rolls-Royce engines.

At this time, flights to Jamaica by Cayman Island Airways also began.

Colombia's national airline 'AVIANCA' which started operations in 1919, (making it the oldest airline in the Americas and the second oldest in the world) was an affiliate of Pan American. The airline inaugurated a Jamaica–New York service in 1954 with the first Lockheed Super-Constellation aircraft to enter the island.

In 1955 BWIA introduced the Vickers Viscount on the Trinidad–Jamaica–Miami route. It was the first pressurized jet-prop plane that also flew from Trinidad to New York with stops in between. For five years it had the prestigious position of being the most modern airplane serving Jamaica until jets made their entrance in 1959/60. Young Senator John F. Kennedy was one of the many celebrities who flew to Jamaica on a Viscount in 1959.

In the mid 1950s, Delta started using a turbo-prop plane, the Constellation between New Orleans and Montego Bay and on to Caracas.

Meanwhile Pan American began using the fully pressurized, fast airplanes and in 1958 British Airways replaced the Boeing Stratocruiser with the "Whispering Giant", the Britannia 312 turbo-prop airplane. That plane flew faster and higher and made the trip from London to Montego Bay via New York, Bermuda and Nassau. Passengers for Kingston were shuttled to Palisadoes airport in BWIA Dakota aircraft which left Montego Bay at 5:35 p.m. and arrived at Palisadoes at 6:20 p.m.

In its ten years in service with BOAC, the Stratocruiser made almost 13,000 Atlantic crossings between London and the USA, Canada and the Caribbean.

Palisadoes itself was in the mid-to-late 1940s the centre of considerable traffic in nonscheduled charter cargo flights—converted United States bombers which flew freight out of Miami to South America and stopped in Jamaica to refuel. Simmons said the airport was so busy that many of its employees worked right through the night as several cargo flights came in as late as three o'clock in the morning. The handling fees, however, were invaluable in keeping the airport solvent. At that time Pan American operated the airport tower at Palisadoes.

Simmons commented that "Jamaica has a remarkable safety record as far as airport mishaps are concerned. Only two major accidents with fatalities stand out. Both occurred in the 1950s. The first involved a CIA Lodestar plane in 1951, the other an AVIANCA flight to Montego Bay in 1959. In the mid 1950s a Pan Am Convair twin-engine aircraft coming in to Palisadoes landed in the harbour some fifty yards from the runway. Fortunately there were no fatalities.

The first BOAC Stratocruiser from London "Canopus" landing at Montego Bay Airport, January 1952.

Avensa came to Jamaica in the 1950s and flew the route from Venezuela to Montego Bay to Miami for several years.

Cuba's national carrier made its inaugural flight to Jamaica in June 1954 for regular bi-weekly service and the following year Panama Airways started flying here.

On July 1959 the Montego Bay terminal building was officially opened, boasting facilities that catered to 500 passengers per hour with parking for seven large aircraft at a time. In that year the first jet flights into Jamaica were made when Pan Am flew a 707 into Montego Bay on a special permit.

Not to be outdone BOAC, the forerunner of British Airways, flew the Comet 4 into Montego Bay from New York in January as, according to the *Gleaner*, 1,500 cheering men, women and children witnessed the event and American singing idol Pat Boone slipped onto the plane before the frenzied teenage fans could get his autograph.

By September of that year BOAC created airline history when it started regular jet service with the Vickers VC10 from London to New York to Kingston on the new runway built up out of the seabed of the Kingston harbour. In August 1961 Palisadoes Airport was officially opened to commercial air traffic. It was later renamed Norman Manley International Airport after one of our National Heroes.

Independent Jamaica's first flying corps was the air wing of the Jamaica Defence Force which was officially established in July 1963. The first aircraft for the airwing came from America under a military agreement.

In the mid-1970s Pan American airlines pulled out precipitously and in 1977 airline connections to Jamaica reached a new low as, except for Eastern Airlines which flew to Montego Bay from Miami and Atlanta, the last of the many air links to the USA ceased to provide service. In spite of this, however, American Airlines made its inaugural New York flight to Jamaica replacing Pan Am in 1977.

The situation brought considerable pressure to bear on Air Jamaica, the national carrier, who took up the slack with increased flights to Miami and New York. In 1977-78 Air Jamaica was carrying 72% of the Jamaican passengers going to the US; Air Jamaica, it was reported, carried 250,000 of the scheduled arrival air-market total 348,000. Twenty years later, in 1998, the USA scheduled air market total arrivals was 1,216,000. Of this figure Air Jamaica carried 655,000 or 54%.

"Rudy" Mantel, who now lives in Florida, played a pioneering role in internal charter-flying in Jamaica. He explained "It was Earl Gardner, a missionary with the Seventh Day Adventist Church in Mandeville who started Jamaica Air Taxi in 1958."

Gardner was instrumental in building the airstrip in Mandeville as well as several airstrips across the island to facilitate the bauxite companies.

Mantel bought the business in 1960 and operated out of Montego Bay. "We took a lot of people to and from Kingston for meetings," he recalled. Many VIPs, tourists, politicians and people employed in the sugar and bauxite industries used the airline.

At the peak of its existence Jamaica Air Taxi had 11 airplanes, 15 pilots and over 100 employees.

In 1974 a newly established company, Trans-Jamaica, owned 75% by the Government, bought out Jamaica Air Taxi which then became a subsidiary operation. Scheduled routes were opened between Tinson Pen, Montego Bay, Negril, Ocho Rios, Pt. Antonio and Mandeville.

Wings Jamaica is one of the pioneers of air service and training. The company was formed with the idea of providing training for Jamaicans who wanted to fly. The company included Charles DePass, "Rudy" Mantel, Carl Webster, Earsley Barnett (the first female pilot in Jamaica) and F. Carl Barnett who learned how to fly by starting with a tiny Cessna 150. In May 1974 Wings Ltd. moved from Palisadoes airport to Tinson Pen aerodrome in the Newport West area.

Air Jamaica, "The Love Bird", began its operation in April 1969. In late 1994, after lengthy negotiations, Air Jamaica was privatized with 70% of the airline owned by the Air Jamaica Acquisition Group with Chairman Gordon "Butch" Stewart. The new Air Jamaica is designed to be professional and profitable with a Jamaican flair.

Trans-Jamaica was also privatized and in 1995 renamed Air Jamaica Express. Wearing the same eye-catching colours as Air Jamaica it became the commuter airline, sister to Air Jamaica.

Today the scheduled carriers in Jamaica are Air Jamaica, American Airlines, Air Canada, Air Europe, ALM, British Airways, BWIA, Cayman Airways, Condor, COPA, Cubana, LTU, Martinair, Northwest Airlines, TWA and US Air.

ORIGINALLY PUBLISHED OCTOBER 2000

Germany in Jamaica

H.P. JACOBS

Residents of Seaford Town, 1986

The visitor to Jamaica will meet many people with German names. Some of them, of course, are Swiss in origin. He may also find many place-names of German derivation.

Indeed, if you go up into the mountains north of the capital—the Blue Mountains, the Port Royal Mountains, the St. Andrew Hills—you just might think you had stumbled into Germany. So much so, that a number of years ago when a visitor, or rather a temporary resident, went to the place called Mavis Bank, he thought, when someone mentioned 'the Harts' place' that he must be approaching the Harz Mountains, not being aware that a Mr. Hart then lived in the area.

He would have thought he was right if he went to the property called Bloxburgh, a corruption of Blocksberg, the name of the highest peak in the Harz Mountains. These were better known as the Brocken and famous for all sorts of witchcraft stories and spectral happenings. The name was evidently given by Jacob Kellerman, who obtained land there soon after the Seven Years' War—probably he had served in the British Army in North America during the War. He became a naturalised British subject in 1762.

Not far away in Halberstadt, Johann Caspar Weise was naturalised in 1764, and a few weeks later obtained 300 acres which became the Halberstadt property. There is no doubt he was from Halberstadt near the Brocken, for he attempted to leave 1,000 dollars for the relief of the Calvinist poor in that city. Mr. Geoffrey Yates, formerly at the Archives in Spanish Town, and who has researched the matter more than anyone else, says that in 1822, sixteen years after Weise's death, the Rector in the German city was still trying to get the money. (In view of Brocken's connection with witches, it is interesting to note that the Jamaican lawyer he asked to handle the case was the uncle of the White Witch of Rose Hall).

To the west of these places is Charlottenburgh, to the north-east Westphalia and Manheim, while well to the north, on the other side of the watershed, is Mount Holstein, and east of that is a pass called Manhertz Gap.

The surname Manhertz is now found on both sides of the mountain, e.g. at Mavis Bank itself. The earliest Manhertz I have traced, John M. Manhertz of Bremen Valley, seems to have disappeared: but it gives a clue to the German home of John Manhertz. Curiously, in the year in which he died mention is made of a slave called Henry Manhertz from the same

Resident of Seaford Town, 1986

area, who was presumably his godson, since a son would most likely have been set free.

The name Weise is not uncommon, with the "W" pronounced as in English and the final letter not pronounced at all. Some of these bearing the name can definitely be traced to the Halberstadt area.

Since so much as been said about superstitions, it may be asked whether these Germans brought the Lorelei of the Rhine to Jamaica. Well, Mavis Bank is the only place in Jamaica where Lorelei is a Christian name, and there used to be a pool in the river there with a river-maamy—Jamaica's fresh-water mermaid. In Jamaica the river-maamy seems to be of Celtic and African origin, but perhaps the Germans were interested in the Mavis Bank river-maamy and helped to keep the belief alive. We know very little of these early settlers except that they must have had very good taste—they chose to live in a wild unsettled country of remarkable beauty—deep valleys and running streams, peaks from which wonderful views could be obtained and woodlands which in those days had a good deal of wild life.

It is still very pleasant, unless of course you dislike scrambling amongst rocks or riding on the edge of sheer precipices on tracks where the horses themselves can seem tired. In some parts there are many mango trees and when the ripe fruit falls, the donkeys that carry loads manage to combine business with pleasure in spite of the steep, rough tracks.

We know even less about the Germans who settled in the parish of Clarendon, very much off the beaten track for the visitor who seldom gets even to Chapleton, which is not very far from Saxony. Chapleton has a church in the nave of which is the gravestone of a man who knew Frederick the Great, 'Jemmy' or 'Jamaica' Dawkins. John 'Gottshalk' owned Saxony (a name I cannot trace in use today) before March of 1815, he too may have been a soldier in the British service. Gottshalk or Godshalk is a fairly common name in Clarendon, but not elsewhere.

On the other hand, a good deal is known about William Lemonius, who did more than anyone else to Germanise Jamaica. He served in the Prussian Army against Napoleon. The late Sir Francis Kerr-Jarrett of Montego Bay (one of his descendants) related a family tradition about the circumstances under which he left Germany. Lemonius and his companions killed their horses on the coast and were taken off by warships, he said. This must mean that Lemonius supported the Duke of Brunswick—'Brunswick's fated chieftain' who fell at Quatre Bras in 1814 in his attempt to rouse Germany against Napoleon in 1809. The Duke was defeated and chased across Germany to the North Sea where he and his men were able to embark on British ships. Lemonius entered the British service.

After settling in Jamaica, he practised his profession of medicine, but had numerous other activities. Following the abolition of slavery, the government was planning the introduction of white people as labourers and small farmers and he was put in charge of this immigration. He concentrated on Germany as a source of such immigrants, and between 1838 and 1854 perhaps as many as 1,500 Germans entered the country.

In people's minds this immigration is important because of the founding of Seaford Town on a property called Montpelier Mountain which Lord Seaford gave as site for a village settlement. Seaford Town is about a dozen miles south of Montego Bay, to the west of the railway line, on the banks of a river. It is still inhabited by people of German descent. But its first days were disastrous. Adequate preparations had not been made for the reception of the settlers: worse still, though the site was scenically attractive, it was very unhealthy, and the mortality was at first very high.

Nor did the place flourish: the settlers kept aloof from their neighbours and were neglected in return. At last the Roman Catholics took the town in hand in 1873, by sending an Austrian, Fr. Tauer, to take charge of a permanent mission station there. He built a stone church, and won over most of the inhabitants to Catholicism—the settlers had been Protestants. His church was wrecked by a hurricane in 1912, but a new one was built. The community numbered about 500, including some old people who still spoke German. The number of family names is limited—one observer says there are only 15; Kamicka (with various spellings) is the most common. Some of the Germans had by then begun to try their fortune outside the village, and in fact a Kamicka in Kingston married a daughter of Prince Clarence, the last chief of the Miskito Indians, who had taken refuge in Jamaica.

But there were other clusters of German settlers, some of which long continued as separate communities. Lemonius himself lived at Stettin (no doubt a name which he gave) in the parish of Trelawny, and there is a 'German Town' in that parish. The late Dr. J. M. Stockhausen, one of the best-known doctors in the island, came from that area. Another group was at Stewart Town, much nearer the sea, and in 1930 there was yet another a few miles to the east in the parish of St. Ann. To the south of Brown's Town was a settlement at Alexandria which had lost its distinctive character—Diedrick is a surname there and in the neighbourhood, the Haltaufderhide is a surname not far away.

The small communities in Trelawny and St. Ann seem to have had more contact with their neighbours than the people of Seaford Town. Forty years ago, the present writer noticed that some folklore tellers knew tales which were not merely of German origin, but must have been told by Germans in Jamaica. The hero of one tale was called Clergyman (which would normally be 'Parson', Minister, or 'Reverend' in country dialect) it must go back straight to the German 'ein kluger Mann' and of course, the hero was a clever fellow.

ORIGINALLY PUBLISHED DECEMBER 1977

The Indian Tradition Lives On

LAXMI MANSINGH
AJAI MANSINGH

On May 10, 1845 the first Indian immigrant, Parameshwar (meaning God in Hindi), arrived in Jamaica. During the next seven decades, 36,411 Indian indentured workers followed.

These first Indian immigrants, their descendants and those who came later have, over the years, woven colourful patterns from the fabric of their rich heritage into the Jamaican tapestry through their contributions to almost every aspect of national life, ranging from agriculture, through handicraft, culinary art, industry and commerce to spirituality.

It all began in 1834 when slavery in Jamaica was finally abolished and a ten-year bonded apprenticeship scheme for the ex-slaves failed. English, German and Portuguese indentured workers were brought in to alleviate labour shortages but due to their lack of knowledge about tropical agriculture and other factors, the scheme failed. And so the British West Indies turned to India where sugar cane cultivation and the sugar industry had originated over 4,000 years ago.

After much deliberation and assurances from the planters for the welfare of the immigrants, and some resistance from the Jamaica Baptist Union who feared for their missionary activities, the British Colonial Office and the then colonial government in India gave their blessings to the indentureship scheme in 1844.

Immediately immigration agents for various West Indian territories were appointed in India for recruiting the voluntary emigrants and recruitment centres were opened across India but mainly in Bihar and Uttar Pradesh. (Over 95% of the emigrants came from Eastern U.P. and Bihar in Northern India, 89% of these being Hindus of all castes and professions, and 11% Muslim.) Indian recruiters would visit village markets and fair grounds to seek "volunteers" by painting Jamaica as the greenest pasture on earth. For a reward of seven pound sterling per head in 1907, they would even kidnap innocent girls and boys and send them overseas, not always without the connivance of higher authorities.

The indentureship contracts were legal documents which initially bound individuals to a specific plantation for one year and to Jamaica for five years, before they were entitled to a return passage. After 1860, the bonding and residency periods were extended to five years each and at the turn of the century, land grants were given in lieu of return passage. Almost all immigrants wished to return home but only 12,109 individuals received their entitlement.

(ABOVE) Two young Jamaican-Indian women dance at the 150th Anniversary celebrations held in 1996. (BELOW) A group of Indian immigrants at a plantation Puja, c. 1890.

The planters were obliged to provide agreed weekly minimum wages for six long days of work, housing (dormitories for bachelors, one room houses for the families), provision land, ethnic groceries and spices, and free medical care. Not all of these commitments were ever fulfilled by any planter. The only "illegal" part of the contract was criminal penalty (imprisonment) for civil offense (absence from work). The self-respecting individuals used to work even when unwell, as sicknesses invisible to the eye were not accepted as an excuse for not working.

(TOP) A recreated scene of a boat carrying a few Indian indentured workers from a ship in Old Harbour to the shore, while hundreds of liberated slaves look on. (ABOVE) Phagwa celebrations in Kingston. (AT RIGHT) Newly weds being blessed in traditional style. (BOTTOM) Tazia (Hosay) procession held in Clarendon, 1978.

Though mostly illiterate, the immigrants had an extreme sense of belonging in time and space, highly confident of their cultural heritage, knowledgeable about the social and economic structure of an Indian society, well-versed in agriculture and farming practices and trained through apprenticeship in their traditional skills such as pottery, carpentry, jewelry making etc. Many were accomplished folk and classical musicians and folk dancers. Some had been small landlords, farmers and businessmen, priests, artisans and labourers.

At least one 1892 immigrant had no such skills. Chandra Kumari (princess of moon), a pretty, delicate and sophisticated young lady refused to do any work as she claimed to be a daughter of the King of Nepal who had eloped with his beloved, a palace guard!

Religion was a way of life for all the immigrants. The Hindus knew of Vedas only as the holiest of scriptures and Geeta and Mahabharata as Lord Krishna's teachings, but regarded Ramayana (Lord Rama's life and philosophy) and Puranas (stories on Vedic philosophy) as the major scriptures. The concepts of the Brahman (The Absolute), Ishwara (Deity with forms and attributes) and deities (transcendental gods and goddesses representing aspects of Ishwara), divinity of soul, reincarnation, Karma and Dharma were deeply ingrained even in the illiterate youths. Brahmin immigrants used to serve as first-time priests. Likewise, the Muslims knew of the Koran and how to offer prayers.

Every individual remembered by heart at least some verses from Tulsidas's Ramayana, Surdas's Sursagar, Kabir's dohas and Meera's bhajans, as well as hoards of folk song and epic tales, which would constantly provide guidance and inspiration at work and in times of depression, which were not infrequent.

The bonds of brotherhood forged on ships created a family atmosphere in plantations where Indians' settlements were kept separate from those of the ex-slaves. Apart from work on the plantations, the daily chores of indentured workers would involve prayers and tending of the children and the garden before and after the long day's work. Evenings were spent singing mystic and folk songs, story-telling, ganja smoking, rum drinking etc. Every weekend would have a regular community puja and katha (prayer meetings) or special ceremonies related with birth (chatti), naming (nawkaran), first hair cut (mundan), marriage, funerals and death anniversaries. Hindu festivals such as Ramnaumi (Rama's birthday), Janamastmi (Krishna's birthday), Shivaratri (Siva's night), Desehra (Rama's return from exile), Diwali (lights), Basant (spring) and Phagwa or Holi (colour), and Islamic festivals of Eid and Moharram were observed regularly.

Assaults however, on Indians and their culture had been incessant. Often individuals were lured to migrate as priests but were forced to work in plantations. At least one of them, Lulua Baba would neither be cheated nor break the legal contract. When brought to the court at the turn of the century on the charges of absence from work, he told the Jamaican magistrate: "If I have to be an invalid to be able to serve my religion and people, then here goes my hand," and chopped off his left hand with a machete.

Furthermore, Hindu and Muslim marriages were not recognized until 1956. Children of such wedlock were declared bastards and could never inherit parental property which was confiscated. Many Indians succumbed to economic and social pressures and became Christians.

Be that as it may, the Indians continued to enjoy and help build Jamaica. Diwali, the festival of lights (which is celebrated in November) and Phagwa (celebrated in March) with music, dances, smearing faces with coloured powder and throwing coloured water on each other) have survived the times and are observed at many homes in Jamaica.

Because of its nature, Hosay, an annual observance of mourning by the Shia sect of Muslims for the murder of the grandson of Prophet Mohammad became the most popular of Indian festivals. From the very inception, it became secularized as all the Hindus helped their Muslim brothers in organization and parade. For nine days, the activities were dominated by three-M's: mourning, mercia (eulogy), singing and meditation while people built Tazia (bamboo and paper replicas of a tomb). On the tenth day, the Tazia was taken to the streets in a procession led by a Tasa drummer playing martial music and followed by sword-, stick- and horse-dancers and hundreds of "mourners." Every plantation in each parish would celebrate Hosay.

Many Afro-Jamaicans would also build Tazias and the process of creolization began. Today Hosay is more like an Indian carnival than anything else. The three-M activities have been replaced by three-D's: drinking, dancing and drumming. The Clarendon Hosay, celebrated in August is an attractive experience even for the old-timers.

Indentureship restrictions and constraints did not deter Indians from making original contributions in agriculture. They introduced the channel irrigation system; succeeded in growing rice in Jamaica (where Americans and the British had failed for a century); established the first rice mill in Jamaica in the 1890s; introduced many vegetables, fruits and other plants and dominated vegetable cultivation in the island until the 1940s. Many original Indian culinary delights such as roti, curry goat and callaloo (a type of spinach) have been so creolized today that they are no longer considered exclusively Indian, but instead, Jamaican in character.

Indians may never be forgiven by some Jamaicans for introducing ganja (an euphoriant which has been an ingredient of Indian culture for millennia) into the island. For decades, the Indians smoked it, or used its young leaves to prepare bhang drink, without creating any social problems. The herb was banned in 1913, after many Jamaicans became addicted to it, and has been haunting the authorities in the recent past.

The indentured workers had always been very enterprising and were censored by the Jamaican Assembly in 1852 for starting small businesses rather than working in plantations. It is indeed amazing that these village folks would be so efficient in dealing with gold and silver. Members of John Hopkins University marine expedition of the 1890s were amazed by the Indian who made "intricate jewellery from the simplest of tools." Indeed, the jewellers among the indentured workers established their craft in the 1860s and organized travelling salesmen who would sell their products all over the island.

Since national independence, dozens of Indo-Jamaican professionals, such as Dr. Prabhusingh, Dr. Persadsingh and the lawyer Mr. Ballysingh, have occupied positions of prominence in almost every field.

Jamaican independence opened up numerous opportunities for the Indian descendants of indentured workers. Many such as Charoos and Chutkans have distinguished themselves as large and medium sized farmers, Pahar Singh and Ramdial own large engineering works, Subraties are among the construction giants, Henry Jaghai is a name in horseracing. Hundreds have lucrative businesses ranging from garages and stores to trucking and busing. Others have entered politics, particularly those from western Jamaica.

Adventurous businessmen like Mr. B. D. Dadlani and Mr. Chandiram, who migrated to Jamaica in 1928 and 1931 respectively, contributed to the economic activity of the country and in later decades, Chatani, Chulani, Vaswani, Tewani, Khemlani, Tulani, Ramchandani, Mahtani, Daswani, Khiatani, Sumtani and others have established a variety of manufacturing, wholesale, retail and in-bond businesses, generating millions of dollars, providing employment to thousands of Jamaicans.

The National Motto of Jamaica is, "Out of Many, One People." One of the "many" is the Indian population, who have made substantial contributions to Jamaica.

ORIGINALLY PUBLISHED NOVEMBER 1993

The Chinese in Jamaica

JULIE CHEN

The Chinese first came to Jamaica nearly 140 years ago. Their story is an interesting saga of courage, hard work and painful adaptation to climate and customs. After years of working as indentured labourers on the island's sugar plantations, they found their niche in the retail grocery trade which they eventually came to dominate. Later, they branched out into other fields: banking, bakeries, ice-cream parlours, factories, gas stations and laundries.

The first Chinese settlers came to Jamaica as early as 1854 and were mainly from the Hakka region of Southern China. Among the first to arrive was a group of nearly 500 men from Panama who were sent here by the Panama Railroad Company in exchange for Jamaican workmen. They however did not live for very long as most arrived in Jamaica ill and emaciated. In the following years small groups of Chinese continued to trickle into the island, but these were mainly re-immigrants from then British Guiana (now Guyana) and Trinidad. They came here on the expiration of their contracts to work on the coconut, banana and sugar plantations which were started here by American companies.

Thirty years were to pass before the second wave of 700 Chinese immigrants landed here. They came on three year contracts to work on the sugar plantations. The arrival of the Chinese in Jamaica triggered feelings of resentment among some sectors of the emancipated slaves and coloureds and attempts were made to restrict the flow of Chinese immigrants to the island. By 1940 all Chinese immigrants with the exception of diplomats, tourists and students were barred from entering the island. Despite the ban, the numbers of Chinese continued to grow steadily. By 1970, the Chinese accounted for seven percent of the population. This dropped sharply in the 1980s when a significant number of the Chinese community migrated to Canada and the United States. Today, there are reported to be some 50-60,000 Chinese in the island, but this figure might be larger given the influx of new Chinese immigrants from Hong Kong who are seeking new avenues of investments and a safe haven as the date for the return of Hong Kong to mainland Chinese rule approaches.

The early Chinese did not remain long on the sugar plantations. As soon as their contracts expired they moved to the towns in search of new employment. Others, however, simply deserted the estates. Most entered the grocery retail business which soon expanded into the wholesale business. A majority of shopkeepers were concentrated in the downtown Kingston area, which became known as Chinatown. There they established

(ABOVE) Pioneer settlers, Mr. William Chin Len Kow from Nu Foo and his wife Marie (nee Lee) landed at Black River, St Elizabeth around 1875. (BELOW) Traditional Chinese dance being performed during Jamaica's 1993 Independence celebrations.

restaurants, shops and bakeries which catered mainly to the Chinese community and those who hankered after "things Chinese."

The success of the Chinese in the grocery trade was due largely to the type of service they offered. They extended credit willingly to favoured customers and sold goods in the small quantities that the majority of shoppers could afford to buy. For the Chinese, it was a chance to work hard and make money. They often lived either behind or above their shops and they provided nearly 24-hour, seven-days-a-week, service. Shops opened as early as 6 am and closed at 8 pm. The inability of the "chineyman" to speak "proper English" was not a hindrance as most kept a long stick in their shops which customers used to point out items on the shelves.

Despite their high profile as shopkeepers and restaurant operators, the early Chinese remained isolated from the rest of the society. They were often accused of being "clannish." Unlike the Chinese in British Guiana and Trinidad, those in Jamaica did not integrate readily with the rest of the society or adopt Western customs. The Jamaican Chinese not only maintained their cultural distinctiveness, but a Jamaican Chinese community began to emerge. This is partly explained by the fact that many of the early Chinese emigrees considered themselves voluntary exiles and therefore clung to the notion of one day returning to the fatherland, China.

The early settlers often sent to China for relatives or friends when they needed more help in their shops. The sons were often sent back to China for enculturation and to find a suitable Chinese bride. They clung to their ethnic identity preserving their customs and language. The

(LEFT) In 1945, the Chee Qung Tung orchestra was formed. They performed Cantonese operas and variety shows for the community at garden parties and at the Ward Theatre. (ABOVE) Lee Tom Yin and Theresa (Dolly) Li, in a 1937 wedding photo. He was the editor of the first Chinese newspaper in Jamaica, *The Chinese Commercial News*, and author of *The Chinese in Jamaica 1957 and 1963*. (BELOW) The all-Chinese Jamaican Home Guard during World War II (c.1943), won awards for the best drilling, according to Joe Young a member of the group.

younger generation were taught Hakka and Mandarin as well as other elements of the Chinese culture. They also formed their own institutions to promote the Chinese culture and even started a Chinese language publication, *Pagoda* and staged the annual Miss Jamaica Chinese beauty pageant.

By the 1940s, however, the descendants of the Chinese pioneers began to chafe at the lifestyle and traditions of their forefathers. Many adopted English names. Learning the Chinese language became less important and very few showed any interest in maintaining strong links with China. Many of the second generation Chinese deserted the family-owned shops choosing instead to enter other professions like medicine, engineering, accounting and commerce. Others became salesmen in non-Chinese firms, some went into manufacturing while a few became active in the arts and theatre.

As the young Jamaican Chinese became aculturated into the Jamaican customs and lifestyles the exclusively Chinese organisations and traditions began to disappear. But in recent years, there has been a resurgence of activity within the Chinese community with the arrival of new immigrants from Hong Kong and Taiwan.

The community continues to celebrate Chinese New Year and the anniversary of the founding of the People's Republic of China. Occasionally other festivals such as the Moon Festival and the Boat Festival are celebrated.

In former days, these festivals were marked by extravagant dinners and fireworks. Today, the celebration is low-keyed and these festivals are marked by garden parties staged jointly by the Chinese Benevolent Society, the Chinese Cultural Association and the Chinese Free Masons. Most Chinese families however prefer to celebrate these occasions in the privacy of their homes with friends and relatives. Chinese traditional dances such as the flag dance and the dragon dance are sometimes performed at public functions including the annual national festival activities.

Unfortunately Chinese peasant religions did not survive the transplantation from China and many Jamaican Chinese converted to Roman Catholicism. A few of the older generation who are still alive worship at the Buddhist temple on South Avenue in Kingston.

Chinatown too has lost its significance as many of the earlier settlers died and their businesses with them. However with the arrival since 1981 of a new wave of Chinese immigrants there has been some revival of Chinese owned and operated businesses in Chinatown. But the area has lost much of the mystique which surrounded it in the earlier days.

There has also been a resurgence of shops and services catering mainly to the Chinese community. Some Chinese products and cooking ingredients are available in many supermarkets. There is a bakery which specialises in Chinese pastries and delicacies and there are occasional classes in Mandarin and Chinese dance. Dim Sum, a traditional Sunday brunch for the Chinese is offered only occasionally by one Chinese restaurant.

(ABOVE) Annual Chinese Benevolent Association's Garden Party 2002,(FROM LEFT) Sam Lyn Shim, president of Chinese Freemason Society; Exley Ho, president of Chinese Cultural Association; Madam Quo, wife of ambassador of the People's Republic of China; Mrs. Sam Lyn Shim; Marjorie Robinson, public relations manager of Air Jamaica; His Excellency Quo Changli, ambassador of the People's Republic of China; Vincent Chang, president Chinese Benevolent Association; Michelle Lyn, president of Caribbean Chinese Association; Unidentified; Michael Lee Chin, chairman of NCB.
(LEFT) Girls who acted in a Hakka play at the Ward Theatre in 1946.

Despite the weakening of the Chinese traditions, the Chinese in Jamaica have never totally severed their links with the motherland. Each year, Jamaicans of Chinese descent visit Hong Kong and China. Some of the older generation still make annual pilgrimages to visit family and friends in their birthplaces.

ORIGINALLY PUBLISHED JANUARY 1994

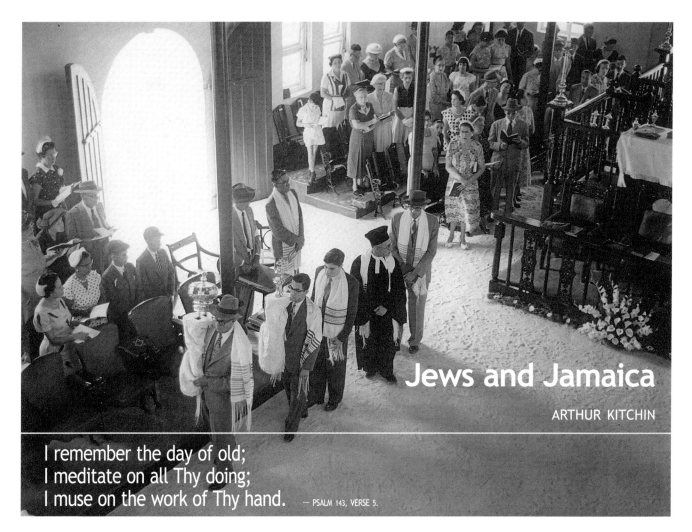

Jews and Jamaica

ARTHUR KITCHIN

> I remember the day of old;
> I meditate on all Thy doing;
> I muse on the work of Thy hand. — PSALM 143, VERSE 5.

Jewish settlers, mainly from Spain and Portugal who feared the dreaded Spanish Inquisition, began to arrive in Jamaica during the Spanish occupation (1494-1655).

These early Jews became known as Marranos or Crypto-Jews as they practised their religion in utmost secrecy while outwardly appearing to conform to the dominant Catholic faith. Some historians believe that Columbus himself was from a Marrano family and judging from the names of his crew, many could also have been Marranos.

Dutch Jews from Pernambuco came to Jamaica in 1654 when the invading Portuguese forced the synagogue at Recife to close its doors. We might add that 23 pioneers reached New Amsterdam and became the founders of Congregation Shearith Israel in New York City, and of the Jewish Community in the United States.

On May 16, 1655, the British landed at Passage Fort in Kingston Harbour and marched towards St. Jago de la Vega (Spanish Town). The Spaniards surrendered the following day and the Marranos, weary of the religious intolerance to which they had been subjected, welcomed the invaders.

(ABOVE) A Synagogue sanctuary scene taken in 1956 with Torah bearers parading past the congregation. (BELOW) A Bar Mitzvah boy prepares to read for the first time from the Torah scrolls.

In fact, the principal pilot upon whom Admiral Penn and General Venables relied during their attack on Jamaica was Captain Campoe Sabbatha, a Marrano Jew. Another Marrano, Acosta, was the chief negotiator in the Spanish surrender.

One of the early leaders of the Jewish colony in England, Simon de Caceres, was advisor to Oliver Cromwell on West Indian projects, and was instrumental in planning the addition of Jamaica as a British possession. Born in Amsterdam, de Caceres had never been a Marrano, he observed his religion openly in London before the official readmission of Jews into England.

Under British rule, the Jewish population in Jamaica steadily increased with immigration from Spain, Portugal, France, England, and the West Indian islands of Curaçao and Barbados. In 1664, the colony at Cayenne was dissolved and transferred to Surinam and several more Jewish families settled in Jamaica. When Surinam succumbed to the Dutch fleet in 1667, the Jamaican colony again increased.

Some Jewish families resided in Jamaica descended from those from Bordeaux; for example, the Brandon, da Costa and Mendes

(CLOCKWISE) A group of Jewish Lads Rovers from 1933; Chanukah celebrations taken in 1955; Governor General the Hon. Florizel Glasspole ON, GCMG, GCVO, CD, (wearing the hat) attending a service at the synagogue; Councillor Senator Hon. Eli Matalon, mayor of Kingston & St Andrew, elected March 1971 and served for two terms until 1973. The following members of the Jewish community also served as mayors of Kingston, Philip Stern (1896-1897) and the Hon. Ernest Altamont daCosta (1925-1927); A wedding contract is signed; The Ark of the Old Sephardic Synagogue, Spanish Town; Sir Neville Noel Ashenheim, CBE, Jamaica's ambassador to America, at Jamaican Independence in 1962, and a member of the Jewish community, presents his credentials to President Kennedy.

families, others came from Bayonne from which a stream of Marranos went from 1520 to the end of the 18th century. They came from Amsterdam—Aaron de Mosseh Tartas in 1694, Moses Peixotto in 1729 and about 30 years later, the Reverend Isaac Touro, father of the philanthropist, Judah Touro, who endowed the old synagogue at Newport, Rhode Island, USA.

Up until the earthquake of 1692, the majority of Jews lived at Port Royal, a pirate stronghold and an open city described as "the wickedest in the world". Although no historian mentions a synagogue, one undoubtedly did exist.

In Deeds 8/86—"John Peeke, Port Royal, sold to the Jews of Port Royal, 29th January, 1676, for £57.0.0, a house and land, 63 ft. by 26 ft., south on Cannon Street, northwest on New Street." One may presume that this purchase was for use as a place of worship.

A synagogue was destroyed in the disastrous earthquake of June 7, 1692, proof of which can be found in a letter written that same day by Edmund Heath, Port Royal, to Dr. Charlette Master of University College, Oxford. "I turned into ye Jewes Street in order to get home, when their Synagogue fell by my side." (Ballard Letters, volume 39, letter number 45. The Bodleian Library).

Interestingly, a Joseph de Costa Alveranga left in his will, dated 1699, a legacy of Ten Pounds to the synagogue at Port Royal for Kaddish (a memorial prayer) to be said for himself and his wife. The synagogue was probably destroyed in the big fire of 1815, after which the Jews in Port Royal rapidly decreased.

The Jews quickly integrated themselves into the life of the island, particularly in the field of commerce. Among those in the sugar and vanilla industry was Abraham Gomex Henriques (died 1673) who owned 3,000 acres of land. Solomon Gabay, a Port Royal merchant, owned a 1,600 acre plantation in 1674; Solomon de Leon possessed 1,000 acres in St. Mary as early as 1672, and David Lopez, 500 acres in St. Andrew in 1692.

Although numbering only 80, the Jewish population paid the largest proportion of taxes in 1700 and the respect they commanded earned them exemption from compulsory military service on the Sabbath, "unless it be when an enemy is in view." In 1831 an important milestone was reached when, due to the efforts of Moses Delgado, Jamaica was the first British territory to abolish political disabilities against Jews—27 years before the abolition took place in England.

By 1849, eight of the 47 members of the House of Assembly were Jewish, with several others appointed as custodes of various parishes. That year, the House adjourned for Yom Kippur by a vote of 19 to 9 as a mark of respect to Jewish members. When the constitution was abolished in 1866, Jewish membership in the House had increased to 13.

The various branches of Judaism introduced here from different parts of the world led to the formation of separate congregations in Spanish Town and Kingston, all acknowledging the 'Unity of God' but with differences in their rituals.

Kingston had two congregations in the early 1700's—the Sephardic synagogue at Princess Street completed in 1750, and the Ashkenazi synagogue consecrated at Orange Street in 1789 and rebuilt in 1837. Funds were voted by the House of Assembly and the Corporation of Kingston to help in the rebuilding as both synagogues were destroyed by fire in 1882.

An amalgamation of the two congregations was sought and in 1885 the Synagogue K.K. Shaare Shalom was built on Luke Street. Many of the estimated 2,500 Jews came together to form "The Amalgamated Congregation of Israelites", but disagreement over the ritual followed and led to the remaining handful of Sephardim building Shangar Hashamayim at 58 East Street in 1884. Some Ashkenazim rebuilt on the former site in Orange Street.

At the end of 1900, the two Sephardi Congregations had merged. The earthquake wrecked the synagogues and many valuable records were destroyed in the subsequent fire. In 1911, the Shaare Shalom was rebuilt on the old site; ten years later the Ashkenazi finally merged with the Sephardic Congregation and this was renamed the United Congregation of Israelites.

Today the Congregation is progressive, based on a Sephardic ritual although aspects of the Ashkenazi ritual are combined to give the service a unique flavour. The Prayer Book was edited and revised by Haham Gaster with some modifications. The old Portuguese melodies have been retained together with some prayers in the vernacular, and a number of English hymns are interspersed in the Hebrew arrangement of prayers.

The synagogue is situated at the corner of Duke and Charles Streets and is roughly the same size as that destroyed in the earthquake. It accommodates some 600 worshippers and instead of a brick structure, it has reinforced concrete with a facade in a style approaching the Spanish colonial period.

The Hechal (Ark) and the Tebah (Reader's Platform) are of polished mahogany and adorned by eight magnificent brass candlesticks donated in 1793 to the Princess Street synagogue. On the floor are blue Wilton carpets with a yellow Magen David design. The Ark contains thirteen scrolls, some more than 200 years old and originally housed in other synagogues on the island.

One unusual feature is the sand on the floor. The only others to follow this practice are those of the Sephardic in Amsterdam, Surinam, Peru, Curaçao, Panama and the Virgin Islands. Some explain this custom as reminding of the sand which covered the floor of the original Tabernacle in the desert. Others suggest that it represents the blessing of God to the Patriarchs that their descendants would be "as the sand on the seashore". Less dramatic would be the interpretation that it deadens the sounds on the wooden floor.

A pipe organ was installed in 1936 and a communal Seder introduced in the grounds of the synagogue which is now an annual event. There is the bar mitzvah (coming of age) for boys and the bat mitzvah for girls which was begun in 1960. The synagogue gardens contain a number of interesting gravestones transferred from old cemetery sites. The oldest denominational cemetery on the island is at Hunts Bay in Kingston. Present cemeteries are at Orange Street and Elletson Road in Kingston.

In 1966, a B'nai Brith Lodge was consecrated as part of the Caribbean District Grand Lodge 23. There is a W.I.Z.O. group for the women. A non-denominational preparatory school, Hillel Academy, was established through a trust by the Jewish community in 1969. Starting with 12 pupils it now has on roll over 400, a high school was added in 1979. A religious school is also held at the synagogue.

Visitors are always welcome at the synagogue, and since the congregation is small, (about 200 today) no admission price is required for the High Holy Days service. Sabbath services are held on Friday nights at 6:00 p.m. and Saturday mornings from 9:30 a.m.

Many religious leaders have preached from the synagogue's pulpit, including the Right Rev. W. G. Hardie, Lord Bishop of Jamaica and later Archbishop of the West Indies. A historic occasion was in January 1964 when after the Second Vatican Council, Bishop John J. McEleney was the first Roman Catholic Bishop in the world to preach in a synagogue. Conversely, rabbis have preached in other churches.

The Jewish community has always been active in social and civic work in Jamaica. Suffice it to say, the torch raised in the past is still held aloft by faithful hands.

ORIGINALLY PUBLISHED OCTOBER 1981

Remembering when the World Was At War

MARC GOODMAN

A visit with Jamaica's last surviving World War I veteran gives a glimpse into history's bloodiest battlefields, and a Jamaica past.

In 1914, Europe decided to have the war it had been expecting for years. A year later, millions lived and died in waterlogged ditches that ran 500 miles from the English Channel to Switzerland, among rats, cats, barbed wire, lice, and corpses. Now, at the other end of the century, a visitor waits on the verandah of a comfortable May Pen house, accompanied by two WWII veterans from the local Jamaica Legion chapter. Nurse Miller-Lewis emerges, walking slowly beside an elderly, merry gentleman in a grey suit pinned with a row of faded ribbons. He is tall, and looks to be about in his 80s. This is 103-year-old Ugent Augustus Clark, the only man left in Jamaica who saw World War I.

At the start of 1916, the 22-year-old Kendal native was living at an aunt's in Kingston and working as a gardener. "Those days, any man in a uniform was a Big Man." There were other reasons to volunteer for the newly-formed British West Indies Regiment, age–old ones. "Adventure," Clark affirms, and loyalty towards the mother country.

The previous autumn, the first Jamaicans preparing to sail to Europe heard a speech delivered by Brigadier-General Blackden that was straight out of Kipling: "Some of you may be killed, many will be wounded, but in bidding you farewell I hope that those who fall may fall gloriously, their faces to the foe, and with victory gleaming on their bayonets."

By March 6, 1916, there were no speeches. Clark boarded HMS *Verdala* at Kingston Harbour with the third contingent of B.W.I.R men. They had been assigned the fight against Turkish forces in Egypt, and after training in England they steamed to Moascar, Egypt past Gibraltar, stopping in Malta, Salonika and Alexandria—heady stuff for Jamaicans who had never left home before.

But "...war hot up in Europe. Must 'e want more men. Our colonel volunteer for us to go up there." To the great disappointment of many in the officer corps, the West Indians were to be used as ammunition carriers. Lt.-Col. C. Wood-Hill, D.S.O. wrote of his efforts to persuade the War Office to let his men fight: "I was informed that it was the considered opinion that the fighting qualities of the West Indians were doubtful and that it was therefore preferred to use them on shell-carrying and labour duties."

By now, though, 178 Jamaicans who had earlier volunteered with British units were being variously decorated with 13 classes of awards. Among those who received a Military Medal was a certain MANLEY, Sergeant N.W., R.I.A., and among the dead was a MANLEY, D.R., Gunner, R.F.A.—Norman's brother, for whom the Prime Minister would wear a black tie for the rest of his life.

But the battalion's fate had been decided, and Clark was immediately sent to the notorious battleground of Ypres. This—a place attacked

Back in Jamaica after the Armistice, there was no hero's welcome. Clark's homecoming was particularly painful. "I did have a girlfriend in the district. As me come down the gangplank me see a friend. Him say, "Clark, you come!....Annie married!"

with a more intensive concentration of explosives than Hiroshima—was the West Indians' first encounter with warfare as it was being practiced in Europe. "When we reach near the front and see dead men, men wounded, men cut up, me remember me fireside a yard! But after you in it for a while it no trouble you."

Reverend J.L. Ramson's contemporary account paints a picture of what conditions were like for units like Ugent Clark's: ..."Rain, rain, rain, sometimes quite tropical in its violence and intensity, and cold winds, and mud such as we in Jamaica only see in cowpens during wet weather...On and on we went, while guns were crashing incessantly; ammunition mules and limbers were going at top speed, and ever and anon a huge column of dirt and debris would rise high into the air from the explosion of a German shell..."

Clark now joined perhaps the most fearsome battle in history, The Battle of the Somme, sounds of whose opening bombardment of two million shells had been heard on London's Hampstead Heath 300 miles away, and in whose first minutes the British Army had lost one-third the number of men as the Americans did in 14 years in Vietnam. Clark remembers, "We had a rugged time. Moxon...from Nassau, was in mud up to his head all day—they had to drag him out. You didn't help the wounded—not your duty. Them have man for that—woman with buggy."

"We have good reputation as soldiers, everywhere we go. When we work in a shell dump, the front say, 'How we get the shells so quick?' " Clark was here witness to gas attacks, and to a small piece of history—the first use of tanks.

A British song of the time bitterly described the typical outcome of a charge against an enemy trench: *"If you want to find the old battalion, I know where they are / Hanging on the old barbed wire."* Like many veterans, Ugent Clark is reluctant to talk about the more painful details of combat. In the field, he remembers, "They speak about (religion) a lot. You feel religion and God. You could dead at any time. You just take it one day at a time."

"War is no good," he says, simply. "It changes things, but in the changing, plenty bad things go on."

Next, in Belgium—the country the war was ostensibly being fought for—attitudes duplicated those at home. "In Belgium they preferred the Germans to us, because we were black. Sometimes them take the handle off their pumps when we go for water. So after a while if we see apples and want them, we cut down the apple tree, we no bother climb it."

Back in Jamaica after the Armistice, there was no hero's welcome. Clark's homecoming was particularly painful. "I did have a girlfriend in the district. As me come down the gangplank me see a friend. Him say, "Clark, you come!....Annie married!"

At this, Nurse Lewis looks up, very interested. "You were coming back to marry her?"

Clark replies, "Well, me no know." 80 years later, his voice breaks a bit. He looks past the gate to the darkening mountains. "But me did love her."

Apart from the offer of a small, unfarmable plot of land in Clarendon, Clark says he received no benefits after the war. He soon left to work on a farm in Cuba with other vets for $1.50 a day, less meals.

He touches the aging ribbons pinned to his jacket. "Me never have an easy time. Anywhere you see the hardest work, look inna that gang you see me."

But the Cuban economy soured too. In 1931 Clark returned to Clarendon. He became a headman at Halse Hall, and then a guard at Vernam Field, the air base.

Now a new chapter in his life was beginning, as he witnessed the emerging political activity of a country beginning to chafe under Britain's rule—and noticed the career of a fellow veteran who had become Jamaica's most brilliant lawyer.

"I saw Manley and Busta (trade unionist and future Prime Minister Sir Alexander Bustamante) all the time. They were heroes. They make Jamaica stand on its feet. Manley was the education man. Busta want you to put something in your belly and put something on your foot so casha don't jook you, and have a good bed to lie down on so when you wake a morning you stronger and can do a better work."

By now a cool breeze is ruffling the tops of the hedges. "Jamaica *has* changed. It better in some ways. Living conditions are better now. You dress more respectable now, look better."

But, he says with a patient smile, "Back then you take off your hat and bow and say good morning to every man. All they respect now is money more than discipline," he says with a twinkle in the eye.

What does he miss about the old days on the island? "Fish! All give 'way free! Things were cheap in those days. Now everything depon price. You used to get three pear for penny, ha'penny or free; a first class shoes for six shillings and six..." The local chapter of the Jamaica Legion recently voted Clark an increase in his monthly pension—to J$1000, or about US$26.

Did he stay in touch with any friends from the war? "No," he says. Then he raises his head and says softly. "I had a good friend in Linstead, Cyril McCarter. I knew him all through the war. I will never forget him regimental number: '3949'..."

A light drizzle has begun. Nurse Velata Lewis has been listening, with kind eyes. "He was a nice, gracious old man. He used to tell my children war stories. After a while I realized he had taken up residence with me. You know how country people stay," she smiles. "If it's 8th cousin it's family. His step-children had all migrated and he was in need of someone to take care, I saw the need for someone to take care of him, and I did."

After the shower is a gentle sunset. Nurse Lewis says, "Pa, see your guest to the gate."

Clark's firm handshake sends off the veterans of another war, the one whose seeds Clark's war planted, and the visitor, into a cool evening. A final glance back from a car window reveals Clark listening, smiling, as Velata turns on a few lights and says something to him from across the verandah.

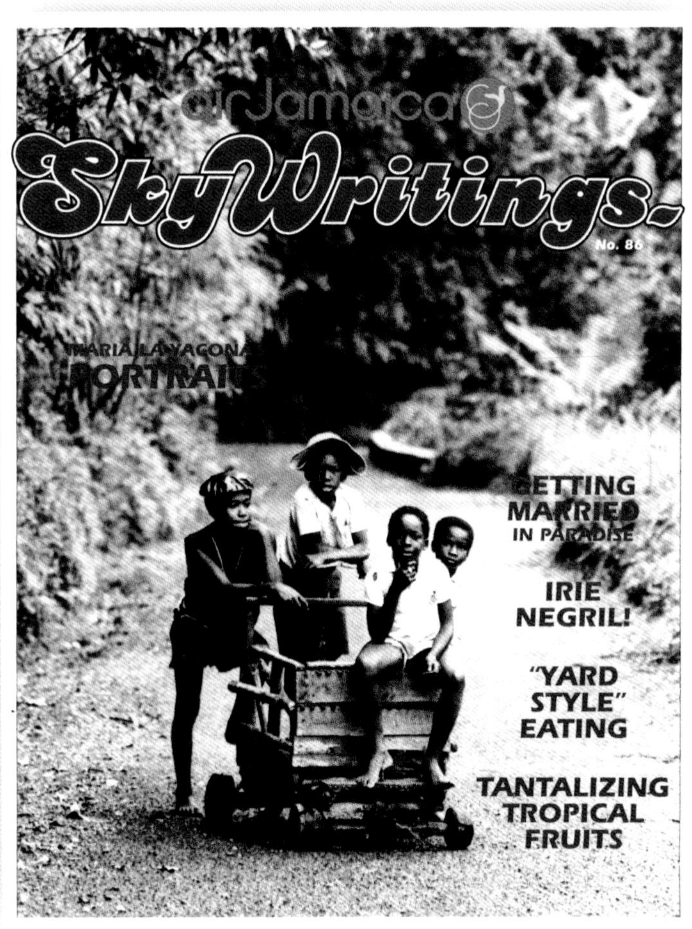

MEMORIES

SKYWRITINGS COVER
May 1993
"Boys in Cart from Green Hill," 1981.
Jamaica, Portraits 1955-1993.

Of Red-eyed Rivers and a Country Childhood

OLIVE SENIOR

There were the rivers we all knew because they were names and blue lines on a classroom map: Mississippi, Yangtze, Ganges. And there were the big rivers of Jamaica which we had never seen but which were forced into our consciousness by repetition and blackboard: Black River, Rio Minho, Cabaritta, Yallahs. And then, there were the little rivers that we ourselves knew intimately, because they were a part of ourselves growing. In our interior farming settlements, we lived with the rivers within us and the mountains around us, and no one ever called these objects by names. Nor could they portray our rivers as blue lines on maps, for there was never any blue about them.

The deeps were the darkest, most mysterious shades of green where the brazilwood overhung with reeds and water grasses. Then, as the river widened and became more shallow, it took the colour of the skies, the trees, our faces, the shape and colour of anything outside of and beyond itself; there was no one colour of the river, But it was always flecked with bits of foam like laughter as it slid over the smooth stones of its bed, gurgled as it sloped round a bend, became a shiny ribbon in a faraway cane field. From high in the hills where we lived we could see the river as a loop of silver snaking through the countryside before it became a dark line, lost, in its wondrous valley. Then it disappeared underground completely, to reappear chattering loudly as it cascaded down a waterfall a few miles away. From there we only knew that it flowed further than we could ever follow, and eventually reached the sea where we had never been.

The road we knew traveled to places we could pinpoint with certainty; the river began and ended in mystery.

"River keep me safe tonight, bring down a special red stone and lay it on the pebbles and show us where the janga is hiding." I would sometimes pray blasphemous, half dreaming, hearing in my imagination the sound of the river faraway and lonely as I fell asleep. And the next day to entertain us, shake up our lonely country childhood of silence and space, the river would playfully whip away a shirt from a washerwomen upstream, hide it in reeds and soapsuds as she, arms outstretched and wailing, would run splashing, stumbling down the river trying vainly to retrieve it. And occasionally the river would leave on our sandy bank a red stone which, we liked to imagine, was precious.

Some days on the river were pure magic. Splashing off the rocks to grab the janga; slyly trying to get bitten by a "bubby biter" which was what made your breasts grow; gathering from the roots of Job's Tears beads for stringing; floating matchboxes and bamboo pieces filled with logwood blossoms to wind their unsteady course beyond our knowing, to float as far perhaps as China, or at least Savanna-la-Mar. Cozy on our dry bed in the bamboo roots, we sat on the banks and waited for the Golden Table of our river legends to appear or for River Mumma, the river maid, to come and sit on the rock and comb her hair, singing. And then, there was the duppy of Cudelia who had drowned in the dark hole upstream which was named for her and whose hair these fifty years was growing still as clinging green moss which hung from the rotting tree trunks. And if any of these creatures of legends, these ghosts and phantoms had appeared, would we have stayed?

For we also feared the river.

There were times when it turned angry and threatening, lost its sparkle, grew dull lead under the lowering skies. Times of flash floods and rainfall, the river swelled with the clay of upstream mountains. The river is crying, we'd say, its eyes are red. This stronger river would gather its strength and force its way among us, dominating our lives, a vast and mighty entity creeping red brown up the valleys, covering the little bridge, sweeping across the roadway. All traffic stopped while the red-eyed river made up its mind whether to go or stay. When it did go, the roadway, the banks, the grasses, the tree trunks remained stained with the red clay which baked and flaked into dust. And into our village the river brought the debris of other people's lives; trees and swollen, dead livestock, bits of houses and chicken coops and sometimes, said our parents, the dead body of a river sacrifice.

Then one day we grew up, learnt that our river had a name, a source and an ending; found that having left it and returned, it had shrunk in our absence. But we also found that everyone else with a country childhood had a secret river too—the Nuevo, Heo, Savanna or One Eye, Mammee, Flora, Sulphur or Cockpit.

All Jamaica's rivers are magical and special. They were here long before roads, bridges, reservoirs and water pipes, before maps, before names. Since the first time of man on this land we have drunk their waters, bathed in them, cried by their banks, watered our animals, baptized our converts, washed our clothes, hunted fish and crayfish, sailed boats and rafts, used up the sands, found beads to string, imbued them with legends and healing qualities, singing our songs.

Dip dem Bedward dip dem
Dip dem in de Healing Stream
Dip dem sweet but not too deep
Dip dem fe cure bad feeling.

Someone had counted 134 rivers in Jamaica; 67 along the south coast and 67 along the north; indeed, one of the translations of the aboriginal name of our island Xaymaca is "land of springs." The central mountain ranges running east to west across the island form a natural watershed and the most powerful rivers rise high on the flanks of these mountains. Instead of keeping a straight course to the sea many rivers sink and reappear, carving out and sometimes abandoning caverns, caves and sinkholes which make our island a speleologist's paradise. The rivers that behave in this way are the ones that flow in the middle of the island, starting their course in an area which is made up of shale and yellow limestone which are impervious.

However, nearer to the coasts are rocks of the more permeable white limestone, and when the rivers meet these, they sink underground,

Then, as the river widened and became more shallow, it took the colour of the skies, the trees, our faces, the shape and colour of anything outside of and beyond itself; there was no one colour of the river.

For we also feared the river.

There were times when it turned angry and threatening, lost its sparkle, grew dull lead under the lowering skies. Times of flash floods and rainfall, the river swelled with the clay of upstream mountains. The river is crying, we'd say, its eyes are red.

some to disappear forever, but many will reappear—frequently with dramatic suddenness at a point where the water gushes out again from the limestone cliffs to form beautiful cascades and waterfalls. A series of such cascades along the north coast give that stretch of coastline the name "Chorreras" meaning "spouts," a name which has since been corrupted to Ocho Rios. Today, the only one of these beautiful falls remaining is Dunn's River which is a noted attraction.

Jamaica's rivers are on the whole deceptive. Who seeing the vast valleys that dissect our mountains, the broad deltas covered in fields of sugar cane and vegetation, the abandoned gully courses that crisscross Kingston, for instance, would connect them with the nearby thin trickles of water often lost in their sandy or stony beds? In our time, many of our rivers have been harnessed for electricity, their waters drained to fill our dams and water taps, used to irrigate our scrubland. The forests at the riverheads have been gradually shorn, the rains have gotten less. The rivers, their mighty job of sculpting the land now over, have gotten smaller. Or maybe we have gotten bigger.

Yet up to a little less than a century ago, before even our major rivers were bridged, they totally dominated our lives. They could only be forded in the dry season and when the rains came, communities on river banks would become separated, families parted, and whole sections of the land completely cut off from others. The Yallahs, for instance, would frequently sever Kingston from the eastern end. Traffic from the western end was frequently halted at May Pen when the Rio Cobre had its way. Indeed, May Pen developed around two inns on either side of the Rio Minho which got enough patronage from marooned travelers.

The clock tower in that town is a memorial to a popular doctor who drowned trying to cross the river while it was in spate or, as we say in Jamaica, when "de ribba ben come dung." "O Rattla, a how you come over?" excited villagers ask the singer in a song about "De Ribba Ben Come Dung" once popular among river communities. In many verses he sings and pantomimes his attempts at crossing until, in triumph, "A rock so, a rock so, a rock it come over." "Whai oh, we glad yu come over," the hearers cry in relief, for all know the danger of such a crossing.

Although there are so many rivers, there is only one well developed river system, the Black River, which flows for 45 miles and in its lower reaches, where it is joined by many tributaries, drains a large area only slightly above sea level. This has created a fascinating morass ecologically rich and botanically exciting, containing mangrove settlements, marsh forests and floating vegetation. Like other morass areas, this once harboured large numbers of crocodiles, but these creatures have become so scarce they have had to be officially protected.

Jamaica's rivers hold in their secret care many strands of our history. Our first people, the Arawak Indians, always lived near to springs and rivers and many of their settlements were on river banks. When the Spaniards came, the first trails they opened up cross-country followed the river valleys and gully; later they were widened to become packhorse trails. A large number of our rivers still bear their Spanish names. When the English settled, it was in the river deltas and rich alluvial valleys that they planted their sugar cane. Where the river permitted, the plantations floated their sugar downstream and built their shipping wharves where it entered the sea.

Many of Jamaica's large towns and settlements are in fact on river banks and all ports near the mouth of rivers from which fresh water could be obtained—Spanish Town, Linstead and Bog Walk on the Rio Cobre; Frankfield, May Pen on the Minho; Savanna-la-Mar on the Cabaritta; Port Morant on the Morant; Rio Bueno on the river of that name. Kingston itself occupies what was once fruitful sugar estate lands watered by a series of 18th century aqueducts bringing water from nearby rivers—Mona and Hope from the Hope River, Constant Spring from the Wag Water.

But if the Europeans and others took to the lower reaches, it was the Africans who made themselves masters of the upper river valleys. The Maroons or runaway slaves, first settled the wild country surrounding the Cave River Valley and Lluidas Vale in the centre of the island. In the east, the Windward Maroons made the whole of the Rio Grande their own, with their foremost citadel of Nanny Town perched on a naturally fortified ridge above the Stony River, a Rio Grande tributary. Richly stocked with fish—calipeva, mountain mullet, hognose tarpon, snook and snapper—the Rio Grande and its many tributaries fed and watered the fugitives. It also made it difficult for the pursuing English soldiers to reach them since the redcoats often had to march in single file up or across rivers and were thus easily picked off; river crossings also made it hard to keep their powder dry. The names of rivers in the east still bear testament to these African runaways—Negro River, Quashie's River and Cottawood. When the enslaved Africans were freed, there was little land left for them along the lower valleys and they too pushed their settlements upwards to the precipitous high valleys, where their generations still cultivate on slopes which sometimes reach 30 degrees.

These slopes are subject to the ravaging effects of erosion, torrential rainfall, slides, and flash floods; in rainstorms and hurricanes, the red-eyed rivers literally bleed Jamaica into the sea.

Yet in the dry season, if you come away off the beaten track, you can still find streams of crystal clear waters, unpolluted, untamed. And on a leaf-dappled and joyous river bank, you too, sitting in the shade of the bamboo roots might spot River Mumma, golden in the afternoon, singing.

ORIGINALLY PUBLISHED JANUARY 1982

PHOTOGRAPH BY FRANZ MARZOUCA AND RICHARD KHOURI, ORIGINALLY PUBLISHED AS A COVER JANUARY 1994.

Reminiscences

JOHN ALLGROVE

There was a sort of special atmosphere, for instance, about going to Mavis Bank early in the morning—six miles away—to catch the truck. I must have been about ten, then, a score of years ago. We would use the plane flying over every morning as our alarm clock. In those days the market truck ran twice a week and when you missed the truck, you walked all the way to Kingston—thirteen miles away. But there was something about going down to the village, so early, with the odd person getting up on his way to the fields; you know, the whole smell of the air, the clarity of the hills, the sun just barely coming over them, all the changing light....

The trucks very seldom left anybody though, and the police were always after them for overloading. But the drivers had all sorts of ruses for picking up people after they'd passed the police station. One time the police were smarter; they stopped the truck a long way out of town. That Friday evening they removed from the transport some thirty-six of us who shouldn't have been there, and left only the forty-four the thing was licensed to carry.

Oh, in those days the vehicles could do some fantastic things—if the driver had to stop on a hill there wasn't any way he could start off again. He'd have to roll backwards to a level place first, down the twisting road.

The nice thing about those market trucks was that all the people knew each other, you see, every week taking their produce to market and going back on Friday evening. The journey might take five hours from Kingston, and we would sing to pass the time away. I mean although you were being squeezed to death, there was a feeling about it. The usual method of collecting the fare for instance was to stop halfway between Gordon Town and Mavis Bank, and the driver would wrangle with the passengers about what the fare should be. It would take an hour or so sometimes, just collecting fares!

Even this has changed. The operators today are much more business-like: pay as you enter. No pay, no trip. They have buses now, and vans and Land Rovers that go all the way up into the hills. A man doesn't think of walking to Kingston these days to sell his produce; not like then. They'd walk both ways sometimes, twenty-odd miles with a donkey or a mule if they had one to carry the produce. Or carry it on their heads.

And the music! That was before the jukebox. A live band is different, you see. There were two bands in Mavis Bank alone. A man might have a flute or a guitar in his pocket or on his shoulder; sometimes both. I had a friend, a forest ranger, used to play his guitar all the way to the Peak, seven miles from Torre Garda where we lived. There was a trumpeter and a banjo player, I remember, in the district; they're playing in a band in Philadelphia now. That's a long way from home.

We'd make our own music too. To make a saxophone you'd find a young bamboo shoot, and you'd load it with a stone, so that it curved down. Then when it started to grow back up again, there you'd have the bottom part of the sax, the bending part. You'd use different sections of the tree to make the instrument, even the reed would be from a sliver of bamboo. And they made clarinets as well, and flutes out of the same bamboo that some called wild cane. At celebrations the bands would play square dances and the schottische and the rhumba—remember that? Everybody would dance, young and old, with the white rum tuning up the homemade saxophones.

I know the hills and the people like the back of my hand. Villages with names like Epping Farm, and Penlyne Castle, where I lived. And places with strange German names like Westphalia, which is below Cinchona Gardens about seven miles away—not as the crow flies, but by our tortuous roads into the valley 3000 feet down, and then that height again up the other side. And Hagley Gap that was far below: the nearest post office town three miles away where I used to go every other day for mail. Population 800.

It was a rough life there, and a good one. I remember things like going to school in Kingston for the first time when I was nearly ten. I had to fight for that. That was a wonderful day. And the time the man who bought the property next door hired an epileptic, and one day the crazy fellow tried to drown me. But he wasn't from there, of course. He was a stranger.

Once however a group of us were cutting down a piece of forest, we were all there, I was about sixteen. You know the usual thing to do: you cut the undergrowth high enough so that you can see the stakes and don't step in them and bore your feet. And then you go through and cut down the bigger trees. I was cutting down a pretty tall fellow, sixty, seventy feet high. This tree grew up the hillside, made a bend, and grew vertical. Now normally you can control the operation—you give the tree a belly in the direction you want it to fall, and then you back it with an axe.

But with this tree there was only one thing to do with it, cut it. It was going to fall on the hillside no matter what you did. So I cut it, and it fell, slid down the hillside between my leg, and then rocked on the part where it bent to grow vertical, and it chucked me about fifteen feet into the air. Well, I dropped in an area completed surrounded by small, sharp stakes. And not one of them touched me! Things like that, we took them as part of life, I guess. Like the loneliness of walking home from Mavis Bank. Five miles of dark and silence, all alone with not a man in sight for miles, when I was ten! The ruins of the old great houses. They had belonged once to the coffee plantations. We said that they were haunted of course! You know the kind of reputation empty houses have. It's difficult to tell who built them or how old they are exactly, but we know that the Spaniards came to these Mountains when they were here, because there are a couple ancient copper mines in the area, which they dug.

Then under the British, at the height of the coffee boom there were some forty properties in those hills, some as large as 1200 acres. Those were wealthy men, they say that Devon House, in Kingston, was built by one of them. It was all part of a competition to see who could put up the handsomest house. One of the men who lost that bet is buried under a bamboo root in Sheldon, the coffee property he owned. John Bull, his name was. You can see the grave there today.

Most of those estates had their own factory, worked by running water; water wheels with great wooden gears, they used, that pulped the coffee and husked it and then polished it and even packaged it. But then time had its way, and there were World Wars One and Two, and, especially, a grass called wynne grass. They brought it into the area in the 1950s, and it spread like wildfire all over the Blue Mountains. Now this grass burns like anything, it really is beautiful fuel; but it grows over everything and strangles it to death. Tall and beautiful. What with this and people farming and using fire to clear their land and the fires getting away and burning the coffee and the windgrass choking what wasn't burnt to death, I guess thousands of acres of coffee were completely obliterated during the last war. And all the coffee in the Blue Mountains today is pretty well on small holdings.

My father lives in one of those houses now. Whitfield Hall. We run a business there. Well, he runs the guest house, and I do a bit of farming, growing coffee; and I enjoy it, you see. I grew up with the land and I love the land. I do a fair amount myself, not all, but things like the pruning I do, and the planting ... It's hard to explain to people who are not of the land, not of the country and the hills. They think you're mad. "After all you're a qualified engineer!" they say. "It's a lot of work, they're a lot more easy ways to make a livelihood."

But there's something about it that holds you, far above what you may make out of it. Where my father is now, we haven't got any electricity, and we don't intend to put in any. We still use Tilley pressure lamps. The hiss of these at night, and the noises outside; the sound of the solitaire, the bird that you hardly ever see, but it whistles a tune that sounds a little like a hymn you've heard; and sometimes the wind blowing the "winter rain" fine and nearly horizontal. There's something very special about it that I can't get where I live in town. And in the country I can open my windows when I want. I walk where I wish.

ORIGINALLY PUBLISHED SEPTEMBER 1972

In the forties, when I was born, my father built a cottage on the sea in Treasure Beach. Primarily chosen for its proximity to Mandeville, "Treasure Cot" as it was called, became the favourite get-away of a mountain family.

In Search of the Sea

SALLY HENZELL

In those days Treasure Beach was lorded over by 'Doctor' Senior, an imposing, good-looking man who wore his stomach over his low-slung pants with the pride of the well to-do. He was the first 'big lobster' in the area and had a pleasant house in Calabash Bay. It was also he who sold the land beside his house to my father and a friend, my father feeling it necessary to have a partner to share the £100 for the acre; in fact the deal nearly fell through when 'Senior' refused to come down to £90.

The road from Gutters to Pedro was unpaved (almost completely sand) and the Great Pedro pond was always full and had crocodiles as well as ducks and other pond birds. The houses here were built of Spanish wall (beams and stone incased in mortar) and had either two or four rooms, some with verandahs, in which the kitchens and priveys were housed separately. Some were painted beautiful bright colours and a few had fretwork. Apart from these, there was only Folichon, owned by a colourful couple, Madame Melasse and her Russian lover, Lola de Balaban, and the Treasure Beach Hotel built in the late twenties and owned by Dicker. The aviatrix, Jean Mountbatten and Megan Thomas the first international ice-skating star, were fixtures for a time, the forerunners of the crowd who are still attracted for the very same reason, the anonymity of a paradise, where hidden from

(ABOVE) Sally Henzell at Jakes, 2001; (BELOW) "Going Fishing," the family at Calabash Bay with Treasure Cot in the background; (OPPOSITE PAGE) "The brackish water-well where we washed-off, in front of Treasure Cot at Calabash Bay.

prying eyes they could do as they pleased. Treasure Beach remained generally isolated in the fifties and even the sixties although by then the second wave of Mandevillians such as the Thelwells, Sir Arthur and Lady Mabel, and 'Dada' Harris had built houses on the strip.

Treasure Cot was our family's favourite place in the whole world and there would be a countdown as the day approached that we would take a trip there. In great excitement the Standard 8 or whatever relic we drove at the time, would be loaded up to the roof and then the four of us, (five, when we were small and Nanny a.k.a. Mrs. Reynolds came too), would squeeze in and set off down Spur Tree hill.

In the car with us would be: Oliver, the pet parrot in his cage; one or two dachshund dogs; fishing rods; snorkeling gear, (for goggle fishing as it was called then); ridiculously few rum bottles filled with drinking water which soon ran out (probably because there were more with rum); food; a vast lump of ice; Daddy's tool kit and banjo; Mummy's wind-up Singer sewing machine; books, games, clothes and other miscellany.

Coming over the hill just below Southfield, a shriek of delight would have us jumping around and tearing off our clothes as the sea came into sight preparing for our family tradition of all four of us running straight from the car into the water, a priority that I find strangely lacking in more subdued and reasoned persons. After all, once cooled and invigorated by the crashing surf, dowsed with a bucket of brackish water from the well dug in our front garden, we could then unload the precious cargo and settle in.

The days ahead started early. My sister and I would follow our father along the reef till we came to Barracuda Hole (where Jakes is now situated), and then we would watch as my father shot breakfast, lunch or dinner, depending on the size of fish. We would be back in the sea before lunch, with our surf boards this time, made from cotton tree planks, light and floatable. We were taught from very young how to cope with them when a rogue wave came bearing down. We would dive till we lay on the sand, our boards still firmly clutched, and wait as the immense body of water crashed and swirled inches above our breathless bodies. We were quick to learn there would be three in succession each more immense and further out than the one before. There were accidents of course, but nothing that iodine and gentian violet, (the mainstay of our medicine cabinet), couldn't cure. For sun our noses were smothered in zinc ointment but with our father being a great admirer of sun-tanned ladies, no further precautions were taken.

In the afternoons we often went out trolling in a canoe and fishing off the reef. The canoes we had were chipped out of cotton tree and had canvas sails and wonderful names. It was fascinating to watch a canoe emerging from a tree trunk through the ancient labour skill of using only simple tools like the adze and hatchet. They had managed to stretch the width of a tree to 7-foot 2-inches by gradually adding wedges along the gunwale, getting that perfect symmetry in the hull by driving pegs of a certain length through from the inside so as to achieve the desired width.

On other days we would go for long donkey rides or shell-collecting walks—jumping down the sand dunes with other kids of our age, digging for crabs by following a trickle of water in damp sand, exploring the tumbledown remains of an old wooden house, or simply running amok, squashing Portuguese man-o-war jellyfish to hear them pop in the sand. Our days would then wind down with the ceremonious lighting of the Tilley-lamp that happened in the early evenings. I was a fascinated observer, as Daddy put on the mantle, gave it a pump, struck a match with at first, nothing. But then after several attempts and some grown up expletives, light would sizzle out and the banjo would come into play. Often he was joined by Martin who is still around with his Hawaiian guitar which he plays on his lap. Sometimes a kalimba box and a pair of maracas would emerge shyly from the shadows and join in.

We would build bonfires on the beach of the driftwood we'd collected, in company of Zim who worked in the yard. He fought a long and courageous battle on behalf of my mother with stray goats who seemed able to scale any wall when the plumbago and bougainvillea were in bloom. He was our constant companion and we were always luring him away to play in the sand dunes or marvel at the miniature sea aquariums of the rock pools.

Starry nights and full moons were much appreciated. Sometimes we hung the huge mosquito net from the 'cacia tree and slept underneath with our friends.

Our parents would give parties and cars would drive up with people bedecked with leis and Hawaiian sarongs (if that was the theme) and they would sit on the grass and eat off banana leaves. I remember the spoil-sport who didn't want to expose himself to the night breeze, being firmly undressed by Mummy until he was suitably naked and in character.

A special place to us, our parents were fairly diligent about keeping the secret of this unsophisticated village to themselves. Now and then someone more progressive or the Tourist Board would try to put Treasure Beach on the map but my mother was quick to respond with letters to the *Gleaner* telling of shark attacks, deadly swift currents, frequent drownings and other largely imaginary off-putting scenarios, so much so that by the beginning of the nineties still little had changed. German back-packers discovered us, they rented inexpensive rooms and stayed as guests in people's houses. Bicar's nightclub appeared, a disco with girls, a pool table and flashing lights. Gone however were the days of the itinerant projectionist with his projector, his generator, his reels of film and a screen made of a sheet that was hastily tacked up at the back of 'Dads Amusement Centre'; at the end of the reel there was an interminable pause while the reel was changed. It may have happened more than once, but I remember the peels of laughter when the lights hit the sheet for the second act and there in the midst of the action and highly illuminated, swayed an inebriated fisherman caught in an awkward pose.

Now we have three hotels and over 30 guesthouses and numerous new buildings going up. We have satellite dishes and cellular phones and helicopters landing with guests for the hotels. We have spanking, newly painted 'fifers' (fibre-glass canoes) with cushioned seats taking tourists up the Black River or to Sunny Island and—for the best crab in the world—'Little Ochi' in Alligator Pond. The road is being resurfaced and the odd famous person can be seen strolling along it.

ORIGINALLY PUBLISHED DECEMBER 2001

The Mango, The Ackee and The Breadfruit

DIANA McCAULEY

This is what I remember of my childhood. First there was a gutter at the back of the house and it was filled with leaves. We used to slide down it and get into trouble with three-toothed nanny because our clothes were dirty. We were all girls, but we never wore skirts. There was a cardboard box that we used to pull each other in, round and round the cherry tree. An empty chicken coop was our clubhouse and we climbed a plum tree. We caught lizards with nooses made from the fibres of a coconut tree, and shot grass quits with slingshots. We tried to catch peenie-wallies to put them in a bottle so we could have lamps, but we never could. We caught wasps instead and often we were stung.

We had a wood stove and there was a place for killing chickens which was always covered in feathers. My father had a rose garden and the chickens from the man next door often came into our garden and dug up the roses. My father shot the chickens and threw them over the privet hedge into the next door yard. We never saw any chickens again.

I remember bicycles, but I was older then. We would start at the top of the garden by the plum tree and race past the chicken coop and the rose garden, down a hill, picking up speed, round the corner where the chickens were killed, then a very sharp corner around the cherry tree and stop. Always we missed the last corner and ended up in the privet hedge—I was usually a mass of cuts and bruises. Beside our house was a gully and I remember the Flora rains when the gully came almost to the level of our lawn and a car was washed away and there was no school for three days. We had a swing and a gardener and a cook and three-toothed nanny. We had huge Sunday lunches of roast beef and rice and peas and yampie and callaloo (which we all hated but had to eat) and plantain.

Every summer we went to San San in Portland. It was an expedition. A van had to take everything we needed for those two weeks—food, drinks, a playpen for my baby sister, games, fishing tackle, buckets and spades and the dinghy. I was always carsick on the way there and my father would stop the car and walk with me until my nausea subsided. I remember his arm across my shoulders as we walked along a country road, the broad, flat banana leaves brushing us as we went by. He told me that he was always carsick when he was a child and he talked of the country then and the donkey he had and he told me duppy stories. I always knew this was my father's country too.

Soon we would drive on and we would sing and we would wait for the moment when we would sweep off the hill and see Blue Hole—then we would be close, very close. Arriving, we would spill out of the car in a tumult, head straight to the beach and there, there was the sea and the little island. I had no words for what I saw then, but I would run straight into the sea, clothes, and all, and jump high and soaking, arms, outstretched to the darkening evening sky. A certain spanking awaited me for getting my clothes wet, but it did not matter.

I will never lose the taste of those summer days no matter how old I am or how far I travel. We built sand castles late in the evening and reinforced them with rocks, sure they would be there in the morning, but always the sea would have taken them away. We woke early and went fishing in the dinghy and our catch would be fried for breakfast. Oh, we ran wild, we children. We snorkeled the reefs from early morning for our aquariums. We swam to the island and climbed to the top and there we could see the miracle of the reef, the deep and the shallow, the coral of every shape and colour, the sea fans, and the endless surge of the surf, rolling over and over and over. Then we would search for soldier crabs in the fallen leaves on the island, the vegetation underfoot thick and wet from Portland's afternoon rain. And we would carry back with us a full bucket of the crabs, a seething mass of infinitely various shells. We had soldier crab races on the beach and the grown-ups would bet match sticks on the crabs.

I remember the cricket matches on the beach and the day my father broke his big toe trying to pole vault with a rotten bamboo pole. I remember the rafts we made with three or four pieces of waterlogged bamboo loosely tied together with string. I remember the hole in the rock at the end of the beach which we grandly called a cave and used for secret meetings, and the underground stream of icy cold fresh water flowing into the sea and fogging our masks as we swam past.

We water skied on the lagoon which we always called Blue Hole. The water in the lagoon was deep and dark, utterly opaque and flat calm, sometimes covered with the blossoms of the flame-of-the-forest trees. We skied out over the light green shallows where the seaweed grew and then over patches of turquoise of a colour no camera or paintbrush could ever catch, over thick white sand far down beneath the water.

We played water polo in the lagoon and we dived from the almond trees that lined the banks. And I remember the evenings after the rain when the sea was green glass, the bush sang with the whistling frogs and the manta rays glided down the channel, exotic underwater birds, their wings spanning wider than our dingy. We feared seeing the rays when we snorkeled, but when we did, they ignored us, gliding by without effort and we knew our swimming to be clumsy.

One afternoon someone skiing discovered a dead piglet in the lagoon and fearing it would attract sharks we all piled into the ski boat to take it far out to sea. We went out so far the sea lost all its colours and became grey and hostile, the small boat wallowed in huge swells and we were all afraid as we watched the land become a smudge on the horizon. My father waited on the dock for our return. He had seen the tiny boat laden with children disappear into the swells. His anger was towering and we were all grounded for the rest of the summer.

On the last day of my childhood a boy and I climbed to the top of Whale Head, an arduous, barefoot climb up a rocky path and we looked down at Dragon Bay, unprotected by a reef as San San Bay was. The sea pounded the beach and spray flew from the rocks. A river flowed cold and green into the sea and coconut trees lashed the sky. Although we were steeped in this beauty, this sunshine, this land and took it for granted, we were silenced then as we looked down on the deserted bay and we stayed there for two hours, not speaking. Once more my father awaited my return, but his anger was worth those two hours I looked down at Dragon Bay for the first time.

When I was ten I went to high school. We moved to a house right under the shadow of Jacks Hill and I looked through my window and saw this green mountain edged shaped against the sky and it was my first sense of God. It has never left me, that moment.

So it was time for high school. The streets were noisy and full of laughter. I took the bus everywhere, too impatient to wait for my parents to collect me. Jolly Joseph we called the buses, dirty and badly driven and crammed with people. There were never any queues, it was just a matter of who pushed hardest and shouted loudest who got on the bus. I was living life it seemed to me then, just approaching adolescence, testing my first choices, and I loved the colour and the clamour of it, the throb of the rock-steady music coming from rum shops, the goats in the streets. I had been born to it, but also I chose it, this Jamaica was mine to the bone.

I learned to play the guitar, but I was tone deaf and I flirted with socialism and never wore shoes except to school. I read poetry and philosophy and made no distinctions between black and brown and white and Chinese and Indian. My father said it was not so simple, but I knew he was wrong. I sat by the poui tree in our garden under the shadow of the mountain and I watched the grass turn brown and die through the great drought in 1967. I watered the few patches of grass that remained on our lawn with dishwater. Every day I prayed for rain, and that summer I fell in love and wrote the story about the squirrel.

Now it is many years later and my childhood is still sharp in my mind. I've left Jamaica and I've come back and my son is growing up and has never prayed for rain or caught a peeni-wallie or snorkeled the reefs. I've been to other countries—England, Canada and the States—and I will not stay there for I am not of them. We are all like that, we West Indians, every one of us a transplant from some other place, every one of us building a jigsaw puzzle culture.

Jamaica is different now. A gardener and a cook and three-toothed nanny have given way to one helper. There are no more Jolly Joseph buses and we haven't had a drought like that one since. Now there is a hotel at Dragon Bay and a restaurant on the very spot where we stood. Now there are drum-pan chicken men and mini-buses and not so many goats, and traffic lights and high-rise buildings in Kingston. Once we had a hurricane and this magnificent land was changed overnight—broken, bare, dirty. But so quickly the trees had new leaves. All the trees: the mango, the ackee and the breadfruit. And the sun shines on us all—still, it shines.

ORIGINALLY PUBLISHED JANUARY 1996

Under Banyan Tree

EASTON LEE

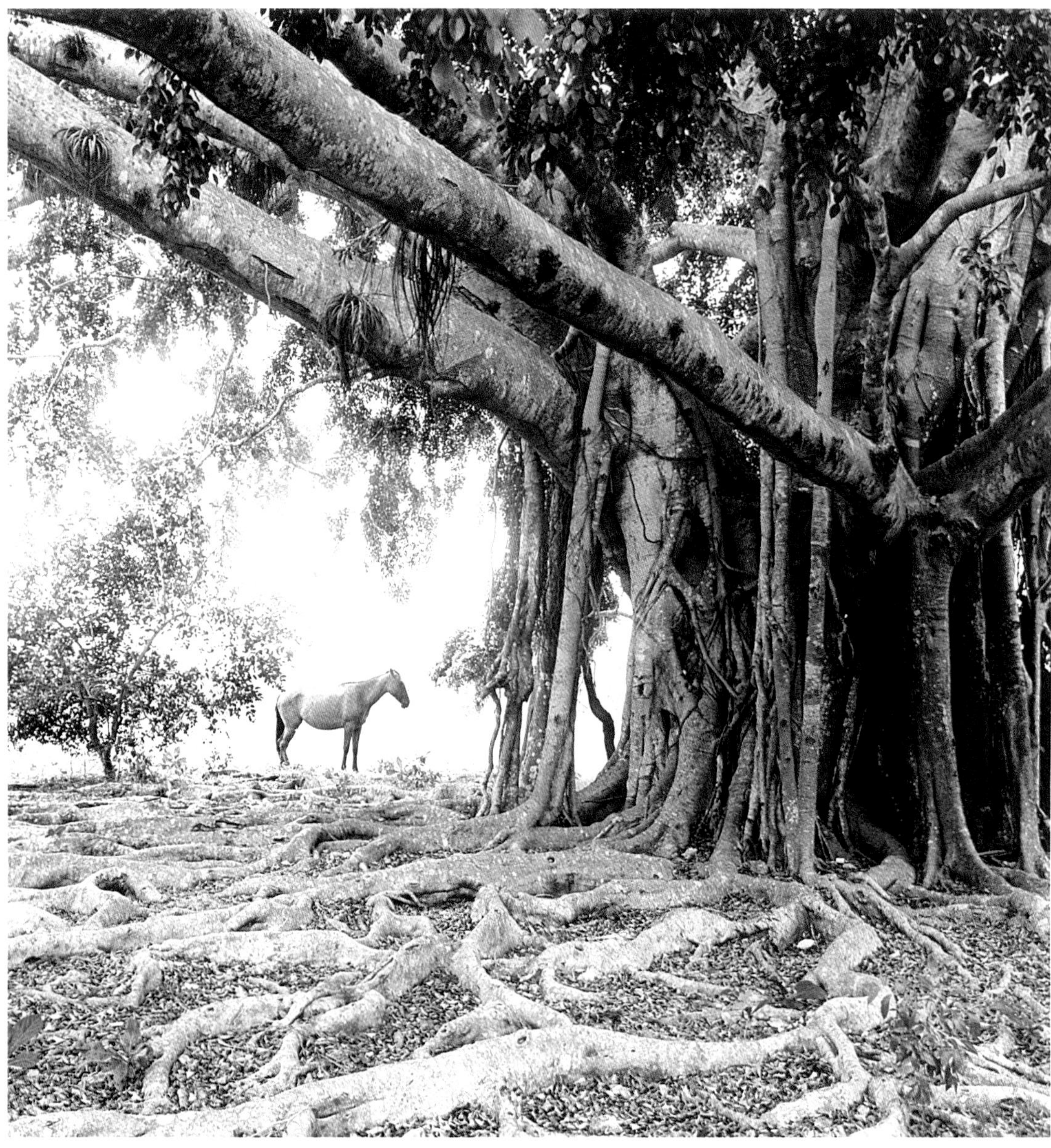

An excerpt from Easton Lee's *From Behind The Counter*, a collection of poems which distill the wisdom, love, survival strategies and humour of old rural Jamaica.

IAN RANDLE PUBLISHERS 1998

This country grown in your gut
like a Banyan tree
spreading strong limbs of hurt and happiness
reaching in the far corners of your insides.
Each branch drops a thousand roots
that knot up your belly bit by bit
tangle your heart-string
and the only thing you can do
is love it.
You find yourself going and coming,
now you live, now you hate and love again
"Me da rock so, you da rock so".
You can't escape it
even when you curse it go away
green-card it to
country grade AA
stow away to the "Mother Land"
or any other place,
the pain and love in your gut get worse and
worse.
You can't understand
for the big fat purse
is no pain killer—no mind healer
"For you da rock so, me da rock so!"
God Almighty!
How do you leave a lover
you know since you know yourself?
Since the first stirring?
You keep remembering the heaven and the
hell
the sweetness and the gall
the long nights
the cool days
the hot loving, burning
the fight and the quarrel
the leaving, the returning
and the peace...
What is it, what is it
will it ever cease?
You don't really want it stop
for this is your life,
the misery, the mystery of it.
More and more the Banyan roots
tighten round your feet
and your heart strings
move into your brain
anchor you to the bedrock
till you become the root,
the tree—the rock itself
you're one with the root
the tree and the rock.
And you know the only place
you'll go in your bed in your head
is six feet under.
"You da rock so
me da rock so
under Banyan tree."

ORIGINALLY PUBLISHED AUGUST 2000

A Rap with Myself

BARBARA GLOUDON

The thing that's bothering me recently is am I contemporary and liberated, or just contemporary or what? Let's take it a bit at a time.

I went to primary school—high school, university of life education. I yearned for and worked for some of the Better Homes and Gardens trappings—including the husband and the two children, and I must confess I quite enjoy them.

Like many of my peers in Jamaica, I go out to work. My job is in a man's world and I suspect men of lesser competence than myself get more salary and perks than I do, but I don't waste too much time bothering myself about that. I enjoy what I do and I've developed a kind of boredom and contempt for the constant money squabble, I can't be bothered to knock myself out on that score. Besides, if I had a lot of money I might turn into one of those ladies from another section of the middle class who bore me to tears, with their endless discussions of what they bought in Miami on the last shopping trip and all the super attachments and furnishings they're going to add to their already overdone houses.

I go out to work and manage to keep my home going with the aid of a helper. For a long time now I've refused to call her a maid. It began one day when I heard my small daughter and friend discussing "their maids". Right then I felt almost sick that there were children, age under five, who could talk about adults in this way, like their own personal chattels. I began to teach my daughter and myself that none of us had maids. We're lucky enough to have helpers, who work longer hours than we would, at salaries which we wouldn't accept, so that we can enjoy the freedom women in other countries can't get. Sounds corny but you know how it is sometimes.

Actually, I'd like to talk about my helper. She's unique in a way. She's one of the few Jamaican women I know who's free and single and proud of it. She's never had a child and has managed to survive the primitive hostilities against the childless woman in the Jamaican society, especially lower on the social scale. I don't know if anybody has ever called her "a mule", which is the favourite epithet for those who have never reproduced.

Sometimes we talk about "modern day youth" and problems like birth control and sex education. My helper won't believe that a lot of our young girls get into trouble (Jamaican euphemism for pregnancy) because they have no idea how their bodies are made and what causes what when what happens. My helper won't buy that at all. She says "dem just bad" and points out that in her day, if she "did get into trouble", her mother would kill her, for her people always had ambition. (Ambition is heavy with all Jamaicans male or female). But my help agrees with women—"taking the birth control", which I suppose is a handy way of putting it, much as my middle class sophisticated friends would announce,"I've my teenage daughter on the Pill." Actually I have never heard one of my friends say that, although some of them swear that as soon as their daughters are big enough, that's just what they are going to do. "I'll hand it to her just like that" they say, I haven't worked out that one for myself yet. To tell the truth, when the showdown comes, I know I won't be able to do it. My mind is made up on that. But I tell you something, I won't make up my mind about the abortion question. I'm kinda religious ...maybe more than kinda, and not being one of the legendary fecund Jamaicans, I have this thing about the sanctity of life. But I refuse to go out on the limb in the pro and anti debates which rage, because it is such a personal thing, I don't feel qualified enough to lecture anybody about what to do with their own body. I guess that rules me out of Women's Lib. To tell the truth, that's not the only thing which rules me out. Between us, I can't abide those women who go around putting down men, I mean like emasculating. I adore male company. I get bored as hell with gaggles of women pattering on about how they're going to change this and that. I'm sick of minutes of the last meeting at coffee meetings and sermons to help the poor and the time has come for the hand that rocks the cradle to rule the world. That's a load of old rubbish. Any smart woman has been doing that long ago, in her own sphere and with a whole lot more people than she'll talk about...smart girl that she is.

There are some platforms of women's lib which I back, but in an action way...like day care centres which, God knows, we need scores and scores of here in Jamaica and not for the American reasons of freeing Mother to do what she wants with her life, like tearing up her Maidenform or going to art classes. Down here Mother has no choice, she's out there working to cope with the cost of living, and somebody has to look after the baby. But Grandma has migrated to Canada to recover her lost youth. And suburban housing estate design has no place for old people in our compact houses anyway. Where's Grand Aunt going to stay, even if she would come in handy to mind the baby? So we need, right now, the day care centres, good ones, where all sorts of children can get a chance to awaken their intelligence in stimulating circumstances and not in a wash pan inside some old lady's yard, or with a part-educated adolescent whom we've acquired through the morning radio programme which also swaps furniture and agapanthus seedlings.

Funny thing is, when I begin to talk with myself, I discover there's a lot of things I get angry about, when it comes to the rights of women and children. But I don't think there's any point in just getting angry and rushing to join one of the many ladies' groups. I'm foolish enough to think that I'd better start working on myself and those within the circle around me and then when moving together, we keep it spreading till we achieve something positive. I suspect that this has done it now. I'm definitely not liberated and not a radical. Where am I?

I'm a Jamaican and I love this country so much it is silly. I bitch about its faults in noisy arguments with my friends, yet I'd hate to leave it to live anywhere else. I travel out a lot (like everybody else) and with each outing, I come back and put my head together and figure out why I wouldn't like to live anywhere else. And I think I'm beginning to get some kind of answer. An island, this island, in a way is like a pregnant womb. It's got all the things I want right near by. I can kick and squirm and beat my way out to face life with friends and those I love around. Does that make sense?

ORIGINALLY PUBLISHED DECEMBER 1972

Being Where I Am

ELAINE PERKINS

People always ask, when they hear that I live in Malvern "But how can you live so far away?" and I invariably reply by asking them, "far away from what? From where?"

A bewildered and confused look often crosses their face then, for what they really mean, but are usually too polite to say, is "why do you choose to live so far away from me and the things that are important to me? You must be crazy."

But I am where I want to be just as they are where they want to be. My family is in Malvern, my house is in Malvern, my garden is here, my books. All the things I love to see and smell and touch are here. I am here. What and where can I be far away from?

Malvern has a mean temperature of about 76 degrees for most months of the year and I've experienced it at 54 degrees and lower in the months between December and February. I love going out into the garden then when the mist comes gliding around the hillsides and soon I find myself enveloped in clouds so thick I can hardly see my own feet. It is as if I am somewhere between earth and sky and I feel wondrously expectant for it seems that almost anything can happen.

But times like that are not often. Mist means damp and Malvern is almost always dry, though cool. And high, more than two thousand feet above sea level. That's one of the reasons, probably the main reason, why so many Europeans settled here in the early days and why asthmatics and those recuperating from diseases of the respiratory system used to take the cure here during the early 1900's and later. People around here say, upon what authority I do not know, that Malvern has one of the best climates in the world. I do think they have something. There can't be many more salubrious climates in the world. It suits me very well.

In my garden I grow sweet pea, hydrangea, day lillies, agapanthus, nasturtium, and other temperate climate plants, as well as bougainvilleas, hibiscus, crotons etc. The soil where I am is very thin, making it necessary to use huge amount of compost and mulch to make soil as well as to retain moisture in view of the low rainfall.

The town, and I so describe it advisedly, because the public and commercial area of Malvern could fit quite comfortably into the length of one Kingston, not to mention one New York City block; closes down about 7 p.m. most weekdays. There are no resident sound systems. No record shops. Hence no excessive noise, save for now and then on a public holiday night. No patty nor any other kind of fast food shop nor restaurant. No cinema. No betting shop. No market. No tennis nor golf clubs. In fact no club at all. I, for one, can live very happily with that.

When folks here who don't have a car, want to have ice cream and patties, visit the cinema, or go to market, they take one of the capriciously-run taxis or mini-buses which ply the route to Santa Cruz. The Malvern terminus is in the middle of the intersection of Mr. Mill's shop and next to the police station, where the road to Santa Cruz joins from Southfield past Munro, Hampton and Bethlehem, through Malvern and on to other parts.

Santa Cruz, the nearest market town about ten miles downhill, hot as hell in marked contrast to cool Malvern, is probably as fast-growing a place as there is in Jamaica; by far outstripping the parish capital Black River, which went to sleep in the late nineteenth century after the Germans destroyed its logwood trade with their invention of chemical dyes, and hasn't woken up since.

I like the Santa Cruz market—foodstuff laid out or piled on crocus bags on the open ground, haggling with the butcher over too much bone in my order of meat—its sprawling, noisy, smelly, rustic ambiance. I enjoy that.

Malvern began life as a dormitory for rich Black River businessmen of the "good old days" and it still has a tranquil, unhurried, "residential" quality, as distinct from the bustle of Santa Cruz, or even the slight commotion of Black River, turning in its sleep, on a market day. It boasts among its residents a few professionals practising law or medicine somewhere in, what someone described as, "that ring of nascent conurbation" that extends from Nain, not far from the foot of Spur Tree Hill, through Junction, Top Hill, Southfield, Flagaman, Pedro Cross all the way back around to Black River and Santa Cruz itself. And then, of course, there are the teachers. The Malvern area boasts, in Munro College for boys and Hampton School for girls, two of the oldest, most reputable educational institutions in the island in addition to which, there is the Bethlehem Teachers' College founded by the Moravians. This is an aspect of the German connection in the southern part of St. Elizabeth, surviving elsewhere in names like Potsdam, and in the startlingly blue eyes so often staring out of brown faces in places like nearby Treasure Beach.

We have our fair share of young people in a population of under five thousand between the town of Malvern and its several outlying districts such as Smoothground, Gingerground, Knole, Elgin, Stanmore, Mt. Plymouth, Retirement, Prosper, Eppington Forest, Joyland, Schoolfield, Leeds and so on... They live their lives as most young people in the rural parts of Jamaica do. They go to school and church and help work the land, they play games at the ball ground and have their love affairs. But there's not too much hanging about on the streets; one tends not to see them playing dominoes on shop piazzas or engaging in boisterous behaviour. I think that's good.

Southern St. Elizabeth is an arid place. Life here used to be harder than in any other part of Jamaica. More than anywhere else in Jamaica, survival was a matter for forethought, of prudence, of discipline, of endurance, of hard work. That has put its stamp upon the people even in these days of sometimes piped water supplies, though almost all householders still depend upon their water tanks. Southern St. Elizabeth farmers are still, by a long shot, the best farmers in Jamaica. A young man or woman from St. Elizabeth, especially from "South" is still the dream of many an employer anywhere from Savanna-la-mar to Morant Bay by whichever route. They are disciplined, hard-working and generally honest. Who wouldn't want to live amongst such people?

At Christmastime and other public holidays or when someone decides to hold a public dance (strangely enough usually on Sunday nights) sound systems come from outside to blare the latest dance hall music. The three most popular dance spots up this way are at "Pipers", "Mass Coolie" and "Ray Charles", which are the names of their proprietors. But, unlike other places I know, even when the boogieing goes on from dusk to dawn, the music does not obtrude; probably because of the beneficient hill that so fortunately stands between our house and the town.

I am not afraid to walk alone up and down the crooked hill and gully roads for I am pretty certain that that person coming towards me, even though I might never have seen his face before, is going about his own business and will not disturb or harm me. In the style of the country, we greet each other as we pass or we might stop a while to chat about the weather, who's sick or dead, (people will attend a "set up" or "wake" even if they are not personally acquainted with the deceased so long as it is being held in the area) who's getting married, who is moving in or out of the town, the price of things, happenings in other places, send our regards to families and friends, and then move on. Good manners count for a lot in these parts and country people seem always to have time for each other.

I feel reasonably secure here. That's really what I like best of all about this place.

ORIGINALLY PUBLISHED SEPTEMBER 1991

All Aboard

CAROL RECKORD

You can travel by air from Kingston to Montego Bay any day of the week in thirty-five or forty minutes! And ordinarily, its no more than three and a half or four hours by pretty good road with some attractive towns and villages along the way!

But with two friends visiting from the eastern Caribbean—and with a long weekend ahead—it seemed to be a good idea to make an early start and spend a leisurely six or seven hours looking at Jamaica's back yards and back gardens and back pastures all the way to Montego Bay. This must be one of the nicest things about railways—they allow you to look over the back fence into the part of the yard where people are relaxed and where all the action is. Whether it is a yard full of people gossiping, cooking, washing...or a brickyard, factory yard, church yard...the railway always manages to give its passengers a ringside seat at the back fence.

Our long weekend was thanks to a public holiday which meant that the Kingston ticket office was doing good business. Fifty Jamaican dollars bought us three one-way tickets. We took another look at the crowd and got cold feet: "Could we get first class tickets, please?" The ticket seller seemed doubtful. We played safe and took the second class tickets. Then, into the line and aboard the train, marching in very close order with many bags, baskets and assorted boxes—and with a somewhat noisy, very good-humoured Jamaican crowd.

As we say in Jamaica, "Every clock minds his own business". Nobody really expects the train to leave at six-fifty a.m. as the crisp railway office lady had promised. But what's half-an-hour between friends?

Even before we left the Kingston station, it became clear that this train on this Saturday morning was not the time nor the place to settle down with a good book. Jamaica's railway coaches are long open affairs with an open door at each end—and a great deal of movement back and forth.

Early in the journey, the train conductor and his assistants did their tour back and forth. The people selling Red Stripe beer and soft drinks were doing business. Our little group—and many other little groups—approved of this. Equally interesting was the appearance of a smiling, plump lady with a big pudding pan—a prince among pudding pans—with a clean white cloth covering up the mysteries underneath. But not for long. Someone beckoned, the lady lowered her pudding pan to rest one side lightly on my shoulder... and lifted the cloth to show her cargo of golden fried fish, blessing our part of the coach with heavenly fragrance. After all, it was breakfast time.

Our train made its short stops at Gregory Park and Grange Lane, both with wooden station buildings constructed in the colonial railway architectural style—remember the movies of the Indian north-west frontier and the Australian outback?

Spanish Town was the first big, busy station yard with a jumble of sheds and small buildings strung out along a couple of hundred yards of track. Sitting in the middle of a large plain where sugar has been grown for hundreds of years, Spanish Town has had a long business partnership with the railway. In fact, Jamaica's rail system depends (as probably do most railways) on commodity haulage—first sugar, then bananas, cattle and, more recently, bauxite and alumina.

If you want to meditate on the changes in farm activity over the past few generations, the level countryside along the railway after Spanish Town is a good place. Hartlands station, where cow's milk in twenty-gallon churns used to be loaded on train for Kingston milk shops every morning. Next is Bushy Park—sugar cane and pasture are giving way to vegetables and ornamentals and (of course) to hundreds of houses where city workers live. Old Harbour is not really a seaport—but the sea is only a few miles down the road.

So we leave Old Harbour, which is the mother and the father of fried-fish selling places in Jamaica and, still in fairly flat country, stop briefly at Inverness siding on our way to May Pen. At Inverness we have come into country which seems to have been taken over by herds of goats; their resourceful owners also make a living by selling charcoal, some honey and thatch palm poles which are slender and straight and very useful as rafters for houses.

This dry, rocky part of the parish of Clarendon was for many generations home to the sisal industry. Along the railway line between Inverness and May Pen, the now-closed Hunt's Pen Cordage factory was owned and run from the 1920s by an enterprising and ingenious Britisher named Addison Lankester.

Thirty-five miles (56 km.) from Kingston, May Pen is an excellent example of a bustling, independent country town. It is the industrial and commercial centre of the prosperous parish of Clarendon, whose hill farmers are successful growers of oranges and yams, tobacco and potatoes, plantains, pumpkins and all sorts of fruit, vegetables and other farm products.

South of May Pen, the vast plains which used to be the parish of Vere are one of the main sugar cane areas of the Island. From time to time, the irrigated and level land of Vere, which typically is owned in large parcels, has attracted crops such as bananas, citrus, and winter vegetables. A few of the projects have done well, some have collapsed—but wherever there is a spread of level land, there will be someone ready to gamble on it.

It took the Kingston crowd a little while to settle down comfortably in their seats. So it must have been somewhere just before (or just after) Spanish Town that the stage was properly set and our first preacher took up his position about two feet from my left ear. The gentleman, in a "full suit of blue", began by reminding us of the 1957 train disaster and its casualties. It didn't seem to be a sporting thing to do to a very captive audience, I thought.

All in all, his message wasn't at all cheerful and we weren't sorry to see him go. By the time he left we were feeling the effect of upholstered seats but it was good to have full leg room and ample seat width.

The variety of vendors' displays began to build up. Spanish Town seemed to contribute a whole platoon of sellers—bangles and watches sno-cones, more fried fish, biscuits and beer. At each station there was fresh fruit and plenty of bammies. But... would anyone really buy a watch from a man on a train? It depends on how much money ... and how many beers you're carrying, doesn't it?

When four large suitcases appeared at one station somewhere along the line, no-one needed to ask what was going on. All Jamaica is now familiar with the signs of the traders—that group of enterprising women (there's hardly a man among them) who fly to Port-au-Prince, Miami, Curacao, Cayman and Panama to buy and bring back goods of plastic, paper and every material under the sun for Jamaicans to wear, use and enjoy. The suitcases blocked a doorway for an hour or so—with their owner never straying far; then they disappeared as suddenly as they had come.

The Montego Bay line travels nearly half of its length without passing the 500-foot contour. Then, at Clarendon Park it begins the slow climb into the hills of central Jamaica. We were now invading the bauxite country—limestone hills with seams and pockets of red earth. The red is, in fact, iron oxides—but the richness is aluminium ore, bauxite. In the old days the chugging and puffing steam locomotive would be joined in tandem by one of its mates. The two would take the laden train over the steepest part of the track—with much hissing and clanking as air-brakes were applied on the downhill sections. With diesel-electric locomotives nowadays, there seems to be less drama—but to the railway enthusiast there's nothing to compare to the clackety-clack of rail travel, especially in hill country where the track makes its graceful sweep around curves while carefully climbing the gradient.

By this we had entertained a second and a third preacher—both with more of cheer and promise than the first. Each gave his message, led a hymn or two—and took up a modest collection before passing on. Most of the hymns were familiar, some were gems of the Moody and Sankey vintage. The passengers clearly had their favourites, in which they joined with energy and generally with harmony. A good time was had by all.

Between May Pen and Montego Bay, the stations are all modest and rustic. Even Williamsfield, which serves the town of Mandeville and its thriving neighbouring villages and towns, manages to hide its light under a bushel—in the way of sober, respectable (and prosperous) country folk.

The up-hill work continued through Williamsfield and Kendal, past some great pasture-land at Grove Place, where the government has a livestock research station with some impressive Jamaica Red cattle. Here and there the train stopped at a siding to disembark a passenger or two... we passed Mile Gully, Comfort Hall, Balaclava. At Greenvale, just before Balaclava, the sign said SUMMIT, Montego Bay Line, 1705 feet above sea level. Here, too, we crossed with the Kingston-bound train; some of our vendors and preachers deserted us for the city-bound crowd.

After Balaclava we were back into sugar-cane country with the sugar factory at Appleton sitting right on the track. By this time the crowd had thinned to a more comfortable—and less sober—number. The down-hill ride offered a chance to make up lost time—and we clanked our merry way through Maggoty, Ipswich, Catadupa and looked at some pretty wild country to the right. Over there the famous Cockpit Country with its strange topography of rounded hills and eroded limestone valleys—Karst country, the geologists call it—seemed to invite exploration. The Cockpit country is especially striking from the air, with its solid vegetation and very few houses and only occasional tracks.

This was the tidying-up stage of our journey—packing away and hair-brushing time and empty-bottle collecting time. For me it was treat time—because our last preacher, who came aboard somewhere near Cambridge, was a cheerful body with a good voice and a wonderful stock of old Sankey hymns. It was a joy to join with many voices in the beautiful, vigorous old tune:

He's the lily of the valley,
the bright and morning star
He's the fairest of ten thousand
in my soul

So we rattled through Cambridge, Montpelier, Anchovy...into Montego Bay station—still singing and humming the old songs. We were saddle sore and hours late and ready to do it again.

ORIGINALLY PUBLISHED APRIL 1988

Kingdom of Green

PETER ABRAHAMS

We are hill people, my wife and I and we have been all our lives.

My earliest and most persistent memories are of the green hills of Africa going away, one after the other, each higher than the one before, as far as the eye could see and beyond into the haze of distance. And for her it is the towering green volcanic mountains of Java among which she spent her formative years. So it was natural that when we came to rest finally, to put down roots and to rear a family, it should be in the hills; and because of our nature and our needs it had to be the hills of St. Andrew in Jamaica, physically as far away from Africa as from Java, yet very reminiscent for each of us of those other faraway hill countries. She grew up eating a succulent-tasting but foul-smelling fruit (when fully ripe) called durian; she met it here half a lifetime later in the shape of the Jamaican jack fruit, and at once the gap of oceans and cultures and time was bridged.

Today, and for the last two weeks, on and off, we have had a high whistling wind coming in across the sea from the south. It reminds me of the Mistral which I encountered many years ago in French Mediterranean hill country; it is also reminiscent of the Harmattan of West Africa, though much gentler on the skin and not as dry. One feels exhilarated watching the John Crows riding the high wind. Suddenly they are the most beautifully graceful creatures in the world; and the most free while riding the wind. It comes as a surprise to find, on going down to the plains, that the wind has passed so high over the city that the people there are hardly aware of it. You have to be somewhere above a thousand feet to begin to feel the wind, we are more than two thousand feet up and on the crest of a hill and with no windbreaker between us and the sea. So we feel it strongly. Behind us are even higher hills and the people who live there feel the force of the wind even more strongly. The land here rises steeply so that less than a mile away from us, as the crow flies, the altitude is 3,300 feet. The road between our hill—and the ones behind that rise to more than 300 feet—is not far off a thousand feet below us, which should give some idea of how steeply the land rises and falls here. Yet because these hills, the Red Hills, are old ones, the rise and fall of the land is not the steepest in the island. In the Blue Mountains which are geologically newer the rise and fall of the land is much steeper. And because of the very high hills and the very deep valleys there are times of the year when you wake up in the morning to look down onto cloud-covered valleys, or when you have to travel through a thick evening fog that reminds one of cold industrial countries; but this is a cleaner,

I have watched this washing away of the good earth during the rainy season when the rivers leading into the sea are swollen with life-giving earth and it has made me despair over the unwisdom of man.

less damaging fog, than the fogs I have known in cold industrial countries. And in the winter, around Christmas time, it can get very cold in these hills; and the higher you go, the colder it can be. So it is not strange, or pretentious, to find, in the hills, homes with fireplaces. But more than anything else, in good weather or bad, whether the wind is high or the air is still, there is the pervasive comforting green of the hills interspersed here and there by riots of colour as when the delicate petals of the yellow poui fall and transform a patch of earth into a joy forever, or as when the ginger lilies and wild orchids and the wild pines are in full bloom. There is the fragrance too, of mango time, of when the citrus are in bloom and the bees and the birds keep up their delightful din from daylight to darkness. Living in these surrounds, whether we appreciate them consciously or whether we take them for granted, does influence the lifestyle of the hill folk and how they look at the world about them.

They are, on the whole, a proud and independent people; they are resilient and clear-eyed realists. The African strain is strong in them, stronger than it is with the folk down on the plains—that is apart from Spanish Town which has always struck me as the most African town in all Jamaica. But no matter how strong the African strain they are distinctively Jamaican, a people unto themselves, bound together by generation of shared living and working in these hills. They all speak the same language which some people call English and others call Jamaican; whatever you call it, it is a kind of free enriched language that does many things that standard English cannot and that is spoken with the kind of lilt you find when Welshmen speak English.

When slavery was ended and the apprenticeship system was brought in and proved largely unsatisfactory, the ancestors of today's hill folk withdrew in large numbers from the life on the plains and created for themselves self-contained and self-sustaining communities in the hills and grew their own food on the hillsides or in the fertile valleys between the high hills. In time they carried food down to the plain to sell in order to earn money to pay the hated taxes or to buy the few things they need from the city. In time, too, and in increasing numbers, the young people refused to remain on the land and work it with their parents. Instead as soon as they could, they joined other young people from all over the island in the drift down to the plains and the city and the bright lights. The result is that today the Jamaican small farmer and the man who works the hillside land in particular is rarely under thirty. More often he is in his forties and fifties.

But we have noticed an interesting new development in the past few years. We have been in our particular little hill community for something like eighteen years now. In that time we have watched many youngsters go to the local village school till they were fifteen and then disappear from the community. Whenever we enquired after these youngsters, parents would tell us they had "Gan a town" Recently, some of these youngsters now grown into young men and women have started returning, often with a partner and a child or two, to their hillside communities. It is a very small heartening sign because unless some of the young people come back we will not have people to work the land when the present generation of small farmers pass from the scene; and if we do not work the land and work so efficiently as to feed our growing population then all the progress we may make in other fields will be reduced to nothing. So the return of at least some of the young people to the hills after they have had their fill of the bright lights of the city is very important. The people who now handle the country's affairs have shown themselves aware of this. They talk and plan now of making small farming a reasonably profitable undertaking, which is what it has not been for the older generation of hill folk. They have begun to offer small farmers guaranteed outlets and guaranteed prices for their crops. They plan, too, to take piped water and electricity to all the villages throughout the country. When these things are done, when electricity will bring the blessings and the curses of radio and television within the reach of each rural hillside home, and when the members of the household will only have to turn a tap to have all the water they need for washing and cooking and watering their crops in dry times, and when these crops bring them enough money to pay for all this and then leave something over for the luxuries that enrich life, only then, it seems to me, will our leaders have any moral right to call on the young people to return to the hills and undertake the backbreaking task of making them what they naturally and logically are and should be which is this island's food basket. To do this we will also have to do a considerable amount of rehabilitation work on our hillside land. The older generation of small farmers have traditionally cleared land by burning it. This is by far the quickest and easiest way to clear difficult terrain of thorny bush. And after the burning you usually get a good first crop of corn or yam or cabbage or pumpkin. The trouble is that when the rain comes, it is torrential and comes very fast down these steep hillsides, and it usually carries all the topsoil away and down to the sea. I have watched this washing away of the good earth during the rainy season when the rivers leading into the sea are swollen with life-giving earth and it has made me despair over the unwisdom of man. We must at the very least arrest this annual erosion of the good Jamaican earth if the hills are to sustain the people of this land. A handful of people are committed to this important job but thus far political considerations have stood in the way of an outright and total prohibition of this destruction of the Jamaican earth through fire by good men who know no better. We must hope that these people who now handle the nation's affairs will see the urgency of this problem and will put a stop to the firing of the land. If the green hills are allowed to turn brown and wither and become barren rock all Jamaica will suffer grievously. There is no need for this. We need the hills for more than just food, though that is crucial. We need the hills for the sturdy breed of balanced human beings they have bred who have had so much to do with this country's stability; and we need them because they help men to be tranquil and at peace in a troubled world.

ORIGINALLY PUBLISHED SEPTEMBER 1972

Christmas Breeze, Mangoes and Moonlight

HILARY SHERLOCK

Like Christmas Breeze it seems to happen suddenly. All at once the lignum vitae trees are covered with smokey, blue blossoms and dancing yellow butterflies. Frail poui trees drop their leaves, showering themselves and the earth below with yellow. Later in the year the poinciana gives us her gift of scarlet, orange or crimson flowers.

Our seasons are subtle, sensual and often highly personal. I have such a distinct memory of a special little girl I knew. Kathy was very smart though her ability to move was restricted by brain injuries. Her mother told me of Kathy's answer to a question on a North American I.Q. Test. Asked to name the four seasons of the year Kathy responded—"Plum, Mango, Guinep and Pear." Incorrect, according to the test, but so true to her and our experience as Caribbean people.

For me the seasons are defined by flowering trees and plants, accompanied by changes in the texture in the air. For others it may be what food or fruit is "coming in"—a longing for breadfruit and pear—what fish are running—have the crabs begun to walk, where are sugar pine and sweet yam. We may greet the seasons with differing emotions as Olive Senior paints in her poem, *Birdshooting Season*:

"We stand quietly on the doorstep shivering. Little boys longing to grow up birdhunters too. Little girls whispering: Fly Birds Fly."

We are not restricted by seasons harshly delineated by weather. Our dry season may often turn out to be wet, in another year it may not rain during the traditional wet season. Every summer is sighed over as "the hottest I can remember." A definite sign that an earthquake must be on the way, immediately. If it arrives three months later we all remember the prophecies and claim them fervently with the familiar—'Me no tell yu so!'

Many farmers still plan their planting cycle by an almanac which is based on the cycles of the moon. The suitable time of the moon governs when the planting is to take place depending on whether the expected crop is to bear above or below the ground. Hopefully our children will know that naseberries and otaheite apples are bearing, not only because they see them being sold in plastic bags along the roadside. That would be to miss the anticipation and joy of seeing the flowering and subsequent growth of the fruit—to guess how many days until the fruit are fit or turn, a very technical difference, to drive or walk over the carpet of pinky red blossoms shed by the otaheite apple trees.

Traditional gardens were planned with seasons in mind, no instant blooming hybrid's answering a sudden call for colour. Several of our plants and trees originally came from abroad and were distributed by keen gardeners and owners of small and large properties. After all, one cannot nurture a garden or a friendship without sharing. Thus, the historian Douglas Hall documents the 18th century activities of Mr. Thistlewood, "a small settler in Western Jamaica."

"The sources of Mr. Thistlewood's supplies are interesting because they indicate his activities as an importer, and illustrate the horticultural interests of local people—estate-owner, settlers and slaves."

Among our best loved trees the yellow poui came from South America, poinciana from Madagascar, mangoes and cassia fistula (showers of gold) from tropical Asia. It would be hard to imagine our islands without these imports.

Given the rampant road rage encountered in Kingston traffic today, I often give thanks to the gardeners of earlier times. How wonderful to turn a corner and be calmed by the lushly flowering bougainvillaea seeming to specially love the Liguanea Plains, returning vibrant colours for neglect, even in a year of drought. When the lignum vitae is in bloom I have a friend who plans her route so that she passes as many of these trees as possible. They remind her of her father, his love for these trees, shared with his love for his family, friends, his home and his garden. For me the yellow poui is very special, blooming around my birthday.

So when we are hushed, let us give thanks for the gardeners of earlier times who like those of today often absorbed their love and respect for other living things from their parents. They join Amy Webster in her classic *Caribbean Gardening* who attributed her love of gardening to her own parents:

"...as soon as my hands could hold a thimblefull of earth and carry a small can of water, my parents made me the slave of flowers" (her mother watered hers)... "In the mornings before daylight... they are still asleep and won't even know they were touched. Father, whose devotion was to flowering trees, many of which he imported from distant lands, used to say that the correct time for gardening is evening. He explained: plants then have the cool of night in which to settle down."

And so like Kathy let us rejoice in our seasons and enjoy them with our beloved Miss Lou (The Hon. Louise Bennett-Coverley, OJ) in her celebration of mangoes, moonlight and love from her poem *Moon an Mango*:

"...Mary me dear, me free from care
Me head an heart is light
For now is mango season an
Tonight is moonlight night.

An everytime a mango drop,
an as me teck a bite,
Me mine just run pon yuh an all
Dem long-time moonlight night.

What more a man can waan fi eat?
What else him waan fi do?
De ongle ting a waan, me likle
Booloolooops, is yuh!"

ORIGINALLY PUBLISHED AUGUST 1999

Remembering Old England
A Scene from the Past

DONETTE ZACCA

It's beautiful to capture a natural and remarkable scene from one's surrounding with little interference from an observer.

I shot this photograph in Lime Tree Garden, St. Ann over eight years ago. The scene was at a friend's funeral and I stood outside the church and observed the people.

As I watched the older men walking across the church lawn, I became struck by the visual similarity of the men. Their attire and mannerisms had been inherited from the many years spent in England. It was evident to me that these men had shared the same past and were present to say farewell to a friend.

This was a special moment to capture because the men represented an era that was gone but remained through memories and years of shared friendship. These were the men who worked on the garbage trucks, buses, factories and railroads in England to improve the lives of their families residing in Jamaica.

It's beautiful to capture a natural and remarkable scene from one's surrounding with little interference from an observer. The magic lies in the peace and serenity that this images exudes. Quiet and strong.

ORIGINALLY PUBLISHED JUNE 2001

The Middleman

DONETTE ZACCA

In busy downtown Kingston where sidewalks overflow with pedestrians, Harold Woodrow Willacey has set up his moveable shop. Says photographer Donnette Zacca, "A friend and I happened to be downtown one Saturday morning taking photos of various activities. It was then that I noticed a little man, white shirt, neck-tie and a hat with a small table supporting a small typewriter—his tiny hands moved quickly along the keys. Resumes, applications, letters of all kinds he types, making his living along the sidewalk of constant hustle and bustle."

Born in 1927 in Manchester, Jamaica, Mr. Willacey recalls that he learnt typing at school. After serving in the Royal Air Force during World War II, he sustained an injury while working in a factory in England and was forced to return home to Jamaica. He then started typing in the streets of Kingston, putting families in touch with each other, helping people apply for jobs, playing the role of a middleman of sorts.

One of his fondest childhood memories is of delivering a letter from his headmaster to Jamaican national hero Marcus Garvey. Mr. Willacey recalls, "I was accompanied by another student named Jack Daniels. We caught the bus to Franklin Town (it cost a penny from downtown). We then proceeded to Liberty Hall where I handed the letter to the gentleman who said, "You boys had any lunch yet?" I can't remember what Jack said to him, but he sat us down at a table and went to the pot and served us a pepperpot dinner. I didn't do so well with my dinner as there was too much pepper in it."

Mr. Willacey also remembers the Coronation of King George VI as, "...the most spectacular thing—I remember all the children were given sweetie pans with the picture of the king and queen painted on them, a serving of lemonade and some bun."

While the Kingston of these memories no longer exists, Harold Willacey remains very much a part of the cityscape.

ORIGINALLY PUBLISHED JUNE 2002

A Debt Remembered

ANTHONY GAMBRILL

A little over a year ago a tall, proud Jamaican farmer by the name of Aston Auther Caballero was buried at The Church of God in Jamaica at Lucky Valley, in the parish of Clarendon. His family, friends and community honoured him in song and speech in a long and emotional church service. But probably missed in the nostalgic recollections was the fact that as a young boy he grew up with his grandfather Abraham, a Cuban exile from his homeland's first war of independence and one of a generation of Cuban tobacco farmers who helped launch the Jamaican tradition of fine cigar-making.

Tobacco had been cultivated in the Caribbean by Taino Indians long before Christopher Columbus arrived. Ingested by inhaling it either smoking it through hollow canes or in the form of snuff, tobacco was believed by the Tainos to have supernatural powers to the extent that it was used in religious rites.

This domestic strain of tobacco, aided probably by the occasional introduction of seed from other tobacco-growing regions, was used for smoking well into the nineteenth century. Known often as "jackass rope", coiled as it was in rope-like lengths, common Jamaican tobacco was harsh on the palate to say the least. It wasn't until Cubans introduced tobacco seed of a vastly superior quality and sophisticated growing, harvesting and processing techniques that a Jamaican cigar industry become a possibility.

As elsewhere in the Caribbean Cuban land owners had concentrated on sugar until the nineteenth century, discouraged by the fact that making tobacco products was a Spanish crown monopoly. Fortunately areas like Vuelta Abajo in Pinar de Rio province and Vuelta Arriba in Camaguey were ideal for tobacco but not sugar. By mid-century Cuba was literally world-renowned for its luxurious Havana cigars.

Whilst sugar maintained a largely rural and capital intensive character, employing slaves and a limited number of artisans and managers, tobacco provided the opportunity for the establishment of small and, increasingly, medium-sized manufacturing enterprises employing an evolving urban middle class.

Service of Thanksgiving
for the life of
Aston Auther Caballero
(Comrade)
(April 19, 1914 – November 30, 1998)
Service at
THE CHURCH OF GOD IN JAMAICA
Lucky Valley, Clarendon
on
WEDNESDAY, DECEMBER 9, 1998
at 11:00 a.m.

The specialized, painstaking and delicate work demanded in cigar-making required skilled workmanship. To relieve the monotony reading "lectores" were introduced into the workplace.

Inevitably the outcome of this component of cigar factory life was to improve the workers' literacy and increase their level of political consciousness. Later the Cuban patriot Jose Marti was to describe the lectores as "an advanced pulpit of liberty."

However the restrictive practices put by Spain on its Caribbean colony created an unmanageable burden on the Cuban economy, including the fledging tobacco industry.

In the 25 years between 1862 and 1887 the number of tobacco farms in Cuba fell from 11,550 to only 4,515 as a result of economic depression, and later, the ravages of war. Many who were active in the separatist movement as well as those sympathetic to the cause were to lose their property through expropriation.

The 1868-1878 Ten Year War of Independence, "La Guerra Grande", is well-documented in Cuban historiography. Although it represented the longest sustained struggle for independence, the Ten Year War never moved beyond being a provincial undertaking with the rebels successfully occupying little more than the eastern third of the island.

During this turbulent decade thousands left Cuba to escape the social upheaval and devastation that was imposed on the land. Whilst many who fled to Jamaica were awaiting the outcome of the rebellion, some became settlers and a large number passed through on their way to the United States and Latin America.

How many Cubans ultimately emigrated to Jamaica and how many settled is yet to be conclusively determined. The governor of Jamaica, Sir Peter John Grant, in 1872 estimated the number to be approximately 1500.

The influx of exiles began at least four years earlier when the *Gleaner* newspaper reported the arrival of the steamer Tampico from Santiago de Cuba "with upwards of 100 men and women, among the ladies and gentlemen, who are fleeing to a place of safety…" As the months and years passed the refugees, from wealthy white creoles and penniless middle class families to black field hands, kept flooding in.

Dr. James Phillippo, in a letter to the *Gleaner* on May 6, 1872, praised the Cubans for their hard work and determination to survive: "On a recent visit to Spanish Town, I saw no less than seven or eight small tobacco plantations, on some of which the planters and their families had built thatched huts in which they are content to reside until better days come."

Over a period the Cubans found the most suitable areas to farm tobacco with their rich loamy soil, ample rainfall and humidity and sufficient sunlight. These included Temple Hall on the banks of the Wag Water River north of Kingston, Colbeck on the St. Catherine plain, the Rio Minho and its tributaries which reach deep into the hills of Clarendon and lands in St. Thomas adjacent to the Plantain, Yallahs and Morant rivers.

The most rewarding of these tobacco-growing areas was the Rio Minho. It was here that Abraham Caballero farmed. He married the daughter of the owner of Lucky Valley where he lived until he died in 1925.

The area included Morant said to be capable of producing a much-prized tobacco wrapper, the districts of Fattening Pastures and Best Well, as well as Woodleigh where Robert Gore still grows tobacco for his May Pen factory, home of the famous Royal Jamaican cigar.

The decade of the 1870s saw Cubans gradually begin to enjoy success as both growers, cigar manufacturers and purveyors.

One of the earliest Cuban settlers, Don Juan Miguel Palomino, brought seedlings to start a new life and begin a dynasty that is still making cigars in Jamaica today. Another legendary name was Machado, farmers and cigar-makers who eventually built a business large enough to sell to Britain's giant British-American Tobacco Company.

The Caballero family are still familiar members of the community largely around the May Pen area. This writer had the privilege of visiting Aston Caballero in his home close to the Pindar's River where life is still guided by old-fashion values and nature's bounty makes it that much more worth living.

ORIGINALLY PUBLISHED FEBRUARY 2000

SUNDAY STROLL

BLACK RIVER SUNSET

MARGARITAVILLE

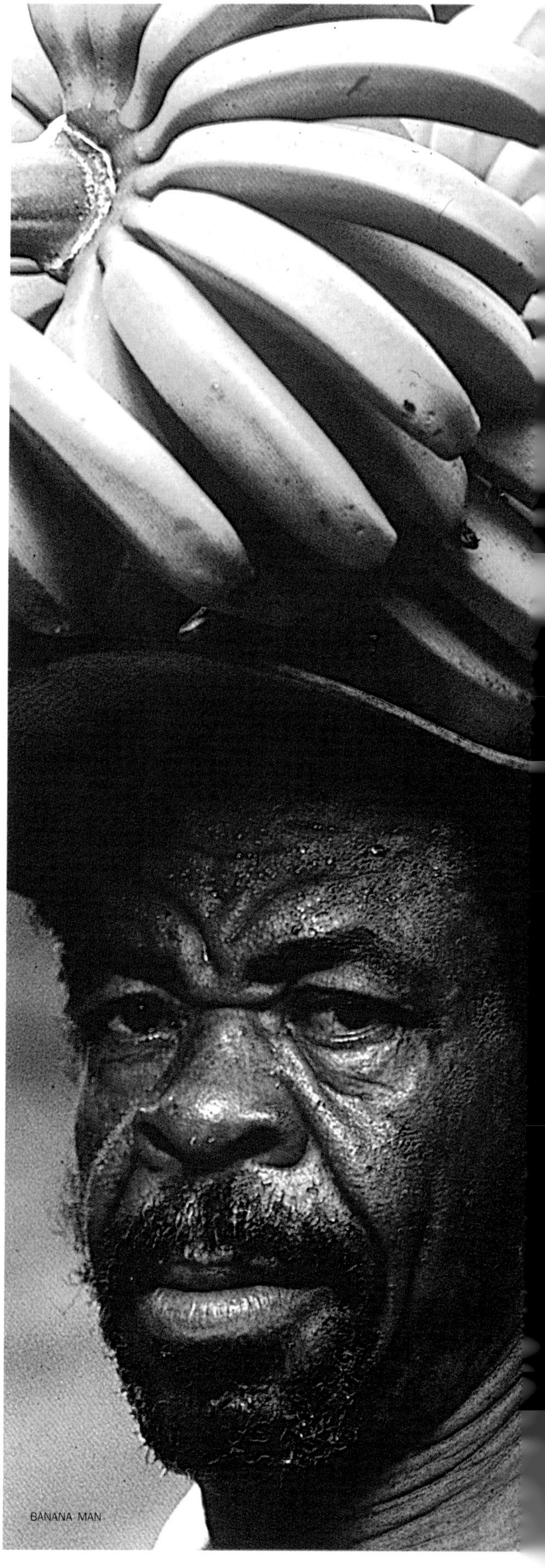

BANANA MAN

Cow Foot For Lunch?

IAN CUMMING

RAFTER'S REST

With a map, camera and spirit of adventure a young lad journeys Jamaica.

Being a fresh faced Brit straight off the airplane it seemed a strange offer, but being able to understand one word in ten of the Jamaican accent, I decided cold food for lunch didn't seem utterly ridiculous.

This was the start of a nine week photographic journey around Jamaica. When there is snow on the ground in London, it doesn't require a great deal of will-power to head for the Caribbean, not unless you have a passion for being cold and wet.

Two months and 150 rolls of film later and my time is up. Although I have looped the country I feel as if there is much more to be covered (an excuse to come back?). Jamaica may be relatively small compared to Britain or the States, but in nine weeks I feel as if I have only scraped the surface. I could keep going round and round this stunning country each time bumping into different people, seeing different sights and maybe just maybe, I will be able to tell the difference between "cold food" and "cow foot."

ORIGINALLY PUBLISHED OCTOBER 1996

PHOTOGRAPHY ©IAN CUMMING

THE LOVE BOATS

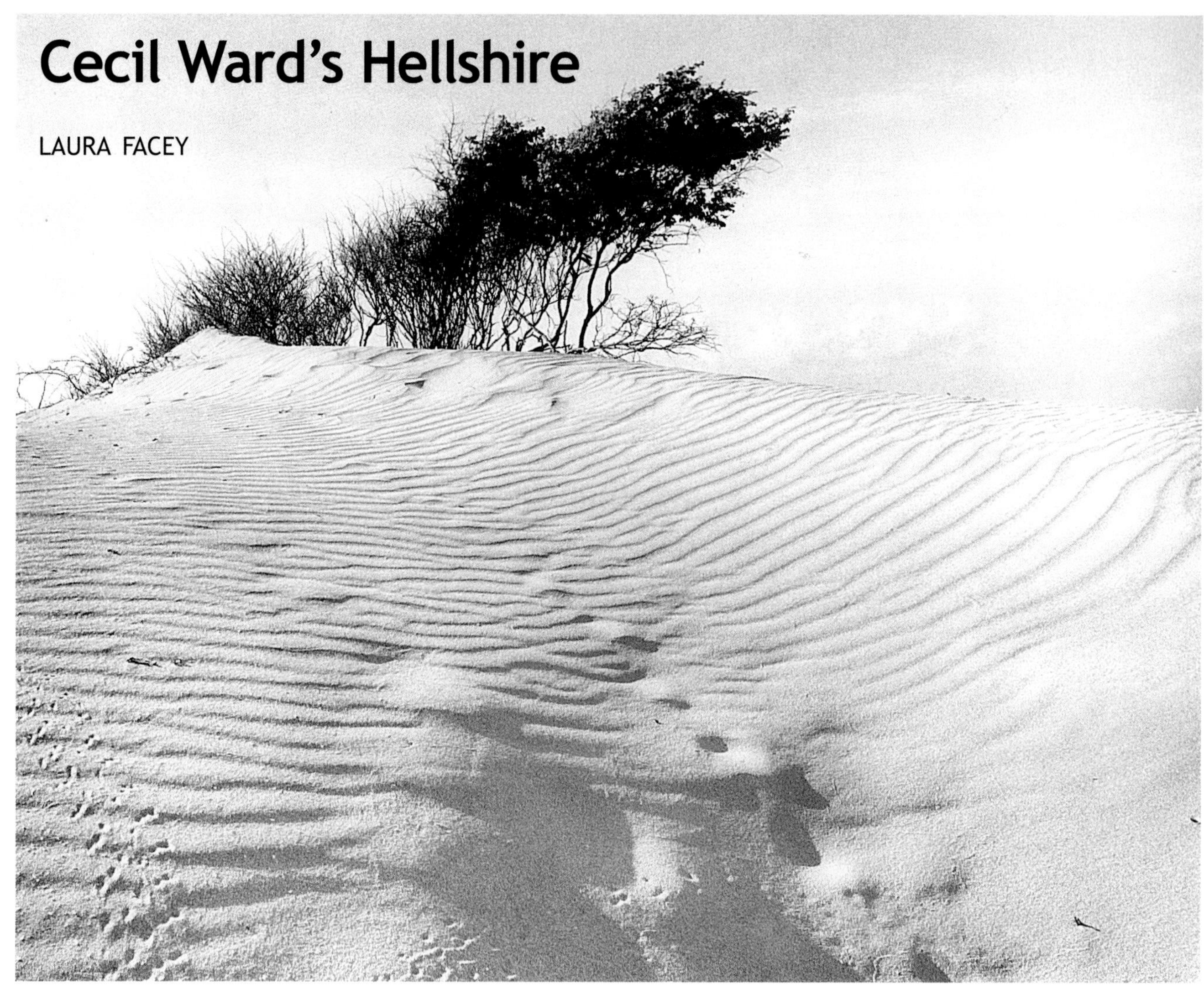

Cecil Ward's Hellshire

LAURA FACEY

The wind blows me all over the land. I can hear the sea not far away.

And once I saw a fisherman when the sun was already high in the sky. He wore a hat for fear he would get "dark eyes" from the blinding sun. I knew he was as old as the sea and that the waves had taught him quiet patience.

And then I visited old house point. The old man still lived there. I drifted through his cool home, brushing the many textures that made up his world. In every nook a found object lay waiting for its day of purpose.

And so I turned to the drying landscape where the surface of the salina had responded to the sun, where it had dried her, pushing apart the marsh into a maze of thousands of pieces.

Without a sound I moved to where mangrove stumps stood. I watched their shadows awhile then went towards distant trees. There as before I found the creek. Sunlight still played on fallen leaves and I felt my soul tangle as it followed roots of the mangroves.

ORIGINALLY PUBLISHED FEBRUARY 1987

Preserving the Fantasy of the Past

Robin Farquharson

As the sun rises beyond the hills, the mist slowly disappears. But in this sugar cane valley the pattern varies—some fields seem to hold the mist much longer it seems.

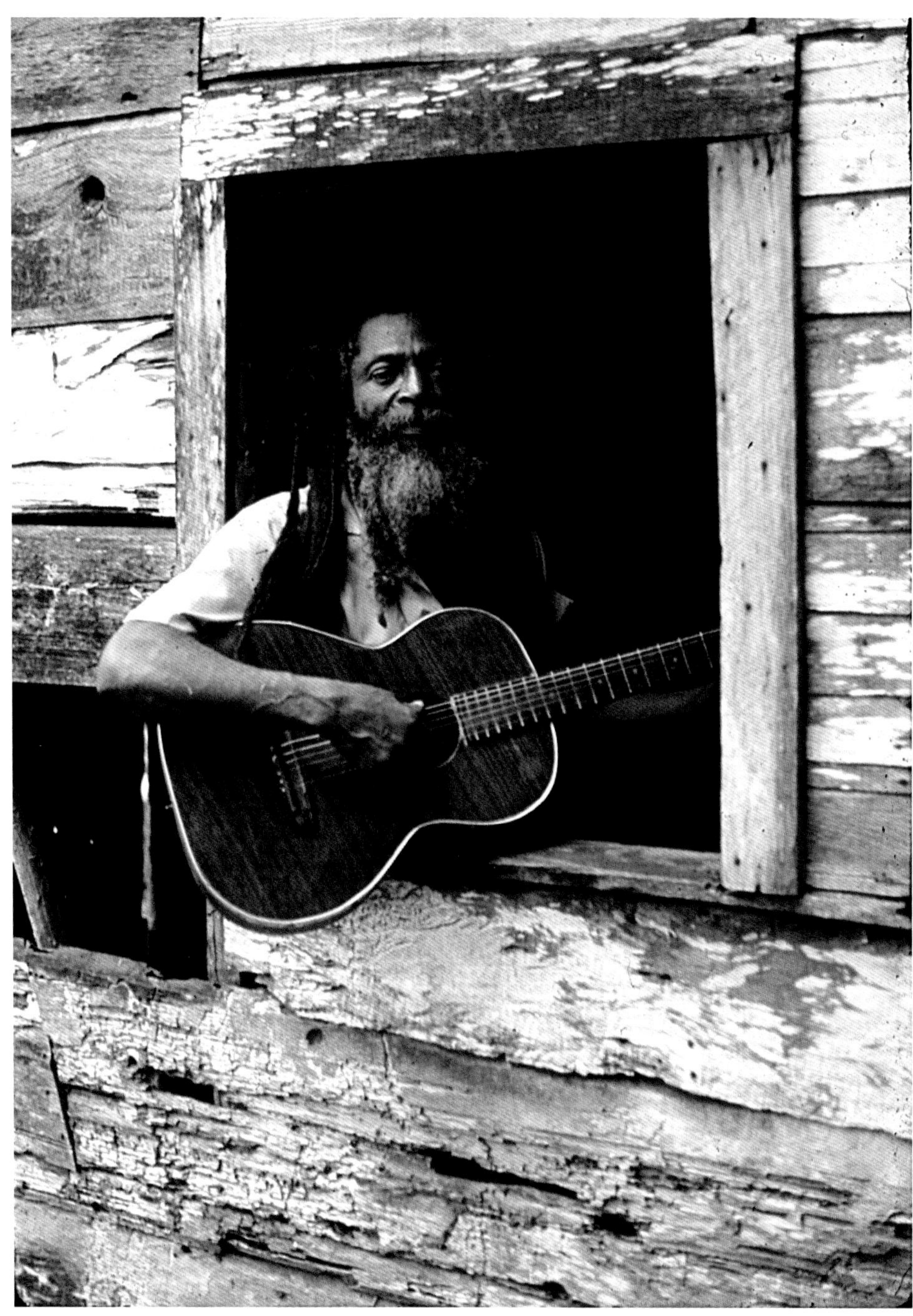

'True Heart,' a blind Rastafarian poses by a window of his house, and he sings to me about the robin and the stranger he welcomes to his house. Beside him a winding country road following the turns of an almost dry river.

The rainstorm was about to break, and the clouds hovered over this old mansion near the seafront at Black River, turning the afternoon into evening. For me this house holds a special fascination, this was the home of the doctor in attendance at my birth.

The night mist slowly sinks by, and the morning dawns fresh, just right for milking the cow.

Driving through St Elizabeth one late afternoon I saw Beatrice Palmer and others by their house, 'cotching' on the verandah rail, resting at the end of the day. She was happy to pose for me. I later learned she was a peanut farmer all her life.

On a bright, sunny day, a Chinese resident of Black River poses at the window of his second floor room. Below, the shop doors are closed, the sidewalk's bare—it's Sunday.

ORIGINALLY PUBLISHED APRIL 1978

Coming Home

NICOLA KELLY

This was one of those quintessential Jamaican moments—I knew it as I stood there, tears rolling down my cheeks, on that rocky hillside slap-bang in the middle of the island—moments that are not contrived, or planned, or rehearsed; they just happen all by themselves and they are real, so real, that they remain with you forever.

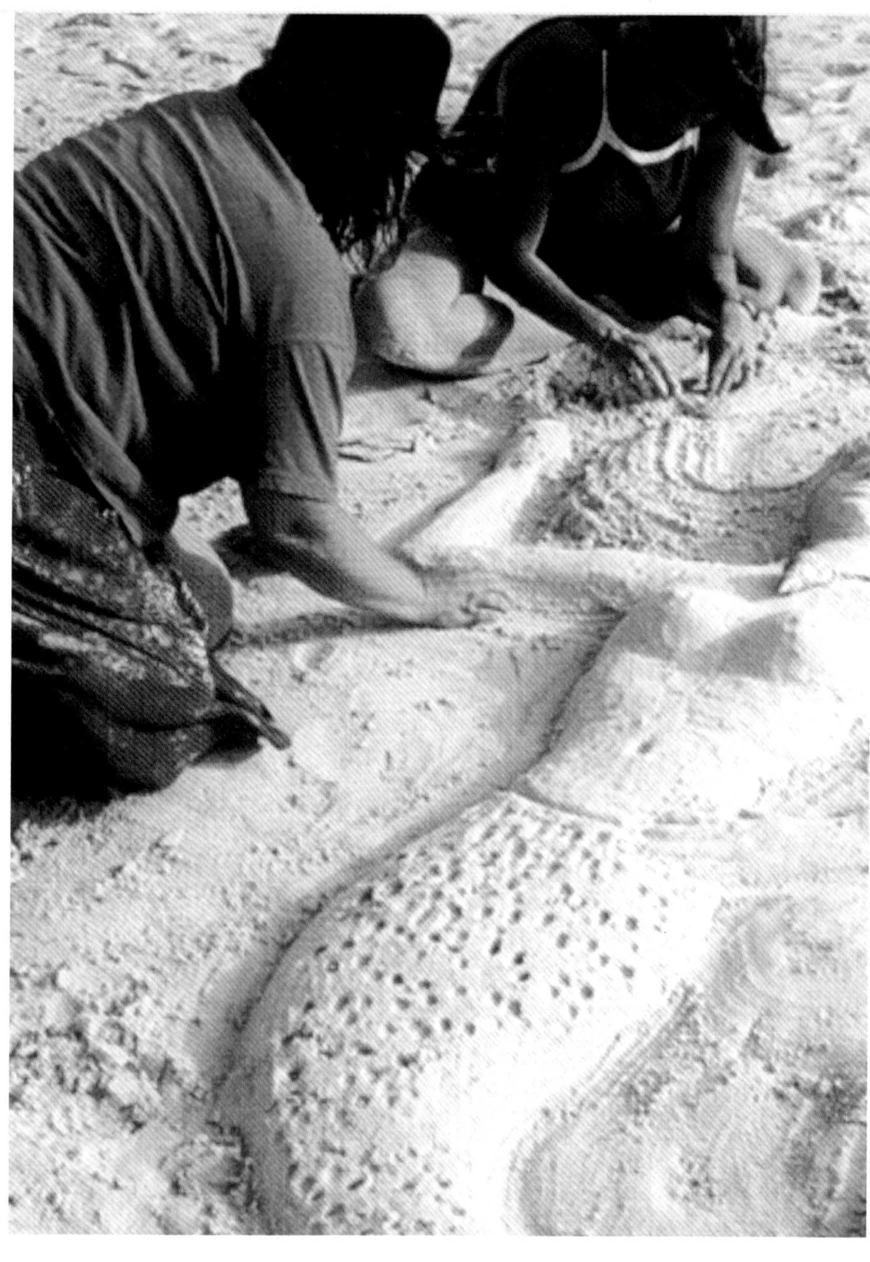

"Remember, man, that thou art dust, and unto dust you shall return"—intoned David Latty, farmer turned minister-of-the-moment, and so it was that we returned Don Pedro's ashes to the red dirt of his Clarendon hilltop. With a limestone outcrop and gangly guava standing sentinel, Uncle Pete can gaze in peace west and north over the green, bumpy Cockpit and south over the valleys of the Mocho Mountains. Cap in hand, machete by his side, Mr. Latty exhorted us in prayer and song as parakeets wheeled and screeched overhead in their final salutation. We found shade afterwards amongst the banana and coffee, quietly sipping our 'Stripe' and munching on patties, bun and mangoes, the woodsmoke from the small fire stinging our already teary eyes.

And there had been plenty of tears already. "Water come a mi eye" even before the plane wheels kissed MoBay's asphalt as first glimpses of the island appeared in the window..."and for those Jamaicans returning to the island—welcome home" said the purser.

Sniffle. We reach! We, in this case meaning me and twenty-three other siblings, cousins, our spouses and children, come to spend two weeks together at Silver Sands in Trelawny. All because I was turning forty and selfishly wanted all my 'brederin' around me, to celebrate our Jamaican childhood and heritage, to figure out whether we can fill the aching gaps left by our parents now all gone, to instill the stories, traditions and deep love of birthplace in our children, going forward in our lives but never letting Jamaica go.

So we're here and we're falling out of vans and cars and running into each others' arms and crying and laughing and shrieking all at the same time. Will we ever stop talking? There just isn't enough time.

The beach and clubhouse bar at Silver Sands becomes our daily meeting place. People come and go but the conversation rolls on. An early morning swim becomes a popular means to jump-starting the day, bobbing about for ages in the beautiful, blue, rejuvenating sea, swimming, body surfing or merely sorting out the problems of the world. The little ones delight in the waves, jumping into the pristine foam or scrunching their toes through the creamy-white talcum powder sand. Heaven. We disperse to our different villas for a substantial Jamaican breakfast—ackee and saltfish, rundown, green banana, johnny cakes, fresh fruit. What joy to suck on a Bombay mango seed and to taste bananas and pineapple that have not been ripened by some synthetic process. Back at my villa "Horizon", Alvin, our 'main man', has already brewed fresh Blue Mountain coffee, which we take outside on the verandah to peruse the *Gleaner* or gaze absently at the brilliantly-coloured hummingbirds and tiny lizards basking in the early morning sun.

Food, with its attendant tastes and smells, is a mainstay of nostalgia and we're lacking in neither! For us Jamaicans, stocking our villas is more of a treat than a chore as we enjoy seeking out the ingredients for favourite dishes in nearby Duncans. Our Jamaican patois re-emerges as we acquaint ourselves with local shopkeepers and marketwomen, amazed at prices expressed in hundreds of dollars and loving every minute as we "feel up, feel up" everything from avocado pears to otaheites. Seats in the cars for market day at Browns Town are hotly contested and menus for dinners for 30-plus people planned with great gusto. On one night "Jamahome" does stew peas, fish and bammy, "Hastings Place" serves up lobster with butter and lime after our long day in Cave Valley. Our villa welcomes everyone with fricassee chicken, rice 'n' peas, plantain and filet steak barbecued to perfection by Alvin accompanied by his delicious bammy. "Kelso" pulls out all the stops with a magnificent curry goat. To hell with diets as every favourite food from childhood is revisited—banana chips, icy mints, pink-on-top, broomstick, gizzadas—even Kisko pops.

Before the invasion of our Kingston relatives and friends for our Saturday night jump-up, the thirteen cousins and spouses retreat for a quiet, sentimental evening, sans enfants, to the nearby Good Hope Great House, an exquisite Georgian plantation home. Arriving close to sundown, we drink in the verdant beauty of the valley below—neat groves of pawpaw and waving sugarcane extending into the distance, ending only in the vastness of the Cockpit Country—a view probably little changed from the 17th century. Manager Blaise Hart, welcomes us, and before long we're sipping rum punches provided by Clint and Clifton who will look after us for the evening. We talk in low voices, soothed by the peace and tranquility settling in the gloaming around us. There is a great sense of familiarity as we wander through the house, sights and smells reminiscent of old places we'd stayed in as children—cedar floors, Berbice chairs, mahogany tables and sideboards, four-poster beds, crooked louvres. We love it. Dinner awaits on an outside terrace, our table arrayed with multi-hued crotons, hibiscus, anthuriums, and scads of bougainvillea, the candlelight from the glass hurricane lamps playing on the faces of these people so dear to me. Another memory, more moments, to file away forever. This is an evening of superb food, wine, stories, toasts, a lot of laughter, some wet eyes. I've put together a family cookbook to which everyone has contributed, each one writing in their own inimitable fashion, adding anecdotes and memories.

World Cup fever has us in its grip in spite of the fact that our "Reggae Boyz" are already out and hence most days we camp close to the beachside bar and its TV set. Ray and Garth demonstrate considerable patience and humour in dealing with our liquid requirements though the kitchen staff just can't seem to comprehend our insatiable demand for patties, both beef and callaloo..."Will there be any more patties today?"..."Yuh still want more?"..."Yes, man!" This goes on day after day. Domino sessions spring up under the almond trees, Kevin sails the Hobie Cat and assorted passengers away to distant beaches, others depart on excursions to Negril and Ocho Rios, the children carve turtles and mermaids out of the sand, we snorkel, chat, swim, drink, chat some more, swim some more, read...fall asleep.

A flurry of activity as family and friends start arriving for the weekend fun. A pre-party party is held up at "Kelso", everyone determined not to get too jammed up before the Saturday night session—"try yuh bes'!" A friend has brought his Campion College yearbook, someone else has a fat stack of old photos and brother Mark has compiled a tape of 'hits' from our early 70s heyday (remember *Band of Gold*!!). People are stacked up in other Silver Sands villas and elsewhere and the next day it's patently obvious that we've invaded the place. There's a lot of hugging and kissing going on as the greater family reconnects spilling over into the evening as even more old faces turn up. The lights twinkle in the trees. Virgo cooks up a wicked jerk chicken on the barbecue and we chat ourselves into oblivion. The kids enjoy soccer and sparklers under the stars whilst some of the more overly-refreshed 'grown-ups' dance to some old Motown number.

Not yet partied out, a couple of nights later Kevin and Chris feel a need for some live music and fix up (through Alvin, a man of many talents) a trio from the Fishermans Beach to give us a session at "Jamahome". Music night is on! After much splicing together of wires and fiddling about with knobs, some serious 'riddims' hit the air and we're skanking and singing, aided and abetted by rum in every shape, form and fashion. Alvin, the lyric master, takes the mike and suddenly another JA moment is born; he lays down a rap about "dis ya family renunion" (sic)..."dem come from Hengland, dem come from Miamee...".

There were too many images, too many unique moments, to mention here. Jamaica, and especially her people, embraced us, caressed us, renewed our souls and let us go again. These memories, these moments, are for us, the building blocks of family strength; our collective past brought together in the here and now, to live within us forever.

ORIGINALLY PUBLISHED DECEMBER 1998

A Cushion for My Dreams

EVAN JONES

I was born two hundred years ago, back in a time before the motor car, before electric light, and telephones, in the days of the coal pot, the wood burning stove and ice cream made in your own bucket. Water ran only in rivers until my father built a tank in the back yard and caught the rain water on the roof.

It was quieter then. Here, where I live now, in London, there is the eternal sound of the internal combustion engine, a helicopter, an airliner, a bus, a car, a motorcycle, a lawn mower, a street sweeper, garbage truck, and a jet-ski on the river. Even when these are quiet, there is no silence, there is the background babel of a great city, and foreground the purr and whine of electric motors, fridges, washing machine, and air-conditioners.

When I was a child in Jamaica you could distinguish sound. You could recognize Uncle Norbert's truck three miles away, and tell by the gear change which corner it was turning. You could hear dogs, and tree frogs, and ghosts in the bush walking and talking, and sometimes, up in the hills the beating of the drums, the rhythm of souls being saved.

Here there is usually a low, grey sky, and always soot on the window sill. In my childhood, there was always a blue sky, piled with towering cumulus, salt on my fingertips, and the never ceasing murmur of the sea. I used to lie on the window sill to watch the sun rise in the morning turning everything to colour. I would watch a green lizard on the quickstick tree sporting his orange tie, and asking the flies to dance. Only occasionally I would try to knock his head off with a stone.

My mother and my father, great important ghosts, move in and out of the room's memory, my mother hymn book in hand on her way to church, my father reciting poetry on the back of his mule. Brothers and sisters, smaller, more active ghosts, play and fight. Real people. But when I first think of childhood in Jamaica, I think of landscape.

I am in love with landscape, and because of Portland, Jamaica, I can never get enough of it. I love the Alps, and the Scottish highlands, the meadows of Dorset, and the acacia dotted plains of Africa. I have seen the moon rise over the Sea of Galilee, and been on a boat at night, over the Cayman Trench, beyond all sight of land, balanced on the dark bubble of the sea with the unsubstantial sky above filled with revolving lights and floating vapours, and seen the redness of approaching dawn and the fading gold of the departing moon.

It was a privilege to begin in Paradise, to be brought up in a Garden of Eden. If one's first memory is the fiery sword then life must seem even more terrible than it is, and the thought of eternity intolerable. Portland, Jamaica gave me a cushion to lie on, a refuge in the mind, a sense of beauty. If I had been born in a concentration camp, in the slums of Calcutta, or in a city razed by nuclear war, I'm not sure I could cope with only that to remember.

I don't much like the works of man, and I think we are a nasty little species of which a God would be ashamed. Our cities are rubbish dumps, and we despoil the earth that we were given. 'Each man kills the thing he loves' is the kindest way of saying it. We are hardest on our selves perverting our own kind, and out of our own greed destroying the lives of others.

Think of an idea, think of its opposite. Think of the beauty made by man, the Parthenon, the dying Gaul, a Madonna of Bellini, or a movie with Marilyn Monroe. Think of a favourite poem, of football and reggae, cricket and calypso, thoroughbred racehorses, gardens, curry goat and rum. Are such things worth one drug-crazed murder, one ravaged child, one starving mother? Do they justify man?

I cannot accept the answers of religion. For me, hypocrites in dog collars, pompous Popes, and mullahs screaming for murder and torturing women are not the answer, but only part of the problem. I can't answer it either. But I should try, as time is getting short. Born two hundred years ago, I can't have that much longer. My grip on the old twig is not so steady. Dear friends keep falling off, dying in the most unpleasant ways. For me to get out of bed, stand straight, and walk out of the room is a big number. If a beautiful girl overtakes me on the street I can't catch up with her, and if I did she'd probably call the police. I can't remember why I came into a room, and so I have to go out again to look for the reason.

So the dark is coming, and no questions answered, and because I cannot see my future as a wisp of spirit shooting through the stars, because I cannot sing or play the harp I must come to some conclusions before I grow dizzy and release my grip.

Will this one do for now? Despite weakness and pain, despite waste and ugliness, shame of myself and scorn of my fellow man, I have been privileged, because I grew up in Jamaica. I lived in Eden before the flaming sword.

ORIGINALLY PUBLISHED FEBRUARY 1999

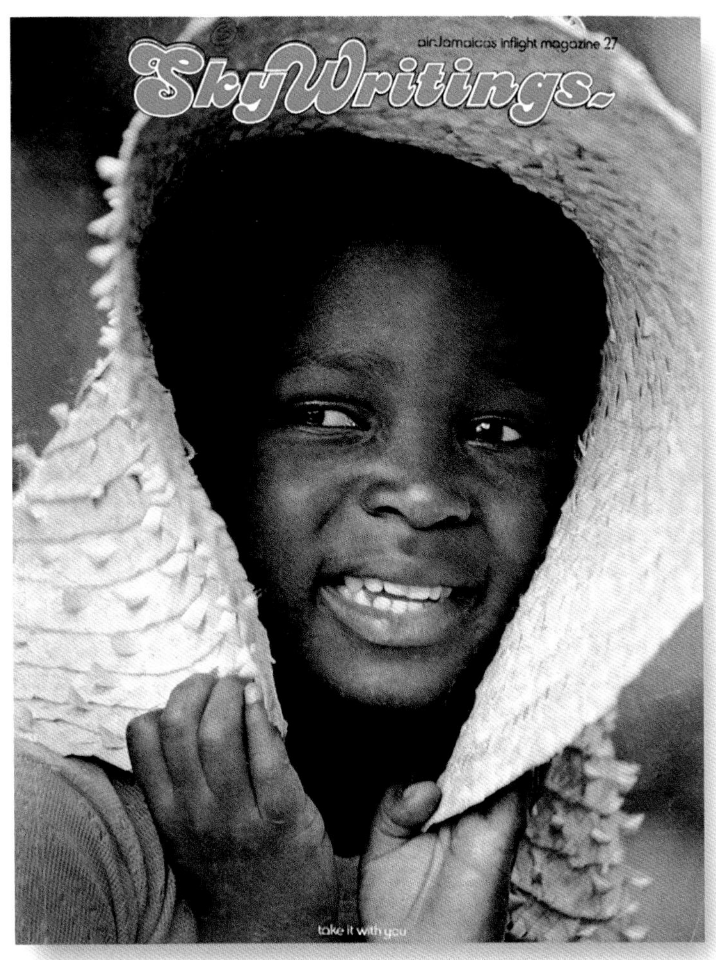

CONTRIBUTORS

SKYWRITINGS COVER
January 1981
A child's smile.

©MARIA LAYACONA

Contributors' Biographies

Tony Aarons is an archaeologist/ anthropologist/preservationist who has practiced for many years in Jamaica and elsewhere in the Caribbean and the Americas, specializing in Amerindian New World cultures.

Peter Abrahams was born in Johannesburg South Africa. He settled in Jamaica in 1956 and is a journalist and author of many books.

Tara Abrahams-Clivio has had a love affair with journalism beginning at school in New Zealand where she completed her BA (University of Auckland) followed by an MSc in Broadcast Journalism at Boston University. She has worked in various fields of communications including radio (United Nations, PBS and ABC affiliates, Boston), as producer of the talk radio show Breakfast Club (Jamaica), in television (CVM, Jamaica) and in pr/marketing (ICD Group and McDonalds, Jamaica). She is now a full-time mother of Sophie and Maximilian.

Nadine Anderson Cheng, art director at *SkyWritings* magazine, graduated from the Edna Manley School for the Visual Arts in 1989 and was voted and featured by *The Jamaican Magazine* as "best student" in her department for that year. She has had a successful career in the fields of fine art and graphic design and was also a former public relations officer for the Jamaican Artists and Craftsmen Guild.

John Allgrove spent his childhood years in the Blue Mountains and now operates Whitfield Hall hostel from where most climbs to the Peak begin. For 22 years he was chief engineer at the UDC.

Ben Barber is currently state department bureau chief for *The Washington Times*. Since 1980 he has reported from Latin America, the Middle East, Africa and Asia for *USA Today*, the *London Observer, Boston Globe, the L.A. Times, Christian Science Monitor* and other publications.

Norma Benghiat is the producer of the "Coalpot Recipe" postcards and the author of *Traditional Jamaican Cookery* (Penguin).

The Hon. **Louise Bennett**-Coverley O.M., O.J., M.B.E., Hon. D. Litt, best known as "Miss Lou" is a legend in her time. The foremost folklorist, poet and writer in dialect in the West Indies. Miss Lou holds an unequalled place of pride and affection in the hearts of all Jamaicans.

Barbara Blake-Hannah is a multi-media journalist and author working in print, film/video, broadcasting and public relations. Her greatest achievement she says, is home-schooling her son, teen technology whiz kid, Makonnen.

Adrian Boot, one of the UK's best known photographers, has done extensive photography of Bob Marley as well as most of Jamaica's leading musicians, extending his list of published books with *Jah Revenge, Bob Marley: Songs of Freedom* and *Bob Marley: Natural Mystic.*

Calvin Bowen was a retired assistant editor of the *Gleaner*. After his retirement, he wrote an opinion column for the paper.

Wenty Bowen is a Jamaican journalist and filmmaker, who taught at the University of the West Indies in the Creative Production and Training Centre and now teaches at Tufts University in Massachusetts.

David Boxer is chief curator of the National Gallery of Jamaica. He is the author of numerous publications on Jamaican art and is one of the country's most celebrated artists.

Ian Boyne is a *Sunday Gleaner* columnist, host of Jamaica's longest-running television interview programme, *Profile*, as well as *Religious Hardtalk* on Radio Jamaica. He has won four journalism awards, the first at 18 for his newspaper profile on the distinguished novelist Peter Abrahams.

Cherry Brady is an attorney-at-law living in Barbados. She holds a Master's degree in journalism, is a frequent contributor to local newspapers and also a published author of several academic articles in learned publications.

Dr. David Buisseret taught history at the University of the West Indies, Mona between 1964 and 1980. Since 1995 he has been Garrett Professor of History at the University of Texas at Arlington.

Bernard Burrell a Jamaican-born print-broadcast journalist and social worker, is the London-based correspondent for Radio Jamaica and a regular panel contributor to BBC World TV current affairs programme, *Dateline London*. He travels widely and is preparing materials for a book, *Images of Moroccan Life and Society.*

Ivy Baxter was a trail-blazing pioneer of the contemporary dance movement and an outstanding educator in the field of dance.

Michael Campbell was born in England and studied at the Wakefield College of Arts & Technology. In the eighties he worked with Michael Woodward Associates Worldwide—a fine arts dealer. Presently he is involved in CG animation.

Morris Cargill, lawyer, landowner, entrepreneur, writer, is ultimately best remembered as a *Daily Gleaner* columnist who believed "a good joke can tell you more about the essential truth of something than an entire volume of academic dissertation."

Jimmy Carnegie is a sports writer and historian who has published several books. He will be working shortly on a history of the Carreras Sports Foundation.

Julie Chen has worked as a reporter, editor and feature writer at major Jamaican newspapers and radio stations. She is completing a Master's Degree in mental health counseling.

Ray Chen a Jamaican-born resident of Montreal, was trained at the New York Institute of Photography. His successful careers in Canada and Jamaica span 36 years with major assignments in Europe, Canada, the US and the Caribbean. He has published two books *Jamaica-The Land and The People* (1984) and *Jamaica-The Beauty & Soul We Love* (1993).

Barry Chevannes' edited collection *Rastafari and Other African Caribbean Worldviews* was nominated for the U.K.'s Katherine Briggs Award. His most recent book is *Learning to Be a Man: Culture, Socialization* and *Gender Identity in Five Caribbean Communities.*

Walter Chin, born in Montego Bay, Jamaica, has had his photographic work reproduced both in the advertising and in editorial pages of almost every glamorous magazine in the U.S. and many in Europe. His exquisite nudes have won him exposure in prestigious books and exhibitions.

Samuel Clayton was born in Kingston, Jamaica in 1937. He is a playwright, dramatist, music teacher, vocational instructor, orator and philosopher.

Steve Cohn is a photographer/art director who contributed to many publications in Jamaica from 1986 to 1995. He is currently living and working as an art director in Bethesda, Maryland.

Karl 'Jerry' Craig, O.D., M.F.A., a leading Jamaican artist and art educator, has been a major force in fostering international appreciation for Jamaican art by organizing traveling exhibitions to the U.S., European and the Caribbean. His own work is in numerous local and international public and private collections.

Marguerite Curtin is a teacher, editor, publisher, artist and researcher. Between 1995 and 2000 she was project co-ordinator at the Hanover Museum in Lucea.

Ian Cumming, an English travel photographer specializing in the Caribbean and Tibet, continues to explore Jamaica from the caves of the Cockpit Country to the dancehalls of Kingston.

Cecille Daley a freelance writer, has contributed articles covering a range of subjects for *SkyWritings* and other Jamaican publications.

Cheryl Daley-Champagnie printmaker, papermaker, Sisterlocks associate/trainer, lives and works in Jamaica with her husband, Patrick, a graphic designer, son Tarick (dog lover) and daughter Kelsey (visionary).

Monica daSilva has been photographing dance in Jamaica for the last 20 years. She currently works at CVM-TV as an editor.

The Honourable **Dr. Omar Davies**, has been Minister of Finance & Planning of Jamaica since December 1993. Dr. Davies follows a wide range of sporting events but his real passion lies in the collection, research and commentary on various musical forms, particularly Jamaican music. Despite all his achievements, Dr. Davies still considers graduating from Glenmuir High School his greatest.

Lorraine Deeks-Murray has contributed several articles to *SkyWritings* over the years and she is the editor of *The Jamaican Magazine*.

Lindy Delapenha spent almost 20 years playing professional football in England and later joined Jamaica Broadcasting Corporation as its sports director.

Ernest deSouza was the spiritual leader of the Jewish Community in Jamaica from 1978–2000. As a professional photographer, his publications include *Pictorial History of the Jewish Community in Jamaica* and *Prayers, Meditations and Order of Services* for the Synagogue.

Odette Dixon Neath is the mother of three sons. In her free-time, she works full-time as the editor of *SkyWritings* magazine.

Enid Donaldson-Mignotte started writing a weekly column for the *Gleaner* and the *Star* 16 years ago. In 1993 her book *The Real Taste of Jamaica* was published by Ian Randle Publishers. A new edition soon followed and it still remains a 'best seller.'

Colonel Allan Douglas, a member of the Jamaica Defence Force for the past 32 years, has published *Newcastle and Its History*.

Dr. Alan Eyre is a geographer and ecologist specializing in environmental systemics, tropical rainforest conservation in Jamaica and the Caribbean. His interest include nature tourism, and the establishment and management of national parks worldwide.

Laura Facey is an artist who lives with her family and works in the hills of St. Ann, Jamaica. She recently completed a life-size carving of Christ for the St. Andrew Parish Church in Kingston, Jamaica.

Robin Farquharson was born in Black River and raised on a family-owned sugar estate in Westmoreland. He studied photography at Rhode Island School of Design. On his return he began photography of *'Old Jamaica'* (memories of childhood)—24 exhibition prints now in the National Gallery collection. He is currently completing an illustrated book on sugar estate life in 1920s Jamaica.

Trevor Fearon has written his first novel, *In These Our Sunshine Years*, which is scheduled for publication in early 2003.

Peter Ferguson turned to commercial photography launching many dynamic projects including *KRIS* magazine and the Studio Art Gallery/Workshop. Peter is currently near completion of a personal project entitled *Change Markers—101 Portraits of Men in Jamaica*, a collection of black and white images.

Warren Field spent over 25 years in the advertising business as an art director and creative director. He is now a freelance illustrator, cartoonist and fine artist.

Claire Forrester is a Jamaican journalist with more than 25 years of experience covering national and international track and field meets and co-authored *Unyielding Spirit*, the authorized biography of Merlene Ottey.

Jeremy Francis developed his love for photography while living in Europe where he was intrigued by the beauty of the landscapes through seasonal changes. After working for 20 years in film and television production in Jamaica, he has now made commercial still photography his main professional activity.

Suzanne Francis-Brown is a freelance writer and editor who recently completed a masters degree in heritage studies. She has four published books, two of which are children's stories.

Anthony Gambrill, founder/publisher of *SkyWritings*, is best known for scripting the *8 O'CLOCK JAMAICA TIME* satirical revue, but has been writing articles for newspapers and magazines for the past 50 years.

Ashley Gambrill, former editor of *SkyWritings*, is a freelance journalist and short story author. She is a graduate of Boston University, and a mother of two handsome boys.

Laura Gambrill is a graduate of New York University. She is *SkyWritings* assistant editor and regularly travels the Caribbean in search of story ideas.

Colin Garland was born in Sydney, Australia and educated at the National School of Art in Sydney. Living in Jamaica since 1962, he was a professor at the Jamaica School of Arts (later the Edna Manley School of Arts) from 1964–1984, where he made important contributions to the dynamic development of the Jamaican art scene.

Neville Garrick graduated from U.C.L.A. in graphic design and toured with Bob Marley as his art director. He is a photographer, writer and filmmaker and designed several of Marley's album covers.

Marguerite Gauron, a resident of Portland and contributor to *SkyWritings* for over 20 years, is a news correspondent for RJR, managing director of Gauron Food Products and president and founder of the Portland Environment Protection Association.

Barbara Gloudon has worked in print and on radio, variously as editor, reporter columnist and commentator. As a playwright she is noted for her work with the Little Theatre Movement, Jamaica's longest established theatre company.

Fiona M. Godfrey, an artist living in Mandeville, teaches painting to children and annually exhibits their work in the well-known "Young at Art" show. She is currently working on a series of large oil paintings.

Danielle Goodman is a writer and editor.

Marc Goodman's pieces for *SkyWritings* have ranged from an interview with Nobel Laureate Derek Walcott to a survey of New York nightlife. He is contributing projects associate at *Vanity Fair* magazine.

Herbie Gordon selcted the camera as his professional tool at the Kingston Senior School's Photographic Club. He joined the *Daily Gleaner* in 1961 as a darkroom technician and then as a newspaper photographer. In 1969 he set up his own photographic service particularly in the field of advertising and public relations.

Sonia Gordon is a freelance writer whose articles have appeared in several Caribbean publications. She has also written a Jamaican travel guide, contributed to others, and authored her first play.

Dr. Douglas Hall was the first West Indian to head the history department at the University of the West Indies. He has authored and co-authored many books including *Free Jamaica, Five of the Leewards, In Miserable Slavery*. Appointed emeritus professor and awarded the Norman Manley Award of Excellence in the field of history (1999), he passed away in November 1999.

William Hames is a Los Angeles based photographer, born and raised in Japan who for 25 years has been photographing the music and entertainment industry. To view more of William's work go to www.williamhamesinc.com

Beverly Hamilton has worked in teaching and journalism, done field research on the Garvey movement for 25 years, written magazine and newspaper articles, lectured and is currently working on a textbook on the topic. She was a researcher for the film *Look for Me in the Whirlwind* shown on PBS.

Guy Harvey is a unique blend of artist, scientist, diver, angler, underwater photographer and adventurer. Best known for his marine wildlife art, Guy has filmed and produced several underwater documentaries and two books, *Santiago's Finest Hour* and most recently his autobiography *Portraits from the Deep*.

Staci Hassan-Fowles has over nine years experience in the graphic design field as an artist/photographer with Jamaican and overseas clients. She was the recipient of the United Nations Art award in 1980 and again in 1984. She is also a member of the National Dance Theatre Company of Jamaica and has been on numerous tours throughout the United States and the Eastern Caribbean with the NDTC.

Alex Hawkes, an American who resided in Jamaica for many years until his death, was a journalist, broadcaster and author of several books on cooking and gardening.

George Hay is one of Jamaica's best known cartoonist. His work has been published extensively, locally and internationally. He currently is a director of GH Associates, a graphic design studio started some nine and a half years ago.

Brian Heap has directed 12 national pantomimes, amongst other productions and acted in many plays. He is an educator in drama at the University of the West Indies, Mona.

Tony Hendriks, Jamaican born and half-bred, is an award-winning actor, writer and comedian. He works all over the world, is loved by people of many nations and wanted by their constabularies.

Sally Henzell started writing in her teens. Her work has been in several publications including *Focus* and *Jamaica Women*. She has recently published *Paper Images*, a collection of love poems.

Ruel Hudson is a graphic artist with a background in advertising who resided in Jamaica in the early days of *SkyWritings*.

Albert Huie was a major figure in Jamaica's early art movement and as a post-impressionist painter, he is recognized as Jamaica's foremost landscape artist. His many honours and awards include the Silver and Gold Musgrave Medal from the Institute of Jamaica and the Jamaican Order of Distinction.

Dermot Hussey is a music director at America's first national reggae radio station, The Joint XM101, XM Satellite Radio, in Washington DC, and has over 30 years media experience.

Paul Issa is a director of the House of Issa group of companies (which includes Couples Resorts). A sometimes writer and actor, he can be seen in the long-running Jamaican TV soap-opera *Royal Palm Estate*.

H.P. Jacobs came to Jamaica as a teacher but made a major contribution to the political evolution of Jamaica as a journalist and editor. By inclination a historian, "H.P." delighted in collecting fascinating facts about the country he adopted.

Michael S. L. Jarrett, journalist and public relations consultant is a former editor of *SkyWritings*. He had a long career in Jamaican radio, television and press, writing under pseudonyms *Mike Jarrett and Ekim* and is Jamaica Festival Gold medal winner (Music in 1968 and Photography in 1978).

Evan Jones is a writer of feature films, television plays, novels, poetry and children's books who has worked in Europe, North American and Australia, and now lives in London.

David Katz, journalist, photographer and deejay, is the author of *People Funny Boy: The Genius of Lee Scratch Perry. Solid Foundation: An Oral History of Reggae*, will be published in 2003.

Nicola Kelly, a busy mother of three, part-time Spanish teacher and currently in the development phase of a book about her mother's life, currently resides in the United States though her heart will forever be in her home, Jamaica.

Cookie Kinkead has spent the past many years photographing boutique hotels and exotic locations for interior and travel publications such as *The World of Interiors, Travel & Leisure* and *Vogue*.

Arthur Kitchin was a freelance journalist and *Daily Gleaner* columnist between 1979 to 1981. He obtained the LL.B. (Hons) Degree and is now an attorney-at-law in private practice.

Susan Koenig received her doctorate in conservation biology from Yale University's School of Forestry and Environmental Studies and is currently director of research for the Windsor Research Centre, located in Jamaica's Cockpit Country.

Christine Kristen is the curator for Burning Man, an annual art event in the Black Rock Desert of Nevada. She was a Peace Corps volunteer in Jamaica from 1979-1981, and now resides in San Francisco.

Ed Kritzler a transplanted New Yorker living in Jamaica, specializes in Caribbean history and Jewish pioneers in the New World. He answers correspondence at edkritzler@yahoo.com

Mary Langford, a former teacher at the Queen's School, has written a *History of Quakers in Jamaica* (published by Friends United Press) and contributes articles to the Natural History Society and the Bulletins of the Jamaican Historical Society.

Maria LaYacona came to Jamaica as a *LIFE* magazine photographer and has stayed for over 50 years. Her widely-acclaimed photographic work has included her National Dance Theatre Company portfolio and her own book of Jamaican personalities published in 2000.

Urban Leandro's cartoons and caricatures were a uniquely popular feature of the pages of the *Gleaner* for 52 years from 1937 until his death.

Easton Lee, poet, playwright, broadcaster, and communications consultant, has published two plays, two volumes of poetry, with a third at the publishers. He is currently working on his first novel. He is an ordained priest in the Anglican Church.

Patrick Lee published the *Canadian Jamaican Chinese 2000,* a pictorial record of over 400 Jamaican Chinese families living in Canada. See www.jamaicanchinese.com

Marlene Lewis (MFA) is an artist and original member of the *SkyWritings* team presently living, teaching and working in New York.

Beatrice Desnoes Lim was a lover of life, nature, ideas and people. She had an innate talent for photography and journalism. Her photos captured the splendours of Jamaica while in print she enthusiastically debated women's rights, the environment and politics.

Mirah Lim, a graduate of Georgetown University, is a freelance writer who has been published in *The Jamaica Observer Arts* magazine and an anthology "the Best of *The Jamaica Observer 2001*".

Nigel Lord, is a freelance photographer who has lived in Jamaica and worked around the world for the past 20 years. His love for Jamaica and photography can be seen in his diverse and eclectic style covering all aspects of this fascinating profession.

Vin Lumsden has spent a lifetime working in agriculture and related fields. Trained at Cambridge University, he has run the gamut from research, lecturing, producing and presenting programmes on radio and television to consulting in agricultural communications.

Phillip Lynch, who has won several awards in national photographic competition, has appeared in advertising campaigns and magazines. When not behind the camera he pursues an active interest in chess and tae-kwondo.

Angus W. MacDonald, M.Arch. BOCA, LGSEA, is an architect in Virginia, USA. He also worked in Jamaica, and has invented the Amcor hurricane resistant panelized construction system of unified steel and cement.

Livingston MacLaren was the cartoonist for the *Daily News* before its demise. His popular cartoons have been published in book form.

Students of politics study **Michael Manley** because of his bold stance against many of the world's injustices. However, it is in his love of cricket that we glimpse the passion of the man who so admired the players of this fascinating sport. (Former Prime Minister of Jamaica 1972-1980, 1989-1992)

Ajai Mansingh holds personal chair of professorship; executive director, natural products institute, UWI; Silver Musgrave medallist; published over 150 scientific and 50 social anthropology articles; co-authored the book *Home Away from Home.*

Laxmi Mansingh holds professor's rank as medical librarian, UWI Mona. She has published extensively on librarianship and cultural history and co-authored the award-winning book *Home Away from Home – 150 Years of Indian Presence in Jamaica.*

Franz Marzouca studied photography in Switzerland and Miami before returning to Jamaica in 1982. Shooting primarily for advertising agencies he has developed a strong reputation for his distinctive energy and style with still-life work with many images appearing on international campaigns.

Francisco Mastalia, a native of Italy and resident of New York, has spent 25 years trotting the globe as a portrait photographer and an enthusiast of documentary photography.

Louis Matalon is a graduate of the Ringling School of Art and Design with a Bachelors Degree in "Illustration". He is an art director at McCann-Erickson Jamaica.

John Maxwell, 50 years in journalism; reporter, editor, commentator, chief subeditor/copytaster BBC World Service News; originated *Public Eye* talk-show; environmental advocate, author of *How To Make Our Own News* (UWI Canoe Press) and *Jamaica Sunday Observer* columnist.

Sandy McIntosh is a specialist writer who works for clients in the human services sector in Kingston. She is a published poet, and recently completed her first collection of short stories.

Franklyn McKnight is the publisher of the *North Coast Times* and director of news and current affairs at IRIE-FM. A veteran journalist, he was an associate editor at The Gleaner Company and founding editor of the *Jamaica Herald.*

Frank McManus at the time of contributing to *SkyWritings* was a public relations consultant to the Jamaica Tourist Board.

Diana McCaulay is an environmentalist, currently the executive director of the Jamaica Environment Trust. She has been a weekly columnist for the Gleaner Company and is now working on a book on the environment.

Patricia Meschino has covered musical events throughout the Caribbean in her six years with *SkyWritings* as senior music writer. Her work has also appeared in several other publications including *Time Out New York, The Source* and *Caribbean Travel and Life.*

Sonia Mills has written for print, radio and television. Come 2003, she will give up full-time paid employment in miscellaneous fields to read more and write more.

Pete Millson is a freelance portrait photographer working for UK broadsheets and magazines, US magazines, and now *SkyWritings.* He's currently exhibiting his work from *The Guardian: Home Entertainment– Black & White Portraits* and lives in North London.

Jean Miranda was a journalist and editor of *Flair* and *SkyWritings.*

Mervyn Morris who wrote *On Reading Louise Bennett, Seriously* in 1963, edited her *Selected Poems* (1982) and *Aunty Roachy Sey* (1993). He teaches at the University of the West Indies, Mona.

Nazma Muller is a Trinidadian writer who has worked in the media at home, in Jamaica and London. Her specialties are people-watching and traveling the world looking for a good lime.

Barbara Nelson, a former teacher, now a freelance journalist and researcher, has written for *SkyWritings*, the *Gleaner* and other Jamaican publications and co-authored a social studies textbook for high school students.

Rex Nettleford, scholar, artist and cultural animateur, is currently vice chancellor of the University of the West Indies. Professor Nettleford is also founder, artistic director and principal choreographer of the internationally acclaimed National Dance Theatre Company of Jamaica.

David Ogden was a British TV commercial producer (including the classic "Life is Just for Living" for Red Stripe), musician, artist and writer whose early death deprived Jamaica of his brilliant creative talent.

Elena Oumano, Ph.D., is the author of 18 books, published in the U.S., Europe, and Asia. She is also a freelance music journalist specializing in reggae, other Caribbean music, world music, and hip hop for *Billboard, The Village Voice, Vibe, The New York Times*, and other publications.

Amador Packer was one of Jamaica's pioneer photographers. His most memorable work includes artistic studies of the island's landscape and portraits of Jamaican people, spanning five decades pre-and post-Independence.

Alfonse Pagano, a New Yorker, turned to photography as an art form in 1994 after a distinguished career as a painter.

Rosemary Parkinson has written *Shake Dat Cocktail* (Macmillan) and *Culinaria: The Caribbean* (Koneman), and is a contributor to *SkyWritings* and the *Daily Gleaner* newspaper. She is currently working on several projects and plans are underfoot for another book.

Elaine Perkins is a housewife and grandmother who currently assists her husband with his talk show programme *Perkins On Line.* She is also writer and producer of Jamaican radio dramas.

Michael Reckord is a writer of poems, plays, stories and articles and a lecturer of writing, speech and public relations. His works have been published in books, newspapers and magazines at home and abroad.

Carol Reckord was a farmer, fisherman, boat builder, photographer and actor as well as a senator, radio and television broadcaster, magazine editor, writer and creator and voice of the radio character, Jack Naseberry.

Keith Reece (Uhuru), is a Jamaican born artist who has worked in the advertising industry in Jamaica and New York as a designer and illustrator. He has designed Jamaican postage stamps and exhibited paintings and sculpture in Jamaica, Washington D.C., Germany, Spain and Hong Kong.

Mallica "Kapo" Reynolds was a self-taught artist and Jamaica's most well-known and respected intuitive artist. He was awarded the Institute of Jamaica's Silver and Gold Musgrave Medals and the Jamaican Order of Distinction.

William Richards lives and works in Jamaica and New York City. His first work in the "Big Apple" began with *Essence* magazine and *Capitol/Blue Note Records.* Since then, William has photographed for: *Motown, The Fader, Island/Ded Jam, Time Life* among others.

Dr. Diane Robertson is the author of two books *Jamaican Herbs* and *Live Longer, Look Younger with Herbs.* She is chairman of the holistic Herbal Association (Jamaica), a prolific writer and lecturer on ethno-medicine.

Carey Robinson, historian and TV producer/director, has written three books dealing with the Maroons. He is currently writing *Jamaican Tales of the Supernatural*, and *Memoirs of a Media-person.*

Ian Robinson came to Jamaica from England in 1968 on Volunteer Service Overseas. He fell in love with the country, people and culture and stayed until his untimely death in 1997.

Dr. Ralph Robinson, head of the department of life sciences at the University of the West Indies, is a certified diving instructor (BS-AC) and has published more than 30 scientific articles in the field of parasitology.

Charles Rousseau, assistant general manager of the Jamaica General Insurance Co. Ltd. is an avid amateur photographer, who works mainly with zoom lenses and loves sports, nature and candid photography.

Heather Royes has been a journalist, international consultant, diplomat and writer. Her poetry has been included in anthologies in the UK and the Caribbean and her manuscript of poems won second prize in the Una Marson 1993 National Literary Awards in Jamaica. In 1996 *The Caribbean Raj* was published and another collection on the Caribbean is to be published soon. She is working on a non-fictional novel about the 1970's.

Cheryl Ryman a former research fellow at the African-Caribbean Institute of Jamaica and tutor and principal dancer with the National Dance Theatre Company. She has published several articles on African-Caribbean dance and culture.

Headley G. Samuels, sports photographer, best known as "**Dellmar**," has won countless awards, had seven successful exhibitions and published a pictorial *Caribbean Cricket Spectacular.* Travelling worldwide with West Indian cricket, he has covered many test matches.

Robert Edison Sandiford is the author of *Winter, Spring, Summer, Fall: Stories* (Empyreal Press/The Independent Press) and two comic collections of erotica, *Attractive Forces* and *Stray Moonbeams* (NBM Publicating).

Dennis Scott, Jamaican poet, playwright, actor, dancer, teacher has published three poetry collections, including the prizewinning *Uncle Time.* His work has appeared in many anthologies. Previously unpublished poems are being considered for a posthumous collection.

Joy Scott is a former journalist with the *Jamaica Daily News* and librarian at the St. Catherine Parish Library. She is currently information resources manager at the Office of the Prime Minister.

Olive Senior is the author of the *Encyclopedia of Jamaican Heritage* and other works on Caribbean culture, three internationally acclaimed works of fiction – *Summer Lightning* (which won the Commonwealth Writers Prize), *Arrival of the Snake-Woman* and *Discerner of Hearts* and two of poetry – *Talking of Trees* and *Gardening in the Tropics.*

Raymond Sharpe was one of Jamaica's leading sports journalists and editors.

Hilary Sherlock, is a teacher of children with special needs, has also worked in rural community development and is an author of a Caribbean Reading book and co-author of a collection of Caribbean folk tales with her father Sir Philip Sherlock.

Sir Philip Sherlock, a founding father and former vice chancellor of the University of the West Indies, was also a historian, storyteller and poet. His last work *The Story of the Jamaican People* was published in 1998.

Andrew P. Smith is a free-lance photographer and writer who focuses on the Caribbean's hidden natural and cultural heritage. He is currently participating in the *Liquid Light* photography exchange programme between the East Midlands in the U.K. and Jamaica.

Maureen Sheridan is a multi-media artist whose songwriting and production, video production and direction, photography and journalism have received international recognition. She is also the author of *Bob Marley, The Wailing Soul,* (Carlton Books).

Patrick Simmons, aviation consultant, started at PanAm and has held managerial positions at BWIA for 20 years. He was company secretary at Air Jamaica from 1966 until retirement.

Noel Snyder is a biologist who has studied endangered species, including the Puerto Rican parrot, the snail kite, the California condor and the thick-billed parrot. He is the author of several books and many scientific publications, and is a cellist. He lives in the Arizona desert.

Kristie Stephenson graduated from Rhode Island School of Design with a Masters Degree in Architecture, in June 1999, and is currently enjoying living and working in Florida in her chosen field.

Paul Stoppi spent years studying architecture, then discovered photography. He lives in Miami Beach and loves taking pictures of hot chicks and clouds.

Laura Tanna, who has a doctorate in African Languages and Literature, writes regularly for the *Gleaner* and is author of *Jamaican Folk Tales* and *Oral Histories* (including video and audio cassettes) and *Baugh: Jamaica's Master Potter.*

Diana Thorburn's writing over the past two years has mainly been in academia, as she is working on completing her doctorate in international political economy at Johns Hopkins University, and teaching part-time at the University of the West Indies, Mona.

Juliet Thorburn is a water colour artist who has had six successful exhibitions to date. She lives on the north coast of Jamaica where she paints.

Jack Tyndale-Biscoe is considered the pioneer of aerial photography in Jamaica and by successive editors of *SkyWritings*, a legend in his time.

Cecil Ward attended the Ecole de Beaux Arts in Quebec City but has lived in and out of Jamaica since childhood. Winner of the Bronze Musgrave Medal for photography in 1987 by the Institute of Jamaica, his work has been exhibited in solo and group shows. He is represented at the National Gallery of Jamaica and in private collections, most notably that of the Urban Development Corporation of Jamaica.

Mark Steven Weinberger, creative director of *SkyWritings,* has been associated with the magazine since its inception in 1972. A transplant New Yorker by way of his Jamaican better half (Marlene Lewis), he has lived in Jamaica off and on for over sixteen years and has helped produce more than 60 issues of the publication. Digital photography is his love. Kingston is his home.

Dwight Whylie was a BBC announcer, and national assignment editor for CBC Radio in Canada, a newspaper columnist and chairman of the Broadcasting Commission in Jamaica.

Marjorie Whylie a popular key artiste, and leader of Whylie Wrhythm, has lectured at Jamaican tertiary institutions for many years, teaches keyboard, voice and percussion and is musical director of the National Dance Theatre Company.

Cynthia Wilmot is a journalist and filmmaker, winner of awards in both print and audio-visual media, including a British Airways prize for travel-writing and the Doctorbird award for a body of work in Caribbean film and video production.

Fred Wilmot, over 50 years a resident in Jamaica, is an editor, radio and TV personality, columnist, writer, public relations pioneer and private pilot. Now retired and living between Jamaica and his native Canada, he is completing a history of Jamaican aviation.

Donnette Zacca, photographic artist, is a tutor at the Edna Manley College of Art. Zacca has had several exhibitions and has won numerous awards in the Jamaica Cultural Development Commission annual photographic competition.

Members of the SkyWritings team from 1972 to 2002

(IN ALPHABETICAL ORDER)

Nadine Anderson Cheng, Catherine Barrett, Leeanne Bayley-Hay, Glen Beckett, Jameel Cargill, Liz Carvalho, Carmen Clarke, Paul Clayton, Margaret Clunis, Pat Colly, Alison Comacho, Deidre DeCourcey, Angela deFreitas, Dennis Dixon, Sundra Dixon, Odette Dixon-Neath, Leroy Edwards, Judy Elliot, Molly Evans, Gillian Fisher, Bert Fowles, Anthony Gambrill, Ashley Gambrill, Laura Gambrill, Linda Gambrill, Carlton Gordon, Sonia Gordon, Tricia Shay Gray, Joyce Gryff, Clifton Hall, Anna Kay Harrison Von Dueszeln, Garth Hendricks, Maria Hoo, Ruel Hudson, Felix Hunter, Mike Jarrett, Katrina Kelly Barnes, Deryck Lesley, Mortimer "Bunny" Levy, Marlene Lewis, Ingrid MacPherson, Andrea McHayle, Jean Miranda, Lorraine Murray, Yvonne Nembhard, Jimmy Olsen, Tracey Payne, Dawn Peña, Marceline Ramsey, Angelique Reid, Betty Reid, Sybil Rendle, Dennis Scott, Mary Sörum, Christine Snaith, Leroy Stapleton, Michael Stasko, Eleanor Sutherland, Cecile Taylor, Pollie Taylor, Eunice Thompson, Juliet Thomas, Juliet Thorburn, Tanja Turner, Mark Steven Weinberger, Karen Weller, Gordon Williams, Jill Williams, Dorothy Witter, Elizabeth Wright.